Last Chorus

HUMPHREY LYTTELTON

Last Chorus

An Autobiographical Medley

Foreword by Stephen Lyttelton

JR BOOKS

For Susan

First published in Great Britain in 2008 by
JR Books, 10 Greenland Street, London NW1 0ND
www.jrbooks.com

First published in paperback, 2009

A catalogue record for this book is available from the British Library.

ISBN 978-1-906779-44-3

3 5 7 9 10 8 6 4 2

Printed by CPI Bookmarque, Croydon, CR0 4TD

Contents

Part 5 That's My Home

Acknowledgments

Producing a book of this nature could not have been achieved without an army of support. For help in compiling, editing, clarifying stories, verifying dates, and supplying photos, emails and written material, I would like to thank the following people: Susan da Costa, Mary Stewart-Cox, Henrietta Lyttelton, Helena Lawrence, Steve Voce, Patricia Woods, Adrian Macintosh, Jimmy Hastings, John Rees-Jones, Norman Giller, Stacey Kent, Elkie Brooks, Trevor and Family, Dave Green, and John and Pat Barnes. A special mention must go to my father's publisher Jeremy Robson and Senior Editor Lesley Wilson without whose help this book would not have been made. And finally, my wife Emma who has supported me throughout this emotional rollercoaster and tolerated the mass of paper and photos that threatened to take over our house.

Foreword

When my father died in April 2008, he had been working on a book about calligraphy – one of his many passions. The book was centred on the collection of handwriting that he had inherited from his own father and had built on himself. He had planned to finish the book in the months of convalescence following his operation for an aneurism. Sadly, this was not to be. When we searched through what he *had* completed it became clear that there was not enough material to justify publishing the book that he had planned.

In the days and weeks following his death we went through the process that everyone in this situation must have to go through. The house needed tidying and we needed to get things in order. For all Dad's many talents filing and organisation was definitely not one of them so this was always going to be a daunting task. However, what did come to light, as we rifled through box files, cleared drawers and emptied Waitrose bags, was an abundance of autobiographical work that had accumulated over 60 years.

This included daily diaries that had been kept assiduously for seven years, a selection of which is included here. Written in his fine italic hand they end as abruptly as they started but provide a detailed insight into his daily life and the social and political landscape of that period. Reading these diaries opened up a wealth of memories. I had forgotten the regular trips out as a family to review restaurants for his column in *Harpers & Queen*. I am not sure how his editor at the time would have reacted had she realised that his monthly contribution relied heavily on the gastronomic tastes of Lyttelton children (aged 19, 17 and 12 year old)! Going out so often was a contradiction for someone so private and every now and then the constant recognition would get the better of Dad. One evening when sitting in a bustling and noisy Italian restaurant in St. John's Wood he became aware of a

German couple a few tables away, staring at him relentlessly. It was clear this was irritating him but we thought nothing of it until Dad very calmly pulled his tie up under his glasses and put one of his size 13 desert boots on his head!

I am sure it will surprise many that my father was, for a period, a keen D.I.Y. enthusiast. As with most things that he took up, he did so with an all-consuming passion so we soon found shelves appearing at will, walls repapered and many other tasks taken on with abandon. This was until an unfortunate experience with a Black and Decker brought things to a sudden end….

We also found a solitary diary written in 1940 (my father was only 19) when he was working in his uncle's steel works in Port Talbot, South Wales. This was written after he had just left Eton but display an innate talent for descriptive writing that he would later exploit. Although he doesn't refer to it in the diary his experiences and the people he met forged my father's socialist outlook and distaste for inequality that remained with him all his life.

In addition to the diaries we discovered a mass of published and unpublished autobiographical work and anecdotal articles. And last but not least his funny and sometimes surreal cartoons.

Reading through the material, it became clear that a large part of my father's life was unknown, even to us, and that we should bring it all together in one complete volume. As children, we had to some extent taken what he did for granted. Trips to see him play were rare although I do remember seeing him at the Festival Hall with Louis Armstrong and we even got to meet Louis afterwards. But it all seemed strangely remote from our daily lives so as not to take on any real importance. We had no inkling of the significance of what he achieved as a pioneer of jazz in the years following the war. For someone to have come from the world that he was born into and end up on stage with some of the all time greats of jazz is difficult to comprehend, even now.

What also shone through his written work and diaries was the incredible relationship he had with his musicians and the music they played. It gave great solace, reading Dad's accounts of his tours and of his great friendships, to know he was doing what he really loved.

And, of course, the ever-present humour and silliness was always there. Dad would always be caricaturing band members including depicting his bassist, Dave Green, as an owl. At times he would go to extraordinary lengths to achieve the right impact. Dave Green recalled the following story to me of when they were on tour. While waiting in a carriage for their train to leave the station, Dad tapped Dave on the shoulder and pointed to the train next to them, as it slowly trundled past. As the last carriage came into view so did a large owl like face drawn in the dirt!

His current Band deserves a special mention in this foreword. Not only are they one of Dad's 'best bands' but also they were like a family to him and gave him a huge amount of love. When he was unable to drive to appearances they took it in turns to drive him around the country. They are a special bunch and it is great to see them still playing Dad's music.

Dad's popularity as Chairman of *I'm Sorry I Haven't A Clue* has at times overshadowed his musical achievements. Jon Naismith, the show's producer, was very conscious of this and would introduce Dad regularly as 'The jazz musicians' jazz musician and game show host' as well as bringing Dad's trumpet playing into the live shows. It was surprising to read in the diaries that, in the early days of *Clue*, my father was more than sceptical as to whether the show would succeed (but then he also gave the Beatles a 'miss' on Juke Box Jury!). Dad especially loved the live shows as much for the travelling and being with the team as for the opportunity to ad lib.

Home life for us was incredibly normal. Supported by our mother, Jill, Dad would immerse himself in family life like any father. He would religiously take us to school when he could while subjecting us to a daily diet of Radio 4. The school we attended could not have been more diametrically opposite to that of his childhood and many a distant ancestor. It was called at the time a 'progressive school' although it would be fair to say that in the years to follow he would often wonder when 'progress' would be made. That said he was keen to be involved and would be an active participant in school activities. I remember the pride I felt when he gave a talk at the school on wind instruments, playing tunes on a kettle and a rubber hose.

His unusual work schedule was so different from that of our friends that it prompted my sister, Georgina, to ask him why he had to go to work one evening. 'To make money', was his reply. 'But you have money', chimed Georgina. 'How do you know that?' he asked. 'I can hear it in your pocket'. Dad's chosen mode of transport was his car and he became synonymous with his trusty Volvo, prompting Georgina to enquire if he was again going to work in his ' vulva!'. He loved to tell, and later hear, these childhood stories

Discipline and dealing with any sort of family conflict was not something that came naturally to Dad who generally elected to delegate this responsibility whenever possible. The design of the family home meant that from his study he was able to see across to the rest of the house. So when a row or disagreement would ensue he would elect to retreat to this vantage point where he would quietly mutter to anyone in earshot, 'Have they finished?'. This ploy would not always work, and on one occasion required a more inventive solution. Christmas was, to all intent and purpose, traditional – turkey, crackers, whoopee cushions, lots of laughter and, of course, a full-blown family row. Once, when the row showed no sign of abating, Dad disappeared for a short while only to reappear in full Egyptian regalia (including fez) and a tray of champagne. The row quickly dissipated and normal service resumed.

Over the years the house would swell with ever more friends. Dad would love nothing more than listening to and telling stories. The local friendships that he made lasted a lifetime and supported him through some difficult periods. None more so than when our mother contracted Progressive Supranuclear Palsy, a cruel disease from which she eventually died. Dad made every effort to ensure that she remained at home and enjoyed the company of friends and family right up to the last weeks of her life. This took an immense toll on him physically and mentally although he would never let that be known.

As proud grandfather to Pep, Pedge, Lucy, Charlie, Oliver and Eve and great grandfather to Elijah, Jacob and Bella he took to the role slowly. On one occasion, as Dad left the stage following a concert, he spotted a young boy looking up at him expectantly and approached him: 'Did you enjoy the music?'. The boy nodded enthusiastically.

The evolution of Humph. H.L.'s signature cartoons – the last drawn one month before he died.

'Do you know who I am?', he asked, to which a voice from behind said 'He should do, he's your great grandson!'. However, with time and some gentle guidance from his daughter-in-law, Emma, he eventually got the hang of it and embraced the responsibilities that went with being 'cool grandad'.

The level to which he maintained his home/work division only really became clear when he died, although we had been given some inkling earlier in the year. In January 2008, he held the first, of what was planned to be a series of small gatherings, where the different sides of his life were to be finally brought together. Little did we know how important this was to become although I suspect *he* had an idea. To meet Susan (da Costa), his manager and later his partner, for the first time and see how much she loved and cared for him was a great comfort to us all, as was meeting some of his band members who were welcomed as family members.

An incredibly fit man, Dad was not immune to the rigours of old age and the threat of illness. Here is an extract, delivered in his characteristically witty prose, from an email he sent to his great friend, singer Stacey Kent, in which he describes the side effects of a treatment he had just received:

> I was warned that among the side-effects expected with the second dose are hot flushes, muscle degeneration and a change in outline to resemble Jane Mansfield more than Gregory Peck, whom Susan believes I resembled in my youth. So far none of this has happened and my lovely band tell me that I am showing more stamina and am playing better that I have for a decade. Trust me not to conform!
>
> I did report to the senior nurse who administers the jab that it was playing havoc with my emotions. 'You mean tearful?' she asked, with the air of someone who already knows the answer. I nodded, biting my lower lip. 'Oh', she said, 'that's the commonest symptom – all our male patients complain about that!' From time to time, I suddenly get a feeling of enormous sadness, and the tears flow. It doesn't last long. OK in private but definitely not in the street, where it frightens the horses. I think it's good for me to let go. In the days when I had a few testosterone hormones wandering aimlessly through my system, I would have told myself to shut up, Lyttelton – you can't carry on like this. I now (uncharacteristically, you may say) as I mop the keyboard before it fuses, say why the fuck not? It's the truth! They tell me that if my count stays down, they will take me off the injections, testosterone will flood back, and I shall resume my role as a menace to the entire female population of Barnet and outlying neighbourhoods. Oh, those check-out ladies at Waitrose.

His descriptive humour and positive approach to adversity can again be seen in another email to Stacey describing an accident he had in January 2008.

In the early hours of Sunday January 27th I returned from the ground-floor toilet in Susan's house (she only has the one) and climbed the twelve steep stairs up to the first floor where the bedroom is. I didn't put the light on, thinking I could see enough from the dim light of an outside street lamp. I had got to the eleventh stair, where the steps part company with the bannister rail as they turn sharp right, when I discovered that I couldn't. Groping for a door-post that could have offered support, I tripped over my feet, which were having some sort of altercation down on the thin end of the stair, and fell backwards into space. A little way down I landed heavily on the base of my spine (I used to have a vestigial tail there, but I think I knocked it off) and skied – yes, I've joined the club – on my ill-covered spine down the rest.

When I reached the bottom, I lay groaning. I felt little pain but, in a rare burst of conformity, I seemed to think subliminally that it's what one should do in the circumstances. Susan, woken from a deep sleep, shouted 'What's the matter?'. Too shaken to come up with the contemporary cliché 'There's no other way to say this…' I shouted bluntly 'I've fallen downstairs!'. When she got to the stairs, she looked down on the sprawling figure of her long-time employer and short-time partner lying below, with his head on the coarse doormat of her hallway-cum-office, his legs entwined on the bottom stairs and his body somehow folded in between.

When she unravelled me and helped me to my feet, I went through the testing of the limbs and extremities (trumpeting fingers first) and found that nothing was broken. At first, when I embarked on a free fall of 270 degrees, I did think fleetingly that my active life, if not life itself, was over. And I've no doubt that when I landed, I went into immediate shock.

After the event, people queued to tell us of friends who had suffered a similar fall, seemingly unhurt, then died suddenly three days later. I was grateful for their thoughtfulness, but didn't go to the doctor next day, preferring to do a gig in Sonning (walking like an unkind take-off of Coleman Hawkins in his last years but playing OK).

When I visited my father in hospital the night before his operation he could not have been in finer spirits: sitting upright in bed wearing his jalibeyah and receiving his many visitors with that characteristic glint in his eye. You would have been forgiven for thinking he was in there for an in-growing toenail rather than a life threatening operation. If he was fearful he kept it to a few private moments, showing more outward concern for his visitors and fellow patients. His last words to me that evening were a testament to his philosophy on life. 'This is a win–win situation for me. If the operation goes to plan then I will wake up with you all around me. If it doesn't then I will know no different but you will all be OK'.

When I saw the many media tributes following his death it was apparent that there was a whole generation, including his grandchildren, who had no real concept of what my father had achieved in his lifetime. Reading all of this material has provided a rounded picture of my father's life that I can add to my own, many faded memories. And I hope that a similar effect will be enjoyed by all his friends and fans who read this book.

As a postscript to all of this, here is an excerpt from an email sent early in 2007:

> I am going to allow Joey Jordan (Elkie's youngest) to take me up paragliding in the spring. He is a fully trained expert and takes his mum aloft regularly, so I have no qualms. What an experience it will be, floating silently above North Devon among the seagulls!

Due to the fact that he was too busy touring he never actually took his inaugural flight. However Dad finally achieved his wish in September 2008 when his ashes were scattered by Elkie and Joey over the North Devon coast.

Stephen Lyttelton

R.I.P. by Humphrey Lyttelton

Humphrey Lyttelton, the well-known Old Etonian ex-Guards Officer jazz trumpeter, was born on 23 May 1921 at Eton, the only son (among four daughters) of an Eton schoolmaster. It was, many observers agree, the turning-point in his career. Up till then he had led what can only be described as a sheltered life, taking little active part in public life and relying heavily in most matters affecting his livelihood upon his mother. It is not known exactly when he came to a decision about a career, but it is safe to say that, at an age when the average, healthy boy is grappling with the choice between growing up to be an engine-driver or a sex maniac, Lyttelton had already decided that for him it was to be a well-known Old Etonian ex-Guards Officer jazz trumpeter.

To be born on 23 May 1921 at Eton, the only son of an Eton schoolmaster, was a brilliant first step in a career marked by many examples of such forethought and inspiration. The location and circumstances speak for themselves. It was one of the dispensations of Henry VI Our Founder, his heirs and successors, that the son of an Eton master should be educated at the College free, gratis and for no more than it takes to equip him with a top hat, a suit of tails, two sets of underwear and an allowance of seven and sixpence a week at the school tuck shop. It follows that, short of accident or miscalculation, such as being born the fifteenth son of a ferret-handler in Thursoe, Lyttelton could scarcely fail to become an Etonian and, in the fullness of time, an Old Etonian.

The date of his birth also displayed that degree of ruthless calculation which was to mark his subsequent career. It ensured that, by the fateful year of 1939, Humphrey would be eighteen years old and of military age. In the carrying out of this phase of his plans, Lyttelton received – and was ever quick to acknowledge in later life – invaluable assistance from the late Adolf Hitler, of whom it has been said, Herr Hitler used his not-inconsiderable influence to make it possible for the young Old Etonian to become a Guards Officer and an ex-Guards Officer within the short space of six years.

At least one authoritative history of World War Two claims that by landing at the Salerno beach-head clutching a trumpet in his hand, Humphrey almost single-handedly brought the Italian campaign to a successful conclusion. It is now thought that his role in the affair has perhaps been exaggerated and that his gallant and persistent trumpeting in the face of the enemy was responsible for fewer German casualties than at first claimed. Nevertheless, he was mentioned frequently in dispatches, leading eventually to his withdrawal from the Front and return to England. The scenes on V.E. Day, when the ex-Guards Officer designate was hoisted on to a handcart and towed, still trumpeting, through Piccadilly to the cheers of grateful Londoners, have been described in vivid detail by an eye-witness.

Within months, Lyttelton, now a successful Old Etonian ex-Guards Officer, was pointed for the most crucial phase in his career. It has been suggested by at least one base calumniator that the road to becoming an Old Etonian ex-Guards Officer jazz trumpeter was a smooth one. It must be borne in mind that the Luttleton family, as it was originally spelt and often still is, goes back a long way into English history.

The Luttletons were sturdy cricketing folk much given to original and fascinating hobbies, and the pages of their family history teem with Archbishop-cricketers, Cabinet Minister-cricketers, Public School Headmaster-cricketers and at least one Old Etonian Chief of the Imperial General Staff-cricketer.

With such a background, there was naturally enough considerable pressure upon young Humphrey to go into the family business. It should not be thought that he was ill-equipped for this. On the playing fields of Eton, he became noted as a fast-bowler of quite unparalleled velocity, trajectory and altitude, a distinction which for many years was marked by a commemorative metal plaque in the knee-joint of a Mr Joby who recklessly sold sweets and soft drinks on the boundary immediately behind the bowler's arm.

It was in 1936 that Lyttelton made perhaps the most coolly-calculated move in the furtherance of his career, going with his mother during the Eton and Harrow cricket match at Lord's to buy his first trumpet, dressed in the full top-hat-silver-waistcoat-tail-coat regalia of the Eton First XI Supporters' Club. One half-hour lesson, a quick flip through the pages of the *Nat Gonella Trumpet Tutor*, a few hours' practice in the lavatory (now preserved for the nation) of his grandfather's house in London, and Humphrey Lyttelton was a trumpet player. But the battle was not yet won.

How near he came to becoming an Old Etonian ex-Guards Officer orchestral trumpeter, doomed to obscurity in the anonymous brass section of a symphony orchestra, can be judged from the words of Dr Mervyn Bruxner, the conductor of the Eton School Orchestra, on hearing Humphrey perform the Jeremiah Clark 'Trumpet Voluntary' within a few weeks of taking up the instrument: 'Good God!' One should mention, too, a later performance, arranged for trumpet, pipe organ and stentorian tenor voice, of the aria 'Sound an Alarm' from Handel's *Judas Maccabaeus*, a musical event which is marked by a commemorative metal plaque erected only recently at the approaches to Eton College which reads 'WINDSOR BRIDGE IS NOW CLOSED TO TRAFFIC DUE TO THE DISCOVERY OF A PERMANENT STRUCTURAL FAULT. NO ACCESS TO WINDSOR VIA ETON HIGH STREET'.

The manner in which Humphrey became an Old Etonian ex-Guards Officer jazz trumpeter is now too well-known to need reiteration. The names of historic stepping-stones – the Nuthouse, Regent Street...the Orange Tree, Friern Barnet...the Red Barn, Bexleyheath – are etched in the annals of jazz history, not to mention his liver. The careful reader will note that as yet the infant Lyttelton's full ambition was unrealized. He had yet to become a *well-known* Old Etonian ex-Guards Officer jazz trumpeter. At this point he met up fortuitously with several people who were to have a considerable influence on his career.

One was Canadian-born jazz clarinettist Wally 'Trog' Fawkes, a member of George Webb's Dixielanders, who persuaded Humphrey to join the band. Shortly afterwards, on the occasion of the first International Jazz Festival at Nice, Canadian-born *Daily Mail* temporary Foreign Correspondent W. E. Fawkes wrote an article for his paper revealing that the young trumpet-player from England who was appearing at the festival was, in fact, an Old Etonian ex-Guards Officer jazz trumpeter whose ancestor, Humphrey Lyttelton, had been an associate of Guy 'Trog' Fawkes in the Gunpowder Plot. Overnight Lyttelton had become well-known.

It wasn't long, however, before Lyttelton confided in friends that life at the top, as a well-known Old Etonian ex-Guards Officer jazz trumpeter, was far from easy. For one thing, there was the competition. Was not Old Stovian ex-Navy author-scriptwriter-art-critic-blues-singer George Melly coming up fast behind him, becoming more well-known every minute? With a ruthless energy unusual in a man of his size (six foot three in his stockinged feet, slightly smaller in shoes) he threw himself into the task of accumulating hyphens.

Within weeks, thanks to a broadcast on what was then the B.B.C. Home Service entitled 'How I bought my first trumpet', he had become a jazz trumpeter-broadcaster. Meeting up fortuitously with Canadian-born clarinettist-journalist-cartoonist 'Trog' of the *Daily Mail*, he became overnight a jazz-trumpeter-broadcaster-cartoonist. He started his own band with Canadian-born former George Webb Dixielander cartoonist-journalist-clarinettist Wally Fawkes, thus turning into a well-known Old Etonian ex-Guards Officer jazz-trumpeter-broadcaster-cartoonist-bandleader.

There seemed no end to the man's achievements. The purchase of a pair of binoculars, a quick tour of fifty London restaurants, the acceptance of an article by *Punch*, an appearance in *Any Questions?* and an interview in *Late Night Line-Up* led to his becoming, by 1972, a well-known Old Etonian ex-Guards Officer jazz-trumpeter-broadcaster-cartoonist-bandleader-bird-watcher-gastronome-humorist-panellist-TV-personality. It was fantastic, incredible, unprecedented….

News Item. At the funeral of Harry Widdicombe, the well-known

Old Etonian ex-Guards Officer jazz-trumpeter-broadcaster-cartoonist-bandleader-bird-watcher-gastronome-humorist-panellist-TV-personality-corpse, an incident occurred when a man ran from a group of onlookers and began to beat with his fists on the side of the hearse, shouting, 'But I need the final chapter for your book this afternoon at the latest!'

PART 1

IT SEEMS LIKE YESTERDAY

Family with a Capital F

I had always been aware from early childhood that I belonged to a Family with a capital F. On both my mother's and my father's side my ancestors go back into history in a line of almost unbroken distinction and worthiness. True, there were one or two bright spots to encourage the rebel. I feel a certain amount of warm affection for a very early ancestor, called Humphrey Littleton (as the name used to be spelt), who contrived to get himself hung, drawn and quartered at Guildford for a rather shady part in the Gunpowder Plot. Mind you the H of P wouldn't be among my targets. As a device for keeping six hundred odd (and some very odd) potentially dangerous persons off the streets, it seems to me worth preserving at all costs. And for Thomas Lord Lyttelton, too, whose hearty disregard for the moral conventions earned him the title of the 'Wicked Lord' and the more informal nickname 'Naughty Tom'. In a biography of Thomas by Mr Reginald Blunt, my aunt Maud Wyndham wrote in her Introduction:

> In his family, 'Naughty Tom' stands out as a spectacular figure, for although in Victorian days the nefarious doings which earned him this soubriquet were not disclosed to the younger scions…we were all familiar with the strange story of his death, and that it was on his account that the name of Thomas, which had been a favoured family name since the days of Thomas Lyttelton the judge, was forthwith dropped like a live coal.

This habit of dropping names which are disgraced seems to have persisted in the Lyttelton family right up to the present generation. My father has often said that his decision to call me Humphrey – a name eschewed by the family since my namesake let the side down in the seventeenth century – was regarded by my grandparents as a rather perverse joke. But his bold example must have broken the ice, because the name Thomas has now been restored too.

The circumstances of Naughty Tom's death, referred to by my aunt, were certainly strange. He was visited one night by an apparition of a Woman in White, who bade him prepare to die. He replied, in a somewhat conversational way for a man who might be expected to be scared out of his wits, 'I hope not soon, not in two months,' to which she answered gloomily, 'Yes, in three days.' At breakfast next morning he laughed the incident off, and was apparently calm enough to go to the House of Lords and make what a contemporary describes as 'a fine speech'. On the night of the third day, he went to bed cheerfully, enquiring of his servant what care had been taken to provide good rolls for his breakfast the next morning. And then, with this mundane thought in his head, he suddenly sank back and expired. A clear case of heart failure, I should say, but it's difficult to explain away the apparition. According to another contemporary chronicler, 'The Lyttelton family, either from constitutional nervous irritability or from other causes, was particularly susceptible of impressions similar to the shock which seems to have produced Lord Lyttelton's death.' I'm not sure that I like that backhanded reference to 'other causes', but we'll let it pass.

As for Naughty Tom's 'nefarious doings', over which the Victorian Lytteltons drew a veil, they don't seem to have amounted to much more than gambling, frivolity and mild seduction. That his contemporaries viewed them with such concern – one young lady on whom he had designs referred to him as 'perhaps the most accomplished libertine that any age or country has produced' – may have been as much a matter of politics and social jealousies as of outraged morality. I think the historian Sir George Trevelyan hit the nail roundly on the head when he referred, in his *American Revolution*, to Tom's reputation as the 'Wicked Lord Lyttelton'. 'He belonged to a family in which such pre-eminence was easily earned. Though much less good than other Lytteltons in his own generation, he seems to have been no worse, and as regards pecuniary matters, considerably more prudent than plenty of other Lords.' In other words, he earned his notoriety not so much by being a wicked *lord* as by being a wicked *Lyttelton*.

And in this, one can feel a certain amount of sympathy for him. For how good those Lytteltons were! Thomas Lyttelton, the fifteenth-century judge, must take the blame for setting the ball rolling. He wrote a judicial work, *Treatise on Tenures*, which has since been described as 'the most perfect and absolute work that ever was wrote in any human science'. I believe it is still regarded as the last word on the subject of tenures – whatever they may be. Coming down through the ages, we find that George, the first Lord Lyttelton and father of poor Tom, earned triple distinction as a littérateur, a poet and a politician. While still a young man, by virtue of a few poems and prose writings and some political orations and activities, he was already being referred to as 'the great Mr Lyttelton'. Which is enough to send any son off the rails. As a poet, he was nothing to write home about, although he did well enough to get a chapter in Dr Johnson's *Lives of the Poets*, and to be represented in *The Oxford Book of English Verse* for a while, until the Editors had to drop him for want of space. Historians seem to agree that, as a politician, he would have been better if he hadn't been quite so good. As one puts it, 'His unimpeachable integrity and honest loyalty to his friends largely disqualified him from taking the leading part in the tangled politics of his day.' And as for his orations, 'they were applauded more from respect for his character than for the value of his arguments'. Little wonder that when, in a temporary lapse from correctness, he once went off to the House of Lords with his nightcap on, Naughty Tom, who saw him leave, kept mum, and was bitterly reprimanded later for so doing.

My great-grandfather, also called George, was the fourth Lord Lyttelton, and maintained the tradition nobly. A distinguished Greek scholar, able politician, authority on Education and the Church, one of the best amateur chess players in the Midland Counties – these are just a few of the achievements listed in the obituary notice which appeared in the *Birmingham Gazette* soon after his death in 1896. He had a port named after him in New Zealand, too. The fourth Lord raised a large family – eight sons and four daughters by his first marriage, three further daughters by his second. Thereby he added further complications to an already tangled family tree. Large families were not new in the Lyttelton family. Earlier Lytteltons had been equally prolific. But hitherto the old, condemned house which was the family seat at Hagley in Worcestershire had, by its draughts and hygienic deficiencies, been effective in curbing the increase. By the fourth Lord's time, a new Hagley Hall had been built, hardly more comfortable than the old but at least habitable. So all his family survived childhood, and most lived to a ripe old age.

The eight sons of the fourth Lord are known to my generation of Lytteltons as the Great Uncles. In them the Lyttelton tradition was consolidated. The eldest was Charles, my grandfather, who, as the eighth Viscount Cobham, became head of the family. He died when I was a small boy and I only know him now as a disembodied head in the one family portrait which my father possesses. The head is disembodied because, due to what I suppose was carelessness on the part of the artist in mixing his paints, all the darker tints in the picture have turned pitch black. Although I never knew my grandfather there has always been something awe-inspiring about that floating head with its vague eyes, high nose and cheekbones and short, grey beard. Most distinguished of the brothers was Great Uncle Alfred, a man of magnificent appearance (but weren't they all?) who became Colonial Secretary under Arthur Balfour and played for England against Australia at cricket. Among all his other distinctions, he made cricket history in 1884, when he was wicket keeper in a Test Match under the captaincy of W.G. Grace. All the regular bowlers had been tried in succession without success, and at last, in desperation, W.G. Grace threw the ball to Great Uncle Alfred telling him to take off his pads and bowl. Great Uncle Alfred bowled under-arm lobs and skittled out the rest of the Australian side. More fuel to the legend. Then there was Great Uncle Neville, a soldier who rose to be Chief of the Imperial General Staff and Governor of the Chelsea Pensioners. I have heard it hinted that he was not a very good Chief of the Imperial General Staff and that it was perhaps a pity that when the German military chiefs were poring over maps of Europe and

turning their minds towards plans for military conquest their counterpart in England seemed to have nothing better to do than write letters to *The Times* about the lbw rule. However, these are questions for the adult mind. To the young it was sufficient that Great Uncle Nevvy was a Field Marshal with a huge military moustache and tier upon tier of medals. Great Uncle Arthur was Suffragan Bishop of Southampton and had a large white beard. Great Uncle Edward was a pillar of Education, becoming Headmaster first of Haileybury College, then of Eton.

The distinctions of the remaining great uncles are rather harder to define. Great Uncle Bob was a very indifferent solicitor, Great Uncle Spencer travelled a lot but did no work, except for a period as Mr Gladstone's private secretary, and Great Uncle Albert was a clergyman, so I am told, with the habit of bridging awkward gaps in the conversation by bursting nervously but rather loudly into song. 'And we, like sheep…' he would boom, stopping suddenly short and coughing noisily when he saw the heads around him jerk up in alarm, for all the world like startled sheep. Nobody ever heard him sing any more than those opening words, and it was rumoured unkindly that he used to turn for spiritual uplift to the index of the hymn book rather than to the hymns themselves, as a sort of short cut to eternal life. None the less, as a body they were a formidable and imposing array. All, without exception, were excellent cricketers, and the pages of *Wisden* are peppered with their names. In music and the arts their tastes were conservative and pronounced. None of them did very much in the executive line, although Great Uncle Edward was a member of an amateur glee singing quartet and Great Uncle Spencer had a rich bass voice. In their own circles they had quite a reputation as amateur music critics, although I have heard it suggested by an irreverent nephew that most of their pronouncements were relayed straight from the lips of Sir Hubert Parry. There is a story about Great Uncle Albert which leads me to think that he at least had his moments of honesty as a critic. He was a clergyman and at one time a missionary in South Africa. Just before he went out there he was taken by a female relative to hear Sir Hubert Parry give a private piano recital. Arriving late, he found himself steered into a seat only a few feet away from the open piano. After the first few crashing chords Great Uncle Albert stood up and set off through the assembled company in the direction of the door. There his female relative overtook him. 'Albert dear, where *are* you going?' 'Africa,' came the unruffled reply. 'Goodbye!' And he left.

Great Uncle Albert was an eccentric. He possessed that kind of eccentricity – a sort of excess of sanity – which can best be summed up in the words of the musical comedy song: 'Doing what comes naturally'. If a thing seemed to him a good thing to do at the time he did it. Once, on a railway station, finding the waiting-room seats uncomfortable, he lay full length on the floor with his head pillowed on his suitcase. As he was six foot three, broad-shouldered and had a large grey beard falling over his clerical dog-collar he attracted a certain amount of attention. A crowd of curious fellow passengers gathered in the doorway. Sensing their presence, Great Uncle Albert opened one eye and explained in a mellow, fluting voice: 'Not drunk – just tired.' Again, when he was in South Africa and about to make a long journey from Cape Town to Johannesburg, he dropped his watch at the last minute, and broke it; so he took the large ornamental clock off the mantelpiece and carried it with the rest of his baggage for several hundred miles across the South African Veldt.

Another of his peculiarities was an insatiable curiosity about public notices. He wanted to know why they had been put up and to him the obvious way of finding out was to disobey them. In his day, the escalators at Underground stations – new-fangled devices which had just come in – were so designed that one had to step off sideways on to the platform. At the bottom of each moving staircase, there was a large notice which said STEP OFF WITH THE RIGHT FOOT. When he first ventured on to the modern contraption, Great Uncle Albert read this notice from a distance and pondered on it throughout the downward journey. Why should the authorities have seen fit to issue such an arbitrary instruction? There must have been a reason, and he proposed to find it out. So when he got to the bottom, he turned to the right and stepped off deliberately with his left foot. The moving staircase carried his right foot on behind it so that when, by natural reflex action, he put that foot forward to complete the disembarkation, his legs were effectively tied in a knot. Momentum threw both temporarily useless limbs into the air and, spinning like a top, Great Uncle Albert was literally projected onto the platform, coming to rest at the feet of a group of waiting travellers whose amazement was heightened by the fact that he was a bearded bishop wearing frock-coat and gaiters.

On another occasion, when Great Uncle Albert stayed with Great Uncle Bob, he found a bathroom geyser with a notice in red letters warning users not to turn a particular tap on while the geyser was alight. Ever eager for knowledge, Great Uncle Albert turned the tap and blew all the windows out.

If there is any clue on the Lyttelton side to my unconventional musical ambition it lies in Great Uncle Albert's habit of doing what comes naturally. In some degree it is found in the next generation in the person of my father's brother, Richard. A prominent executive in the steel industry and manifestly sane from every point of view, Uncle Richard was known to have caused raised eyebrows by doing what to him seemed a perfectly logical thing. During the war when clothing became scarce he gave up wearing socks altogether, and travelled into the City on the Tube with a large area of naked skin showing below the bottom of his pinstripe trousers. I remember going to dinner with him once – a formal dressed-up affair. While I and several other guests were waiting in the porch to be let in we were intrigued by a curious rasping noise coming from inside. When the door was opened we found our host, in white tie and tails, sawing firewood in the hall.

There is very little in the musical history of the Lytteltons which explains why, after all these years, they should have produced a jazz trumpeter. The tradition for amateur music in its very mild form was carried on in my father's own generation. While at Cambridge my father himself learned the 'cello, but according to a contemporary report nobody got very much enjoyment out of it except himself. I doubt whether his other recreation – that of winning innumerable medals for Putting the Weight – did much to enhance his touch.

The 'cello seems to have been a popular instrument among amateurs towards the end of the last century. My mother's father, in whose upstairs lavatory I began my life as a trumpeter, was also a keen 'cellist. To his small grandchildren he was a terrifying figure, although my mother tells me that his fierceness had mellowed considerably by the time we came to know him. As a type I suppose one could class him as a peppery colonel with a touch of the stern Victorian father thrown in. But this gives a false picture of him because it neglects a robust, almost childish, sense of humour which was one of his most attractive features. Rubber fruit which squeaked, joke cushions which made rude noises when you sat on them – these novelties were absolutely made for him. I can remember my mother once persuading me to put a squeaking rubber apple in the fruit bowl at lunch. Babraham Hall lunches were, for us children, formidable affairs with an army of footmen and maids, under the generalship of the head butler, padding round with an endless succession of courses. The children used to sit through the meal in apprehensive silence, to the eventual fury of my grandfather, who would explode from time to time with an impatient: 'Why don't you say something?' Having been persuaded by my mother to put the joke apple in the fruit bowl against my better judgement, I spent the meal in a fever of apprehension. But she was right: it was the success of the week. It was all my grandmother could do to prevent him going to a Council Meeting in Cambridge with it secreted under his waistcoat so that it would let out a shrill bleat when he bowed to the Mayor. He was an odd mixture of martinet and rebel. There came a time towards the end of his life when a number of his friends passed away in quick succession. Each time, my grandmother suggested that he ought perhaps to go to the funeral, but he made some excuse. Eventually a close relative died. 'Of course you will be going to the funeral this time, dear?' He banged his fist down on the breakfast table: 'I really cannot go to all these funerals!'

His amateur 'cello playing was something of an ordeal for his daughters, who were ordered in rotation to accompany him on the piano. All mistakes on his part were angrily blamed on them and they knew better than to argue. He put a lot of feeling into his playing, striking a pose like that of Madame Suggia in the Augustus John painting, and breathing fiercely through his bristly white moustache just like one of the old bulls on his farm. As far as I remember, his actual performance was poor, but he had fun.

I have skimmed rather lightly over my family history for, to tell the truth, it is not a subject to which I have ever given much study. To explore fully the whole Lyttelton family on one side and Adeane family on the other would be a life's work. If I have stressed the examples of eccentricity and non-conformity, it is because in them I find the only clues to the situation in which I find myself.

My Father

There's a subtle distinction between what you remember about your father and what you have learned. I know that George Lyttelton was a distinguished and inspired teacher of English literature at Eton, because many people, in all walks of life, who feel that he opened their eyes and ears to Shakespeare and Milton and Dickens have told me so. He wrote lengthy and superb letters to a vast number of recipients, contributed cricket reports to *The Times* and composed (in longhand and with laborious care) quite a number of articles, papers and essays which were published. He could not have been a journalist – it took him days to polish and rephrase a thousand-word piece in his elegant (and painstakingly-acquired) handwriting. His friends often tried to goad him into writing a book. I remember him once gnashing his teeth with genuine rage (distinguishable from the petrifying but often simulated fury which we knew as children) at the implication that he shied from authorship because of laziness. 'You blithering idiots!' he cried at the world at large, 'Does it not occur to you that I might not *want* to write a book?'

The memories I have of G.W.L. are mostly lighthearted if not actually frivolous. In the family circle his sense of fun went back beyond the schoolboy stage to a sort of nursery innocence. He was scrupulous in not uttering rude words, even of a mild lavatorial kind, in the hearing of my mother and sisters. One morning at the time of the Korean War, he was reading his *Times* at the breakfast table when he was suddenly overtaken by convulsions. Pressed from all sides to share the joke, he resolutely refused until at last he agreed to write it on a piece of paper for my eyes alone. The note, carefully folded several times and passed down the table with much adjuration to secrecy, read 'THE SOUTH KOREAN DEPUTY PRIME MINISTER'S NAME IS MR BUM SUK LEE'.

At meals, especially when all the family were together on holiday, he was by any nursery standards badly behaved. I'm talking now of when he was about fifty and the oldest of us were just entering our teens. One might have expected a revered schoolmaster of awesome repute to have brought a certain restrained dignity to the dinner-table. One of his favourite games, in which everyone but my mother joined enthusiastically, was to beat a rhythmic tattoo in 6/8 time on the table – da-dum da-dum, da-di-di-di-dum – starting very stealthily and then getting louder and louder until the cutlery and glasses jumped about. If asked to pass anything like a bread roll or an orange, he would ask 'Tunnicliffe or Denton?' and withhold it until he got an answer. This was a Lyttelton family joke. Tunnicliffe and Denton were cricketers, one famous for his slip-catches, the other renowned for his work in the deep-field. I don't recall which was which, but if you were lucky enough to nominate the deep-fielder, the object would be lobbed over gently. The wrong choice brought it thudding into your chest or, more often, ricocheting round the room.

I should say here that outbreaks like this were strictly rationed and offset at other times by a profound, but no less entertaining, pessimism. In times of uncertainty, this bordered on the masochistic. Any suggestion that things might get better next year met with the cavernously gloomy response '…if there *is* a next year!'. He had little fragments of song which would suddenly pop up during lulls in the conversation – one of the jolliest began 'Born one day when his mother was away…' and ended 'No wonder Little Billy Blunder went stark, staring mad!' More often he would intone, in a sepulchral voice, a sombre ditty that went – 'Days and moments quickly flying...blend the living with the dead...soon will you and I be lying...each within his narrow bed.' He didn't half liven up Sunday dinner!

It may be that my own invincible optimism derives from a youthful observation that few, if any, of his gloomy prognostications ever came to the sort of fulfilment that he expected. 'I suppose you all realize', he announced one lunchtime in the late 'thirties, 'that in five years' time I shall be unable to move a muscle, with the possible exception of my eyeballs.' He was in his middle fifties then, and despite a rheumatic disease which slowed him up a bit, he remained active enough to fall out of a tree at sixty-seven, get knocked off his bike by a careless motorcyclist at seventy-two and be jolted off the top of a bus when not far short of eighty. Whenever we talked of doing something 'next year' he would add in a voice of doom '...if there *is* a next year'. Yet the years came and went without one, so far as I recollect, ever being cancelled.

Short of a recurrence of the Flood, the thing he dreaded most was a Run On The Pound. We had an Impending Financial Crisis in our house long before anyone else even began to suspect that there was something wrong, and I grew up in the belief that the fall of a couple of notches in the exchange rate of the pound brought the workhouse several streets nearer. Today I can look back with equanimity on a succession of runs on the pound which amount to nothing less than monetary diarrhoea, and the only time it ever had a noticeable affect on me was when a fee contracted in Deutschmarks for an engagement in Germany suddenly inflated behind my back.

It would be grotesque to use the word 'pig' in respect of one as sensitive and, despite his huge frame, graceful as my father. But I suppose he was, by today's stern standards, a male chauvinist. In the old Eton days there were servants. When he and my mother moved to Suffolk after his retirement, he quite enjoyed doing not the actual washing-up but the drying-up afterwards. He took it very seriously, completely reorganizing the box in which the knives and forks were kept and making, we thought, rather a fuss if someone put a small fork where a large fork should go.

He was no cook. By this I mean not that he didn't cook well, but

G.W.L. invents an OATCAKE

that he didn't cook *anything*. From the cradle, his upbringing was founded on one unshakeble article of faith – that God would provide, not only food, but someone to cook it. Only once in his life did he have reason to doubt this. It was after they moved to Suffolk, where my mother cooked breakfast and supper and a daily help took care of the midday meal. Once my mother went away on a short visit without him, having carefully arranged things so that he would only have to get himself breakfast. As he was quite happy with nothing more than a bowl of porridge, there seemed to be no problem. Before she went, she wrote out, in words of one syllable, instructions on how to make overnight porridge – how much oatmeal and water to put in the casserole, which oven to leave it in till morning.

When he came to interpret these instructions, a thought occurred to him. What possible reason could there be, other than a characteristically feminine awe of convention, for making the porridge in a casserole and then decanting it into a soup plate? Chuckling, no doubt, at the illogicality of women and their capacity for making work, he put a handful of oats straight into the soup plate, added water and put it uncovered into the oven. Next morning, he discovered that he had invented an oatcake – no delicacy, it must be admitted, but compact and quite suitable as hard, not to say indestructible, rations for a polar expedition.

When I was young, one of the high spots of our family life involved helping my father make the Cider Cup.

As Housemaster at Eton, one of his duties was to entertain a host of parents on the Fourth of June, a day of festivity in honour of Henry VI, Our Founder. Feeding the throng was no problem – we had a cook who churned out chicken-in-aspic by the ton. But Father took upon himself the onus of generating a festive spirit without too great a strain on the budget.

The answer was Cider Cup, a beverage which looks rather dull in the recipe books but which offers almost unlimited scope for improvisation. Huge earthenware vessels were trundled out, fruit was sliced, quart bottles of cider were opened, soda siphons were lined up.

Freud no doubt had a word for what ensued, but 'sploshing' is the one that comes most readily to mind. A squad of hit-men on a 'rubbing out' operation can scarcely have looked more aggressively zealous than the Lyttelton Gang when, after an orgy of sploshing from the cider flagons, we opened up with soda siphons fired from the hip. The result was a fairly innocuous brew but, after all the heady excitement of concocting it, the permitted tumblerful of the stuff never failed to give me, at eleven or twelve years old, quite a frisky buzz.

I don't know what secret ingredient it was that sent his guests out into the playing fields of Eton with such silly grins. But I did notice that he wasn't too careful with the ash from his pipe.

When it came to food, he was a man of simple tastes, although my mother always regarded with deep scepticism his oft-repeated avowal that 'bread and cheese will do me perfectly well'. She noted that whenever she provided some alternative to bread and cheese – a steak and kidney pie, say, with two veg and apple pie with thick cream to follow – he attacked it with all the enthusiasm of a man who has just been rescued after six months on a barren island. But it's true to say that he didn't go very much for rich and alcoholic feasting. I remember the day he came back from having lunch with a relation who was a tycoon of global, if not cosmic, influence. He always dreaded these occasions, being a man of measured habits whose curriculum made no allowances for the crippling midday meal or the recuperative afternoon nap.

On the day in question, he was immensely relieved when the tycoon, pleading pressure of appointments on which, it appeared, the future of the world hung, announced at the outset that they would have to eat a truncated meal in his office instead of going out. Waving aside the apologies with genuine unconcern, my father relaxed in the comforting expectation of a cheese sandwich – with some pickle, perhaps – brought in by a panting office-boy.

Some minutes later, an official looking disturbingly like a butler insinuated himself into the room and passed to the captain of industry a murmured message. To my father eavesdropping uneasily on the other side of the huge executive desk, it seemed to convey the dreaded information that luncheon was served. Gliding across the opulent carpet, the official then flung open two sleekly-panelled doors to reveal, in the adjoining room, a vast boardroom table bow-legged under the weight of food. To use my father's own awe-struck words, there were acres of caviar, smoked salmon, game pie and mousse, picketed by magnums of champagne and decanters of port. That night, home again, he sat in his armchair trying to read, breathing more heavily than usual and occasionally giving a convulsive shudder at the thought of what he would have had to put away had not the critical state of international high finance demanded a snack in the office.

As the second son of a ninth viscount, he had considerable experience of meals in stately homes. When I look back myself to childhood holidays spent with innumerable cousins at Babraham Hall or Longford Castle, my first memory is of sitting at a huge dining-room table at lunch, watching with some awe as a human conveyor belt of maids and footmen brought course after course to the table. I can see my father sitting opposite, massively polite but revealing mounting impatience through the movement of his eyebrows. They were superb eyebrows – bristling reddish antennae set at a downward-sloping angle, capable of beetling prodigiously but at their most eloquent when they began moving up his huge brow through degrees ranging from surprise to utter disbelief at the folly of mankind.

He always liked to be out and about on holidays and, in the country, was a great one for lopping, sawing and otherwise maiming trees. As lunch dragged on towards three o'clock with no apparent slackening in the flow of food to the table, the eyebrows would reach full stretch as though about to take off and go flapping away through the window in an independent bid for freedom. On one memorable occasion he took direct action, though he always protested afterwards that it was an accident. Near the end of one gastronomic marathon, a colossal bunch of grapes was carried round, its great weight supported by a curved silver bracket from which also hung a pair of embossed scissors. When it reached him on its imperial passage round the table, he took the scissors and applied them with all the delicate precision of an operating surgeon to one of the stalks. As it happens, it was the main stalk, and with one snip the whole massive bunch fell to the floor with a moist thud, leaving three or four grapes suspended rather foolishly from the bracket. In the ensuing confusion, with his family and nephews and nieces unable to contain themselves, a motion to adjourn the meal was carried without a vote.

I have one curious trait which I believe to be inherited from my father and which may explain his lack of stamina at formal affairs. Whenever ten or more people are gathered together in one room, chattering away like broiler-fowl at feeding-time, I go deaf. It is as if the input channels of my ears become overloaded and automatically cut out as a precaution against short-circuiting and bursting into flames. For me, social convocations for drinks or meals turn, when warmed up and under way, into surrealistic happenings in which lips move, tongues wag, eyebrows plunge and soar but nothing that could remotely be described as human speech reaches me.

At family gatherings, when questions, answers, anecdotes and reminiscences were crossing at all angles like a conversational Crewe Junction, my father often betrayed the symptoms. His face would assume a bland, withdrawn expression and he would start talking to the dog, a sure sign that, for the moment, human intercourse had become impracticable. On one startling occasion, he was brought back into the conversation by a question about the weather they had been having in East Anglia. 'Mrs who?' was his discouraging response.

I remember him telling me once about an MCC lunch which he attended with his cousin and great friend, Father Ted Talbot of the Mirfield Brotherhood of the Resurrection. My father often made after-dinner speeches at the MCC. All we at home knew of the events was when he returned with his breast pocket stuffed with cigars which he had scooped with his great shovel of a hand out of the box that circulated at the end of the meal. He rarely smoked them himself, but they came in handy for guests. At the lunch in question, he and Ted Talbot sat next to each other. Halfway through the meal, he bellowed into the reverend's ear that he had never in his life heard such a hubbub of conversation. Father Talbot in turn put his mouth to my father's ear and suggested that they should try a simple experiment. If they burst into song, how long would it be before they were detected? Thereupon the two of them, towering, bespectacled schoolmaster and craggy, befrocked cleric, began to sing, 'O God, Our Help In Ages Past…', *mezzo forte* and *con spirito*. They got through three verses quite unnoticed before they collapsed in unseemly giggles.

Most of the enduring things I learnt from my father were by example rather than precept. His 'serious talk' with me as I approached puberty lingers in my mind solely for its almost startling brevity. He was standing in the traditional position with his back to the fireplace and he uttered the injunction in a strong, resonant voice with a stern lowering of the massive eyebrows, as if to make up in portentousness what his message lacked in length and detail. 'Eschew evil!' he boomed, then gave me a heavy paternal bang on the shoulder and left the room, humming to himself.

Nanny Viggers

I can still relive every frustrating second of the time when I didn't see a runaway horse. We were staying with my grandparents in Cambridgeshire, and at the end of one of the long gravel drives which radiated from Babraham Hall, I was just emerging, strapped in a push-chair amidst an entourage of nannies and nurserymaids, into the main road when somebody shouted, 'It's a runaway horse!' The nurserymaid in control of my push-chair was a quick thinker, damn her, and she shoved me immediately out of harm's way – which happened to be deep into a rhododendron bush, face foremost. There I was, strapped and impotent in the darkness of a bush while the most exciting moment ever to happen in five years of sheltered existence came and went in a clatter of hooves and confusion of shouts. What made it infinitely worse was that my older sister, who at that age represented everything in life that had to be fought and outwitted, saw it all.

When I think back to childhood at home, my mind alights, for no obvious reason, on the day that fairies didn't appear at the bottom of our garden. My father took over a boys' House at Eton when I was four, and from that time until the end of the war, 'home' was a great barrack of a place called Warre House, at the end of Common Lane. Warre House was too big to recall in its entirety. Indeed, there were some parts of it that I never saw. To us, the 'boys' side' was out of bounds, and I remember it only as a clatter of boots and hubbub of shouts by day, and, by night, as a delirium of voices, from piping treble through cracked yodel to mature baritone, which maintained a dusk chorus outside my bedroom window as I went to sleep. The private side of the house was centred mainly around the well of a broad, green-carpeted staircase which stratified it into landings. My parents worked on the prevailing upper/middle class principle that if you bred a family of five or six children and added a nurserymaid to look after the nanny and a 'daily' to look after everyone, you had a self-contained unit which, given suitably remote *lebensraum*, could safely be left to its own devices. So the top landing was our territory – and by 'us' I mean my older sister, myself and three other sisters who joined the cast at regular intervals. I have a dim recollection of ladies in large hats being brought up the last flight of stairs to see us, saying 'There they are!' as they first perceived us peering like caged beasts through the banisters.

The second landing is chiefly associated in my mind with my father. We didn't see much of him as small children, except on holidays. His study was on the second landing, a huge room full of books – from wall to ceiling on shelves, stacked in piles on every flat surface and moving like an invading army across the floor. Along the same landing, next to their bedroom, was his dressing-room, a place of some importance in our lives since the first step towards emancipation from nanny's rule was being allowed to have a bath downstairs in the dressing-room. This room I associate most closely with my father. It had a flowered carpet, a well-stacked bookshelf at one end, golf clubs and a cricket bat in the corner of the bookshelf, golf balls and tees, and, for no reason I ever discovered, a large bottle of vinegar on the huge mantelpiece, photos of old school and university friends, mostly in athletic postures, everywhere and, on the dressing table under a mirror on the wall, a bookrest on a pedestal so that he could read and memorize poetry while he shaved. There was also a distinctive bottle of hair-cream, of a brand to which he remained faithful throughout his life, which smelt 'like Father' and which, as I discovered after some furtive experiment, flattened one's hair back in congealed strands, solid as wire, and gave one a very grown-up look. The bath was the biggest in the world, and a sort of ottoman with a cork top had to be put up against it to enable us to climb in.

If the second landing was established in my mind as my father's territory, then the ground floor, with its long drawing-room leading off the hall, belonged to my mother. As very small children, we used to be brought down after tea to the drawing-room to spend an hour with my mother. It was an hour spent in reading aloud or in hobbies. My lasting memory of that drawing-room is not of the elegant furniture, the silver ornaments, the flowers, the piano, the big mantelpiece with the two blue-and-gold vases and the ornate gilt clock. It is of my mother sitting on the rug in front of the hearth, with her legs splayed out from the knee in a sort of inside-out Yoga posture like a capital W, surrounded by the debris of some hobby – rug-making, stuffing home-made toys, painting lampshades, framing her own oil-paintings, making things out of shells, pebbles or matchboxes or cutting out clothes for fancy dress or theatricals. When Scotty's School put on a performance of *A Midsummer Night's Dream*, my mother was for weeks in position on the hearthrug, mouth full of needles and thread and inundated to the waist with flimsy material of arboreal green.

Scotty's School was our one outpost on the ground floor. In a big room which we knew as 'the schoolroom' long after we grew up, a Miss Scott ran a kindergarten to which children came not only from other Eton families, but also from far afield in Datchet and Windsor. Scotty was a lady of tense nervous energy, betrayed by a permanent furrow above the sharp nose. She had amazing teeth, of proportions which would have been beyond a joke in a Christmas stocking, and she wore snakeskin shoes. She taught us the alphabet, numbers, the days of the week, the months of the year and singing. And she produced *A Midsummer Night's Dream* one midsummer's day on the lawn at Warre House. Only isolated facts about this production stay in my mind. Titania was to have been played by Celia Spurling, a dazzling beauty from Datchet who fell through the roof of a greenhouse shortly before the big day and had to withdraw, a mass of cuts and bruises. So Suzanne Cook, a dazzling beauty from Windsor, stepped into the part. Joanie Allington, a daughter of the Headmaster and a distant cousin of mine, played a rather watery Oberon. She was a big girl of ruddy complexion who relieved the very earliest signs of tension by bursting into tears. A girl called Miriam played Bottom, a piece of casting which seemed to us all eminently just. As an inhibited actor, I was cast wisely as Snug the Joiner, a modest part from which I can still recall one line. It was 'What say you, Bottom?' – a thoughtless line to give a shy boy of six.

I don't know if the production was good or bad, if the assembled parents sitting round the lawn on canvas chairs applauded satisfactorily, if I remembered my lines or dried up when the cue came for 'What say you, Bottom?'. But in the middle of this vagueness, one moment stands out clearly, in the recollection of which I can smell the hay lying in the big field that stretched out beyond the lawn, count the red berries on the evergreen bush that punctuated a wall running beside the 'stage' and feel the texture of the jerkin of arboreal green which my mother made, with a zig-zag hem laboriously scissored round the bottom. It was a moment of supreme insignificance. As producer-cum-prompter, Scotty was in position behind a bush, stage left. From this point of supposed concealment, her forceful contralto voice reinforced the singing of the choruses, some of which had been imported from other

Shakespeare plays to give the fairies something to do other than just run about trailing muslin. Behind another, larger bush, a group of fairies was supposed, at some stage, to trip out daintily, singing the familiar setting of 'Where the bee sucks, there suck I'. My younger sister – I had only two at the time – had rehearsed this song endlessly in the nursery, under the supervision of Nanny Viggers, who was shaped like a cottage loaf, wore one of those black shiny nanny's hats which we always believed were made of squashed beetles, and was at this moment in time watching the performance with the nurserymaid at a respectful distance from the mothers. For some completely inexplicable reason, the juxtaposition of the syllables in the line 'Where the bee sucks, there suck I' struck us children as uproariously funny. We had only to sing it, to its naïve little tune, for life to be temporarily suspended by helpless giggles. Apparently, this weakness was infectious. For when the cue came for the appearance of the fairies, singing prettily, from behind their bush, nothing was seen or heard except a few squeaks and Scotty's solo contralto. A second start was equally unproductive. And then there was Scotty, in full view of the audience, standing over the fairies' bush, brow furrowed, teeth akimbo, uttering the peaceful words 'Where the bee sucks, there suck I' as though they were a trumpet call to battle. Who knows what evocative ingredient imprinted the scene on my mind? The smell of hessian scenery, perhaps, or the frail melody of that song. Or the unexpected appearance of snakeskin shoes in 'a wood near Athens'.

My mother began to take an interest in my artistic and musical activities. Being a proficient amateur artist herself, she had high hopes of me in that direction, and plied me with drawing books and coloured chalks almost as soon as my eyes began to focus. She preserved a collection of my earliest work, and claims that it shows promise of a flair for comic art which has since been fulfilled. I have studied the drawings carefully, and they seem to me curiously undistinguished even for a child of two. There is one lifelike study of a particularly shapeless potato which, with childish impudence, I had boldly entitled MAN. Another, called LADY, is obviously the same potato from a different angle. Mothers are never very sound critics. Nor, in the old days, were nannies.

It was Nanny Viggers who first 'discovered' me as a musical prodigy by spreading it about the Playing Fields that, at the age of three and a half, I had picked out 'The Whistler and His Dog' on the dulcimer. The dulcimer was my very first musical instrument – a collection of graduated metal plates mounted in a scale on wood and played with two little mallets like a xylophone. Oddly enough, this early musical performance is one of the few childhood memories which have stuck in my head. I fancy I remember exactly where and how I was sitting, up in the Warre House nursery, when I banged out what Nanny Viggers took to be an accurate rendering of 'The Whistler'. I was hammering away quite happily in accompaniment to the nursery gramophone when I heard her tell the nurserymaid in a loud whisper, 'Listen! He's picking it out perfectly!' I must have had a better ear for music at three and a half than Nanny Viggers had at fifty, because I was quite well aware that she was wrong. I doubt if I could pick out 'The Whistler and His Dog' on a dulcimer today without a bit of private rehearsal first, and the most I was doing then was just following the direction of the tune without regard to detail. I have been chary of critics ever since.

-- Pamela Adeane (she wasn't Lyttelton then)

H.L.'s mother.

The dulcimer whetted my appetite for musical instruments and I began to demand them every Christmas. None of them lasted very long, but on each one I managed to make a little more musical progress.

My first 'real' instrument was a banjolele, a hybrid affair looking like a banjo and sounding like a ukelele. I think it was a popular minstrel show on the radio which put the idea into my head. My mother finally bought me the instrument in exchange for my tonsils, which were taken from me when I was seven. I had the operation in a nursing home in London, occupying a private ward in solitary state. When I came round from the anaesthetic, the first thing I did was to cast a bleary glance under the bedside table. And there sure enough was the promised banjolele, wrapped up in brown paper and string. I got into such a wild state of excitement that it was thought best to postpone the opening of the parcel until I had regained my strength after the operation. But after a few tantalizing days I could wait no longer and hauled the package up on to the bed.

Inside, the banjolele was fastened away in a black mock-leather case. I remember that case with affection. It had a peculiar smell which I can recall to this day in bouts of nostalgia. I have quite a collection of memorable smells stored away in my head, and the most evocative of them are those which belonged to musical-instrument cases, and which I associate with the agonizing excitement of new possession. There is the delicate scent of the rosewood box holding my first mouth-organ; the pungent aroma of the imitation plush in which my streamlined 'Manhattan' trumpet nestled; the deliciously dry, horsey smell of the canvas holdall in which my first drum arrived; and the whiff of black mock-leather which cut through all the clinical smells of the sick room and sent my temperature soaring with blissful anticipation. Unfortunately I can remember rather less about the banjolele itself. The minstrel team on the radio had misled me, and the instrument turned out to be not up my street. True, I enjoyed gazing at it as I lay in my nursing home bed, imagining the wonderful sounds which I should soon be coaxing from it. But when I returned home and began lessons, the magic went. A faded woman with a faded mandolin festooned with faded ribbons came down from Windsor to teach me, and we sat for hours a day picking away on the drawing-room sofa. It all seemed so remote from the rollicking noises which I had heard over the radio that I soon lost heart, and the instrument disappeared into a cupboard in its black mock-leather case, to be later sold.

After nursery rhymes and the classical selections provided by our musical box, the first music which really attracted me was military band music. With the Guards stationed at Windsor and the Eton Officers' Training Corps constantly marching up and down behind a band, I heard plenty of it. When I was five, the boys in my father's House presented me with a miniature OTC uniform – mulberry-coloured jacket and knickerbockers, peaked cap and small puttees. I was never much interested in the military significance of my new uniform, and whenever I went out in it with Nanny Viggers to watch an OTC parade, I always identified myself with the band.

As soon as I was liberated from the perpetual custody of Nanny or nurserymaid, I began to make regular visits to Windsor to follow the Changing of the Guard. But while other small boys whooped and frolicked round the marching troops with toy swords and rifles, I concentrated on the band. It became a regular routine for me to cycle up to Victoria Barracks at 10.15 every morning and accompany the Guard on foot up to Windsor Castle and back. Normally, the parade was led by the Battalion band of drums and fifes, but when the Royal Family were in residence, the full Regimental Band came down from London and we had the luxury of two bands playing alternately. I always made these excursions on my own – none of my sisters were interested, and being of a fundamentally unsociable disposition, I did nothing to encourage my local playmates to come with me. They were a hearty, bumptious lot, and they would only have distracted me.

As it was, I began to acquire quite a specialized knowledge of marching music. When the band took time off, during the formalities of Changing the Guard, to indulge in excerpts from the popular classics, my interest died instantly. I was, and still am, something of a purist when it comes to military bands. To my mind they exist for one purpose only – to accompany troops on the march with rousing music. When they start tinkering about with Rossini overtures and extracts from Gilbert and Sullivan, they are an abomination. I can't see why military bands make such persistent efforts to better themselves. Within their limitations, and in the hands of the best march composers like Sousa and Alford, military marches have a value outside the purely functional one of keeping the troops in step. One of the few things which reconciled me to army life during the war was the opportunity for marching along behind a band and the thrill of responding, in the increased jauntiness of step and uplift of spirit, to the music of masterpieces like 'On the Quarterdeck', 'The Standard of St George' and 'The Thin Red Line'. On my treks to

Victoria Barracks, I came to know the characteristic form of the modern military march.

I suspect that it was the American John Philip Sousa who first consolidated this march form. Of his enormous output of marches, most conform to it rigidly. And no doubt it was through Sousa's influence that the form is present in some early ragtime pieces and cakewalks, and in the first jazz music in New Orleans. (James Scott's 'Grace and Beauty', Charles Daniels's 'Hiawatha' and Abe Holzmann's 'Smokey Mokes' are all good examples of the march influence in ragtime and cakewalk music.) The repertoire of New Orleans jazz is full of tunes in march form, and it's difficult nowadays to tell which are fresh compositions and which were taken over lock, stock and barrel from existing marches and rehashed by the street parade musicians in New Orleans. The layout of tunes like 'High Society', 'Fidgetty Feet', 'Chattanooga Stomp', 'South Rampart Street Parade', 'Buddy's Habits' and, among Jelly Roll Morton's compositions, 'King Porter Stomp' and 'Frog-I-More Rag' can be compared with the summary I have given above without showing very much divergence. There is plenty of room for research into the march influence on early jazz material. Perhaps I will undertake it one day, but not here. I have mentioned it in this context because it explains, to my satisfaction, why, when I became attracted to jazz, I felt a special warmth – of nostalgia, perhaps – towards the old jazz with its march flavour.

Meanwhile, I was persevering with my music 'studies', making very much more progress on my own than I did at music lessons. At music lessons, I was a failure. Others since Scotty have tried to teach me the piano, but no one has succeeded in steering me past a particularly knotty piece called 'The Jolly Farmer'. I hated that Jolly

Farmer with a bitter hatred, and still do. A man who causes so much human suffering has no right to be jolly.

As a result of my failure at piano lessons, I have never learnt to read music properly. I know the position of all the notes on the written stave, and given an hour or two and absolute silence, I can sort them all out. But I can no more sight-read than speak Russian. Once when I was a schoolboy, I sought to impress my friends by going to symphony concerts armed with miniature scores. I kept this up for some time without being found out, but only by subterfuge. Whenever I got lost, which was usually somewhere about page three, I would wait until the orchestra came to a particularly loud and busy passage, and would then rustle through my score until I found the dots beginning to lie thick on the page. Then I knew I was in the right area, and it only needed some landmark like a horn solo or a rapid tattoo on the drums for me to be able to plot my position exactly. In this way, I almost always avoided the embarrassment of arriving at the end of the score one whole movement ahead of the orchestra, with no more pages to turn and my friends eyeing me suspiciously.

In jazz, I have never found the inability to read music at sight more than an occasional inconvenience. Jazz is an aural tradition depending mainly on impromptu performance. Themes are learnt by ear and then given extempore variations. And furthermore, the music has qualities of tone and inflection which cannot be conveyed on paper. A transcription of a trumpet solo by Louis Armstrong, however detailed, cannot convey any idea of the actual performance on record. And no orchestral trumpeter reading it off could bring it to life, because so much of its quality lies in the originator's personal tone and sense of timing. The same goes for band performances. The jazz tradition has been spread in the past mainly through the medium of gramophone records. Written music is used only as a convenience, for conveying and 'fixing' musical ideas and for outlining arrangements. And even in this it is not essential – there are alternative methods which are just as practical.

I can understand this attitude perfectly. It must be extremely galling for someone who has spent much time and energy learning the complex technicalities of European conservatory music to see people earning money and acclaim quite comfortably without it. But I have absolutely no sympathy with the proposition that music is a sort of exclusive club open only to those who pass difficult initiation tests. The best comment on the subject of reading music was made in the 'twenties by a jazz band leader who was ordered by a nightclub proprietor to cut out the jazz and stick to written arrangements. 'Heck!' he said. 'What do we do if the lights go out?'

I was lucky as a child, because I always had plenty of opportunity to play instruments and enjoy myself with music without too much adult interference. The nursery was remote enough from the grown-ups' rooms to allow me to blow and bang away to my heart's content, and Nanny Viggers was tolerant, in the knowledge that she would gain considerable kudos in the Playing Fields if she could point to one of her charges as a musical prodigy. So by the time I was subjected at a ridiculously early age to Miss Scott's formal music lessons, I had already discovered that music was fun. And Scotty's efforts to prove, with her five-finger exercises and sight-reading tests, that it really was a serious business calling for endurance and drudgery failed to scare me off. The only concrete result of my music lessons was that they instilled in me such a dislike for all the academic hocus pocus that, when I reached an age when I could have taken the technicalities in my stride (and I would put that at any age between twelve and eighteen), I avoided them like the plague. The result, as I have said, has caused me some inconvenience. But looking back, I would sooner have it this way than the other way around. I can at least keep on playing when the lights go out.

In my explorations in the musical-instrument field, I was led eventually to the drum, as a direct result of my passion for martial music. My father's brother, the Reverend Caryl Lyttelton, had a living in the East End of London. And seeing my enthusiasm for military bands, he managed to procure for me an old discarded side-drum from one of the local Boys' Brigades. I had picked up a few rudiments from watching the drummers at Windsor, and soon I had made enough headway to warrant proper lessons. After some enquiries, my mother ran to ground an ex-Coldstream Guards drum-major who lived in Windsor and gave tuition. I remember the day Mr Glass came to the house for an interview. He was a man of rather forbidding appearance, having been disfigured in the First War by a bullet wound in the mouth which gave him a very exaggerated hare lip. When my mother said tentatively that I had managed to pick up quite a lot on my own, his answer was brisk. 'Never mind,' he said, 'we'll soon unlearn him all that.'

Mr Glass was a fine teacher, and we became great pals. It says a lot for his teaching methods that he had me practising for hours a day at exercises which, for sheer tedium, beat anything I had ever suffered at the piano. The basis of all drumming is the roll, a beat which most people recognize as the preliminary to 'God Save the Queen'. The early stages of the roll are learned by hitting the drum twice with each stick in an exercise described phonetically as 'Daddy-Mummy'. I daddy-mummied religiously for hours a day, and it is a further tribute to my parents' tolerance in these matters that I didn't daddy-mummy them out of their senses. Mr Glass believed, with a sure instinct, in the carrot-in-front-of-the-nose technique when it came to teaching me. Each lesson was divided into two periods. The first was occupied with hard practice on the technical side. The second was set aside for practical application. I had quite a collection of marches on gramophone records, and we used to put these on and drum away together just for the fun of it.

Mr Glass was a member of various amateur orchestras in Windsor, and once he allowed me to sit next to him in the orchestra pit at a performance of *The Mikado* by a Windsor company. Mr Glass sat in the middle of an enormous array of assorted instruments – kettle drums, bells, xylophone, and goodness knows what. I sat beside him, enormously impressed and hoping that everyone in the theatre could see me. I didn't see much of *The Mikado* – from the orchestra pit, only a small portion of the stage was visible and even then one had to lean forward uncomfortably. I tried this at first, but I leaned too far and got a crack on the head from the butt end of a bass trombone as the player brought it up to play. So I satisfied myself with watching Mr Glass in action. When the time came for 'God Save the King' he handed me the sticks and said, 'Go on – roll 'em up!' There was no time for argument, so roll 'em up I did until my wrists ached. After that I went home with a bump on my head from the trombone and a feeling of pride in having given my first public performance.

At the age of nine, my education took a further step and I went to Sunningdale Preparatory School. I have no lurid tales to tell of my life at Preparatory School. There were no sadistic masters, no roastings over the study fire by school bullies, nothing, in fact, but what I take to be an average, normal private-school life. Of course we had our legends, which were quickly passed back home through the medium of the Sunday letter. One of the masters used to allow himself the mild luxury of a glass of stout every day at lunch in the communal dining room. Within no time he was labelled 'the Master Who is Drunk in Class'. Then there was 'the Oldest Master in England', 'the Best Latin Master in Europe' and, best of all, 'the Tallest Master in the World'. We also clung to a romantic belief that the head gardener, whose name was Smith, was the same Smith who had been our Headmaster's predecessor, and we wove elaborate stories about the 'Headmaster Who Became the Head Gardener'. When I went to Sunningdale I was allowed to take Mr Glass with me, since there was no drum teacher on the staff. He made the eight-mile journey from Windsor twice a week to give me drum lessons. At first there was very little opportunity of doing any drumming outside of these lessons. The Headmaster when I first went to the School was Mr Crabtree, a bluff, rubicund, choleric old man with a rheumatic limp and a volatile temper. He was the conventional type of Headmaster, without any very unusual ideas on education. On the disciplinary side he wielded the cane ferociously, but there was plenty of warmth and understanding in his dealings with the boys. When he read aloud to us in the evenings, it was from the established classics. (I still remember his terrifying impersonation of Fagin in *Oliver Twist*.) And his direction of the end-of-term concerts followed the time-honoured private-school pattern. We had no school band of any sort, and the musical items consisted of solos and duets by the star instrumentalists and singers, and madrigals for the choir. Not much scope for drumming.

But after a year or so, Mr Crabtree retired and was succeeded by Mr

Fox. Mr Fox had several strong views of his own about the recreational activities of the boys in his care, and they were not by any means conventional. While keeping up the Dickens and Shakespeare readings, he leavened them with lighter stuff from contemporary literature. He also revolutionized the School Concerts, introducing the principle that they should not be just showcases for the star turns, but ambitious entertainments in which every boy in the school should play some part. Individual performers outside of the normal musical and scholastic run were encouraged to contribute, and that was where I and my drums came in. In my first concert under Mr Fox's direction I played the drum in a piece called the 'Parade of the Tin Soldiers', with a chorus of boys doing toy soldier drill on either side of me. My debut almost ended disastrously. A few minutes before the tin soldiers were due to go on I lost my drumsticks. I searched in a panic but could not find them anywhere. When I finally appeared on the stage I was playing my drum with two fluted laths hurriedly cut by the School carpenter. They got me through all right, but I was glad that Mr Glass had been unable to come.

After this I appeared often in the school concerts, not always in a musical capacity. In the drawing class I had already shown a leaning towards caricature, and so I was put on the stage as a lighting caricaturist. At that time the Lightning Caricature act was very popular in the music hall. It consisted of an artist, with a lay-out pad propped on an easel, dashing off caricatures of well-known public figures suggested by the audience. This impromptu method was considered rather risky with an embryo caricaturist such as myself. So, instead, I drew a selection of familiar faces – Mr Baldwin, Gandhi, etc., etc., and at the same time recited verses about them composed by Mr Fox. Before the names were revealed the audience was invited to shout them out. When I drew Adolf Hitler, they all yelled 'Charlie Chaplin'. For Mahatma Gandhi, they cried 'Schnozzle', referring to Jimmy Durante, with one voice. I felt something of the bitter disillusionment of the misunderstood artist, but blamed it on their ignorance of international affairs. Perhaps I aimed a bit too high.

In the last concert at Sunningdale we had a jazz band. That is what we called it, anyway, and it was certainly nearer to a jazz band than anything which had appeared on the stage there before. It was composed of three or four boys playing kazoos, a master on the Swannee whistle and myself on the drum. I had no idea then that my career would ever lie in the direction of jazz, but I must have been impressed because I remember our jazz band more clearly than anything else. The tune we played was 'Whispering', well-known in those days as the signature tune of Roy Fox and his Band. It is a tune with a simple melody and even simpler words. After that concert performance it stuck in my mind so firmly that when I formed a real jazz band of my own at Eton two or three years later, 'Whispering' was the first tune we played. In fact, for a long time it was the only tune we played, whenever we met and practised.

I spent four years at Sunningdale School. I did not distinguish myself particularly in any of the normal fields, although for a while I was thought to be a promising high jumper. At the age of twelve I was overgrown, and most of my abnormal height was leg. Until I grew a bit more into proportion, I found that I could jump over the horizontal bar with comparative ease. I never learned proper high jumping techniques like the Eastern roll – for me it was just a matter of running up to the bar and stepping over it. At cricket and football I was poor but enthusiastic. My chief hate in the athletic department was swimming, not through any hydrophobic tendencies, but because of the methods used by the swimming instructor to teach diving. He used to get us to jump off the end of the high board, and then grabbed our ankles at the last minute in an effort to invert us. As often as not he grabbed too early, and brought us crashing down on our knees on the rough coconut matting. Then it was off to Matron for iodine treatment. This primitive method of instruction made no headway with me, and to this day I still choose to jump into the water as Nature intended, with my nose clasped between finger and thumb.

At this time I had an operation for hammer toes, which meant wearing knee-high plaster of Paris boots for six weeks. My parents hired me a bath-chair, the sort that one could propel by working two levers with the arms. It was really quite an advanced contraption for its day, with steering worked by twisting the right-hand lever and three-speed gears operated by a wobbly lever on the left. It had no brakes, the idea being that one should use one's arms in a pumping movement to accelerate or slow down. My model was further adapted with planks of wood, so that my plastered legs stuck out horizontally in front of me, converting the whole machine into a sort of primitive battering ram.

I had always been one for cycling far and wide on my own, and once my arms had put on a bit of muscle, I began to take my bath-chair further and further afield. Thus, one afternoon, having travelled a circuitous route up gentle and manageable gradients, I found that my return journey took in Windsor Hill, one in nine at its steepest point and, with its sharp right-hand bend, a challenge to any red-blooded bath-chairist. A few yards down the hill, the braking power of my arms gave out. I was no longer pumping the arm-levers, they were pumping me. Shoppers on the hill leapt clear as I hurtled down, my arms now a barely visible blur. When Windsor Hill turned right, I went straight on, to be catapulted out of my capsizing vehicle at the feet of a lady who was just coming out of E.V. Tull's.

It cannot have been other than a traumatic experience for her, emerging into the light with half-a-pound of assorted centres, to have a skinny schoolboy half encased in plaster thud heavily at her feet with a terrible clatter of ironmongery. And what about E.V. Tull, just about to tip a tray of milk chocolate cats' tongues on to the scales when, glancing out of the window, he sees this juggernaut of iron, wickerwork and wood bearing down on his plate-glass window with its pilot in his gleaming crash-boots flailing away like a demon to work up speed.

Scholastically, I was not very distinguished as a prep-school boy, being ill-equipped with the power of concentration. But I did succeed in learning the rudiments of Latin and Greek, a smattering of history, one or two elementary facts about mathematics and some French. I was taught French for a short time at school by an inspired teacher called Monty Evans who spoke in a Welsh accent tinged with French, a blend of Emlyn Williams and Charles Boyer. From the Welsh side he had inherited a fine sense of verbal drama, with a spectacular line in reproof. 'Lyttelton,' he cried once in a passion, 'if this was Russia you'd be found in the river in the morning, headless and flo-o-o-o-ating downstream!!' By such awe-inspiring methods he taught me enough French to get by if I have to adopt it as an official working language, on the clear understanding that any official who addresses me should do so, like the late General de Gaulle, at dictation speed.

It was an explosive event at school that persuaded me, and those entrusted with my education, that I was not cut out for a scientific career. I ignored the precept that lies at the very heart of scientific investigation – Always Follow Up An Experiment. Confronted with a vast complex of retorts, phials and glass tubing in which liquid bubbled and steam whirled, I inserted a cork firmly into the open end of a tube, on the quite reasonable and rather altruistic grounds that it was the only opening that didn't have a cork. Far from following up the experiment, I was half a mile away in a different classroom, listening to a lecture on Garibaldi, when the entire apparatus blew up in a holocaust of splintered glass and flying corks.

I had another attempt at learning the piano, but failed again. To some extent this was the fault of the teacher, an octogenarian lady whose teaching methods were as old as herself. Like the diving instructor, she believed that pain is the surest way of getting results. When one of her pupils played a wrong note, she grasped his finger and stubbed it down on the right one until the end went blue. Sometimes she would conduct one's playing with a heavy pencil which did double service as a baton and a truncheon for the immediate correction of mistakes. How well I remember the dreadful duets, the nerve-wracking misery of sitting next to her at the keyboard, fumbling through the treble part while she hammered out the bass, counting the bars ferociously and lashing out with a ring-encrusted hand at every slip! After a few terms, I protested to my parents and the piano lessons were discontinued.

In the summer of 1934, I left Sunningdale. I have been back to the school once or twice since then, and have passed it often on the railway line which runs right by it. Like many childhood scenes revisited, it has shrunk considerably. I used to think that the school house was a vast, impressive building, rather on the lines of

Buckingham Palace in scale. But now it turns out to be just a medium-sized and very ugly house of red brick. And as for the great desert of grass on which we used to play cricket and football, you have to look snappy as the train goes by or you'll miss it altogether! I think that it was a pity to go back. I am sorry now that I ever discovered that 'the Tallest Master in the World' is shorter than I am.

Eton: Swing Swing Together

At the end of my last term at Sunningdale, I went through the ordeal of the Common Entrance Examination for Eton. Exams were never my strong point. I always scored low marks, and found it difficult to explain to my parents and masters that I really knew more than I was able to convey on paper.

I once achieved the almost impossible by scoring two out of a hundred for arithmetic. Looking back on it, I can't see how I managed this. Nowadays I can add, subtract, multiply and divide quite well, and I sometimes surprise myself by recalling, from the dim recesses of my memory, a system of discovering how long it takes six men to dig eight ditches if it takes two men a fortnight to dig one. I really don't see how the examiners whittled my score down to two. When I took the School Certificate exam at the age of sixteen, I almost went grey during the period between the end of the exam and the announcement of the results. Every day I went over the papers in my mind, and each time I came to a more depressing conclusion as to my chances. Eventually, I decided miserably that I must have failed on all but one subject. I practically fainted with shock when I learnt that I had scored a 'credit' on all seven subjects. In view of this astonishing success, it's a bit annoying that no one has since shown the slightest interest in the Certificate which I won.

To increase the anguish, there was a system at Sunningdale

whereby the results were displayed on a blackboard for the whole school to see. So the whole issue became a public matter involving the honour of the school. It was all right for the brainy boys. They scored their inevitable scholarships and found themselves school heroes. But the poor fellows who, in spite of gruelling efforts, only notched the lower forms had to bear not only their personal failure, but the stigma of having let the school down. I was lucky and earned a safe position in Upper Fourth.

Eton is an open school without gates or boundaries and the High Street, though out of bounds to smaller fry for most of the time, played an important part in school life. I was fitted for my top-hat at New & Lingwood's, who had the top-hat market pretty well sewn up. I seem to recall a legend that one of their proud possessions was a block made specially for a scion of the Royal Family whose head was of such pin-like proportions that the smallest hat in stock fell over his ears.

Over the road the hairdressers was called Thomas's although George Thomas, a portly Don Ameche whose own hair gleamed with a dressing that smelled like gin and orange, has long been promoted to that great Salon in the Sky. With an iron hand thinly disguised in a deferential velvet glove, he interpreted the perennial wishes of parents for a short-back-and-sides severe enough to last till the end of term and through the holidays. Over each chair there was a pulley that operated a sort of whirring kerb-sweeper called an Automatic Brush. I have always attributed my bald patch to George Thomas's punitive zeal with this devilish device.

Farther up on the same side was The Cockpit, an olde-worlde burrow in whose timbered nooks and crannies generations of visiting parents have stuffed their faintly embarrassed offspring with Sunday teas and pumped them unavailingly for news of their progress. I remember The Cockpit for its Devonshire cream, which we lathered on to scones and covered with raspberry jam. It had a taste not to be found or even suspected in the callously mass-produced 'clotted cream' which is nowadays touted. The Cockpit was for special occasions.

Our serious noshing was done at Rowlands, within the legal school bounds. Breakfast at Eton was about 8.30a.m. and 'Boys' Dinner' not until 1.45p.m. Five hours was a long time for growing lads, and we bridged the gap in Rowlands with 'three on a raft' (three fried eggs on a great square of toast) and a majestic Banana Mess that involved two bananas and two blobs of ice-cream, with a generous blanket of double cream over the lot. Rowlands was a monument to the digestive stamina of our privileged classes.

When I began my Eton career, my father had been a Housemaster for many years. But there was never any question of my boarding at his House, since there was a rule against sons becoming their fathers' House-pupils. It was a good rule which was accepted readily by all parties – especially by the sons. As an added insurance against my home and school life becoming too confused, my father laid down that, for the first year or two, my visits to his house should be restricted to Sunday tea. So, when I eventually said a nervous goodbye to my parents and walked the three hundred yards to Mr Butterwick's House, with the odd-job man wheeling my trunk along on a hand-cart beside me, I felt that I was making another definite break with home.

At Butterwick's, the emphasis was on games. And not only on playing games, but on *winning* them. I also had to contend with the theory that violence and assault, not to say murder, on the field of sport dispel aggression which might without it be directed towards lynching the masters or toasting small boys over the fire. At Eton, they have a traditional spectacle called the Wall Game which must have been specially designed to fulfil this purpose, combining as it does the merits of rugger, soccer, boxing, tag wrestling, weight-lifting and open-cast mining. It's essentially a low-budget sport – all you need is a wall, a ball and a strip of mud.

Actually, the ball is expendable, as my father in his Eton days discovered one afternoon when things were a bit quiet in the middle of the scrum (they call it a 'bully', which figures). By way of a scientific experiment, he scooped a deep hole in the mud, put the ball in it and shovelled and patted the mud back into place. He then set about making the sort of encouraging noises appropriate to a player in possession. 'Heave up, you chaps!... We're gaining ground on the rotters!… Pass it back, Wynnington-Smythe, you duffer!' The great human mass went on heaving and pummelling and grunting heroically. They were still at it when the whistle blew for time. And the contestants went trotting off to their baths and their high tea without a backward glance at the tell-tale mound in midfield.

With the ball playing such a negligible part in the proceedings, it's hardly necessary to have any rules, which is just as well since it is not every referee, lying flat on his face to insert the ball in the bully for kick-off, who manages to extricate himself in time.

After the game had been established for several centuries, it was found necessary to insist that those whose ears and temples were in constant abrasive contact with the wall should wear a thickly padded headpiece, to protect the brickwork. And at some stage there grew up a sort of gentleman's agreement that, while it is quite legal to knead, squash, knuckle and generally rearrange the face of the opponent nearest to you in order to weaken his resolve and his foothold in the mud, eye-gouging is bad form.

Fortunately, at six foot three and thirteen stone I was too small to play the Wall Game. In the earliest House photograph in which I appear as a stringy thirteen-year-old, Cyril Butterwick and the House Captain are sitting on either side of a table piled high with cups and trophies – something like fifteen or sixteen in all. By the time I had reached the eminence of House Captain, the table had been replaced by a small stool and the number of cups had dwindled to four. But that was not through want of trying. Whether we were successful or not we remained an athletic House. I do not wish to imply that our Housemaster cared for nothing but breeding athletic toughs. Indeed, Cyril Butterwick had a keen and perceptive taste for the arts and literature; his special hobby was collecting silver, and he made himself such an expert on the subject that when he retired as a schoolmaster, he was able to take up a job at once with Sotheby's, the auctioneering firm. In all the private tuition which he gave to his pupils, he did much to encourage an interest in art and literature, and to dispense culture in general. And his enthusiasm for success and glory on the playing fields was not, after all, unusual in a school which aims at producing sound leaders of men with healthy minds in healthy bodies, rather than artists and poets and musicians and other dubious eccentrics of that sort. None the less, the fact remains that the grim pursuit of athletic honours occupied so much of one's time at Butterwick's that there wasn't much left for indulging artistic and musical inclinations.

I started keenly enough by joining the Eton School Orchestra as a tympanist. The Orchestra was not given much official encouragement, being allowed to rehearse only once a week. And I'm sorry to say that, in my day, it was generally regarded as a huge joke. At the School concerts, the very sight of its preparations to play brought forth expectant giggles from the audience. The strings, reinforced by masters' wives and local amateurs, were treated with some respect. But with every note from the windwood and brass, the hall resounded with irreverent glee. And with good reason, it must be admitted. The responsibility for teaching the wind instruments rested on one harassed man, an ex-instructor at the Military School of Music at Kneller Hall.

With Kneller Hall behind him he must at one stage have had considerable qualifications as a bandmaster. But years of trying to teach Etonians to play the trombone and the bassoon during the odd moments when they could escape from the playing-fields had undermined his confidence and broken his nerve. By the time I came in contact with him, he had given up the struggle. The result was that the standard of playing in the wind department of the School Orchestra was dismal. Never mind – the audience found the terrible spluttering noises richly comical, and pieces in which the trumpets and trombones and bassoons were prominently featured in their full horror were greeted with tumultuous encores.

In general charge of Eton music, and conductor-in-chief of the School Orchestra, was the Precentor, Dr Henry Ley, a small round, lame man with an uncanny resemblance to the *Daily Sketch* strip character Pop. He used to play the organ in College Chapel, which the upper half of the school attended every morning and twice on Sundays. He was an inspiring organist, but he played louder than anyone I have ever heard. When he let himself go, the congregation of five hundred lusty boys all singing at full lung-stretch was

Eton schoolmaster, Bloody Bill, who wore a signet ring that doubled as a knuckleduster. After bamboozling HL with numbers, he'd bring him back to basics with the words 'what is one'.

completely engulfed in the roaring torrent of sound, and great buzzing noises started up in odd corners of the Chapel as the masonry began to shudder in sympathy. He was an enormously popular figure, and his appearance on the rostrum always roused the audience to a tumult of affectionate applause. In return, he beamed indulgently when they greeted the orchestra's efforts with mirth. He himself had a keen and robust sense of humour. I always remember the delight with which he used to tell his favourite story of the chorister in St George's Chapel who got his finger stuck in a hole in the carved pew. After a desperate struggle the poor boy burst into tears, and the second male tenor was sent out to fetch assistance. He came back with the verger, who examined the situation and then went out, with the tenor, to return after a minute with a carpenter. The carpenter sawed off a part of the pew, his activity drowned by a congregational hymn. Unfortunately the section of pew removed incorporated a candle-holder and a large two-foot candle. When the removal was completed, a little procession moved off down the aisle – the verger in front, the tenor and the carpenter in the rear, and in the middle the diminutive chorister in tears, with a piece of carved pew and a candle half as big as himself still stuck on the end of his right index finger. Whenever Henry Ley recalled this scene, he pummelled himself with glee.

The 'Bolero' was a sure stand-by in emergency. Once we had a visit from the Radley School Orchestra which, by school standards, was very, very good. Inevitably, the Eton Orchestra was invited to give a return concert, and there was much alarm among the more sensitive players as to how we should make out. But there was really no problem. We had one or two good singers and soloists to pad out the programme, and for the Orchestra – there was the 'Bolero'. In the performance at Radley, I played the big drum. Ludovic Kennedy was our side drummer. He has since distinguished himself in other fields, writing books, broadcasting and marrying Moira Shearer. At that time, he specialized in the side-drum part in the 'Bolero'. Our cymbal player was taken ill at the last minute, so a friend of mine who was featured elsewhere on the piano was hurriedly called in. Henry Savile had never played the cymbals before in his life. But the honour of the School was at stake, and he rallied round nobly.

Alas! Unknown to him, there is a special technique for the cymbals. They must be hit with a glancing blow. Henry Savile's methods, strictly in the light of nature, was to crash them together head on. In the climax of the 'Bolero', with the conductor exhorting us to play 'Louder! LOUDER! *LOUDER*', Henry Savile knocked his cymbals inside out. The sight of the instruments, convex when they should have been concave, was quite disastrous, and the orchestra rode out the final bars with the percussion department having hysterics behind the big drum.

Outside the school orchestra, my musical inclinations found other outlets. It's not much fun playing the drum all by yourself, so I took up the mouth-organ. In itself this isn't very unusual for a schoolboy, but I think I took it more seriously than most. I saved up for a super De Luxe model with a button at one end for making sharps and flats, and I practised incessantly. Hitherto I had never gone in for idols very much, unless you count such corporate bodies as the drummers of the Grenadier Guards or the Kentucky Minstrels who inspired my tentative efforts at the banjolele. But once I had embarked on the mouth-organ I became a devotee of Larry Adler, the Number One Virtuoso of the Harmonica from America, whose records I collected avidly. In his hands the humble mouth-organ became an instrument as technically complex as any of those in the modern orchestra, and I very soon put aside all thought of mastering all the tricky sucking and blowing necessary to play in different keys. But I became quite agile in the instrument's basic key of C. One day I saw Larry Adler in a film at the local cinema. From then on I played with a stylish, snaky movement of the fingers which much impressed my friends.

Round about this time, there began to appear in me a streak of professionalism which had hitherto been absent. When my first mouth-organ wore out, I canvassed my contemporaries at Butterwick's, suggesting that as I entertained them so frequently for absolutely no charge, the least they could do was to contribute towards a new instrument. I rather expected them to react in characteristic public-school fashion by forcibly removing my trousers. But surprisingly, they paid up.

Soon I found the mouth-organ becoming popular on OTC [Officer Training Corps] Field days. I had a good repertoire of marches dating from the childhood treks to Windsor Barracks to watch the Changing of the Guard. So, whenever there was any marching to do, I struck up. My company commander was a mathematics master with an unorthodox approach to soldiering. He used to haul me out of the ranks and plant me at the head of the Company to act as the band. Schoolboy mouth-organists have no Musicians' Union to protect them – they must look after themselves. I refused to play unless someone else carried my rifle and equipment. So a bargain was struck, and everyone was happy – except the disgruntled boy who found himself marching along under a double load of impedimenta. I hope my music helped him.

In spite of the various comforts which it brought with it, acting as military band for the whole company equipped only with a mouth-organ was tough going, and sowed the seeds of a hankering after a more powerful instrument.

My dissatisfaction with the mouth-organ was further aggravated when, at the age of about fifteen or so, I discovered jazz – I speak now of jazz in its narrow sense. I already knew quite a lot about dance music. It had been introduced into the nursery when I was still quite young by the procession of dance-band-struck nurserymaids who had crooned the latest hits over me in my bath. And when I became old enough to lay my hands on the family radio set, I began to listen regularly to the broadcasts by Jack Payne and Henry Hall. My interest in dance music never rivalled my love of military bands, but it kept me abreast of the times.

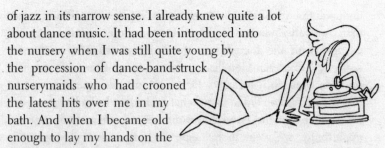

I reached jazz – proper jazz – in several easy progressions. From Jack Payne and Henry Hall to Harry Roy and his lively Rag Bag selections, next to Nat Gonella and His Georgians, then to Louis Armstrong. The first dance-music records I ever collected with any enthusiasm were those by Nat Gonella. They were the nearest thing to 'the real stuff' which had yet been produced in England, and although at that time I didn't know what the real stuff was, I recognized the Georgians as my cup of tea. Gramophones and wireless sets were not allowed in boys' rooms at Eton. Some of the more adventurous spirits used to keep in touch with the outside world by making home-made crystal sets and hiding them in the walls behind their boot cupboards like members of an underground movement. But for the rest, it was difficult to pursue an interest in such a mundane subject as jazz during term-time.

My friends and I used to pay regular visits to the school watchmaker's shop to listen to the latest Nat Gonella records in the gramophone department. Then one day, one of our group came back from having 'flu in the School Sanatorium in a state of great excitement, having heard a record on the wireless by Louis Armstrong which had knocked him sideways. The tune was 'Basin Street Blues', and we went straight up to the record shop to order it. Service there was leisurely and we had to wait several weeks for the record to arrive. By this time we were in such a state of excited anticipation after our friend's build-up that anything but the greatest and most dramatic jazz record of all time would have come as a disappointment. But Louis Armstrong's 'Basin Street Blues' is just that. And after playing it fifteen times we tottered out into the daylight with the incredulous stunned expressions of the newly converted. Poor Nat Gonella's number was up. From that moment on, we were fully-initiated Jazz Lovers. The manager of the watchmaker's shop didn't know what he had let himself in for when he handed over the Louis Armstrong record. Henceforth, at every opportunity, we went to his shop to hear records. We gave up ordering from him, getting the new records quicker in Windsor. But we went on using his record booth for playing over our new acquisitions, buying a cheap record from him once a month to keep him happy. Many a hot summer's day, when our parents and masters fondly believed us to be taking healthy outdoor exercise, we were crammed, seven or eight at a time, in the unhygienic little cubicle listening to jazz. The first Saturday in every month was a red letter day for us. The new monthly record releases were out, and we used to dash off immediately after the last morning class to Dyson's on Windsor Hill to buy them up. While Mrs Dyson tried in vain to keep law and order, we crawled about over the floor and the shelves and in between the legs of the other customers, whooping with excitement at every find.

The natural outcome of this new-found enthusiasm was the formation of a jazz band. Solo mouth-organ might have been all right for marches, but for jazz you had to have a band. So I scraped around, and eventually got together a quartet consisting of mouth-organ, ukelele, piano and drums. By this time the ban on visits home had been lifted, and I was able to go there with my band on wet half-holiday afternoons to play in the now unoccupied schoolroom where Scotty had once held her kindergarten. For a time, we got along quite happily, giving a rough impression on our odd instruments of the noises which we heard Benny Goodman and Louis Armstrong and Fats Waller make on records. By an odd coincidence, one of our earliest recorded favourites was a version by Benny Goodman's Quartet of 'Whispering', the tune which the Sunningdale School 'Jazz Band' had featured several years earlier. It was a natural for our band – no other tune seemed to go quite so well. So my father's long ordeal began – gently at first, because our early versions of 'Whispering' were not really very loud.

It was this deficiency in volume which at last made us dissatisfied with the instruments we had – all except the pianist, that is, who had the only proper instrument in the band, and who was anyway rather a lukewarm jazz player. It was time to jettison the mouth-organ for the trumpet. One weekend in 1936, I went up to Lord's Cricket Ground to see the Eton and Harrow match. At Eton, we used to call the event just 'Lord's', with the implication that anything else which went on at the ground during the summer was relatively unimportant. (We were the drybobs, of course – the wetbobs had 'Henley'.) In accordance with strict family tradition, I was a drybob, although not among the Lytteltons whose names recur incessantly through the history of the Eton and Harrow Match. My recollections of 'Lord's' are strictly those of a spectator – and not a very ardent spectator at that.

On the first day of the match the decisive step of my life was taken. My father, as befitted a member of the clan and the brother of the reigning Treasurer of the M.C.C., was in the Pavilion writing notes for his report in *The Times*, for which paper he was for many years the Special 'Lord's' Correspondent. I was not a member of the M.C.C. My father had put my name down for the Club at birth and then, having seen how I was shaping as a cricket-enthusiast at school, had very wisely withdrawn it. So my mother and I, excluded from the Pavilion, settled down in the Rover seats to watch the game. I should have had a special interest in this particular match because four members of my own House were playing in the Eton XI. But my mind was on other things. Some time in the previous holidays my mother had promised to buy me a trumpet. Ever since childhood I had established the taking up of musical instruments as my chief hobby, and in this my mother had always given me generous encouragement. When I was still at the crawling age, she gave me a dulcimer and from then on it was a toy saxophone, a concertina, innumerable penny whistles, a banjolele, an accordion, a mouth organ and a drum. By the time it occurred to me that I wanted a trumpet, buying instruments for me had become a habit with her, and she could not break it. We had tentatively arranged to go off and buy it on the first free shopping day of the Lord's weekend. It was tacitly assumed that I should perform my duties as a drybob on the Friday and Saturday, so Monday seemed to be the day. But once we reached London, the tantalizing three days' wait was too much for me to bear. After watching an hour's play on the Friday, I became restless and turned the persuasive heat on my mother. Who would know if we went off then and there, bought the trumpet and slipped back into Lord's? She did not take much persuading, being no sort of a cricket enthusiast herself. So we set off like conspirators, mingled with the crowd behind the stands until we came to a suitable exit, and then bolted.

I had my detailed plans ready. As an ardent reader of the *Melody Maker*, then the leading dance-band paper, I knew the ropes and told my mother to drive straight to Charing Cross Road.

Ever since the growth of the modern type of popular dance music, Charing Cross Road has been to the music publishing business what Fleet Street is to journalism. Rubbing shoulders with the publishing houses and instrument shops are Gents' Outfitters specializing in American wear of the most eccentric kind. Into this stronghold of Americana I strode in my top hat and tails, with my mother hurrying along behind – a little nervous now.

The odd thing is that I have no recollection of any feeling of discomfort or self-consciousness. I'm certain the whole population of Charing Cross Road stopped and stared, and equally sure that there must have been some ribald comment. Like most fifteen-year-old schoolboys I was extremely susceptible to embarrassment and given to furious blushing at the least provocation, and I can only think that on this occasion the thoughts of my mission drove everything else out of my head. Hurrying my mother along, I sought out the largest and most extravagantly chromium-plated music shop, marched straight up to the counter and said to the startled assistant: 'I want a trumpet.' I must say here that my mother had never been in whole-hearted agreement with my choice of a trumpet as my next instrument. Apart from the prospect of having a learner-trumpeter in the house, I think she still nursed frail hopes of my musical interests taking a turn in the classical direction. Anyway, right up until the last moment she kept up a gallant rearguard action in favour of something a little softer. Even when we were inside the shop and I was already inspecting the selection of trumpets produced by the assistant, she roamed among the display cases vainly pointing out the attractions of the flutes, oboes and clarinets. But when the trumpet had been selected and it came to writing out the cheque she accepted fate bravely, just wincing a little when she saw the De Luxe streamlined 'Manhattan' model which I had selected. This model was one of the cheapest on the pre-war market. But at that time I thought it the most beautiful thing I had ever seen.

Having clinched the deal we drove back to Lord's, myself with the trumpet case open on my knee, goggling enraptured at my new possession. Once back at Lord's I had to part with it. It might have attracted attention and unwelcome enquiries. With four members of my House in the Eton XI it wouldn't do for anyone to find out that I had 'shirked Lord's' even for an hour. So I left it in the gents' cloakroom, going back from time to time throughout the day just to have another look at it. By a great stroke of luck heavy rain clouds blew up early in the afternoon and put a speedy end to the day's play.

That night I hardly slept at all. I had the trumpet on a chair by my bed and throughout the night I kept picking it up, fondling it and going through the motions of playing. What with one thing and another it wasn't until the next day that I had a chance to blow it. We were staying in London with my maternal grandfather, Colonel Charles Adeane, C.B., C.B.E., the Lord Lieutenant of Cambridgeshire, and a figure of awe to all his grandchildren. He and my grandmother were not in residence at the time, but even so, the house was not an encouraging place for anyone planning to blow a trumpet. It was in Great Cumberland Place, one of those tall, narrow terraced houses which seem to go on upwards for ever. Indoors, the prevailing atmosphere was one of absolute peace and calm. The ground floor consisted of several elegantly furnished and thickly carpeted rooms smelling faintly of pot-pourri. At the windows, heavy lace curtains and banks of flowers from the gardens at Babraham Hall, the country seat in Cambridgeshire, shut out the sounds of the street outside. Sometimes, silent figures would appear from 'below stairs' bringing trays of China tea and frail cucumber sandwiches for the guests, or tiptoeing over to the fireplace to put coals noiselessly on the little fire with velvet-gloved hands.

There was absolutely no question of shattering the calm with a trumpet blast. So, when rain put paid to the Saturday's cricket, I set off upstairs with my trumpet, and a cheap '*Tutor*' which I had bought with it, to explore the house. The serenity of the ground floor spread to the bedrooms upstairs, and it wasn't until I had climbed to the very top of the house that I found, tucked right under the roof, a tiny, remote lavatory which seemed to suit my purpose admirably. The furnishing was sparse, but by sitting on the seat and propping my book of instruction between the taps of the washbasin I managed to get fairly comfortable.

To be quite frank I did not anticipate any difficulty. After a day and night in contemplation of the trumpet I had acquired the conviction that from the first nothing but the most exquisite sound could possibly emerge from an object so beautiful. I almost threw the *Trumpet Tutor* out of the window into Great Cumberland Place. There wouldn't be any need of it after all. All I had to do was supply the air and the instrument would play itself! In happy anticipation I took it out of its case. I knew the right pose to strike from the photographs in jazz magazines – head tilted back, trumpet pointed skywards, fingers waving sensuously over the valves. I checked in the shaving mirror to see that I had just the right expression of inspired concentration on my face, and then I blew out. Nothing happened. Not a sound. In the awful silence I could hear a pigeon chuckling to itself in the guttering above the window. The cistern above my head gave a little derisive gurgle. Never mind, I thought, obviously I hadn't blown hard enough. I had another shot, straining until the veins stood out on my forehead. This time there *was* a sound: a very, very small hiss from the far end of the instrument, like a distant train letting off steam. Something was obviously wrong. Could it be that the salesman in Charing Cross Road had pulled a fast one on me and sold me a dud instrument! I anxiously consulted the *Trumpet Tutor* and, to my relief, discovered that I was going about things the wrong way. I had been blowing 'as one would inflate a balloon'. Instead of this I should have been 'sharply withdrawing the tongue from between the lips as though spitting out a fragment of tobacco'.

After one or two practice spits I took up the trumpet again, drew in a terrific breath and spat viciously into the mouthpiece. Before the noise which resulted all my illusions about the infallibility of the instrument tumbled like the walls of Jericho. I should like to be able to say that I had blown my first note. But that wouldn't be strictly accurate because, in that first explosion, at least sixteen separate notes must have burst simultaneously from the bell of the trumpet. There was a great clattering of wings from overhead as my audience set off at high speed towards Marble Arch. Some anonymous footsteps hurried up the stairs, hovered outside the door and then went rather uncertainly away.

When the echoes of that first hideous noise had died, I sat still for a moment trying to readjust my mind to the realities of the situation. Then, turning to page one of my *Tutor*, I settled down to learn the hard way. Rain having written off the cricket match at Lord's, I practised for the rest of the Saturday and all the next day in my hideout at the top of my grandfather's house. After the first disillusionment I made fairly quick progress and by Monday could climb painfully up and down the scale of C in the low register. On the Monday morning I went back to the shop where I had bought the trumpet to have my first and, as it turned out, my only lesson.

My teacher was a trumpeter from the Mayfair Dance Orchestra called Sim Saville, a stocky little man with rimless spectacles and a permanent look of deadpan resignation. As one who already had thoughts of becoming a hot trumpeter, I was not encouraged by his appearance. He wore the standard uniform of the 'straight' dance musician – white shirt, nondescript tie and the sort of black suit which could be converted, simply by the substitution of a bow tie, into a 'tuxedo' for the evening's work. From my slender knowledge of jazz types gleaned from the trade magazines, I could see at a glance that Sim Saville was not 'hep'. However, at that stage in the proceedings it did not much matter. I played him over my scale of C and it was clear from his reaction that it was very much more than he expected from me. He was not to know what hard practice I had put in in my grandfather's lavatory. He was under the impression that I was playing the instrument for the first time and was shaken considerably by my achievements. By the end of the hour's lesson he was enthusiastic enough to say that if I continued at the same rate I would eventually 'go places'. I came away glowing with pride, although it is fair to say that I did not take his forecast very seriously.

I had no great ambition to 'go places' in the sense he meant. In my daydreams, I never visualized myself as a musical star with my name in lights. I was a jazz fan, and jazz had never held out to its devotees much promise of fame and fortune. Jazz lovers as a whole, and young jazz lovers in particular, tend to have a rather arty, starvation-in-a-garret approach to the object of their devotions, and all forms of commercial success are highly suspect. I knew what Sim Saville meant by 'going places', and in my schoolboy's mind I put the suggestion out of my head with a mental curling of the lip. But it wasn't only youthful priggishness. At fifteen, one can afford to keep one's ambitions abstract, and to me, learning to be a jazz trumpeter was an end in itself. There was no thought in my mind of jazz ever becoming anything like a career for me. People sometimes ask me, 'What*ever* made you take up the trumpet, Mr Lyttelton?' Looking back over the chain of events since the Lord's weekend when I first bought the instrument, I can only say that it looks more as if the trumpet took *me* up!

In keeping with my amateur approach to trumpet playing, I gave up having lessons after the first session with Sim Saville. Back at Eton the two other frustrated musicians in the band had got to work on their parents, with the result that the ukelele-player turned up one day with a full-blown guitar, and the drummer, who had up to now made do with a solitary snare-drum and a pair of wire brushes, eventually blossomed out into a full-kit with affairs whose exact function I have never really discovered. With this new set-up, we really began to do justice to 'Whispering', and our renderings of it began to drift up into my father's study on the floor above – and beyond, into the neighbours' earshot. One of the decisive factors in my musical career has been my father's ability to shut out distracting sounds while he is working. And although 'Whispering' penetrated into his head enough for him to remember the tune for many years afterwards, it never roused him to more than the mildest protest. With the neighbours, it was different, and we had complaints. However we kept them at bay with a few small concessions like the shutting of windows, and our sessions were allowed to continue.

During the intensified practice in the little lavatory at Great Cumberland Place, I had discovered that the chorus of 'Basin Street Blues' can be played, without too much drastic alteration, on the bottom three notes of the scale of C. So we played 'Basin Street Blues' for a week or two. As my trumpeting became more ambitious, we added new tunes – of four, five and even six notes – until I began to acquire some fluency.

I wouldn't recommend this slipshod method of learning the trumpet to anyone. I was lucky in my interpretation of the instructions in my cheap *Tutor*, and got through the early stages without picking up any fatally bad habits.

One of the essential items of a trumpet learner's equipment is a mirror. Anyone who reads musical magazines knows what a trumpet player in action *should* look like. And by constant reference to a mirror during practice, the learner can see at once if he has the right appearance. As soon as he sees his eyes beginning to bulge and apoplectic veins standing out all over his face, he can then hurry off to a teacher to have the fault remedied.

Profiting from the experience provided by the amenities in my grandfather's upstairs room, I got into the habit of doing all my practice in front of a mirror. This gave our housemaid at home some anxiety at first, and she reported to my mother, in her own words, that she was afraid I was developing narcissistic tendencies. I don't think the explanation really convinced her, and from then on, she gave me odd looks. But I couldn't bother about her. I was prepared to face greater hazards than that in pursuit of my ambition to be a jazz trumpeter.

At Eton, jazz was ignored. But thanks to the proximity of Scotty's old schoolroom, it was possible for those of us whose interests lay in the direction of jazz to meet regularly and let off steam without being molested. We used to hold public sessions on Sunday afternoons, and

when we had become fairly proficient and able to play one or two tunes other than 'Whispering', we attracted a considerable following. Those were carefree days. We learnt our repertoire from a great variety of records which we had collected between us, ranging from early Louis Armstrong classics to the latest recorded jam sessions. Anything which was played by a small band and was improvised 'from the heart' was 'pure' jazz to us. We didn't know or care anything about 'authenticity' – we just played for fun and that was that. The tradition for Sunday sessions at Warre House continued for some years after I left the school. When I joined the army and went to Windsor as a young Grenadier Officer, I assembled a group of Etonians on the same lines as my previous quartet, and started the weekly meetings up again. We went up to London during one school holiday when I was on leave and made a set of private recordings. The titles give some idea of the catholic range of our repertoire – 'Tin Roof Blues', 'Ain't Misbehavin'', 'I May be Wrong' and 'Mr Five by Five'. By this time, the school authorities, while still looking askance at jazz, eased up the cold war to the extent of allowing us to play at School dances. As far as I remember, these dances were a wartime innovation, but they afforded a small degree of official recognition for the jazz band.

My own jazz activities at school did not, however, put an end entirely to my association with the official School Concerts. When I had to some extent mastered the trumpet, I took part in a performance of the aria 'Sound an Alarm' from Handel's oratorio *Judas Maccabaeus*. It all started when I was called in to give trumpet support to a singer called David Bruce in the Inter-House singing competition. He didn't win the prize, but our joint efforts caused such an uproar that our 'act' was put into the programme for the next end-of-term concert. And we were highly honoured when no less a person than Dr Henry Ley himself decided to complete the trio on the School Hall organ. I don't know whether we were put in as a serious contribution or comic relief, but I have my suspicions. David Bruce had a voice roughly described as tenor which, on a clear day, could be heard in Maidenhead. I have already paid tribute to Dr Ley's capacity for extracting volume from the organ. In the School Hall that night they both excelled themselves. But I pride myself that, when it came to the point at which David Bruce called upon me at the top of his voice to 'Sound an Alarm', I let fly a fanfare which drowned the pair of them. Needless to say, this extraordinary performance met with the unqualified approval of the School Concert audience, and the applause and laughter carried on well into the middle of the orchestra's next piece.

Apart from this single concert appearance, I took part in several of the House instrumental competitions. The prize on these occasions was usually carried off by one or other of the musical Houses, who swept into the field with string quartets and miniature chamber orchestras. Butterwick's was not a musical House, and our contributions were usually on the frivolous side. Most ambitious and slapstick of all our efforts was an arrangement of the Rossini overture 'William Tell' for two pianos, trumpet, flute, 'cello and xylophone. At the last moment before we were due to appear before the judge, someone hung an 'L' plate on the 'cello – a fair comment but, in the circumstances, unkind – and the assembled audience was howling with laughter before we even began. The judge, in his summing-up, commended us for enterprise and originality. But he didn't give us the prize.

I was a poor games player and athlete, but enthusiastic enough to get by. Once, when all the star athletes were away doing an exam, I won every single event in the Junior House Sports. The cup which I bought out of my prize money is the only one I possess. At cricket I was an unqualified failure, the highest score I ever made being 25. I could have been a good fast bowler if I had ever discovered the right moment to release the ball. As it was, the greater proportion of my deliveries either flew out backwards and hit the umpire, thudded into the ground dangerously near my own feet, or sailed away to the boundary high over the wicket-keeper's head. I got out of a lot of cricket by bribing the scorer to put me down as 8 not out – through which I achieved a reputation, not for skill, but for commendable consistence.

Of course for those who did not care for cricket, there was always the alternative of rowing. During my last term I was persuaded against my better judgement to fill a vacant place in the House Bumping Four. For some odd reason, four competent oarsmen could not be found and it was considered that even a passenger in the boat would be better than the disgrace of falling to 'the Bottom of the River' through the inability to provide a crew.

These bumping races were quite an occasion at Eton. Almost the entire school turned out to follow the race from the towpath, jumping at the excuse to play hunting horns, wave rattles and create an unholy hubbub. Out in the middle of the river the race was a more serious affair; in fact I can record it as being among the most ghastly experiences that I have ever endured. The course was one and a half miles long, and it was a matter of going flat out from start to finish. And this not on one single occasion only but on four successive evenings. Each time before we had gone a hundred yards I found myself praying for death.

By some curious miscarriage of justice, our scrap crew managed to avoid being bumped. In fact we actually executed a bump ourselves though it was hardly a triumph. The cox of the boat in front jumped so much when he heard the starting gun that he dropped his rudder strings into the water and was still fishing for them when we rowed peacefully by. On another day, our coach lost control of his bicycle and plunged head first into the river. It was interesting to discover that we could do just as well without him.

As far as scholastic side went, I was sound without being distinguished. Eventually I achieved the position of House Captain and a member of Sixth Form. Neither of these achievements was as impressive as it may sound, being more the result of perseverance and tenacity than of brilliance. If one started high enough up the school, passed all one's exams en route and stayed on long enough, sooner or later one reached Sixth Form. And the post of House Captain was achieved in much the same way.

To this latter post there are various administrative duties attached, as well as the responsibility of caning the wrong-doers. For the caner, there were unexpected hazards. A friend of mine in another House had occasion to chastise a junior member of the Royal Family. On the upward swing of his first stroke, he burst the only electric light bulb in the room. And from then on he scattered his blows by guesswork all over the royal anatomy.

For me, a much worse punishment than caning was the confiscation of my trumpet, which happened whenever my work was unsatisfactory or I made too much noise with it in the House. For a while, these constant interruptions threatened to cripple my progress, until I hit on the simple answer. Whenever Mr Butterwick pronounced the grim sentence 'Bring me that trumpet!' I would hand over my trumpet with every appearance of regret. But it was only a spare – a cheap model kept specially for use as a hostage. This was locked away in a cupboard, and I would go elsewhere to practise on my carefully-guarded proper instrument.

Membership of Sixth Form meant being among the top twenty boys of the school. Its privileges included a stick-up collar and walking in the Ram. 'The Ram' was the name given to the procession of Sixth Formers which preceded the choir into College Chapel at the beginning of each service, and followed them out again at the end. This procession moved in single file, slow-marching on the way in, and striding along at a brisk quick march on the way out. The first two or three 'Rams' were terrifying to the newcomer to Sixth Form, especially if he was the junior member and had to lead the procession. If anything in my school life served to inoculate me against any future attacks of stage fright, it was the experience of slow marching quite alone (there were seven or eight feet between each member of the Ram) into a Chapel full of five hundred boys, each one delighting in one's discomfort. They were not disappointed when, getting dressed on a Sunday morning, I mislaid my underpants. Being late for chapel I grabbed another pair from the drawer, finished dressing and dashed out as the bell stopped ringing.

It was about halfway down the aisle that the errant underpants made their presence felt, sliding down one trouser leg where they had been lurking all the time. With protocol demanding that my arms should stay rigidly by my sides, there was nothing I could do, and seconds later the entire upper school saw what must have looked for a moment like ectoplasm emerge from my trouser leg and trail along behind me for the rest of my miserable journey.

PART 2
THE SOLDIER'S LAMENT

Land of My Fathers

By the time I reached Sixth Form I was almost nineteen. For some time school life had been disrupted by the war preparations which began soon after Munich. I don't think I or my own circle of contemporaries really took in Munich. We were driven out to the airport to see Neville Chamberlain return with his little piece of paper by a senior master who impressed us all by saying to me, 'You realize, Lyttelton, that this means peace in your lifetime?' Eton had not taught me to have very profound views on anything, so I just said, 'Oh.' Next morning, my Latin master came into the class with his eyes full of tears and announced that he felt ashamed to be an Englishman. We all looked at each other and said 'oh' again. We were equally placid when sandbag filling and stirrup-pump practice became a regular part of the school curriculum. In fact, we were perfect potential cannon-fodder, and our motto was 'Ours not to reason why…'.

In this spirit we accepted the outbreak of war with only a mild tremor of apprehension, and trooped up to London to enlist. We enlisted early – Friday, 13 October 1939, to be exact. I don't think any of us felt particularly patriotic or bellicose at that time. But the herd instinct is strong in the public schoolboy and we were all desperately anxious to do the right thing. One of our particular gang had a father who had been a Grenadier in the First War, another knew the Grenadier Guards Adjutant – so we all chose the Grenadier Guards.

I very nearly didn't make it. Up at the Regimental Headquarters at Wellington Barracks we waited in an anteroom for our interviews with the Regimental Lieutenant Colonel. The walls were covered with Regimental photographs, and there were two big glass-fronted cabinets in the room full of silver cups and trophies. All round us, there was a great deal of stamping and saluting, and from time to time fearsome-looking men with spiky waxed moustaches and lion-tamers' eyes would stalk in and give us the once-over. Then we were summoned, one by one, into the Presence. When I went in and confronted the Colonel, he fixed me with a searching gaze for a full minute and then snapped, 'Sit down, young man…now then…how's y'father?' Well, I thought, if all the questions are going to be as easy as this…. But then the grilling began in earnest.

'Eton, eh?'

'Yes, sir.'

'Eleven?'

'No, sir.'

'Twenty Two?'

'No, sir.'

'Middle League?'

'No, sir.'

'Upper Sixpenny?'

'No, sir.'

For the lay reader I must explain that these strange names which the Colonel kept firing at me are the names of Eton cricket teams in order of merit and distinction. And as he continued on down the list, I saw my chances of becoming a Guardee receding. Eventually, with my head bowed and my eyes roaming shiftily over the carpet, I mumbled the truth – that I was nowhere in Eton cricket at all, a complete dud. There was a dreadful silence while the Colonel wrestled with himself. Then…

'All right, we'll take you…give my regards to y'father when you see him.' The interview was over and I was in. Next port of call was the medical board, for which we had to troop off to some barracks on the other side of London. Here, I met with a further obstacle. I had always had a certain amount of foot trouble in childhood, springing from congenital hammer toes. In 1933, at the age of twelve, I was operated on by one of the leading orthopaedic surgeons of the day, who aimed to straighten my toes out. When the great man had performed, sure enough my toes were miraculously straight. But then, after six weeks, my plaster of Paris boots were removed, and it was found that the toes on my left foot had responded so enthusiastically to treatment that they now actually bent upwards. This unorthodoxy obviously puzzled the Medical Board, and there was a moment of hideous doubt as to whether I was up to army footslogging. But like the Colonel of the Grenadiers, they came to the conclusion that one couldn't be too particular in wartime, and I got through again. All that remained then was for me to swear allegiance and sign on the dotted line. And when I rejoined my friends on the train back to Eton, there was much jubilation. We were in the Army now. Although I enlisted in October 1939, there was no immediate prospect of call up. The Guards in peacetime are domestic troops with very low strength, and after the outbreak of war, it took some time to build them up to fighting strength. So there was a long waiting list of officers at first. When I left Eton in the summer of 1940, I was told that I should not be wanted for at least a year.

The problem arose – what to do? Some of my contemporaries in the same position went to Cambridge or Oxford on a year's short course, but there didn't seem much sense in that. Then one of my uncles, who was an executive in the steel industry, came forward with the suggestion that I, and a cousin of mine who was in the same quandary, should do a course as students in his firm's steel works in Port Talbot, South Wales.

Horror of Welsh housewife at the unexpected arrival of a whistling time bomb in her sink

The idea didn't appeal to us at once. Neither I nor my cousin Anthony were mechanically-minded, and I think steel-working came fairly high on the list of Jobs We Would Rather Be Seen Dead Than Doing. But in the end we decided to go – we had to do *something* and we persuaded ourselves that it would be enterprising to take the plunge straight from Eton into industrial life. If we had known in advance that our decision would take us away from the London area for the duration of the Blitz, we would probably have made up our minds a bit sooner! We were signed on at fifteen bob a week, which in those days took care of digs with all expenses *and* a weekly visit to the movies.

Anthony Lyttelton was really more of a brother-once-removed than a cousin to me, because our mothers are sisters and our fathers were brothers. We first met when I was eight and I disliked him so intensely at first sight that it was clear that we were either going to be deadly enemies or close friends. It turned out to be close friends. Our lives ran parallel – Sunningdale School, Eton, Wales and the Grenadiers – until he was killed on the Anzio beach-head in 1944.

Our landlady in Tan-y-groes Street, Port Talbot, was a mum to us, easing us into our new life on a cushion of almost incessant conversation. She had a lung capacity like blacksmith's bellows and kept up the flow of words until the last cubic millimetre of breath was expended, replenishing the supply with an intake that nearly dragged the tasselled crochet cover off the sideboard. She initiated us at once into the mysteries of high tea. In our hitherto sheltered lives we had known only 'supper' or, on posh occasions, 'dinner'. The first time the mongrel blend of afternoon tea and supper appeared on the table at half past six, I spread strawberry jam all over the cold meats, taking it to be chutney.

It was a rackety life at Tan-y-groes Street. The landlady's husband was bedridden upstairs with the after-effects of a stroke, one of which was that he snored incessantly and, what was worse, irregularly day and night. You never knew when the next burst was coming.

There was another lodger, a Mrs Mullens, in whom our arrival triggered off acute paranoia. She wore what, as children, we used to call 'dribbling glasses' – gold-rimmed pince-nez secured to her corsage by a thin chain which wobbled like saliva when she bristled indignantly, which she did whenever she clapped eyes on us. Within a week she became convinced that we had engineered a plot to keep her out of the bathroom. If she saw the bathroom door closed, she assumed that one of us was inside, thwarting her hygienic purposes. We would watch her through the chink in our bedroom door, stalking like an enraged hen up and down outside the empty bathroom, her pince-nez dribbling furiously, muttering, 'I know they're in there!' She never actually tried the door-handle, preferring instead to make her presence known by continually pulling the chain of the lavatory next door.

Life as a student in the steel works wasn't initially very exciting. The managers in the various departments were too busy promoting the war effort to give us more than cursory instruction, so we drifted about drawing diagrams in notebooks. I could still give you a rough idea of how a Coke Oven works.

Until I had drawn diagrams of about three hundred pipes and their destinations, I hadn't realized how many by-products come from the coking process. On one occasion, in order to convince us and himself that we were doing something useful, the manager put us on a night-shift in the laboratory where, judging by the pervading smell of naphthalene, they extracted from coal gas the basic ingredient for mothballs. We sat up all night wielding a dip-stick and making crucial tests on the liquid at clearly specified intervals. Or rather, we would have done had we not rather carelessly dropped off at around midnight, waking up in the first light of dawn to the realization that several critical points in the process had come and gone unrecorded, with heaven knows what consequences.

We hadn't been equipped for life at an expensive public school for nothing, so we dug out the records for the previous week and fudged a convincing-looking entry from them. If you happen to recall a purchase of mothballs, round about Christmas 1940, which stripped the paper off the bedroom walls, burnt a twelve-inch hole in the back of Dad's Sunday suit and anaesthetized the family cat, I'd be rather obliged if you would keep it quiet.

It took a long and notably friendless time for it to become known to us that, to the workers, the two strangers haunting the manager's office and snooping about writing in notebooks were clearly spies for the management. We were not helped by the very new-looking cloth caps and dungarees supplied to us by Mr Lewis in the High Street who, I hardly dare say it, would persist in referring to the latter as 'dungs'. Even after we had surreptitiously sprawled about in coal dust to take the newness out of them, we still felt conspicuous outsiders.

Our status changed when we graduated to the Melting Shop. Here we were discovered by Fred Hurley, a Londoner who, at work, was the charge-hand of the labourers' gang, and in his spare time was the local secretary of Toc H – at the time a club for servicemen but it has since become a charity for young people – and what was then the British Empire Leprosy Relief Association. He found out somehow that we were distantly related to Gilbert Talbot, in whose memory Toc H had been founded. From that point on he befriended us with such dynamic ruthlessness that we were soon engulfed in altruistic activity – canvassing door-to-door in an Ask-A-Soldier-To-Tea campaign, writing home to Eton to rustle up second-hand books for our lads at sea, even soliciting second-hand pipes from former schoolmasters to send to leper colonies in Africa. Anyone who has ever witnessed the many functions of a schoolmaster's pipe – an instrument for chewing ferociously, waggling facetiously, prodding sagely, puffing ruminatively – will guess that this turned out to be a gruesome collection, but we were assured that they worked wonders in pacifying the patients.

As a counterbalance to these seemingly pious activities, Fred, who had a well-worked and notably unpious repertoire of expletives, introduced us to the beer-drinking marathons at the Velindre Working Men's Club. I have the fondest memories of our Saturday night circle at the V.W.M.C.

Harry, Fred's father-in-law, was one of the club's elders, a handsome old brigand, tall and straight with a white Clark Gable moustache and a devilishly wild eye in which Fred had learnt to gauge the exact moment in a heavy evening when Harry's mood changed from ripely good-humoured to 'cankerous'. There was old Tom, the perfect foil for the stentorian Harry – round, purple, wheezy and inaudible, with a laugh like a prolonged sneeze. And there was Len, one of your saturnine Welshmen, whose limbs after a pint or two began to wave about, all angular indecision, like those of a puppet. Like all Welshmen, Len was prone to burst into song at the drop of a drop. Unlike most Welshmen, he was quite incapable of singing two consecutive notes in tune. When at the appointed hour he raised his puppet's arms aloft to conduct and launched into his favourite song – a tune of the moment called 'Don't Pass Me By' – Harry would be precipitated into his cankerous phase prematurely. 'Sing a toon, mun, sing a toon!' he would cry, eyes blazing with offended propriety. And old Tom would go blue and start sneezing.

As for the club itself at that time, I can only recall a bare sort of place in which one sat at wooden tables while pints of wallop, headless, dark brown and lethal, multiplied in front of one as if by trick photography. On most Saturday nights, if the assembled company was in the mood, there would be a 'free and easy'. A chairman for the night would be appointed and would call on those known to have a talent in some form of entertainment to give a turn. There was strict tribal etiquette on these occasions. Ostracism or a heavy toll in free drinks awaited anyone who declined to answer the call when it came. As for the chairman of the night, his standing in the community if not his very manhood depended upon the way he maintained control.

One night, only a short while after we had been introduced into the club, a 'free and easy' materialized. A man in a flat cap, toothbrush moustache bristling in a promisingly authoritarian fashion, put himself forward as chairman and, having been duly acclaimed, began calling on the entertainers. A young man with no teeth and a cavernous mouth sang 'I mutht go down to the thea again, the lonely thea and the thky…' while the front row dodged and weaved and wished themselves in oilskins and sou'westers. Singers predominated, although someone did play 'All Through the Night' on a musical saw.

When it came to old Tom's turn, the mountain had to come to Mohammed, for his speciality was, like the rest of his personality, inaudible. Against occasions such as this he kept a small tin spoon in his breast pocket with his reading glasses. He remained stolidly in his chair and, as every head in the room bent towards him in rapt attention, he put the rounded back of the spoon against his teeth and strummed with his fingers on the handle to produce a mouse-like jig.

To Fred, partially deaf since the First War, all the fluttering activity beneath Tom's puce pin-cushion of a nose produced no sound whatsoever, and he began to giggle noisily. When he got up and left the group, I thought it was to compose himself outside. He was in fact making use of the diversion to have a private word with the chairman, with what can only be called malicious intent. Heaven knows what garbled version of my biography he fed into the man's ear or in what scrambled form it finally penetrated his brain. I only know that, when Tom's miniature recital was over, the man in the flat cap banged the table with the flat of his hand and cried, 'I now call upon a Member of Parliament, Lord Humphrey Lyttelton!'

I should say here that I had no musical instrument with me in Port Talbot at that time, nor was I known to any of my immediate associates there as a musician. Fred's putting forward of my name to the chairman had been conceived and carried out as a joke. In a moment of desperation, I remembered suddenly a sideline with which I had had a modest success at school.

Basically it can be described as animal imitations, with a few film stars thrown in. Partly for dramatic effect and partly to satisfy an overwhelming urge at that moment to shriek, I started with my parrot, following it up for contrast with my goldfish. Seeing old Tom apparently in the throes of hay-fever in the corner, I was encouraged to romp through the whole repertoire – tortoise, cassowary, stork and finally chimpanzee, at which point, overcome by a sort of stage-struck hysteria, I ran amok through the room and took a flying leap on to old Tom's lap.

Modesty prompts me to mince words, but it can be put in no other way. I stopped the show. Indeed, so much beer was needed to revive the gasping audience that the evening fell apart with astonishing speed. Fred's attempt to try the same trick on my cousin failed for the simple reason that the chairman's computer had by now broken down completely beneath the flat cap. Fed with the name 'Mr Anthony Lyttelton' it hiccupped, blinked, swallowed convulsively, shut its eyes in prolonged concentration and uttered the words, 'I now call upon Mr Rock!!!' Several people began to sing at once in different parts of the room. 'Sing a toon!' bellowed Harry, by now cankerous beyond the reach of all reason. Len, on his way back from his fifteenth expedition to the Gents, took this as his cue and, waving his spidery arms aloft, delivered himself of the words 'Don't pass me by...' in the declamatory style later made famous by Rex Harrison, before falling sideways over a table loaded with glasses.

By now the chairman, staring failure in the face, was clinging to Harry's waistcoat and crying like a baby, and Fred, rather overawed by the holocaust that he had unleashed, suggested we should all go home. Our troubles were not quite over. Once outside, Len weaved across to the nearest shadowy lamppost and began to relieve himself against it, singing loud enough to wake the dead. Halfway through the operation, the lamppost switched on a torch and arrested him.

Fred Hurley, his wife May, their children and her parents all became our family while we were in Wales. We used to go round to the Hurleys on Sundays – May would serve a vast lunch, after which Fred would take us round to visit his friends. At each house they would express their hospitality with apple or bilberry pies. We would look at Fred in desperation, Fred would seize an opportunity to whisper hoarsely that they would be very offended if we didn't eat a slice or two. By six o'clock it had invariably reached a point of stark choice between eating or breathing. Happily there was a time-limit to this forced-feeding. We had to get back to May – and supper.

As he got to know us, Fred rapidly formed the opinion that it was no bloody good our wandering about the bloody works bloody scribbling in notebooks. The gang of which he was in charge shovelled and humped the ingredients which went into the steel-making furnaces – they had names like dolomite and manganese, but they all looked like grey gravel to us. Under his quite unauthorized guidance we put away our notebooks and set to with shovels. Of all the processes, the Melting Shop, where pig-iron and scrap, seasoned with dolomite and manganese, was brewed into steel, held the most fascination for me. Experts called sample-passers (Oh Lord, here we go again!) could peer into a briefly-opened furnace through hand-held windows of blue glass and tell from the hue of the bubbling mass inside if it was cooking to specification. An élite team of furnacemen, with towels round their necks and little blue spectacles to protect their eyes, 'fettled' the furnace expertly, shovelling up grey gravel and hurling it through the small oven door in one rhythmic movement. They let us fettle a furnace once or twice, demonstrating the technique of which the late Duke Ellington, in another sphere, knew the secret – 'it don't mean a thing if it ain't got that swing'. The crane-drivers who lifted the doors only kept them open for a short time, to conserve heat. Interrupt the rhythm, mess up the footwork, and you sent a stream of gravel splatting against the closed door. The first time I tried I forgot to keep a straight shovel and practically decimated the work-force with flying buck-shot.

Our days as outsiders were over. At break-times, we could sit around with the others in the glow of the furnaces, arguing about Churchill, spreading careless talk about where the bombs fell last night and listening to the shop-floor philosopher holding forth. Old William Evans, who looked like Rudyard Kipling, was semi-retired and on light work, so he had plenty of time to wander about refereeing arguments. He had clearly put in a vast amount of reading in his time and had absorbed the gist, if not the actual pronunciation, of a great deal of Western philosophy. If a discussion became too heated, he would douse it by holding up a finger and saying, 'As so-and-so said in his great book, *State, Ecclesiasastical and Whaddyercall...*'

If my life can be said to have had a single turning-point, the short time in South Wales was it. I came out of it deeply imbued with romantic socialism – a rush of Keir Hardies to the head which I have never lost. There were warm friendships, too, cemented over dominoes at the Velindre Club while up to fifteen pints of beer on a good night gurgled merrily on their way.

Extracts from Humphs diary written in 1940, aged 19

Monday 19 August

This morning found me full of doubt and trepidation. Today I was going into a life of which I had no previous experience, and I could only imagine what it would be like. Consequently, it was with some misgivings that I took the train up to London, after various farewells, to lunch with Uncle Richard before embarking, as it were, upon a journey to what seemed a foreign land. After a good lunch and encouraging words from Uncle R., however, spirits began to rise, and Chucks [Cousin Anthony Lyttelton] and I took up our positions in a 1st class carriage, buoyed up by hopeful anticipation.

We arrived in Port Talbot in this mood, and were met by Mr Archie Evans, a pleasant but typically reticent Welshman, who had with much difficulty found us some lodgings. These consisted of two bedrooms and a sitting room and were kept by a friendly but extremely garrulous lady called Mrs Burke. She had a husband upstairs laid low with a seizure, and a substantial daughter, aged eleven. We left our luggage and set out to explore the neighbourhood. Port Talbot is a large town running along the foot of a mountain of meagre proportions, and situated between this mountain and the sea. Gloom descended upon us once again, as we ran the gauntlet of many pairs of eyes and glances which, because they were not noticeably friendly, we imagined to be hostile. We were also rather doubtful about our visit to the managing director next morning. However, when we returned to a meagre meal of tea and biscuits, the comedy of the situation forced itself upon us, and we went to bed by candlelight (P.T. is ill-equipped with electricity) in fairly cheerful spirits. Sirens wailed persistently and there was gunfire etc. all round but fatigue and the knowledge of a long day before us prevailed and the last two warnings fell on deaf ears.

Tuesday 20 *August*

The bed was very comfortable, and I woke refreshed, but again assailed by fearful early-morning doubts. Cold water in the bath did little to help but breakfast and a comfortable pipe brought short reassurance. Archie Evans came at nine, and took us off to see Mr Hollings. The latter is an elderly heavy-looking man, who seemed to think that we had come intent upon 'skylarking'; however, we assured him that this was not the case, and we were allowed to venture out together. Mr Victory gave us some very technical instruction, which was rather above our heads; we left the works at four and went into P.T. to do some shopping. We returned to a fine meal served up by Mrs B. at 5.45, after which, replete and contented, we settled down to write letters. Tomorrow, we shall venture forth in dungarees and cheap caps, to brave the dust and coal of the washery. No sirens tonight.

Wednesday 21 *August*

Off to the works at 9 o'clock, feeling, and probably looking, very amateurish in creased dungarees and unsoiled caps. We need not have worried, for on arrival, we met Mr Blacklegs, the manager of the coke-ovens, who sent us off to study the washery. Frank Roberts took us up there, expressing the desire to see us black from head to foot, and left us with one of the men. He explained everything and then we walked round, picking up knowledge and coal-dust (the latter in greater quantity) until we had mastered the washing system and satisfactorily blacked our caps and 'dungs'. A siren interrupted our studies. We were shown to a shelter, to which we went, and in which we spent an amusing half-hour. The language of some of the men was very instructive, and we returned to the washery on the 'all-clear' with an enlarged vocabulary.

Thursday 22 *August*

In the morning, we had our first intimate conversation with Mr Blacklegs. We sat in his office while he made some telephone calls and a very interesting experience it was. He bellows down the mouthpiece with his mouth right in it, as though mindful of the distance between himself and the man at the other end, who I imagine puts the receiver down and stands back several yards to avoid being deafened. He employs such expressions as 'Lord bless my life and soul', which must add considerably to the telephone rates. He took us round the tippers and crushers (technical terms, of course, for things that tip and crush), and then, providing books and pencils etc., set us the task of drawing diagrams of the washery, tippery, crushery and hoppery. During this, Frank came in, and was very amused to see us scratching our heads over blank sheets of paper. All very like school!!

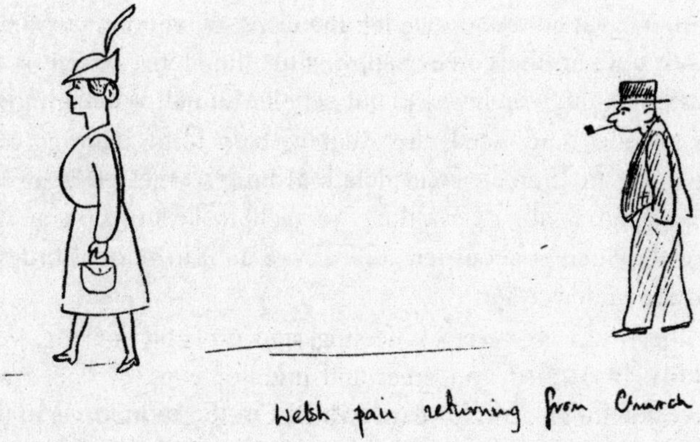
Welsh pair returning from Church

Home again to sausages and fancy cakes for tea. Delicious, if bizarre. Then more letters, all in the hope of speedy answers.

True story told at lunch:–

Two women overheard discussing invasion possibilities.

First woman: I hear that if the Nazis come here, they'll turn us all into maternity cases.

Second woman: I don't mind that, but it's that stallion from Russia that worries me!

This is but a tame example of the average Mess story and, I think, is redeemed by its authenticity.

Friday* 23 *August

There were three sirens last night, but I slept through two of them satisfactorily. Amusing letter from Father this morning, describing his exploits in the Home Guard. Having slept through his dawn patrol last week, he was determined this week to see to the winding of the alarm clock himself. However, his mishap of the previous week was almost repeated, as, after winding the alarm to bursting-point, he forgot to wind the clock! All was well, however, as the clock struggled on till 3.40, ten minutes after the time for patrol!!

Good musical programmes on the wireless don't exist in wartime. There is nothing but eternal comedy cross-talk acts and nauseating dance-music. Good orchestral and good jazz music are sacrificed to keep 'our boys' in the Forces happy, while the Home service is too busy with talks on which way to put on your tin hat! What a war!!

We sat and reminisced after supper until 11.30, passing from Sunningdale to Eton in great detail. I think we get off at twelve tomorrow, and, weather permitting, we might make an excursion into Porthcawl, which is about ten miles away, and, in normal times, a flourishing holiday-resort.

Saturday 24 August

Another quiet night. Very nearly overslept in the morning. Mrs B.'s cursory knock is hardly adequate, but Chucks comes in if I do not appear for some time. 9 o'clock found us in Blacklegs's office, and once again listening to a bellowed telephone conversation. It is now established that he is a Yorkshireman and, therefore, needless to say, a great cricket-fan. Chucks and he held a vast discussion on the subject of cricket until 10 o'clock, when it was decided that we should finish off our coke-oven diagrams.

Had lunch at the lodgings, during which we decided to go to a film in the afternoon. The cinema was very smart and provincial but for such a populated town, surprisingly empty. There was a party behind us which saw fit to clap every appearance of a British ship on the screen (and, being a sea film, such appearances were frequent), and the corner of the cinema in which they were operating was rudely termed 'the cowshed' by C. and self.

6.30. Tea, after which a soft chair and a book. We had a short musical interlude, with self on trumpet and Chucks droning an original and entirely independent second part.

A descant was provided by the siren (Wailing Willie) and after a bit, we heard 'Jerry' above. A whistler bomb, apparently dud, came down within hearing. Terrifying ten seconds, waiting for shattering explosion. A few minutes later tremendous A.A. and bomb activity shook the house.

The wireless has excelled itself. We turned on for a Symphony Concert by the L.P.O., to find it faded down to a mere murmur. Through this we could detect the 'Peer Gynt Suite' (Greig) and the

'Unfinished Symphony' (Schubert). We switched off amid oaths and, ? hours later, turned on to find the wireless playing the last few bars of *Tannhaüser* at full strength!! We go to bed cursing the B.B.C., 'Jerry', the wireless and the war.

Sunday 25 August

I spent an idle day, reading and smoking in a chair until lunch; then reading and smoking in a chair until tea. Chucks went to church in the evening, but I was so firmly fixed in my chair that I preferred to worship in the 'vast cathedral of immensity', to borrow Father's phrase. So I sat reading and smoking in a chain until supper. No, that is wrong – I did go for a short stroll down the road. I noticed that the Welsh, smart in their Sunday best, have a curious formation when walking home from church: the men walk together and the women walk together, but the man and wife move in column – wife first, husband ten yards behind. I wonder if they converge when they get home, or whether meals are eaten in adjoining rooms. The barrage-balloons stand out against the grey sky like great evil slugs today – not the shiny, comforting creatures of a fine day.

Went into the bathroom to find Chucks rinsing his head in the bath from outside!! His slipper was lying on the floor but the temptation to seize it and deal him a stinging blow (a temptation which, a year ago, would have been followed by instant action) was easily resisted as I glanced in the mirror and beheld the first, faint vestige of a moustache!!! I have kept this a secret up to now (it was started last Wednesday); but how can I keep secret what daily forces itself more and more prominently into the range of the human eye. Soon it will be a film-star moustache; then a Hitler; then perhaps, a 'knightly growth'; until, at last, the goal is reached, and I am the proud possessor of a 'walrus'! That day is as yet far off – perhaps it will never come. Can I face the ill-concealed smiles of friends and relations who know me as clean-shaven? Time will show.

Siren has just gone, two minutes after the passing of an obviously German plane!!

Monday 26 August

Letter from Ma. Eton has apparently heard its first A.A. guns. Hon G. [father] all set to repel invaders!

Tuesday 27 August

Uncle Richard says that he might murmur something about our wages, which will be welcome. Mr Bowen is the man who will eventually provide our pay. We shall have to laugh extra loud at his jokes in future.

Made arrangements about buying a gramophone (an expediency for long winter evenings).

Wednesday 28 August

Returned to town and bought a gramophone, and some records of marches to cheer our evenings. Also *William Tell* and a Gigli. Tea of cauliflower au gratin, piled high on a plate, after which, replete to bursting-point, we played our records with loud needles, causing every beam and window pane to bend outwards perceptibly. Mrs B. panted in halfway through the evening with some very old records, which, being chiefly of the tinny Hawaiian variety, almost blasted us out of the window. During dinner, we played *William Tell* at full blast, conducting wildly with knives and forks. I expect we shall soon galvanize poor Mr B. upstairs into some sort of action – he must have been vibrating like a jelly all the evening.

Thursday 29 August

Everything went wrong today from the first. We found none of the letters which we expected, and spent breakfast cursing everyone from the postman to the Postmaster General. Chucks rose from the table in a fury and caught his head a tremendous crack on the gas chandelier, breaking the mantle into a thousand fragments. We arrived late at the works and went into the lab for more experiments and tests.

Played *William Tell* at full blast again and, when it ended, we heard the siren going. It's nice to know that the gramophone drowns the siren! There are 'Jerrys' booming overhead now, amid the boom of A.A. guns. There goes that infernal 'All-Clear'. It always goes just as I am finished the day's entry. Maybe if I wrote less it would go sooner. I'll try one day.

Friday 30 August

Lunch and some pay. Mr Bowen has turned up trumps and went into a safe, singing, for some reason, 'and we like sheep…' (he doesn't appear to know any more than that) and produced two small packages, which we accepted gratefully.

Saturday 31 August

We set out on bicycles to the Pyle and Kenfig golf course, to spend a pleasant afternoon free from the revolting odours in which we spent the last week. Mrs B. said that it was a five-minute bike ride to the course; she was wrong – it took about forty minutes. However, we got there eventually, to find a very smart clubhouse, complete with the regiment of staring imbeciles without which no clubhouse can rightly claim to be a clubhouse. They stared solidly as we went in, stared solidly as we came out, fat overdressed men and fat overpainted women with eyes like unsympathetic prawns.

After nine holes, we felt that, with a long bicycle ride before us, we had had enough, so we sat reminiscing over gin and gingers outside the clubhouse, feeling like H.G. Wells's Traveller in Time must have felt when surrounded by the little people of 8202 AD. We might have been two double-headed gorillas such was the interest which we aroused in the population of the clubhouse. At length, thinking we'd given them enough for their money, we mounted our bicycles and pedalled wearily home.

Sunday 1 September

The day has been an uneventful one. I read until about 12, when, feeling the urge to do a little trumpet practice, and not wishing to disturb Chucks, who was deep in *Gone with the Wind*, I retired to the only room in the house where I could be comfortable and, at the same time, comparatively unheard. Viz: the lavatory. Here I played away until lunch when, feeling rather cramped, I returned to civilization and a hearty meal.

After tea, Chucks went off to church, while I made a pretence at writing some letters. Drew a few soothing pictures, and then returned to the sagging chair for a short doze.

Bed. (I have drawn night shift tomorrow [10p.m.–6a.m.!]. Diary entries will be irregular until next Thursday.)

Monday 8 September

Monday night. I went to the lab to find Trev and Mr Cook, a burly young Scot, playing darts on the door, aided by a piece of chalk.

Mr Cook is charming but obviously out for enjoying himself in as 'broadminded' a way as possible. He told us that he would never marry – women were too soft for him; in fact, in the whole of history, only three women qualified for the position of Mrs Cook – Marie Antoinette, Cleopatra, and Bloody Mary. 'I shan't marry till I'm earning £1500 a year – then, when I get that, I shan't marry till I get £3,000 a year – and when I get that, I'll say "Cook, you're — lucky; keep away from women!"'.

At about 12, I realized with horror that I was to be left alone till morning, to carry out test which, if bungled, would throw the whole works into utter confusion and chaos.

Thursday 11 September

The *Daily Express*, always reliable for pretty amusing misprints, excelled itself today. 'A stick of bombs landed in a Jewish street. I asked a number of people around here how they reacted. The answer was simple. They behaved just like cickneys.' I make no comment!!!

Thursday 12 September

Mr Jolly, as I say, turned up trumps, and gave us our information. His name is curiously inappropriate, for a more gloomy and weary-looking man would be hard to find. However, he is very helpful and pleasant, and altogether a better proposition, as far as fatherly advice is concerned, than old Pooh-bah Hollings.

Friday 13 September

Friday 13th! The day was certainly unlucky as regards the post.

Nothing all day! And some records we ordered hadn't come. Apart from these trivialities the day has passed smoothly. We went to the top of the coal- storage bunker this morning, a vast concrete tower of considerable height, from the top of which the whole works can be seen. We were horrified to see men working on ladders suspended from the edge by a piece of wire rope. They climbed about like monkeys, sliding down ladders which I should be unwilling to walk down.

After lunch, we climbed to the top of the bunker again, with Frank. They were testing the machinery, and it was very amusing to see Frank gazing at the vast engine, which was new to him, as a child would look at a car for the first time. He spat from the top of the building, and shook with laughter when he discovered that there was a man below!!

There was no post, except one bill. However, I found, to my gratification, that a letter of mine had been printed in the *Melody Maker*!!

Saturday 14 September

The rest of Saturday was spent in cinema and lodgings. The films were good this week, even though every programme is marred by that intolerable bounder R.E. Jeffrey, and by the Cowshed Clappers. By the way, Frank's little parting joke in the morning was to stick a card saying 'For sale, cash only, no dealers, sold in parts,' on to our bikes. At first, we did not know who had done it, but when Frank emerged from his hut shaking with silent laughter we knew at once.

After pedalling against the wind to the gramophone shop, to find no records, we arrived, hot and angry, at the lodgings, to find that Mrs Burke had, in the kindness of her heart, piled a vast fire in the grate!! We spent the evening simmering in the corners of the room furthest from the fire, and stumped to bed early.

Sunday 22 September

The Blast Furnaces

The last three days have been spent in the Furnaces. Our first introduction to the B.F.s (by which name, for brevity's sake, they must perforce be known) led to inevitable comparisons with the Coke Ovens – companions which were not favourable to the B.F.s. To begin with, the manager, Mr Frost, is very pleasant and amiable, but compared with the dynamic Mr Blacklegs, he is very small beer, to use a rather meaningless expression. Nervous and with an air of permanent embarrassment, he gives the impression of being constantly in a state of panic about something. When we entered his office, he was telephoning frantically in his high voice (which sounds as though he had a mouthful of shrimps), and even after he had hung up the receiver, he was still in what might, in modern language, be described as a dither. He shook hands with us, twitching all over as though galvanized, and then immediately handed us over to his assistant, since when we've seen him twice at a distance.

Mr Smith is a disconcerting young man. He has a characteristic of never doing anything by halves; he is not content to come in smiling and chewing gum, or frowning and smoking a pipe, but must/needs to come in smiling and frowning, smoking and chewing *all simultaneously*. We're not sure whether we like Mr Smith.

A very funny thing happened at lunch today. Towards the end of the meal, Mr Bowen suddenly sat up, sniffed, and announced, 'Somebody's socks are on fire!' On investigation, it transpired that the smell which was worrying Mr Bowen was that of Chucks's Turkish cigarette!

Monday 23 September

I had to walk halfway to the works this morning to pick up my bike which was being done up at the local bicycle shop. The wild-eyed, farouche- looking mechanic, who had sworn he would be there at 9 o'clock, pedalled furiously up at 9.20, apologizing profusely, and explaining that he would have arrived earlier had not his own bicycle collapsed beneath him when he mounted it at five to nine.

Tuesday 24 September

We spent the morning in Mr Smith's stifling office. Chucks, wishing to draw a diagram, looked about for a ruler; and his eye fell upon a rather battered wooden slide-rule on Mr Smith's desk. He had just drawn a line and set the rule aside, when Mr S. entered, saw the rule lying there, and sprung upon it with a cry of horror. 'Don't use that, man, it's a slide rule!!' he cried, and hugged it to his chest. He then said that it had been given to him by a former manager, who had died before he could show Mr S. how it worked. So Mr S. didn't know how to work the rule, but bitterly resented it being used as a ruler! Had the manager not died, he would probably have explained to Mr S. that among the many uses the versatile instrument could be put, that of a common or garden ruler was prominent.

Meanwhile our gramophone has quietly and surreptitiously gone off its head. It has taken to thumping inside suddenly, not only when a record is playing, but also in the middle of the evening when we are sitting back in silence, reading. It usually chooses a moment when Mrs Burke, cleaning away the tea-things, has her back to it, and jumps visibly when a sudden metallic clang goes off behind her. And, stranger still, when Chucks was in the middle of a tirade against life in general, it suddenly began quietly revolving as he reached the climax of his speech! Nothing is more damping when one is at the crux of a flow of oratory than to have a gramophone turntable revolving as one's only applause. No one was within yards of it, and yet, with the brake on, it chose to revolve. It all goes to show…!

Wednesday 25 September

My *bicycle* has now gone off its head. On the way to the works, it began making a noise like a mowing machine, which was, to say the least of it, very embarrassing. Down the street I went. Calank-calank-calank, while windows flew up, doors flew open, and old men paused in their ceaseless chewing to gaze as I passed. Calank-calank-calank – on I pedalled, praying that the bike wouldn't disintegrate before I got to the works. It was bad enough calanking down the high street before a crowd of octogenarians and red-elbowed women, without falling in a heap amidst cogs, spokes and chains with half a mile to walk with the wreckage! However, I managed to reach the works intact, and by the time lunch came round, the bike had recovered, and the canteen was reached without even so much as a squeak.

After lunch it started again with renewed vigour, and reached the stage when pressure on the pedal ends in a crunch and sickening lurch forward. Every nut and bolt quivered as I staggered along before an even larger midday audience than that of the morning, pretending that I didn't notice the noise.

The bike returned to the wild mechanic this evening, and he will, before tomorrow dawns, have probed the mysteries which lie within the gear-box, and will silence for ever the calankers.

No sign of Uncle R. today. Hopes sink.

Bed.

P.S. Les Smith blanched on entering his office to find it full of Chucks's Turkish tobacco-smoke. The Welsh seem unfamiliar with the brand, which they seem to look upon as opium or burning socks!

Thursday 26 September

Thursday is always a bad day and today was no exception. There was no post this morning and I had to walk halfway to the works again to pick up my temperamental bicycle from the wild mechanic. I padded into his shop very silently in my rubber shoes, just as he emerged from a back room engrossed in a letter. He leaped a mile when I suddenly boomed 'Good morning', and looked even wilder and more extraordinary than ever. My bike ran smoothly and silently to the works (except for a comfortable creaking of the saddle springs) and I hope it will remain intact for a time now.

Friday 27 September

Friday is, on the other hand, a good day, with two great features – pay and a good lunch at the canteen. The Friday fish at the canteen is without exception the best meal, and what's more, everybody knows it, so we arrived very early for lunch today.

Monday 30 September

During these last few days, a new arrival (temporary) has presented itself at 37 Tan-y-groes. This is a vast, wooden structure which professes to be a wireless. Our regular wireless having run down, and being in a state of recuperation, I delved about in Port Talbot, and at length ran this monstrosity to ground. It has all its 'guts' outside, and spreads them round the room like tentacles. The main thing is, it plays, even without an aerial, the lack of which the electrician who supplied it viewed with grave concern. 'It won't play loud,' he said, shaking his head. It plays quite loud enough!!

Lunch at the canteen has been, as usual, very entertaining. Bowen told a story the other day which reduced everyone to helpless laughter. He took a pair of trousers to be altered, and the old tailor looked at them and scratched his head. 'No!' he muttered. 'I can't see what's wrong with them.' Suddenly his face lit up. 'Ay! I've got it!' he cried. 'These trousers 'ave got two left legs!!' Mr B. then went to Burfoots to be fitted for an overcoat. 'Do you want to measure me?' he asked. 'No,' the tailor said. 'We'll take the measurements from your coat.' 'But', argued Bowen, 'you can't put a thing inside a thing that's the same size as the first thing!' In spite of this overwhelming logic, the tailors were persistent. So now, when Mr Bowen wants to put on his overcoat, he has to take his jacket off!!

And then, of course, there's Toomph. I don't think you know Toomph, so a word must be said here to introduce him. Every day at 5 o'clock, as we are returning from work, we meet him coming resolutely down the railway line, now gazing steadfastly before him, now intent upon the ground. His face is red, his eyes protuberant, and his jaw set in the manner of one who is determined to get home, whether anyone likes it or not. But his most striking feature, and that which has earned him his name, is his gait. His legs are short; they would be longer had they chosen to reach their destinations – the respective feet – as the crow flies. As it is, they take a devious route, forming together an almost geometrically accurate circle. It is assumed, though no one has actually made the experiment, that, given favourable weather conditions, a well-trained pilot could steer a Spitfire through them without risk of damaging either the legs or the plane; and it is a known fact that when he rides a bicycle, the right foot presses on the left pedal and vice versa. This curious formation of the legs necessitates an even more bizarre walking action. In order to avoid the feet springing across one another and tying themselves in an inextricable knot, every step must be made with exaggerated firmness and uncommon speed, which in their turn cause a galvanic action of the body. This, in itself, would look funny enough, but Toomph is not satisfied; he must (needs?) put the finishing touches to it by clasping his hands behind his back *beneath* his coat, so that the latter sticks out like the tail of an indignant sparrow. Various accessories, such as lunch-tin, mug and gas-mask container, are all piled up behind, so as to leave the front clear for the violent 'toomphing' action of the legs. Every evening, he pounds towards his tea, giving no thought to what lies on either flank, but gazing intently at the railroad track, now and then raising his eyes to avoid a collision. Toomph-toomph-toomph on he goes, until he is swallowed up in the forest of cycles and men which throng the gates.

Mr Shaw referred to Queen Victoria as being 'a bit of a lad in her day'!!

Monday 4 November

I am now saving up my dough to cover the cost of the clarinet which I bought soon after the weekend. I call it Lucy, a name which owes its origin to a curious dream which I had last Easter. I am becoming fairly adept on my Lucy now, but it is a difficult instrument. As I struggle on, I am amused to recall that it was once Derek Flannery's intention to learn the clarinet!!

(Entry concluded on Sunday 11 November)

We've met another tremendous character – Fred Hurley, who is foreman of the labourers in the shop. He is a member of Toc H, and a tremendous social worker. We've been to tea with him already (after three days' acquaintance), and are now firm friends.

Thursday 12 December

We went off to St Fagan's, seat of the Earl of Plymouth. I viewed the whole thing with mistrust, especially as mention had been made by 'Bibs' Plymouth (our hostess) of dancing! However, it turned out to be great fun, although as far as a rest from our labours was concerned, we'd have done better on a camp-bed in the Blast Furnaces. The only fly in the ointment was the dancing – we went to a club near Cardiff, which provided a good band, a filthy supper and some of the most incredible-looking patrons as ever existed outside the pages of *Punch*. I spent most of the dance chatting with the bandsmen, but couldn't avoid a few dances. We were back in the castle by twelve. Coffee in the kitchen was the next item on the programme, followed by rye whisky and ginger ale in the drawing room. What with more dancing, games, discussions and gramophone, we were not in bed till 5.45am. Sunday was spent in armchairs.

The week following was spent chez Blacklegs, and, being packed with incident, went by like lightning.

The other day we were wandering around the P.T. melting shop, gazing in mute admiration at the gas-producers, when a fairly ordinary-looking man emerged from their midst and engaged us in conversation of a commonplace nature. Suddenly he advanced a pace or two, and in a confidential way, asked if it would be all right if he came round that evening on a spot of business. We said 'yes', and spent the rest of the day wondering what form his business would take. (This was a Monday.) The evening arrived, and no one came. After Tuesday, Wednesday, Thursday passed without any sign of anyone, let alone an ordinary-looking man on business, we came to the conclusion that the man was a bit dotty, and the matter passed from our minds. On Friday evening there came a knock on the door which lacked the finality which signifies the approach of la Mullens, and Mr Lewis was ushered in. Sitting gingerly on the very edge of the sofa, he poured forth such a story of woe as is rarely heard outside the pages of the Parish magazine. His sister, he said, was lying in a hospital in N. Wales with one leg some inches shorter than the other; irons for support of one of the legs – I don't know which – were essential, but Ed Lewis, sole supporter of his family and half his father-in-law's, had not the wherewithal. Could we lend him 25/- which he would pay back in instalments of 10/- every Friday? To cut a short story long, we doled out 25/- shillings and were given in return a completely illegible I.O.U. Next Friday came round and so did Ed, but not with ten shillings. Instead, he produced a sister-in-law (not in person) who is lying in a nearby hospital with an ear complaint which threatened her brain. What with her and rent etc, Ed found himself unable to find our ten bob, and faced with dry bread for a week unless he could somehow find another half-sovereign. Out came another 10/- note, and blessings from Ed. Then the mystery started. On our return from a weekend at Llandaf with the Geoffrey Lytteltons, Mrs Burke said that Mr Lewis had called on the Saturday and would call again that evening (Sunday). No sign of Ed throughout the day. Oh, I almost forgot – during his Friday visit, he promised to give us each a woollen jersey as a Christmas present. We saw him next on the Tuesday following, and barely recognized him. The old boots which he had displayed to us on his first visit, were replaced by smart black shoes. Over these hung a pair of immaculately creased morning-trousers. Only a rather soiled pullover and a scraggy tie betrayed the fact that he was a workman and not a stockbroker! We hailed him, and expected an explanation of his weekend visit. But – the mystery deepens! – he made no reference to it!

And this is where there appears to be something suggestive of fishiness; when he visited us the previous Friday, he said that he'd just had a day off to see his sister-in-law, and he obviously hadn't been working this Tuesday.

So the questions at once spring to the mind:–

a) Can a man who is eating dry bread afford two days off in a week?

b) Can a man who is eating dry bread afford morning trousers?

c) Can a man who is eating dry bread afford two woollen jumpers with zip-fastener collars?

A rum business, you say. But even rummer is the subsequent disappearance of Ed! We haven't seen him at the works, and he didn't appear with jumpers or 10/- last Friday. If he is genuine, he is to be pitied. If not, he has given us a story which is almost worth 35/-!!

Tomorrow is Friday – we shall know then whether our money has gone towards Miss Lewis's leg-irons or Ed Lewis's leg-wear. I can't help hoping slightly that it's the latter – it will ruin the story if he turns up.

Christmas Day 1940

Chucks was still a bit on the queer side (internally) this morning, so once again I stumbled off to the works alone. It was all very much the same as any other day, except that the men in the Melting Shop were singing as they fettled the furnaces, which was quite impressive. As the canteen was shut today, and the office was closing at twelve, I didn't see why I shouldn't have a half day off, so I returned to Tan-y-groes Street for lunch. And what an extraordinary lunch it was too! Elizabeth Burke had had a glass of cider just before, so that her walk was a bit wobbly when she brought our lunch in. All went well until she reached the bread-sauce stage and then disaster befell her. There was a crash and I looked up to see bread-sauce on the floor, on the windows, on the curtains and even on the ceiling! Miss B. fled in confusion and wisely left the rest of the serving to her mother. The meal consisted of turkey (Mrs Burke), Christmas pudding (Warre House) and champagne (!!) (Aunt Sibell). Almost up to Longford Castle standards!

After an afternoon in armchairs, we set out to spend the evening at Fred's. I took along Lucy and some gramophone records, hearing that Mr Dyer, the local organist, would be there. (I think I've mentioned him before.) Sure enough, there he was, and Mrs Dyer too, a vast, comfortable red woman with horn-rims and a grape-laden hat. Mrs Fred produced some incredible wine with which we opened the evening – I think its name was Segavin (!!) and that it came from the local chemist. Then Dai Dyer sat down at the piano, Lucy was assembled, and a search was made for a suitable tune for a duet. At last, a battered copy of a tune called 'Mello Cello' was produced, and Dai played it over while I picked it up. At last all was ready, and with a flourish of chords, we swept into the tune. Carried away by his enthusiasm, Dai burst into song, shouting from time to time such encouragements as 'Good boy! That's it! Down here – up here!'.

Having made a start we raced ahead, through 'Swanee River', 'Abide With Me', 'All Through the Night' until, both exhausted, we decided to have a rest. Beer was produced and rapidly disposed of. In the course of the evening, the local barber, Stan Locke, dropped in, and took us over to his house for half-an-hour. There we met his father (who was out of work and trying to get a job in the works) and a series of shrieking, giggling women whose identity we never discovered. They were all related to Stan Locke, but beyond that we could get no further. The evening, or perhaps I should say the following morning, was ended back at Fred's with everyone in high spirits. Margaret Hurley and young man, George Moreton, came in to swell the crowd and the party eventually broke up at about 2.00a.m. with Fred in his shirtsleeves smoking an enormous cigar!

Colonel Bogey

On 6 June 1941, just about the time that Hitler invaded Russia, I joined the army. Anthony and I met again on the platform at Victoria Station on our way to the Guards Depot at Caterham. When we got on to the train, we discovered quite a collection of our school friends heading the same way and it was a gay if rather nervous party which arrived at the Depot and reported at the main gate.

The Caterham initiation into the Brigade of Guards is famous. Nowadays it is still spoken of, by those who know, in the same breath as the Foreign Legion. 'We make 'em or break 'em' should have been the motto on the crest over the main gates. Our reception that first evening was deceptive. When we arrived, we were shown round the camp by a very mild and polite company officer who might have been conducting a party of tourists. Then we were handed over to one of the 'Nannies' – regular Guardsmen known technically as 'trained soldiers' who were put in charge of recruit squads to show them the ropes. He took us straight to the NAAFI (canteen) and we spent most of the rest of the day drinking cups of tea and rather nervously repeating to each other that Caterham did not seem so bad after all.

Next morning the fun began. With a sure instinct in the most effective forms of mental torture, the first blow was struck at our vanity. We were marched off to the barber's shop where, with quite undisguised glee, the Corporal-Barber got to work on us with the clippers and shaved our hair off almost to the roots, except for a very small tuft in front. When we first saw ourselves in the mirror, we nearly cried. Then we did the next best thing and laughed heartily – if a little hysterically. We could take a joke! The next step in the breaking-in process was a medical parade in which we were given a series of injections and vaccinations which made us feel very ill, and brought our spirits down to zero. Then off we marched to the Quartermaster's Stores, where we collected our uniforms and equipment. In order to make things harder, everything was issued in small pieces. The cap, for instance, was broken down into its components parts, each of which was given to us separately – the cap itself, the buttons, the badge and the strap. When we had our arms full of assorted fragments of equipment, we were told that the loss of any one article would bring down on us the direst penalties stopping short only at court martial, and were marched back to our barrack room at the double so that, in spite of all our efforts, we dropped a lot of the stuff en route. I lost one button. And so effective were the threats directed at us in our demoralized state that I spent hours of agony worrying about that button. In the end they gave me a new one – just like that. But I had paid for it.

It's hard even for me to believe now that after about three weeks at Caterham, I was a fanatic about my toe-caps. The treatment which we meted out to those poor boots hardly bears description. It involved 'boning' them with the handle of a toothbrush to iron out the pores of the leather, smearing them with boot-polish and setting fire to it to harden the surface and – a real old soldier's dodge, this one – peeing in them and leaving them overnight to marinate, as it were, until the leather became brittle and receptive to the polish. After the war had been going on for a year or two, some perceptive fellow at the War

Office noticed that the requisition for new boots from the Brigade of Guards exceeded those of the rest of the British Army put together. It took no more than a brief test on one ammoniated boot to find out why, so the order went out that boots were to be shiny no longer. But not before I had discovered that three weeks was all it needed to mould me into a mindless zombie who thought nothing of piddling in his boots.

Looking back, it strikes me that most of the people one encountered in the army were stark, staring mad. Sometimes, supervising a parade as an officer and watching drill-sergeants and sergeant-majors going through extraordinary paroxysms and facial contortions, it occurred to me that, in civilian life, people were shut away for much less. It was clear that the maintenance of discipline required a total suspension of a sense of humour. When I was stationed as a lieutenant at Wellington Barracks – the place from which the troops emerge for the world-famous Changing of the Guard – a quite serious crisis of discipline occurred over an incident which, to most of us part-timers, seemed trivial and mildly hilarious.

It was discovered, at crack of dawn, that someone had, in the euphemistic language of Army Regulations, committed a nuisance in the middle of the parade ground. No one knew when it had happened but, when daylight broke and soldiers began to turn out for the early parade, there it was, quite substantial and for all to see. Hasty work with a shovel would, one might think, have been the simplest way of, well, clearing up the matter. But before this could be done, the Regimental Sergeant-Major had come on to the scene and had been, to put it mildly, appalled. To him, the offending object in the parade ground was not simply a nuisance – it was a symbol of defiance, an act of mutiny, a studied and deliberate insult to Her Majesty's tarmac.

Before the sun had risen above the cookhouse block, a culprit had been persuaded to confess and was duly marched in front of the Commanding Officer. He gave the only possible explanation in the circumstances – that, having drunk some beer in a pub which had upset his digestion, he had been taken short halfway across the parade ground with an attack of the 'runs'. The R.S.M. would have none of this. 'I thank you, sir, for leave to speak!' he bellowed in the lunatic formula required. 'Sir, I personally hexamined the nuisance with my pace-stick and found it hard and hobviously made with a heffort!'

We moved from Caterham to Sandhurst and having been there a short time and taken the lie of the land, I sent home for my trumpet. There were one or two accomplished musicians in my company and it wasn't long before I had a band going. Every Tuesday night the evening meal was given an air of formality. The officers would wear their mess uniforms and the Sandhurst military band would play music during the meal. Afterwards my jazz band used to take over and play an informal session for the rest of the evening. These Tuesday sessions became a regular thing, patronized by both officers and cadets. And when it came to the final concert on Passing Out Night we were naturally invited to play. Passing Out Night was something of an event at Sandhurst. It took place on the eve of the Passing Out Parade, when the company which had finished its four months' course of training took leave of the rest of the unit. Originally, Passing Out Night had been a formal occasion comprising a Dinner at which the company commander could address his troops for the last time, and an elaborately staged entertainment.

But this arrangement had proved unsatisfactory. The concerts were ambitious affairs and a lot of work and talent was put into them. But the occasion was also one for celebration – especially by those who had passed their exams contrary to expectation. So the show was invariably interrupted, and sometimes stopped altogether, by rioting in the audience. For this reason, Passing Out Night was eventually split into two parts. The formal concert took place early in the last week, before feelings ran too high. And the night before the Passing Out Parade was left clear for the Dinner, an informal entertainment on a low level (vulgar songs and jazz bands) and the Riot.

And what a riot it was too! With unbelievable foolishness, the authorities had decreed that any damage done by a company on its Passing Out Night after all its bills were paid up should be paid for by the company which came in its place. As soon as a new cadet arrived therefore, he found on his mess bill an entry of several pounds relating to the Passing Out excesses of the previous company. Having thus paid damages in advance, he was determined when his night arrived to have his money's worth. There was also, no doubt, a certain amount of sadistic glee in the thought of the sum which the next company would have to fork out. It is difficult to arrive at statistics on such an occasion, but I do know that my own company smashed almost every one of the 300 glasses in the canteen, pushed all the windows out of the dining room, tore away woodwork and reduced tables and chairs to match-wood. I claim an alibi to prove my innocence in this general destruction because at the time it was at its height my band was playing on the stage. Perhaps, on second thoughts, we were partly to blame for whipping up the audience into such a frenzy. Obeying a golden rule for musicians in moments of danger, we kept on playing – until, quite by accident, a flying bottle crashed into the open front of the piano and severed every single one of the strings. Then, as the battle was still raging, we hid our instruments and plunged into the fray. Next day, for many an officer cadet, the parade signified a passing out in more senses than one.

On the whole, the course at Sandhurst was a dull one. I found that I had no great aptitude for military tactics, especially that particular form of exercise known as a TEWT – Tactical Exercise Without Troops. Standing out in a biting wind on the top of a hill and trying to answer hypothetical questions about an enemy that was supposed to be lurking behind a distant bushy-topped tree never inspired me with any sort of enthusiasm. But our training did have its light relief, usually drawn from the misadventures of less adaptable colleagues. The star-turn in our company was Cadet Officer Beadle, a Grenadier candidate who was what the Americans call a 'fall guy'. Everything happened to him. Whenever he marked time on the parade ground his gaiters came unfastened and flew off. In the weapon training periods he was a constant danger. His rifle was always going off when he least expected it, and when he first fired a burst from a tommy gun the target remained unscathed but a heavy branch came crashing down from the top of a nearby pine tree. When we had an exercise to do any distance away from the college we rode out on bicycles.

Beadle could just about ride a bicycle but he couldn't get on or off it. The army made things more difficult for him by insisting that bicycles should be mounted and dismounted in a drill. This was a hangover from the days when they rode everywhere on horseback, and, in fact, the words of command were lifted straight from the *Manual of Horse Drill*: 'Prepare to mount…' (one foot on the pedal here)…'Mount!' (over with the leg and into the saddle). Beadle never mastered the complications of bicycle drill. He could manage the 'Prepare to mount' part of it but on the command 'Mount!' the bicycle used to topple away from him, bringing him crashing down on top of it. The process of dismissing was even more hazardous for all concerned. Our parade ground was at the bottom of a long, steep hill, and the usual routine was for the company to free-wheel down the hill, form up in line on the parade ground and dismiss formally. The success of this manoeuvre naturally depended on the ability of the troops to stop their bicycles once they reached the parade ground. And this was where Beadle came unstuck. The first time he tried it he came whizzing down the hill just as everyone else had formed up, and ploughed through the ranks like a bulldozer, knocking cadets and bicycles flying. From then on he was allowed to skip the formal dismissal and keep going until he reached the bicycle shed, where a great crashing and tinkling of scattered bicycles announced his arrival. But of course, even in this unusual case, the military formalities had to be observed, and as he whizzed past the company commander at thirty miles an hour he could be heard shrieking for 'Leave to dismiss, please, sir?'.

Every phase of Sandhurst training was enlivened by Beadle's antics. Beadle on a motorcycle, rearing and bucking all over the track and finally shooting off it altogether and disappearing through a hedge; Beadle at the wheel of a 15cwt truck, Beadle with a hand-grenade. But enough! This is where we must draw a veil. It came as a surprise when he passed at the end of the course. Not everyone did, even among the Guards candidates (who were no better as soldiers than the others, but stood a better chance with the Guards instructors on the principle that dog doesn't eat dog). Failures were 'back-company-ed' which meant that they had to drop back into a junior company to do the course again – rather like Snakes and Ladders. If proof were needed of the partiality of the Brigade of Guards staff it may be found in the fact that, after sleeping my way through the lectures and exercises at Sandhurst, I was finally passed with an A grading, which labelled me as an outstanding cadet. And with Anthony, Beadle and the Grenadier contingent I moved on to the next phase – the Grenadier Guards Training Battalion at Windsor.

I arrived at Victoria Barracks, Windsor, the goal of my childhood excursions to hear the band, as a Second Lieutenant in the Grenadier Guards. After the carefree days at Sandhurst, where one's hybrid status of half officer, half recruit gave one a certain amount of immunity from many of the discomforts of army life, Windsor was a definite turn for the worse. In the Brigade of Guards there are two species which share the position of the lowest form of military life – young corporals and young officers. The guardsman without rank is, by comparison, a lordly being, entirely without responsibilities, and with a reputation for stupidity behind which he can shelter comfortably. Once he becomes a corporal he sheds this protection, and becomes an object to be chivvied and harassed by every rank from sergeant upwards. Young officers are, if anything, in a worse position still because they are open to attack from above and below. The senior N.C.O.s saluted us, called us 'sir' and abused us as roundly as they had done at Caterham and Sandhurst. And the officers, from newly promoted Lieutenants up, made it quite clear that, in their view, young officers should be seen but not heard. Some of the 'young officers' in my batch were fast approaching forty, but it made no difference. On parade we were taught drill and weapon training and platoon tactics. In the Mess, we were taught the elementary facts of Guards life – *eg*: that a telephone is a telephone and never a ''phone', and that a man who calls for 'a beer' instead of 'a glass of beer' is quite lacking in education and decorum.

After a time, if one passed all the tests, one was allowed to drop the prefix 'Young', and become a real officer. After that, life at Windsor settled down to a level routine of parades, guard duties, lectures, courses and inspections, all leading up to posting to a service battalion.

During my stint with the Training Battalion I did a course in signalling at Catterick (and formed a band there), became for a while Education Officer at Windsor (and formed a band there) and spent a lot of time at home down in Eton (and formed a band there). I also went to the Wingfield Morris Hospital at Oxford for another operation on the feet to prepare me for active service. (No band there.)

All the time at Windsor, drafts were leaving for the battalions overseas, and lists were posted, amid much excitement and suspense, on the notice-board in the Officers' Mess giving the names of those who were to go on draft-leave forthwith. In their reactions to the prospect of going to the fighting line, officers at Windsor fell into three distinct categories. There were the few who were genuinely excited and stimulated by the thought of fighting; the 'get-at-the-Boche' boys who professed, rather too often and too eagerly, that they were itching to have a crack at Jerry; and the rest who accepted the inevitability of it all without complaint but without enthusiasm. I belonged to the last category. I had no illusions myself about the glamour or thrill of front-line fighting. If, by some oversight not in my control, my name had never appeared on a draft list at all, I should privately have been extremely pleased. When it finally did appear, however, I read it with a feeling of relief – the sort of relief mixed with apprehension which I had often experienced at the dentist's, when the assistant finally put her head round the waiting-room door and said: 'You're next, Mr Lyttelton.'

The trip across from Tripoli to Salerno took five days. I have an idea that the boats which we travelled in were called L.C.T.s but I have no recollection what the initials stood for. All I remember is that they were hideously crowded and that the troops' quarters below deck had been fitted by some over-thoughtful administrative mind with seats which prevented anybody from lying down. The officers had tiny quarters below but having inspected them for comfort we decided unanimously to sleep out on deck. Except for one choppy day the weather was fair, which in the light of the average guardsman's capacity for being seasick at the slightest undulation, was a fortunate thing. On the evening of the last day we heard the news over the ship's wireless of the surrender of Italy. In some naïve way we thought at first that this would completely alter the circumstances of our landing, and the ship resounded with cheers. It was even wildly suggested that we should march from the landing stage straight through to Naples without opposition. Well, the surrender of Italy did affect our invasion, but not in the way we thought. It merely meant that the demoralized Italian coastal defences were replaced at once by German troops, whose attitude to the forthcoming intrusion was far more businesslike. This possibility was foreseen by the more strategically-minded officers among us, and by nightfall a cloud of misgiving and foreboding had fallen again over the huddled figures on the top deck. Down below on the troop deck, however, the general misconception remained and it did, in fact, have a beneficial effect in that it enabled the soldiers to sleep as peacefully as their uncomfortable quarters allowed.

There is something about our approach to Salerno which had always puzzled me. Before the invasion set off from Tripoli there had, of course, been elaborate security precautions, and these were maintained during the journey across. It seems odd, therefore, that we arrived within sight of the mainland – and presumably visible from there – in broad daylight on the evening of Wednesday, 8 September 1943, and remained there at anchor until darkness. What was not surprising in the light of this was that three times during the night we were visited by bombers. The invasion fleet retaliated with red tracer bullets which under any other circumstances would have made a very attractive and edifying firework display. One or two ships went up in flames, but the troop-carriers were not hit. All I can remember of the actual landing was that it began in such chaos that it is a wonder anybody got ashore at all. Ships milled around in the harbour trying to find their right places in the queue, and senior officers in charge of operations bellowed abuse to all and sundry through megaphones. The initial landing was made at 3.30 and my own boat-load disembarked at 7.25. Long after I had returned to England at the end of my service abroad I found in an old copy of *The Illustrated London News* a double-spread artist's impression of the Salerno landing. It made my back hairs stand on end. There we all were, British and American troops shoulder to shoulder up to our chests in water, holding our rifles and equipment above our heads and struggling towards a beach which was alive with exploding shells, bombs and land mines. Aeroplanes zoomed down on us from above, and behind us, in the harbour, great columns of smoke rose heavenwards as our ships went up in flames. Fortunately, reality was less horrific. When I walked down the gangplank on to the narrow stretch of beach four hours after the invasion had begun, with my pistol in one hand and my trumpet wrapped in a sandbag in the other, the beach was empty except for one man standing with his back to the enemy and calmly performing a function which in more peaceful circumstances would have earned him fourteen days C.B. for 'committing a nuisance in a public place'. Shell fire from the enemy was concentrated not on us but on the barrage balloons put up by our fleet. This seemed to us strangely frivolous at the time and to this day I am not quite sure what its object was. One by one the poor balloons collapsed flaming into the sea, but no aeroplanes came in to take advantage of their destruction. I heard it said later on that the German plan was to leave the invading troops unmolested until they had all landed and then to move in and cut them up. At any rate, there was no beach-head battle at first.

As the day wore on, however, resistance toughened. We were all detailed to assemble in a specially predestined area as soon as we had landed but the company commander who was supposed to occupy the forward end of the assembly area found when he got there that he was in the front line and under mortar fire. So it was decided on the spur of the moment to assemble somewhere else. All morning we waited for instructions and at about midday the Brigadier was told to advance and see if he could reach Battipaglia, about three miles inland.

The Sixth Battalion led the advance, which took us 300 yards before we were brought up short by enemy resistance. As Signals Officer I was not in the forefront of the advance and to tell the truth I had very little idea of what I was supposed to be doing at this time. Wireless communication was limited, and anyway the fighting area was so small that runners were the quickest method of passing messages. My first personal experience of animosity from the German side came when I was wandering rather vaguely about in the middle of a tobacco field. Quite suddenly there was a whining 'ping!' and a tall tobacco plant a yard to my left was crisply decapitated. It says a lot for my trusting nature and for the slow way in which things dawned on one at this time that I didn't realize at first that I had actually been sniped at. When I did I hurried off into cover – not at a run, I hasten to add. This has nothing to do with courage or coolness in the face of danger. It is just that my training at Eton and in the Guards had instilled in me a notion that to run is somehow undignified. I believe I was actually afraid of being laughed at by the sniper who had spotted me, if I allowed myself to break into a run. So I stalked with dignity into a ditch, and then broke out in a cold sweat. Life had suddenly become quite unreal. At first the unreality was not unpleasant – rather stimulating, in fact. Then the stretchers began to come back to Battalion Headquarters and the vague dream turned into a nightmare.

Walking wounded in various stages of distress began to drift back from the front line, some escorted by comrades, others alone and pathetically lost. One of our men climbed to the belfry of a church tower to guide some mortar fire. I saw him silhouetted against the light in a little window for a few seconds, and then the top of the tower vanished in a whirl of dust and smoke, hit fair and square by an enemy shell. A party went up to bring the man down, but what was left hardly made the journey worthwhile. Rumours of terrible losses and setbacks began to fly, often exaggerated but sometimes confirmed by a thickening of the stream of stretchers. Once I came across two men in a lane, one staggering about stupidly with his arm round a companion's shoulders. They looked like two pals rolling home after a night at the local, and I was green enough to think that one of them was in fact dead drunk. A minute later I was ashamed of

the thought when it dawned on me that the man was shell-shocked. In a short time I had seen enough of these dazed, shambling figures to recognize the symptoms of 'bomb-happiness' only too well.

There wasn't much question of sleep the first night, although at one point I did drop off, huddled in my overcoat bang in the middle of the main inland road. I was awakened by the driver of a lorry who saluted respectfully and asked if I would mind moving into the gutter.

By the time the full implication of the situation had sunk in – that I was in the middle of a full-scale battle – fatigue had to some extent come to the rescue, deadening the senses. Even so, I can remember the first chilling impact of seeing a brother officer brought in dead on a stretcher and I remember, too, being absurdly shocked when older hands made brittle jokes as the stretcher party went by. I hadn't yet discovered the vital necessity of shrouding oneself in a protective blanket of callousness.

As a signals officer I was pretty well anchored to Battalion Headquarters, which, although they were only a few hundred yards behind the front line, were not often concerned in actual face-to-face fighting. But I did go 'over the top' once, an experience which, from the point of view of studying one's own reaction to events, was most interesting – the more so because, although we did not know it at the time, the whole thing was a false alarm.

The Battalion was halted just behind a high railway embankment and, owing to some misunderstanding, our Commanding Officer was led to believe that an enemy counter-attack had reached positions just over the other side. So he decided to rally all the available manpower for a good old-fashioned death-and-glory charge over the embankment. Everybody was conscripted for this: medical orderlies, batmen and all the miscellaneous bodies to be found hanging about Battalion Headquarters.

My own hastily assembled platoon consisted of two men wearing canvas plimsolls who had been put temporarily on the sick list with bad feet, a Quartermaster Sergeant who had been unlucky enough to choose this moment to visit us from the administrative section further back, and two diminutive men from the Royal Corps of Signals. They had very bad luck, I must say. They had become separated from their own unit and called in at our Headquarters to find out how to get back. All they wanted us to do was show them the way to go home. Instead, they found themselves roped in to a miniature Charge of the Light Brigade. With this curious collection we lined out alongside of the embankment.

I wasn't scared, just a little numb. You only get really frightened if you think, and I made a point of not thinking. I slipped my brain into neutral and concentrated on rallying my motley troops. Then the Commanding Officer blew a whistle and we charged over the railway lines yelling belligerent phrases at the top of our voices – 'Come on the Grenadiers!' and 'Let 'em have it!'. We did this not so much to frighten the enemy as to comfort ourselves. Somehow it is easier to go to one's death shouting and yelling like a mad thing – it relieves the feelings. When we reached the other side and found that we were not mown down by a hail of machine-gun fire as expected, our shouting took on a slightly querulous tone. And as we advanced further and further without seeing a vestige of the enemy, our bellicose slogans were replaced by the most terrible oaths, uttered half in relief and half in anger at having wound ourselves up to such a pitch of self-control to no purpose. We returned to H.Q. feeling glad to be alive, but a little sheepish.

The pattern of attack and counter-attack around Battipaglia was maintained with very little let-up for three weeks. Sometimes, the battalion was pulled back into reserve, and although that only meant withdrawing a few hundred yards from the front line to positions still within shelling range, the few hours of respite were like a holiday. Games of football would start up, and there would be boar-hunts after pigs which were running loose among the ruined farms. On these occasions I would get out the trumpet and sit and practise under a fig tree. But there wasn't really much time for music. In the circumstances, however, we found that all sorts of mundane noises came as the sweetest music to our ears: the sound of the shells from the naval guns in the harbour swishing and roaring over our heads like express trains; and the evening concert of sustained fire from the machine-gun regiment next door, which rattled away for fifteen or twenty minutes on end without, I believe, doing much damage to the enemy but with the healthiest effect on our morale.

Then there were the raids by American aircraft – although, at first, when the battle line was confused, these proved a somewhat dubious blessing. The very first flight of U.S. bombers that came over flew round the back of the enemy lines and roared into attack from behind them in the hope that they would be mistaken for German aircraft. When they released their bombs several seconds too late and nearly blew up our own Brigade Headquarters the general opinion was that they had carried the pretence too far. On this occasion we suffered two casualties in our own Battalion Headquarters. One man was watching the raid from an upstairs window in the farmhouse we had requisitioned and when he saw a bomb detach itself from the leading plane his first thought was to get in the open to avoid being buried under masonry. Another man watching from outside thought it safest to get under cover. Travelling at high speed, they collided in the door of the farmhouse and knocked each other out. In the prevailing atmosphere of nervous tension minor accidents like this were seized on as comic relief. Indeed, fairly serious wounds often took on a relatively frivolous aspect in the heat of battle. I remember coming on a sergeant sitting in a shell hole wryly contemplating his ankle from which the foot had just been severed. In spite of the pain and the shock he looked up at me with a wry grin and said: 'If only Mum could see me now!'

The village of Battipaglia was eventually taken after a crippling bombing raid which practically levelled it to the ground. After that, we advanced as far as Salerno itself. The town had been completely evacuated by the civilian population, which had moved out into the open country. Our Battalion Headquarters set itself up in a large house which, judging from the few books still remaining in the shattered bookshelves, belonged to an architect. The Germans had been in possession before us and had apparently looted the place bare before we arrived.

We hadn't been in occupation more than an hour or so before the owner and his wife, a young Italian couple, came back to see what was left of their home. It was pathetic to see them wandering from cupboard to cupboard and discovering the loss of all their cherished belongings. The Germans, for no reason that one could see, had apparently destroyed all the wife's clothing and furs and the husband's collection of architectural books. Apart from a few sticks of battered furniture all that was left was the telephone, which we had commandeered and converted into a field telephone by detaching it from the wall and connecting to our own lines. It was this minor and, one might say, purely tactical encroachment on their property which they seemed to resent more than all the Germans' destruction. I suppose that telephone represented their last stake in the battered shell which had been their home. Anyway, the sight of it torn from its moorings seemed to upset them enormously. As signals officer I was detailed to cope with them and I spent a very sticky hour getting the unhappy pair off the premises.

In my experience the lot of a signals officer in a Guards infantry battalion was not a very happy one. He had, of course, the physical advantage of being attached to Battalion Headquarters, which meant that he was rarely called upon to spend much time in the forefront of the fighting. On the other hand he had the moral discomfort of being responsible to company commanders whose knowledge of modern methods of communication was nil. In many respects I was a failure at the job, through my own lack of concentration and administrative ability. But I was not nearly as incompetent and uncooperative as most of the Battalion's senior officers thought me to be. At one stage a patrol was sent forward into No Man's Land and I was ordered to maintain contact with it by signalling from an upstairs window of Battalion Headquarters. When I confessed to the senior officer who gave the command that all the signalling lamp batteries had been sent away in error on a truck he soundly reprimanded me as a bungling idiot. He didn't know that I had sent the batteries away on purpose, in order to avoid committing not only my own suicide but that of the entire Battalion Headquarters by flashing a lamp from an upstairs window in the direction of the enemy's artillery batteries. Some of the last-minute brainwaves which were conceived by the company commanders and passed to the wretched signals officer to carry out had to be heard to be believed.

On the eve of one advance the officer commanding the leading company decided that new-fangled radio communication was too unreliable, so he demanded to be kept in constant *telephone* communication with Battalion Headquarters. When I pointed out that the telephone lines were not elastic and could therefore hardly be used by troops on the move, he had the bright idea of commissioning two of my signallers to advance with him over hill and dale carrying an enormous roll of telephone line between them on a drum. Nothing would persuade him that this was impractical – nothing, that is, until the two sweating and stumbling men were suddenly pulled up short by the cable coming abruptly to an end. By dodging backwards and forwards in the company commander's wake they had expended about four miles of line in 300 yards, weaving a sort of cat's cradle among the bushes and vines. The experiment was not repeated.

In the Salerno position we had another spell of fierce fighting. By this time our casualties were mounting up, particularly among the officers. The Guards have a proud tradition for steadfastness and coolness in action. One has only to cite the occasion at Dunkirk, when they marched on to the jetty at the height of the bombardment in perfect parade-ground formation and inspired the battered troops on the beaches by their example, to show that their reputation is justified. But there are times in battle when blind, foolhardy courage is not the best, nor the only, solution to the problem.

I often found it difficult to reconcile myself to the 'do-or-die' atmosphere which encouraged officers – some of them young boys of nineteen – to march at the head of their platoons straight into enemy fire without observing the elementary rules of field-craft. If the Guards' tradition had only incorporated cunning and quick thinking to go with the bravery, many young lives would not have been thrown away for nothing. As it was, the draining away of platoon and company officers was appalling. While we were at Salerno, we had our first reinforcements from Africa – officers and men who were left behind when the invasion set sail to come on later as reserves. Those of us who had been fighting from the start had come to take the casualties as a matter of course. But many of the newcomers broke down and wept when they learnt how many of their friends had gone. If I had to live that time over again and was given the choice, I think I would choose to fight from the beginning again rather than arrive, unprepared and untoughened, in the middle of the horror, as they did.

All this time we were striving to continue the advance northwest out of Salerno. The main road ran between a series of little pimply hills which were held by the Germans. Every time we showed signs of moving they planted an artillery and mortar barrage down on the road and destroyed it. One day, to our horror, the order came from the Divisional Commander for a general advance up the road. Battalion Headquarters was then a railway tunnel, one end of which was safely tucked away behind a hill, the other looking forward up the road towards the enemy. As soon as the advance began the whole length of road became one mass of explosions. We crouched at the forward end of the tunnel waiting to move off and taking in the scene. Someone has made a terrible mistake, we thought. But orders must be obeyed, so there was nothing to be done except go to our deaths courageously. Unfortunately, there was plenty of time to think this time, and I was cold with fear. My signal truck had no armament. It was just a plain car like a civilian bread-van, and I had no doubt that if I started off down that road in it, I was a goner. At the last minute a brass hat from Divisional Headquarters came forward to our position and our Commanding Officer took him to the business end of the tunnel to show him the view. He went pale and hurried away.

Shortly afterwards, the order came forward for the advance to be halted and for the leading troops to take cover in the hills. We were saved! There was only one snag. One platoon was already advancing and could not be contacted except by personal envoy. Someone had to set off down the road to bring them back. At the time there was only one officer available at Battalion Headquarters and that was me. Without feeling in the least bit courageous or heroic I volunteered for the job, and a few minutes later set off on a bicycle for the main road.

I pedalled furiously along until I reached a point where I could see along the road for some distance.

There was no sign of the advancing platoon. So I left the bicycle and, with some relief, ran off the road down an embankment to some low ground with a few scattered bushes for cover. They could only have advanced this way so I began calling the platoon officer's name. But there was no answer. I careered on in a series of short sharp spurts, cowering in the bushes whenever I heard the hiss of an approaching mortar bomb. Some distance off the road there was a river running parallel to it and I crept forward along the bank. Suddenly there was a whoosh! and a deafening roar. Something caught me a stinging blow in the face. I lay half dazed for a minute, my whole face burning and smarting. Then I put up a tentative hand. My fingers contacted something warm and sticky.

I went suddenly weak and sick with apprehension, not daring to open my caked eyelids and inspect the damage. When I did pluck up the courage to look at my hand, I saw that it was covered, not in blood, but in a blackish-brown mess with a few traces of green weed. Mud! A mortar bomb had exploded on the bank of the river not far off, and had spattered me with a stinging shower of mud, and nothing more.

After this shock I felt a wave of impatience towards the platoon on whose behalf I was going through all these hazards. When I found them eventually walking chin-deep in water along the river bed – an unusual display of fieldcraft for the Guards – I took a certain amount of pleasure in telling them to turn round and walk all the way back.

Before the advance was resumed the Battalion was given three days' complete rest in the town of Salerno, and in accordance with Brigade of Guards tradition a ceremonial parade was ordered. I have criticized some aspects of the Guards tradition. But on this occasion the sudden introduction of a spit-and-polish parade into the unreal atmosphere of battle was a masterstroke of psychology. Men who had been barely able to wash their hands and faces for over three weeks were suddenly faced with the mundane and everyday task of polishing brasses and Blancoing belts. And never has a battalion marched with such a swagger as ours did on that parade.

It was during this three days' rest period at Salerno that I began to feel symptoms of illness which could not entirely be put down to prolonged fatigue. I began having violent headaches and spasms of alternate shivering and sweating. Quite early on I recognized these as the signs of malaria, but for some curious reason I did not welcome them. Although I had found nothing stimulating or exalting about my three weeks' experience of battle, I felt very depressed at the thought of leaving the Battalion at this point. Danger breeds esprit de corps in the most unlikely places and, whatever the exact psychological reason, the fact remains that, having got so far, I was passionately anxious not to have to leave the scene. I had a vague idea that if I kept out of the way of the Medical Officer I could ride out this bout of malaria without anybody knowing. This I managed to do up to a point when the new advance had just begun. I can remember lying on an extremely uncomfortable bed of corn cobs in the first stages of the advance, feeling so ill that I hardly noticed that an enemy artillery barrage was knocking great hunks of masonry off the barn in which I lay. Eventually the Medical Officer caught me shivering, whipped out a thermometer and that was that. I was bundled straight off to an emergency hospital behind the lines and from there to a hospital ship which took me back to Africa. I didn't know it then (and would have regretted it bitterly if I had) but my active service days were over.

Dr Jazz

Having left the fighting zone, I was passed back through a series of stages to a field hospital near the shore. But this time I was right in the throes of malaria, sweating one minute and racked with shivers the next. So I wasn't taking much notice of my surroundings. The shore hospital was very overworked and under-equipped. It had no beds, so the patients brought in by each ambulance convoy were just stacked along the walls on their stretchers. After a night here we were carried on board a hospital ship and put in a hold which was honeycombed with tiers of bunks.

Clean sheets! Cool, comforting pillows! Life suddenly became civilized again on that ship.

After the diet of soya link sausages and M. & V. (meat and vegetables) on which we had been living for the past months, the food was positively Ritzy. When platefuls of chicken, roast potatoes and peas first made their appearance my companions, all suffering from malaria, let out cries of ecstasy and fell upon them enthusiastically. For some frustrating reason which I could not understand I didn't share their enthusiasm. I could not raise even the smallest appetite. This seemed to puzzle the medical staff, because loss of appetite is not one of the symptoms of malaria, and having got over the first bout of fever, I should have been feeling quite peckish. On the second day out to sea, however, a slight yellowing of the whites of my eyes and other less printable symptoms revealed that on top of malaria I had also managed to acquire jaundice. I didn't know until several months later that I was also harbouring a latent form of dysentery at that time. But never mind – jaundice and malaria were enough to be going on with. The hospital ship took us back to Africa and we moved into a more permanent hospital at Philippeville. Owing to the diverse nature of my two complaints they had to be treated separately, so the doctors tackled the malaria first and then turned their attention to the jaundice. The latter treatment consisted of being on a fat-free diet for about three weeks, and what with the total loss of appetite on board and the enforced diet in hospital, my eating habits didn't return to normal for some weeks after I had left the front. All this time I continued to feel a strange nostalgia for the fighting line and the Battalion which was now battling its way towards Naples. Whenever reports of action came in I got an angry sort of feeling that I should be there.

This had nothing to do with belligerence – I was never one of the 'Get-at-the-Boche' boys. And although I am as prone as anyone to terrible rushes of anger to the head when I read about concentration camps or mass-murders, I had no feelings of any sort about the German soldiers opposite me in the field. They were just objects, as abstract as the elements, which had to be fought and outwitted. As signals officer based at Battalion Headquarters, I didn't meet many Germans face-to-face – just a few prisoners and one soldier whom I came on suddenly crouching in a trench. I was following a telephone line looking for a fault and as I rounded a corner, there he was, staring straight at me. The shock of seeing him was followed by a worse one when, in the middle of challenging him, I realized that he was dead. Dead Germans and captured Germans – those were all I saw. I never had to fire my pistol and I can't help being glad of that. No, my anxiety to be back in the fighting arose from feelings less objective than hate or revenge or even patriotism. And by the time my jaundice had been conquered and I had been moved, with my appetite restored, to a luxurious convalescent camp outside Algiers this hankering after the life of action had been replaced by the familiar pre-drafting partiality for peace and safety. The knot which had tied me to the Battalion in times of danger and discomfort gradually loosened and then fell apart.

The convalescent camp outside Algiers was an extraordinary place, not in the least bit designed to keep one's battle enthusiasm in top gear. The camp was spread along the shore of a lagoon and consisted of a main building and a collection of little chalets in which each patient had a room. The main building looked out through huge windows over the bay, and there we ate and played in the communal recreation and dining rooms. Apart from a physical training session in the afternoon there was nothing to do in the daytime except lie about on the beach reading and writing long-overdue letters home. In the evening there were dances, debates and whist drives. And there were enough enthusiastic musicians there for me to form a rough-and-ready band. It was such a peaceful, idyllic existence that I would have been quite happy to have stayed there for the rest of the war. But before I had been there very long I had to report sick again with some internal trouble which baffled the camp doctor. So back I went to hospital for investigation.

The army General Hospital provided several more links with normal existence. The colonel who examined me on arrival recognized my name and recalled that he had once operated on one of my great-uncles for gall stones. Colonel Lester was a strange man. He seemed to be firmly convinced that my trouble was a nervous one and he clung to his belief tenaciously. We had quite a battle as I lay on the couch in his office and he kneaded my stomach meditatively.

'How are your nerves?' he asked, looking at me very hard.

Having not so long ago got through a month of hard fighting without any serious upset of the nerves I felt justified in saying that they were good.

He smiled a disbelieving smile.

'But not very good – eh?'

'Excellent!' I said, emphatically.

'Come now!' he said. 'We'll get nowhere if you don't admit it – you've always had bad nerves, haven't you?'

'No, never!' I cried, refusing to budge an inch.

He let the matter rest for the time being but brought it up again with every examination. Once when I was sitting on the hospital lawn in a deck chair quietly reading, he crept up behind me on tiptoe and suddenly boomed 'Lyttelton!' in a loud voice. When he saw me give a slight start he was overjoyed. 'There!' he cried. 'You jumped!'

'Of course I did, sir, I wasn't expecting you.'

'Do you always jump at slight noises?' he enquired – and the battle was on again.

Even when he diagnosed gall stones as my complaint (wrongly as it turned out) and ordered me to be flown back to England he still clung to the idea that some profound nervous disorder was at the back of it all. From others I discovered that he applied this approach to all of his patients, whether they were suffering from undefined stomach trouble or straightforward fractured limbs. We had in our ward some of the toughest eggs I have ever come across, men who were recovering from almost incredible injuries without batting an eyelid. He tried to persuade them each in turn that their nerves were in a terrible state. When I was back in England months later, I met someone who had just returned from Africa and the army General Hospital. He reported that while he was there, Colonel Lester had become a hospital patient himself – in the psychiatric ward!

The thing which really brought life back to normal for me at the

General Hospital was the presence there of a resident band. When I left Salerno with malaria I had to leave my kit behind to be sent on later, but they hadn't been able to prise my trumpet away from me and through all the succession of hospital moves I had it clutched in my hand in its sandbag. So when I at last came upon this group of musicians I was ready for action. It wasn't exactly a jazz band, consisting of piano, drums, several saxophonists and a violin, but after nearly two months without any real playing I was in no mood to be particular. With this band I did one or two jobs at local camps. One which sticks in my memory was at a dance for American troops. On this occasion we had as our leader a G.I. clarinettist called Goldberg, who claimed to have been in Artie Shaw's band back in the States. Artie Shaw was then the fashionable bandleader and every American soldier-musician I came across over in North Africa from learners upward had at one time or another played in his band – all except one, a trumpet-player who was not only a lifelong member of Harry James's orchestra but actually 'ghosted' all Harry James's own solos on record. The nearest Goldberg had ever been to Artie Shaw's band, I reckon, was the front row of the stalls in his local cinema. He couldn't play the clarinet at all well but he had style. The way he wandered about among the musicians with his instrument raised on high was most impressive. At the end of the session he informed us that he was the Musical Director of the local U.S. Army Broadcasting Station and he wanted us all there the following week to take part in one of his jazz broadcasts. He then took me to one side and told me in the strictest confidence that he was also an important foreign correspondent for the American musical magazine *Down Beat*, and he was intending to write a big article about me for that paper.

'Man,' he said, patting me affectionately on the arm, 'you've arrived!'

Unfortunately neither the broadcast nor the eulogistic article ever materialized. For all I know Goldberg may have been perfectly genuine in all his roles, but I wasn't in Africa long enough to find out. Three days later, on 23 December 1943, I was bundled, labelled GALL STONES, on to a hospital plane and flown back to England. I arrived home at about seven o'clock, putting my head round the drawing-room door just as my parents were preparing to take a dinner party in to dinner. It must have been rather a shock for them to see me because I did not have the opportunity to let them know that I was flying home and they had, only a few minutes before, been speculating as to my whereabouts. Apparently their conclusions had been that I must have left hospital and rejoined the Battalion in Italy.

I was home on leave for a month before being committed to the Royal Masonic Hospital in West London for investigation into my alleged gall stones. The first thing they discovered was that I had no gall stones. And from there they embarked on a series of (for me) uncomfortable and humiliating experiments to try and discover what I did have. They took a month to find out that it was dysentery and a further two months to cure it. In the course of X-ray examinations, they discovered, quite by the way, that I have eighteen inches of intestine more than most people have, a fact which I am always ready to explain to those who think I eat too much.

The Royal Masonic Hospital was then half military, half civilian. It made some pretence at following the military hospital routine but not enough to matter. Inspections were the only annoyance – we were inspected by matrons, inspected by chief medical officers, inspected by generals and on one occasion inspected by H.R.H. the Duchess of Kent. Before each of these state visits the decks had to be cleared completely of any symptoms of civilized life. Books, games, writing paper and personal belongings of every kind had to be out of sight, and as there was nowhere else to put them we had to bundle them into our beds with us. When the inspecting visitors arrived, bedside tables were bare except for such necessities of life as enamel kidney basins, wooden spatulas, thermometers and bottles of medicine, and the patients would be sitting up in their neat beds as motionless as dummies, hardly daring to breathe in case a chance movement should unloose a cascade of books and jigsaw puzzles at the feet of the visitor. Most of the personages inspecting took all this as a matter of course, but the Duchess of Kent endeared herself to all of us in the ward when, after walking round and addressing a few words to each of us, she turned to the attendant matron and asked: 'What on *earth* do they do all day?'

At the end of the course of treatment at the Royal Masonic Hospital, I went home on sick leave pronounced cured, but the unorthodox symptoms persisted and when I went to a medical board at Victoria Barracks for a check-up their verdict was 'hospitalization' again.

This time the hospital was at Shenley in Hertfordshire. The military section of it consisted of two or three requisitioned blocks in the middle of the Shenley Lunatic Asylum. It was not perhaps the ideal place for invalids but then I suppose space was short in those days and military hospitals had to go where they could. The remaining two-thirds of the establishment continued to operate as a mental institution and we shared the grounds with the inmates. This was a very unhappy arrangement. Apart from occasional alarms when a dangerous lunatic was reported at large in the precincts, the constant proximity of men and women in all the different degrees of idiocy and derangement didn't help battle-weary soldiers to get well. One of the military blocks was given over to shell-shock and psychiatric cases. Their chances of recovery were, I am sure, considerably impaired by the sights and sounds of the mental home and I can't conceive anything more callous and foolish than to put them there. I must confess that after four months I was very glad to get away from it myself. I went to Shenley originally for further investigation into my internal complaint, but while there I indulged in two further bouts of malaria and another operation on my recalcitrant left foot. Two eminent orthopaedic surgeons had hitherto performed on it without success. Now it began to give trouble again, so I showed it to the resident surgeon at Shenley, describing its history. He was a major in the R.A.M.C. and the possibility of succeeding where two star performers had failed obviously tickled him. Anyway, he decided to have a go. For a month, while the malaria and dysentery treatment proceeded, I lay with my foot encased in a plaster of Paris boot. When this was removed and the foot was examined the verdict was once again – No Change. The little major shrugged his shoulders with a nothing-ventured-nothing-gained air and abandoned the struggle. Since then my foot has remained in its unorthodox shape – I haven't bothered it and since I have given up marching about in heavy army boots, it hasn't bothered me.

1944 was a bad year for trumpet-playing. Since leaving Algiers I had been unable to practise at all. Trumpeting was not encouraged in the hospitals, least of all at Shenley, where the first few blasts might have thrown the inmates into unmanageable confusion. But at the end of the year things improved. After being discharged from Shenley a fit man I found myself posted back to the Guards Depot at Caterham.

Caterham was more comfortable for an officer than it had been for a recruit, although the boredom was deadly. Recruits arrived in a constant stream, and a first-day squad could always be recognized by the complete absence of symmetry in its appearance on the parade ground. There were fat men, thin men, square men, round men, men tilting over to right or left, splay-footed men, pigeon-toed men – in fact men of every shape and size. Miraculously there began to appear some sort of uniformity of shape after a few weeks, and by the end of the course they were all just guardsmen. Every now and then, of course, an incurable individualist turned up who couldn't be shaped into the mould. These misfits ranged from men with an ineradicable grudge against authority to men whose limbs just wouldn't obey the rules. They were all dealt with in exactly the same way, being sent straight off to a psychiatrist, who found them unfit for service in the Guards.

At Caterham with me was a Scots Guards officer called Hugo Charteris, a distant relation of mine and something of a kindred spirit. The boredom and frustration at Caterham ate deeper into Hugo's soul than it did into mine. He was always getting into terrible scrapes. Once, deeply disturbed by a conversation with a brother-officer in an Armoured Battalion about the deficiencies of British tanks, he sent an anonymous letter to the Minister of War upbraiding him for the smugness of his attitude. Characteristically, he wrote the letter on Guards Depot notepaper and put his initials on the envelope. So when the Minister took a heavy view of the incident and reported it to the Major-General commanding the Brigade of Guards, a little simple detective work led to Hugo being put in open arrest. The matter finally fizzled out with a reprimand, but not until a vast dossier had been filed on the case at Brigade Headquarters.

During my spell at the Guards Depot I began to brush up my trumpet-playing. Apart from the opportunity for practice provided by the long periods of inactivity, there were also quite a regular number of dances held in the main gymnasium. For these functions a unit from the regimental Band of the Grenadier Guards used to provide the dance music. The standard was high, which is not surprising, because during the war many of the leading jazz and dance musicians were enlisted into the Household Brigade bands. Names like Harry Hayes, Lad Busby and George Evans could be found in the rosters. Although these regimental bandsmen were attested and enlisted like ordinary recruits they were really semi-pro soldiers who were free to carry on their engagements in London theatres and dance orchestras once their military duties were done. So throughout the war many idols of the followers of popular music could be seen trudging along at the head of a column of guardsmen. At one of the dances at Caterham I sat in on trumpet with the band. Being struck by the clarinet-playing of the bandsman sitting next to me I asked him what his name was. When he said: 'Nat Temple, sir,' I very nearly stood to attention and saluted.

On 8 May 1945, V.E. Day, there was an atmosphere of excitement from early dawn. I had no official duty to perform that day, so around noon I took the train up to London, joined some friends and headed for Buckingham Palace where over one hundred thousand people had assembled by lunchtime. Never one to pass up an opportunity for an impromptu 'blow', I had my trumpet at the ready.

I let fly with jazzed-up versions of 'Run, Rabbit, Run' and 'We're Gonna Hang Out the Washing on the Siegfried Line'. People began singing and a tiny space was formed in the crowd for dancing. It wasn't long before I had a band. A man appeared with a trombone, someone else turned up with a big drum and, finally, a sailor joined us who just happened to have brought along the huge horn from an old-fashioned gramophone. Into this, tuba-fashion, he blew some ripe raspberries.

Throughout the day the Royal Family appeared on the balcony of the Palace and each time we serenaded them. Towards evening, some people turned up with a rickety hand-cart, and that was when my friends really landed me in it. Literally. They hoisted me into the cart and I was pushed at terrifying speed down The Mall, with the rest of the band puffing along behind.

Like Boadicea in her chariot, I led the procession up St James's Street and into Piccadilly. I must have gone through every tune in my then limited repertoire. Just outside Simpson's I spotted two of my senior officers stalking along the pavement. But this was, after all, V.E. Day, and they took the sight of one of their juniors making an exhibition of himself with admirable aplomb.

In later years, I wondered if I had dreamt all this. Then, to my delight, a friend unearthed a B.B.C. tape of a commentary by Howard Marshall in which I get a mention. Admittedly not by name, but he does say, 'And as we return you to the studio, somebody down there is playing a trumpet....'

It was me, it was me – and there's a Louis Armstrong-style flourish at the end of 'Roll Out the Barrel' to prove it!

Back at the Palace there was more dancing and a further appearance of the Royal Family on the balcony. I dimly remember blasting a chorus of 'For He's a Jolly Good Fellow' in the direction of His Majesty. After that, with lungs aching and lips red and raw from so much trumpeting, I went to bed.

Soon after V.E. Day I was transferred from Caterham to Chelsea Barracks. From that point on my military life was really no more than a marking time until my demobilization. Soldiering at Chelsea Barracks was, if anything, duller than at Caterham. The Guards Depot did at least have a function. Chelsea had none – it was, in every sense, a dump. Officers seconded to outside units such as the War Office and London District Command Headquarters used it as a hotel. Soldiers for whom there was no immediate use were posted there until they could be fitted in somewhere else. Medically unfit men were sent there to await discharge. The barracks were equipped with a rough court-room which did a brisk business in courts-martial, the prisoners being housed in the officers' or other ranks' quarters according to their status.

I was posted to Chelsea as a company officer in the unit which staffed the barracks. My men performed all the essential functions such as whitewashing the window-sills and sweeping the barrack square. Of course they did parades too, starting at 6.30 in the morning and going on intermittently all through the day. Each parade had to be equipped with an officer, whose role was to walk about swishing a stick and thinking his own thoughts until the forty-five-minute period was over, when he was needed to give the sergeant-major leave to dismiss the troops. Sometimes there was a misunderstanding and an officer would inadvertently miss a parade. In this event everything went on exactly as if he had been there, the sergeant-major dismissing the troops on his own initiative and everybody being quite happy except the truant, who found himself carpeted for dereliction of duty. With me as a company officer at Chelsea was George Lascelles, now the Earl of Harewood. It was the job of one or other of us to attend the first early-morning parade, and we were left to arrange it between ourselves. Somehow we had an infallible knack of misunderstanding the arrangements so that when the parade formed up in the morning, both Lyttelton and Lascelles were usually tucked up in bed snoring off the effects of a late night. We became a familiar team on the Adjutant's disciplinary parade.

Apart from parades, there was no life at all in Chelsea Barracks. Most of the regular Guards officers had a routine which they had grown into since their young officer days and which kept them quite happily employed throughout the day. It can be summarized as follows: get up – go on parade – have breakfast – go on parade – return to mess for mid-morning sherry or pink gin – go on parade – return to mess for more sherry or gin – have lunch – sit in mess reading papers and magazines and drinking port or gin – go on parade – return to mess for mid-afternoon sherry or gin – go on parade – return to mess for tea – sit and gossip until time for sherry or gin – have dinner – sit in mess drinking port or gin until bed-time. On days when there were no parades, the routine was the same except for the deletion of the words 'go on parade'.

There is no limit to the opportunities for social advancement that I have passed up through innate unclubbability. As a young Guards

Officer at large in London after the war, with so many eligible young men still posted overseas, I was strongly in the running as a Debuntantes' Delight. Instead of which, whenever Ball Committees met and invitation lists were drawn up, the order went forth, 'Don't ask that young man with the big feet who stands by the band all night long!'

There were Royal occasions, too, when a finger seemed to beckon me through half-open doors towards that most exclusive of clubs which surrounded the young princesses. I still have, in a drawerful of oddments, an invitation by Royal Command to 'a small informal dance at Windsor Castle on Thursday, 25 March 1943'. Not one of your great faceless, impersonal State Balls, mark you, but an informal dance, and a small one at that. Just George, Elizabeth, Lillibet, Margaret and me, with perhaps a couple of hundred odds and sods thrown in to make up the numbers.

Before going into the ballroom, we were briefed by a court official on such details as how to bow to the Royal Family on presentation, not bending from the waist in an ostentatious fashion but letting the head loll forward as though the neck muscles had momentarily given way. Since I was six foot three and Princess Margaret was three foot six, the exercise was rather more complicated than the court official made out, but by bending the knees surreptitiously, I think I carried it off all right. It was the band that let me down. It was Geraldo's Orchestra, at that time liberally peppered with names held in awe by youthful readers of the *Melody Maker* and *Rhythm*. The late Ted Heath was on trombone, Nat Temple sat in the saxophone section and the star trumpet soloist was Leslie 'Jiver' Hutchinson, a particular idol of mine.

The whole dance ended on a rather unpropitious note. Some of the copious supply of champagne found its way down below to the guardroom where some guardsmen in my company were on duty as firewatchers. Leaving their inhibitions below stairs among the firebuckets and stirrup-pumps, they surfaced in a state of some disarray to watch the guests departing. Two of them went so far as to line up unsteadily alongside the Royal party, presenting arms with their incendiary-bomb shovels and grinning inanely.

Once settled in at Chelsea, I began to explore the London jazz world. In those days the task of a jazz hunter was harder than it is now. The only jazz club resembling those which abound today was the Feldman Swing Club functioning every Sunday night at 100 Oxford Street. Here Mr and Mrs Joe Feldman, a friendly Jewish couple, used to preside over jam sessions featuring the avant-garde of London's jazz musicians. Their elder sons, Robert and Monty, kept a knowledgeable watch on the musical side of the establishment, but the apple of their eye was the youngest, Victor, who at the age of ten performed prodigiously on the drums. To his credit, Victor Feldman survived being an infant prodigy and became one of Britain's leading modern musicians, playing piano and vibraphone as well as the drums.

In providing jazz music for dancing between the practical hours of 7 and 10.30p.m. the Feldman Club can claim to be the forerunner of today's clubs. Apart from Feldman's there were countless small local rhythm and hot clubs meeting in pubs and back rooms all over London, sometimes with a 'live' band, sometimes relying entirely on gramophone records. I shall have more to say later about these rhythm clubs. The point I want to make now is that they were local, private gatherings, without much attraction for the enthusiast in search of 'live' jazz. For him, outside of the Feldman Club Jam Sessions, there were only the nightclubs. And free-and-easy informal nightclubs with a jazz atmosphere were hard to find in London just after the war. The old haunts – the Florida, the Paradise, the Nest, where American visitors of the calibre of Coleman Hawkins, 'Fats' Waller and Benny Carter used to sit in with the local musicians whenever they came to London – had disappeared. In 1935, the British Musicians' Union and the American Federation of Musicians fell out. America clamped down on the free entry of British bands to the States, and our own Union reciprocated by banning the entry of American musicians into Great Britain. Of course, jazz fans over here got the thin end of the carrot, because all the great jazz stars come from America, and there was a greater demand for them in Britain than for our musicians in the U.S.A.. The ban created a situation which gave all American jazzmen a rarity value.

I became a jazz enthusiast too late to savour the pre-war atmosphere. Once, while I was still a seventeen-year-old at Eton, I did make a pilgrimage to London to take in the Bag O' Nails and the Nest Club. Breaking out of the school and slinking up to London nightclubs was a popular sport among sophisticated Etonians, although I think more of them *talked* about it than actually did it. My own visit was not a midnight escapade. I went with another jazz-minded schoolmate during one of the midterm weekend holidays known as Long Leave. Altogether our initiation into London nightlife was dreadfully respectable. At the Bag O' Nails rows of 'hostesses' sat round and gazed at us like birds of prey as we sipped our drinks, but our eyes were on the band, and we could not spare them a glance. If this strikes you as odd, then you have never seen a dedicated jazz fan. We were hearing jazz – in the flesh – for the first time – the rest could wait!

But to come back to Chelsea. When my post-war explorations began the only jazz nightclub resembling the pre-war pattern was a place in Regent Street called the Nuthouse. By being the favourite haunt of visiting American service musicians it managed to recapture some of the quality of unexpectedness which the old free-and-easy clubs possessed. There was always the chance that some well-known musician from Sam Donahue's U.S. Navy Band or the Glenn Miller Orchestra would drop in for a bit of off-duty playing.

The clientele was a mixed one. There were plenty of G.I.'s, quite a number of Guards and Cavalry Officers on a slumming kick and the usual floating population of night owls – men and women of doubtful occupation who only appear at large after dark. The band had a characteristic nightclub line-up – three saxophones, trumpet and a rhythm section of piano, double-bass and drums – but it had a solid core of jazz musicians. The leader of the band, and its drummer, was Carlo Krahmer, a rare mixture of professional musician and jazz record-collector. Carlo was then the sort of unofficial Dean of the London jazz world. In the basement of his flat in Bedford Avenue he had a gramophone room lined from ceiling to floor with one of the largest record collections in the world. Every day some session would be in progress down there, with musicians and jazz lovers of all tastes sitting round listening to their favourite music. Carlo was always on the lookout for new talent in the jazz field, and ready with his advice and assistance.

If anybody can claim the dubious credit for having 'discovered' me it is Carlo Krahmer. On one of my first visits to the Nuthouse I took my trumpet along and, encouraged by my friends, asked if I could sit in with the band. There passed over the musicians' faces an expression which in later years I have come to know well. It is a special look, registering consent with the minimum degree of encouragement, which musicians reserve for Society types who ask if they can have a go with the band. I was never a Society type, but I was on this occasion wearing the uniform of a Grenadier Captain, which to them amounted to very much the same thing. Mind you, there was some justification for their suspicion. The brother officer who had first introduced me to the Nuthouse was a mad peer in the Irish Guards, who, among his other delusions, imagined that he could play the drums. It being the policy of nightclub managements everywhere to humour and cherish their patrons, especially if they are in the Guards *and* the peerage, my eccentric friend always had to have his little spell behind the drums. He could play a few rudimentary beats on the drum, and if he had concentrated on just beating time he would have not made so many deadly enemies in the band.

Unfortunately, he had seen too many Gene Krupa films, and clearly identified himself with the American drum virtuoso. As he thrashed about him with the sticks, he mumbled to himself, writhed about in terrible contortions, shook his hair down over his eyes, and in moments of special excitement flung the sticks up in the air so that they fell into the piano, on to the dance floor, even into the drinks of the people sitting near the stand – anywhere, in fact, but back into his hands. It was little wonder that the band regarded him and his drumming as an affliction sent deliberately to try them. Some of the musicians have told me since that when I first appeared in front of them with my trumpet and in my uniform their hearts sank. They nodded glumly in answer to my request, so I climbed up on to the stand and suggested one of the standard jazz tunes.

I won't say that my playing brought them all to their feet cheering

and applauding, but it was certainly better than they had expected, and from that time on I was allowed – even invited – to sit in quite regularly. Apart from the regular practice which it gave me at playing in a band, this privilege came in useful in other respects. The Nuthouse was a tough little club in which fights were common. These fights usually spread quickly, because the G.I. population could never let even the smallest outbreak go without joining in, whether they knew what the issue was or not. Consequently, small arguments in distant corners of the room were apt to develop quickly into wholesale rough houses.

There is an unwritten law on these occasions that as long as the band keeps playing it shall remain unmolested. So whenever trouble broke out my first emergency action was always to take up my trumpet and scurry on to the bandstand, leaving my less fortunate friends to fend for themselves. The Guards are famous for their courage and steadfastness in the field, but in a nightclub roughhouse they are absolutely useless. I remember one tremendous fight in which broken bottles and razors were used. The band, including myself, played 'Who's Sorry Now?' flat out, for half an hour, in self-defence. Halfway through I looked across to see how the gallant company of majors and captains at my table were faring. They were crouching on the floor under the table, clasping their unfinished bottles of gin to their breasts like mothers defending their children, and trembling with apprehension.

Through these appearances at the Nuthouse, I was befriended by Carlo Krahmer, and he became my guide in a further exploration of the jazz-cum-dance-music world. It was while I was still an officer at Chelsea Barracks that, under Carlo's wing, I did my first 'gig'. Archer Street, then the unofficial headquarters and meeting place of London's dance musicians, was the market place for gigs. On Thursdays, business was at its most brisk, and the whole area of Archer Street was thick with musicians looking for work, and agents and bandleaders looking for musicians.

Officers in the Brigade of Guards were not encouraged to hang about Archer Street touting for gigs, and anyway, I was not a professional musician in need of a livelihood. So I didn't pick up my first gig in 'The Street'.

It came about in a more roundabout way. A black bandleader and entertainer who ran an agency for black artists was approached to produce a band for a British Empire Victory Ball in Mayfair. The hostess was the ex-wife of a distinguished peer – let's call her Lady B. As often happens on these occasions, the bandleader in question had no band, and so he went down to Archer Street and roped in one or two musicians of his acquaintance, asking them to bring along any other instrumentalists they knew. Carlo was picked as the drummer and he brought me. I approached this first gig with a certain amount of trepidation. To begin with, I had been stationed for some time at Chelsea Barracks and my face was quite well known there. Supposing one of my senior officers – the Commanding Officer himself perhaps – appeared as a guest at Lady B.'s British Empire Ball? Would he take kindly to the appearance of one of his captains in a tuxedo and made-up tie, playing the trumpet in the band? I decided to take the risk. But when I let myself out of the back entrance of the Officers' Mess at Chelsea Barracks I was disguised as much as possible in civvies and my oldest and grubbiest mackintosh. After V.J. [victory over Japan] Day, officers could wear what they liked when off-duty. The pre-war rules which insisted on Guards Officers wearing an off-duty 'uniform' of bowler hat and Guards tie, and which forbade them to travel on buses or tubes, or to carry a parcel in the street – these were relaxed in deference to post-war austerity conditions. And lucky for me they were, or I should never have been able to embark on my Jekyll-and-Hyde existence at Chelsea.

Having left the Barracks, I met Carlo at his home and we made our way to the large house in Mayfair where we were to play. The door was open and we could see one or two liveried flunkeys passing to and fro inside. They seemed to be fully occupied so we found our own way up the broad, velvet-carpeted staircase to the ballroom. Halfway across the floor we were intercepted by a short, diamond-studded and very angry figure. It was Lady B. herself, bristling with indignation.

'What on earth do you mean by walking in here in your mackintoshes?' she cried. 'Go outside and take them off.' As we turned away with our tails between our legs, she said as an afterthought, 'And anyway, I thought you were supposed to be black.' Apparently, she was under the impression that she had ordered a 'coloured' band, which she presumably thought appropriate to a British Empire Ball. We made a few weak, mumbled excuses for being the wrong colour and hurried out to leave our mackintoshes in the pantry. Soon the whole band was assembled. No doubt to her ladyship's chagrin, all of us were white except the leader. As far as I remember, we had two trumpets, a tenor saxophone and rhythm section. There was no music. We just 'busked' through all the obvious tunes and as many of the contemporary dance hits as we could. During the intervals we were herded off discreetly into the kitchen quarters behind the green baize door. There we had sandwiches and drank vast quantities of the liquor intended for her ladyship's guests. This we did at the instigation of the head butler, a treacherous old tyrant, whose main aim seemed to be to sabotage the dance by reducing the band, the staff and the guests to incapability.

After Lady B.'s Victory Ball it was back to Chelsea Barracks for me, and the normal round of garrison duties. There were one or two more gigs with Carlo Krahmer, but none of them compared with the first one for interest and excitement. While at Chelsea I did one other strange job in a rather different sphere. Eton College runs a Mission in Hackney Wick, staffed by a Missioner appointed by the College and financed by the School. One day I had a letter from one of the Eton masters asking me to play the trumpet at their annual Easter Service of Witness. Playing the trumpet in church was no new experience for me – I had, in the past, made quite a speciality of churning out the 'Trumpet Voluntary' at family weddings. But this one was to be different, I gathered, in that it was to be held in the open air. At first I demurred. The idea of standing out trumpeting hymns in Hackney Wick was rather forbidding. But in the end the Great Uncle Albert in me prevailed and I asked myself – 'Why not?'. Finding no good answer, I wrote back agreeing to appear. There was a brother officer at Chelsea who was interested in the religious aspect of the occasion and I took him along on the day to give me moral support.

When I got to Hackney Wick I discovered that the part of the service in which I was to function consisted of a procession through the streets of Hackney Wick led by me playing hymns, and punctuated by a series of 'whistle stops' at which the Missioner and sundry volunteers stood in turns on a chair and addressed the populace. The Chelsea contingent rose superbly to the occasion, though I say it myself. I gave spirited renderings of 'There Is a Green Hill' and 'Onward Christian Soldiers' and my brother officer abandoned his role of spectator halfway through the procession and leaped on to the chair to give an impromptu address. The idea of the procession was to collect a crowd and lead them back to the church for the service. We did collect quite a considerable following of curious children, but, alas! as most of them were on roller skates, they were ill-equipped for church and all of them vanished noisily as we approached the church door. Apart from them there was nobody, but we had done our best.

PART 3
LONDON JAZZ

Unbooted Character

My army career ended on a surrealistic note when I was appointed Adjutant of an Army Mobile Demonstration column. This was a sort of circus which toured England showing off the army in all its most colourful and interesting aspects. We lumbered off round the country like Billy Smart's in khaki, setting up in fields and on football grounds where the P.T. boys did gymnastics, the military police performed on motorbikes, the artillery and the tank chaps let kids swarm all over their guns and tanks, and the dental corps, by way of a side-show, demonstrated how they made military false teeth. Though I say it myself (and as Adjutant to the whole show I was responsible for the fact that, four out of five times, we hit the right town at the right time) it was rather impressive. It was said when we got back that we had attracted one recruit but that three of our chaps had deserted. I think it was only a rumour. However, at the end of five years in the army and with release now in sight, I can't say that the failure of the demonstration column cost its Adjutant much sleep. I was more concerned at the time about what I was going to do when I left the army.

When I was about sixteen, there was a plan afoot in my family to put me into shipping. It was a notion born of desperation. Some years before, while still at a private school, I had gone through a nautical phase, sparked off by a guided tour over the luxury liner *Olympic*, in dry-dock at Southampton. Fired fleetingly with the spirit of Drake and Nelson, I took home all the give-away leaflets and subsequently wrote off in all directions for brochures. The literature about world tours which arrived in due course, hopefully addressed 'Dear Mr Lyttelton', soon assuaged my wanderlust. When you've seen one wide-angle photo of an empty luxury dining-room, you've seen them all, and I went on to film stars, whose photos showed slightly more variety.

When the question of a career arose, this passing interest in seafaring, though a thing of the past, was nonetheless a straw at which my parents clutched eagerly. Through a relative in the City, an introduction was arranged with a big shipping magnate. My father and I went to have lunch with him at Simpson's-in-the-Strand, just the place for momentous, man-to-man decisions. Sir John talked about shipping and its multiplicity of drawbacks for a young man in search of a career. My father listened with all the interest he could muster, showing, as the talk of clerking, overseas postings and promotional prospects unfolded, intense relief that it was my career and not his that was under discussion. And I just sat, revealing, I suspect, rather less animation than the great carcasses of meat that trundled past under their silver domes.

The point came when Sir John was interrupted in the middle of a long anecdote by the arrival of the cheese trolley. He seemed very particular about the condition of his cheese and took some time selecting not only his own portion but ours as well. At the end of this prolonged hiatus, he turned to my father and said, 'Now then, where was I?' My father looked blank for a moment, then turned to me with eyebrows raised. I desperately searched my mind for threads, but every one I grasped seemed involved with cheese. From that point on, the conversation took an abstract turn. Details about shipping as a career seemed by general consent to have become irrelevant. And whenever I see a photograph of Aristotle Onassis on his yacht surrounded by pulchritude, I murmur to myself: 'There, but for an attack of amnesia at Simpson's, go I.'

During the uneventful period at Chelsea I had decided that I would be a schoolmaster in my father's footsteps. This was a fairly natural choice, since I had lived in the scholastic atmosphere of Eton College since birth, and even when I left school to join the army long periods at Windsor had kept me under its spell. Also I had discovered while I was an officer instructor that I quite enjoyed lecturing, even on such uninspiring subjects as 'The History of the Grenadier Guards' or 'Military Law'. Having come to my decision and communicated it to my father, I got under way quickly. First I went to Eton for an interview with the Headmaster. I don't know what it is like now, but at that time, when scholastic manpower was short, Old Etonians were constantly being encouraged, almost urged, to return to the school as masters, and as the son of a Housemaster and great nephew of the last Headmaster but one I had all the right superficial qualifications. While at Eton I had specialized in classics. I was not particularly good at classics but I was better at them than anything else. So I suggested to the Headmaster that classics was the subject for me. He took the suggestion calmly, telling me to go away and brush up my Latin and Greek and come back when I was confident that I could teach them. And then he uttered the words which turned out later to be decisive. 'Geography', he said, 'is the subject of the future and I should like you to teach that too.'

Now, at the time those words didn't strike me as being very important. When I was at Eton geography was an insignificant subject, being tacked on to the history classes almost as an afterthought. The word 'geography' has always been associated in my mind with such easily-assimilated details as capital cities, mountain ranges, raw products and the idiosyncrasies of the Gulf Stream. After my interview with the Headmaster of Eton I went back to London with a light heart. All I had to do was to brush up my classics and rustle up a few facts about raw products and there I was, settled for life – an assistant master first, then a Housemaster and perhaps, eventually, Headmaster!

The trumpet played very little part in my plans and daydreams. I still thought of it purely as a hobby, in spite of the few paid engagements which I had undertaken in my spare time at Chelsea Barracks. Not that I ever thought of dropping it – a trumpet-playing Headmaster struck me as being no more out of the question than a trumpet-playing Captain in the Guards. When I got back to London things began to move. In order to satisfy the Headmaster of Eton of my capacity to teach geography I had to take a diploma, so I wrote off to London University for a prospectus and entry form. Meanwhile, an interview was arranged for me with one of the classics lecturers from Birkbeck College. We had lunch together and somewhere between the soup and the coffee I discovered that brushing up the classics was going to be a tougher job than I had thought – if indeed I had thought at all, which in retrospect seems unlikely. The lecturer was very tactful and understanding but the more he showered me with classical allusions and quotations, the more I realized that the little knowledge I had gained as a specialist at Eton had now completely and utterly disappeared. For the first time I became uneasy about the future and uneasiness turned to horror when the prospectus for the geography diploma arrived from London University. It ran into several pages and appeared to cover every single material aspect of the creation, ranging from astronomy to a detailed investigation into the earth's crust. I had two years in which to take the diploma. It seemed to me that twenty would be a more reasonable proposition, and even then I doubt if I would ever have acquired more than a nodding acquaintance with the earth's crust.

This put a different complexion on things. I spent several sleepless nights reshuffling my ideas on the future. Then I sent the prospectus off to my father and waited for his reaction. His part in the discussions and decisions about my career had been a model one. I know that he would have liked to see me follow in his footsteps. But his policy had always been to stand back until I had made my own decision and then to come forward with help and advice. He had done a lot of groundwork in preparing me for my refresher course in the classics, recommending and providing books and writing off to various influential people. I was therefore nervous of introducing an element of doubt into the proceedings at this late stage. Some time after sending him the geography prospectus I went down to see him at Eton. After a certain amount of vague talk I took a deep breath and said tentatively: 'Sometimes I wonder whether I shall ever make it.' He was plainly relieved that I had broached the subject.

'That', he said, 'is a thought which has occurred to me too.' He then confessed that he was as dubious as I was about my learning up all that geography.

From that point it was only a short stage to agreeing that I should throw in the sponge – and the earth's crust – without further ado, and to discussing what I should take up instead. I had thought about this and had come to the conclusion that there was only one thing I could do, and that was to exploit my talent for drawing. I had very little idea how this was to be done. I had no experience in drawing for publications outside of a few contributions to school and army magazines, and I knew nothing about the commercial art world. However, it provided a frail alternative to the earth's crust and I clutched at it. Then, as in previous discussions about the future, the trumpet and music played absolutely no part. The family tradition, upheld for generation after generation, which looked upon music as a spare-time luxury not to be countenanced as a profession, still exercised an influence over my thoughts. As it was I was taking quite a serious enough step in contemplating art as a profession.

Having decided to aim at a career which fell vaguely under the heading of Art, it remained for me to get a foot in the door as soon as possible. The Ministry of Education gave grants to ex-servicemen in those days to cover every sort of study and I managed to secure one amounting to £163 a year to go to art school. I enrolled at the Camberwell School of Arts and Crafts. I had a pretty shrewd idea in which field of the graphic arts my own talent lay, having dabbled in caricature and light illustration at school and in the army. If I hadn't known this when I started I should have very soon found it out. From the start I studied illustration under John Minton, who derived an endless amount of amusement from my pen-and-ink illustrations. This would have been more gratifying if they had been intentionally humorous. But it was my attempts at dramatic and romantic illustrations of such books as *The Mill on the Floss* and *Dr Jekyll and Mr Hyde* which made him laugh most uproariously. In my first term I entered for the illustration competition with some serious drawings – stark, spine-chilling studies in black-and-white of incidents from Edgar Allan Poe. 'You can't show those!' cried John Minton. 'They're funny!' So, quite early in my art school career, I made up my mind to concentrate on comic art. Consequently my interest in the architecture and anatomy classes, never much above zero, flickered out altogether.

At this time I started rooming with another ex-Grenadier in his mother's house somewhere off the Buckingham Palace Road, but it soon transpired that we were not on the same wavelength. To underline the point, it was about thirty years before I saw him again, when he popped up on the television as a deputy chairman of the Conservative Party Conference. So I moved into a bed-sitter in a rooming-house run by a gay couple in Smith Street, Chelsea.

After a sheltered life on the borders of Bucks and Berks, and despite six years in the army, my awareness of homosexuality was confined to the rather hearty goings-on embodied in public-school gossip. I spent the winter of 1947 – allegedly the coldest since the century began – huddled in an overcoat in my top-floor room, deterred by all the giggling and romping behind the landlords' door from asking how the meter worked.

To anyone who knows the King's Road today, with its boutiques opening and closing like nervous eyelids and every Saturday looking like the annual conference of the Last of the Mohicans, it may seem odd that my abiding memory was of the quietness. The dead of night in Smith Street was punctuated by sudden sounds from afar – a brawl at World's End, squabbling cats in Sloane Square. Once I was woken by the sound of female weeping and the crescendo and diminuendo of a voice repeating 'David…oh, David' in tones of deep tragedy. It was probably just an overwrought deb tottering home brainless after a flop party, but to my active imagination she was heading, Ophelia-like, for the river.

It was a period of reaction from five years of army life and whatever my shortcomings may have been on the academic side, in every other respect I was a model art student. Within a few weeks of leaving the army I grew a beard and renounced all intention of visiting a barber more than twice a year.

In matters of clothes I threw myself heartily into the art students' tradition, assuming a personal and original ensemble composed of my army battledress dyed dark blue, with an expanse of grey sweater showing below the waist line of the jacket. In retrospect, I think I must have looked more like an auxiliary fireman than a Bohemian. But at the time I gloried in the freedom, after years of khaki, to wear what I thought I liked.

In other mild ways I celebrated my release from army control. Those of us who came through the war in the armed forces received an official gratuity at the end, a tip for services rendered. Mine amounted to £88, and I spent every penny of it on Chinese food. That was quite a feat when you recall that, in 1946, a substantial meal at the Universal Chinese Restaurant in Denmark Street – my favourite haunt – would leave change out of a pound note. I was introduced to it by fellow musician John Dankworth, and became instantly hooked – so much so that I recklessly invited my parents to join me on one of their visits to London. My father got on all right, simply observing dryly that, if he were a cow, there was nothing in the fried mixed vegetables that he would not expect from a well-stocked meadow.

My mother, after a few mouthfuls, covered everything so deep in salt that the pancake roll looked like a yule-log. With her, it was a sure sign that her suspicions had been aroused. But then, she came from a background and a generation that regarded all Chinese people as 'sinister'. She clearly identified the waiters with those furtive oriental menservants who glided silently and inscrutably in and out of the pages of old thrillers – always in the employ of the villain, of course.

While at Camberwell I made a journey down to Bexleyheath in Kent to hear a band which had achieved an extraordinary reputation playing in the hitherto unheard New Orleans style of jazz. This band was George Webb's Dixielanders, an amateur group which held weekly sessions in a public house near Bexleyheath. In order to convey the whole significance of this little amateur band, I must take time off for a short excursion into jazz history.

When I first began to play the trumpet, the word 'jazz' was still quite a simple term, roughly describing the 'hot' dance music coming from America. The jazz fan of the 'thirties didn't bother much with definitions, apart from vaguely distinguishing the music of the large bands which he called 'swing' from that of the small improvising bands and informal jam session groups which he called 'pure jazz'. But in the second half of the 'thirties jazz critics and record-collectors who had dug up twenty-year-old recordings of the early jazz bands began to proclaim their discoveries from the roof tops, saying quite reasonably that a lot of this early music was better than the stuff being currently played and, what is more, it deserved attention as being the prototype of American jazz and therefore having a higher claim to authenticity than its later derivatives. After a certain amount of crying in the wilderness they managed to attract some adherence to their point of view. And there was born a movement which has since been called the New Orleans Revival. In England it was not so much a revival as a revelation, because much of the jazz music brought to light had never been heard here before. It wasn't until the New Orleans Revival started that the majority of jazz enthusiasts in England came to know what the original jazz of New Orleans sounded like. The revival began almost simultaneously in America, France and England, and the most important fact about it, with reference to my story, is that jazz enthusiasts who were attracted to the rediscovered music began to learn instruments and form bands with the express intention of reproducing the New Orleans style of jazz which they heard on their old records.

The first of these 'revivalist' bands was American – the Yerba Buena Jazz Band, led by Lu Watters. This band operated in San Francisco and after a few false starts suddenly caught the imagination of the American jazz public and achieved a nationwide reputation. In England the Yerba Buena Band had their counterpart in George Webb's Dixielanders. They came together in 1942, a group of amateur musicians, some of them barely through the learning stage, all keen on reproducing this newly discovered authentic jazz. Apart from George Webb himself, the prime movers in the enterprise were two jazz fans from a local factory, Wally Fawkes and Eddie Harvey. On clarinet and trombone respectively they formed the nucleus of the band's New Orleans line-up. Having collected from among local jazz enthusiasts two cornet-players, a banjo-player, a drummer and a tuba-player – George Webb himself played the piano – they started rehearsing and were soon producing a noise which, it can safely be said, was quite unique and unknown in the history of British dance music. It was a rough-and-ready sound, often ragged at the edges and out-of-tune, but with a vitality and energy which was quite startling to those who were used to the polite and effete noise which had hitherto passed for genuine jazz.

At the beginning George Webb's musicians were completely amateur in status, playing entirely for their own amusement and that of their friends. But gradually the situation changed. Finding themselves acquiring a following, they began to undertake club engagements and after a time they managed to secure a room for themselves in The Red Barn, a public house in Barnehurst, Kent. The Red Barn became the focal point of the New Orleans Revival in England. The meetings were informal and, at first, almost family affairs attended by the band's local supporters. There was no dancing. Jazz was serious music to be studied, and you could not give it full attention when you were being buffeted and trampled underfoot by dancers. At the Red Barn, people who jigged about in their chairs too vigorously were discovered by petulant frowns from their neighbours. Nevertheless the atmosphere was a happy one, and the surroundings were congenial.

The Red Barn meetings on Monday nights lasted from 7 o'clock until 10.30. Perched on a narrow rostrum at one end of the room, the band, with George Webb down in front of them at the piano, let fly with all the vitality of men playing for love. The tunes they played were drawn, via gramophone records, from the repertoire of early New Orleans jazz. Theirs was not just another way of playing dance music, it was virtually a brand-new music in itself, and it attracted many adherents. The bar under the Red Barn began to fill up, the local following being augmented by pilgrims from London and beyond.

As I have said, the music played by the George Webb Dixielanders was rough-and-ready, and by the best standards of today it was undoubtedly primitive. Yet it had the spirit of real jazz, which was lacking from the music of the professional dance musicians.

I joined George Webb's Dixielanders in 1947. Although still amateur in spirit, they had by this time risen financially to the status of semi-professionals – i.e., part-time musicians who were paid for whatever work they did. The following for jazz in those days, although remarkable in its enthusiasm, was not large or concentrated enough to make semi-professional jazz a very profitable pastime. The George Webb band was cooperative, splitting the profits equally and putting something aside for the day when they could rent, buy or build their own headquarters in London.

I came into the New Orleans revival after it had been under way for some years. While at the Camberwell Art School, I began to play quite regularly at the Feldman Swing Club, of which Carlo Krahmer was the unofficial musical director, and I went off to Friern Barnet every Sunday, where informal jam sessions were held in a pub called the Orange Tree. One day a delegation from George Webb's band came out to the Orange Tree – Jim Godbolt, manager of the band, and Wally Fawkes the clarinettist. They asked me to visit the Red Barn with my trumpet, and suggested that I might appear as a guest in one of the Hot Club of London concerts. I felt a terrible new-boy when I first went off to rehearsal on a Sunday morning to the Red Barn. I wore my dyed battledress and my beard and my sandals – full-dress art student's uniform – and I think they thought me an odd fish.

When I first discovered jazz at Eton there had been no such thing as the New Orleans Revival and jazz appreciation was a simple and haphazard affair amounting to just 'knowing what one liked'. My earliest record collection ranged over every jazz style, without any rhyme or reason outside of my own personal taste. By pure coincidence it contained quite a lot of jazz by such men as Louis Armstrong, Johnnie Dodds and Sidney Bechet, who were later to be regarded as the High Priests of the Revival. The beginnings of the movement – the critical cryings in the wilderness and attacks on current taste – went right over my head, so that by the time I reached Camberwell and began to look around the jazz world I was by no means a purist.

I first heard the George Webb band in 1944 at a concert at the Toynbee Hall. I sat three rows back in the stalls and wallowed in the great flood of brassy sound from the two cornets and trombone. But I didn't really attach any particular significance to it. I liked George Webb's band but I liked Count Basie and his swing band too – and that, in those days, marked me as a deviationist quite beyond the pale. So I was rather cautious on my first visits to the Red Barn. The Webb band used to rehearse on Sunday mornings in the bar-room which had been put at their disposal. It was February when I made my first appearance there. Snow lay on the crazy paving outside, and in the bar, the band crouched around a small fire which the unofficial manager, Jim Godbolt, kept stoking energetically with pieces of driftwood. We supplied ourselves with beer from the saloon bar upstairs and then got to work. I didn't join the band at once. My first engagements with them were as a guest-artist or a deputy for one of the cornet-players. It took me some time to get into their way of playing, but at length I settled in enough to persuade them that I was worth taking on permanently.

Life in the jazz business has been so full of excitement that my memory of early thrills has become obliterated. But I am quite sure that the evening when George Webb bought me a beer and asked me to join his band ranks high among them. I accepted, but with severe qualms. Apart from my quartet at Eton and the sort of one-night engagements which I had been doing with pick-up bands, I had never played in a band before, and for my initiation I was joining one which had a considerable reputation in a highly specialized field. I had passed the band's scrutiny, but what about the fans? I was certain that the new-boy would be given the once-over very thoroughly by the band's regular supporters, who had come to look upon it as the guardian of all that is purest in jazz. When I first appeared before them, one Monday night in February, they listened very intently. Pints were sipped and pipes were puffed with more than usual deliberation that night.

What the earnest listeners heard was a young musician with the indiscipline of one who had hitherto always played on his own, with a very scanty idea of the 'pure' New Orleans trumpet style in its narrowest sense, and with an awful lot of steam to let off. Opinions were clearly divided from the first. Some were enthusiastic, some reserved judgement and some were shocked and horrified at hearing such liberties taken.

Inside the band the atmosphere was much more congenial. Musicians who actually have the task of producing the music are always more inclined towards tolerance than the non-playing listeners.

I joined the band to replace the first cornet-player, Reg Rigden, forming, at first, a two-cornet team with his old partner, Owen Bryce.

I discovered at once that they had evolved a very rigid method of playing together in harmony, with each one playing his proper part and no messing about. My style of trumpet-playing was more fluid than this and poor Owen Bryce had terrible difficulty in keeping me to the straight-and-narrow path. Every time I cut loose he was left stranded, playing a second part which had no relation to anything. We both tried hard to come to terms. At one stage he hit on the idea of indicating my part with sharp jabs of his elbow. Every detail of phrasing and syncopation was conveyed to me through the medium of my left ribs. Owen Bryce was a vegetarian of sturdy but ungenerous build, and he had elbows like marlin-spikes. On physical grounds alone I was relieved when he decided to give up the struggle and retire from the band. That left the conventional New Orleans line-up of clarinet, trumpet and trombone, with the rhythm section led by George Webb himself at the piano.

The other dominant personality in the George Webb band when I first joined it was Wally Fawkes, the clarinettist. Wally is a Canadian by birth, having come to England when he was seven. In the Webb band he was the very opposite of the volatile George – tall, placid and easy-going, with a deep-rooted aversion to anything which threatened to make life complicated. When I first met him, he occupied a single room in a flat in Rowland Gardens belonging to some friends. The room was barely furnished with a wardrobe, a table, a small cupboard, one or two kitchen chairs, a bed and a gramophone. Records, jazz magazines, books, shoes and cricket gear were all stacked against the wall in a great mountain. At the head of the bed, a poster advertising a Hot Club of London concert was pinned, to prevent his head from marking the wall. Clarinets of all ages and shapes stood around the floor like saplings in a plantation. And the space behind the wardrobe was crammed thick with income tax forms, bills, bank statements and sundry official communications, some of them still in their envelopes, which he had stuffed out of sight and out of mind as soon as they appeared. He treated tiresome and disturbing thoughts in the same way, pushing them right away behind some mental wardrobe. Relaxation was his watchword, and he never cluttered up his head with problems or thoughts which were not his immediate concern. Nor did he believe in speaking one word when none would do. This careful economy of energy was mistaken by some for slow-wittedness; others regarded it as enigmatic. It was neither, but a definite policy – a design for living.

On one occasion Wally and I travelled together to a studio near Victoria Station, London, to record a session for Radio Luxembourg. Knowing the area quite well, I led the way confidently to the address we had been given. There was no brass plate beside the door, no indication that the house was or ever had been a recording studio. A bang on the door drew no response. Believing that we had the number wrong, we decided to separate and, starting at opposite ends of the street, to look at each doorway to find some clue as to where we should be. Arriving at my end, I looked up and saw that my memory had let me down. I called to Wally and, as he approached at a trot, gave him the news. 'We're in the wrong street.' His answer persuaded me that I had teamed up with someone whose humour, as well as his musical ideas, matched mine. He said, 'Good job we didn't find it, then.'

Humph Meets Trog

If we were light-hearted and carefree about our adventures and mishaps in George Webb's Dixielanders, we were in deadly earnest about our jazz. Every job was followed by an intense post-mortem in which faults in our performance were picked out and examined, and resolutions were made to put them right in rehearsal. I was no less keen than the others. Gradually my trumpet-playing had come to occupy more of my time and thoughts. With the opportunity of regular playing, it developed in rapid stages from a hobby into something more like a vocation. But still I pushed away any thought of it as a profession. In the sphere of music in which I was interested, George Webb's band was at the top of the tree. And in spite of its great

Humph's first published cartoon.
(Courtesy of his daughter, Henrietta Lyttelton.)

intensity and enthusiasm, their following was still very restricted. Even if I had entertained the thought of music as a career, I could never have made a living playing jazz alone. And the idea of working out an apprenticeship in a dance band didn't appeal to me at all. So I remained an amateur in every sense, and in the moments when I wasn't thinking about music, I continued to regard commercial art as my chosen career.

The musical jaunts with the Dixielanders were undertaken by me in my spare time from my art studies – though perhaps art studies is rather a high- sounding phrase for my activities at Camberwell. I have said earlier that I very soon decided on cartooning and caricature as my artistic metier and thenceforward I mentally wrote off the National Diploma Examination as being a waste of energy. On the other hand, until something else came along I was quite happy to continue drawing my grant from the Government. If ever my conscience was troubled by this mild form of false pretences, I pacified it by arguing that the fundamental aim of the grant was to assist me to earn my living, and how I set about this myself was really my own affair. After two years, I decided that the masquerade had gone far enough. Not that I had concrete plans for the future. For some time I had been canvassing the weekly and monthly magazines with cartoons and I had had one success in *Men Only*. This loomed so large beside all the countless failures that I was encouraged to regard myself as an established cartoonist and to write to the Ministry of Education saying that, as I had already embarked on a career, I shouldn't really need a National Diploma after all. They accepted this impudence quite mildly and refrained from demanding their money back.

One of H.L's early drawings as a professional cartoonist.

There followed a lean year during which I was very glad of the pocket-money which my trumpet-playing brought in. At length, after a few false starts, I got a regular job in Fleet Street. Jobs in Fleet Street, as anywhere else, depend largely on contacts. And by joining the George Webb Dixielanders I acquired a ready-made contact in the form of Wally Fawkes. Wally had studied commercial art at Sidcup Art School, and there he had been 'discovered' as a promising artist by Leslie Illingworth, then the political cartoonist on the *Daily Mail* and *Punch*.

Leslie Illingworth was one of the hubs of Fleet Street. For many years he sat in his office at the top of the *Daily Mail* building drawing his cartoons and exerting a kind of involuntary magnetism which attracted visitors of every type, occupation and nationality to him in a constant stream. Before Wally Fawkes joined the ranks of Illingworth's regular visitors, he went to an advertising agency. And then one day he got an urgent message from Leslie. The *Daily Mail* had decided to introduce decorative drawings into its Features page on the lines of those used in the *New Yorker*. Rumour had spread round the office that an offer was going to be sent to Saul Steinberg in America. This news was quickly transmitted by Illingworth to Wally Fawkes, who came up straight away with a selection of Steinberg-type drawings. Whether or not the proposed offer to Steinberg was ever seriously considered I don't know, but when Wally Fawkes produced his drawings nothing more was heard of it. Under the pen name of 'Trog', Wally was engaged by the *Daily Mail* to draw column breakers. Oddly enough the name 'Trog' originated with the George Webb Dixielanders, who had at an early stage in their career been labelled 'Troglodytes' by an acid critic because of the allegedly prehistoric nature of their music. The shortened version 'Trog' was adopted by the band as a mutual term of address, and when Wally Fawkes came to require a nom-de-plume, 'Trog' was a natural choice.

Trog's drawings were essentially modern in conception, at first sticking closely to the Steinberg pattern but gradually acquiring a look of their own. They employed a large degree of grotesque distortion, and some of the *Daily Mail*'s long-standing readers rushed into the correspondence column with cries of protest when they first saw the weird little Trog men and women peering out at them over the breakfast table. But soon the new style caught on and Trog's column-breakers became one of the paper's most popular features.

Trog spent three years breaking columns. Then events took another turn which brought Lyttelton into the picture. The powers that be sent for Trog and told him that he was to be promoted to a full-size strip cartoon. Whereupon he got on the telephone to me and tipped me the wink that the job of column-breaking was shortly to be vacant. This was right up my street. Apart from the experience and variety which the job offered, I had noticed that it left Trog plenty of spare time for his clarinet-playing. There were no office hours. As soon as the commissioned drawings were done the artist could go home. Within two days of getting Trog's message, I had a collection of Trog-style drawings ready. And they did the trick. I was taken on by Ronnie Collier, the Features page editor, as a freelance column-breaker, being paid by the drawing. Searching round for a pen name for myself I chose Humph, because that's what most people had called me, and I felt that if I was going to be landed with a pseudonym as Trog had been – he often received letters addressed to Mr Trog, *Daily Mail* – I might as well choose one that was familiar. It took some time to establish this new name on the *Daily Mail* and after several weeks the art room boys were still coming in to ask if I had my 'Trog drawings' ready yet. It was a great day, and a milestone in my artistic career, when they first began to call them 'Humph drawings' or even just 'Humphs'. Nowadays the Humph pseudonym has spread into all my various activities. Having misspelt my surname consistently for years, the musical papers seized on 'Humph' with obvious relief, and now they rarely call me anything else. Unfortunately, autograph-hunters still insist on the full version, and the only time I ever tried to get away with 'Humph' in an autograph book I was nearly lynched. Autographs present a constant danger to me. I once almost made an enemy for life by signing my official signature – a pompous 'H.R.A. Lyttelton' – in someone's book. They glared at it so hard afterwards that I asked to see what I had put, and hurriedly substituted something a little less formal. When I started my cartooning career as 'Humph' and took on yet another regular signature, I had to keep my wits about me.

I began at the *Daily Mail* as a freelance. This system had its pros and cons. High among the cons was the ever-present risk that some momentous event or the sudden death of a public figure would drive all humour from the paper and leave me temporarily out of work. Nobody was more solicitous about the health and welfare of the Royal Family or the heads of state than I was at that time. The chief pro was the fact that there was no limit to my potential earnings. As the idea of column-breakers gradually caught on, editors of pages other than the Features page began to hanker after them too. For one happy period, 'Humphs' came up all over the paper like a rash, and I made hay. I look back on those column-breaking days with considerable nostalgia.

After a time, however, these carefree days came to an end. The editorship of the paper changed hands, and the policy of the paper changed with it. For a time there was an uneasy period when it became clear that the post of column-breaker was about to become redundant. The Correspondence Column was shut down, and when it reappeared, it was cast in a new mould which excluded light-hearted illustrations. Gradually my little postage-stamp drawings disappeared, one at a time, from the articles in which they had made their regular home since 'Trog drawings' became 'Humphs'. I thought my days were numbered, and began to contemplate setting out in search of fresh columns to break. Then, at the last minute, reprieve came. I was promoted to pocket cartoonist.

Like the Column-breaking Era, the Pocket Cartoon Era came to an end, and for much the same reason. The *Daily Mail* took another turn in the more serious direction, and pocket cartoons were out. I was transferred to my old status of freelance, but that turned out to be a polite way of turning me out to graze. At that point, my career as a cartoonist, which I had pursued for just on five years, came for the time being to a full stop. But I had been associated with the *Daily Mail* in other ways besides that of resident artist.

Before the end of the Column-breaking Era – in other words before the general policy of sobering up the paper had come into effect – I spent a year as reviewer of gramophone records. In the first place the idea was that I should deal with the jazz and dance music recordings only, but naturally the paper was keen, if possible, to have one man doing the whole lot, so they tentatively suggested that I might take in the classical records as well. This was a poser. In jazz and 'popular' music I knew my way about quite well. But I was no sort of an authority on 'serious' music. Like many outer-fringe music-lovers I knew what I liked and liked what I knew. My general knowledge was good, but as a specialist I was nowhere. In taking on the job of reviewing classical recordings I was acting under false pretences. On the other hand, I was quite a diligent and painstaking fraud. I invested in the six volumes of *Grove's Dictionary* to help me out on the historical and factual side, and I made a point of checking my critical conclusions with the better-informed opinions which appeared in the musical monthlies. I don't mean to say that I actually *copied*. I had opinions of my own but I was not quite bare-faced enough to let them go without first corroborating them. In this way I think I got through my first journalistic venture without making any very serious blunders or giving the game away.

My record reviews were among the items, deemed 'frivolous', which were swept out with the column-breakers when the paper's policy changed. I made no more literary contributions after that – not until I received a call from the strip department of the paper to provide them with a story for Trog's 'Rufus' strip. This came just after my expulsion as a pocket cartoonist, at a time when it looked as if diplomatic relations between me and the *Daily Mail* were on the point of ceasing altogether. Writing for strip-cartoons is a craft which I have heard dismissed contemptuously as 'filling in balloons'. There is a bit more to it than that. What was demanded of me was a synopsis showing the outline of my story, and then a day-to-day 'shooting script' with specific details of each panel for the artist. I approached the task with diffidence. My predecessor on the 'Rufus' strip had been Sir Compton Mackenzie [Scottish novelist], a star turn specially imported by the *Mail* into the strip world. My experience as a story-teller was negligible. And besides, there were all the subtleties peculiar to the craft. The knack of creating suspense and sustaining it from breakfast time to breakfast time; the necessity for keeping the plot obvious from day to day so that a chance reader who comes across the strip wrapped round his vegetables one day has a chance to become enthralled. However, I relished the idea of extending my collaboration with Wally (Trog) into the journalistic field, and he in his turn saw the advantages of having a collaborator who was constantly at his right hand on the bandstand. Often at the jazz club, when our audience saw us talking together animatedly on the stand and assumed that we were discussing the tempo and interpretation of the next number, we were actually exchanging ideas on the future of Flook or Bodger (Trog characters). Sometimes people would come up and suggest to us ideas for the following day's strip, not knowing that it is actually written and drawn several weeks in advance. Once, when the central character, Flook, was about to inspect the troops at the Changing of the Guard, we received an urgent invitation to drinks at the Officers' Mess at St James's Palace. The Captain of the Guards and his junior officers were all Flook fans, and greeted us with hospitality. But it turned out that the main object of the invitation was that we might be told, as gently and amiably as possible, that the Queen's Guard wasn't mounting next day, and that if we portrayed Flook inspecting them, we should commit a gaffe which would resound through every mess and barrack-room in the Brigade of Guards. Luckily Flook *wasn't* inspecting the Guard the very next day, but if he had been, we could have done nothing to stop him.

Flook's adventures were planned minutely in a weekly strip-conference at the *Daily Mail*, attended by the Strip Editor, Trog and me. I would produce the story and the 'shooting script' and they would inspect them from their particular viewpoints and make amendments where necessary. Trog kept a careful eye on the script to see that it remained 'visual' and not too literary; and he also kept a watching brief as the representative of Flook. Having originated the character and lived with him for four and a half years, he knew him better than anyone else. And there was a tendency for all three of us to refer to Flook as if he were real and sitting next door in the outer office.

'Flook comes round the corner and says, "What's going on?"' I read from my script.

'He wouldn't say that,' chips in Trog.

The Strip Editor jumps in as referee.

'Surely it doesn't matter if he says it here?'

'But he wouldn't,' insists Trog and the discussion continues, amounting in the end to a complete psycho-analysis of Flook to get the little balloon perfectly in character.

In spite of the care with which details of the story were thrashed out, there were times when we were taken by surprise. Once, in order to see if the readers were on their toes, I introduced a character who spoke in code. It was a very simple code, and I expected that we should have a flow of letters in the day after it appeared in the paper giving the solution. The response fulfilled my expectations. Letters flowed in with every post – and all in code! I spent several afternoons up in the *Daily Mail* office helping the secretary to decipher them.

To pick up the thread of my musical life I must go back to 1947 and the disbanding of George Webb's Dixielanders. During my time with the George Webb band I had formulated in my mind a fairly definite idea of the sort of music I wanted to play, and that in its turn fostered an ambition, almost subconscious at first, to lead a band of my own. When I handed in my notice to George Webb in November 1947, I did so without any definite plans for starting on my own. But I knew in my heart of hearts that it was going to happen somehow.

I think Wally Fawkes knew it too. We continued to see a lot of each other after I had ceased to be a Dixielander, and most of the time we talked jazz. He came out to the Camberwell Art School for weekly illustration classes, and it was during one of these, as we sat idly cross-hatching in Indian ink and exchanging ideas on playing jazz, that it suddenly became clear to me that we were both moving, in a series of veiled hints, towards one conclusion – that I was going to start a band and that Wally Fawkes was going to be in it. A plan was concocted, but it was several weeks before anything came of it. Wally had been with George for about five years, all through the early crusading years of the revival, and there was a strong tug of war between his loyalty to the Dixielanders and his musical aspirations. As for me, I wasn't impatient. Although the prospect was exciting, it didn't overawe me because there was nothing at stake. My reputation as a jazz trumpeter was a minute local one acquired during eight months at the Red Barn. And financially, the whole project was on a part-time semi-professional basis. Since we didn't depend on income, we didn't need capital. Plans were very short-term – to collect some musicians together and rehearse in our spare time. Outside of this, the future could take care of itself.

The band materialized in January 1948. With Wally Fawkes's departure, George Webb's Dixielanders finally broke up, and we inherited Harry the trombonist. John, our seventeen-year-old drummer, was discovered by Wally on the staff of the *Daily Mail*, and the pianist and guitarist both came in from another band which had recently disintegrated. We rehearsed in a room in Great Windmill Street which was aptly called The Cave. It operated periodically as a nightclub, and was done up to look like the inside of a cave. The walls were painted with green and rust-coloured slime, and hessian stalactites hung from the ceiling. In these sombre surroundings we started to practise. During the first meeting, a figure carrying a double bass with only three strings appeared in the doorway and asked if we wanted a bassist. We never discovered where he came from, but we needed a bass, so we took him on there and then. He plucked away at his three strings for several months, and then retired again into the limbo. He once confided to another member of the band that he was a 'Bohemium'. It must be confessed that he became more and more Bohemium as time went on. He grew a pale yellow beard and wore shaggy leather jackets with the works of Henry Miller peeping out of the pockets. When he eventually left the band it was because he had become manifestly unhappy in the company of us 'part-time Bohemiums'.

The band did its first public engagement on 22 February 1948, at a club in North London. We split the £10 fee seven ways – twenty-five shillings each and twenty-five for the band fund, a reserve for paying for rehearsal-rooms and other incidental expenses. The fans were enthusiastic, but the critics reserved judgement, saying kindly that they were sure the band would be fine once it was licked into shape.

However, offers for other engagements began to come in and to cope with them we took on a part-time manager. Lyn Dutton had appeared on the jazz scene during the last days of the Dixielanders. He worked by day in an advertising firm, and in the evenings, he gave lectures on jazz under the auspices of the Workers Musical Association, with the George Webb band providing 'live' examples. Since the idea of my band was first mooted he had given it enthusiastic encouragement and when it became clear that someone would be needed to handle the administrative side of the band, Lyn was the obvious choice. He agreed to join the band as a non-playing member, looking after the administrative side in his spare time. His experience in accountancy came in useful, although I must say it wasn't taxed very severely in those early days. Nevertheless, with a manager, a typewriter and a tin cashbox, we were all set to go.

In March 1948 we had our first lucky break. We were engaged as stand-ins for Graeme Bell's Australian Jazz Band at the newly formed Leicester Square Jazz Club. The premises were hired from the

NSPCC for every Monday night, and the younger generation of jazz fans turned up there to let off steam. Many of them were students from the art schools and from the various branches of London University, and they had unlimited reserves of steam. Young people came too from shops and offices, seizing the opportunity to assert themselves by dressing up in bright, highly original fashions and letting their hair down. No one knew anything about the dances which were originally danced to the music in New Orleans at the beginning of the century. So the dancers at the Leicester Square Jazz Club just invented steps of their own. Led by the art school contingent – the least inhibited of those present – they flung themselves on to the floor and just did the first thing that came into their heads. No doubt it was a terrifying spectacle and there were moments when the band began to look anxiously towards the fire escape. What the diners in the Café de l'Europe below thought about it has never been ascertained.

The Leicester Square Jazz Club gave us our first regular engagement, deputizing for Graeme Bell's Band when they went on tour. We brought along with us a strong contingent from Camberwell Art School, and John Minton, now recognized as a distinguished painter, was among the most formidable and dangerous of the first school of dancers. A reporter from *The Leader* magazine came once to do an editorial feature on the new phenomenon and these were his impressions:

> 'It's gala night at the Jazz Club. New Looks swirl, shirt tails fly. Feet stamp, hands flutter. Hair-do's tumble in ruins. Youths close their eyes and twitch to the savage rhythms. A naval officer throws back his head and howls like a wolf. Soldiers, solicitors, art students and barrow-boys sway to the beat. A bearded artist hurls his partner halfway across the room....'

The Leader magazine reporter committed the indiscretion of mentioning the N.S.P.C.C. in connection with the wild scenes described. Next week when the band arrived to play and the fans arrived to dance, the entrance was chained and padlocked.

With the sudden demise of the Leicester Square Jazz Club the

Graeme Bell Band and the Humphrey Lyttelton Band moved over to the London Jazz Club, a newly formed club with a jazz-for-dancing policy. The meetings here were twice a week, held in a large rehearsal room underneath Jack Solomon's Gym.

Our move to the outer fringes of Soho gave more ammunition to the journalists, who, from time to time, wrote up our activities as a glimpse into the seamier side of London life. When we moved into Great Windmill Street we became automatically one of the 'Soho Jazz Haunts' referred to in every newspaper report on drug addiction and West End vice. Compared to these highly-coloured reports I am afraid we were really a very tame crew.

Anyone with a romantic idea of jazz as an accompaniment to low-life and vice would have found the tweedy, pipe-smoking Australians and Britishers with their happy extrovert music very unpromising. As for us, we had no inclination to become involved in the underworld. Thanks to all these contributory factors, we established in the early days an atmosphere which was discouraging to the spiv and the dance-hall parasite. I did once detect a man in the crowd who gave me serious misgivings. He looked the real gang-leader, with an immaculate Edwardian suit, carefully curled hair and a suspicion of side-whiskers. He came several nights running and stood just over to the right of the band, eyeing us with a drooping, insolent eye. One night he sauntered casually over to me as we were stepping down for an interval. He was a big man and I glanced quickly round to see if all the commissionaires were handy. When he spoke, it was through narrow lips.

'What are you goin' to do about this place?' he asked.

That is it, I thought – the kiss of death. He was demanding protection money, obviously. The place was probably teeming with his 'boys'.

'Do?' I said weakly.

'Yes, do,' he said and then he came a bit closer. 'It's gettin' terrible…full o' spivs…not like the old days at all…any more o' this and I'm staying at home with me records!'

Soon after the band had settled into its resident job, we had our second stroke of luck. An International Jazz Festival was held at Nice, and I was invited to go as trumpet-player with the English band. This was a scratch group collected together for the occasion under the leadership of saxophonist Derek Neville. Carlo Krahmer was on drums and I think it was through his instigation that I was chosen.

I did have one member of my band to keep me company at Nice. In his capacity of Trog of the *Daily Mail*, Wally Fawkes came too – as a foreign correspondent! If in those days Wally was a man of few words conversationally, on paper he was a man of none. Pencils, paper and ink were things to draw with. For any other purpose they were a snare and a delusion to be spurned at all costs. However, this was a special occasion – the Nice Festival had enough jazz Olympians on its bill to tempt an ardent jazz lover to swim the Channel to get there. Wally tried something which was, on the face of it, equally impossible. He walked into the Foreign Editor's office and volunteered to cover the Festival for the *Daily Mail* as a reporter. He came out again looking dazed but delighted, with a detailed brief and an expense account to cover the trip.

We flew to Nice, in a state of delirious excitement. Up above the clouds, with the sun shining into the heated cabin and the snow-covered French Alps appearing through gaps in the white blanket, we relaxed like opium-dreamers, luxuriating in the prospect before us. The list of the great American musicians whom we were going to see reads like one of those ideal teams which jazz fans – like their counterparts in cricket – are always compiling. Louis Armstrong, Jack Teagarden, Earl Hines, Barney Bigard, Sid Catlett, Sandy Williams, Rex Stewart, Mezz Mezzrow, Pops Foster, Baby Dodds – they were enough to be going on with. To appreciate our feelings on going to Nice, you must imagine a minor musician in the classical field suddenly being summoned into the reincarnated presence of Bach, Haydn, Mozart, Beethoven and Brahms.

It was a good thing that we relaxed on the plane, because once we had landed all relaxation ceased. The Festival was a ten-day affair financed by the French Government and organized by the Pope of European jazz criticism, Hugues Panassié and his Hot Club of France. Once established in the Plaza Hotel, the English contingent slipped into a routine which was maintained right up to the end of the Festival. Playing time in the evenings usually stretched from 9p.m. until 1a.m.. If we weren't playing ourselves we were at the Casino or the Opera House listening to the stars. Afterwards there were informal sessions at the Queen's Hotel or the Havana and Monte Carlo nightclubs, lasting until morning.

The French Government official in overall charge of the Festival flung himself into the unorthodox job with true bureaucratic zeal. Memos came pouring out of his office imposing minor restrictions on the musicians, among which the most unpopular was one forbidding impromptu jam sessions. Getting together informally after working hours and swapping musical ideas has always been common practice among jazz musicians – it's the truly amateur side of jazz coming uppermost – and this official edict was a severe blow. Under normal circumstances it could never have been enforced at all; but authority had taken the precaution of withholding all the return fares, so that rebels were threatened with having to pay their own way home. The Europeans taking part – British, French, Belgian and Swiss – could afford to call this bluff, but for the Americans it was another matter. Nevertheless, some of them broke out occasionally and we heard, and took part in, jam sessions involving Rex Stewart, Jack Teagarden, Earl Hines and Sid Catlett.

It was a great disappointment to everyone that Louis Armstrong did not appear at any of these rendezvous after playing. But even if there had been no ban, I doubt if he would have played. Louis was the real King of Jazz and, like all Royalty, he wasn't able to move around as he pleased. At Nice, he had only to emerge from his hotel into the street for a thousand fans to materialize from nowhere clamouring for autographs. Wherever he went, he was surrounded and protected by an entourage of managers, jazz notabilities and sycophants. Formality dogged him. When he first arrived there was a big reception held in his honour. (It was during this that I tottered out to the nearest Bureau de Poste and wired my first wife Patricia with the succinct message 'Have shaken hands with Louis Armstrong'.) And when we all met for the first rehearsal, the proceedings were held up indefinitely while musicians and organizers crammed into his dressing room to listen to him just warming up.

I shall not attempt to describe my feelings on hearing Louis Armstrong play for the first time. I am not the swooning type (Hugo Charteris once wrote to me, 'Saying something sentimental to you is like making a sudden movement near a flock of crows') and I don't feel that I could do justice in words to the quality of sound which came from Louis's trumpet as he blew the first few practice arpeggios. Perhaps I can best sum up the effect it had on us all by reporting that it drew from a normally sane English critic the silliest comment I have ever heard. Louis Armstrong has an embouchure like a rat trap, the strength of his lip equalled only by the power of his lungs. Consequently on this occasion, when he attacked the higher notes, little jets of saliva spurted out around the mouthpiece. Seeing this, the critic leant across to me, his eyes dewy with emotion. 'Poor old Louis,' he said in a hoarse stage whisper, 'he's losing a lot of saliva these days.'

We usually turned in to our hotel beds at about seven o'clock after the all-night revelry. But we didn't sleep for long. It must be remembered that this was in 1948 when England was still suffering from war hangover and one of the main attractions of the Continent was the unlimited amount of food. At that time, a breakfast of two eggs on a thick slice of gammon was not a thing to be lightly ignored, so we left strict instructions at the hotel desk that we were to be called without fail at ten o'clock for a large, pre-war English breakfast. Once this was polished off it was a risky business to go back to sleep again – one might miss lunch! Sometimes we would go out for a drink, although it was usually safer to stay in the hotel. We had very little money and advantage was taken of our financial difficulties by a little French chemist who, as a side line, carried on the illicit sale of 'pastis' – a home-brewed and potent form of absinthe.

This sinister figure dogged us everywhere, slyly producing little medicine bottles from his sleeve and chanting 'Pastis?' in a tempting voice. He himself was a living warning against drinking the stuff. Everything about him was red – his hands, his face, his hair, his eyes – there was even a suspicion of rosiness about his teeth. One of our party fell for his sales talk early one evening. He disappeared, and we didn't see him again until four o'clock the next day when he tottered into the hotel lounge deathly pale and croaking and trembling like an old man of eighty. At first we had doubts about his prospect of survival. But by nine o'clock in the evening when we were due to play he had recovered enough to drag himself on to the stage. It was another two days before he was really himself again, and even then, a murmur of 'Pastis?' in a high voice was liable to send him into terrible jitters.

The first few days at Nice were punctuated by urgent requests from the London *Daily Mail* for the story which Trog had promised them. This was an eventuality which Trog had not thought about up to now, but as the demands became more insistent he had to give his role of news-hound more serious attention. He spent an agonized afternoon on his story, at the end of which he had managed to cover the back of one small, tattered envelope. At the last minute, when he was thinking of admitting defeat and refunding his expenses, the Paris office of the *Daily Mail* came to the rescue. They rang him up at Nice, extracted his impressions from him, and then put one of their staff men on the job. The following morning a story appeared in the *Daily Mail*. The larger part of the story concerned me. But this was not through any undue partiality on Trog's part. He had mentioned, in his telephone conversation with the Paris office, that I was an Old Etonian, and forthwith they had pounced on me as 'news'. In common with the Duke who Turns Dustman and the Cobbler who Inherits Baronetcy, I was found to have snob-value. Soon my prowess at Nice, highly coloured and grossly exaggerated, spread into all the papers. I was the Old-Etonian-ex-Guards-Officer-Viscount's-nephew-trumpeter who set Nice on fire and, it was hinted, gave Louis Armstrong himself reason to contemplate retirement!

My name was frequently linked with that of Captain Oliver Lyttelton, the wartime Minister of Production and then a prominent member of the Opposition in Parliament. Our press cuttings would tend to overlap occasionally, and all told, there was scarcely a relationship which hadn't been attributed to us, from father and son downwards. For the record, Oliver Lyttelton was the son of my Great Uncle Alfred which made him my father's first cousin and my first cousin once removed. His sons – my second cousins – were at school with me, and I met him once. He was once nominated the Best Dressed MP; I can claim no such distinction even in a profession where the standard is low. People often ask me if he approved of my activities; they never asked me if I approved of his. And there it all is in a nutshell.

For Dancers Only

When my one and only trumpet teacher, Sim Saville, prophesied that I should one day 'go places' as a trumpeter, he was talking in terms of the bright lights and the big money. In this respect, I have chosen a path which has led to less spectacular results. But in the literal sense, he was right.

After Nice, my band began to get into its stride. We played at the London Jazz Club every Monday and Saturday to an average of seven or eight hundred dancers and listeners. And, when summer came, the club organizers, Stan and Bert Wilcox, chartered a steamer and sent us off with a boat-load of fans down the river to Chertsey. These Riverboat Shuffles, as they were called after Hoagy Carmichael's tune of that name, had become a tradition in London jazz since the Hot Club of London days. Jazz fans, critics and musicians piled on board one of the little Thames steamers and sailed off for the day with instruments blaring and dancers pounding the deck. Whenever the boat stopped in a lock, everybody spilled ashore, and startled passers-by enjoying a quiet Sunday walk along the towpath suddenly found themselves in the middle of scores of prancing couples in vivid tartan shirts and jeans. At Chertsey there was picnicking and bathing, and then the boat sailed back to Westminster Pier or Richmond and discharged its weary, sunburnt cargo ashore.

Most of the engagements undertaken by the band were for the jazz public. But occasionally the organizers of non-jazz functions have taken it into their heads to book a jazz band by way of a novelty. One of the first engagements outside the jazz field came up soon after my return from Nice. It was to play at a dance at Cambridge's most exclusive political club, the Pitt Club. My second cousin Anthony – the son of Oliver Lyttelton, not the first cousin Anthony mentioned earlier – was some sort of officer in the club at the time and I think it was through him that we were approached. Cambridge has always had a weakness for jazz bands, and the Pitt Club function was the beginning of a long association between us and the University. On our part, we have always been struck by the hospitality extended to us on our visits – and never more forcibly than on this first occasion.

I travelled up separately from the band, so I wasn't there when they were received by the organizing committee at the station and presented with a bottle of gin, a bottle of brandy and a bottle of champagne, just to get them in the mood before the dance began. When I arrived none of them were to be found. On enquiry I discovered that they were being marched round the town to work off the effects of their welcome. When they returned they were grinning happily, but just about fit for action. Throughout the evening the hospitality continued as it had begun, and before long, in spite of a mild request that we should 'tone it down a bit' in view of the smallness of the room and the mixed attendance, we were really rocking in every sense. The guests took it well, except for one dignified-looking young man who, in the middle of a spirited 'Tiger Rag', stood in front of the band and shook his fist at us before sweeping out with his lady on his arm. Towards the end of the night the hospitality began to take its toll. In the middle of one number featuring some agile work on the trombone, Harry, our trombone player, lost his grip on the slide, which flew off across the floor under the feet of the dancers. He set off unsteadily to retrieve it and that was the last we saw of him till next morning. For the last half-hour we received no support from our 'Bohemium' bassist, who stood draped around the neck of his instrument sound asleep. After the guests had gone the Committee gave us a breakfast of fried egg and bacon in the library. When the Bohemium opened his eyes and saw a plate full of eggs in front of him he came suddenly to life and flung the lot at the nearest bookshelf. Our hosts were not in the least daunted by this ungenerous act and as we all trooped off to bed they invited us to drinks the following morning. We discovered that 'drinks' meant several bottles of champagne left over from the night before. And so it all began again.

In August 1948 we made a trip to Brussels to take part in another Jazz Festival. This was a smaller affair than Nice, involving only bands from European countries. The organizer was a Napoleonic character whom we will call Wilhelm. He seemed to make a great point of the fact that we should arrive properly equipped with uniforms, which, he insisted, '*doit être* IMPECCABLE *et* TRÈS SOIGNÉE'. At that time the band had very little money in the kitty and when we played engagements which demanded uniforms we wore a rig of our own devising, consisting of white shirts, green ties, brown slacks and Government surplus windjammers. These last were like mackintosh golfing jackets with zip fasteners down the front and pockets everywhere. With a bit of care, we thought, we can at least make them look '*impeccable*', if not '*soignée*'. Anyway, they were all we had. In answer to Wilhelm's anxious enquiries, we wrote back assuring him that we would arrive fully equipped with uniforms, but we thought it best not to dwell on the '*soignée*' angle. When we arrived at Ostend, Wilhelm met us and conducted us to the Casino at Knocke, where the Festival was to be held. In appearance he was bald and olive-skinned, like an Italian tenor, and just as excitable. I don't think he knew or cared very much about jazz, but he took an almost megalomaniac pride in the fact that he ran almost all the jazz clubs in Belgium single-handed. He handled the musicians under his control at the Knocke Festival more like a generalissimo than an impresario. The slightest hint of insubordination and he would fly into a tantrum, striking absurd operatic poses and frowning prodigiously. As we were a ribald and irreverent lot, he was doing this most of the time. He took us to our dressing room at the Knocke Casino and we proudly displayed our 'uniforms' for his approval. When he saw the pathetically crumpled mackintosh golfing jackets he threw his hands in the air and fell back on to a settee feigning unconsciousness. Then he flung himself into such an orgy of dramatics that we thought he had gone off his head. From all this we gathered that our uniforms were just about the least '*soignée*' objects he had ever seen.

Financially and artistically the Festival was a flop. On the other hand, as a Continental jaunt for the band, with expenses paid and few responsibilities, it was a roaring success. We were there for a week of summer weather with nothing to do all day except sit on the front drinking iced chocolate or sleep off the effects of the previous night's entertainment.

Back in England our spare-time playing began to increase. With the Jazz Club and rehearsals, we played regularly two or three evenings a week and fulfilled other engagements at weekends.

In 1948, within a year of its inception, my band started making gramophone records, rather tentatively at first. Our early recording experiences were eventful. One day in the Glasshouse Street studio, as we were listening to playbacks of two of our London Jazz recordings, Wally Fawkes, then a smoker, casually flicked some ash into what he took to be an ordinary waste-bin and ignited a bundle of the highly-inflammable by-product of the recording process known, I think, as 'swarf'. Within seconds both the control room and the studio were engulfed in white smoke. Coughing and spluttering and weeping, we all escaped into a little anteroom. From there we had to plan an operation to rescue the non-portable instruments. We had an engagement that night and the studio manager announced gloomily that it would take several hours to get rid of the smoke. As the smoke gradually rose to about a foot from the floor, we sent the smallest member of the band, George Webb, in on all fours like an Indian scout, to collect and pass back bits of the drum kit one by one, giving him primitive artificial respiration in between each sortie. We made the gig!

In 1949, the band played on records and at a concert with one of the greatest New Orleans jazzmen of all – soprano-saxophonist Sidney Bechet. Late in '49, the organizers of the Jazz Club, Stan and Bert Wilcox, decided to defy the ban and present Bechet at a concert in London. He flew in to London one Saturday evening, and a deputation from the club met him at his London hotel. We found a tightly-knit, athletic-looking old man of indeterminate age – he is either vague or secretive about his date of birth, and theories as to his age ranged from fifty-three to well over sixty. He had a warm, light-brown complexion which looked as if it had faded in the Southern sun, and a rich, spicy voice to match. He greeted us with mellow dignity, a mood which he sustained all through a hurried Chinese meal and a visit to the packed jazz club, where autograph-hunters almost trampled him to death. During lulls in the assault from the fans, he cocked an ear at the band. At the end he said that he looked forward to recording with us, and gave me a list of tunes which he proposed to play. Next morning, he arrived at the little studio chosen for the recording, and, having apparently forgotten his conversation of the night before, produced four more tunes for us to play. In the end we made six sides, none of which were on either of the previous lists. I have an idea that this chopping and changing of the plans – which I diagnosed as failing memory – was in fact a cunning ruse to keep us on our toes.

The circumstances of the recording session were nerve-wracking. As Bechet was one of the most celebrated and important jazz musicians to set foot in England, every critic, collector and man-about-jazz in London who knew of the event turned up to see him. At one end of the small recording studio the atmosphere was like a cocktail party, with people milling about excitedly and chattering to each other. At the other end Bechet and the band were busy trying to make records. There were times when he and I, discussing the arrangements, were forced to shout at each other in order to make ourselves heard. To complicate the situation further, the studio engineer had devised a microphone set-up which divided the rhythm section of drums, banjo, bass and piano from the rest of the band by a thick screen. I don't know what the advantage of this was from the technical point of view, but it certainly made matters more difficult for the unfortunate musicians, who could see neither the green starting light nor Bechet's signalled instructions. In the end, however, the session got under way and we began to make some recordings. Sidney Bechet took great pains over the preliminary rehearsals of each number. We had rather a cumbersome band – four other melody instruments besides himself on soprano saxophone – and he rehearsed us very strictly before we cut each record so that all of us knew what part we were to play. He was patient but firm with us, and once we had got over an understandable tendency to listen to him instead of concentrating on our own playing, we settled down to work. After the first master was cut we all prepared ourselves for the playback and the inevitable post-mortem. At Parlophone we had become used to hearing our performance back and discussing it hypercritically before passing or rejecting it. So it came as a shock to our highly self-conscious amateur instincts when Sidney Bechet declined to hear even one playback of the records we had made. After the first cutting the session supervisor came in and suggested to Bechet that he should listen to the results.

'Why should I?' he said – 'That don't do me no good.'

I don't believe he ever heard one of those records, although he expressed to me later the opinion that one of them – 'When It's Sleepy Time Down South' – was a masterpiece!

The concert in the evening remains blurred in my memory. The band jittered through a few introductory numbers and then Sidney Bechet came on playing to a roar of greeting from the audience which drowned the strident notes of his saxophone even for us standing a few feet away. It was a great honour and distinction for us to be on that platform playing with him, but sometimes I wish I could have relaxed in a seat in the stalls and just listened.

After the concert, Bechet called me into his dressing room and gave me a pep-talk about the band, assessing the faults and merits of each of us in detail. Of all the great American masters, Sidney Bechet seems to have realized most the nature and significance of the New Orleans Revival and his responsibilities towards the young musicians engaged in it. When he came to live in Europe a few years later he made it his business to advise and train those with whom he came in contact, an attitude which is refreshing and unique. As for his own playing, I can only say that it almost swept us right off the stage at the Winter Garden into the orchestra pit. For me, its energy and power are symbolized in my memory of the knot in his tie, which jumped up and down like a piston-head over his Adam's apple as he blew.

With regular broadcasts, regular recordings on a major label and regular tours into the provinces at weekends, the band started to increase its following to a degree which was far beyond our dreams in the old crusading days. The first time I really grasped the full extent of my notoriety was when I heard that my cousin Charles, the tenth Viscount Cobham and Lord of Hagley Hall in Worcestershire, had received an under-the-counter portion of steak in a Birmingham restaurant on the strength of being Humphrey Lyttelton's first cousin.

As a result of the increased demand for our services, we became more ambitious in our activities. We took an office in London, and Lyn Dutton abandoned his daytime job to take up residence there as a full-time manager. We remained spare-time musicians, however, and at one time we had on our strength George Hopkinson, Income Tax man and drummer; Wally Fawkes, cartoonist and clarinettist; Ian Christie, photography student and clarinettist; Keith Christie, RAF 'erk' and trombonist; George Webb, engineer and pianist; Buddy Vallis, Insurance agent and banjoist, and Micky Ashman, aircraft-factory clerk and bass-player. We continued to treat our music seriously and our band engagements with levity. The advantage of remaining semi-professional was that we could afford to remain specialists in the music we enjoyed. And although there were ups and downs, music remained for us a source of enjoyment instead of becoming routine work. There was a freshness about every job on which we met which kept our spirits high – sometimes too high.

There was one dance at the US Officers' Club in Regent's Park when riot broke out in our ranks. It was held in Winfield House, which belonged once to Barbara Hutton until she gave it to the U.S. Army during the war. We were set up in a smart ballroom which was linked to another buffet room by a corridor. We played in the ballroom all night – and the guests remained in the buffet, eating and drinking and talking foreign politics and ignoring us (I don't think they wanted a jazz band – I don't think they even wanted a dance). At first we were on our best behaviour, and when the caretaker asked us to be very careful not to scratch or stain the floor or disturb the décor, we listened sympathetically. But the loneliness of that empty ballroom finally wore us down, and we broke loose. It was the whisky that started it. They brought a bottle and some cardboard mugs to drink it in. The spirit poured straight out of the bottom of the mugs on to the parquet floor, and the strain of trying to salvage the precious stuff before it all ran away made us rather hysterical. Soda siphons were brought into play, and the culminating point came when Ian Christie, our clarinettist, leapt on a chair like a ballet-dancer, grabbed the nearest support to stop himself overbalancing and brought the Star-spangled Banner crashing down on his head. After this we packed up our instruments, abandoned the empty ballroom and joined the guests in the buffet. There we found a friend – a British Army officer who said that he was a jazz fan and that he had enjoyed our playing thoroughly. For those few kind words we loved him, and when some of the band came back from the cloakroom after a brisk game of football with a bowler-hat, it was a pity it turned out to be his.

Our club activities were simple enough. In 1951 we parted company with the London Jazz Club and started our own jazz-for-dancing club in the same Oxford Street premises on a different night of the week. To build up our finances we had to work hard, travelling out of London almost every weekend. And this became very tough on the members of the band who had to return on night trains after a Sunday concert to be at their office desks at 8.30 on Monday morning. (In this respect, Wally Fawkes and I both gained from the fact that Fleet Street didn't wake up until 11 o'clock in the morning.) In the end, we came face to face with the fact that we should have to choose between taking up jazz professionally or curtailing our activities.

In the winter of 1953, the final decision was made. We reverted to a completely semi-professional status, confining our work chiefly to the club on two weekday evenings a week and to an occasional weekend jaunt out of town. Our wives, bless them, sent up audible sighs of relief. They had, after all, married cartoonists and draughtsmen and Income Tax clerks, and it was understandably not in their scheme of things to find themselves almost full-time orchestra widows!

Hitherto, jazz clubs in general had been almost completely ignored in the Press except for a few highly coloured features and some nasty hints in the reports on drug cases. We came into the category of low dives, none the more popular to newsmen for being uneventful and dull. Then all of a sudden, the angle changed. Overnight, we became socially significant, a post-war phenomenon, something to be studied and psychoanalysed. It was quite a pleasant change. There were of course a variety of interpretations. From the *Daily Worker* we gathered the comfortable impression that our customers were solid, dependable proletarian types, the salt of the earth, whose coloured shirts and erratic dancing were simply an expression of revolt against the drab, soul-destroying grind for existence in a capitalist Hell. We even rather fancied the artist's sketch of the band which portrayed us as rugged working types in seamen's jerseys and heavy boots. It only needed a bit of string knotted under each knee to complete the impression. Then along came a special correspondent from *The Times* to put us right. Our clients were not really proletarians and honest toilers after all, but 'public school men and undergraduates', 'enthusiasts from Wellington and Clifton', 'Oxford men', 'a youth from Rugby'. Not 'blokes' at all, but 'chaps' – horrid, hearty 'hoorays' in little corduroy caps. 'Once, when things were cheaper, it was fast cars and roadhouses.' No wonder *The Times* gently reproved us for not understanding the young in heart. In our innocence we had always regarded our patrons as an oddly assorted, heterogeneous, unpredictable mob, as motley a crew as the Foreign Legion itself, who came to the club because they liked to dance – and listen – to jazz. Naïve old sillies that we were, we failed to spot that they were in fact hotheaded blue-bloods in disguise.

For the first thirty years of its life, jazz got along very nicely without suffering any inferiority complex about its status. In New Orleans and Chicago, the populace lived, laughed and loved to jazz music, neither knowing nor caring that they were in the presence of a budding art-form. Then, thanks to the gramophone, jazz spread into the culture-conscious world. Inevitably there emerged an élite, consisting of 'serious' jazz students, musicologists, record-collectors and critics. They wrote critical theses, compiled complex record catalogues (called 'discographies') and generally established themselves as arbiters of taste. In 1934, M. Hugues Panassié – a sort of jazz Ernest Newman – published in France the first important book of jazz criticism, delightfully called *Le Jazz Hot*. All this was quite excellent and salutary. In the 'thirties, when jazz was sucked into the maelstrom of the American music industry, the critics and 'serious' jazz-lovers undoubtedly helped to preserve its identity. But in the process they tried to lift jazz above its station, to make a respectable woman of it. And there began a tendency to try to foist on it all the trappings and paraphernalia of 'serious' music. It has met with some success, especially in Britain, where we no doubt take more readily to the dignifying process. For example, the jazz concert, where no one seems to find it odd that dance music should be trotted out before a seated audience. It is considered an extra feather in the cap of jazz if it can be presented in a hall normally reserved exclusively for serious music – like the Festival Hall in London or the Philharmonic Hall in Liverpool. And it's fascinating to see how the jazz audience, once allowed into these august surroundings, takes on an aspect practically indistinguishable from the 'classical' audience – even down to the empty seats in front reserved for the critics when they should be finished at the bar.

Two incidents demonstrated the gulf which then existed, not only between the élite and the general jazz public, but also between the élite and the musicians who produced the music. Early in 1956, Louis Armstrong and His All Stars came to Britain for a tour – Armstrong's first appearance here for twenty years. They presented the sort of show which they normally put on in America, which is, in effect, a sort of jazz-based variety show with comedy routines, solo specialities and jazz classics all bundled in together. The 'serious' jazz enthusiasts were greatly disturbed. They had gone to hear a jazz concert and were treated to high-spirited clowning and gallery-fetching showmanship. Was this the Louis Armstrong whom they had worshipped on records all these years? Why couldn't he put on a 'serious' jazz concert, as Nature intended? In their dilemma, they searched for scapegoats. It was all the fault of his agent, his publicity manager, the concert promoters – they were forcing him to 'play down' to his audience against his will. Then one night, after the show,

Concert programme designed and drawn by Humph.
Wally Fawkes is drawn as Flook from Trog's series of cartoons.

he and a handful of his musicians came down to my club in Oxford Street. It was a private session – no managers or agents in sight. When Louis and the rest decided to play for us, there was no compulsion for them to play anything they didn't want to play. They got up on the stand and put on a miniature version of their stage show, comedy vocals, drum solos and all. This incident proved to me something that I had always suspected – that to Louis Armstrong there was no distinction between jazz and popular entertainment.

The idea that there might be some highbrow form of jazz, divorced from showmanship and entertainment in the broad sense, was quite beyond his experience or comprehension. And he was not alone. When Lionel Hampton brought his orchestra to Britain later in the year, events repeated themselves. Hampton's band was a dance band specializing in a rugged, exciting brand of jazz. Wherever they played, there were scenes of wild enthusiasm, verging on riot. The obvious and natural habitat for a band of this sort is in the dance hall, where the audience can respond freely to the compelling swing of the music. In Europe, they were booked for concert appearances, and the effect of the supercharged dance music on an audience compelled to remain seated often led to sudden eruptions of pent-up exuberance, sometimes calling for the intervention of the police. When this happened in England, the 'serious' jazz lovers were duly dismayed. People getting up and dancing to jazz? Such vulgarity! They were surprised and hurt that a great musician like Lionel Hampton should countenance such a thing.

Two organizations, the Visiting Orchestras Appreciation Society and the National Jazz Federation, arranged to present a midnight concert at the Royal Festival Hall 'especially for musicians and "serious" jazz lovers'. It was promised that Lionel Hampton would drop his usual presentation and put on a concert of highbrow jazz for the *cognoscenti*. When he turned up and presented his normal stage show with all the trimmings, there was a furious outcry. Nobody quite knew what they had expected, but it wasn't this. Hampton had insulted the jazz lovers! But it was really the other way round – the jazz lovers had insulted Hampton by trying to impose their wishes and demands on him without bothering to find out how he felt about it. They had assumed that he would leap at the chance to turn his back on the public and play something special for the élite. It was quite clear that he had no wish to do anything of the sort. He was bewildered by the whole proceedings and looked thoroughly unhappy and ill at ease until some members of the *hoi polloi* who had impudently gained admission began to clap and whistle and stamp their feet!

The moral to all this is that if you want music for eggheads, you must find eggheads to play it. If you start to apply the same treatment, the same critical approach to jazz as that which is traditionally applied to serious music, sooner or later you will run into absurdity. Let me tell one more cautionary tale. Towards the end of 1956, a concert was staged at the Royal Festival Hall in aid of the Lord Mayor of London's Hungarian Relief Fund. Someone hit on the excellent idea of inviting Louis Armstrong to appear with the Royal Philharmonic Orchestra under Norman Del Mar, to play, among other things, the version of 'St Louis Blues' which he had already played in New York with the New York Philharmonic.

Louis cancelled his engagements in the States and flew over for the event. He picked a British group to take the place of his own All Stars, and went into hurried rehearsal with Norman Del Mar. At the time in Britain we were at a disadvantage. We had few, if any, conductors who were familiar with the jazz idiom. Leonard Bernstein, who conducted the orchestra for the New York concert, was able to converse with Louis in the technical jargon of jazz. When a passage turned up for the small jazz band to play on their own, he had only to ask Louis 'How many choruses, Pops?' for the whole thing to be settled. In this respect, poor Norman Del Mar was at sea. At the first rehearsal he bounced about on the piano stool like an agitated Teddy Bear. 'Stop, stop, stop! I realize you fellows are flexible, but I must know where I am to bring in my chaps!' It was impossible to leave a gap in the score for the little group to fill in. Every bar that was to be played had to be marked on the score. Where a jazz player would recognize, by ear, the exact point at which he should come in, the conductor had to have it down in black-and-white or he was lost. Louis himself was all calm and reassurance at the rehearsal. He addressed Mr Del Mar indulgently as 'Professor', 'Daddy' and, on one occasion, 'Fats'. When Norman Del Mar, pounding out the orchestral part of the piano, roared out a desperate inquiry about the tempo, Louis put a hand on his shoulder. 'Hold that one, Daddy…you got a good tempo there, boy!'

When the concert time came round next day, the Royal Festival Hall was filled to capacity with the most heterogeneous audience it has ever seen. Dinner jackets, fur stoles, white-tie-and-tails rubbed shoulders with duffel coats, sweaters and jeans. The occasion was charged with the sort of bogus dignity at which the British excel. One glance at the programme showed that trouble was in store. For the organizing committee had insisted on putting the Second 'Hungarian Rhapsody' in the programme after Louis Armstrong. In the planning of orchestral concerts, it is quite usual – almost traditional, in fact – to have an orchestral finale after the solo artist has appeared. But this was something different. Louis Armstrong was an artist of world fame, unique in his own field. To hear him in London was a rare experience. And since he was billed as the main attraction, it was a safe bet that the large majority of the audience, formally attired or otherwise, had come to hear him. As it was, the concert opened with two orchestral pieces, accompanied by all the usual symphony concert flou-flah – the procession on to the stage of leader, then conductor; the solemn bowing, the whole air of puffed-up restraint. When Louis eventually stalked on with his jaunty, stiff-backed walk, the whole auditorium erupted in a thunderous welcome. He grinned at the audience, looked down with mock pride at his brand-new suit of midnight blue, then turned and roared a greeting to the musicians behind him. Immediately, the atmosphere changed, became warm and relaxed. And when, after a lengthy orchestral introduction, Louis's gingery-toned trumpet swept in to lead the little jazz group into the 'St Louis Blues', it was as though a spring had been released. From that moment on, Louis Armstrong dominated the concert.

Good jazz has never been ashamed to aim its attack on the senses first and foremost at the feet. It always amazes me how many jazz pundits, who write at length about the degree of 'beat' or 'swing' in a jazz performance, can stand and listen to it with statuesque immobility, apparently not even wiggling their toes in response. There are still jazz enthusiasts who regard the activities of the dancers at a jazz club as some sort of sacrilege. More than once, when I have written an article about dancing to jazz, I have received indignant letters informing me, in as many words, that 'jazz was never intended for dancing'. Intended by whom? The players who originated it? If they had any higher intentions for their music than the mundane functions – dances, picnics, parades and funerals – which it accompanied, they must have been sadly disillusioned men. For during the formative years in New Orleans, the jazz critic, the serious student, the collector, the 'intelligent jazz appreciator' was an unknown species. No pundits were on hand to help Buddy Bolden or King Oliver or Jelly Roll Morton or the young Louis Armstrong along the straight-and-narrow path of 'pure' jazz. Their only guides were the dancers, who applauded them if the music was good to dance to – and flung them off the stand if it wasn't. The relics of that era which are preserved on record suggest that, far from being debased by its dependence on public approval, the music actually flourished on it. And, paradoxically, those who deplore the whole notion of dancing to jazz are the first to refer to the first New Orleans era, when jazz was solely a functional music, as the Golden Age.

In Britain, jazz-club dancing began around 1948. Nobody will pretend that, in those days, it reached a high standard of grace and beauty. But it started under a severe disadvantage. The music was 'Revivalist' in nature at that time – its style and format were lifted from gramophone records of the 'twenties. The poor dancers who were cajoled into taking the floor at the Leicester Square or the London Jazz Club had no records to turn to for guidance. Thirty years separated them from the dances – the Bunny Hugg, the Black Bottom, the Charleston – which were originally designed for the music. So they had to start from scratch. At first, they set about it in the way some adventurous people learn to swim – by jumping in at the deep end and threshing about for dear life. Those were the days when curious onlookers used to make special visits to the clubs to watch the extraordinary antics of the dancers, and anxious Pressmen boggled and predicted the utter collapse of our civilization. It was certainly a hazardous business for all concerned, including the musicians. On more than one occasion in those early days, a flailing arm became engaged in the slide of Keith Christie's trombone and whisked it off under the feet of the dancers. Eventually we had to reverse the normal set-up on the bandstand, withdrawing the more vulnerable front line behind a protective screen of drums, guitar and bass.

In the course of time, some sort of style in jazz dancing began to emerge. The basis of that style was the 'jive' – a modified form of the 'jitterbug' dancing which swept America during the 'swing' craze of the 'thirties. Jiving was introduced into British dance halls by the American troops during the war. And it began to infiltrate into the jazz clubs when young people – not necessarily dedicated jazz fans –

began to desert the big dance halls for the more informal jazz club atmosphere. Basically, jiving is not a very elevating or inspiring dance formula. Its attraction to jazz dancers is that it gives wide scope for individual interpretation. In fact, it allows the dancer as much freedom of improvisation as the musicians on the bandstand enjoy. The male is attached to the female by the slenderest of links – a single handclasp at arm's length – which gives great freedom of movement. Jiving brought some sort of basic form to the anarchy of jazz club dancing in its early days. On the simple foundation that it provided, all sorts of personal styles could be based. Another big influence came from Paris. There, they handled their post-war jazz revival more professionally than we did in London. At the clubs where Claude Luter played the French brand of New Orleans-style jazz, drinks were boosted up to the most unspeakable prices and students who could dance well were admitted free to give atmosphere and attract the tourists. A high standard of dancing emerged, more spectacular and gymnastic than anything known in Britain. The French style was imported into our clubs directly by visiting French students, and indirectly by our own jazz-clubbers who came back from holidays in Paris and tried to emulate what they had seen at the Club Lorientais or the Vieux Colombier.

So jazz dancing in Britain began to acquire some shape. I have no doubt myself that the style of dancing which emerged had some influence on the development of the music.

Apart from the introduction of jiving as a basis for jazz dancing, there has not been any noticeable collective trend. Styles have come and gone. At one stage, when the jazz clubs were even more deeply embroiled in coffee-bar culture, there was a marked ballet influence. The girls took to wearing ballet shoes and black tights, the men to blue jeans several sizes smaller than Nature intended. And instead of plodding manfully around like the rest, they glided and pranced about on toe-point with much expressive gesture of the hands. This practice receded in time due to the serious overcrowding on the dance floors. It was the survival of the fittest on the parquet, and it's little wonder that the style which prevailed belonged more to the rugger field than the ballet stage.

The female jazz dancer was usually less adventurous than the male. Most of her variations were based on familiar undulatory patterns taken from stage or films. Once again, it was in the Hooray sphere that one finds the most startling eccentricity. The Hooray female was notoriously submissive and yielded to male domination on the dance floor with remarkable stoicism. Hardened by generations of stiff training – jostling in the crowds at rugger matches, sloshing through the mud at pheasant shoots, being kneaded and gnawed at on the miniature dance floors in murky nightclubs – she even managed to muster some show of enthusiasm as she was flung about the floor like a rag doll, her clothing awry, her hair-do in ruins. To the Hooray male, jiving was something to be done with heart and soul, with blood, sweat and toil – like the Eton Wall Game.

Sometimes, in the London season, timorous hostesses succumbed to the demands of their young guests and engaged a jazz band for a coming-out dance. We have played at quite a number of deb dances – and I can say without hesitation that they are more frightening than any other function I have ever attended. Whenever possible, I would go along beforehand to inspect the lie of the land. I was usually shown into an elegant, beautifully ceilinged room which would, at a pinch, accommodate twenty couples. Family portraits glare down, priceless vases stand precariously on pedestals around the walls. There is no bandstand – we are simply to set up in a corner, occupying as little space as possible. The hostess is in a dither of anxiety – is the room big enough? Will the band be too loud? I reassure her with promises that we will at any rate *start* pianissimo, but I can almost hear her saying to herself: 'Why, why did I ever listen to those children – there was never any of this worry with dear, nice Mr Geoffrey Howard!' (Geoffrey Howard was a specialist in deb dances – in his band there's always a man who stands in front and plays the violin and smiles.) When the big day arrives, we troop in with our instruments. Having arrived at the house and shed our coats, we set up in the allotted corner of the room, watched with curiosity by the handful of early arrivals – and with anxiety now bordering on panic by the hostess. Some care had to be given to the opening numbers, in the light of my assurance that we will start with something soft. What is 'soft' in a jazz club would splinter the chandeliers in a miniature society ballroom. We would usually ease in gently with some solo numbers, seeing to it that no two melody instruments play together at the same time, that the brass is tightly muted and that the drummer is playing with wire brushes and not sticks. As likely as not, the hostess would hurry up halfway through the first tune to beg for mercy, and we play the rest of it with our faces to the wall.

Things improve when the guests begin to arrive. Those who know us and have heard us play in our natural surroundings soon chafe at the subdued sound, and requests start rolling in for 'something hot'. It's a tug-of-war between the jazz fans and the hostess, with the band in the middle. Sooner or later, something snaps, and it's almost certainly us. Out come the mutes, the drummer grabs the sticks and begins to lay about him, and we abandon all restraint in an ensemble version of 'Royal Garden Blues'. From that point on, youth is at the helm. The hostess and her contemporaries vanish to commiserate with each other in some distant room. Except in matters of dress, the dance floor becomes indistinguishable from any jazz club, except that the Dervishes are out in strength. Familiar faces whiz by, registering every variation of human emotion from ecstasy to numb terror. Gradually the older members of the party drop out, and the pace gets faster and furiouser. Tail coats are discarded, all caution in matters sartorial is thrown away. As off-the-shoulder evening gowns are twisted and jerked more and more out of alignment, one begins to see why they called it a coming-out dance.

A few days later we receive a cheque and a letter of thanks from the hostess. The dance, she says, was an enormous success, entirely due to us. Many of her guests have written to say how much they enjoyed us. And there the matter ends. Next year, it's back to Geoffrey Howard.

In 1951, Graeme Bell's Australian Jazz Band made a return visit to Britain. They had been here before in 1947, during which time we shared with them the residency of the London Jazz Club and struck up many personal friendships. When they returned, I invited Graeme himself and his wife and small daughter to take up residence in the two big rooms which were then lying empty in my large maisonette at Swiss Cottage. I withdrew to the basement, while the Bell *ménage* took over the ground floor (my own status at the time being bachelordom tottering on the verge of marriage). Their arrival marked the beginning of a happy but turbulent epoch in the history of No. 67 Belsize Park.

At the time I was not well acquainted with the customs and conventions of Australian life. I have since been told by an Australian friend that it is quite common in Melbourne, say, for a long-lost friend to arrive unannounced at a household, to be put up for the night on a mattress in the living-room and, having next day imported a packing case to serve as bedside table, to remain comfortably installed there for months. This may be an exaggeration. I can only say that, within weeks of the Bells' arrival, I met an Australian artist on the stairs, who, it seems, had been living for some days in my front room. Peter Glass became a permanent resident, becoming so much 'one of the family' that he eventually officiated as best man at my wedding.

When the Bells left, he stayed on, maintaining the tradition by importing an Australian doctor – and subsequently the doctor's brother – into the house. In addition to the residents, there was a constant stream of visitors during the Bells' tenancy, the arrival of each being the cue for a party. The parties were usually held in my living-room downstairs, because it was large and insulated for sound from the rest of the house. From my point of view it had a further advantage. Having, in the distant past, been the kitchen for the whole house, it had a stone floor which, in those bachelor days, I had neither the urge nor the money to cover. So all I had to do was push the more vulnerable furniture against the wall and I had nothing to fear – nothing, that is, that a large mop and a few blobs of cement couldn't cure.

Carousals recalled after the event are often tedious – and unflattering to the participants as well. I will say no more than that the Bell parties were real marathons. Usually my band as well as Graeme's would be in attendance, with instruments. The liquor was imported in bottles, not only protruding from every overcoat pocket, but also filling as many suitcases and hold-alls as could be called into service. Graeme himself was a prodigious party man. On a good night he would maintain the pace from dusk till dawn, when all but the sturdiest had succumbed. If he was travel-weary from touring and not quite at his best, he would withdraw to a quiet corner and doze during the height of the party. Then, when everyone else was bleary-eyed and spent and thinking longingly of bed, he would re-emerge refreshed, querulously demanding, 'What's the matter with everybody?' And back they had to go into the fray. As frequent host, I discovered that there was only one way of emptying the room – and that was to appear in the doorway in my overcoat and announce that I was going out to breakfast. Then we'd all troop out and drive to an all-night restaurant in Baker Street for eggs and bacon.

Naturally, there was always a jam session on these occasions. And it was during these informal get-togethers that Graeme and I hatched the idea of making some records with an augmented band taken from the two groups. We both recorded for the same record company at the time, so there was no difficulty in getting permission. The idea was to hatch up some simple arrangements, leaving plenty of scope for solo work and maintaining in essence the styles of our two bands. The line-up for the first recordings was Wally Fawkes, George Hopkinson and myself from my band, Keith Christie, who had recently left me to form his own group, and Ade Monsbrough, Pixie Roberts, Graeme Bell, Lou Silbereisen and Bud Baker from the Bell Band. Our instrumentation was trumpet, clarinet, alto sax, tenor sax, trombone, piano, banjo, bass and drums. We called it the Bell-Lyttelton Jazz Nine. I wrote a tune for one side, Graeme one for the other. Graeme called his 'Take a Note from the South'. In the light of my domestic circumstances, I called mine 'Open House'. We rehearsed in my living-room, the music propped up on upturned instrument cases and our only audience the silent array of quart bottles. There was a faintly conspiratorial air about the whole proceedings. Nine men playing jazz together from written arrangements is not exactly a revolutionary notion – but at that time, with Revivalist ardour still burning high in local jazz club circles, it amounted to subversion. It's a funny thing about written music – its psychological effect upon the average jazz fan is violent and profound. He has been brought up on the doctrine that jazz is improvised, and that while your dance band hack is a slave to the 'dots', your jazz man is free to play the way he feels. And to a great extent this is true. But all jazz is arranged to some degree.

The Jazz Twelve records were not as satisfying to me as their less ambitious predecessors. But once again they were great fun to do, and that's really all that we were concerned about. We didn't expect the records to sell, and we were right. It was about this time that we first added a saxophone to the regular line-up of the band. The saxophone was to the traditionalist the arch-villain of the piece. The reason for this is that the instrument came into jazz late in the day. There is a legend that jazz bands were forced to use saxes by hard-headed and philistine dance-hall proprietors because glittering saxophones impressed the public. Knowing from the inside how musicians' minds work, I take this with a hunk of rock salt. At any rate, the jazzmen from New Orleans showed no marked reluctance to make use of the new instrument. King Oliver was using one in 1919, Jimmy Noone adopted a sax and clarinet front line in the early 'twenties, Jelly Roll Morton often featured saxes on recording sessions at which he had a free hand.

Adrian Monsbrough played alto sax, clarinet, trumpet and trombone at various times with the Graeme Bell Band. When they returned in 1951, he was specializing in alto sax. His face, with its short aggressive nose, fiercely bulging eyes and long upper lip, had in repose an expression of benign and disdainful pugnacity, like a Boxer puppy. He wore his thinning hair in an oddly distributed thatch over his brow. In conversation he was monosyllabic and blunt, and his offstage air of relaxation (it earned him the nickname 'Lazy Ade') gave an impression of nonchalance bordering on ennui. Despite this, he was the most sensitive and talented musician among the Australians, and the one who inspired the most confidence as a jazzman. Technically, he was not highly accomplished. He and his alto sax lived on terms of mutual distrust and non-cooperation. Every note he played seemed to be torn grudgingly from the instrument, with which he literally grappled, heaving and lurching about like a man trying to extract one of his own teeth. The music that emerged, under protest, was very different from that originally envisaged by Adolph Sax, but it was none the less strikingly effective.

I think it was originally Ade's idea that he should make some records with us. With only two men in the regular front line, it was a simple matter to incorporate the alto sax of Ade Monsbrough on our recording sessions.

In return, I made a couple of sides with Lazy Ade's Late Hour Boys – a contingent from the Bell Band. I have a special reason to recall this session. The previous night, in a mild binge at the Studio Club in Swallow Street, some uncouth draught cider crept up on me and laid me out. It appears to have inflicted me with delusions of grandeur. It doesn't do to rely too much on hearsay, but I am told that, having left my overcoat behind in the club, I sent Bob Raymond, then a freelance journalist and a keen jazz fan, back to fetch it. Three times he brought it up, and three times I sent it back insisting that it wasn't mine. The coat in question was made for my father in 1908, and is the only one of its kind in the country, if not the world. It seems that I was at great pains to explain this, not only to poor Bob, but also to every passer-by in Swallow Street. At length I agreed that the coat was mine, and clambered into a cab, directing the driver to Buckingham Palace. Someone must have put him right, because I awoke next morning in my own bed, feeling anything but regal. When Graeme Bell looked in later in the morning, I asked anxiously if I had disturbed him when I came in. 'You were all right,' he said, 'I didn't hear you – but those ten drunks you brought with you made the hell of a noise.'

We were due to leave together for the recording studios, but I broke it to him that it was unlikely that I should see the day out, lying motionless in bed, and the prospect of my finding the strength to reach the Abbey Road studios was poor. However, by mid-afternoon I began to feel the presence of my spine once again, and I ventured out. They were just coming to the tail-end of their session when I arrived. Without removing my 1908 overcoat I joined them and made two records which must be among the most relaxed in jazz history. I had a large, lead ball-bearing lodged at the back of my head which rolled forward and hit me right behind the eyes every time I got too enthusiastic. And one eye gleamed an angry red from a burst blood-vessel. I still have a copy of 'Back Room Joys' and 'Hook, Line and Sinker', but it makes me a little queasy to play it.

Graeme's band had a line in Public Relations which didn't exclude a little pugilism when the occasion demanded. There used to be a ballroom in Glasgow called Barrowlands where, as the curtains parted, the visiting band was confronted with the reassuring sight of a row of massive 'chuckers-out' standing shoulder to shoulder in front of the stand *and facing the audience*. The Bell boys heeded with relish and some involuntary clenching of the fists the warning that, quite often, Glaswegians bent upon expressing themselves in direct action would evade the bodyguards and commit mayhem among the music stands.

In the event, their session at Barrowlands started disconcertingly quiet. Apart from an occasional wild cry and the sound of shattering glass from the body of the hall, no kind of fun seemed to be brewing. Then, at the height of the evening, Graeme Bell himself, seated at the piano, saw in the corner of his eye a figure mount the stage and approach him from behind. With an exultant Antipodean roar he leapt up and, without pausing, let fly with a wild right-hander. An autograph book flew in one direction, a pencil in the other, and a bespectacled young man who, up until the moment of impact had been an Ardent Fan, lay spread-eagled on the dance floor.

When the Bell Band went home, we almost prevailed upon Ade Monsbrough to stay here and join us. For domestic reasons he had to go back to Australia, although he hoped to be able to return here within a short time. Several times since then he has been on the point of sailing for England, but twelve thousand miles is a big gulf across

A monthly bulletin designed and written by Humph. This was sent out to members of the Humphrey Lyttelton Club – president Sidney Bechet.

which to conduct negotiations, and nothing came of them. Then in 1952 we enrolled Bruce Turner as regular altoist.

Bruce is something of a legend in the jazz world. There are two theories about him. One is that underneath a vague and absent-minded exterior there is a hard-headed, practical fellow who knows just what's what and upon whom there are no flies. The other, to which I subscribe, is that underneath a vague, absent-minded exterior lurks that rare being, a genuine eccentric. When Bruce joined us, he had just bought a second-hand car from the friend of a friend of a friend. Proudly he showed it off to a pal who knew something about cars. The pal looked it over, sat in the driving seat and tried the controls. 'How much did you pay for this?' he asked.

'Two hundred pounds, Dad.' (To Bruce everyone is Dad.)

'You fool! It's not even in running order! Why didn't you ask someone who knows about cars before you bought it?'

'I did, Dad. The man who sold it to me knows about cars.'

The car sat for three years in a garage. Then Bruce offered it to them for sale, and a deal was struck. When the garage fees were totted up, Bruce had to pay *them*.

It took us some time to get accustomed to Bruce's eccentricities. There was the vocabulary – a sort of extreme basic English with solitary words to cover every sentiment and opinion. Thus 'Great!' for approval, 'Stinks!' for disapproval, 'Ughff!' for disgust, 'Never!' for disagreement, 'But…' for doubt and so on. It wasn't until he had been with us for some time that we found out that he could write and lecture fluently, and that he is a widely read and well-informed student of politics and philosophy. He did his best at all times to cover up these practical traits. During his last few months with the band he took to reading an atlas on long train journeys, poring deeply over SOUTH AMERICA or THE MALAYAN PENINSULA and sometimes memorizing the index by way of a change. On one occasion two girls sitting opposite attracted his eye. With admirable chivalry he proffered his atlas. 'Would you care to look at this?' They were too polite to refuse, and spent an uncomfortable half-hour thumbing through the pages, feigning interest.

Then there was his diet. He had a headful of theories, most of them with a strong 'Back to Nature' bias. He wouldn't touch alcohol or tobacco, and liked to bring his own food on tour with him. This consisted of the most depressing assortment of raw vegetables which he consumed with every outward appearance of relish. No doubt it was very good for him, but its beneficial effect must have been counteracted by the craving for cream buns, chocolates and all kinds of sugary concoctions which he freely indulged. A man of tender susceptibilities, he could never eat meat unless it was so heavily disguised as to leave no trace of its past history. I have good reason for saying that this was no affectation.

After one of our Continental tours, he stayed over with myself, my wife and Wally Fawkes for a day or two in Paris. One morning, in a little café in Montmartre, we ordered bouillabaisse. Bruce was too busy making approbatory noises in the direction of the waitress to take in what was happening, so we ordered it for him too. While it was being prepared, Bruce was full of apprehension. 'Will I like it, Dad?' We did our best to set him at ease, although we didn't quite know what to expect ourselves. When the waitress returned and put in front of him a clattering bowl of marine corpses, all claw and antennae and spiky fins, Bruce was for once at a loss for a word. He just turned green, got up and walked out. We saw him again five days later, in Glasgow. He had made straight for the nearest seaport and come home.

By digressing about Bruce Turner, I have skipped one of the most adventurous experiments in which we indulged. It happened before Bruce joined the band and not very long after the Bell–Lyttelton affair. Once again, it happened quite by accident. A Mardi Gras celebration was held in an hotel off Russell Square in the February of 1952. Since the Mardi Gras carnival is an event common to the West Indies and to New Orleans, the idea was to have a combined celebration with my band furnishing New Orleans-type jazz and a group of London-based West Indian musicians playing the music of the Caribbean. There was a mild calypso vogue on in London at the time, and two stars in the calypso field – Lord Beginner and Lord Kitchener – were on the bill, too. For most of the evening the bands played alternately, but towards the end we had a merger – a wild jam session in which anyone who could shake a maraca or strike bottle and spoon together joined in. The result was sensational. Some of the simpler New Orleans tunes which we played came vividly to life in the clattering rhythmic surroundings. After the rugged four-to-a-bar of the conventional 'traditional' rhythm section of that time, the shifting rhythms were highly stimulating. And the evening rose to a climax with everyone, including some of the serious jazz students who had come along to give the proceedings their critical appraisal, coiling around the floor in a long, hilarious procession.

The upshot of it all was that I felt the urge to do something more along the same lines. In collaboration with record supervisor Denis Preston, who was then handling most of the West Indian recording artists, and Freddy Grant, one of the leading West Indian musicians in London, plans were laid for a recording session. And the Grant-Lyttelton Paseo Jazz Band came into being. The word 'Paseo', a

Trinidad dance, was chosen to distinguish the group from my regular band. My idea was twofold: to reintroduce the rhythmic variety of Creole jazz into our music, and also to inject new life into the worn jazz repertoire by drawing on the folk-music material, still quite contemporary and fresh, which existed in the West Indian community.

Reactions to the Paseo recordings were very similar to those which followed the Bell-Lytteltons, although there was a small quarter in which genuine enthusiasm was aroused for the idea. The sale of our Paseo records was healthy enough to encourage us to incorporate the West Indian section in our regular touring band show. We devised a show which offered straight jazz from my band, straight West Indian music from Freddy Grant's boys and some Paseo jazz from the combined teams.

The Paseo show lasted about six months before the money ran out. We had a heavy wage bill, and although the show was quite favourably received wherever it went, we couldn't keep it going. It was fun while it lasted, and it did us all good to extend our musical horizons a bit beyond the conventional jazz boundaries.

I gave up balloon-filling for the *Daily Mail* Flook cartoon soon after we turned full-time. Wally 'Trog' Fawkes left the band after eight (for me) happy years, finding that the strain of contributing the daily strip cartoon and taking part in the band's blossoming activities was too much. When I found myself confronted with the same dilemma a month or two later, I jumped the other way. There's a nightmare quality about turning out a strip cartoon, rather like the bad dream in which some indefinable Thing is chasing you and your feet turn to lead. However hard you work to build up a stockpile, the insatiable daily consumption by the newspaper wears it ruthlessly down. It caught up on me in the middle of a tour which we did with Sidney Bechet. What with all the work and excitement of preparing for the tour, I had no time to amass the required number of day-by-day 'shooting scripts' – i.e. dialogue for the balloons – to keep Wally going while I was away. I had to try to keep pace with it *en route*. It was impossible to work on the crowded coach, and for most of the tour we had long journeys to cover which meant an early start in the morning. So I found myself trying to work after the two nightly shows – which meant starting round about 12.30a.m. After a few days of this I threw in the towel.

This was not the end of journalism for me, but I found writing pieces for various journals or magazines far less harassing than balloon filling. Material for discussion is constantly presenting itself. What's more, the hardest part about writing is hitting on a theme and developing it. This requires a period of gestation before you actually start thrashing away at the typewriter. (My wife finds this a hard fact to grasp and is inclined to interrupt my ruminative exercises – lying on the bed staring at the ceiling, blowing the trumpet, throwing away the scrap paper on my desk – with 'I thought you said you were going to work'.) Fortunately, a lot of the mulling-over of a weekly jazz piece can be done in the car driving to or from work or on a train when other members of the band have relapsed into sleep. So when it comes to writing the piece, it rarely takes me longer than it needs to type it out. Editors who read this may ask themselves why my copy was always several days late. Well, that's another story.

Between Friends

Under the guidance – some might say the Papal decree – of Hugues Panassié and his central 'Ot Cloob de France, 'Ot Cloobs all over Europe spread the word that anyone who had ever been remotely connected with a jazz band in America was a '*grande vedette*' or big star. To be able to put the words 'Jazz' and 'American' together on a poster, especially with the suffix '*noir*', was to ensure ecstatic crowds and a certain amount of mayhem around the box office.

Very soon the French liner *Île de France* had assumed a role almost as important in jazz history as those Mississippi boats that took jazz up-river from New Orleans to Chicago. On every transatlantic trip she brought over at least one American musician who was delighted to find himself received like royalty.

I am happy to say that we in Britain held ourselves somewhat aloof from these hysterical goings-on. For one thing, we had our Musicians' Union to protect our interests by keeping all American musicians out between 1935 and 1956. Then we wisely rejected ze 'Ot Cloob as being an unreliable Froggy institution, redolent of inefficiency and garlic. Instead, we had Rhythm Clubs, which are rather easier to pronounce with a stiff upper lip. Furthermore, we do not as a nation go in much for treating people as royalty. We have our own royalty, thank you, and we don't even treat them as royalty.

For all these reasons, American jazz musicians at the time tended to remain tourists in this country rather than residents. Some outdid the tourists in their reaction to our institutions. Bud Freeman was a great jazz saxophone player, a veteran of the white Chicago school of the late 'twenties, and a lifelong Anglophile. In the company of the gum-chewing, whisky-bashing, wise-cracking Chicagoans who pivoted around guitarist Eddie Condon in the 'thirties and 'forties, Bud's refined speech, neat Ronald Colman moustache and proclivity towards Shakespeare and plus-fours always stuck out like an elegantly manicured thumb.

In 1963, Bud made his first trip to England, to play at a big festival at Belle Vue, Manchester. On the committee of this festival was the Hon. Gerald Lascelles, the Queen's cousin and an ardent admirer of Bud Freeman and the school of jazz which he represents. Through him, it came about that Bud and his fellow-musicians were met at London Airport by a liveried chauffeur at the wheel of a vast Rolls Royce. Sinking back into its soft leather upholstery, he looked out enraptured as the pinnacled roof of Eton College Chapel, the fairy-story silhouette of Windsor Castle and verdant glimpses of Runnymede and Virginia Water flashed past the window. At the Lascelles home of Fort Belvedere, there was a reception in the great drawing room followed by a photographic session on the sweeping lawns outside. In the middle of it all, Bud came across and put a confidential arm round my shoulder. 'Humphrey, old boy,' he said, 'you've no idea what this means to me. After all these years of dreaming, England is exactly as I always imagined it.'

It only needs to be added that the euphoria engendered by the sudden realization of all his dreams of England sustained Bud

Freeman through a coach trip next day that took in the less romantic lower reaches of London, Birmingham and Manchester.

In the early 'thirties, when jazz visits had become commonplace, our royalty had to get used to a certain absence of protocol when confronted by the jazz aristocracy. George V, who seems to have been quite a jazz buff in his own quiet way, must have felt a twinge of astonishment when, at a Command Performance, young Louis Armstrong unleashed a red-hot trumpet solo at him with the words, 'This one's for you, Rex!'

Around the same time, Lord Beaverbrook gave a party for the then Prince of Wales at which the visiting Duke Ellington band played the music. The Duke of York, later George VI, asked Duke Ellington to do a solo of 'Swampy River' which was in the royal record collection. Ellington didn't recognize him and gave him what he later described as 'the light fluff'. It wasn't the Duke of York's night. Later the band left to go on to a recording studio, taking many of the guests with them. But the Scotland Yard detective wouldn't let him go because of the crush. For some reason the Prince of Wales got through the security net and, at some stage when, alas, the record machine wasn't operating, sat in on drums. As Duke Ellington recalled, 'We expected some little Lord Fauntleroy stuff but he really gave out with some lowdown Charleston.' As the Charleston went out of fashion some ten years earlier, we may draw our own conclusions.

My own recollection of the old European jazz scene in all its splendid absurdity centres upon a concert in Paris in the late 'fifties. It was held in the vast Palais des Sports, where they used to end the six-day bicycle race. The star of the concert was, by a delicious irony, the man who, on a first visit to France in 1929, had put Hugues Panassié straight about jazz – the self-confessed one-time opium-smoker, small-time gangster, dope-peddler and clarinettist Mezz Mezzrow. While the capacity audience blew whistles and shook rattles upstairs, fifteen bands, comprising upwards of a hundred and fifty musicians, were marshalled by hysterical stewards in the concrete passages below, in order to emerge from below ground in an opening parade.

It is impossible to describe the din when, in the echoing, pipelined labyrinth under the stadium, we struck up at a given signal with 'High Society'. Mezzrow set off at the head of the procession with a steward steering him at each elbow. They went too fast and disappeared from sight, at which point those following took a wrong turning and led us all into a cul-de-sac, playing 'High Society' and swearing alternately. Responding to cries of 'turn back' in six different languages, a bass drummer at the rear did a military countermarch and got himself stuck sideways-on in the narrow passage, trapping us all. While an inferno raged beneath, Mezz Mezzrow in the meantime had reached the steps leading up into the auditorium. Piping away manfully on the clarinet, he emerged, not at the head of a triumphant parade, but entirely alone.

Anywhere else in the world it would have been a grotesque anticlimax. But it seemed that the massed 'Ot Cloobs of the entire universe were there, fully-primed. Hitler arriving in the Nuremberg Stadium never knew the ovation that they gave the solitary Mezzrow that night.

Since those early days, improvement in, and recognition for, British jazz has led to a collaboration on a more equal basis, and many of my happiest memories are of tours with, and alongside, American jazzmen.

Sidney Bechet

Sidney Bechet had curious links with Britain over the years. A travelling man for most of his life, he was one of the first jazz musicians to come here, as long ago as 1919. His early impression of England underwent a traumatic metamorphosis. He was then with Will Marion Cook's Southern Syncopated Orchestra, and, during its season at the Philharmonic Hall in London, the band was commanded to send a small contingent along to play at Buckingham Palace for King George V, who has been noted earlier as being quite a jazzer in his own quiet way.

Bechet doesn't seem to have been overawed by the interior of the Palace – 'it was like Grand Central Station with a lot of carpets and things on the walls'. What impressed him most was the sight of the monarch, in the flesh and large as life – or small as life, if we are to be strictly accurate. In his autobiography *Treat it Gentle* Bechet wrote, 'It was the first time I ever got to recognize someone from having seen his picture on my money…it was a funny thing, looking at your money and seeing someone you know!'

It was only a matter of months before he was to hurl all that money overboard into the Atlantic as a gesture of disgust for all things British. As a result of a bedroom fracas with a prostitute – his account of it suggests a sort of escalating slap and tickle which ended with the lady screaming murder and rape out of the window – he was arrested. Although he was cleared of attempted rape and assault and battery, he was ordered to be deported as an 'undesirable alien'. It was on the way home that he decided to sever relations by flinging the assorted likenesses of George V into the sea.

Returning exactly thirty years later, Sidney still found the occasion nerve-wracking. Mind you, there was more than just the hangover of that court case to worry about. In 1949 the reciprocal embargo between the British and American Musicians' Unions was still in force. Some British promoters decided to defy it, and Bechet and Coleman Hawkins were each brought in as 'tourists' with the specific aim of featuring them in separate concerts. In the face of the combined opposition of the Musicians' Union and the Ministry of Labour, the ruse by which Bechet was presented to the public was a naïve one. My band was booked to give a concert at the Winter Gardens Theatre in London. In the middle of the concert, surprise, surprise, Sidney Bechet was picked out by a spotlight in a box near the stage, and was prevailed upon by the compere and audience together to join us on stage for a few numbers. Two days later I made a feeble attempt to persuade a Scotland Yard inspector who called at my house that the two-hour rehearsal which we had gone through with Sidney in the afternoon was not a rehearsal at all but a social gathering at which, quite by chance, some music was played. The promoters were summoned and fined £100 for employing aliens without a work permit. I suppose I was lucky not to be had up as an accessory before, during and after the event. Of course there was no question of bribery and corruption, but I do recall that, having taken down my statement in laborious longhand and obtained my signature to it, the inspector asked for my autograph on behalf of his daughter, who was a fan.

By the time the case came up, Bechet was back home in America, no doubt happy to have escaped more legal trouble but satisfied that the 'rape' incident of thirty years earlier had been expunged from the bureaucratic memory. The concert had been a great triumph for him. A new-found interest in the sound and history of New Orleans jazz was then at its height in Britain, and when Sidney was introduced and walked on stage playing his soprano saxophone, the great roar from the audience completely drowned the music.

At that meeting and at a recording session which we did on the previous day, we got on well with Bechet who, in turn, was in a mellow mood. It wasn't always so. Wally Fawkes, then with me on clarinet, left the band in the early 'fifties on a four-week sabbatical to play in a European band assembled by Bechet in Geneva. He told us on his return of a first rehearsal at which the maestro, suddenly flying into a violent rage, castigated the eager young Europeans so ferociously that their insides turned to water. Afterwards Wally, not a man to be long overawed, asked him if the band had really been as bad as he had said. 'Oh, the band's fine,' said Sidney, 'I just did that to be sure you'd work hard!'

By this time, Bechet had taken up permanent residence in Paris. His early experiences in France were as unpromising as those in Britain. In 1929, during a row in the street with some other expatriate American musicians, Bechet drew a gun and pumped bullets in all directions, one of which found its final resting-place in the flesh of a French woman who was watching the extraordinary Wild West scene at what she thought was a safe distance. For this outburst, Bechet was sent to prison for eleven months. The story was once rife in the jazz magazines that it was this experience that turned his hair prematurely white, a theory which is modified, if not discounted altogether, by subsequent photographs in the 'forties showing a greying but not snowy head. Anyway, it was clear when Bechet returned to post-war France, first as a visitor and later to live, that, as in Britain, all was forgotten and forgiven.

It's a common and understandable wish among jazz fans through the ages that their idols should be lovable. Many of the people who were able to meet Bechet often after he came to Europe, and who experienced his courteous, soft-spoken and considerate manner on social occasions, speak of him still in terms of cuddly affection. My experience is that jazzmen, particularly those who have fought their way almost single-handed to the top of their profession, are as cuddly as man-eating tigers. Bechet wrote of himself, 'I can be mean. It takes an awful lot: someone's got to do a lot to me. But when I do get mean, I can be powerful mean.' In its American sense, 'mean' covers many shades of temperament from evil temper to mere cussedness. It was these lower reaches of meanness which I saw most often in Bechet – and found, as someone never at any time on the receiving end, strongly endearing. I like my heroes to be men of iron, not of cotton-wool and fur. Indeed, it would have astounded and appalled me to discover that music of such passion, command, ferocity and seductiveness had emanated from a teddy bear.

Once Bechet was established in France, he became a national hero. His wedding in 1951, to a German lady, was in his own words 'one of the biggest things that's ever been seen since Aly Khan's marriage'. Held in Antibes, it took the form of a New Orleans Mardi Gras parade, with bride and bridegroom in an open landau followed by a retinue of bands. It helped to establish Sidney in France as a superstar in the Chevalier/Piaf category. Two or three years after his state wedding I visited him in Paris, in a second home which he had established across the other side of the city with a second 'wife', a girl of seventeen, by whom he had then a small son. I was told that he commuted, allegedly 'on tour', between these two households. When I called on him unexpectedly at this second home, our conversation was punctuated by the scolding of his young mistress who had discovered a third liaison with a girl in Lausanne.

That Bechet had not lost his sexual attractiveness at an age estimated at somewhere between fifty-five and sixty became apparent from an episode in the now defunct Queens Hotel in Birmingham during his 1956 tour here. A lady knocked on the door of his room at a late hour, saying that she had been a fan of his for many years and would like a talk with him. 'Take off your clothes and we'll talk,' was

Bechet's unsubtle reply. Next morning he picked up the phone in his single room and ordered breakfast for two.

On that tour, Bechet was the guest soloist with a French band led by André Reweliotty, and my own band toured with them, opening the show for an hour and coming back on for the finale. There is a saying that an Alsatian dog is perfectly safe and harmless unless you show it that you are frightened, at which point it is liable to take your arm off at the elbow. The same, in that late stage in his life, can be said of Sidney Bechet.

Bechet had the French boys strictly disciplined. He liked to have them always under his eye, and when the concerts were over it was a regular routine for them to join him in a meal and then go quietly to bed. Sidney was a man of charming manner but explosive temper, and the truth is that he took undisguised glee in making them tremble. Although we were on the same show, he had no direct control over us, and we went our own way in off-duty hours. The only nonconformist in the French band was Eddie Bernard, the diminutive, excitable and eccentric pianist. If ever a party was afoot, Eddie was on tenterhooks of excitement. Disaster overtook him at Glasgow. It has become a tradition that whenever we visit the city, we attend afterwards at the house of Norman McSwan, a jazz-loving doctor who, with his wife, provides for visiting musicians a fathomless well of hospitality. That night we took Eddie Bernard with us, and sat long into the morning sampling the doctor's whisky and listening to jazz records. We got back to the hotel at 7a.m. Our train was due out two hours later. By an odd mischance, Eddie had changed his hotel room for some reason just before going out, and the night porter had failed to make a note of it. So when we assembled in the morning and Bernard was missing, nobody knew where he was. They knocked on the door of the room into which he had registered, and an angry female voice demanded to know what they wanted. The hotel was the largest in Glasgow, and somewhere in the remaining 474 rooms Bernard was fast asleep. They ran him to ground in time to catch the train by a few seconds' margin. On the train Bechet castigated him roundly. For a day or two it was the end of parties for Eddie Bernard. Then, at Liverpool, a bumper party loomed at the home of one of the local musicians. We promised Eddie that we would take him along *and* deliver him on to the train next morning. All day he was practically airborne with excitement. But, as we assembled outside the concert hall that night, and the French boys embarked in their coach to go back to the hotel, I saw Bechet watching him suspiciously from a rear window. Then their road manager called from the coach door. 'Eddie Bernard! *Un moment*....' Eddie went across and was instantly seized by four pairs of hands and hauled into the coach, which drove off. Kidnapped! We discussed the situation over a Chinese meal before going to the party, and decided on counter-action. A raiding party was sent to the hotel. Bechet's party had just finished their meal and were leaving the table. Our raiders seized Eddie Bernard bodily from under Bechet's nose and hauled him off to a waiting taxi. Next morning, I joined Sidney in a late-morning coffee. After some desultory conversation, he looked at me with a wicked twinkle in his eye.

'I hear Eddie enjoyed his party last night.'

I was cautious. 'Yes, I believe he had a good time.'

'Well, you know something. If I hadn't been tired and ready for sleep, I'd have followed that taxi and come and fetched him myself!'

It was clear from his expression that he was by no means annoyed that his authority had been challenged. Notwithstanding the avuncular appearance and the gentle manner, Sidney Bechet was a fighter by nature. And I have a feeling that he relished our spirited opposition.

Buck Clayton

Buck Clayton was remarkably handsome even, as he was then, in his middle fifties, with the unique blue eyes lending to his face the alert yet sensuous look of a cat. He always chose his clothes with care, sporting in one phase of his visit an English look complete with waistcoat and bowler hat, in which he looked superb. Always the courtly ladies' man, he liked to make for sophisticated nightspots after his work was done, making many friends outside the circle of musicians and fans who surrounded him wherever he played.

When he toured with my band in the early 'sixties he made it clear from the outset that he didn't want to work as a 'star' soloist but as a member of the band. Before his first tour, he sent over some arrangements and compositions at my requests, and I noticed that he had written himself second trumpet parts throughout. His reasons were a characteristic blend of politeness and practicality – as leader of the band I should have the first part, which would also ensure that we could continue to play the arrangements after he had left us. In view of the fact that the first parts were higher and more punishing, I'm not sure there wasn't a wrestler's trick lurking in there somewhere, that is to say, feigning weakness and incapacity until his opponent relaxed and then leaping in with a paralysing half-Nelson.

I must explain. In the course of working with American musicians I have discovered the fundamental difference between the British and American philosophy of life. The Briton maintains a stiff upper lip and says 'Never kick a man when he's down'. The American juts his jaw and says 'Always kick a man when he's down – it may be the last chance you'll get'. During one of Buck's tours with us we played at a big festival in Manchester, at which Dizzy Gillespie was also appearing as soloist with the John Dankworth Orchestra. In the finale, Buck was to join Dizzy and the orchestra in a last appearance. For reasons not wholly unconnected with over-indulgence on a grand scale, Dizzy had incapacitated himself that night to the point where he really could not play at all. The familiar embouchure, bolstered by cheeks puffed up like aubergines, was drained of strength – a situation easily brought on by digestive overstrain, and dreaded by trumpet-players. Earlier in the festival, he had annoyed Buck by wandering onstage and clowning during our set. When Buck joined Dizzy at the end of a set which had been, for everyone, a painful embarrassment, he was in tigerish form, playing so superbly that members of the Dankworth Orchestra forgot their gentlemanly allegiance to their own guest and applauded him wildly. Afterwards, Buck denied having done a hatchet job on a defenceless Dizzy, but, consciously or not, the deed had been done.

At our concerts, Buck and I often engaged in trumpet exchanges. In range and stamina Buck had the edge on me most of the time. Nevertheless he would often murmur, 'Take it easy tonight, Humph –

my chops are in poor shape,' just before we embarked on our special trumpet duet called 'Me and Buck'. As befits an Old Etonian and former officer in Her Majesty's First Regiment of Foot Guards, I behaved in a gentlemanly manner, avoiding any display of fireworks which might put my American friend at a disadvantage and dismissing all base suspicions when, invariably, his ailing chops made a dramatic recovery just as it was his turn to play. One night he went too far. We always ended our performances with Irving Berlin's 'The Song Is Ended', over which I made the closing announcement. As the honoured guest Buck would play the final cadenza, climbing up to an impressive high F. At the Manchester Sports Guild, after a hard and hot session, he made the climb up to E and then turned and pointed to me. Unprepared, the lips relaxed after playing a second part in the low register, I had to hit a high F out of the blue. In the agonised rush of wind there was a high F somewhere to be heard but it was more of a cry for help than a musical note.

humph
Humphrey
LYTTELTON
Club
WEDNESDAY at the MARQUEE
presents from America the fabulous trumpet of
BUCK CLAYTON
OCTOBER 14, 21, 28.
DOORS OPEN 8.0 p.m. till 11.30 p.m. Members 6/- Guests 7/6
MARQUEE 90 WARDOUR STREET, LONDON, W.1.

After that I openly accused Buck of playing wrestler's tricks. He laughed a lot at the suggestion but didn't actually deny it. A few nights later he whispered, as I called our duet, 'Take it easy on me tonight, Humph – I left my jock-strap back in the hotel.' Jock-strap or no, I played flat out. Since that time, our firm friendship was cemented on a keen mutual awareness of wrestler's tricks (we recorded an original tune with that title), when Buck suffered a cruel series of illnesses which forced him to stop playing. It was inconceivable that the close association with the band built up in the 'sixties should cease, so, when I heard that he was beginning to turn his attention to writing, I commissioned some compositions from him which we eventually recorded with Buddy Tate as guest and tenor saxist. When I glanced through them and saw that Buck had designated me to play first clarinet in a number at breakneck speed, I knew that he had not packed the wrestler's tricks away with his horn. I play clarinet slowly, in one key.

As men who have had to make their own way in the world with stiff competition from all comers, jazz musicians tend to develop a Machiavellian sense of humour. Buck was never happier, when we drove round that country together, than when I recounted disasters that involved his American friends and colleagues – how Henry Allen and my band had a row onstage in Manchester, and how Ben Webster was ejected by the police from the Nottingham club where he was appearing as star soloist, and asked the young policeman who had him in an armlock, 'Did you ever know Art Tatum?' Ben Webster was part-Red Indian and, below a certain specific gravity, the sweetest man who ever walked. When flash level was reached, he developed a suicidal tendency to attack anyone in official uniform. Stories of Ben ending a foray with a squad of policemen or hotel night staff sitting on his protesting head would always get the same gleeful but affectionate response from Buck, 'Yeah, that's Ben.'

As a part-Indian himself, Buck has always asserted that 'Indians always fight when they get drunk'. I never knew Buck himself get more than mildly grumpy, though he told of an epic fight in his Basie band youth with fellow-trumpeter Ed Lewis which took place on a sidewalk after a small difference of opinion and lasted forty-five minutes until they were both arrested. When Buck woke up in jail next morning the first thing he saw was a shoe wedged in the bars of the cell window.

Only once did I personally suffer from Buck's relish for catastrophe. I was briefed to organize a concert at the Royal Festival Hall which, in addition to my own band and two British rhythm sections, was to star five visiting Americans – Buck Clayton, Ben Webster, Ruby Braff the cornettist, Vic Dickenson the trombonist, and Big Joe Turner. I decided to split the instrumentalists into small groups, adding Bruce Turner to make up one of the front lines. On the way back from a gig the night before I told Buck my plans. When I talked of putting Vic and Ruby together with Bruce in one group, Buck's only response was a low chuckle. Had I said something funny? 'No, it's nothing,' said Buck, chuckling again. I pressed him. 'Well, it's just that when I last saw Vic he said that never again in his *life* would he work with Ruby.' 'Oh,' I said. Then I told him that I would like him to appear with Ben and Vic. This time it was more of a belly-laugh than a chuckle. 'Don't tell me you won't work with them!' I cried. 'Hell, no,' he said, 'but when Ben and Vic last worked together in the States, they ended up having a fight. Boy, did they *fight*!'

I have never liked the Royal Festival Hall. Every performer has a jinx place that makes him nervous, and for me, the Festival Hall is it. I once used to have a recurring nightmare before every appearance there. In it the hall was roofless under a blue sky. At the back of the furthest stalls was a Dali-esque viaduct and beyond it more audience stretched away to hazy infinity. When I went onstage before this vast audience I found that all I could do was hum through the trumpet as if it were a kazoo. While I hummed inaudibly the audience, all ten million of them, would get up one by one and walk out. And I would wake up sweating – and humming. Before the all-star concert in question I spent an entirely sleepless night, thanks to Buck. There was nothing I could do about altering the programme – when I had suggested putting Ben on with Ruby, Buck nearly fell out of the car.

As it turned out, I could have slept like a baby. When they arrived at the Festival Hall for rehearsal, the Americans fell into each other's arms in great brotherly embraces. In the ever-open backstage bar all was sweetness and light and at least one can say that the concert made up in camaraderie what it lacked in coherence. When I announced Ben Webster's re-appearance for the finale and was told, in stentorian whispers from the wings, that he had gone home, I felt thankful for small mercies. At least he hadn't attacked an official!

Big Joe Turner

By the time Big Joe Turner came to work with us in 1965 the longstanding prefix 'Big' had come to denote more than his considerable height. He was by then Vast Joe Turner and was one of the most prodigious eaters I ever met (six foot and twenty-four stone, as a matter of fact). When he toured with me, we stopped one morning in North London, on the way home, so that he could buy himself a steak for lunch. The butcher brought out a long strip of rump and, hovering over it with a knife, asked how big a steak he wanted. 'I'll take it all,' was the reply, and this huge mattress of meat was rolled up and put in a bag. The story has an appalling sequel. Getting back to his apartment, he lit the electric stove and put the steak (folded three ways, no doubt) under the grill. He then lay on the bed and went to sleep for two hours, with results on which we need not dwell.

When Joe bought a sports jacket at the specialist Big Man's shop on the Edgware Road they had to insert a lanyard with a button at each end to bring it together across his middle. It was hard at first sight to reconcile the huge, genial man with his eager boy's face and rather worried, insecure temperament with that forthright voice, full of masculine assertiveness, that belted out penetrating and quite sophisticated blues lyrics of his own devising on so many cherished records.

On one of our early journeys out of town while on tour with Buck Clayton we pulled up at some traffic lights alongside a radio shop.

'Man,' said Joe to Buck, 'I'd like to get me one of them little English radios to take home.' 'Why? You can get radios like that anywhere in the States,' Buck pointed out. 'Yeah,' said Joe, 'but I sure like the programmes they get.' On another occasion he announced, as we passed a gardening shop, 'I think I'll take home one of those lawn-mowers.' The prospect of Joe, encumbered already with a hold-all the size and weight of a rolled-up rhinoceros, checking in at Heathrow with a lawn-mower reduced Buck and me to a stunned silence. 'Yeah,' mused Joe, 'I'm gonna be the only guy in my street who has a lawn-mower with an English accent!' Here we were getting a little closer to the blues man whose original line of thought had introduced such contemporary 'props' of T.V. and RADAR into his lyrics.

Fortunately the logistics of exporting a lawn-mower eventually deterred him. He was not a man for meeting the complexities of life halfway. Once he got me to stop the car on the outskirts of Manchester. He had spotted a camera shop and wanted to buy a camera – 'I don't want one of them complicated things, just sump'n' I can put up to my eye and shoot.' I conveyed this wish to the salesman, who showed him the newest thing in instant automatic cameras. Halfway through the explanation about cartridge-loading, self-focusing, automatic exposure and fool-proof wind-on, Joe took fright: 'Man, you gotta go to *school* to work this!' he cried as he beat a lumbering retreat.

Buck treated Joe with affectionate indulgence and occasional incredulity. Whenever we went into a roadside store for refreshment, Joe, whose almost consonant-free dialect was hard enough to understand at the best of times, would confuse the person behind the sweet counter even more by asking for a 'soda pop'. Buck shook his head in wonderment. 'You know, back home I never heard anyone talk about a soda pop for *thirty years*!' It was only when Joe's dependence on Buck intruded upon the latter's social life that things became a little strained. Joe, who wore his trilby hat squarely on the back of his head and sported a huge camel-hair coat that reached down to his massive ankles, hardly fitted in with Buck's nocturnal plans, and there was a hint of exasperation in Buck's voice when he described how, night after night, he would tiptoe, dressed to kill, past

Joe's hotel door only to hear it open as he passed to reveal Joe, trilby and top-coat already on, asking, 'Where we goin' tonight, Buck?'

In matters of low finance, too, Joe often took on the role of innocent abroad. On his very first night here we went to Annie's Room, Annie Ross's short-lived nightclub. Outside in Russell Street, we were approached by one of those down-and-outs who materialize, when you are quite successfully parking your car, to encumber you with help. Joe reached into his pocket to reward him for his antics, but I assured him it wasn't necessary. After a festive hour or two during which Buck and Joe both sat in with Annie and the band, we emerged to find the self-appointed attendant still there, now weaving and lurching even more obviously. This time there was no deterring Joe. As the man touched his cap and bobbed obsequiously, Joe put his hand into his trouser pocket, scooped out a fistful of loose change amounting on my reckoning to several pounds and deposited the lot in the man's hastily outstretched hand.

A week or two later we did a television programme from a studio in Westbourne Grove. In the pub nearby at lunchtime we were entertained by an amateur folk-group. Towards the end of their set a girl came round with a pint glass collecting contributions. I put in a coin and then said to her, 'Go straight to that big man in the corner – I think you'll get a pleasant surprise.' Buck and I watched as she spoke to Joe. We couldn't see exactly what happened, but we guessed. The girl came back, her glass brimming with assorted coins. 'Gosh!' she said, 'you were right – but don't you think I should give some back? He emptied both pockets and it looks like about £8!' We told her not to bother.

Onstage, Joe Turner occasionally showed the insecurity which seemed to dog his incursions into unfamiliar surroundings. He sang almost every one of his blues and standard pop songs in the key of C. It became a matter of reflex action for us to lead into an introduction in C. Having done so for about six nights in a row, it was not unusual for us to hear Joe, on the seventh night, lamenting 'Wrong key, wrong key!' as soon as we started. He had a stock phrase, a hangover from the rhyming hip jargon of the 'forties, to express his periodical – and always unfounded – conviction that things had gone wrong. 'We're in a world of trouble,' he would cry. 'Someone took a pin and busted the bubble!' But when he was confident and in congenial company, the big penetrating voice assumed an air of massive authority.

To some listeners over here, weaned on rock 'n' roll and theatrically extrovert 'rhythm 'n' blues', his manner of delivery, standing foursquare with the huge frame bent forward slightly and little movement beyond the snapping of finger and thumb, was disappointingly short of frenetic, as was his limiting of his vocal range for the most part to four or five notes. They missed the passionate intensity which lay beneath the repetitive phrases and the dramatic effect achieved when, by changing just one beautifully-judged note, he gave a stanza an unexpected emotional jolt. Joe Turner, the singer of powerful sexually-assertive, sometimes quite cynical blues ('baby you're so beautiful but you gotta die someday') personifies for me the jazz fan's perennial problem – how to reconcile two often irreconcilable halves of a musician, his music and his overt personality. For me there were two Joe Turners, and I loved them both.

Eddie Condon

Eddie Condon was a very funny man. He was also, on his own ready admission, a boozer. Perhaps his greatest claim to distinction, apart from the devoted and tireless work which he put into the cause of jazz over the whole of his lifetime, was the ability to be drunk and funny at the same time. Indeed, in the short time that I knew him, when my band toured Britain with his in the 'fifties, I never really discovered whether he could be sober and funny.

The advance publicity for his tour stressed exclusively the tough, hard drinking Chicagoan, and his arrival personified it. A team of British musicians, myself included, went out to the airport to meet him. With us was singer Beryl Bryden, a big girl in heart and personality as well as in frame, and a boundless enthusiast for jazz wherever it was played in the world. Beryl had brought her washboard along to supplement the rhythm section. Eddie Condon and drummer George Wettling emerged together from the airport building, having manifestly spent the journey from New York drowning their mutual dislike of air-travel. The first thing that Eddie saw, in a Britain which was totally new to him, was a large lady thrashing a washboard. It stopped him in his tracks and for a few minutes he and George had to lean against each other for support. In the general hubbub of greetings he recovered himself and was next seen disappearing head-first into the pitch-black baggage compartment of an airport bus, mumbling, 'There must be a bed in here somewhere!'

At the Cumberland Hotel, a crowd of musicians and reporters assembled in Eddie Condon's room. A huge tray of multiple Scotches was sent up and an informal Press conference began, with the principal subject of it lying in a crumpled heap face-down on the bed. For a while the questions of the gentlemen of the Press were answered from the muffled depths of a pillow, until one rather needled young man from the *Daily Express* asked with some acidity if Mr Condon could possibly sit up. 'Sure,' said Mr Condon, turning the right way round with some difficulty, '...but you know, I'm no athlete.'

Later the same day, Eddie, having abandoned all hope of recuperative sleep, was hustled off to Lime Grove to take part in an interview with Geoffrey Johnson-Smith in the B.B.C. *Tonight* programme. The resulting chat, captured on scores of amateur tape-recordings, has long been a collector's piece among connoisseurs of the surrealistic. At one point Eddie floored his interviewer by dredging up from somewhere in his fuddled subconscious a word that can't have been in general usage since Doctor Johnson's day. 'Look,' he said, 'I don't want to veridicalize any pronouns....' Later, when Eddie explained that his hands were too small for piano-playing, Geoffrey Johnson-Smith said, rather weakly, 'So that's why you stick to the guitar.' Eddie affected a startled look. 'Do I stick to my guitar?' At the end, a relieved Johnson-Smith said, 'I'm not sure that I've been with you all the way, but thank you.'

After the B.B.C. interview there was a formal Press conference and jam session at a London restaurant. Cornettist Wild Bill Davison, whose hobby of antique-collecting afforded Eddie much scope for sardonic wit, was late arriving. 'Where is Mr Davison?' somebody asked. 'I don't know,' barked Eddie. 'He's probably out unscrewing Big Ben.'

We travelled for most of our three-week tour in a coach, each man with a personal bottle of Scotch, renewed at the start of each day and reinforced with bottled beer from crates stashed in every available nook. As we ate – or rather drank – up the miles, it was interesting to compare the musicians' reaction to what was almost non-stop refuelling. The trombonist Cutty Cuttshall, a big, quiet-mannered man of Red Indian descent with one of the most impressive abdomens ever seen since man began to walk upright, would sit quietly most of the day until the alcohol reached a critical level, at which point he would let out a fearsome Indian war-whoop to let everyone know that, whatever action might transpire, he was ready for it. George Wettling, one of the great drummers in jazz, would gradually turn from a sociable and humorous Dr Jekyll into an argumentative and 'salty' Mr Hyde, finding particular provocation in the unruffled back view of Wild Bill Davison's head a few seats in front of him. His theme in this mood was usually that, without his guiding and goading beat behind them, none of the other musicians could really play at all. 'You hear them high notes he plays,' he would wheeze, jabbing a finger in the direction of Wild Bill, 'he doesn't play them, *I do*!!' This crescendo of disaffection usually reached the same climax. George would get out into the aisle, ready, it seemed, to take on anyone. He would find his way blocked by the full-frontal authority of Cutty Cuttshall, looming over him, his big-checked lumberjack shirt bulging threateningly. The confrontation was rather a sweet one. 'George,' Cutty would say quite quietly, 'be nice!' And George, with no physique to match the red-checked protuberance that barred his way, would sit down.

Eddie Condon didn't always travel with us on the coach. When he did, he rarely had more than one eye open, with which he surveyed the passing British countryside with profound disbelief. Once we stopped at a West Country pub and straggled into the public bar for a lunch break. Along the walls, rheumy-eyed locals surveyed us silently. Eddie Condon, furnished with a large Scotch, went over to fraternize. For a minute or so he stood, hat rakishly on the back of his head, and matched their stares. Then he rapped out an opening gambit. 'Are you guys poachers?'

British jazz fans are oddly puritan. They lap up the tales of speakeasies and the Prohibition era with relish – so long as it's history. Confronted with this personification of the tough, Chicago-jazz era, they were bewildered and rather shocked. 'Why don't you play a guitar solo?' The act which was legendary in the States, the ultra-informal presentation with Condon swapping wisecracks with the audience, directing the musicians in a jam session, wandering about the stage and into the wings (and occasionally strumming his guitar), flopped badly, especially in the provinces. And it's a pity that the public was told so much about Condon the character and so little about Condon the champion of Dixieland jazz, by whose almost single-handed efforts this boisterous down-to-earth music was kept alive before and during the war. They might have shown more sympathy towards the informality.

As Sidney Bechet once noted – and he didn't usually lavish praise on those on the entrepreneurial side of the fence – Eddie did more for jazz than most, worked hard for it all his life, played it on his four-string guitar better than anyone imagined and remained, withal, 'a nice little guy'.

Louis Armstrong

Louis Armstrong was born on 4 August 1901. He always recalled his childhood as carefree and happy, though he grew up in circumstances of stark poverty, far removed from the life he would eventually lead. Nevertheless, his experience of growing up in New Orleans became intrinsic to the man he became.

Whenever interviewers asked me, 'Did you know Louis Armstrong?' I had no idea what to say. I saw him often, spent quite a lot of time in his company and was, I think, looked upon by him as one of a handful of close friends in Britain. But I doubt if anyone knew him. To friend and foe alike there was, deep below the surface of companionship and bonhomie, an impenetrable wall in which every stone was an enigma. Did the genius who endowed jazz with new dimensions in musical range and emotional depth really aspire no higher than the chocolate-box sentimentality of Guy Lombardo, his favourite band? Were slogans like 'You gotta stay in front of the public' and 'All I want to do is just keep hittin' those notes' truly at the root of his creative philosophy? What made a man who clearly cared nothing for wealth and possessions (he was forty-two before he bought his first modest home, and he died in it twenty-nine years later) pursue commercial success with such rigorous single-mindedness? And how does one reconcile a ruthless success story with the love, warmth and sheer happiness which were generously dispensed by its central character and which were returned to him with interest by all who heard him? One might assume from a casual observation of Louis in action on stage that here was a simple, frivolous, happy-go-lucky character, to be laughed at, applauded and patronized rather than respected. And indeed, the illusion has sometimes puzzled and disturbed jazz fans familiar with his music on record, who cannot reconcile the grimacing clown with the profound and immensely powerful music which he produces.

In fact, the superficial impression is quite false. Behind the public façade was a character of great strength, which manifested itself in many different ways. If you saw him often enough on the stage, you would begin to feel it. There was the ease with which the rowdiest audience was kept in check, sometimes by a sort of veiled look, avuncular but slightly menacing, sometimes by a warning word: 'Take it easy, Daddy!' (In his New York Town Hall recording of 'Back o' Town Blues' he silences a tiresome rowdy with a crisp 'Shut up, boy!' in mid-lyric, to the delight of the rest of the audience.) And there's the command which he has over his musicians, no matter what their own experience or standing. When I first saw him at the Nice Jazz Festival, in 1948, he was in command of a sizeable chunk of jazz history – Earl Hines, Sid Catlett, Jack Teagarden, Barney Bigard. Each of these was a jazz giant, and two of them had been for some years bandleaders in their own right. I stood right behind the bandstand one night while they played. And more than once I found myself quaking at the ferocity with which he directed the band. If Sid Catlett's drums started to intrude too heavily upon a solo, Louis would turn and hiss at him

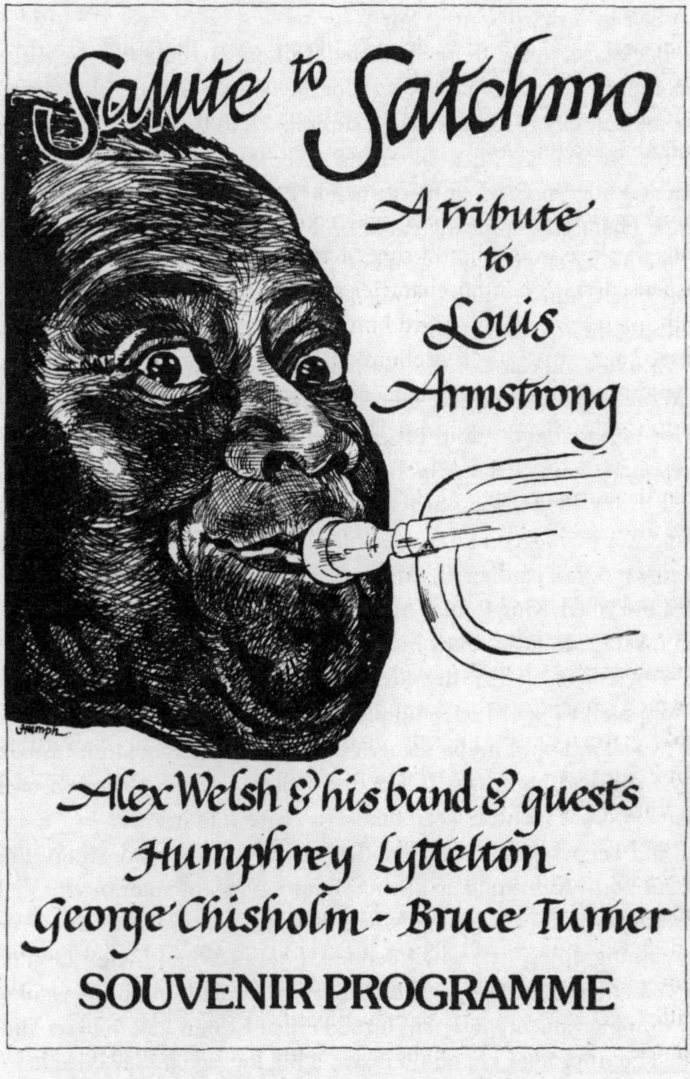

This programme was designed and drawn by Humph for the Salute to Satchmo Tour in 1978.

like a snake. And more than once Earl Hines's exuberance was curbed by a sharp 'Cut it, boy!'.

Backstage, this authority persisted. In London, dukes, earls, V.I.P.s, nobs and bigwigs from every walk of life queued outside his dressing-room each night like schoolboys summoned to the Head. Inside, you would invariably find a fair quota of bores, cranks and loquacious hangers-on. Once, when he seemed to be particularly beleaguered by these characters, someone came up to his friend and publicity man Ernie Anderson and said: 'Can't we get Pops away from these people – they'll talk him to death!' Replied Ernie: 'If you take him away, he'll only ask them to come too!'

Another indicator of the strength of Louis Armstrong's character was his unshakable loyalty towards those he regarded as his friends. I have personal and proud experience of the warmth with which he responds to any action which he regards as a favour to him. At the end of his 1956 season at the Empress Hall in London, when my band was privileged to share the bill, I spent a couple of days making a crown out of cardboard, Woolworth jewellery and ping-pong balls, and inscribed 'King Louis'. At the end of the show, when I was called up on stage to take a bow in the finale, I made the announcement: 'On behalf of all British musicians, I crown Louis Armstrong the undisputed King of Jazz,' and plonked the crown on his head. A day or two later, I saw him backstage at Manchester. I asked him casually if he still had his crown. 'Of course I have – I had it shipped back home today. I'll always keep that – you gave it to me.'

And keep it he did. For another refreshing and endearing thing about Louis Armstrong, in an entertainment world notorious for slick assurances and easy promises, was that he never said he would do something unless he really intended to do it. When he left London after a concert he gave for the Hungarian Relief Fund in November 1956, a big gang of musicians turned out at Euston station to see him off. The impromptu band set up on a big luggage trolley outside his carriage window and played an appropriate selection for him: 'The Song Is Ended', 'After You've Gone', 'Farewell Blues' and a tune which Louis recorded some years ago called 'That's My Home'. When I went to the window to say a final goodbye, Louis told me that he was going to record a big album of all his old numbers when he got back to the States, with some talk about each one. 'And when I record "That's My Home", I'm gonna tell them about this send-off you've given me.' I confess I didn't pay much attention to this at the time. However sincere it was, I felt it extremely unlikely that, when it came down to it, he would single out this occasion from his great store of reminiscences. I should have known better. Ten months later, a friend said to me: 'I've just got hold of the "Louis Musical Autobiography" album from the States. Did you know he mentions you in it? Something about "That's My Home"....'

If one were looking for a dominant trait in Louis Armstrong's character as a performer – something which might give the key to his general approach – I would plump for his professionalism. Louis was a professional in the best sense. Somebody asked him once about other trumpet-players and mentioned Bunny Berigan, who burnt himself out at the age of thirty-six. 'Bunny was great – but he had no business dying that young!' was Armstrong's answer. It may seem harsh but it was a simple statement of his belief.

The character of the itinerant jazz musician in general and Louis Armstrong in particular has a certain Wild West flavour about it. Have trumpet, will travel. From the moment when, as a boy in New Orleans, he turned away from incipient delinquency towards a career in music, his life was spent with a trumpet in his hand. Subsidiary talents – as singer, entertainer, movie actor – manifested themselves later, but Louis and the trumpet were indivisible.

He looked after both with care bordering on hypochondria. Once, on arrival at London Airport, he borrowed a trumpet from Spike MacIntosh (himself a fine performer and Armstrong devotee), his own instrument having been whisked away with the band's baggage. When Louis had ripped off a few characteristic phrases for the cameramen, he returned the instrument to Spike, who asked eagerly how it had played. 'That's a good horn,' said Louis, 'but you need to put some of the hot water through it...get rid of all them newts and saveloys!'

Louis Armstrong's attentiveness to his own plumbing had become legendary by the end of his life. After a charity appearance for the Playing Fields Association in London in 1970, he was given a small token gift by the Duke of Edinburgh at a special presentation to mark the occasion. Louis gave the Duke in return a pocket of Swiss Kriss (a herbal laxative manufactured in Milwaukee), explaining its purpose and function in a forthright and sibilant monosyllable.

The stuff is certainly effective. The late Duggie Tobutt, road-manager to the Harold Davison Office and a man beloved of every visiting American jazz musician, once succumbed to Louis's insistence and took the prescribed dessertspoonful of Swiss Kriss last thing before retiring. At noon the following day, the telephone rang in Louis's hotel room. It was Duggie, ringing to enquire, in a voice which he dared not project above a whisper, if there was 'any antidote to this stuff'.

There can have been few trumpet-players on the face of the globe who did not come away from a visit to Louis regaled with a typewritten diet sheet, several tins of Louis Armstrong's lip salve and enough Swiss Kriss to evacuate an army. Though I must confess that in the bottom left-hand drawer of my desk there are no less than two dozen little sample packets of Kriss, amassed during Louis's 1956 tour here. It's just that I've never seemed to be able to pluck up courage to 'start blasting', as Louis put it so vividly on his diet sheet!

During that 1956 tour I noticed that, for a period before the first concert and between shows, visitors would be ushered away from his dressing-room and even his wife Lucille would withdraw. It wasn't until the band left London on tour and I travelled out to see them in Manchester that I discovered what ritual took place behind that closed and closely-guarded door. The backstage area at Bellevue was deserted during the two shows, and Louis's valet Doc Pugh, reporting to Louis that I was there, was sent to summon me to the dressing-room. Louis was relaxing between shows, stark naked except for a handkerchief bound round his head to keep his hair in place, and a complex jock-strap. I quickly sensed that my presence alone was enough for him – he rarely called upon his friends to say or do anything, but simply to *be* there. Conversation anyway was ruled out, because while I sat and watched he massaged creamy lip salve into the famous embattled 'chops' and then covered them, top and bottom, with gauze. I believe he did say something when the dressing was completed, but that well-known astrakhan voice, vibrating loosely in relaxation and emerging from a thick sandwich of gauze, conveyed no more than a cavernous growl of greeting.

Of course, giving attention to the serious business – in Louis's mind, even duty – of staying alive and in good working order, was a means to survival. So, too, was the perfecting and burnishing of his trumpet technique. He was not, strictly speaking, a self-taught musician. The rudiments of the instrument were taught to him in the Waifs' Home in New Orleans to which he was sent for a year or two in his early teens, and subsequently he had to master sight-reading to cope with work in big organized bands like Fletcher Henderson's Orchestra and Erskine Tate's Theatre Orchestra.

We have the evidence of Lil Hardin, Armstrong's second wife and one of the major influences on his career, that in his mid-twenties in Chicago, the young Louis did a considerable amount of practising at home. In her own recorded reminiscences, she tells how, when Louis was working with Erskine Tate's Orchestra at the Vendome Theatre and doing a feature number on stage, he staggered his listeners by occasionally hitting high F on the trumpet, well above the instrument's normal range. After a while he began to feel the pressure. 'Folks are coming to the theatre every night just to hear me miss that F!' he complained to his wife. She was a trained and experienced musician herself. 'All right, so you start hittin' Gs around the house, then you won't worry about missin' F in the theatre!' was her advice. The trouble was that Louis in his youth was a gambler, and it wasn't long before he was aiming for Gs in public. His formidable stamina pulled him through, but, for most mortal trumpet-players, that way lies a double hernia.

It's obvious that from the first lessons in the New Orleans Waifs' Home onwards he must have worked hard to build the technique and the embouchure to produce the effortless playing which we first hear on record in 1923. But it's equally clear that producing music from the cornet came easy to him, and after the first arduous practice under Mr Peter Davis, his tutor, he embarked on no lifelong routine of systematic practice. A trumpeter in a symphony orchestra – or a modern dance band, for that matter – will warm up before a concert with chromatic runs, sustained notes and arpeggios all scientifically designed to loosen up the muscles and make the lip flexible. Louis always had his own way, as anyone who ever lingered enraptured outside his dressing-room door before a concert will know. Indeed, I always looked forward to eavesdropping on this warming-up routine, which was a concert in itself, a free-form potpourri of soaring arpeggios, random quotations from familiar tunes and crackling high notes.

For a musician in the emerging jungle of jazz music in the 'twenties, however supreme his talent, survival meant being prepared at all times to do battle with predatory rivals. There are many tales of the formidable young Louis demolishing the opposition of men like Buddy Petit, Jabbo Smith and 'Hot Lips' Page. My own favourite was again provided by Lil Armstrong. She tells of a night in a Chicago club – in the mid-'twenties, I would guess – when Freddie Keppard, an established hero from New Orleans, tried to teach Louis a lesson. After listening to Louis for a while, he said, 'Boy, let me have that trumpet.' Then according to Lil, he 'blew and he blew and at the end the people gave him a nice hand. Then he handed the trumpet back to Louis and I said "Get 'im! Get 'im!" Oooh! Never in my life did I hear such trumpet-playing. If you want to hear Louis play, hear him when he's angry! Boy, he blew and people started standing up on tables and chairs, screamin'. And Freddie, he just *eased* out!'

Louis did not regard himself as an artist – nor would he have behaved like one if he did. The nearest he ever came to a pronouncement on his art was 'Man, you don't pose, never!'. The jazz music of Louis Armstrong is closer to folk art than to sophisticated art. Just as the simple country blues singers of the Mississippi Valley managed to express, in the flimsiest little ditties, all the sorrow and poignancy of their state, in a manner which no sophisticated composer has ever succeeded in capturing, so did Armstrong imbue with deep and powerful emotion what is, on the surface, simply rhythmic dance music. He had no need to devise ways of expressing the sorrows of his race. It was there, built into every musical utterance of his.

To many jazz fans who cherish conventional notions of jazz – 'I play the way I feel', art for art's sake, let's all get together in a back room – the Louis Armstrong odyssey presents itself as a steady decline into commercialism. Some musicians, too – notably Sidney Bechet, Louis's friend and colleague of the early years – have commented sadly on the course which Louis took. Yet all admit, somewhat grudgingly, that the trumpet-playing, in popular-song recordings, hill-billy hits, Hollywood soundtracks and what-not, retained a remarkable integrity and staying power. They talked as if this were almost an accident, and they may possibly be right. I see it as the end to which Louis Armstrong lived his life – survival. Not the survival of Louis the big star, certainly not of Louis the rich man, but of Louis, the man with a trumpet in his hand. Matching a lifetime of playing music through the trumpet with never a tasteless note, never a maladjusted phrase, against the performance of those who died, lapsed into obscurity, burned themselves out or earned their packet and retired, Louis Armstrong's career was a remarkable and formidable exercise of will. In the last years it overcame recurrent illness and the cruel demands of 'show business' in which it was ensnared.

In the light of all this, Louis Armstrong's final appearance in Britain, witnessed in all its detail by his friends here, assumed the elements of Greek tragedy.

When Louis had appeared at the Batley Variety Club in 1968, the fight for survival was still on, though it had become a grim struggle. Reports had filtered down to London after his opening nights that his trumpet-playing had become purely vestigial, not more than a few short solo spots in which the tone and timing were all that remained of former glory. Some days later, I was astonished to arrive at the club a few minutes late after tearing up from an engagement in Leeds to hear the familiar solo in 'Indiana', rippling high notes and all, blasting out across the huge auditorium.

Two years and one desperate and weakening illness later, Louis Armstrong came to London for a David Frost charity concert. To me, he seemed for the first time an old man. The always jaunty, stiff-limbed walk had a frail jerkiness about it and in repose his face wore a crumpled, defeated look. In conversation with friends and in front of an audience, Louis's face always gave an impression of youth, even boyishness. A television interview filmed during his convalescence in 1969 had shown him sitting at his desk looking reassuringly plump in the face and animated. Yet Geoffrey Haydon who conducted the B.B.C. interview said on his return that he had been shocked at the laborious way in which Louis had walked across the room to take a book from the bookshelf, shuffling across the floor without lifting his heels from the ground. When he arrived in London, this frailty was marked – it seemed as if the head of a fifty-year-old was perched on the body of a man of ninety.

Consequently, I was staggered to see him arrive the next morning at the theatre at 11.30, trumpet case not far behind in the hands of a member of his retinue, all ready to rehearse with the orchestra. Now the trumpet notes really were laboured and the effort needed to produce them obviously painful. It is hard to imagine any other artist of international repute in his old age being subjected – or perhaps in Armstrong's case we should still say subjecting himself – to the routine of that day. He had brought Tyree Glenn, the trombonist in his American All Stars, to act as musical director. But it was still Louis who played through all the routines with the orchestra, putting such unconserved energy into his singing that the camera crews, theatre staff and spectators gathered round the stage applauded spontaneously.

At 1.30p.m., when rehearsal break arrived, he was hurried to his car and driven to Trafalgar Square so that a film team making a documentary on his progress in collaboration with the Glaser Office – 'my own film', Louis called it, to distinguish it from previous documentaries – could shoot him feeding the pigeons. In the Square, there was a repeat of the phenomenon which, at Batley two years earlier, was graphically described by Duggie Tobutt. We were all sitting backstage one day waiting to leave the club when Louis had finished holding court in his dressing room. Duggie shook his head in bewilderment. 'I don't know,' he said, 'here's a guy who goes out and does a show. When he comes off that stage he's just like me at the end of the day – a mean, miserable old bastard who can't wait to get out of the place. But everyone who comes backstage has someone – a sister with three legs, a brother with no arms – and they bring 'em to see him and he says "Yeah!" and they feel great. What is it with this guy?' In Trafalgar Square, old ladies, bowler-hatted city men and bobbies on the beat, possibly none of whom had ever consciously listened to two bars of jazz, gathered around to shake Louis's hand and tell him about their sons and daughters and sisters and aunts. He was jostled here and there, patted on the back, tugged by the sleeve. At no time was the broad, patient smile switched off or the ear turned away.

Eventually, his managers managed to prize Louis Armstrong away from the crowd in Trafalgar Square and take him back to the Astoria Theatre for further rehearsal. It was after 7p.m. when he got away after several run-throughs of the complete show. And by 8.45p.m., he was back ready to go on. No admirer of the genius of Louis Armstrong ever came away from a show without having received some refreshment of the spirit and lightening of the heart. And when Louis talked with David Frost and sang, the old boyishness returned despite signs of strain even in the voice.

It was the professional all the time, the man whose whole life revolved around those few hours when he was up on the stage blowing. As he put it himself: 'Some of these guys spend too long away from their instruments, gettin' out front and waggling that stick, they forget how to play. One thing you can be sure of – when you hear "Sleepy Time Down South" and that curtain goes up, I'll be right up there blowin'.'

Nevertheless, overall, that Frost concert was a saddening occasion. The gaudy and elaborate stage-setting involved raised glass platforms lit from beneath, across which he had to walk to reach the microphone. Stepping down to floor level, his legs momentarily gave way and he staggered, almost falling over. His show-business reflexes came to the rescue and he covered up with a crack to the effect of 'You want to watch that step!'. But he was clearly shaken. And worse was to come. When he started to play the trumpet, it must have been apparent to him before anyone else that the renowned 'chops' had no strength left in them. And the man who caused Freddie Keppard to ease out of that club in Chicago some forty-five years before, and whose majesty on the instrument had never been challenged by any other trumpet-player, surrendered to a ruthless and irresistible opponent and played the trumpet with his back to the audience.

PART 4
TOUR DE FORCE

Now that We're Here, Let's Go

Some years ago I had to go to Bradford University for a concert. Knowing that the 'new' universities are usually sited on the fringe of the city, I stopped on the ring road and called out to an aged bystander, 'Where is Bradford University, please?' 'There isn't one,' was the instant reply. Thinking he had misheard me I repeated the question, wording it rather differently. The answer came back verbatim, but angry this time. 'There *isn't* one!' Getting a bit shirty myself, I shouted back, 'There must be one – I have an engagement there tonight.' His furious response brought us abruptly back to Square One. '*Well, where is it then???*'

Asking-the-way jokes go back to the early days of *Punch*, but modern town planning has turned the simplest journey into an elaborate game of Find Your Destination. There is a village called Birtle in the North of England which must qualify as Lancashire's best-kept secret. It is only two and a half miles from Bury, but there is obviously someone in the Roads Department of Bury who believes that the war is still on and that the whereabouts of Birtle must be kept at all costs from the enemy. If you are lucky enough to find anyone in Bury who has been in the town longer than twelve hours, they will pucker the brow, stroke the chin and then send you off on a complex round trip which, if you follow it scrupulously, will bring you back in half-an-hour to the exact spot in which they are standing. We suffer particularly from the staff in small hotels who seem, as often as not, to exult in finding, in these sluggards who lie a-bed all morning and keep demanding food and drink at all hours, orders lower than themselves. Usually, the sadistic refusal of night-porters to cooperate in providing refreshment late at night simply makes for ugliness and bad feeling.

But there was something faintly endearing about the snowy-haired retainer at a hotel in North Wales who insisted, in accents of deep regret, that he could not lay his hands on so much as a bottle of light ale. It was only midnight so we pressed our rights as bona fide travellers. 'There's nothing I can do, sir!' he said. 'The manager has the key to the drink cupboard and he has gone to bed.' 'Then wake him up!' we cried to a man. The old boy started back in horror. 'Don't ask me to do that, sir,' he begged. 'The manager's had a hard life!'

Chambermaids, too, succumb to latent sadism whenever they suspect that one would like to sleep into the morning after working late. The British chambermaid, like the British music hall, is a unique and moribund institution. I bring in the British music hall deliberately, for it has long been clear to me, as a persistent traveller on the one- and two-star hotel circuit, that our chambermaids belong to the same proud tradition. Elsewhere in the world, beds are made, towels replaced and carpets Hoovered with uncanny stealth, irrespective of when you crawl from the room or slink back into it. They have a set routine for flushing late-risers out from between the sheets. It begins with persistent knocking until the victim shows himself by muffled protests to be awake. Then a bunch of keys are brought into action, to be rattled meaningfully in the lock, accompanied by mutinous muttering. There's always an aggrieved soprano who does most of the talking, and a sympathetic contralto who intones the responses and acts as a 'feed'. Most of the material concerns some off-stage 'she' – a manageress, perhaps, or a truculent guest – with whom the principal performer has had a row. The script is ridden with clichés like '…so I told 'er straight, I said…' or '…and d'you know what she 'ad the cheek to turn round and tell me?' In all my travels, I can claim to have heard only one inspired line. This was when I woke in a hotel in Shropshire just in time to hear a shrill voice proclaim, 'Well, I looked 'er straight in the face and said don't you turn your back on me!!!' I always feel rather sorry for the contralto stooge, who is lumbered with material that would defeat a Vanessa Redgrave or Maggie Smith. 'Yes, well, there you are, you see…' '…ooh, she never!' and sometimes just a repetitive 'Mmmm…Mmmm…Mmmm…' like a broody pigeon.

Some minutes later the uneasy doze which has now replaced sleep will be shattered by an ear-splitting burst from the bedside telephone. It is the receptionist who has now been brought in as reinforcement. 'Did you ask for a call, sir?' she asks ingenuously. I once had a tenacious lady follow up my anguished denial with another call to say, 'It's all right, sir – it wasn't your call, it was for No. 9!'

It was the late Gerard Hoffnung who first exploited the musical potential of the vacuum cleaner. But with all respect to his efforts to promote it to the orchestral platform, it is, and always will be, a folk instrument. Like the bagpipes, to which it is clearly closely related, it is best heard on its native landing accompanied not by banks of violins and violas and woodwind but by one solitary, unschooled, ear-splitting female voice. If I were asked to pick a classic, a sort of desert island disc, in the chambermaid-and-Hoover genre, I would go unhesitatingly for 'Around the World in Eighty Days'. It has everything to keep an audience not only on its toes but curling them in anguish. In any regional accent you choose between Arrroond the Wurrrld to Araaahn the Woald, the opening line with its broad vowels answers to perfection the twin demands of voice production and dramatic interpretation. Timing is essential to putting across a song with Hoover accompaniment. The full potential of the instrument will never be fully explored unless long pauses are left in which the rise and fall of its siren-call and the percussive effects of its blunt nose nudging the wainscoting and bumping into doors can be heard.

The traditional climax to a British chambermaid performance is when the whole cast goes out amongst the audience with the express aim of depriving the customers of their bedclothes. It's a sort of striptease in reverse, really. The routine in this part of the show is kept fairly free, so that each performer can approach it according to her particular talents. Some favour the 'cheeky chappie' angle, like the lady who once roused me from five hours' sleep with the words 'Come on, be a sport – let's 'ave yer sheets!'. Others favour the dramatic climax, bursting into rooms without knocking and reacting, in true R.A.D.A. style, to whatever meets the eye. Since shrieking hysteria worthy of Lady Macbeth is the standard reaction to a bare torso at the shaving mirror, I must leave to your imagination the *coup de théâtre* which I was lucky enough to witness not long ago. Just along the corridor from me, two chambermaids – Elsie and Doris, perhaps – walked unannounced and simultaneously into the room of a colleague of mine. Unencumbered by vestments of any kind, he was on all fours with his back to the door, doing his exercises with the aid of one of those patent weight-reducing wheels. I can't begin to describe the duet that rent the air, but it would not have been out of place at Glyndebourne. And it certainly brought the audience to its feet.

Two or three times a year we used to undertake a short tour with an American band or artist touring the UK or venturing forth into Europe. As each European tour was confirmed and with the same regularity, I would resolve to learn German. The book I bought for the purpose seemed to be obsessed with money. The hero, Mr Clark, was always rapping on about his agent in London and his horrid house in the suburbs, and couldn't even take his wife out for a birthday meal without totting up the bill out loud and crowing, 'Eight pounds fifty! We had put aside nine pounds for the evening!' The language problem reached a crisis one night when a German fan backstage asked me why a series of broadcasts which I used to do had come to an end. Rashly, I made what I thought would be quite a transitory joke. 'I was fired,' I said, hoping that my expression would convey to him that it was a jest. He looked blank. 'You know,' I ploughed on, 'the bullet.' 'Fired? Bullet?' He looked vaguely alarmed. At this point it occurred to me that my English vocabulary has a gaping hole in it where a conventional, non-slang word for 'unilateral and abrupt termination of employment' should be. I began to feel like a Wodehouse character as I floundered on. 'The boot, old chap…the jolly old elbow…the sack….' He was now looking appalled. Here was a man grinning all over his face and apparently recounting how his employers, for what ghastly misdemeanour we can only guess, had fired bullets at his boots, hit his elbow and bundled him out of the building in a sack. Someone interrupted at this point and I left him to work it out for himself.

As far as the foreign travel is concerned, we have a standing joke that, wherever we may be planning to go, we shall inevitably wind up in Zürich. This is because, on more than one occasion, an exciting trip – to Italy, to Scandinavia, to Austria – has fallen through and we have been switched to Switzerland, where there has always been a ready public for our music. Swiss jazz audiences vary from one area to another. In the French part, everything is done on French lines. A concert billed to start at nine o'clock may well be delayed, for no special reason, until nine forty-five. The interval is similarly protracted, so that the whole show tends to sprawl lackadaisically half through the night. The audiences are vociferous throughout the performance – a solo or a long final ensemble which catches their fancy is liable to be swamped in clapping, stamping and assorted clamour long before it is over. In German Switzerland, everything is far more methodical. If the music is not under way one minute after the scheduled starting time, the audience starts to mark time noisily, and the promoter is apt to burst into tears of impotent rage. Once we played in Zürich at the tail-end of a tour. There is much local rivalry in Switzerland, and the young man who was running our concerts, who came from Zürich, would add a rider to his congratulations after each show: 'But you will play better still in Zürich.' He was particularly contemptuous of the organization down in the French zone. 'In Zürich, the concert will start on time!' When we eventually reached Zürich, on the afternoon of the show, he put us in the charge of an associate of his, an exquisite young man called Walther, who understood very little of what we said but laughed uproariously at it all and generally took a relaxed view of life. Since Walther was a member of the organizing committee we put ourselves entirely in his hands. So nobody sought to question it when the starting time of the concert came round and we were still tucking into steak and chips and red wine in a local café under his benevolent eye. When we got to the hall, the audience had practically penetrated the floor-boards and the promoter's cheeks were awash. We were bombarded with reproaches. In Berne it would not have been so bad, in Geneva no more than they deserve, but in Zürich! How could we do this in Zürich? To make matters worse, Walther then went on to compere the show, and introduced the whole bill back to front. A Swiss trombonist due to make a guest appearance halfway through the show was standing next to me in his coat and hat when he suddenly heard himself announced. He almost did himself an injury trying to assemble his trombone and take off his mackintosh at the same time. Once we were on stage, the concert went with a bang. But I don't believe our young promoter ever quite got over the humiliation.

By contrast, the French rarely start a concert on time. We were to experience this at first hand when we made several visits to France. One of these was a one-night sortie across the border from Switzerland to Mulhouse in eastern France. The Hot Club of Mulhouse was a sort of junior organization, with no patriarchal president to impose discipline. We arrived in the town in late afternoon and were collected in a scarifying assortment of derelict French cars with what one might call universal university types in charge. They hurtled us at high speed and with reckless abandon (the Citroën I was in had a mild fracas with another car *en route*) to a pub, where we were told to make ourselves comfortable until they returned. We drank Pernod for two hours until they came back and ushered us into a private room upstairs for dinner. We had a multi-course meal washed down with quantities of red wine and liqueurs and were just ready to sink into a post-prandial stupor when someone remembered that we had a concert to play. The organizers seemed unperturbed by the fact that the show should have begun forty-five minutes ago. Indeed, from what I can recall of the audience, they too seemed to be quite sunnily disposed towards the whole thing in general and us in particular. Perhaps they were swimming with Pernod and red wine themselves. All I remembered of the show itself was that at one stage I twirled the trumpet around and it flew from my crook'd little finger and executed a graceful parabola across the stage. Fortune was on our side that night. Apart from a superficial wound, it was undamaged and still playable. The audience applauded wildly as though it were some special piece of showmanship. I recall a similar success at Rouen, where I stamped in a number right on the neck of Freddy Legon's banjo and smashed it to smithereens. On that occasion the front rows actually rose to their feet and accorded me a special ovation. Afterwards, in the dressing room, one of them shook my hand vigorously and gave his opinion of the stunt: '*Formidable* – but expenseef, no?'

In Germany, a slow handclap at the beginning means 'You will make concert right away! The pooblick haf been waiting…', while a slow handclap at the end means 'We haf ways of making you play an encore!'. On my first tour to Germany, everything seemed calm and orderly – we shared the bill with Big Bill Broonzy and Lil Armstrong – but only a week or two before they had risen and bombarded the stage with chairs because Louis Armstrong finished a concert early. It wasn't Louis's fault. With four thousand people waiting outside for the second show, the authorities insisted on the first house being curtailed. We overran by half-an-hour.

The most exacting job I have ever undertaken was an all-night carnival in Munich. We flew over just for one night. At the airport we were met in broad daylight by a crowd in fancy dress. It looked like an alfresco Chelsea Arts Ball. They presented us each with a foaming *stein* of ale, and then drove us into town in a procession of the oldest and smallest motor-cars I have ever seen. They were all painted bright red and plastered with posters for the evening's ball. The festivities began at eight thirty. We were told that we should be playing on a revolving stage, alternating with another band at half-hour intervals. In a sort of crow's nest above the stage sat an elderly German stage-hand, whose function was to press a button and revolve the stage every half-hour. He did this with punctilious zeal.

To encounter *Braunwinsorzuppe* on a train journey between Hamburg and Wiesbaden is an experience akin to finding a colony of rare Malaysian tree ants in a wardrobe in Pinner. It is startling, mystifying and deeply sinister in its implications. For those with an imperfect ear for German pronunciation, I had better explain that we are discussing Brown Windsor Soup, a liquid which, together with diesel oil – to which it bears a striking similarity in taste and appearance – lies at the very heart of the British railway system. I know little of the origins of Brown Windsor Soup or of its connection with the otherwise distinguished Royal Borough in which, as it happens, I was born. I know only too well its acrid, meaty smell which seems to permeate the very carpets and wallpaper in seedier provincial hotels. And the regular appearance, amounting almost to permanent residence, of Brown Windsor Soup in railway menus is one persuasive reason why I travel everywhere by car.

On a three-day band tour in Germany we were driven to an engagement by a young German promoter who owned a vast and ferocious car. *En route* a stone shattered the windscreen and we swerved to a halt. It was a classic example of the malevolence of Things. By working smoothly and efficiently for months, the treacherous machine had lulled the young man into believing himself a technocrat of high order. Then, with one (literally) shattering blow it revealed him for what he is, a technoserf of snivelling subservience. In short, he didn't know what to do. Knowing from experience that there are times when one must fight back, I brushed aside his tremulous warnings and punched a round hole in the windscreen through which he could see to drive. As we moved off gingerly, you never saw a man in such a state of abject timidity, crouching forward in his seat and peering apprehensively through the hole in the shattered glass. You could almost feel the car bunching up, waiting for its moment to strike. That moment came after a few miles when the petrified driver, feeling a speck of rain on his protruding forehead, thoughtlessly turned on the windscreen wipers. Rasping viciously across the network of tiny cracks, the left-hand wiper came in through the hole and struck him on the nose.

Germans still believe that a musician who performs a two-hour concert and then goes back to his hotel to relax has not really earned his living. While you are still bathed in perspiration after four encores of 'When the Saints Go Marching In', a promoter or president of the local Hot Club will present himself in the bandroom with the dreaded words, 'And now, we make cham session, hein?' There is a contradiction in terms here, of course. The original idea of a jam session was that musicians of like mind who had been working separately in commercial and often boring dance bands got together voluntarily to make music for their own enjoyment. Jam sessions are not made – they happen, or not as the case may be. German efforts to make cham sessions have implicated me more than once in diplomatic incidents of some heat. In Dusseldorf a few years ago, American trumpeter Buck Clayton and I were invited after our concert to be the guests of honour at the local New Orleans jazz club. We accepted the invitation, but decided to go somewhere to eat first. The delegates from the jazz club clung to us like bodyguards, watching our leisurely meal with growing concern and much anxious scrutinizing of wrist watches. As soon as the meal was over we were hustled into cars and driven at speed to the club, where an overwrought proprietor was waiting. 'Mr Clayton, Mr Lyttelton, please – you make cham session right away! The pooblick haf been waiting since elefen o'clock!' How he explained our precipitate departure to the pooblick we never found out.

Touring at home is on the whole less strenuous. Bands which are on the road all the time usually travel by coach. In the early days of our sporadic sorties out of town, it was more economical and quicker to go by train. Musicians have perhaps more curious experiences on trains than ordinary people. Ticket collectors, sleeping-car attendants and guards have only to spot an instrument case in the rack to be smitten suddenly with violent persecution mania. One morning, having been called with tea, I dozed off again, to be woken a few minutes later by a vigorous shake. 'Yer tea's gettin' cold!' I gave a non-committal grunt. 'Very well, then, if you don't drink yer tea, I'll report yer!' I doubt whether anyone but a musician has ever been threatened with a report to the stationmaster at Euston for allowing his tea to get cold! Eddie Thompson, a blind pianist, once had trouble getting his guide dog on board a sleeper in the North. An argument developed around the carriage door. Kenny Graham, a bandleader of independent spirit and formidable appearance – with his prickly auburn beard he could be mistaken, in a bad light, for Charles Laughton in a beachcomber role – remonstrated vigorously with the attendant. 'I'm sorry,' said the man, 'I'm responsible for the other passengers, yer know. Supposing he bit somebody?' Kenny's beard jutted. 'How d'you know *I* won't bite somebody?' In the end, by rousing from their beds the city police chief and the stationmaster, authority was given for the dog to be allowed on board. As far as is known, neither he nor Kenny bit anyone during the night.

We made our first prolonged acquaintance with the Condon Band on the midnight train up to Glasgow, where our tour started. Eddie himself wasn't with us – he flew up separately the next day. But the rest of the band was there in full strength – six men and six bottles of whisky. Veteran drummer George Wettling had spent the day in London buying new clothes. He had a check overcoat in which the predominant colour was light red bordering on orange, and a cap to match. Altogether, he cut a figure more appropriate to an English country estate than to a touring jazz band. He was inordinately proud of his new coat, and everyone within earshot on the platform at King's Cross was sooner or later called upon to witness that he had made a 'good buy'. Once on the train, miniature parties got under way in each sleeping compartment (we had a whole car to ourselves) and the conversation went on long into the night. At about 4a.m. things began to subside. Gene Schroeder, the piano-player, had a compartment next to George. Last thing, he gently opened the communicating door and peered in to see if George was asleep. He was. The sheets were pulled up under his chin, and he was still wearing his cap and overcoat.

Some years ago, when we were recording a television series for Granada, we had occasion to travel up overnight by train to Manchester, arriving on a damp Friday morning at 7a.m. I had booked myself a room at one of the big hotels, so as to get a little sleep before the afternoon rehearsal. I suggested that any of the band who were tired could doss down in the armchair or on the floor. I arrived at the hotel before the others, and retired to my room, carefully hanging the 'Do not disturb' notice outside to keep off marauding chambermaids. A few minutes later, Tony Coe, who had spent most of the train journey writing out arrangements, came upstairs, heavy with sleep. Seeing the notice, he thought it unsafe to disturb me. So he went along the corridor to the first public bathroom, changed into his pyjamas, spread his overcoat in the bottom of the bath and climbed in. When the maid found him half an hour later, he was sound asleep. Wakened by her shrieks of alarm, he sat up. 'What's the matter, Dad? Aren't I supposed to be here?'

There are many jobs within the field of entertainment promotion which are inspiring, creative and rewarding, but acting as the temporary mother and father of a touring jazz band is not one of them. It calls for the combined talents of a lion-tamer, guide-dog, psychiatrist, mind-reader, bodyguard and miracle-worker. The best I ever knew was Duggie Tobutt who looked after visiting American musicians on behalf of the Harold Davison Agency. His secret was that he loved it, and he had it reduced to a fine art. As soon as the band coach arrived at its destination, Duggie would heave his burly but invariably dapper form upright and address his distinguished and stellar charges with the words, 'Now, hear this....' All the details for the gig, overnight stay and departure next day would then follow concisely and nothing was ever said twice. With his bald head, well-padded shoulders and ever-twinkling, sceptical eyes, he looked the epitome of the 'wide boy', but there wasn't a phoney or snide bone in his body. He was no judge of jazz. Often he would come across backstage when some jazz giant of irrefutable eminence was playing and ask me, 'What d'you think, then – is he any good?'

To Duggie, genius was no excuse or even explanation for unprofessional conduct or bad time-keeping. In Cambridge once, two shaggy student devotees of the profound and eccentric pianist Thelonious Monk managed to get into the Students' Union to hear the master rehearse for a T.V. show, only to find that after a perfunctory sound-check he had walked out of the building and disappeared. Disappointed, they asked Duggie Tobutt, 'Will Mr Monk be coming back?' and were visibly shocked by the blunt answer, 'How should I know? When you're dealing with Thelonious Monk, you're dealing with an idiot.' Louis, Basie, Duke – possibly Monk, too – all loved him and specifically asked for him on their tours. It was after he had left his prescribed desk-job – he had heart trouble – and returned to the road that he collapsed and died in the manager's office at Batley Variety Club, where Louis was playing.

In the early days, American musicians coming to Europe have always been astonished, and sometimes dismayed, to find that every fan-in-the-street has a sort of data bank on his recording activities in the distant past. It may be this ruthless investigatory zeal that made some visiting jazzmen of advanced age adopt evasive or even sealed-lips tactics towards their admirers.

During a season by the late Coleman Hawkins at Ronnie Scott's Club in London, I was sitting with Ben Webster one night when Hawkins came up to join us. The relationship between the two great American tenor saxists was one of master and pupil and Ben, though a master in his own right, clearly held the older man in some awe. Certainly Coleman Hawkins, with his baleful eye and straggly, Jomo Kenyatta beard, was a formidable old lion for whom the youthful nickname 'Bean' had become quite inappropriate. The two men sat exchanging casual badinage until an aristocratic-looking Englishman approached, elegant wife in tow. The man introduced himself as Lord Someone-or-other, presented his wife and reminded Ben that they had met fleetingly before. 'I wonder', he said, 'if you would do us the great honour of introducing us to Mr Hawkins.' Ben Webster duly obliged, the couple sat down next to Mr Hawkins, and there descended upon our little group a fathomless and seemingly eternal silence. It was eventually broken by Ben in what he seemed to imagine was a confidential whisper for my ears alone. 'Ever'body waitin' for Bean to talk,' he bellowed. Then, even louder '…he ain't gonna talk!!!' And talk he didn't.

On my band's first tour of the States I did not take to America on sight. For one thing, New York was enjoying one of its autumnal bouts of humidity and when we stepped out of the plane it was like walking straight into a warm, damp blanket. For the three days before we left on tour, life beyond the range of an air-conditioner was very uncomfortable. Naturally we spent most nights exploring the jazz spots, so fatigue was added to discomfort. By day there was a certain amount of hustling – interviews with journalists, one or two radio shows and so on.

I had to go with the tour promoter, Jay Weston, to meet a newspaperman from *Time* magazine in a smart bar somewhere around Fifth Avenue. The temperature was in the nineties with humidity to match, and I walked in without a jacket. The journalist was clearly a cherished regular, so the management leant over backwards to be polite in telling me that I could not sit and drink without a jacket on. They even produced one for me – a pale, lightweight affair that had apparently been made to measure for a jockey suffering from a wasting disease. The jacket buttons were not even on waving, let alone speaking, terms with their buttonholes across my middle, and the sleeves barely covered my elbows. As he crammed me into it, the manager explained apologetically that the rule was enforced to discourage any kind of riff-raff from walking in off the sidewalk. In my borrowed straitjacket with its sleeves gripping my forearms like tourniquets, I would not have been out of place in the exercise yard at Alcatraz, but it was too hot to argue.

Broadway was a disappointment. From all those popular songs I had envisaged a sort of theatrical Champs Elysées, and the quite narrow and, by day, tatty street was a let-down.

The jazz haunts, on the other hand, were a jazz fan's dream. At Birdland, now alas defunct, we heard Buddy Rich, Art Blakey, Maynard Ferguson – and we almost heard Miles Davis, whose Quintet was billed to appear but who had got involved in a birthday celebration for Ella Fitzgerald up at the bar and declined the piercing invitation of Pee-Wee Marquette, the club's diminutive emcee, to return to the stand for his second set. The Metropole was another place to be visited as soon as possible. Henry 'Red' Allen led the band there, towering majestically over the imbibing customers on the extraordinary bandstand which ranged along behind the bar. Sometimes in the daytime there was a Dixieland session led by an extrovert and gymnastic trombonist called Conrad Janis. We never went to one of those sessions. We didn't have to – if we opened our bedroom windows at the President Hotel three blocks away, we heard it all.

My favourite place was Basie's Bar, to which I was first taken by John Hammond one night after a delicious meal, seasoned with the music of Roy Eldridge, at a restaurant called the Allegro. Basie's was a long bar, not by any means large, with the band along one wall standing eyeball to eyeball with the customers perched at the bar counter. We went there several times, to enjoy the music of 'Sir Charles' Thompson's Trio and, when Jimmy Rushing was in our company, to join him in demolishing pork chops provided by a massive lady beside whom Jim looked merely plump. They always told me that everything in America is much bigger and that certainly goes for the fatties.

It was at Basie's one night that Tony Coe borrowed a clarinet, sat in with the trio and had the cool Harlem bar-flies literally jumping with astonishment. English critics, both professional and amateur, suffer from a compulsion to compare or qualify whenever they are confronted with British jazz. 'Who does he sound like?' is the first thing they ask themselves, searching for some established American name against whom to measure the home product. The predominately black clientele at Basie's – not in those embryonic days of Black Power notably affectionate towards whites – expressed, in a sybillant and monosyllabic four-letter word that rustled from one end of the bar to the other, the unstinting view that, wherever Tony came from, here was one hell of a clarinet-player.

The readiness to communicate with all-comers is one of the fruits of a virtually classless and protocol-free society. And the alleged rudeness of Americans springs from the same source. I can still recall the shock when I discovered that, as well as having no 'manners' themselves, the Americans actively resented mine.

On a particularly hot and humid autumn day when my sensitivity was already sharpened by the feeling that a wet St Bernard was sitting on my head, I showed the hall porter at the President Hotel a mountain of band and personal baggage and asked with some diffidence if he would take the bags up to the rooms, please. He could not have taken more offence at the word 'please' if I had called him 'my man'. 'Sure I take the bags up!' he snapped. 'I'm the porter, ain't I?' Brought up to say please and thank you and to know just how much food to leave behind on my plate for Mr Manners without at the same time depriving starving children in Russia, I found it hard to adapt. But adapt I did, and when we came back to the President Hotel after a three-week tour, my curt jerk of the thumb and 'Hey c'mon, feller, the bags!' regained his respect and persuaded him that I was not some kind of a fag. I think I even called him 'Mack'.

As one who believes fervently that, for all its shortcomings, Britain is in everyday matters the most quietly efficient country in the world, I do not subscribe to the myth that life in the U.S. runs like a hyper-effective supercharged machine. Our own tour was a catalogue of extraordinary mishaps. We had to assemble at Columbus Circle at 7a.m. for the entire package show to board two Greyhound buses. There were two bands from England in a line-up that included singer Anita O'Day, the Lennie Tristano Quintet, the Thelonious Monk Quartet and George Shearing's Big Band with the Adderley brothers as guest soloists. In charge of the tour was a mild-mannered, bespectacled man called Arnold London, an accountant by profession who had taken on the tour as a favour to the promoter. He lived to rue the day he opened his big mouth.

Arnie's troubles began right there at Columbus Circle. The English contingent arrived slightly before seven, to avoid the catastrophe of being late and seeing the coaches glide sleekly away dead on time. One by one the rest of the cast assembled so that by 9a.m. almost everyone was there. Everyone but Thelonious Monk. Monk, a founding father of Modern Jazz, has a well-publicized reputation as an eccentric, so we had hardly expected to see him bustle up on the stroke of seven, but by ten o'clock it had become apparent that he wasn't going to arrive at all of his own volition. After some agitated phoning, Arnie herded us on board and we made a trip into the suburbs to pick him up. We pulled out of New York at 11a.m. bound for Columbus, Ohio.

Honourable mention should be made here of Thelonious Monk's hat. It plays a leading part in this story because, according to Arnold London's astonished report, Monk was sitting up in bed wearing it when a deputation from the road management called upon him with an invitation to join us all on the bus. The hat had been given to him by an admirer. It was a sort of wickerwork lampshade, or inverted fruit basket, probably Chinese in origin, with long straps which dangled over the ears. We got to know that hat well since at no time in the day (or, presumably, night) did Monk remove it. For ten days it was a fixture. Then on the eleventh day, boarding the coach in Boston, Massachusetts, Monk appeared in a different hat. It was a grey, bulbous affair which mystified us until we recognized it as a homburg in the state in which it was stored on the hatter's shelf, before a gentle karate chop had given it the conventional dent in the top. 'Hey, Monk, you've changed your hat!' someone cried in amazement. 'Sure,' said Monk without a flicker, 'you can't wear the same hat all the time.'

It was on the bus on the way to Columbus that it was discovered that Anita O'Day had no accompanist for the tour. She had relied upon enrolling one of the pianists in the package, but all the pianists bar one were bandleaders with their own star spots on the bill. The exception was my pianist, Ian Armit, who was leaned on heavily by a distraught management to step in and assist her. For Ian, the acute first-night nerves which we were all suffering were augmented by the task of learning Anita's arrangements at a few moments' notice. Before the show she agreed to simplify her breakneck version of 'Tea for Two', full of complex bits of arrangement, so as not to make things too hard for him. When he went on stage at the start of her spot, he found that the stage lighting didn't allow him to see the music. He struggled through the early songs pretty well, but when it came to 'Tea for Two', Miss O'Day either forgot or ignored the pre-arranged plan and reverted to a routine which he didn't know. To make matters worse, she signalled to him to take a piano solo at the hair-raising tempo. Sitting out front, the rest of our band watched with sinking hearts, and were immensely cheered when, in mid-solo, he stopped playing and shattered the awesome atmosphere with a stentorian Scottish cry of 'Oh, shit!!!'. Afterwards, Anita O'Day took the episode with remarkably bad grace, complaining to everyone she met backstage, 'Did you see what they did to me? They gave me a *Dixieland* piano-player!' We became fair friends with Anita on the tour – friendly enough to remind her that nobody had *given* her a piano-player. She'd commandeered one and had no right to complain.

I missed the journey from Boston to New York in which the coaches couldn't find their way on to the motorway and fumbled through the night and long into the morning along minor roads. I had been sent ahead by plane to make a promotional television appearance. On the plane, a stewardess, after peering at me long and hard every time she passed, eventually came up and said, with great charm, 'Pardon my intrusion, but are you by any chance related to Claude Raines?' As a boy I had been movie-crazy and was well-acquainted with the sardonic face of Claude Raines, whom I took to be no more than about five foot three and knocking on a bit even in those days. So I made a rather surprised denial. 'Gee, that's funny,' she said. 'You look so like him I thought you must be his brother.'

The hectic rush to the airport, the solitary journey and the mistaken identification with one of Hollywood's more venerable citizens put me generally in a disgruntled mood and it is my cherished belief that I out-nastied Henry Morgan, a T.V. anchor-man of, apparently, great popularity in the States at that time, whose stock-in-trade was a studied, smirking offensiveness to everyone in range. They put me at ease just before the show by telling me that he had crucified Andy Williams the night before. When I went on he tried to needle me by asking, in a tone of amused surprise, what an Englishman was doing playing jazz in America. Just the same, I said, as Americans are doing speaking English in England. After that the interview rambled along fairly tamely and quite soon, Henry moved on to the next item, which so far as I recall was an abortive phone-call to Mr Krushchev, then on a state visit in Washington, to ask him what he had for supper.

The evening concert at the New York Town Hall was a nerve-wracking occasion. For one thing, the Town Hall is almost as hallowed in jazz history as the Carnegie Hall itself. It was from there that Eddie Condon's famous jam sessions of the mid-'forties were broadcast to England, and it was there, too, that Louis Armstrong made a significant and historic appearance in 1947, playing after years of big-band work with a small, improvising outfit which paved the way for his subsequent All Stars. What made the event even more awesome for me was that our show's compere, Willis Connover, familiar the world over as the voice on the *Voice of America Jazz Hour*, had left the package and the management decided that I should introduce the show. News came backstage that Benny Goodman was in the audience, not to mention several of the heavy guns among the New York critical fraternity, men with resounding names like Whitney Balliett and John S. Wilson. Fortunately, the band was in especially good fettle on the night and bagged most of the good reviews.

The New York Town Hall concert ended in a shambles. George Shearing's Big Band used to finish the show, with Julian 'Cannonball' Adderley and his brother Nat making their guest appearance in the first set. The stage-manager at the Town Hall was it seems, a Jobsworth of a kind thought to thrive only in Britain. Over here we're used to recalcitrant officials with unbending ways. (My whole band was once refused re-admission to a theatre in Blackpool after a visit to the nearest pub in the interval, even though we were due onstage at the start of the second half. 'I *know* who you are,' the old walrus at the stage-door reiterated, 'but my strict orders are "no readmission during the concert!" It's as much as my job's worth….') We didn't expect to find similar obstructiveness in the Land of Opportunity. But on the stroke of ten thirty, when our concert was due to finish, the stage-manager of the New York Town Hall dropped the curtain. To make matters worse, he dropped it on top of George Shearing, who had stepped forward from the piano to announce the Adderley brothers. George, who is of course blind, must have thought that the skies had fallen in on him. Despite pleas from the concert promoters, the man refused to allow the concert to go on a minute longer, and the night ended in a babel of recriminations and abuse.

The upshot was that George Shearing, who I think had had about enough of the rigours of this particular tour, pulled his whole band off the show. We set off for Pittsburgh next morning without them – and without Thelonious Monk, too, who had decided to charter a

A drawing by H.L. for his book Best of Jazz.

plane so that he could stay a little longer in New York. We were still without them when the concert started – ironically, the first and only total sell-out of the tour. Frantic negotiations had failed to pacify George Shearing in time for him to make the show, and, we learned later, Thelonious Monk was at Pittsburgh Airport in time, but for some reason wasn't allowed to disembark. So in place of the usual climax to the concert, a jam session was hastily assembled from volunteers from the cast.

That the version we played of 'All The Things You Are' lasted interminably was no fault of mine. Lennie Tristano, who was at the piano, has always been one of the most advanced musical theorists in jazz. (He also proved a smart tactician at cards. Being blind, he made certain that his sighted opponents gained no advantage. One of my band, going to the coach at night to fetch something, tripped over the Lennie Tristano Quintet. They were playing poker in the pitch dark with Braille cards.) Lennie's colleagues, saxophonists Lee Konitz and Warne Marsh, had come up in the same experimental musical school. Britishers like Jimmy Skidmore and Ronnie Ross could keep up with them. I couldn't, so I stood on stage holding my trumpet, admiring the ingenious complexities of their improvizations and watching the audience, many of whom had come to hear George Shearing, stream out in their hundreds.

The most lasting friendship we made on the tour was with Charlie Rouse, the tenor saxist with the Thelonious Monk Quartet. Through him I managed to pierce at least the outer layer of the enigmatic armour in which Thelonious has encased himself. Monk belongs to a long line of jazz nonconformists, musicians who have achieved original self-expression by hacking out a difficult and uncharted route of their own. Standing in the wings listening to Monk night after night, watching him wander off around the stage while Charlie Rouse was soloing and occasionally execute a little lumbering dance for his own private amusement, I acquired a strong affection for that prodding, unseductive piano style which, according to Charlie, constantly sent out startling messages to his musicians to keep them on their mettle. Jabbing away at the keyboard, sometimes appearing to hit two notes at once by accident and then to return to them to repeat the effect, Monk always seemed to me to play the piano like a man who had only that day discovered the instrument for the first time. As a man I never got close to him, although we did achieve a strange sort of reticent rapport. 'Humphrey, I got you covered,' he said when we were making our farewells. It was the verbal equivalent of a wink and a thumbs-up, and said everything.

On his subsequent visits to England I saw him and the Quartet whenever possible, once going out to Heathrow to meet him. On that occasion, the airport Press photographer tried to set up a photograph with Monk and myself. He wanted a conventional jolly picture and asked me to fling my arms around Monk in a gesture of welcome. It was not a gesture that came naturally to either of us, so the photographer tried a solo shot instead. 'Raise your cap, Mr Monk,' he kept saying. 'Look as if you're saying "Hello, England!".' Monk was wearing a conventional flat cap on this occasion and, with a sleepy expression of compliance, he raised it – but from behind! There were no pictures of Monk's arrival in the evening papers that night.

When I flew back from America after just three weeks in the place, I was bursting with get-up-and-go. Life in little ol' England wuz – sorry, was – going to be different from now on! For about two weeks astonished friends and colleagues were subjected to merciless hustling, accompanied by impatient snapping of the fingers to signify that I expected things to move – where to, I didn't care, so long as they got up and went! It didn't last long. Quite soon I had settled back into the familiar pace at which I have been content to cruise along ever since.

Zwotties

[When touring with the band, Humph kept a diary. The following entries were made on a visit to Poland – and later, Turkey and the Middle East.]

Thursday 21 October 1976, Warsaw

We are met at Warsaw Airport by a young member of the Polish Jazz Festival organization. He introduces himself as Mark, though it later transpires that he spells it Marek. A pleasant-looking blond with a ready grin, though there is something curiously lop-sided about his jaw-line. In him we have our first encounter with the Polish sense of humour, quite similar to the English in its self-deprecating and faintly surrealistic leanings. He says that for the next five days he will be our mother and father.

From the airport we are driven to the Europejski Hotel which is alleged to be extremely comfortable. Unfortunately, the foyer is all we see of it, since they know nothing of our booking. All cock-ups begin at Calais! Mark walks us across the road to the Bristol Hotel, where they are expecting us. Mick Pyne, our piano-player, among whose hobbies is the collecting of books, recorded speeches and other archive material relating to World War II, remembers with some excitement that it was here that Hitler had his headquarters in 1939 at the culmination of the Polish campaign. It now looks ripe for demolition, some parts of the façade having jumped the gun and fallen off spontaneously.

The Polish Jazz Festival has grown from small beginnings in the 'fifties to become one of the largest in Europe, with bands from both sides of the Iron Curtain assembling during the five days. Hitler failed to suppress the underground jazz movements in the occupied countries during the war, and similar attempts by the post-war Communist regimes to ban the 'decadent product of an artistically bankrupt capitalist system' have had to give way in the face of the fanatical dedication and enthusiasm of generations of young fans. (I remember giving an informal lecture to some members of the visiting Red Army Orchestra in the late 'fifties. They showed polite interest in the urban folk-jazz of such proletarian heroes as George Lewis and Bunk Johnson, but perked up mightily when I came to Benny Goodman and Glenn Miller.) Once the official ban on jazz was lifted in 1955, Poland caught up with fifty-odd years of jazz history in one mad spring. Everything from basic Dixieland to extreme avant-garde now flourishes.

We have each been given a wad of Polish zlotys to cover expenses. Before we left England, we received enigmatic advice to take with us the full visitors' allowance of twenty-five pounds sterling. I can't see why – it looks as if our expense allowance is going to be more than ample. And it's easier to pronounce 'zlotys' (we must learn to say 'zwotties') than to find out what they represent in English money.

They say that the food at the Bristol Hotel is the best in Warsaw, so we eat in the massive, 'thirties-style dining-room. I am normally allergic to waiters who hover. Ours, an olive-skinned fatty who would not have been out of place in an Edward G. Robinson gangster movie, practically alights in my lap. As he serves coffee the waiter, with whom we have hitherto conversed in a mixture of pidgin English and sign language, bends over us conspiratorially and says, in perfect English, 'Surely you have some money to change – pounds or dollars?' 'Yes,' we mumble, matching his furtiveness. 'Fold them in your napkin,' he whispers before gliding away. After some debate we decide to risk all – theft, fraud, arrest, deportation – and follow his instructions. When he has cleared away the coffee cups and departed, we peek rather nervously into the folds of the napkin. Hey presto! Twenty-five English pounds have turned into three thousand,

Humph's first photo taken in 1921 aged 3 months (in mother Pamela's arms). His father, or 'Fa' as he was known for most of his life, is standing behind.

Family with a capital F. This photo was taken at Holland House, Eton, in 1960 to celebrate the birth of the twentieth grandson, Humph's nephew Charlie Stewart-Cox.

Left HL aged 18 months. The interesting contraption on his head was intended to remedy 'sticky out ears'. Contrary to what one might expect, he was very proud of them and they helped prepare him for his future life in the studio!

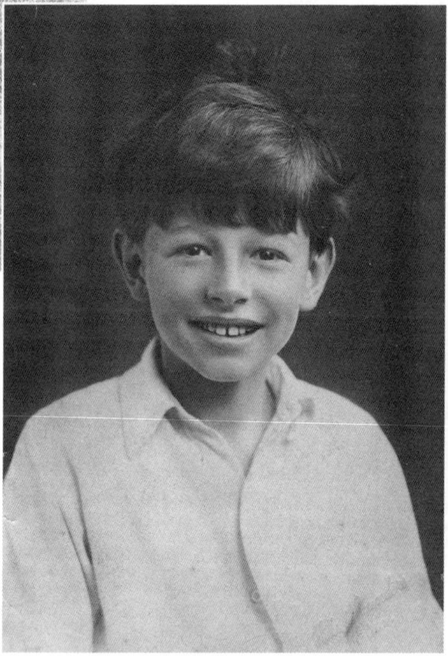

Right A picture of HL at Sunningdale in 1930, aged nine.

Right HL with mother and sisters Diana, Mary, Helena and Rose. The pony was in lieu of a pram as wheels were of no use in the Harlech dunes – the pony was then tethered in a grassy dell by the beach until they went home.

Right Humph duets with sister Helena while on holiday in Harlech.

Above Playing the fool on Snowdon (1938). HL would frequently walk up Snowdon on his many holidays to Harlech, in Wales.

Right HL digs another 'elephant trap' on Harlech beach with cousin Anthony ('Chucks') while sister Mary and Shan Tung look on.

Left HL, with cousin Anthony sitting bottom right, in the sixth form at Eton.

Right Later, again with Anthony, to the left, in a no less intimidating uniform while training at Caterham.

Left Humph gives instruction to the Home Guard (summer 1940) prior to leaving for Port Talbot in August of the same year.

Right Ade Monsburgh, HL, Pixie Roberts, Jack Varney, Lou Silbereisen, Dave Carey and Graeme Bell. First visit of Graeme Bell's Australian band, 1947–48.

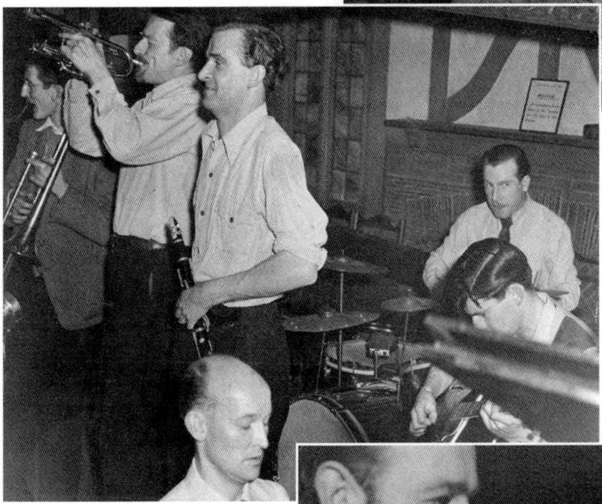

Left Keith Christie, HL, Wally Fawkes, George Webb, Dave Carey and Neville Skimshire. The London Jazz Club Christmas Party, 1948.

Right HL (with Shakespearean beard) goes eyeball to eyeball with Sidney Bechet.

Left What a handsome fellow – an unusually glamorous HL in a Hollywood pose.

Right Humph with his first wife Patricia and daughter Henrietta in 1949.

HL and the Band with singer Jimmy Rushing (Mr five-by-five) in 1957.

Right This picture was taken at the Dorchester. The photographer wanted Duke Ellington to pose doing something 'English'.

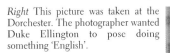

Left HL meets Monk (Thelonious Monk) at Heathrow in 1960, having toured the U.S. with him the previous year.

Right Big Joe Turner, Joe Temperley and HL in Joe's garden. Joe Temperley played in Humph's first eight-piece band, standing in for Jimmy Skidmore who was ill. When Jimmy returned HL was left with a dilemma. After much deliberation HL approached Joe and asked if he played baritone sax. 'It's my main instrument,' replied Joe. And so he was hired and a lifelong friendship was sealed. Humph was later to find out that Joe had not been near a baritone sax for some years!

Left Louis wrote this message to Humph when HL missed a reception for Louis after the death of his father.

Right Humph with Louis. Humph was not only inspired by Louis but they also built up a genuine friendship and respect for each other. Humph was grief stricken when Louis died. When Humph was to do a special tribute for his *Best Of Jazz* programme he substituted the theme tune with Louis' 'Flee As A Bird To The Mountain'. Concerned that he would break down producer Keith Stewart agreed to record the opening of the show (the show was live in those days).

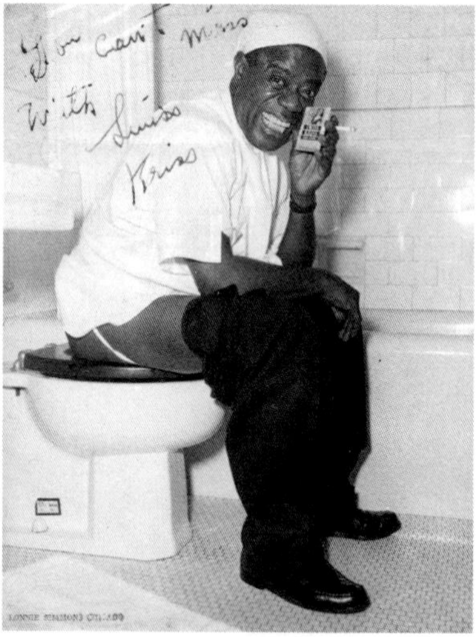

Left This photo was sent by Louis to Humph together with a detailed diet sheet on how to use Swiss Kriss. Directions for use included: 'At bedtime your dose will be real heavy, in order to start blasting right away and get the ball rolling.' It signs off with a 'Satch' slogan – 'the more you s**t the thinner you git'.

Right This photo was taken on Humph's U.S. Tour in 1959. Left to right: Eddie Taylor, HL, Charlie Rouse (saxophonist with the great Thelonious Monk Quartet) and Jimmy Skidmore.

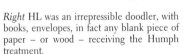

Left Humph shares a joke with American jazz guitarist and bandleader Eddie Condon.

Right HL was an irrepressible doodler, with books, envelopes, in fact any blank piece of paper – or wood – receiving the Humph treatment.

Left Humph in full flow with an appreciative Lionel Hampton looking on. Picture taken at the South African Treason Trial Concert.

Left Family photo taken for a 'rare' publicity shot at home in Alyn Close. Left to right: HL with Snuff the dog, Jill with Brandy, David, Georgina and Stephen with Whiskey!

Right Humph swings out with daughter Georgina c. 1965.

Left Humph plays trains instead of trumpet, with sons Stephen and David, c. 1961.

Above HL often made his children's costumes for the annual King Alfred School competition (winning the first prize many times). The crown he made and presented to Louis at the Empress Hall in 1956 became a treasured memento of Louis.

Left This is the house that Humph built. HL with architect John Voelcker, discussing the plans. Some months earlier there was a set-back when it was discovered that the foundations were three yards too far to the east!

Right The family would take annual holidays to Harlech, Wales. When the days of grey cloud became too much to tolerate the Lyttelton family would jump in the car and embark on an often fruitless quest chasing distant rays of sunlight on the horizon. On this occasion the effort paid off.

Left HL and band supporting Elkie Brooks at the Bull's Head in Barnes. Elkie sang with Humph on many occasions and they recorded an album together. A close friend, Elkie sang 'Trouble in Mind' at HL's funeral.

Right Humph would take his binoculars with him everywhere. On one of his Middle East tours he grabbed a rare opportunity to bird-watch at the municipal dump and sewage overflow in Jeddah.

Above A very rare picture of Humph on horseback while visiting the Lost City of Stone in Petra (Jordan).

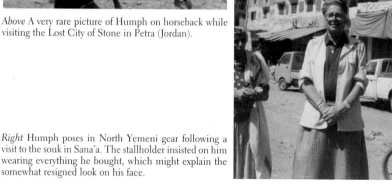

Right Humph poses in North Yemeni gear following a visit to the souk in Sana'a. The stallholder insisted on him wearing everything he bought, which might explain the somewhat resigned look on his face.

Right HL and Buck Clayton were the greatest of friends and also collaborated on a number of albums. When this picture was taken in 1985, Humph had invited Buck over for a holiday as his health was failing and he was no longer playing.

Left 1984 line-up at the Bull's Head with, left to right: Pete Strange, Paul Bridge, Adrian Macintosh, HL, Bruce Turner, Mick Pyne and John Barnes.

Right HL marches out for the cause with Bruce Turner on sax and Georgina on tambourine. (Labour Party march in Barnet, 1974.)

Left Humph recording *I'm Sorry I Haven't a Clue* in 2006 with producer Jon Naismith ('He's not your son Humph, he's the producer'). It was his 85th birthday and he was presented with a cake while the audience of the Birmingham Hippodrome sang happy birthday.

Right Humph with manager (and later partner) Susan da Costa on a visit to Edinburgh Zoo.

Left Jeremy Hardy, Colin Sell, Tim Brooke-Taylor, HL, Graeme Garden and Barry Cryer, backstage for a 'live' *Clue* show in Brighton, 2007. As usual the team hang on The Chairman's every word.

Right HL recording his last *Best of Jazz* programme in March 2008 after 40 years on the air. The show won many awards, including a prestigious Sony award for specialist music in 1992.

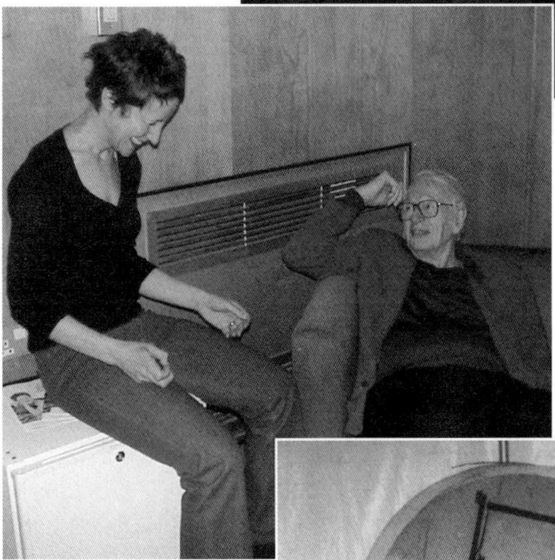

Left Backstage with great friend Stacey Kent. They had unintentionally arrived for the gig in matching clothes. HL recorded an album with Stacey and her husband Jim Tomlinson called *Between Friends* in 2000.

Right From a 1999 calendar 'Oh The Glamour Of It All' showing photos of backstage, taken by Humph's saxophonist, Jimmy Hastings.

The Band 2007: Karen Sharp, Adrian Macintosh, Jimmy Hastings, HL, John Rees-Jones, Ted Beament, Ray Wordsworth and Robert Fowler. Humph would regularly acclaim this band as being one of his very best.

Humph in a typically silly mood. Taken by the band's bassist John Rees-Jones in 2007 at Hever Castle.

seven hundred and fifty zlotys, at the rate of 150 ZL to the pound. No wonder Mark was reluctant to see us change money through the usual channels!

Back at the Kongress Hall we wait our turn to go on. We are told that there will be five thousand people in on every one of the five nights, and ticket prices are soaring on the black market. I have chosen three originals of mine plus Duke Ellington's 'Creole Love Call', and we do 'St Louis Blues' for an encore, which the audience demands from us as they did from the far-out German band.

Friday** 22 **October** 1976, **Warsaw

Ham and eggs at 10a.m. in the breakfast-room, which turns out to be the very room from which Hitler emerged on to the balcony to review his triumphant troops. As we stand on it looking down into the broad street below, by coincidence a small parade marches by led by a military band. We resist the urge to give it the benedictory Hitler salute. An eerie experience.

After breakfast we wander out towards the city centre, loaded with zlotys and bent upon shedding some of them. It is clearly easier for the foreigner to acquire them than to spend them.

It soon transpires that Warsaw is not the place for a shopping spree. Even Kathy Stobart, who could write a directory of the department stores of the world and whose appearance on homebound aircraft, festooned with clanking plastic shopping bags, gives her fellow-travellers serious concern about the feasibility of take-off, finds little joy in the Warsaw equivalent of Marks and Sparks. Bruce Turner, a staunch communist, is the only one of us not dismayed by the general shoddiness of the goods, but he pitches his sights low. All he wants to buy is a Chinese-style Mao Tse-tung jacket. Why he should expect to find one in Warsaw I don't know, but in the event he fails, walking out muttering, 'They won't sell me a Mao jacket, they won't sell me a Mao jacket.'

Bruce's eccentricity is legendary in the jazz world. A lot of it, no doubt, is a sedulously-acquired cloak to conceal a natural diffidence. But in most of the extraordinary utterances there is a genuinely original flair for, and enjoyment of, words. In Turnerese, the

American saxophonist Lucky Thompson becomes Fortunate Thompson, and the series of recordings featuring Buck Clayton Jam Sessions are spoonerized into the Jack Clayton Bum Sessions. A now-forgotten American movie comedian called Hugh Herbert instilled in him years ago the habit of saying everything twice. From early comics and Billy Bunter stories came the ludicrously archaic phrases – 'Some fun I'd say' (abbreviated now to 'Some fun, some fun'), 'This is the life for a chap, life for a chap' or 'Gosh, thanks' – which take the place of more humdrum clichés. Sometimes apparent gibberish turns out to be a conventional phrase mangled in deliberate, usually rhythmic, mispronunciation. Fans or promoters who invite him out after a concert are often bewildered to have their invitation declined in what sounds like a mixture of Swahili and scat-singing. 'Gudder gudder be-DERLY, gudder gudder be-DERLY.' It is left to us to explain, after he has hurried away to his hotel room, that what he said was 'Got to go to bed early'.

I call on the man from the British Council – our sponsors for this tour – who tells me that leather and amber are the only two commodities likely to attract the visitor from the West.

It was back in 1956, when I was on tour with Sidney Bechet and simultaneously trying to write and send off story material for the *Daily Mail* comic strip 'Flook', that I first practised the relaxation exercises in Dr Grantly Dick-Read's book (or some article that I've read since), which suggested that it helps if you lie spread-eagled on the bed and concentrate on the sensation of falling. I go one better, imagining myself to be King Kong, in the final scene from the eponymous movie, falling from the Empire State Building *and still twenty feet from the pavement*. It works a treat. Apart from providing easy cat-naps, it accounts for the fact that I have driven an average of forty thousand miles a year for twenty years or more without once, touch wood, having fallen asleep at the wheel. A rapidly-induced ten minutes' kip in a lay-by gives one an hour-and-a-half of driving free from the numb head and the swivelling eyes.

Saturday 23 October 1976, Warsaw

Two Swedish promoters come to the hotel this morning to discuss the possibility of a tour of the Swedish Folk Parks by the band next year. One of them is called Ake Forsberg, a name that could have come from one of those 'forties swing band personnels which my father used to get me to read out to him whenever he felt in need of entertainment. He hated swing music but loved the personnels and selected reading from *Hot Discography*. One of his favourites was Sam Donohue's Navy Band in 1945. By the time I had got through Conrad Gozzo, Tasso Harris, Dick Le Fave, Tak Takvorian, Joe Aglora, Al Horish, Barney Spieler and Buz Sithens he would be mopping his eyes. He is the only person I ever knew who, at the end of a movie, would not make a dash for the cinema exit once the credits began rolling. He stayed in his seat, glued to the screen, enjoying the rich variety of American names which, he insisted, must have derived from anagrams concocted around the font.

As always on tour, there is a lot of sitting around. The foyer of the Bristol Hotel offers plenty of entertainment of a faintly sleazy but intriguing kind. We are fascinated by the activities of one small, ferrety man who seems to be permanently attached to the place. He is perpetually on the go, circulating among the guests as they check in and out. We think we have nailed him as the local 'fixer' – cameras, girls, currency, you name it. It was he, we reckon, who rang Mick Pyne's room at random in the middle of last night and asked thickly, 'You like man?'

Mark had arranged to take us to the old town at 3p.m. but he arrives at the hotel an hour late and looking ashen, having had what he describes cryptically as a 'life crash'. Without explaining further he goes off again, so we make our way to the old town on our own. On this rather hurried trip we are here not to sightsee but to off-load our embarrassment of zlotys.

Our evening concert is in another students' hall further out of town, a barn-like room with poor acoustics. Several bands are crammed into one communal dressing-room and one of them, called the Vistula River Jazz Band (trad jazz names are the same the world over), sets up in a corner and plays at us relentlessly all night, except for a brief moment of respite when they are actually onstage playing for the public.

During our set (well received) I am somewhat startled by the sudden appearance in the wings of a tramp, long-haired and wispy-bearded, who waves and beams at me as if he knows me well. And indeed he does – it turns out to be Barrett Deems, who was neatly crew-cut when he was over with Louis Armstrong in 1956, but who now looks like Jimmy Durante with a Rasputin hair-do. He and Buddy Tate are over for the Festival with Benny Goodman, and have decided to pay us a surprise visit. Despite the Vistula River Jazz Band we have a good chat in the band room. Buddy says that he endures some ribbing from other musicians because he seems to know someone in every town, city or country that he visits. This time, he told them, 'I'm sure I'm not gonna know anybody in Warsaw' – but when they all trooped out of the airport, somebody walked straight up to him and said, 'You know, Humphrey's in town.'

Sunday 24 October 1976, Warsaw

A beautiful sunny day with a clear sky and all the buildings standing out with that razor-edged definition that late autumn sunshine bestows. Nothing of the dour, Eastern European servile state here. Indeed, the almost tangible spirit of Warsaw is of a robust and often humorous independence.

Mark is sufficiently recovered from shock to divulge that his 'life crash' involved leaving his small leather bag containing around 32,000 ZL of box-office 'take' in the taxi that took him home on Friday night. He reckons it will take him eighteen months to pay it back. We are not materially affected, but the incident spreads despondency and some remorse among members of the band who have been rather too quick to take him to task for every lapse or breakdown in organization.

This afternoon at 2 o'clock we assemble to go by coach, with several other bands, to Lodz or, as the Poles have it, Woodge. There is a Hungarian group, a Polish trad band who will back the American trumpeter Wallace Davenport, an American-led avant-garde band, and us. Summoned by Mark, we troop out of the hotel to see, standing outside, the oldest bus ever seen outside a museum. Wallace Davenport is offered a lift in a private car and gratefully accepts. After many years on the road with Lionel Hampton and a recent severe illness, he has recently returned to take life more easily in his native city of New Orleans. So what is he doing here in Warsaw? His chronic look of deep gloom suggests that he is asking himself the same question.

It's a measure of the efficiency of our valiant bus that it takes four freezing and jolting hours to cover the eighty-two miles to Lodz, through dull, homogeneous farmland that offers little diversion. Even the one or two amateur ornithologists among us are doomed to boredom, with nothing to spot but the occasional hooded crow. Handsome birds with their grey velvet doublets, but when you've seen one. Because the journey took so long, there is too little time to eat before the show. This doesn't prevent the whole cast from trooping across the road to a smart modern hotel for a meal. The promoter from the Filharmonia runs in on the verge of heart-failure, but the Hungarian band that is due to open is still unfed and refuses to budge.

Having at least had our starters, we do the British thing and volunteer to open the show instead. The audience is cheerful and enthusiastic, and having got our set out of the way we can listen to some of the other music. Wallace Davenport is a fine player, though his true forte is as a section leader.

I have a chat with Wallace after his set. Without prompting, he harks back to the occasion in 1967 when the Hampton band went on strike over one of my compositions. Lionel Hampton heard us play a piece called 'Blues in Bolero' at a Jazz Expo concert at which he topped the bill. In his usual excitable way (with Hamp, hysteria is never far below the surface), he grabbed me as I came off stage. 'Hey, Humphrey, bring that blues number down to Ronnie Scott's in the morning – I'm gonna play it on T.V.' I thought the whole thing was highly improbable, but I had the piece copied out and duly reported at Ronnie's in the morning. The band was already rehearsing for their B.B.C.-T.V. show, so I sat in the shadows enjoying the music and little bothered that they seemed to have the programme set without my contribution. The last number they rehearsed was Hamp's theme tune, 'Flyin' Home', during which he led a visibly reluctant band off the stand for a parade round the room. As he passed me, waving vibraphone mallets in the air and braying in ecstasy, he seemed totally carried away. Then he spotted me in the gloom. 'Did you bring that number, have you got that tune? We'll do it next!' His enthusiasm, alas, was not shared by the rest of the band. The piece has a drum introduction in bolero rhythm, and his drummer couldn't make it. 'I can't do what your guy does,' he kept saying to me, and I accepted it as a well-deserved compliment to Spike Wells, who was working with me at the time. Hamp looked at me as if expecting me to take charge and run the band through it, a job for which, in Lester Young parlance, I had 'no eyes'. Fortunately, the matter was resolved when the whole band, led by Wallace Davenport, got up without a word and made for the bar, indicating that the rehearsal was over.

I have always assumed that, like me, they instantly put the matter behind them and gave it no further thought. But tonight, Wallace Davenport goes to some lengths to explain that the action was no reflection on myself or my tune, but that having rehearsed numbers that they *knew* all morning, they were in no mood to learn something completely new. I urge him to believe that I would have done the same myself and bear no grudge. His insistence on making amends for the trivial incident distracts me from asking him whether it is really true that, playing for a private boat party on Lake Potomac, Lionel lashed the band into such a frenzy on 'Flyin' Home' that the saxophone section unquestioningly obeyed his exhortations and jumped into the lake, still blowing the compelling riffs. My guess is that the story is about as reliable as the one about Buddy Bolden being heard across Lake Pontchartrain on a clear night. On the other hand, I can testify, having worked with Hamp on stage, that he has a remarkably low frenzy threshold. A few well-timed off-beats from the drums and he's in vertical take-off.

After the concert, we re-embark on the refugee wagon, piling on the overcoats and settling down in the now more generous space into separate, mute mounds of long-suffering. The Hungarian band are more resilient and decide to launch an impromptu concert of Hungarian folksong, belting out a succession of songs all of which reach a predictable accelerating climax with frenetic hand-clapping and shouts of 'Oi!'. I'm ashamed to say that the response among the British contingent is to nestle, like startled hamsters, further into the protective overcoats. The leader of the Hungarians is a young man with frizzy hair and the manic look of Tom Baker's 'Doctor Who'.

When the Polish band joins in with a couple of their own songs, the scenario acquires a certain inevitability. Doctor Who suddenly claps his hands for silence and announces: 'And now, some singings from the English party!' From each mound of overcoat a balloon emerges bearing the words: 'Oh, God!' The shouts of encouragement become so insistent that I foresee an international 'incident'. Suddenly Harvey Weston, who is our bass-player for the tour, emerges from his cocoon and, with startling verve, launches into 'My old man said follow the van…'. Harvey might be said to be of studious rather than extrovert appearance, so there's clearly an element of self-sacrifice in his sudden entry into the fray. Encouraged by it, we gradually surface and join in, while the Hungarians listen in awe.

'Let's all go down the Strand', 'Two lovely black eyes', 'Don't 'ave any more, Mrs Moore' – they follow each other with a vigour born of desperation. During 'Mrs Moore', the only one of which I know the words throughout, Doctor Who hops across and interrupts me. 'You know, these folk-musics are very interesting for us – from what part of England do they come?' 'From the old city of London,' I shout back, and off he goes to impart the information to his compatriots. The four-hour journey seems to take no time at all. As we disembark at our hotel, Doctor Who says, 'When I get home, I will try and arrange that you come to Hungary.' 'That will be nice,' I say, 'we've never played in Hungary.' 'Not to play,' he cries. 'To sing!'

Monday 25 October 1976, Warsaw

This morning, the foyer of the Bristol Hotel is suddenly invaded by what appears to be an entire tribe of peasants having, like out-of-towners everywhere, a look of bewilderment tempered by confidence in their numbers. There must be four generations represented, and from the oldest to the youngest they have the same powerful, proud, bottom-heavy faces of hewn stone that suggest that they would be more at home on horseback, fur-clad and scanning the plains, than perched on sofas and armchairs in a hotel foyer. Wherever they come from, it is clearly a society in which authority is invested in age and seniority. It's uncomfortable to compare the demeanour of these elders – strong, composed and formidable – with the anxious, defensive look of so many old people back home. Not all – my own upper-class grandparents remained figures of awe and authority until the day they died, and the steel-working and coal-mining communities of South Wales and the North are still dominated by the older generation in domestic affairs. It's in the large and ever-increasing urban area in the middle where loneliness is endemic that we seem to have gone badly wrong.

At 11 o'clock, a sleeker coach arrives at the hotel to take us to Crakow for our last concert.

It's a smooth but boring journey to Crakow. The hearts of the hedonistically-inclined are uplifted when we are signed into a smart American-style hotel in which we can wash, brush up and relax until we return to Warsaw late tonight. We are still heavily loaded with zlotys which we must get rid of before going through customs tomorrow. There is a free hour in which we can visit the shops, so it's a near thing.

Going straight to the concert-hall from the shops, I find that the audience is already assembling in the huge foyer. Can't attract anyone's attention at the stage-door, which is locked, so I have to go in through the front, breaking my lifelong rule not to clap eyes on an audience before a show. This has nothing to do with aloofness or showbiz mumbo-jumbo, but for the more down-to-earth reason that it scares me to death. Tonight is a case in point – by the time I have blundered through the hordes of predominantly youthful strangers, trying to find the way through to the back, I am convinced that we are in for an indifferent, if not hostile, reception. As a result, I am clammy with nerves before our set, which is the last one before the interval. We walk on to a warm ovation and a sea of smiles and at the end could cheerfully have done three or four encores.

After us, the show goes on till midnight, so we go back to the hotel for an end-of-term meal. In a burst of confidentiality, Mark tells me that he has only recently been released from a spell in prison for political activity. His family is both dissident and aristocratic, an unpopular combination. In the course of one interrogation, his inquisitor pointed at the telephone on the desk and asked, 'What is that?' When Mark laughed incredulously at the pointless question, the man seized the handset and smashed it across his face, fracturing his jaw and knocking out several teeth. The episode explains Mark's occasional lapses in concentration and also the lack of symmetry in his jaw-line which we noticed when we first saw him at the airport.

We embus for Warsaw soon after midnight. A few hours later we say farewell to Mark, who is now green with fatigue, and fly home.

Sir Humph's Delight

Wednesday 14 November 1979

Alarm call at 5.45. Did all the packing last night, so got off at 6.15 for Heathrow. Relying on a hire car to turn up at this hour of the morning is too nerve-wracking. The last one I had turned out to have a regular contract to take a small girl to school, so I was taken on a round trip of the leafy avenues of Stanmore with a mute, uniformed nine-year-old in the back seat while the minutes to check-in time ticked by.

This time there are no hitches, and we take off at around 9a.m., losing three hours en route and arriving at Istanbul at 3.30.

The show tomorrow is in Ankara, so we have to change planes in Istanbul. We are met by a large, red-bearded man in a flat cap who is

Clive Gobby, the assistant British Council representative. With him, the first move is made in a game which is to elate or depress us at each stage in the tour. In countries with strict currency controls, there are problems over transferable fees for touring bands; suffice it to say that a deal has been worked out at home and day-to-day subsistence is our only concern. As we arrive in each new country we shall be given expenses in the local currency to pay for our hotels and meals. We have been assured that they will meet all costs and, allowing for invitations to meals or receptions, may well leave us something to spare for shopping. With all the strange, unconvincing-looking paper money, it promises to be every bit as exciting as Monopoly, with similar bonuses and forfeits according to the throw of the dice.

We have a wait of forty-five minutes before flying on to Ankara.

After another forty-five minutes aloft, we arrive at Ankara. We're met by a bearded young man who introduces himself as Francis Jurksaitis and hurries on to explain that he is, in fact, English. He is the British Council second-in-command, and his first official function is to hand over our expenses for the two nights in Ankara, which he does with a rueful expression and the hope, expressed none too convincingly, that they will cover everything. He also gives us foolscap sheets with our itinerary for the next thirty-six hours. They are perused in stunned silence, then somebody says, 'Christ!'

We check into the Bulvar Palas Hotel. We have now been on the go for about twelve hours, but there is time only for a quick shower before the social events of the day start. When you work for the British Council it is on a quasi-diplomatic level, which means that all parties and receptions listed on the itinerary are obligatory. As most of them involve a buffet meal and therefore count as bonus points in the expenses game, we have no complaints. First event this evening is a get-together with top British Council man Jeremy Barnet and his wife Maureen in the lounge of the Bulvar Palas. With them is a Turkish bass-player, Selçuk Sun (pronounced Selchook Soon), who, we are told, is one of the handful of accomplished and knowledgeable jazz musicians that Turkey has so far produced. He is full of excitement at the prospect of a party at his house tomorrow.

Don't remember seeing it on the bandcall, which seemed to me to be choc-a-bloc from lunchtime onwards. So I ask innocently, 'When is that?' 'Tomorrow morning,' he cries, 'immediately after your rehearsal!' A nervous glance at the itinerary confirms that a rehearsal is scheduled for 9.30a.m., followed by drinks at the house of Mr Sun. A quick word with Francis scotches the rehearsal, but we can't disappoint Selçuk. Nor can we prepare for what promises to be a marathon by having an early night, as there is still a reception at the British Ambassador's before today is out.

Taking account of the three hours that we dropped on the long flight from Heathrow to Istanbul it is still twelve hours since my alarm call this morning. What's more, we have had no opportunity to eat since the meal on the plane at lunchtime. So what remains of today has a dream-like quality. Sir Derek and Lady Dodson are charming in the face of the dislocation caused by the late arrival of seven musicians all clamouring for food.

Sir Derek is soon to retire and seems, in our brief conversation, to have more than half a mind on that blessed moment. I sympathize with him entirely – a deputation from outer-space would be harder to converse with in the late hours than a group of travel-weary jazz musicians. Dave Green has brought an electric bass on this trip to make the travelling easier and safer – it's a thick, elongated affair that stands on a spike like the conventional bass, which is why it's nicknamed a 'pogo-stick' in the trade. I mentioned this to Sir Derek when we're talking about the rigours of touring. 'That's funny,' he said, 'I came across that term for the first time the other day. What exactly *is* a pogo-stick?' At 12.30 at night after a day's travelling, loaded to the gills with battered courgettes and Buck's Fizz, one could as easily explain Einstein's Theory of Relativity. Fortunately, the conversation seemed to fizzle out at that point....

Thursday 15 November 1979, Istanbul

This morning, we're all shattered. Disconcertingly, the acrid pall of wood-smoke has penetrated the hotel, and we walk to the breakfast room with handkerchiefs over our faces.

At 10.30a.m. we are picked up to go to the party at Selçuk's house,

somewhere out in the suburbs. There we meet another leading Turkish musician, drummer Erol Pekcan (pronounced Pekjan), who introduces himself to me as 'your Turkish counterpart'. It transpires that he leads a band and presents jazz on radio and T.V. Tallish, bald and pear-shaped, he looks like a cuddly version of the sinister actor Eric Pohlman. We listen to records, talk jazz and drink coffee, tea and, among the more reckless souls, the Turkish drink raki which belongs to the Pernod family and, like Pernod, brings one's forehead out in a not altogether unpleasant cold sweat after a sip or two.

Fortunately, there is no time to embark on a lost weekend since we are late for the sound-check at the concert hall and must be hustled once again into cars.

The run-up to the concert exerts its usual revitalizing effect. It's a splendid, dignified hall normally used for symphony concerts. There is an air of excitement backstage – and some curiosity, too, since

Ankara is less hip in jazz matters than Istanbul. For us, Turkey offers the perfect arena. It has had some contact with jazz over the post-war years, both 'live' and on record. But unlike Britain and Western Europe, it has not been saturated in it. A two-day visit in 1978 revealed that, in some mysterious way, we have acquired a following here so the shows have a special atmosphere of excitement.

After the concert, we're once again pretty hungry, since there was time only for a hurried bowl of soup beforehand. Fortunately, there are two functions scheduled tonight – a reception in the foyer of the concert hall, with drinks and snacks, followed by a party with buffet supper at Jeremy and Maureen Barnet's house. I talk myself and everyone else into the ground at each. It is well after midnight when we get back to the hotel, and we have a 7a.m. call in the morning to fly to Istanbul. My father, faced with a prospect of fine but excessive eating (and using an old-fashioned term for 'to diet') used to say, 'Have we not all eternity to bant in?' I feel the same about sleep when encountering new places and people. Anyway, five and a half hours is enough.

Friday 16 November 1979, Istanbul

At Istanbul we are met by Clive Gobby who, we discover, takes a somewhat lugubrious view of life. Driving into the city in his car, I tell him that we are glad to leave the polluted atmosphere of Ankara. 'It'll be worse here,' he says, pointing to a great swathe of blue-black smoke on the horizon. It appears that two tankers, Romanian and Greek, have recently collided in the Bosphorus, and the former has been ablaze for two days, sending up a pall of smoke which, Clive judges, should engulf the Sheraton Hotel with the wind in its present position. We are staying at the Sheraton. When we get there, we find that the cloud misses it by half a mile or so. Some of the band travelling in another car arrive pale and shaken. Seeing a crowd peering over the sea wall by the harbour, their driver stopped to investigate. On the rocks below the wall, a dead sailor rocked gently on the tide, stiff with rigor mortis.

Musicians are adept at extracting the maximum nourishment from the minimum outlay. Peasant soups full of chunks of meat and vegetables are always a good bet. Here, kebabs with mountains of rice and salad on the side commend themselves. The meat is a bit scrawny, but there's loads of ballast. Halfway through the meal, Dave Green bites into an innocent-looking chilli and turns such an interesting shade of mottled red that I have to capture the moment with a quick caricature on a table napkin. Am spotted by our waiter, who brings up another napkin and points at himself, asking for the same treatment. His colleagues follow suit, dumping paper in front of me and striking macho poses that somehow miss the point of the exercise. When the rest of the band leave for the hotel and a much-needed rest, I'm still there like Toulouse-Lautrec, working away. I wouldn't mind if they hadn't then presented me with my bill in full. I'm sure Lautrec got a discount.

Our concert this evening is in a cinema over the way from the hotel. The San Cinema holds nine hundred, and is completely sold out.

Saturday 17 November 1979, Istanbul

No need for an alarm clock in Istanbul. Even seven or eight floors above street level, the dawn chorus of car-horns is impressive.

So it's a high-spirited concert at the San Cinema this evening, once again sold out. Afterwards, David Evans, the senior British Council representative, invites us out, so it's off to the banks of the Bosphorus to a restaurant in a narrow street away from the water.

Towards the end of the meal, when raki and wine have flowed freely, surrealism takes over. Across the room, three young Turkish couples at one table are becoming increasingly noisy. Suddenly, one of the young men throws back his head and begins a sustained howling on one undulating note. Food poisoning? Epilepsy? Metamorphosis into a werewolf? A glance at the ecstatic expression of a girl sitting opposite him discloses that he is singing her a love song. The performance draws applause not only from those round his table but others sitting nearby. Supercilious glances are cast in the direction of the phlegmatic and staid Britons across the room. National honour has been challenged. Happily we are equipped to respond. After thirteen or so years in the band of Alex Welsh, Roy Williams and John Barnes have accumulated a strong repertoire of party pieces, one of which is a duet, à la Bob and Alf Pearson, called 'Barefoot Days'. They believe the song's origins to be in Mancunian pub singalongs, but counterclaims have been made that it is sung in the South, too. Certainly the North Country elongation of syllables such as 'nook' and 'hook' give it a special flavour.

The burst of song from an unexpected quarter silences the opposition. Indeed, when John Barnes, flushed with success, stands on a chair and intones an entire Stanley Holloway monologue (another of his specialities), the Turkish party beats a retreat, sportingly shaking our hands as they file past to the exit.

We fly to Damascus by the Bulgarian Balkan Airline. Bruce Turner, the most unlikely-looking Stalinist at large, comes in for some ribbing on the supposition that he will get V.I.P. treatment.

We're all fairly jugged when we reach the Omayyad Hotel. Richard Hitchcock, the British Council representative, has met us at the airport and now takes me into a corner to transact business. Am able to tell the rest that, in the Expenses Game, we are on to a winning streak in Syria. By putting us into a medium-priced Arab hotel instead of one of the big internationals, Richard has seen to it that our daily allowance, more generous than in Turkey, will leave plenty for shopping.

After eating we go to the hall – more a small lecture room than a theatre, seating about 300, which means that we can do the show without amplification. The audience tonight looks from the stage to be a cosmopolitan lot. Syria is less jazz-orientated than Turkey, so my announcements have to be rather more informative than at a normal concert. But all goes well, and we get an enthusiastic reception.

'Ow Abaht it, Mush?

Monday 19 November 1979, Damascus

Another enjoyable concert in the Little Theatre. Richard Hitchcock estimates that about 50 per cent of our audiences have been Syrian, the rest part of the international community. After the concert, we are invited to a party given by Bob Straker-Smith and his wife Dawn.

The party establishes a pattern with which, I suspect, we shall be all too familiar before the tour ends. 'Where have you come from? Where are you going next? How on earth do you manage to transport all the instruments? The last time I saw you was at 100 Oxford Street in, let me see….' The cocktail party was conceived as the perfect way to bring together a large number of people who have nothing whatever to say to each other and couldn't possibly hear it if they had. In our drummer Alan Jackson's phrase, 'It's G.B.H. of the eardrums, innit!' The cul-de-sac style of conversation reminds me of my father's complaint against an elderly friend of his, that she would insist on hailing him across a busy street with 'You must come over and meet Mr So-and-So – he's going to Asia Minor tomorrow for five years'. I am not a party man but, once there, can be relied upon to see it through to the bitter end, holding forth ceaselessly. In other words, all the foregoing is humbug. I get on famously with a lady who shares my interest in calligraphy, stuff myself to bursting point from the delicious Indian-style buffet, and corrugate every ear in the room before being dragged away to catch the transport back to the hotel.

Tuesday 20 November 1979, Damascus

We don't have to leave until 4p.m. and are well furnished with spare cash, so return to the souk area for shopping. Richard Hitchcock has recommended a general store opposite the Omayyad Mosque whose owner is known to him (and trusted by him). It's a tall building of several floors all looking over into a central well. In the middle of the ground floor a fountain plays, coming, the owner tells us, from a natural spring beneath the building. He offers us tea before we start our shopping and we drink it black and sweet from handle-less cups. His trading honesty reveals itself when somebody asks if the white pieces on the mosaic boxes are genuine ivory. 'Ivory, bone, plastic, who can tell these days? But if you don't know, you don't care?'

Afterwards, a roam through the covered souk produces a classic bargaining exchange between A.J. and a shop-keeper called Victor, a stocky Damascan who claims to have visited England many times but who seems to have learnt most of his English from British soldiers from every region. His opening gambit is, 'Nice to see you, to see you, nice...'Ow you doin', all right?' The subsequent conversation is peppered with English colloquialisms, the perfect foil for A.J.'s cockney jargon. The object of the haggling is a large pot or jug of indeterminate metal for which Victor wants a hundred pounds. ''Ow abaht it, mush?' A.J. offers fifty pounds. 'Do us a fyvour...One hundred pounds!' 'I can't, my son, that's all the money I've got.' 'This is much better than money – is GORGEOUS!' To Victor's suggestion that when he gets to Kuwait, A.J. can get the money without problem from his company or business associates, Alan says, 'But we're not rich men.' 'You don't 'ave to be rich!' explodes Victor, then, waxing philosophical: 'You know, the English, they used to be rich...I used to make a fortune out of English...Before – you weren't born, I think – they used to spend money without thinking...like this, up, down, left right...but now, they can't...they have to be careful.' But he's soon back on his sales pitch, holding the pot up on one hand. 'You can see the harmony of the shape...this is good for a gentleman like you, a musician, who knows abaht it...you have to put in your house, is very noice...you can sell it for two hundred English quid in England...what you say?'

Alan now lowers his offer to forty pounds, which offends Victor's sense of fair dealing. 'You said just a while fifty pounds an' I don't accept it...now you must say over fifty!' A.J. is adamant, Victor appeals to us. 'I don't know what kind of a chance I've got with your friend – he is absolutely squeezing my neck. I have no bloody chance at all!' Eventually, Alan withdraws from the fray with, 'We'll 'ave to call it a day, my friend,' and Victor reciprocates: 'You are very welcome in Damascus...you are very nice people and we hope to see you many days in Damascus and I wish you nice journey.'

We troop out and set off through the crowds. Suddenly there's a shout of 'Oi!' from the distance. It's Victor, yelling 'Fifty pounds!' from his shop doorway. Without stopping, A.J. bellows 'Forty!' over his shoulder. Over a widening distance the exchange goes on. 'Fifty!' 'Forty!' 'Fifty!' There's the sound of pattering feet, and Victor runs up. 'It's OK – forty.' They go back to the shop to clinch the deal. Victor is subdued but satisfied. 'Me, I see the eggs now and not the chicken tomorrow.' It's a scrambled metaphor but we know what he means. 'As we say in England – small profit, quick return.' After some more amicable chat and a promise from A.J. to send Victor two Tootal ties for Christmas, farewells are exchanged. Walking through the souk, A.J. peers into the bag. 'Actually, I really dig this thing,' he says, with about forty pounds' worth of conviction.

I shall be sorry to leave Damascus. My sense of history is weak, but here the 'aroma of the past' is strong and irresistible. When our guide the other day casually pointed out the Street Called Straight, where Paul preached, and the East Wall over which he was lowered in a basket to escape persecution, my mind was assailed, if not by the blinding light of conversion then at least by the strong recollection of soggy ginger biscuit dunked in milk and the shiny black books smelling faintly of petrol from which we learnt our Scriptures before breakfast at Sunningdale School.

When it comes to checking out of the Omayyad Hotel, a ticklish situation develops. As the day has progressed, our passage to and from our hotel rooms has been dogged by members of the hotel staff, who indicate by wary and suspicious looks that they think we are about to do a daylight flit. The problem is that we have dissipated most of our temporary wealth and, furthermore, tipping comes under the heading of 'internal travel', which is the responsibility of the British Council. Richard Hitchcock will deal with it eventually, but he is not here yet. I try to sidestep the problem by carrying my own heavy bags to the lift. But as soon as I step outside the room a swarthy chambermaid darts from the shadows and tries to wrest them from me. Shouting at each other in two different languages, we do a sort of paso doble down the corridor and, at the lift, I try to extricate myself from an increasingly ugly situation by pressing what's left of my Syrian money into her hand. In the gloom of the corridor it's hard to be sure, but I have an idea that she spits. By now a male colleague has joined her, and when the lift arrives, they both get in with me, the lady now screeching with indignation over this furtive foreigner who has tried to leave without paying his dues. Down in the foyer the entire complement of chambermaids, porters, cleaners and bottle-washers has assembled, standing grimly round our luggage like guards surrounding the hostages of war. When we try to escape from embarrassment by going into the restaurant and ordering tea from our pooled resources, they post a look-out at the door in case we climb out of the window. Richard Hitchcock arrives at the very last minute and sends in his assistant Ehmad – the Arab 'fixer' with which every British Council outpost in this part of the world must be equipped if it is to function at all – to buy off the guards and release our luggage.

After farewells at the airport, we join a scrum at the boarding gates to get on the Boeing 707 to Kuwait. Men one side, women the other, use your elbows! After the comparatively libertarian ambience of Istanbul and Damascus, we are now entering the – for us – uncharted and unpredictable waters of Islam.

We are met by a large, jovial Englishman called Ken Rasdall, whose speciality is supervising the opening of new airports all over the world. Kuwait has just built a whopper. Whilst uttering prudent and diplomatic reservations about his ability to work wonders, Ken does just that, wafting us past customs and jostling queues of immigrants to where a deputation from the British Council is waiting to greet us. An assistant representative, a Dubliner called Leo O'Keeffe, hands us each a bulky sheaf of pages which turn out to contain our programme of events for the next six days. No time to read it, as we pile into a minibus to drive to the Marriott Marina Hotel.

Nothing in the itinerary nor in Leo's conversation prepares us for the pure Hollywood sight that greets us when we drive round Kuwait and reach the shores of the Persian Gulf. The Marriott Marina is a former ocean liner, now immobilized in concrete at the quayside and floodlit from end to end. A more detailed look at the itinerary shows that it is peppered with heavy-point-scoring receptions and lunch invitations. One entry is mystifying – 'Friday 23 November: day off. Lunch with Miss Juanita Monteiro, followed by hockey match.' Glamorous expectations aroused and then nipped in the bud, all in the same sentence.

Wednesday 21 November 1979, Kuwait

Woken at 9a.m. by the telephone. It is Miss Juanita Monteiro, who introduces herself and tells me that she used to work with my old friend Sid Dirks in what was Trans-Canadian Airlines. She will call round later to meet us in person. After a leisurely breakfast I meet the others in the foyer or fo'c'sle or whatever, for a briefing from the chief British Council representative. John Munby is an impressive talker, and the rush of words, often uttered while he circles one as if preparing to cut off all avenues of escape, express an energy and enthusiasm that are highly infectious. Kuwait is going to be fun.

It's a pleasant, sunny day with the temperature in the seventies, so we go to the upper deck at noon for a swim in the small pool. I spot a figure beckoning to me from the shadows near the entrance. It is an Indian lady of matronly build in snazzy dark glasses, floral shirt and tightly upholstered white slacks. I go over to see what she wants. 'Remember me? I called you earlier.' It is Miss Juanita Monteiro.

She has been in Kuwait for seventeen years, and has become a member of the prosperous Indian business community. She doesn't boast to this effect, but I deduce it. In fact, she appears less flamboyant and self-assertive than her build-up in the itinerary has suggested, and she clearly wants to be as helpful as possible. We arrange to spend the day with her and her family on our rest day on Friday, and I think I have planted a fruitful seed of dissent about the hockey match.

The catering manager at the Marriott Marina Hotel has organized tonight's barbecue beside the large swimming pool outside the hotel. There's an audience of about 300 of all nationalities, though they say that the nearest we come to 'local' support is a large and scattered contingent of Egyptians from the diplomatic and banking community. But there's quite a peppering of gleaming white Kuwaiti 'dishdashers' amongst the informal Western-style dress. Surveying the candle-lit scene, Bruce Turner is heard to say, 'Life for a chap, life for a chap – glamorous, glamorous.' Confronted with any kind of Hollywood lavishness, the film buff in him has little difficulty in suppressing the Stalinist.

Glamorous it may be, it also gets decidedly chilly as midnight approaches. We notice that many of the male guests appear to have come straight from work, still carrying their briefcases, which they lodge under the tables. As the night breeze begins to chill the jugs of soft drinks on the bar-table, they find it more and more necessary to duck under the tablecloths to consult their documents, emerging refreshed and heart-warmed by a quick glimpse of balance sheet or sales return.

Musically, it's a somewhat hybrid affair for us, since we have to temper the informative, British-orientated programme which the British Council has asked for with some of the boisterous Dixieland standards appropriate to a festive pool-side occasion. Thanks to the briefcases and their stimulating contents, we go down increasingly well as the night progresses.

Thursday 22 November 1979, Kuwait

Nothing to do today except go over to the British Embassy Club for a drink at midday and repeat the barbecue concert at the hotel tonight. Go up to the pool early.

In leisure moments such as this morning round the pool, a team of disparate, often weary and sometimes disgruntled individuals becomes a street theatre of manic invention, augmented by fantasy characters. Much of the elaboration emanates from Mick Pyne, a devastating mimic and talented amateur cartoonist. Some years ago, on tour in Switzerland, I was passing the time in a hotel lounge doing caricatures of all and sundry. Dave Green rashly came out with: 'It's a funny thing, nobody's ever been able to do a caricature of me.' It took a few minutes' practice to remedy the deficiency with an arrangement of circles that suggested Dave in a moment of pop-eyed indignation. From then on, it became a habit to subject Dave to mild persecution by drawing the owl-like cipher in all sorts of unexpected places. The very first evening, when we were waiting for the night plane out of Basel, he visited the men's loo in the airport and encountered it staring up at him from below the water-line in the bog, where I'd scribbled it with a felt pen a few minutes earlier. I once adapted the centre-fold of a *Playboy* magazine into a Dave

Green, using the boobs as bulbous eyes, and sent it to him. And every Christmas for years he has had a card from me with some kind of owl motif.

It was this spherical, glaring face that became the prototype for a character called Grosser Green, immortalized in Lyttelton Band folklore. Somewhere along the line, Mick spotted that Dave sets great store by the routine highlights of touring life, whether it's a tasty schnitzel and/or *grosser Bier* in a German or Swiss café, or a visit to the souk in the Middle East. Having set his heart on a plan, he announces it loudly and repeatedly in the hope of bringing everyone else in, but can be as quickly deflected from it by a dissenting voice. So a typical dialogue after checking in at a hotel might run:

DAVE: 'Right, fellas…*grosser, grosser*!'
SOMEONE: 'I'd sooner have a wash and a kip first…'
DAVE: 'Yeah, I feel a bit shattered, too…right, bed, bed!'

It was from this that Grosser Green was born – a loud, barging, rotund figure with the pop-eyed, owlish features, rampaging around the world from one disaster to another. The Grosser saga has been fuelled by Dave's actual mishaps. He was once nicknamed 'Mister Bratwurst' by a German coach driver because of his reluctance to venture further afield among the mysteries of German menus. Endless deliberation and vacillation at the table would always end with: 'No, I think I'll just have a Bratwurst.' It was a red-letter day when he decided to give himself a treat, plumping for something German in the fish section which, for sheer weight of consonants and syllables, promised to be substantial. The metamorphosis into Grosser, all saucer eyes and indignant cries of 'WHA-A-A-AT???', was instantaneous when the waiter arrived with two cold rollmops on a plate. Thence-forward, in restaurants all over the world, the words 'I've done it again' have disclosed that Grosser has once more backed a loser. The whole of this is a foul calumny on Dave's sensitive, talented and long-suffering nature, but he takes it well and indeed acts up to it.

Friday 23 November 1979, Kuwait

Our free day. Juanita arrives at 11a.m. to take us out for the day, driving a handsome Buick. John has been booked for the day with the minibus so we travel in convoy to what would have been a leafy suburb of Kuwait had there been a leaf in sight. We have drinks round a cocktail bar festooned with comic pub notices from England, saucy slogans in framed Gothic script or poker-work.

Ozzie, an elegant figure in early middle-age with greyish-white hair, tells me that he was at the Regal Cinema, Edmonton, in 1957 on the night I sat in for a number with Lionel Hampton's Band, wearing a fashionable Edwardian-style suit that prompted one Teddy Boy punter to say, 'That 'Umphrey – 'e's one of us!' Ozzie had a front-row seat in the reserved V.I.P. section. He was still wondering why they had ushered him there without even looking at his ticket when the curtain went up, and he saw the whole Lionel Hampton Band dressed in blue gaberdine suits identical to his. He had been taken for one of their entourage and favoured accordingly.

Other guests are expected for lunch, so we go down to a games room in the basement and play darts, table tennis and billiards while we wait. They don't turn up, so, suitably exercised, we return upstairs and sit down to a sumptuous Indian banquet.

Happily, the delayed lunch has put the hockey match out of the question, so we debate what we will do with the rest of the afternoon. Some are so crippled by vindaloo and dhansak that they choose to retire with John and the minibus to the hotel. John Barnes, Alan Jackson and I decide that we would like to see 'the desert', envisaging that somewhere beyond the outskirts of town there must be arid dunes and camels and Ronald Colman. Juanita volunteers to drive us out there, suggesting, somewhat vainly, that we might like to take in a guided tour of an oil refinery too. After driving for about forty minutes we reach a point where, if you stand with your back to an unsightly oil installation on the horizon, the remaining three-quarters of the vista is uninterrupted desert. It's still rather disappointing – very flat and with dirty-grey, scrubby sand, nothing like the Sahara.

Back at the hotel around 6 o'clock, we get ready to go to a reception at John Munby's house. A swinging affair, thanks to John and Lilian M.'s energy as hosts and a lanky and highly-strung Palestinian doctor who has brought along an armful of Louis Armstrong records.

A dominant figure at the party is another berobed Arab, an outsize version of Dizzy Gillespie with the same swivel-eyed look that contrives to blend mockery with innocence. When I first encounter him, he is in earnest conversation with a man from the B.B.C. to whom I am introduced. I linger on to eavesdrop. Dizzy is explaining that, 'though it is not in our culture to show off', his family should rightfully be ruling Kuwait. While he talks, the B.B.C. man studies his face intently, presumably trying to divine whether he is hearing the truth or an outrageous 'line'. Dizzy's swivelling eyes give nothing away.

Later, I ask John Munby who he is. 'We're not absolutely sure,' he says. 'He turns up at all the parties, and I think he works for the Ministry of Education. We suspect he might be deputed to keep a benevolent but watchful eye on us.' Dizzy certainly likes to give that impression. When he is later introduced to us all, the eyes roll across to give us a knowing sideways look. 'I have seen most of you before,' he says. 'You left the hotel yesterday at 11 o'clock, a lady was with you.' The Marriott Hotel stands aloof from other buildings. To have seen us leave with Juanita, he must either have been lurking behind potted palms in the foyer or perched high on a distant skyscraper with binoculars. I tell him that I am giving an illustrated talk tomorrow in which I shall solicit questions from the audience. Round come the eyes again. 'I shall be there. Expect a question.'

In mid-morning, Juanita turns up, bringing me a large floppy textbook on colloquial Arabic which the Kuwait Oil Company issues to its foreign employees. After she's left, I study the first few pages, and end up with a string of words which, the book assures me, represent an appropriate greeting.

At lunch over a club sandwich I try '*Shukran*' ('Thank you') out on the waiter. He responds with what sounds like ''Ave one', a dangerous invitation to travelling Brits. A riffle through the book reveals that he is saying '*Afwan*', rather improbably translated as 'Not at all'. At least they don't say 'You're welcome'!

We have to go to the Mousetrap Theatre in the English School to set up for tonight's lecture.

The Mousetrap Theatre is inside a compound, approached across a wide expanse of dusty open space. A tiny staircase leads down to the backstage area. The cars have to park outside the compound, so all the gear has to be taken over by hand. A gnarled and wiry Arab caretaker is sent across to help. The drums are no problem, but Dave Green's electric 'pogo stick' bass is transported in a narrow rectangular box over six feet long and weighing a ton. Having reconnoitred the tiny entrance, I collect a few helpers to go and fetch it. Approaching us across the quadrangle is a strange apparition, half man, half sideboard. It's the caretaker, bent in a right angle at the waist, with Dave's case on his back. All we can see of him is a pair of matchstick legs, bowing slightly under the weight. Brushing aside our offers of help, he teeters on single-handed, leaving us to speculate as to how he got the thing on his back in the first place.

Apart from an opening gambit I have nothing prepared – my usual technique in 'talks' is to rely on questions, and if nobody asks any, to pose them myself and to go on to answer them…e.g. 'I can see you're wondering how we know when to stop and start' or 'you may well ask how much of our performance is improvised and how much prepared'.

In the event, there are quite a few spontaneous questions along those lines – though the loaded and possibly incriminating question that Dizzy seemed to be threatening last night doesn't materialize, as he fails to show up.

Sunday 25 November 1979, Kuwait

We leave the hotel at 11a.m. to go with the instruments to the Telecommunications Centre, where tonight's last concert is to be held. We fear a rather stuffy, formal affair, since bigwigs from the local banking and diplomatic community are going to be there. It turns out to be the opposite – a queue-up-and-help-yourself buffet (curry again – my taste buds are now permanently steaming) – with John Cambridge, a lively and unstuffy bachelor, greeting everyone with 'Jackets off – it's far too hot to wear jackets!'. There is a lot of talk about the tense situation in Saudi Arabia to which we listen with ears flapping since we are due to fly in there in three days' time. No one seems to think we have a hope in hell of being let in, and I must say that the idea of a British jazz band breezing into a situation that the local Press is describing variously as 'a land-mine', 'a tinder box' and a 'knife's edge' does seem rather far-fetched. But in Arabia nothing is predictable, and from our British Council mentors in London not a word has been heard.

Monday 26 November 1979, Kuwait

We don't have to leave for Dubai until around 4 o'clock this afternoon, so there is time for a shopping expedition.

We have been told that the gold souk is something to see, but even so it takes us by surprise. I succumb to gold fever and buy myself an 18-carat ring. I've never worn a ring in my life, but the opportunity to look flash for a mere £20 outlay can't be passed up. When I buy a bracelet, too, to take home, I am brought heavily down to earth as the rather supercilious Indian behind the counter asks, 'Only one?' I know what he means – in the street and at the airport we have seen

Arab women wearing a dozen or so on each wrist, the flashing gold against the sombre black shrouds indicating a compact between God and mammon.

John Barnes stops off at a menswear stall to equip himself, from head to foot, with Arab gear. The salesman takes great delight in dressing him up, there and then, and at the end J.B. looks quite convincing with his dark glasses and jutting beard.

It's late evening when we go to Kuwait Airport for the flight to Dubai. I feel slightly end-of-the-hols about leaving Kuwait – under John Munby's aegis it's been a stimulating week.

This feeling is accentuated when we get to Dubai. We're met by several young men from the Jebel Ali Club, where we are to play tomorrow. The club has hired us from the British Council for this gig, and I soon gather from Dave, the club secretary, that this will be a predominantly expatriate audience. I've begun to enjoy the quasi-diplomatic aspect of our tour, and my feeling is that there'll be little scope for it here.

Tuesday 27 *November* 1979, *Dubai*

The weather this morning is English summerish, hot but with no humidity. There's a swimming pool alongside the club, empty like the pools in Kuwait because the residents think it's cold. We lounge around it during the morning. Bruce Turner, who would as soon buy a phial of liquid gold as a bottle of sun oil, burnt himself in patches in Kuwait, so he lies on the slatted sun-bed here with the affected parts covered by bits of his discarded clothing – T-shirt over the forehead, underpants round the neck, socks draped over the tops of the feet. He looks like a mummy that's come unwrapped.

Over in the souk there's a mixture of the exotic and the trashy similar to that which we found in Kuwait. I complete my Arab wardrobe by buying a full head-dress assembly.

The evening concert is in the tarmacked forecourt of the club, open to the skies except for a covered bandstand. The club forecourt is packed with an almost exclusively British expatriate audience most of whom, judging from snatches of conversation en route to the stage and during the interval, passed through the Humphrey Lyttelton

Club at 100 Oxford Street during the 'fifties. This is encouraging and at the same time daunting, since some Oxford Street veterans believe that the modest entrance fee to Mack's Restaurant bought them a lifetime's guarantee that my music would never change so much as a dotted quaver. Fortunately, it's rarity that's the winning card tonight, and the very fact that we suddenly materialize in their midst is enough to unleash cheering euphoria.

Wednesday 28 November 1979, Dubai

We have still had no word from the British Council in London about our imminent trip to Jeddah. Most people here think that, with fundamentalist fever affecting even such easy-going places as Kuwait and Dubai, the notion of our playing in the grounds of the British Embassy in Jeddah is unlikely to say the least. However, we shall match London's stiff upper lip when we leave for Saudi Arabia tonight.

The exit customs at Dubai airport are the toughest yet. They search all the hand-baggage thoroughly, turning out everything on to the counter and leaving us to put it all back. Passing under the metal-detector arch I set off a burst of urgent bleeping caused, it transpires, by my wine-waiter's knife, a constant companion. I use it most at home for cutting calligraphy pens from garden cane, so it does have a very sharp and dangerous blade. On the other hand, Arab writing is done with a 'reed' pen exactly like my homemade product, so they should know all about pen-knives. And presumably the senior official to whom the matter is referred does, because I get the knife back. Dave Green doesn't materialize on the plane, and we fear we may have lost him. He eventually arrives in full Grosser manifestation, eyes popping with indignation. The customs man has just prised open several of his boxes of Turkish Delight which have been intact since Istanbul.

We have to break our journey and go through more customs at Dahran, and Dave's face as he emerges from inspection tells us that more of his Turkish Delight has been vandalized.

A quiet young Scot called Jim McGrath welcomes us, and takes us to the Sands Hotel, which will be our home for the next four days.

There is a general air of depression around today, compounded of tiredness, a feeling of anticlimax after the lively social atmosphere in both Kuwait and Dubai, and a consciousness not hitherto felt of being in an alien and not very hospitable culture. In other words, the vibes are not good.

Later in the morning we are driven half a mile along a dusty road to the Embassy where there is a scaffolded stage just inside the main gate. Other members of the concert committee are there, including the British representative Tim King, who anticipates a large crowd tonight.

As far as anyone on the concert committee knows, we are the first 'Western' band of any kind ever to perform so publicly in Saudi Arabia, where music plays no part in their culture. No one quite knows what the official view is, but they suspect that if the audience response is too riotous, the police will move in and put a stop to everything. By the end of the concert, however, inhibitions – and the police cars – vanish and everyone whoops and yells.

Friday 30 November 1979, Jeddah

Today being the Arab 'Sunday', we have a day off. We have an open invitation from several committee members to spend the day at the Red Sea Sailing Club, a few miles out of the city.

Thirty minutes out of Jeddah in Tim's car, we dive off the main road and cross the sand to an enclosed compound on the sea shore. We go into a clubhouse and change for the beach, emerging on to a scene resembling a rather overdone parody of a Rubens painting. The strict Islamic law that forbids women to appear in public unless covered down to the wrists and ankles is in abeyance here, since the club is for Europeans only. The result is an explosion of liberated flesh which the flimsiest of bikinis make no serious effort to contain. Stalking out into this undulating landscape, I'm aware that I cut an odd figure. Tim King has warned us that on the Red Sea beach there are creatures – whether fish or insect I didn't take in – that lurk under the sand projecting a poisonous spear upwards which, if trodden on with a bare foot, will put one in hospital if not the mortuary. My sandals came adrift days ago and, having size thirteen feet, I can't just walk into a shop and replace them. So I have come to the beach in ordinary black shoes, all right when partly shrouded by trouser bottoms, but painfully conspicuous at the end of bare legs. However, I'm reassured by the sights around me that the prevailing mood is 'What the hell!' and stride forth unabashed.

It's a pleasant holiday atmosphere on the beach – we sit on rugs, sip soft drinks and watch the finals of the small-boat race.

Afterwards, in the interests of experience, I allow Tim to take me out in a craft which is only marginally larger than one of my shoes. Before we scud off into deep waters, he explains to me about 'tacking'. 'When I say "Get down!", crouch as low as you can in the boat – otherwise the boom will swing across and hit you.' Tim has not secured advancement in the diplomatic service for nothing. He is eminently unflappable, and when he first says 'Get down' it's in such a calm, everyday voice that I pay no attention. The boom is light aluminium, but even so it moves fast and can give you a fair whack on the side of the head. I get a few more clobbers before we're through as I'm not the shape to be furled quickly into a space the size of a small hip bath. I get back to the jetty bruised, drenched but exhilarated.

Saturday 1 December 1979, Jeddah

Today we have our first health crisis. John Barnes, having had two nasty-looking insect bites on his wrist, reveals red tracks extending up his arm, a clear sign of poisoning. We send him to the Embassy nurse, who in turn packs him off to a doctor in town. He returns with a bum punctured by a penicillin injection and strict instructions not to play tonight. They *think* they have intercepted septicaemia in time, but he has to go back at 4.15 for a check-up.

Sunday 2 December 1979, Jeddah

Another lazy day at the pool. John goes again to the doctor, returns with a clean bill of health. The tracking marks are still there, but they are receding, and he can play tonight. In the evening Helmut turns up to drive some of us to the souk.

The British in general, and myself in particular, are hopeless

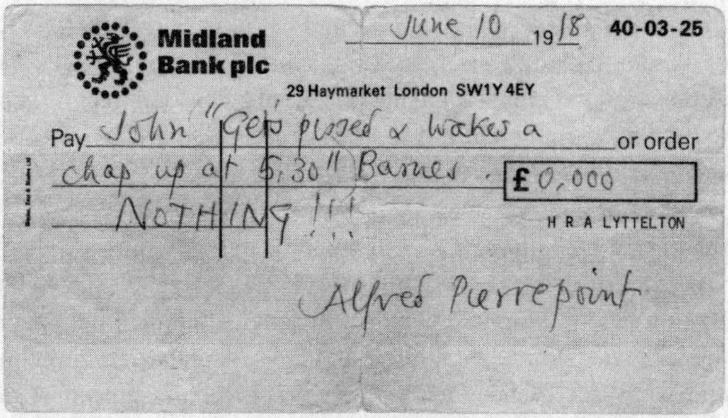

Midland Bank plc
June 10 1918 40-03-25
29 Haymarket London SW1Y 4EY
Pay John "Gets pissed & wakes a chap up at 5.30" Barnes. or order
NOTHING!!! £0,000
H R A LYTTELTON
Alfred Pierrepoint

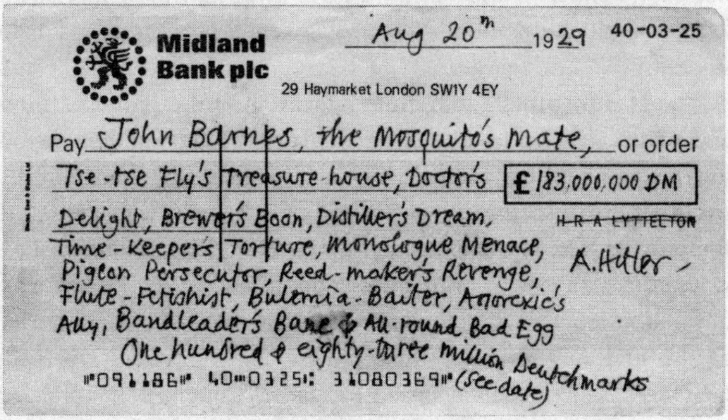

Midland Bank plc
Aug 20th 1929 40-03-25
29 Haymarket London SW1Y 4EY
Pay John Barnes, the Mosquito's mate, or order
Tse-tse Fly's Treasure-house, Doctor's Delight, Brewer's Boon, Distiller's Dream, Time-Keepers Torture, Monologue Menace, Pigeon Persecutor, Reed-maker's Revenge, Flute-Fetishist, Bulemia-Baiter, Anorexic's Ally, Bandleader's Bane & All-round Bad Egg
One hundred & eighty-three million Deutchmarks (see date)
£183,000,000 DM
~~H R A LYTTELTON~~
A. Hitler
⑈091186⑈ 40⑆03251⑆ 31080369⑈

Humph's cheques to band member, John Barnes. 'Pissed' was the first cheque issued after four of the band had an impromptu party in John's room next to Humph! In the Middle East, John was so badly bitten by mosquitos he was pulled out of a concert.

hagglers. It's the acting that's the stumbling block – the derisive shout of laughter when the first figure is quoted, the pretence that something that you've expressly gone into the shop to buy is a load of junk worth half the price at most, the walking away at regular intervals with the jaw jutting resolutely but the ears flapping for the inevitable recall for further bargaining. Trade union leaders no doubt find it all in a day's work, but I cave in with the first final offer.

On the way back, where the old and newer markets join, we have to paddle round a foul-smelling morass where a sewer has overflowed. A whiff of frankincense would come in handy here. Another good concert at full strength in the evening, then a formal reception at Tim King's house in the Embassy.

Monday 3 December 1979, Amman

Having extricated ourselves from the hotel, we are driven to the airport to fly to Amman. A bearded British Council man meets us at Amman, and introduces himself as John Chapman. He gives out itineraries which tell us that, after a twenty-minute stop-off at the hotel for a check-in and wash, we leave by bus for the University of Yarmouk, ninety minutes' drive away, to do a short concert for the students.

The bumpy trundle to Yarmouk takes all of the promised hour-and-a-half, and by the time we've unloaded the instruments we are forty-five minutes late for the concert. It's with some trepidation that we troop into a lecture room full to bursting point with vociferous students. As soon as we appear a huge cheer goes up and the place is clamorous with expectation as we set up on stage. What, I am forced to wonder, are they all cheering? I am none the wiser when we start to play and an enormous swell of noise and movement greets the opening bars. We blow against a barrage of clapping, shouting and jostling, but there are friendly smiles everywhere and a pervading atmosphere of goodwill.

The wild enthusiasm is maintained right up until the last number. Had we been pop idols of their own age at the end of a three-hour concert, we could not have been received with more genuine warmth and enthusiasm. As they gather round and talk to us at the end, a young man comes over to me and introduces the only note of dissension. He pumps my hand and, in tones of ecstasy, cries, 'Sir, we have very much enjoyed your concert of Western music. But why no Beethoven?' I begin to explain that there are different kinds of Western music, but he will have none of it. 'No, sir, you should have played Beethoven's Fifth Symphony, but I do not complain. You are the king of music!'

Tuesday 4 December 1979, Amman

This morning the Jordan *Times* has a write-up of last night's concert at Yarmouk, headlined 'HUMPHREY LYTTELTON PUTS ON A ROUSING JAZZ SHOW'. It explains the good humour when we arrived late by saying that the 400–500 students and university staff 'had been entertaining each other by telling jokes at the microphones'. Later it reports that 'all the swinging jazz pieces were acclaimed by deafening clapping, whistles, shouting and the traditional Bedouin ululating call. The final number of the show, "Fish Seller", was most wildly applauded by students clapping and shouting "Eh-la!". During the number's percussion interlude, the enthusiastic students jumped on to the stage and began performing a traditional Bedouin dance...The rousing success of the concert produced what is, for Jordan, a very rare sight – after the show, a group of fans and autograph-hunters mobbed the players. Clearly, Humphrey Lyttelton is a musician who knows how to reach his audience.' And vice versa.

The evening begins badly. Dressing after a shower, I suddenly notice that the gold ring which I bought in Kuwait is missing from my finger. It was a little loose, especially since we came to the cooler temperature of Amman, but surely not loose enough to have just dropped off in the street or taxi. I assume that all the flailing about getting in and out of shirts has dislodged it, so get down on hands and knees and search every inch of the wall-to-wall carpeted floor, moving all the furniture about. Nothing. Common sense urges me to be philosophical. It has fallen off somewhere and is gone, so forget it. You have lived for fifty-eight years without wearing a ring, you can surely stagger through the next fifty-eight similarly unencumbered. People who are meant to wear rings don't lose them. You bought it with joke money anyway, so just lie down, have a rest before the show and think of something else. But this is ridiculous, I shout back at my distraught image in the bedroom mirror – things don't just disappear. The next minute I am clawing away at the fixed bed-head which comes away from the wall surprisingly easily for such a patently new fitting. Apart from a row of grinning nails, it reveals nothing.

There's something unsettling about losing things. Having put the room back together, I go down to the bus, feeling disgruntled and glum. The concern does nothing to cheer me up. I have to memorize an opening speech which John gives me, thanking the government for inviting us, the British Council for arranging things and the Minister for coming. There's nothing like the vibrant expectancy of Yarmouk, but we get a good ovation when we walk on and there's no reason to suppose that the show will not produce an exhilarating climax to the tour. But as soon as we start to play, we realize that there is something seriously wrong with the sound. It becomes clear that, while on stage our brains are being scrambled by noise, nothing very coherent or compact is getting across to the audience, whose applause is generous but short of ecstatic.

By the interval I am gibbering. The T.V. producer is brought backstage to persuade me that the sound is perfect. John makes soothing noises, assuring me that the audience is loving every minute of it. I feel the desperation of a hospital patient being told that the pain that is bending him double doesn't exist. Just before we go on, a message comes back that, yes, they *have* found a fault in the sound circuit. I go back on to find that everything is, indeed, vastly improved. Unfortunately, our nerves are now shot. A.J., in particular, has sought refuge from frustration among the refreshments in the band-room and is not wholly in touch. In other circumstances, his climactic drum solo would have been hilarious. Always a master of light and shade, he takes thing to extremes tonight, at one stage embarking on a long passage with both sticks pressed silently into the head of the snare-drum, only the rhythmic movements of his arms and shoulders revealing what musical thoughts are going on in his head. Then, instead of giving us our cue to come back in, he stops, carefully puts the sticks in their sling and stands up, arms raised towards the audience in a gesture of peace and benediction. He gets huge applause, and the concert ends with prolonged clapping and cheering. But it's been a nightmare to me.

Back in the hotel, I am stripping off for final ablutions when something tinkles on to the tiled floor. It is my gold ring. Ever since I first noticed its disappearance it has been lodged smugly in a fold at the top of my underpants.

Wednesday 5 December 1979, Amman
Leave the hotel at 9.30 for the airport. John Chapman shows us a write-up in the paper. It gives a glowing account of our performance, with special praise for our tonal finesse and overall balance. A.J.'s drum solo is singled out as a high spot, especially for its subtlety in the quiet passages – lost, says the reviewer, on some of the restless elements in the audience. So that's all right.

Toot'n in Kamen

Sunday 3 January 1982, Kuwait
Alarm call at 6.15. Day starts with a panic – I've hired an Avis Ford Fiesta to go to Heathrow, and packed trumpet, suitcase, bag with passport, traveller's cheques etc. into the boot last night so I wouldn't forget them. Discover this morning that I don't know how the boot opens – a straightforward turn of the key doesn't achieve anything. A day's supply of adrenalin is expended before I discover the knack.

In the departure lounge we meet Sian Griffiths, from the music department of the British Council – a tall, boyish-looking lady out of the Joyce Grenfell box of soldiers, a fact of which she must be aware, as her conversation frequently lapses into Grenfellese.

Arrive in Kuwait at 7p.m., met by British Council man Bruce Brown and by Tony Barlow, who is the manager of the Messila Beach Hotel where we are playing this time.

Tuesday 5 January 1982, Kuwait
Cloudy today with rain about. Get up around ten but take my time dressing as we have nothing to do this morning. Picked up at 1 o'clock by a stocky, dignified British Embassy driver whom I remember from last time. En route to our lunch date with the Ambassador, he tells me that he has been with the Embassy twenty-five years. The imminent prospect of a gold watch and testimonial has no restraining effect on his driving – we hurtle along at 80 m.p.h.,

braking at roundabouts with a force that threatens to catapult everyone into the front seat.

John Cambridge is still in residence as Ambassador, much thinner now after a severe illness but just as sprightly and hospitable. The lunch is a replica of our last visit – stand-up drinks, queue along the buffet, disperse to tables to eat, short mill-about afterwards. Food rather more ordinary this time – a new chef, or Thatcherite spending cuts making their distant presence felt? Her Minister of State for Transport is among the gathering, here on an official visit. We are introduced – his name is Kenneth Clarke (the Creator's lack of inventiveness with regard to human faces is matched by man's limited imagination over names) and he turns out to be a jazz fan. Blond, chubby-faced and unpompous, he looks a bright hope. Well, a genuinely hip Prime Minister wouldn't be bad – Harold Wilson tried, but there was a square underneath.

The concert tonight is a repeat of last night, but with an even larger crowd. Informed opinion is that the predominantly European dress is misleading, as Kuwait's educational and commercial establishments are full of Egyptians, Iraqis, Syrians and the like, and they are well represented in the crowd.

Wednesday 6 January 1982, Kuwait

Another good sleep, broken only by a massive thunderstorm at about 7a.m. It cleared the air and today is fine and warm. Had an omelette and croissants at the Coffee Shop at 11.30, then we are taken at twelve to the Embassy Club at the invitation of the amiable double act Iraqi Nuri Alvarez and Pakistani Sarwah (known in Arabic as Siru) whom we met here last time. Mr Siru promises to get me some cassettes of Arabic music, about which I learnt very little last time. I ask him especially for examples of Kuwaiti music, which has an African percussive element that brings it closer to jazz than most of the familiar minor-key wailing.

After the show, we are invited to a party at the home of Mr Twiggers, the administrator of the theatre. He remembers me telling him at a reception last time we were here that we hadn't met very many Kuwaitis, so he has assembled a roomful of them, including a band – four or five drums of assorted sizes and a lute (the penny has finally dropped on this trip that the word 'lute' derives directly from the Arab name for the instrument, '*el oud*'). When the delicious and sumptuous buffet is disposed of, there is a full-blown musical soirée. In accordance with Arab custom the Kuwaiti attendance is all male – that's the reason, someone explains, why Bedouin dancing is so extraordinarily camp, with effeminate hip-swaying and eye-rolling. Since women take no part in music or dancing, Bedouin male dancing must imitate the female role. To my horror, I am singled out by a group of Kuwaitis to receive a lesson in the subject. Someone borrows a spare dishdasher, which is draped over me and surmounted by the head-dress assembly. Bursting out of this gear, which is five sizes too small, I am led on to the 'dance floor' by a plump and shining young man called Khaled and encouraged to shake a hip. They have a technique of finger-snapping which contributes occasional pistol-cracks to the percussive music – he tries to teach me, but it nearly breaks my fingers and achieves no more than a damp 'flip'. Anyone from home witnessing the scene might fairly have taken it as an exercise in humiliation, the baiting of a village idiot. But it's quite clearly a friendly and complimentary gesture, so I fling myself in the routine with abandon. But one can take the ambassador bit too far.

At the end of the night it's a dishevelled band that returns to the hotel. Roy Williams says that, passing the kitchen door to pick up his jacket, he hears our hostess saying, 'Frankly, I think they're all a lot of poofs.' We don't know if she is referring to the hip-swaying Kuwaiti dancers or us.

Thursday** 7 **January** 1982, **Kuwait

Tonight we have another 'lecture' at the Mousetrap Theatre, on the lines of the one arranged by John Munby last time. This time, we take the instruments in the morning, do a quick sound-check (no problem as there is only one microphone), and then are collected by the redoubtable Juanita Monteiro for lunch at her new house. When she rang through with the invitation, she asked if we would bring our instruments to surprise her sick mother with a serenade outside her bedroom door. I can think of no quicker way to propel the poor lady into whatever next world she may be called, and am therefore relieved to be able to say that, alas, the instruments are all under lock and key at the Mousetrap. Once again J. provides a superb Indian meal in pleasant company, her brother Joe calling in while we are eating.

This evening, preparing to go on at the Mousetrap, we have a surprise visit from Edward Heath, who is in Kuwait for talks associated with the Brandt Commission. The British Council has sent him an invitation as a matter of courtesy and he turns up, to the obvious concern of his tour organizers, who have to get him to a dinner later on. He walks straight into the band-room to say 'Hello'. I was introduced to him at a *Punch* lunch when he was Prime Minister, but we exchanged few words and this visit can only have arisen from a thoughtful desire on his part to encourage the British Council's activities – and some fellow-musicians in the process. His politics are not mine, and many times I have ground my teeth to dust listening to his Prime Ministerial speeches. But contrary to the media image of an embittered Achilles sulking in his tent, he seems to present nowadays a far jollier, less frosty front, with a nice line in self-deprecatory humour. He tells us how he was serenaded over breakfast this morning by a Filipino band 'in pyjamas – I like breakfast to myself, don't you? I always hate working breakfasts with colleagues – not that they happen very often these days.' He says he'll have to leave the concert after fifteen minutes or so 'to go to this bloody dinner', but in the event hangs on for about half an hour, to the manifest consternation of his minders. Afterwards, even Bruce Turner the Stalinist was heard to say, 'Nice chap, nice chap.'

I ad-lib the whole lecture as before, and it goes well. Afterwards, there's a reception at the home of British Council chief Tom White and his French wife, Gabrielle. Sit-down meal for a change – I am next to Mr Rajabi, the Arab husband of the English lady who runs the Mousetrap Theatre – he founded the English-Speaking School. Very informative, and with a sharp 'English' sense of humour. While we're talking about Kuwaiti music, jazz etc. I find myself thinking what a large part clothing plays in our perception of each other. If the B.B.C. motto were amended from 'Nation shall speak unto nation' to

'Trousers shall speak unto nightgown, belt shall speak unto braces…' it would give a better idea of the job to be done.

Here I am, finding myself surprised at holding an easy, relaxed and mutually-comprehending conversation with someone whom I had assumed would be different, awkward and alien, just because I am wearing collar, tie and jacket while he is in robe and head-dress. We might as well be wearing lapel-tags saying 'WILY ARAB' and 'BUTTONED-UP ENGLISHMAN'….

Friday 8 January 1982, Bahrain

Arriving in Bahrain, we are met by the British Council representative, a middle-aged, military-looking gent (with the sprawling name of Henry Bryce Bending. We assume it's double-barrelled, but he says, 'Call me Bryce.' He is accompanied by his assistant, Roy Kannemeyer (from South Africa) and Arab driver-cum-Mr-Fixit, Abbas.

John Barnes and I decide to accept Roy Kannemeyer's invitation to a look around the island and hospitality at his place, on the grounds that if we crash into a deep sleep at five in the evening, it will throw our whole routine out for days.

Going back into the hotel, we meet Bryce Bending in the foyer, who has come to tell us that a T.V. session arranged for this afternoon has had to be postponed until tomorrow because the studio isn't ready. I spend the afternoon stretched out like a gorged python on the bed, getting up in time to go with the others to a recommended emporium called the Nip In Liquor Store to further thwart the mini-bar. Alcoholic sales are allowed in Bahrain, but only in these special stores which are discreetly located away from the centre of town.

We play tonight in the hotel ballroom, to a largely expatriate audience. The atmosphere is quiet at first – the room is one of those huge, ocean-liner affairs, and I have a feeling that the sound isn't reaching every corner. A large bespectacled Englishman at a table on our right decides to take it upon himself to jolly things up, and starts some benign heckling in a booming voice. In my announcements I sometimes refer to the band sardonically as 'The Orchestra', which prompts him to bellow at one point, 'Mr Lyttelton, can you tell us exactly when a band becomes an orchestra?' It's clear as we go on that he is one of the Nip In Store's most loyal customers. Hearing me refer to the 'front line of the band', he comes across, commandeers a microphone and makes a speech about farting and the superior noise emanating from 'the back end of the band'. I thank him for raising the cultural tone and leave it to his manifestly embarrassed wife and friends to shut him up, which they do successfully.

The postponed T.V. show is on this afternoon. Bryce and Abbas pick us up to take us to the studio. The studio is surrounded by heavy security, a sequel to the attempted coup by fundamentalists that was discovered and thwarted a few months ago. The locals refer to it as the Problem, in the way the Irish talk about the Troubles.

Inside we meet a lady, introduced as Miss Ziyani, who is said to be a famous T.V. director in Bahrain. In leather trousers and with long black hair, she looks decidedly slinky. She was trained in the United States and has a strong American accent to show for it. Why is it that an American accent superimposed on broken English spells bullshit? We have arrived at 2.45p.m. to find the studio empty. It is only just finished, hence the postponement from yesterday. There is an expensive-looking composite floor as smooth as untrodden snow, and it is Mike Paxton who points out that if he drives the spurs of his drum kit into it, it will probably do thousands of pounds of damage. Someone is sent to find a piece of rug or matting on which the kit can be set up. Mick Pyne goes to the piano to try it out and finds it locked. Everyone in sight is asked who has the key, and it turns out to be someone who is off for the afternoon. Meanwhile Arab studio hands arrive with a huge Persian carpet the size of a squash court for the drums. They unroll it, and Mike prepares to set up his drums.

An hour goes by before the search party returns with the piano key. 'I guess we have to hurry,' says Miss Ziyani, heedless of the fact that there are still no microphones set up. At 4 o'clock, the sound men return, with what appear to be newly-purchased microphones in boxes marked Amateur Sound Kit. We have to be finished by 4.45 at the latest, so once the amateur kit is assembled, we reel off six numbers straight to camera without rehearsal or sound-check. Sian, who watches it all on the control-room monitors, reports that every time a camera alights out of focus on the wrong musician or has its view blocked by another camera in transit, Miss Ziyani says 'Whoops!'.

Monday 11 January 1982, Doha

We are met at Doha Airport by Clive Bruton from the British Council, who hands out itineraries for the thirty-six-hour stay. We shall be quite busy here – there's an official reception chez Clive and Carol Bruton tonight, and tomorrow morning, a one-hour concert for school children prior to the full evening concert.

Tuesday 12 January 1983, Doha

Mindful of the long day ahead, I left the party at midnight, the rest of the band staying on. Apparently things warmed up considerably, judging by the balloon-like swelling round John Barnes' ankle this morning. You can always tell when J.B. is getting into the spirit of things. Last night, when these were expended, he went on to demonstrate to the official from the Department of Culture the technique of Will Gaines, the black American tap-dancing wizard who was discovered some time ago working as a housepainter in Rotherham, England. Will has the fastest feet in the Western Hemisphere. J.B. has not, and they got entangled and brought him down, badly twisting his ankle in the process.

An assortment of cars arrive at the Ramada Hotel at 9.30 to take us to the children's concert this morning. I have, lodged in my memory, a routine for talking about jazz to children put together some years ago for a couple of schools lectures. While we're setting up and having a cup of tea, I collect together sundry props from the Theatre kitchen – a large tin teapot, some empty tins and a Coca Cola bottle. When we're ready, about 400 children of all nationalities and colours troop in. We start with a short number, then I go through all the instruments, explaining how we get sounds out of them. When it comes to the brass instruments I get them all making the buzzing noises into imaginary mouthpieces. Four hundred children blowing raspberries sounds quite impressive. With the teapot I show how a tune can be got out of any metal object that involves tubing, and the tins and bottles demonstrate the idiosyncratic sounds that jazz players produce. Then we go on to build a conventional 'Dixieland' ensemble on the theme of 'Jingle Bells', working up to a jam session in which they all join in. Finally, a resumé of jazz origins leads to a march around the stage to 'High Society'. In the middle of this, a storm of whoops and giggles breaks out. I have forgotten about John's bad ankle, and the sight of him hobbling along painfully in the rear, baritone sax aloft, breaks the place up. John, the kindest and most congenial of men, hasn't a drop of false dignity in him, and he comes off, beard jutting with glee at the sensation he has caused. Given half a chance, he would have laid a monologue on them.

The concert in the evening is a great success. As a matter of courtesy I start with the '*marhaba…masa' al-kher…ahlan wa sahlan*' routine that I learnt on the last trip, and an uncouth British voice shouts, 'Talk bloody English!' Talking to Clive Bruton afterwards, he says that this sort of resistance by British expatriates to any movement towards the Arabs and Arab culture is the British Council's biggest problem.

Wednesday 13 January 1982, Abu Dhabi

These starts get earlier and earlier. Up at 5.30 this morning – the flight's not till 8.15 but we have to be prepared for the lengthy negotiations to get the baggage on.

There's a reception at Clive Mogford's tonight, but we're not sure how substantial the food will be, so I have a precautionary snack in the Coffee Shop at six. At 7.30 a car collects us to take us to Clive's place.

There are lots of V.I.P.s at the party, including the British Ambassador. I am invited by the Pakistani Regional Manager of the Khaleed *Times* for lunch on Friday, an invitation which is extended recklessly to the whole band before the party's over. The purpose appears to be for us to lend a professional ear to his twelve-year-old son playing the organ. He is, we are given to understand, a prodigy.

One never knows how firm these party-time invitations are, but the R.M. is very insistent, giving me his card which reveals that his name is Arshad Sami Khan. No far-fetched mnemonic needed here – from now on he will be Sammy Cahn.

Thursday 14 January 1982, Abu Dhabi

Tonight is the hotel's informal 'do', with the audience at tables, a buffet supper halfway through, and dancing if they want to. Our band-room is a small, curtained-off cubby-hole behind the stage, at the opposite end of the ballroom from the one exit. At the finish, there is such a prolonged uproar of appreciation that the only way we can get out and up to bed is to strike up 'When the Saints Go Marching In', march through the cheering crowds, out of the far door and straight into the lift.

Friday 15 January 1982, Abu Dhabi

The Sheraton staff are all smiles this morning after the scenes last night, especially as it was their function. We are now people of some importance. As befits V.I.P.s, we spend the day lounging arrogantly by the pool.

At 5p.m. I'm picked up by Sammy Cahn and taken to his house. Over tea and sweetmeats, I listen to his plump twelve-year-old son play the organ. Fortunately for me, the boy is extremely good – his repertoire is cocktail-bar music with no scope for originality but his harmonies and 'time' are perfect. There is talk of him going to America and, since he already has an American accent and a self-confident air, I am able to say with sincerity that he should do well there. If Sammy Cahn junior becomes famous, I shall claim that I discovered him.

Monday 18 January 1982, Jeddah

Leave Jebel Ali for Dubai Airport at 6.30a.m. to fly to Jeddah. A circuitous route this time, changing planes at Bahrain and stopping off at Dahran in Saudi Arabia to queue into, and then out of, immigration before re-embarking. On the last lap, berobed male Arab passengers keep disappearing into the toilets, to emerge later clad in gleaming white high-quality towelling, sans head-dress. These, it transpires, are pilgrims en route to Mecca and the posh towelling represents the humble sackcloth of tradition. Arriving at Jeddah at 12.45 local time, at the immigration desk, Michael from the British Consulate warns us not to say that we are here to play music, but simply to put 'Guests of the British Ambassador' as the purpose of our visit. They seem quite happy to accept that guests of the Ambassador customarily arrive with musical instruments, including a double bass and complete set of drums.

Tuesday 19 January 1982, Jeddah

The concert tonight is in a big gymnasium with acoustics that swallow up most of my announcements. At one point I am surrounded by a group of young people all eager to discover the rules of 'Mornington Crescent'. This enigmatic party game from the B.B.C. radio quiz *I'm Sorry, I Haven't a Clue*, of which I am the hapless chairman, has exercised the minds of listeners over the eight years or so since we first started the show. On its first appearance, I introduced it as 'the children's' game which all of us have played in our time'. Thenceforward, we have not thought it necessary to explain the rules on which the team-members Tim Brooke-Taylor, Willie Rushton, Barry Cryer and Graeme Garden base their carefully considered moves from one London Tube Station or street location to another towards the winning destination, Mornington Crescent. Consequently, we have all of us received a steady stream of letters saying, in effect, 'You may have played "Mornington Crescent" in your childhood, but some of us haven't...' and demanding an explanation. We think it's more fun to let people work it out for themselves, and it's gratifying to know that, in many households, maps of the London streets and Underground system are unfolded and laid out whenever the programme comes on the air. It's giving away no secrets, I believe, to say that we once did a spoof version – a Pro-Celebrity game in which I pretended to introduce one of the distinguished knights of the British theatre. As a non-existent figure made his way to the stage, our well-briefed studio audience gave 'him' a rapturous welcome. Addressing an empty chair deferentially as 'sir', I explained that he would take his turn after Willie Rushton, fifth in the order of play. When it came to Willie's turn, he cried 'Mornington Crescent!' triumphantly, bringing the game to an end. With profuse apologies I sent our 'guest' back to his seat, omitting throughout to give the listening audience his name. A few weeks later, when the show was on the air, I received a letter at the B.B.C. which, in apoplectic terms, accused me, the producer and the B.B.C. of the grossest discourtesy to one of our most distinguished actors. The producer had one or two similar complaints, and I've no doubt some went straight to the Director General. It was intriguing to discover that all the writers identified the 'guest', who naturally made no utterance during the programme but seemingly accepted his humiliation with the greatest dignity, as Sir Alec Guinness!

Wednesday 20 January 1982, Jeddah

Visit to the souk in the morning – buy yet another Bedouin head-dress – a red-and-white check this time, Saudi style.

Yesterday, Chris and Primrose Anander offered to take the bird-watching enthusiasts among us out to look at flamingo and black kites. The sewage outlet and the rubbish tip didn't sound quite so enticing as, say, Minsmere or the Ouse Washes back home, and they did ask rather anxiously if we are sensitive to smells. We accepted without reservation, and they pick us up after lunch. The first port of call is a bit strong, a huge, malodorous swamp steaming slightly under the afternoon sun, but offering in compensation a fine view of scores of pale-pink, Arabian-type flamingo, as well as more familiar sanderling, redshank, curlew, sand-piper and little plover in scurrying abundance. From the sewage outlet we drive further out to the rubbish tip – a spectacular journey, since the road eventually peters out into a sand-track, while remaining ostensibly a big dual carriageway. Apart from us, the traffic consists exclusively of lorries and juggernauts, most of which pound in both directions along the comparatively smooth central reservation, swerving like huge dodgem cars to avoid collision. This road out to the tip is lined by a veritable shanty-city of dumped containers, some of which have been adapted, with windows and doors cut out, for some kind of nomadic human occupation.

But the sights en route are nothing compared to the first view of the tip itself. I am prepared for a sort of glorified municipal dump, the usual conglomeration of household refuse, soggy cardboard boxes, indestructible plastic objects and broken bottles. What confronts us on arrival at the tip is a vast and picturesque lagoon, a vista of lakes, beaches and islands in handsome monochrome under the late afternoon sun. It's only when we get out and walk about, binoculars at the ready, that we find out that the beaches consist of a shingle of rusty soft-drink cans – millions and millions of them – and the islands are made up of the decomposing bodies of old cars and trucks. The place is alive with birds, not all easy to spot among the debris. Black kites are commonplace, and we are more excited spotting waders, varieties of heron, and black-winged stilts trailing their fragile legs behind them in flight like streamers. At one point, focusing on a pair of heron on a distant 'island', I spot a movement in a car wreck in the middle distance and discover a bird – shaped like a bittern but more probably a squacco heron – preening itself on the steering wheel. We could have stayed there for hours, but after a while a persistent itching around the ankles and moving up the trouser legs suggests that the lagoon's insect life is as interested in us as we are in the birds, and we beat a reluctant retreat. The journey back along the desert road is even hairier than the outward journey. Though there are two carriageways, the general rule seems to be that if the southbound road proves too deeply pot-holed, it's OK to veer across to the northbound lane and carry on against the tide. In a small saloon car, it must be like finding oneself in the path of stampeding elephants.

Thursday 21 January 1982, Sana'a

At the airport we check in the baggage, then sit down for buns and coffee in the small cafeteria.

We're met at Sana'a's airport by Ken Rasdall. We have told him in advance that we have a new drummer this time. When introduced to Sian in her travelling 'uniform' of open-neck shirt and jeans, he says,

'And this is the new man, eh?' Sian is the antithesis of 'butch', but the combination of jeans, height and shortish curly hair sometimes confuses. I don't know which makes her crosser – being addressed as 'Monsieur' or 'Sair' by hotel porters or persistently as 'Sean' ('Shawn') by male British Council colleagues. (She is 'Sharn'.) Incidentally, Arab porters really do say 'sair' for 'sir', as in old *Punch* cartoons.

One of the reception committee, a big, lumbering man called Bob, is delegated to drive two or three of us to the hotel in a rattling Land Rover. Just outside the airport he decides to take a short cut along a bit of one-way road. Round a bend he meets a shrieking convoy of police motor cycles escorting a black Mercedes. They part to avoid him but drive on. 'Whoops,' he says, 'that was the President.'

Sana'a is 9,000 feet above sea-level and the air is rarified. When we check in at the newly-built Sheraton Hotel, they warn us to take the lift at all times – walking upstairs can leave you gasping for oxygen. After an hour's rest go on to Ken Rasdall's house, as guests at his birthday party. He and his wife Anne also live in a traditional Yemeni house with barely-furnished, cell-like rooms which would seem chilly and uninviting but for the consistently warm climate that rules out the need for floor, wall and window coverings. The Rasdalls' friends swarm like gannets round a sensational assortment of curries, salads and sweets. I remember Ken's curries from our '79 Kuwait trip, but here he surpasses himself. A lady called Rosa dispenses mulled claret of her own making using, so far as I can tell, the concoction of red wine, brandy, Cusenier, water, sugar, cinnamon and cloves which I splosh together for Christmas parties at home. I have always thought it a mild brew, but combined with the rarified air it has obviously acquired lethal powers, knocking out Mick Pyne, Theresa Clark and finally – and dramatically – Rosa herself, who actually hits the floor. A wonderful evening.

Friday 22 January 1982, Sana'a

Am taken sightseeing in the morning by an American couple, John and Susan Giusti, with their two children. The expatriate community here is far smaller than that in the oil countries and seems to be limited to diplomats, cultural representatives and teachers. We go to the souk and are immediately immersed in Arabia – the real thing, as opposed to 'the Gulf' or 'the Middle East'. I buy a thick bracelet bearing the authentic mark of a Jewish silver-smith and enough knobs, blobs and excrescences on it to fell an assailant with one blow. For myself, there are more articles of clothing to be bought for my Arab wardrobe – a terracotta square for the turban and a rather natty grey worsted skirt or *footah*.

There's such a cheerful, anything-goes atmosphere in the souk that I am emboldened to put on the skirt and turban there and then. The store-holder volunteers to knot the turban for me in an authentic style, and seems unperturbed when I put the skirt on over my trousers. John Giusti tells me that there are several regional variations in the way the turban is tied – a fact that's confirmed when I walk off down the street and am confronted almost at once by a portly Yemenite who stops in front of me with arms outstretched in greeting and bellows the name of his village several times, pointing at my head-dress. All along the way my eccentric attire inspires smiles and salutations, a change from the Gulf atmosphere in which the wearing of Arab gear by Europeans invites often justified suspicion.

The concert tonight in the Sheraton Hotel has a small and select audience of about 150, including a party of twenty or so Yemeni students from the English school. It's true what they said about the air up here. From the start it's clear that we're going to have to adjust our breathing. A lungful lasts a fraction of the normal time, and when we come to the first slow number, with a lot of sustained notes, phrases can be heard petering out all over the shop. It's a good, lively concert, and afterwards we meet the audience in an adjacent bar. One of the young Yemeni students asks me reverentially how old I am. When I answer, 'Sixty,' he looks duly awestruck and then says, 'Ah, well…you have the experience to make up for it.'

Have prevailed upon a hirsute teacher called Dave to take myself and John Barnes to the souk at 9.30 this morning. I deeply suspect that J.B. is about to pull a stroke in our perennial battle of the dishdashers. He has had a look in his eye ever since Carl Robert gave me the grey and embroidered Sunday-best affair in Kuwait. Since then he's been determined to outdo me with something flashier. At the souk we dash off in different directions in search of our respective quarry. At the appointed meeting place J.B. turns up, jutting gleefully, with a loose parcel under his arm. As I suspected, he has trumped my Kuwait acquisition with a silky robe in black-and-white stripes.

We rush back to the Sheraton just in time to perform a midday concert for schoolchildren. There are 200 of them of all ages and nationalities with one language – twangy American – in common. Once again it's a lot of fun, and they blow some fine raspberries during the brass instrument demonstration.

At the concert tonight, Peter Clark says it would be a good idea if I were to wear my Yemeni outfit, dagger and all, on stage. He says it will go down well, especially with the indigenous population. John Barnes has a head-dress, so after a bit of 'If you will, I will', we agree to dress up for the second half. Peter's Yemenite assistant ties the turbans for us authentically, and I don the skirt and dagger. J.B. goes on first to test the water and receives an acclaim just short of a standing ovation, so I emerge with confidence. Pavlova stepping on stage for her farewell performance could hardly have been more rapturously received. As I bow low in acknowledgement, the dagger digs deep into my crutch, bringing me effectively down to earth. The audience remains euphoric to the end, but I don't think I shall adopt it as a band uniform. The skirt is very comfortable and loose, but with bare legs and sandals below I am very conscious of my size thirteen feet. Unshrouded by sagging trouser hem they feel like skis. Afterwards, going into the men's loo still in my rig-out, I am ecstatically embraced and kissed by a gnarled Yemenite with decimated teeth and five days' growth of beard. When I relate this in the band-room, Peter Clark says enigmatically, 'Hmm – that can be interpreted in several ways.' I hurriedly change back into my trousers.

Sunday 24 January 1982, Cairo

Another early start. Call at 6 a.m. for a pick up at 7 o'clock. The rather ethereal sense of fantasy that our Sana'a sojourn has engendered is capped by my hotel bill, made out by the Filipino cashier and enchantingly headed 'Mr Little Son'.

We're met at Cairo Airport by British Council representative Peter Thompson, aquiline and bearded. 'A typical trad jazz face,' someone remarks, to discover minutes later that he used to play piano in the Leeds University Jazz Band. He tells me that he has a tape somewhere of the band performing with its resident singer, Barry Cryer. I must have a copy – it will enhance my authority as chairman of *I'm Sorry, I Haven't a Clue* to have such a skeleton from Barry's past in hand.

Cairo at first sight threatens to be a nightmare. Cairo seems shrouded in a kind of seedy and grasping cynicism. Even the international banks in the airport tout for business, their clerks calling and beckoning from the exchange booths like the ladies in Hamburg's Herbertstrasse. 'Hold on to your wallets and don't take your eye off the baggage for a moment,' is Peter Thompson's advice as we wait for our transport.

We've checked in at Shepheard's Hotel. The hotel staff are all dressed for a provincial production of Aladdin, and they hover like vultures. 'Tips with everything' is clearly the motto here.

Halfway through the first day in Cairo my diary suddenly peters out, partly because of an itinerary over the following two days that barely gave us time to eat and sleep, let alone scribble a journal, but also perhaps due to my feeling that the best of this particular tour was over. I recall, in the evening of the first day, going for a casual walk through the city with some of the others and being assailed on all sides by shopkeepers importuning for business. One of them actually seized Mick Pyne's arm and hauled him into a shop to sample perfume. The routine is always the same: 'You American?…German?…Engleesh? Ah, I am in England two weeks ago…Piccadilly Circus…Lycester Square…Hyde Park…you see, I know them, eh?' Had we confessed to being American or German, the guide-book list of locations would have been just as pat. After a few blocks our nerves began to fray – it had been a long day – and one or two worthy and enterprising traders were told, in vain, to piss off!

On Monday 25 January we left early for Alexandria, where the first concert took place. There are two routes, one across the desert and the other longer one along the Nile. We decided to go for the quicker route, which would take us past the Sphinx and the Pyramids at Giza for a quick glimpse, but as we approached it we became bogged down in an impenetrable traffic jam, through which the message came that the road was closed. So we trundled for something like five hours through one village after another, stopping for food in a sort of amusement park. En route we passed houses with camel and donkey fodder stacked on the flat roofs, combining the functions of hay-stack and insulation. I have no recollection of the concert so it must have been uneventful.

Next day we returned to Cairo by the desert road. Writers sometimes refer to great monuments 'looking down' on the tiny, temporal beings below, but it's worse than that. They don't look at you at all, but stare out over your head like venerable lions at the zoo, leaving you feeling totally irrelevant and rather silly.

The Sphinx may well have imparted the same feeling, but we only passed it on the road. We didn't really give it a chance to impress, because by this time we were in a hurry to get into Cairo and make use of the late afternoon for hurried sightseeing. The choice available in the time was either a quick visit to the Museum or a dash to the bazaar. Predictably, I suppose, John Barnes and I chose the latter, being escorted by a man from the British Embassy who knew the best shops to visit. It was a sight to see – a maze of little streets and alleys lined by one Aladdin's cave after another of more exotic, sophisticated and expensive treasures than in any of the Gulf souks. A sort of labyrinthine Bond Street in which we bought some silver bits and pieces to take home, and some more robes. They stopped being dishdashers when we crossed from the Gulf to the Red Sea, becoming '*thobes*' in Saudi Arabia and '*jellabas*' here. It'll be all one when we get home. After the '79 tour I sent one of them to the laundry in Barnet, writing 'dishdasher' on the list. It came back with the word crossed out and 'night-dress' substituted.

At one point, back in the hotel, I was staring out of my bedroom window over the Nile, thinking that I was beginning to enjoy Cairo now that it was almost time to go home, when I turned to see a sort of Grand Vizier standing in the room. His turban and robes were a

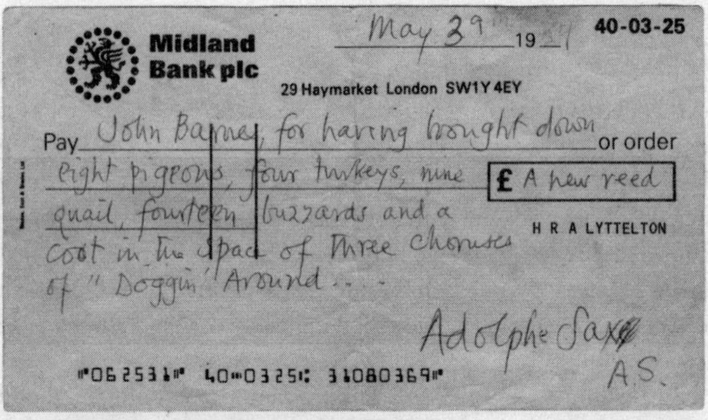

Midland Bank plc

May 29th 19

40-03-25

29 Haymarket London SW1Y 4EY

Pay John Barnes, for having brought down eight pigeons, four turkeys, nine quail, fourteen buzzards and a coot in the space of three choruses of "Doggin' Around... or order

£ A new reed

H R A LYTTELTON

Adolphe Saxe

A.S.

062531 40 0325 31080369

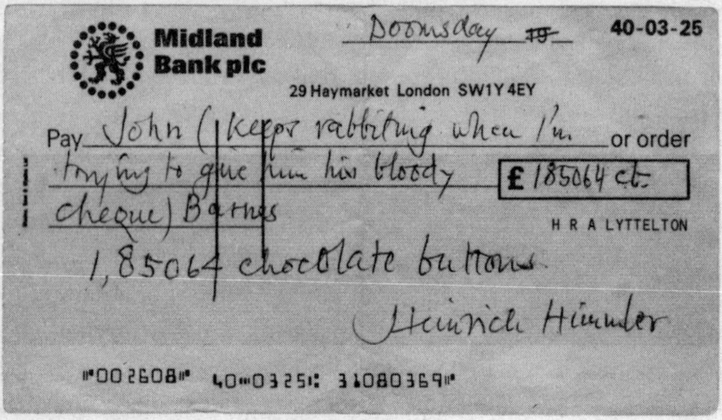

Midland Bank plc

Doomsday 19

40-03-25

29 Haymarket London SW1Y 4EY

Pay John (keeps rabbiting when I'm trying to give him his bloody cheque) Barnes or order

£ 185064 ct.

H R A LYTTELTON

1,85064 chocolate buttons

Heinrich Himmler

002608 40 0325 31080369

More hilarious payment cheques to band member, John Barnes. Pigeons refers to squeaks on the baritone sax that sounds like birds in pain.

rich damson colour and I can't be sure, but I think his shoes curled up at the toe. With long drooping nose and wisp of grey beard he might have looked impressive, but it was the wheedling look that gave away his purpose. 'You are leaving tomorrow, sair,' he said. I nodded. 'I shall not be here when you go.' 'Oh,' I said, 'I'm sorry about that,' and turned back to the Nile. He was obviously some kind of head porter or commissionaire, but having for two days tipped somebody whenever I so much as walked down the corridor, I didn't see why I should now reward a total stranger. After what seemed like five minutes I turned back into the room, to find him still there, a silent and immobile presence. I am normally a push-over for buying a quiet life with largesse, but this time irritation at the sheer blatancy of the demand took precedence. I busied myself pointedly with sorting postcards and folding clothes while he continued to stand there. At long last he gave a theatrical shrug and stalked off with that measured and wary gait with which cats extricate themselves from a confrontation. I half expected him to point at me from the door with forked lightning darting from his fingertips to turn me into a toad, but he went ambling off leaving me feeling pleased with – and surprised at – myself.

By the time we've done a good concert and enjoyed another hospitable reception afterwards, I am convinced that I could grow to love Cairo.

Monday 8 March 1982, Beirut

Up at 5.45a.m. to get to Heathrow for the 9.35 flight to Beirut.

All goes smoothly, and we have an uneventful flight to Beirut where, as always, there's a British Council man to welcome us. This time it's a small gingery Scotsman with a pepper-and-salt beard who introduces himself as Farquar Grant. We start addressing him as 'Fark-war' but he corrects us, saying that the correct Scottish pronunciation is 'Farker'. Not the sort of name you can comfortably shout across a crowded room. (It reminds me of a colleague in the wartime army whose name was – and I hope still is – Johnny Bastard. The Grenadier Guardsmen, whose barrack-room conversation was strung together by four-letter words, came over coy when called upon to address him, altering the name to 'Mr B'stard' with heavy emphasis on the second syllable. He would have none of it, shouting 'Bastard, Bastard!' to their intense embarrassment.)

We are staying at the Mayflower Hotel, not far from the American University in West Beirut. It looks homely and familiar, wouldn't be out of place in Guildford High Street – the bar even has a pub sign, 'The Duke of Wellington', over its street entrance. As soon as we check in, we are invited by the manager to go straight into the bar for a welcoming drink on the house. Sitting there, I ask Farquar just what the political situation is at the moment. He draws sharply on the ubiquitous fag and indicates with a sidelong look that it's not the sort of thing you discuss in a crowded bar. But he does inform us that we'll probably hear plenty of gunfire during the night, but not to worry. Bullet holes in the big mirror behind the Duke of Wellington's counter suggest that the gunfire may not be all that distant.

Later in the evening, we all walk for ten minutes down to a restaurant called El Pacha. It's just the sort of place in which musicians feel at home – a glorified students' 'caff' buzzing with life where one can shout and laugh and swap noisy reminiscences without inhibition. Early bed and a good sleep, despite some desultory gunfire in the distance.

Tuesday 9 March 1982

After breakfast in the basement restaurant (nobody but us there), we are taken down to the American University to set up for tonight's concert. An eager young Lebanese called John is in charge of the P.A.. Initially, he has the sound jacked up so high that our opening must have been heard in the foothills of the Shouf mountains forty miles away. I don't want to upset him – as a Lebanese he has enough problems. So with infinite patience I get the volume gradually reduced until we have all we need in the small hall. It's a familiar problem. Ever since the invention of the electric guitar, the electrical engineers who used just to provide microphones and speakers have acquired delusions of grandeur. They call themselves 'sound mixers', with the implication that musicians and bands are simply there to provide the raw materials for their creative talents. They sit behind the huge consoles at the back of the auditorium, hairy, skinny young men wearing jeans like tourniquets and huge headphones, twiddling with knobs and fiddling with faders so that the soft bits are loud and the loud bits are deafening.

We're picked up at 5.15 for the concert – an early affair starting at 6 o'clock since people don't like to be wandering about late. A grey-haired, lugubrious but distinguished-looking gentleman called Mr Nebeel Ashcar is Beirut's leading jazz authority and critic – it's somehow reassuring to discover that even embattled Beirut resembles every city and town in the jazz-speaking world in having a doyen among jazz buffs! This evening, as soon as I arrive, he comes across to urge me to dispense with all amplification – he clearly has as little confidence in John the Marconi as I have. And how right he is! The students whom we saw arriving with additional sound equipment this morning have since erected it, and all our carefully acquired sound balance turns out to have been scrambled, apparently to suit the needs of a team from the University whom I have given permission to film the concert for their archives. The first half is an acoustic disaster. In the front row, Nebeel Ashcar's face elongates, registering alarm and despondency. At half-time I stage a temperament, diplomacy having failed. By striding rapidly up and down the band-room with arms flailing, I persuade John that I am serious in my wish to have all microphones and speakers swept away. As a result the second half is perfect, Nebeel perks up and the international – predominantly student – audience erupts, keeping us at it until around 8.45.

Wednesday 10 March 1982

At about 8.30 this morning, there's a knock on my door. I call out cheerily, 'Shan't be long!' assuming that it's a chambermaid after the bed linen, but a muffled voice says, 'I have a gift from the Manager'. I open the door to find a maid bearing flowers and a box of chocolate truffles. Nice – but what for? After breakfast, I go to the reception desk to thank the Manager, who tells me that the presentation was from Mr Mounir Sama'a, the owner of the hotel, who would like to see me in his office. There I find a small, dapper, middle-aged man who sits me down and makes an emotionally-charged and rather moving speech, thanking me for last night's concert and trying to express what it meant to him and his fellow-citizens. 'Like all our country I am in a hell of a mess psychologically,' he explains, 'and for two hours last night we are completely transported away from all our troubles.' He comes near to tears when he talks about Beirut's glittering past as the Paris of the Arab world. 'You wouldn't believe how beautiful our city was, and now look at it – all broken.' As a further practical gesture of appreciation, he rings through to reception and has my room changed, moving me to what turns out to be a sort of bridal suite in front of the hotel, away from the romping schoolchildren and that damn bird. And he invites all the band to have champagne with him later in the day. I feel great sadness for him and his compatriots, without being any the wiser as to the reasons why they are tearing each other and their prized city to bits. It's very similar to the surface situation in Northern Ireland, where everyone you speak to appears to be a neutral victim of the troubles and you get no hint of the allegiances that must lurk underneath.

Tonight's concert, again at the American University, is a success from start to finish, with the amplifiers and their problems banished.

Thursday 11 March 1982, Brummana

We have a concert tonight at Brummana, a village up in the mountains about twelve miles from Beirut.

There's a hairy moment en route. We're driving along a cliff road looking straight out over the sea, with Roy Williams, Dave Green and Mike Paxton in the leading cab when, suddenly, those of us following see a soldier leap out into the road and take aim at their rear window with an automatic rifle. Our driver hoots frantically and they pull up, to be surrounded by shouting soldiers. We stop in front to investigate. What has happened is that, in answer to a query about his camera by Mike Paxton, Roy has put it to his eye to demonstrate just as the cab drove past an army post. He was simply pointing the camera out to sea without any thought of taking a picture, but the soldiers thought otherwise. At first they make as if to confiscate the whole camera, but after intercession by the two cab drivers – no doubt on the lines that we are mad but harmless Englishmen – they content themselves with ripping out the film. Unfortunately, it was near the end of the reel and contained all his shots from January's tour as well, but Roy is nothing if not philosophical, especially in the knowledge that, not two minutes earlier, a wild-eyed sentry has been taking careful aim at the back of his head.

We all hide our cameras under the seats for the rest of the trip, especially as we drive down into the heavily-devastated area on the boundary of West and East Beirut. Here we come into contact with recent history as seen on the T.V. newsreels at home. There are the gutted ruins of the Holiday Inn Hotel in which British tourists and newsmen were holed up for days in the first outbreak of civil war in '76.

At Brummana, we go straight to the Tivoli Cinema where we are to play tonight. By Odeon standards it's modest – no need for microphones in the smallish rectangular basement. While we're setting up and hanging about down there, we're introduced to an imposing man of Orson Wellesian girth with the face of an amiable toad – he's Mr Albert Rizk, the owner of the cinema and of a restaurant upstairs, to which he invites us all to a meal as soon as we're ready. Here, in a bright, vine-festooned dining-room with a view across to the mountains, we have a chance to take in the much-vaunted beauty of Lebanon. With snow-capped mountains in the distance, cattle grazing on the nearby slopes and firs, cypresses and stone pines softening the rocky outlines, the panorama combines the best of Switzerland and Italy. We're in the wrong place for the famous cedars of Lebanon, but this ambiance will do for the time being.

At Albert's table we gorge ourselves with dish upon dish of varied dips and stuffed leaves and meatballs. This feast, apparently, was merely the hors d'oeuvres – a procession of even larger dishes arrives at the table, mostly based on lumps of deliciously-marinated lamb, to be followed by a cream and syrup sweet which sends Bruce Turner into ecstasies. As we walk stiffly out of the restaurant at the end, vowing that this will be our last meal for forty-eight hours, Albert calls after us: 'Of course, you will be my guests at dinner after the concert tonight!'

We're staying at the Al Bustan Hotel in Beit Mery, a little village further up the hills.

After a brief nap, it's back to the Tivoli for tonight's concert. Still groaning from the extended lunch, we're not exactly straining at the leash, but we find a wonderful atmosphere in the cinema, with a large, cheerfully noisy and predominantly young audience giving us a fine reception. We can't be sure whether it's for our music or simply for our presence there. In the interval and afterwards, we encounter again the question with which we've become familiar on trips to Northern Ireland. 'Why have you come here?' they ask in genuine wonderment that anyone from a relatively safe and orderly part of the world would be so reckless.

Friday 12 March 1982, Beit Mery

We don't have to leave for Beirut Airport until 3 o'clock this afternoon, thus enabling the hospitable and expansive Albert Rizk to issue another invitation for lunch at the Tivoli at 12.30. Forewarned, we skip breakfast and set off in various directions for a brisk morning walk. My route takes me, on a tip-off from someone at the hotel, to some magnificent Roman ruins about half a mile up the hill behind the hotel.

It's another enormous lunch with Albert, who is clearly a magnificent survivor. To hear him talk of the splendid food and wine available in Lebanon in general and his own restaurants in particular (he has another in the heart of Beirut), you would not even suspect that the country has just suffered a destructive civil war and is poised precariously on the brink of another. At one point he sweeps away all conflicting considerations with the ripe pronouncement, 'There's no doubt about it – food is one of the pillars of *joi de vivre* – it's true, why talk about it?' With which he scoops up a dollop of houmous with a shovel of pitta bread and engulfs it. Before the end of the meal he presents me with a cookery book – *A Gourmet's Delight: Selected Recipes from the Haute Cuisine of the Arab World* by Aida Karaoglan – which he says contains several recipes from the chefs of his Al-Barmaki Restaurant in Beirut. He inscribes it, 'To Humphrey. A Fine Gourmet.' His card reveals that he is President of the Federation of Tourist Syndicates of Lebanon. A great man – may he long survive. We drag ourselves away at 3p.m.

Once checked in, Sian, Martin and I gather for a brief conference about our itinerary. Apart from full-blown concerts in Aqaba and Amman, our contract here involves several days of filming for Jordanian television – some kind of documentary in which we shall be shown sightseeing and performing in sundry places of interest. The plan, when first mooted, was generally popular all round, since the venues comprised the Roman amphitheatre in Amman, the Roman remains at Jerash (around which we pranced at midnight on the '79 tour) and above all, the Lost City of Petra which we were all set on seeing this time. Now it transpires that the lady producer and instigator of the documentary has gone off to Germany for some pressing reasons of her own, and her bosses and Martin between them have taken the opportunity to scotch the whole idea, with which they were less than enchanted in the first place. In short, the filming is off, but we shall still be taken sightseeing. At school, the announcement of an unexpected two-and-a-half days' holiday would have been the cue for whooping and capering but, I think to Martin's surprise, we all feel rather deflated. After Lebanon we're all primed for action and I was looking forward to our being the first jazz band to shiver the crumbling pillars and pediments of Petra with an alfresco blast. There's something sloppy and untidy about the alacrity with which the whole thing's been abandoned that smacks of intrigue, about which I don't wish to know.

Sunday 14 March 1982, Amman

Set off in the minibus at 10.30 to drive to Jerash for today's sightseeing. Things are different now from our nocturnal visit two years ago when we wandered at will among the Roman remains. There is now a big car-park and reception building at the entrance, and we are stopped by a guide dressed like a policeman (or maybe vice versa) who tells the driver where to park and then marshals us all behind him for a guided tour. As if impelled to assert our British independence, we decide that after the journey we need a cup of tea first so we make him wait while we stream off to the rest-house.

Back in the hotel, totally whacked, I look forward to an early night after our communal meal in the restaurant. A message arrives to say Victoria, the errant T.V. producer, has arrived back and wants to see me, so I go and wait for her in the foyer. She is a raven-haired, sultry-looking lady made up, with black-rimmed eyes and vermilion lipstick, as if for a silent movie. It's a face made for smouldering – and when she asks how the filming has gone and I tell her that it hasn't, she smoulders prodigiously on the settee opposite me. She goes off to telephone her office and I have to sit up long past my planned early bed-time watching her pacing gloweringly up and down outside the phone kiosk as she waits for response from them. Eventually she comes across to ask, 'What time do you leave in the morning for Petra?' When we answer 'Seven o'clock' she says, 'I will be there with my camera crew – all is arranged.' Relieved to have turned aside a tempest, I totter off to bed.

Monday 15 March 1982, Amman

We assemble blearily at 7a.m. Neither Victoria nor her camera crew are to be seen so, not to be done out of our day at Petra, we wait just a short time and then drive off, assuming that they'll make their own way. At a high point in the road near our destination, we stop at a solitary shop by the roadside. A notice alongside it reads: WELCOME TO PETRA SOUVENIR SHOP. FROM THIS POINT YOU HAVE A GOOD VIEW OF PETRA MOUNTAINS. NICE PICTURES CAN BE BOUGHT HERE, ALSO FILM, SLIDES AND OTHER ACCESSORIES. We duly peer through our binoculars at the mountains, but Petra did not remain a lost city for centuries by showing off to the outside world, and we see little other than a craggy outline, so we press on impatiently.

The whole area is teeming with American coach parties. A young guide steps forward to take charge of us – no one can remember the names of the two guides recommended to us by Akhram in Jerash, so somewhat naïvely we ask him if he is acquinted with Akhram. The answer rebounds with the speed of a squash ball. 'Of course – he is my brother!' He introduces himself as Ahmed.

We hire him anyway and he goes off to buy our tickets for seven horses – Bruce's response to the offer of a mount is, 'Sooner have a tooth pulled,' so he will walk the three kilometres through the ravine to Petra itself. Our guide returns with the tickets, but says there is an hour's wait. When we vote to get our money back and walk, horses suddenly materialize – docile, broad-backed animals saddled with blankets and with an Arab groom in charge. I haven't been on a horse since 1931 and regarded it as dangerous and foolhardy then. Under pressure of my 15½ stone, my animal embarks on a 'go slow' strike, picking its way among the boulders with infuriating precision, its head drooping stubbornly. The Arab groom hands over to a small boy of ten who, armed with a switch from a tree, periodically galvanizes the animal into a craggy trot that seriously endangers my manhood. The others seem to have compliant beasts that keep going at a steady pace, although they seem to be doing no more than me, which is to sit inertly like a bag of sprouts with the reins dangling. We make an odd cavalcade, with Lord de Vere looking positively Wellingtonian in the saddle, Mike Paxton, with his long hair, Zapata moustache and coat-hanger shoulders looking like some ancient Scottish war-lord leading his men in a spot of marauding, and Grosser startling his horse every few yards with stentorian cries of 'wh-a-a-at?'.

The surroundings grow more and more fantastic as we descend. As we near the bottom, Greco-Roman porticoes carved around cave mouths high in the walls give a hint of wonders to come.

Every brochure and travel book on Jordan contains a photograph of the entrance to the city, the narrow gash of light at the end of the ravine through which a sunlit segment of bright terracotta façade can be glimpsed. Even so, the sight makes one gasp with surprise. Across an open space, carved into the side of a sheer red cliff, is the intricate frontage of a Roman temple, complete in every detail – pillars, Corinthian capitals, embossed pediment and all. As we dismount and stand gaping, a contralto American voice, planking like a banjo, exclaims, 'Is that IT?'

The American coach parties, after a quick lecture from their guides and a photosession in front of the Treasury, remount and depart noisily back up the ravine, so we are left with the place virtually to ourselves except for the Bedouin entrepreneurs who swarm around trying to sell us priceless relics that have been excavated that very morning. One of them chases me at a run all over the rock-face – we must have looked like two mountain goats at courtship – waving fistfuls of beads. There's no escape, so I end up haggling over a Bedouin necklace of orange beads that look like suppositories and feel like plastic to me. I beat him down from the equivalent of fifteen pounds to five, which I look on more as a modest ransom for my escape than an exorbitant price for junk.

The return journey is no more comfortable. The small boy leading my horse has sussed that I am not keen on trotting and takes malicious delight in wielding the switch and goading the animal on into jolting animation. As we walk up to the restaurant, there is a cry of 'Yoo hoo!' from the balcony. It is Victoria, announcing that she has arrived. 'Bad luck!' we cry in unison. 'You've missed it all!'

While we eat, Victoria sits next to me rolling her eyes in a series of theatrical expressions ranging from entreaty to despair. She is trying to get us to go back down the ravine and go through the sightseeing all over again, for the benefit of her tardy cameras. I am holding out well until she pulls a fast one, intercepting all the bills on the way to the table and paying them behind our backs. Who was it who defined 'putting an ob' on someone as one of the essential ploys in the art of life? An 'ob' is short for an obligation, and Victoria has effectively planted one on us while our guard was down. By way of compromise, I suggest that, since the Nabataeans forgot to carve a grand piano out of the rock and there is no easy way of getting bass and drums down the ravine, the front line – i.e. myself, Bruce Turner, John Barnes and Roy Williams – should pop down again for some quick filming. Immediately, the creative producer in her surfaces and she launches us into a scenario. First, it's up to the reception area to film us buying, and being draped in, Arab headgear. Meanwhile, she commandeers four horses to take us down the ravine again. By this time, the regular old plodders have been put out to graze. So it's a matter of bribing horsemen who are galloping up and down the ravine to hand over their mounts for an hour. The animal I get belongs to a boy in his early teens who was last seen careering over the rocks like the Lone Ranger in a chase scene. Up to this moment I always thought that smoke coming out of equine nostrils was no more than an artist's device to denote power and a fiery temperament.

Victoria is already in a state of incipient panic over the light, so there's no time to look around for something more docile. I am hoisted into a saddle that has been polished as slippery as ice and has stirrups so short that I immediately adopt the Lester Piggott position. Dimly-remembered instructions about gripping with the knees are useless, as my knees are up by my ears. As Victoria and her cameras lead off in their truck, she screeches at us to follow and to act as if we were taking in the wonders for the first time. My horse doesn't walk, it tap-dances, and the only way to stay on is to hang on grimly to the front of the saddle. When I start to act, I become aware that my face is locked in a rictus of sheer terror. And as we come to the first carved façades up in the cliff sides, Victoria's imagination runs riot. 'Sing something!' she cries. 'Sing some jazz as you look at the caves!' No activity has yet been devised that John Barnes won't fling himself into with enthusiasm, so he starts scat singing – 'Zazu zazu zey, ba ba rebop…' – his beard jutting skywards. We all follow suit, boop-a-dooping up at the cliffside like raving madmen. A trick rider in a circus would find it a difficult routine to squat on top of a tap-dancing horse while at the same time scat singing towards the heavens, and I am suddenly overtaken by a pulsating rush of anger to the head. Sliding to the ground, I stomp across to Victoria in her truck, shouting, 'This is bloody ridiculous – I'm not breaking my neck for you or your bloody film!' She is visibly impressed and I get a lift to the bottom while she continues to film the others. It's only now that I get a chance to take in the sight of Bruce Turner on horseback, a startling tribute to Victoria's powers of persuasion. As he comes close, I ask, 'How you doing, Bruce?' 'Some fun, I'd say,' he answers without conviction.

With light fading, we hurry on to the open theatre, where she has us perched like statues on four widely-spaced plinths, playing 'Big Butter and Egg Man' to the amazement of the Bedouin cave-squatters who appear like gannets on the overlooking cliffs.

It's late and quite dark when we check in at the Alkazar Hotel. We are somewhat relieved that Victoria is staying elsewhere, but before our meal is over, she arrives full of plans for the filming tomorrow. It seems that she has arranged for us to go in the morning to a local music shop where we shall be filmed enjoying a jam session with some local musicians. We shall then go to the beach for some fanciful shots which will include Roy Williams playing the trombone up to his neck in the briny. At this point, supported by Martin Savage, with whom we have restored contact, I put my foot down. With a concert in the evening we are not going to spend all day doing silly things for her cameras. We shall go the beach to relax, and she can come along and get what shots she can, but there will be no acting.

We have arranged that Victoria will be at the beach at 10a.m. True to form, she arrives with her camera crew at 11.30. By now she is wary of this highly-temperamental bandleader, and she keeps her distance, presumably photographing our leisurely activities through a telescopic lens.

The concert this evening is in a bizarre but romantic setting – stage and chairs are set up in a well, open to the sky, in the centre of the hotel. We're overlooked on three sides by three storeys of balconies that run outside the hotel bedrooms. The audience is predominantly British, European and American, although the Governor of Aqaba and his 'cabinet' are in the front row. During the interval I am presented to him and we chat about Jordanian music. I manage to keep a perfectly straight face when he extols the virtues of a Jordanian bazouki-player seemingly called Jamal Arse. A heady show, very well received, which Victoria captures on film.

Next stop, Chesham High School on Friday.

PART 5
THAT'S MY HOME

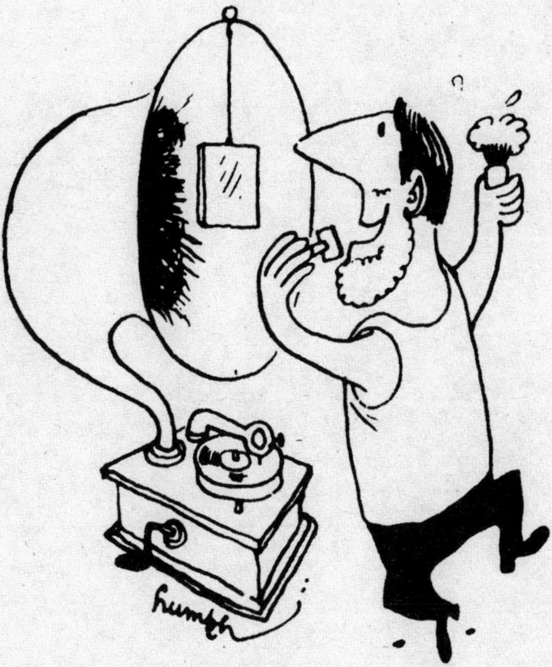

The House that Humph Built

When we decided to build our own house, it was by no means the culmination of a long-held ambition. Having lived for some years in Northwest London, we naturally gravitated northwards, bearing in mind that access to the West End from the North is very much quicker than through the impenetrable fortifications of Streatham or Woolwich to the South. So we collected fistfuls of sheets from the estate agents and went house-hunting, striking north up the Finchley Road and setting course for the Green Belt uplands of South Hertfordshire. I don't suppose we were easy clients. Life at Belsize Park, where rooms once designed as lofty drawing-room, stone-floored kitchen and 'below stairs' hinterland presented exciting problems of interior decoration, had given us a taste for the bizarre which was scarcely titillated by the standard 'bijou' or 'golf-course Tudor' residences which we were sent to see. One estate agent misread our requirements with embarrassing results. Abandoning his office for an afternoon, he took us in his car to see some properties which he felt were just up our street. First we drove some distance out into Hertfordshire, turning to our alarm through an imposing gateway into an interminable winding drive flanked and almost swamped by rhododendrons. The house did justice, in size and dignity, to its approaches. It was, in fact, a mansion – an edifice that had failed, through some unexplained defect of pedigree of character, to become a stately home, and had died of a broken heart because of it.

In front of its flaking French windows, stone urns, crudely sandpapered by time and weather, marked the outline of a terrace which, despite evidence of quite recent occupation, was already in the process of being hungrily reclaimed by Nature. Inside, family portraits reduced almost to a monochrome by dust and neglect still lined the panelled walls of the dining-room. Ornaments stood about and there was silver lying in a heap on the dining-room table. So little sign was there of contemporary living that I conceived the fantasy that the owners, having dissipated the family fortunes in riotous living, had the previous day been whisked off to Newgate, leaving the house and its contents to be carved up among their creditors. The agent had very little idea what to do with the house. He was prepared to sell us all of it plus the surrounding estate, all of it plus the terrace for conversion into a garden, or (seeing no trace of enthusiasm in our faces) half of it with a small plot outside the French windows. When all seemed lost, he produced what he took to be his trump card. Flinging open the huge oak doors at the end of the dining-room, he revealed a vast ballroom, with parquet flooring, glittering chandeliers and a small rostrum at one end suitable for accommodating a string band or harpsichord ensemble. From the expression on his face as he ushered us in, he clearly felt that here was an inducement which a slightly mad Old Etonian, ex-Guards Officer jazz-trumpet-player would find it hard to resist.

It was probably the experience of that day, and others similar to it, which persuaded us to look for a plot of land on which to have our own house built. Before very long, we were offered a rectangle of undeveloped land near Elstree. The front of it was on a road, the back sloped steeply down into a valley across which the Northwest winds would blow. Through a friend, we were put in touch with an architect reputed to have fresh and imaginative ideas. John Voelcker's appearance confirmed the reputation. An El Greco gauntness, a certain wildness in the eye, something about the way in which the black hair sprouted vigorously from the forehead in an equine forelock showed that we had chosen a man of high enthusiasm and artistic temperament. We were lucky in our choice. In the circumstances which followed, I doubt if he felt the same about his clients. He came out to look at the strip of land, and eventually proposed a design reminiscent of an Arab fortress, built round three sides of a rectangular courtyard and enclosed by a wall in front. The

Throughout his life Humph would use his cartooning skills to personalize invitation and christmas cards.

idea was that the outside of the house should have the minimum of window area, to protect us from the cold winds which would sweep up from the valley, and that we should look instead through large windows on to our own courtyard. Since the land sloped away steeply towards the rear of the plot, it was planned to have two storeys at the back of the building, with garage space below the rear rooms. We were beginning to get excited about the prospect when a phone call from the estate agent told us, apologetically, that there was no planning permission for the land in question, and that, unless we wanted it for grazing cattle, we would have to look elsewhere.

Some days later, we found a plot in Arkley, near Barnet. The garden of a large house (called Alyn House) was being sold off in half-acre strips, and there were two left. The strip which we chose was shielded from the road by two layers of trees, and had on it the remains of some kind of outhouse, possibly a solid greenhouse. John

Voelcker came out to look at it, and in discussion, the existence of the second row of trees, firs set at an angle across the strip, gave us the idea of keeping the design which he had roughed out for the other plot, but using the fir trees in place of the front wall. The idea commended itself to us for two special reasons. By building the house around three sides of a courtyard, we brought into use in the middle of the house about 800 square feet which, in a conventionally designed house, would be largely wasted and overshadowed areas on either side of the building. And secondly, we felt that a single-storey structure, totally concealed from the road by trees, would preserve the proportions and the general appearance of the original estate, with its dominating big house and smaller out-buildings. Unfortunately, the local council had already given planning permission for two bulky conventional houses of uninspired design to be built on the two strips furthest from the large house. But a single-storey building was already proposed on the strip which separated our land from the big house, and John Voelcker took immense trouble to consult the architect of our neighbour's house so that the two houses would blend and relate to each other.

As soon as I entered into the necessary negotiations with the local council about building my house, it became clear to me that I had seriously handicapped myself by engaging an architect at all. Elaborate machinery was set in motion for the sole purpose, as far as I could see, of thwarting him. His plans were not only rejected, but criticised and openly derided on practical grounds by people with less qualifications to judge them than me. At a public hearing to appeal against the decision of the council, men of supreme insignificance were enabled with impunity to cast doubt upon his professional ability, notwithstanding the fact that he possesses all the necessary qualifications of his profession. And even the Minister of Housing's findings, reversing the council's decision in our favour, were couched in terms of condescension, as though the Ministry was reluctantly unable to find good cause to stop the building. I doubt if the fertile imagination of Beachcomber could devise a more richly farcical situation. Architects are trained in every up-to-date facet of their work – design, function, materials and so on. Once they are qualified, their professional work is handed over for judgement to persons of no comparable qualification, whose ignorance is matched only by their prejudice. As a result, Britain is still, in the main, an architectural wasteland. Under the conditions in which John Voelcker, my architect, had to work, I should long since have been ushered gently away by men in white, leaving a trail of mutilated borough councillors in my wake. I hope I was not instrumental in adding to his difficulties. As a client, my attitude to my architect was much the same as my attitude to my dentist. Having chosen a dentist because I believe he will do the job well, I lie back, open my mouth and leave the rest to him. So it was with my architect – except that, when in doubt, I kept my mouth shut.

Bye Bye Blackbird

When we had our house built we put a small square window in the dining room at knee level. It turned out to be quite a good idea, really – sitting on the settee you can look out at the back garden at ground level, so to speak, and see what Nature's up to. It was in these circumstances in the early 'sixties that I caught a bird watching me.

Mind you, it's not always easy to know when a bird is watching you. For instance, a woodcock has a range of vision of almost 360 degrees, which is jolly convenient for the woodcock but a damn nuisance for a bloke who likes his privacy. The nosey creature can be watching your every move while facing in the opposite direction, like the bounder you catch staring at your reflection in a train window. But we are not here to talk about the woodcock. A bird which, with all that going for it, still ends up on a raft of toast on some company director's expense account menu is hardly worth prolonged consideration. I didn't know at the time what bird it was that was rubbernecking at me through the dining-room window. It was just a sort of bird-shaped thing of indeterminate colour with an inquisitive profile and a beady eye that was without doubt fixed on me. What's more, when it opened its beak to chirrup a comment to an unseen mate, I felt my ears burning. So it was in a retaliatory mood that I there and then took up bird-watching.

What, you might ask, is there to take up? Is it not just a simple matter of 'First find your bird and then watch it'? It is not, matey. Apart from anything else, it is essential to know what you're watching. The interests of science are poorly served by the bird-watcher who studies the behaviour of a hedge sparrow believing it to be a female robin. And when you go on to discover that a hedge sparrow, not content with not being a female robin, isn't even a sparrow, then it's obvious that what you need is a Book On The Subject. And this isn't as easy as it sounds, either. At the last count there were at least fifty bird-books on the market, ranging from cheap and unreliable pocket books to highly-priced artistic books. As someone who owns all fifty of them (it's amazing how quickly news of a new hobby gets round among the relatives, especially at Christmas time) I can offer at least one piece of basic advice. If you pick up one of the cheaper books and want to test its accuracy, look up 'Jackdaw' in the index and turn to the illustration. If it shows a bird with a royal blue body and a powder blue head, put it down quickly. An artist or printer who can depict a jackdaw looking like the Queen Mother at Ascot is no man to be let loose among yellow hammer and bullfinches. I favour the books that show the birds just standing broadside on, a dozen or so to the page, all facing the same way, like the pictures in those books on battleships that we used to read at school.

I discovered quite early on that even the most objective and accurate bird-book sometimes misleads. On holiday in Wales shortly after I became a bird-watcher, I spent half a day watching a flock of small birds that obstinately refused to conform to any illustration in the book. Crouching in a gorse bush, I scrutinized them in close-up through binoculars, growing increasingly frustrated and uncomfortable. By a process of elimination I ruled out the linnet, the redpoll, the little bunting, the juvenile Cretzschmar's bunting, the rock sparrow, several varieties of flycatcher and the whitethroat, arriving eventually at the twite. But 'the male has a pinkish rump', and not a pinkish rump could I see. Indeed, the only pinkish rump within miles was mine, and I was growing more aware of it every minute. It wasn't until, creaking homeward, I found a dead one by the side of the road that the obvious truth dawned. A healthy male twite in the field, mucking about by dusty roadsides, is a very different customer from the male model in the text books, whom he no doubt regards as a right twite with his poncey pink rump and fancy ways. You might as well try to identify one of our scruffier Cabinet Ministers from a photograph by Vivienne.

Bird-watching has its own snobberies, or pecking order, as we say. I know bird-watchers who like to call themselves amateur ornithologists, although what they know of the actual science of birds wouldn't fill a wren's egg, the stuck-up things. On the other hand, one way to insult a self-respecting bird-watcher is to call him a bird-spotter or, worst still, a tally-spotter or tick-hunter. The latter even sounds like an insult in the Somerset Maugham vein. 'Get out, you rotten little tick-hunter!' Tick-hunters are in fact people who indulge in the seemingly innocent pastime of spotting as many different species as they can and ticking them off on a list. I did it for a while, but found it bad for the character. It's rather like scoring for yourself at golf. The temptation to cheat – to overlook those few 'practice' swipes in the bunker or, in the case of tick-hunting, to mark off that distant soarer as a marsh harrier when you know it could be a seagull – would corrupt a saint. And ironically, bird-spotters are listed by the Royal Society for the Protection of Birds as one of the numerous hazards from which birds have to be protected today. More than once recently a rare bird has alighted in this country only to be scared away almost at once by the thunder of heavy boots as tick-hunters converged upon it from all over the British Isles. Goodness knows how they found out about it – perhaps a little bird told them.

It must be said here that a bird-watcher isn't the same as a bird-lover, either. Bird-lovers have anthropomorphic tendencies which are quite unscientific. For example, a sparrow got into my kitchen the other morning, exciting the dog and generally barging about. When it saw me coming it began to hurl itself at the windows, making a terrible racket among the Venetian blinds. With the calm nerve and steady hand for which your British bird-watcher is famous, I raised the latch of the window and opened it gradually until the bird got out. It flew off to a hospitable tree at the bottom of the garden where it sat for a moment, tweeting prodigiously. At this point your bird-lover, attributing to it a human character, would say, 'Ah, look – he's saying "Thank you"!' As a hard-headed birdwatcher, I knew better. He was saying '?*@!!**@!!!' and I don't blame him. He must have picked up some nasty bruises amongst those blinds.

Some time later I came home from work one Sunday midday to be told by the children with great excitement that a red-legged partridge had turned up in the back garden overnight. (We have a bird-spotting book in every room and nothing that lands in our back garden remains anonymous for very long.) Sure enough, there it was – a greyish bird the size of a domestic hen, with rather handsome red stripes around the chest and the vermilion Manchester United stockings that give it its name. It was stalking around the lawn with a proprietary air, tame as they come and showing a remarkable turn of speed whenever food appeared. It stayed with us all day, eventually flapping up on to our neighbours' roof for a brief reconnaissance before setting off for its more conventional habitat.

As a member of the R.S.P.B., I was flattered to think that, in the course of some ill-charted flight, it had chosen our North London garden for sanctuary. But this is beside the point. During its stay, in a quiet moment in mid-afternoon when it was swaying somnolently on one leg outside the kitchen window, I happened to notice that it was going through some rather odd contortions in the area of the head and neck. First it stretched its neck to the limits of its not-inconsiderable length. Then it drew its head backwards and downwards, opening its beak wide and expanding its throat into an impressive goitre.

My first thought, born of guilt at having overindulged it in an unhealthy partiality for sliced bread, was that it was choking. Seeing that, in intervals between this silent retching, it showed no signs of distress – no bulging of the eyes or purpling of the legs – I began to wonder if it was perhaps short-sighted and was going through some elaborate courtship display for the benefit of the lawn-sprinkler.

It was in pursuit of this line of inquiry that I turned to my bird-

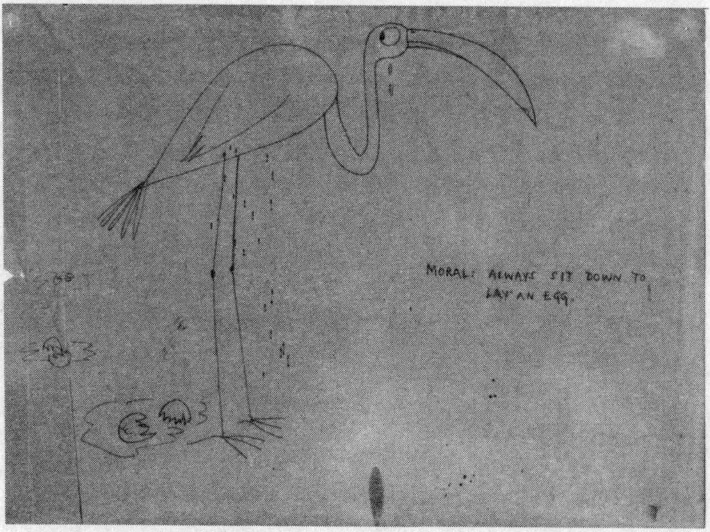

When asked by his Nephew Rupert Stewart-Cox (then aged 7) to 'Draw me a picture' Humph produced this sketch on a piece of scrap paper that has survived over 45 years! (Courtesy of Rupert Stewart-Cox.)

books and discovered what I might perhaps have guessed. Despite the absence of any sound compatible with the human eardrum, the bird was singing. It seems that, had I been prepared to risk losing an ear by putting my head close to its beak, I would have heard deep down in the recesses of its oesophagus a sound like 'the whetting of a scythe, or a decrepit steam locomotive'.

What arises from this is that Nature, Providence, the Deity or whatever else you like to call the force that shapes our destinies, has a sounder judgement than you or I in matters of music. Having inadvertently created a bird with a singing voice like someone whetting a scythe (and you can't win 'em all even if you are the Deity, as a quick glance around God's creatures will confirm) it thoughtfully refrained from letting it off the assembly line without first disconnecting its loudspeaker. None of your egalitarian nonsense about every bird's right to sing. Two decrepit puffs of the steam locomotive and it's switched off at the mains!

Some years ago, I made the mistake of going in for a garden pond. Actually, it was a passing thought rather than a conscious decision, but I happened to mention it to Mr Jenkins, a venerable enthusiast who came in of a Friday to help with our garden. On the following Friday we came back from a family outing to find that he had excavated what appeared to be an elephant trap in the lawn. Not since Stalag VII can there have been such purposeful and energetic digging.

Once the gaping hole was polythene-lined and cemented – a double insurance against seepage and, if the worst came to the worst, earthquake – I had to think about what to put in it. Having let it stand all winter to let the tap-water mature, like the book said, I hurried off in April to a local aqua horticulturalist's to stock up. For a while it was spring all the way as I planted out the Bog Primula and the Water Mint, the Lavender Musk and the Water Forget-me-not. Into the matured water headfirst went Golden Orfes, Comets, Nymphs, Fantails and a green tench or two to do the scavenging. That first spring I gave up watching television altogether and just sat by the pond, frozen stiff and waiting for the miracle of Nature to unfold.

It was the following spring that things began to go wrong. Several of the fish, emerging from their winter torpor, appeared to be having navigational trouble, keeling over sideways like U-boats under attack. One even inflated like a huge zeppelin and kept looming into view from behind the oxygenating plants, threatening to explode. On the banks the Water Mint, hell-bent on territorial expansion, smothered everything and I couldn't for the life of me remember where I'd planted the Water Forget-me-not.

One day a friend, peering ruminatively into the depths, said, 'You know you've got *Dytiscus marginalis*, don't you?' 'Great heavens!' I cried, prodding various parts of my anatomy in search of telltale symptoms. 'Look, there!' He pointed into the murk. 'A Great Diving Beetle, heading for your green tench!' To the layman, the Diving Beetle no doubt presents rather a jolly sight, like someone rowing upside down in a dinghy. But we pond-watchers know better. As well as the carnivorous adult, there is a dreaded larva, like a large, articulated earwig, that goes through your fish stock like a scourge, nibbling bits off them when they're asleep.

Quite frankly, it all became a bit of a worry, especially in the spring. Frogs arrived, leaving great blobs of tapioca in the water and giving more cause for concern. I don't know if you realize it, but a severe frost in April can play havoc with your tadpoles. The first year, I fished all the spawn out with a shrimp net and put it to hatch in a separate tank on the edge of the pond. Metamorphosis took place according to plan beneath my very eyes, and I even reached the point of collecting greenfly grubs from the back of leaves every day to feed the captive froglets.

My dream of rearing a family of super-frogs ran into difficulties when it was time to go away on holiday and the minute creatures were clearly not ready to fend for themselves among the *Dytisci marginalis*. Someone who professed to know all about it suggested that I should leave some raw meat in the tank which would then breed maggots for the frogs to eat until my return. I am not much of a bio-chemist, and I can only guess that at some juncture the maggots turned the tables on the frogs. We won't go into details, but it was not a pretty sight, and the smell was worse.

Mainly Traditional

Some years after moving into the house my wife gave me a power drill for Christmas. 'A man and his Black and Decker…' the T.V. advert used to intone, showing a lantern-jawed he-man of the outer suburbs advancing, power-drill jutting menacingly at the hip, upon some quaking piece of home-repair. It became impossible to sit gazing idly into space without the eye alighting and focusing reluctantly upon some defect in the domestic environment which could be put right immediately by the simple expedient of boring a neat hole.

So there I was, when, with a certain inevitability, the insidious thought intruded that a batten screwed to the wall over the oven wouldn't half be useful. It was the work of a moment to assemble the power drill, plug in, switch on and commence drilling a neat hole right through the middle of the oven cable. One minute the drill was biting smoothly into the masonry under the firm but sensitive grip of a master craftsman, the next there was a blue flash, a small explosion, and in place of the rampant Tungsten Carbide Tipped Masonry Drill No. 8, a remnant of charred metal drooped impotently. With the shops shut till Tuesday, ten tons of frozen provisions in the fridge and a severed electrical artery buried beyond reach of Do It Yourself in the walls, the inner and outer voices in favour of Dad getting down to some useful jobs over the holidays were instantly stifled.

Christmas was more fun when we were young, and will always be so. I have forty-two first cousins at the last count, and a heavy contingent of us used to assemble at the stately home of an aunt and uncle in Wiltshire for the holiday. The focal point of the day was not the meal, but the burning of an enormous bonfire in the grounds. I didn't know then that we were performing an ancient rite devised by our sun-worshipping ancestors to give the weak and wintry sun a bit of assistance. Hurling logs on to the blazing pyre just seemed a good way to work off the lunch and to persuade the Christmas pudding to move over and make room for the Christmas cake.

I have a lasting and fond memory of one such family gathering many Christmases ago. The scene was after the Christmas dinner, when the 'big presents' had been opened by countless offspring, nephews and nieces, and were in the process of being lost, fought over and trodden on. Screams and accusations rent the air. In the middle of it all, my father, then well advanced into his seventies and to all intents *hors de combat*, had found one of those duffel-bags full of hygienically-polished wooden shapes that one of the younger children had been given. Knee-deep in wrapping-paper and brawling descendants and oblivious of the mayhem around him, he was deeply absorbed in building a stately cathedral on the drawing-room table.

My own role on Christmas Day was a limited one. I was in charge of drinks, turkey and stockings which, were I not able to persuade Santa to keep them under lock and key until 7.30 at the earliest,

For many years, Humph would create Christmas cards for his band.

would merge imperceptibly with the parcel-wrapping of the night before.

We were always told that if we dared to wake up and open our eyes, Father Christmas would hurry away without leaving anything. I was always fully awake, every nerve jangling. But avarice overcame curiosity and I kept my eyes tight shut, so I never actually discovered which of my parents it was who undertook the furtive impersonation. I think it must have been my mother. My father usually left that kind of thing to her. Besides, he was six foot three, weighed eighteen stone and had a hip complaint which made him something less than agile. Had he undertaken the chore, there would surely have been crashing and banging to waken the dead.

I'm afraid a Dr Spock piece on Christmas would make most of us feel terribly guilty. It's the fault of inflation, of course. When I was a child, the Christmas stocking was a sort of appetizer, a collection of amusing and trashy little objects costing no more than one or two pence each. Nowadays, it's hard to find anything trashy that costs less than a fiver. What with T.V. advertising and opulent shop-window displays, the expectations of our children soar far above the little packets of sweets and harmless jokes that we used to be happy to get. I must be absolutely fair and say that the expectations of parents are considerably higher, too.

Had he been around at the time, Dr Spock would have had nothing but praise for the way in which my sisters and I were encouraged to make our Christmas presents. Year after year, with admirably feigned surprise and delight, my poor father would open scruffy little packages containing either a pen-wiper made of circles of coloured felt crudely stitched at the centre, or a box of matches over which cut-out pieces of glossy coloured paper had been inexpertly gummed. At least, when my turn came, there was Art Work at school from which a slightly higher standard of artefact emerged. I have done my duty. On my desk, as I write, there is an ashtray which my daughter manufactured for me when she was about six. It is made of assorted lumps of clay pummelled into a crude saucer shape, fired in the school kiln and glazed a rich, reddish brown. She is old enough now not to take offence when I say that it looks exactly like one of those Dirty Fido practical jokes which my children so often welcomed in *their* stockings.

But enough of this crusty harking back. The truth of the matter is that Christmas was more fun as children because we didn't have to do the work.

After stocking duties, my next responsibility was for the drinks. In this department, I had no high ambitions. One year, succumbing to a vague urge to go in for some wassailing in style, I made a hot punch, with old ale, brown sugar, cinnamon, the lot. Some people can do this sort of thing with the cleanness and efficiency of a dispensing chemist. I am not one of them, and it was Twelfth Night before I got rid of the sensation that my elbows were sticking to the lining of my jacket. If one is in the habit of taking a glass of wine with meals, then to make Christmas special one is faced with the choice of drinking something different or simply drinking more. Without any further effort or expenditure, the latter contingency was taken care of by my wife's brandy butter which, in every respect other than taste, was indistinguishable from gelignite. So I tended to go for something which we have no occasion to drink – or cannot afford – at other times. At this point, modesty can no longer be allowed to conceal that, if I am cack-handed with the hot punch, I am a craftsman with the Gaelic coffee. So unerring is my manipulation of the double cream over the back of the spoon that my wife's mother once assumed that I was handing her a perfectly-poured Guinness and had a rather nasty shock. Incidentally, purists always insist, with that blinkered obstinacy peculiar to purists, that Irish whiskey must be used. I make my Christmas Gaelic coffee with Scotch malt whisky, which apart from anything else is a lot nicer to drink neat after the coffee is finished.

And that brings us to my only other official function of the day, the carving of the turkey. And let me say at once that I do not subscribe to the authoritarian view that carving is the prerogative of the head of the family. I simply did it because every one else was too busy juggling with chipolatas, roast potatoes and bread sauce. There are in the old English vocabulary specific terms for the carving of different birds – to spoil a hen, for example, and to unbrace a mallard, unjoint a bittern, unlatch a curlew, sauce a capon, allay a pheasant, display a quail, thigh a woodcock, disfigure a peacock. I can find nothing about turkeys, but my wife's assessment of my annual performance seemed to lie somewhere between the spoiling of a hen and the disfiguring of a peacock. I admit that I lack finesse. More conscientious carvers than I will start at the blunt end with little rounded slices and work up from there. I subscribe to the opposite school which eyes the bird keenly for a moment like Douglas Fairbanks Snr preparing to administer the *coup de grâce* and then lunges in with great swashbuckling swipes. The end product is huge planks of breast on which all the other good things can be shovelled.

We have now arrived at the crux of the matter – the true function of the turkey. Jean Anthelme Brillat-Savarin, the eighteenth-century magistrate, politician and noted gastronome, described the turkey as 'certainly one of the finest gifts made by the New World to the Old'. Now, everyone is entitled to his opinion, especially if he is an eighteenth-century magistrate, politician and noted gastronome. But I have always loved to look upon the monstrous freak, with its bosom of a dowager and thighs of a soccer full-back, as an early testimony of the Americans' obsession with packaging at the expense of content. What other bird offers such a cavernous interior for the stuffing of sage, sausage meat, chestnuts, chopped bacon and anything else that comes to hand? And what other bird can claim so little positive flavour to interfere with, or blunt the appetite for, these tasty contents? I note with some triumph that when Brillat-Savarin himself killed and cooked a wild turkey in America, he felt called upon to serve partridge wings *en papillote* and grey squirrels in a Madeira *court-bouillon* at the same time. Being a politician and a magistrate, he was probably too fastidious to reveal to the world one of the basic truths about turkey – that no slice carved from it with all due majesty before the meal tastes half as good as the bits torn from it surreptitiously when you are supposed to be taking it back to the larder afterwards.

Get Ready to Fly

We were never much of a travelling family – as a family, that is. In an old scrapbook, there are photographs of my father, a devotee of the classics, 'doing' Greece, sitting about on mountain crags looking earnestly statuesque. And in World War I, my mother ran away from home to join Queen Alexandra's Nurses on the Western Front. She had, in truth, a very happy home, but in those days eldest daughters were expected to stay at home helping to run things and look after Father when he came back on leave. Her view, in a nutshell, was that Father could look after himself, so off she went under a temporary cloud.

Apart from this, it can't be said that either of them qualified for the Roaring Twenties equivalent of the Jet Set. Indeed, when I was a child, our holiday routine could fairly be called stodgy. Summer holidays were migrations to the same spot each year. I dimly remember names like Overstrand and Happisburgh (pronounced Hazeborough) as regular Norfolk summering places. Then, when I was eight my parents started taking us to Wales and kept it up until war broke out. Many of my most vivid childhood memories are therefore set in Harlech, where we took a house each summer.

It was in Harlech in 1935 that I dug a deep hole outside our bathing hut and got rid of our Nanny. With pride rather than bones shattered by a sudden four-foot drop into a well-concealed elephant trap, she gave notice next morning.

It was in Harlech too, a few years earlier, that I nearly drowned in the sea, paddling into an unsuspected dip and finding myself out of my depth. My screams were heard by Captain Hughes, who kept a soft-drinks stall in the sand-dunes and was a semi-official beach-guard. He reacted with an alacrity born of a lifetime's experience of the sea and its treachery. Dashing down from a high dune as fast as astonishingly bow legs would carry him, he collided with a beach hut, giving himself a severe nosebleed.

Meanwhile, in a few traumatic seconds, I had discovered that I could swim.

I have inherited, I believe, a bleak attitude to foreign travel which both my parents shared. Robert Louis Stevenson notwithstanding, they believed that to arrive was all right, but it was the 'travelling hopefully' – hoping that the tickets were not still on the hall table, that the luggage would turn up before it was time to go home, that the green-looking fellow-traveller at the steamer rail would move to leeward before the worst happened – that made the whole business insufferable. Neither of them really took to aeroplanes. When my father was prevailed upon, during his retirement, to visit an old, housebound friend in Italy, it took twice as much effort and nervous strain to get him airborne as to put two men on the moon. Of course, he loved it when he got there. I still have a postcard from him which reported, 'In the morning I breakfast in bed (under mosquito net) and then read. The afternoon is less strenuous however.'

It's little wonder – and to me, a matter of some relief – that as children we were not lugged about all over the Continent and beyond. Children have a healthily sceptical attitude to travel anyway. They know instinctively that, when it comes to 'seeing the world', there are more discoveries to be made mucking about in an overgrown duck pond than hopping about on aeroplanes. And it's healthier, too. Can *you* remember a holiday abroad when you didn't spend half the time nursing an upset tummy, a scorched back or some malignant insect-bite? In a moment of misplaced guilt, I once suggested to my twelve-year-old daughter that we might all pop over to France for a week. 'No thanks,' she said emphatically, 'I don't want to get rabies!' Wise girl.

I was about that age when my parents, possibly labouring under the same feeling of guilt, took my eldest sister and me on our first trip abroad. With educational intent they chose the town of Bruges in Belgium, surrounded by historic sites of what used to be called the Great War and within easy reach of the art galleries and museums of Brussels. Great precautions were taken to avoid unpleasantness on the Channel crossing. Before we left home at Eton, my mother dispensed anti-seasickness pills which had to be taken several hours before the journey. I'm rather surprised that my father went along with this. One of his favourite stories was of a schoolmaster colleague on whom the prophylactic pills had such a profound psychological effect that he was violently ill out of the window of the stationary boat-train at Victoria. In the event, our crossing was absolutely smooth – boringly so, from the point of view of these recollections. I have never been a particularly good sailor, although on the few bad crossings that I have endured, others have always been in more dire straits.

From one particularly choppy trip, I recall the picture of a row of huddled schoolgirls, indigo of countenance, utterly concentrated on the fight to retain their dignity. Then along the row, like a priest lighting candles, came a well-meaning but fatuous teacher, peering into each tightly-buttoned face and asking, 'Are you all right?' As anyone with an inkling of psychology could have guessed, the kindly words acted as a catalyst, and one by one, the girls gave up the battle and heaved. I'm sure that, had there been the slightest undulation on our trip from Dover to Ostend, I would have remembered it.

Having ridden headlong, if a trifle circuitously, into my narrative, I must now rein in and confess that my actual memory of the unforgettable first trip abroad is rather patchy. I would like to believe that I was thrilled and starry-eyed enough to satisfy my parents that it was all worthwhile, but I have my doubts. I think I was twelve years old then, and it may be of some comfort to harassed parents of today to know that the loathsome adolescent is not a new or indeed modern invention. It worries me slightly to this day that the one anecdote from that holiday which achieved legendary proportions through constant repetition depicted me throwing a moody during an excursion into Brussels and stumping off into the busy side streets of a totally strange capital with the defiant words 'I'm going home'. Since 'home' was at best fifty miles away in Bruges, and at worst across the Channel in the Home Counties, my sudden departure caused something of a family trauma. They regarded it, with touching faith, as little short of a miracle that I was eventually found, but I have little doubt that I was loathsome enough to maintain them safely in sight throughout.

There were jolly moments, too. We used to travel from Bruges into Brussels on long-distance tram cars and those rackety, hurtling journeys through fields and along hedgerows did provide a memorable thrill. On one of our days in Brussels, my father conceived an elaborate joke. With a solemn face, he read from the guide-book about a celebrated statue called the Mannikin, carefully omitting any details which might give us an inkling of what to expect. Primed by his insistence on its cultural importance and legendary significance, we searched through the streets with mounting curiosity. When we were suddenly confronted by the naked cherub urinating ceaselessly into a fountain, our reaction of giggling shock did not disappoint him. Indeed, the simple joke had a more rewarding pay-off than he could possibly have expected, for, to compound our embarrassment (we had enjoyed a sheltered upbringing), our arrival on the scene coincided with that of a party of nuns.

If anyone enjoyed that Belgian holiday unconditionally, it was my father. Our hotel in Bruges was just across from the clock tower of the market-hall which housed the famous carrillons. During dinner, when the concert of chiming bells started up across the square, he froze into immobility, knife and fork raised, to make sure we didn't miss a single note. He took us all up that belfry tower one day, enthusiastically counting the number of steps while we trailed up behind him. He had a certain feeling for the macabre, and, as we looked out over the town with a mixture of awe and vertigo, he regaled us with gruesome statistics – how a penny dropped from the summit could split a man's head in two, or how wrongdoers of old were hurled over the edge, their limbs attached to ropes which ended abruptly some ten feet from the ground. When we visited the Great War battlefields and saw one of the guns that had shelled England – it could have been Big Bertha herself or a smaller sister – he was totally captivated by her vital and awe-inspiring measurements.

As a schoolboy, it was natural that I found the battlefields exciting. But it is here that I have to pause and question my memory. Can it really be that visitors to the preserved trenches and escarpments of Hill 60 were able to buy souvenirs? I have this strong recollection of shops with shell cases, pieces of shrapnel and other items of grim bric-à-brac on sale, and of a particular brass bullet-case which was for many years a treasured schoolboy possession. But perhaps I am straying into fantasy. If I have judged my age at that time correctly, the year would have been 1933. Less than five hundred miles away, in Munich, a man with a dropping forelock and a Charlie Chaplin moustache was at that very time laying plans to enter the souvenir trade himself. It was thanks to him that I made my second trip abroad in 1943. But we're not going there again....

As a family man I've never had much success with holidays. I've tried. I have chased toddlers all over Heathrow departure lounges, nursed them through seasickness, trekked overland with what has seemed like a car-load of monkeys.

'Lyttelton,' my old staff sergeant in the army used to say, 'you'll never make a soldier – no method, no method at all.' Well, I fancy he would think again if he could have seen me back in the 'sixties marshalling the family for our annual visit to North Wales. Each year was more impressive. 'Make your plan and stick to it' was one maxim that lodged in my subconscious at some stage in my officer training. With this in mind I always informed the troo...sorry, the family, that we would mobilize promptly at 10.00hrs on the Tuesday. A cynic watching us trundle off down the drive at precisely 11.47hrs on the Wednesday might say that my plan had misfired. I can tell him that it was thanks to my clear and decisive battle orders that we got off before the weekend. As my wife used to say in tones which came perilously close to mutiny, packing for five people for a fortnight in a place where sunny spells, sea mists, snow, heatwave, hail, hurricane and humidity can all occur in one day, and usually do, is no pushover and I ought to try it one day.

I always left out of my reckoning, too, the inexorable way in which toys which had lain dormant in the remote recesses of cupboards for years suddenly became indispensable items of the children's equipment. In the back of my mind, I suppose, was the thrust from Battipaglia to Salerno in 1943 when, under my supervision as signals officer to the 6th Battalion, Grenadier Guards, the signals truck was packed full of diverse equipment with a jigsaw precision that left the inspecting C.O. speechless – a phenomenon which cannot be attributed entirely to his discovery that the batteries for the signalling lamps had been left behind.

It was with something of the same feeling of pride that I surveyed the neatly stacked car boot at zero hour (amended) minus two, only to see it disrupted by the last-minute and apparently urgent inclusion of roller skates, a headless Teddy Bear in the throes of sawdustectomy, two plastic walkie-talkie sets minus batteries (ah! shades of Salerno!), a battered box of Monopoly distributing counterfeit largesse in all directions, several cameras with vital spools missing, a lidless tin full of broken crayons and clogged pencil-sharpeners, an ill-assorted rabble of plastic animals that would have given Noah hysterics and innumerable inflatable rubber objects with their stoppers missing. At one stage in the packing process I was tempted to resort to one of the more ghastly clichés of authority by crying 'If you play ball with me, I'll play ball with you!', foreseeing in the nick of time that it would be taken literally with whoops of delight and further loss of time.

It became a matter of tradition that, every year, we packed the car and travelled to Wales in relentless rain. This made planning and foresight all the more essential. One year an improvised tarpaulin with which I covered the roofrack leaked and driving rain infiltrated a suitcase, transferring the Caribbean motif of a rather snazzy beachshirt of mine on to all my plain shirts, vests, pants and even pyjamas. To this day, the local residents of Harlech know me as the man who anticipated the Flower People by several years. After that, of course, my tarpaulin drill was impeccable. We used to have one of those 'spiders' with elastic tentacles that stretch over the luggage and sometimes release their hold and smash your glasses while you're taking the strain. On one trip some dozy individual (no, of course it wasn't me!) stuck the hooks *through* the tarpaulin, weakening it in the face of a stiff headwind. Still, I think my old staff sergeant would have been proud to see us thundering off up the M1, no more than twenty-six hours behind schedule, with great fronds of tarpaulin flying like proud pennants behind us.

I am as non-violent and pacifist as the next man, but there's something about a seaside holiday that never fails to rekindle a dormant bellicosity. Perhaps it's the sight, at breakfast-time, of the rival armies making their plans and dispositions, thermos-flasks at the ready, maps unfurled and propped against the marmalade pots. It may be the routine of the nightly briefing in the T.V. lounge, when the rival commanders make their silent Appreciation of the Situation while the briefing officer at the London Weather Centre warns of deep depressions advancing from the west and cold fronts holding static positions on a line from Northeast Scotland to the Wash.

Certainly no man with red blood in his veins can fail to shiver with the thrill of battle when, advancing upon the beach, he hears from his advance scouts the sudden challenging cry, 'Mum! Dad! There's somebody sitting in OUR PLACE!!!'

It throws a revealing light on man's chronic inability to live at peace with his neighbour that, given a beach large enough to provide perfectly adequate *lebensraum* for everyone, some ruthless aggressor will always plant himself and his barbaric family on the one spot which by tradition, pride of place, Squatters' Rights and sheer, straightforward justice, clearly belongs to you. Of course, seasoned campaigners will not be unprepared for this eventuality. In my experience, the most effective weapon for dislodging an enemy from prepared positions is a baby, preferably one that has reached the crawling stage. No giant tank was ever built more impregnable and unstoppable than a baby hell-bent on appropriating a bucket and spade or demolishing a sand-castle. All you have to do is point it in the right direction and let go.

I realize that it is not every family that can rustle up a baby at short notice, and there are very effective alternatives – a small boy with a plunging kite, for instance, or a roving dog that has been sedulously trained throughout the winter to cock its leg against anything that looks like a gaily-coloured canvas windshield. I must confess to reservations about the latter. It should perhaps be kept in reserve for an enemy who blatantly defies the Geneva Convention by opening up with a transistor radio, say, or sending ingratiating children to establish a Fifth Column in your midst.

Of course, not all of your problems will stem from an external enemy. There is the question of man-management, of controlling and inspiring your own troops. In this respect, perhaps I might underline a basic principle with a cautionary tale from my own experience. It was as a newly-fledged second-lieutenant at Victoria Barracks, Windsor, that I learnt, in an initiation lecture, never to qualify or explain an order. It only invites argument and tempts disobedience. What I should have said to my daughter Georgina was, 'Come out of the sea now…why?…because I say so!' It might have earned me a look of dumb insolence and a black mark from Dr

Spock, but it would have achieved results. What I actually said was '...because your teeth are chattering' – and back came the answer like a boomerang...'Oh, that's all right – only my teeth are cold!'

We started going to Wales after a series of holidays abroad from which we returned physically shattered and mentally in urgent need of a rest-cure. They were so fraught with calamity that, to turn disappointment into fulfilment, failure into success, I started to keep a holiday diary. I don't mean one of your 'Arrived at 3p.m....unpacked...weather good...' telegraphic affairs, but a full, comprehensive chronicle of events.

You have to admit it's good thinking. For the price of a solid notebook and a reliable ballpoint, you are transformed from the helpless victim of circumstances into one who preys upon them. You have become, in the very literal sense, a journalist, eager to be where the action is and hungry for copy. From now on, the plane that arrives uneventfully on time, the hotel that lives up to the brochure's Utopian promise, the weather that furnishes a backdrop of unremitting blue sky and sunshine – these all become items on the debit side of a holiday, boring and undiaryworthy non-events.

I suppose it was World War II that first seriously dented the myth of the *sole Italiano*. When we heard of all those military advances bogged down in monsoon-like rain, of all those tanks wallowing axle-deep in mud from October onwards, it was hard to retain the notion of a benign sun beaming down incessantly upon a favoured land.

What the war left undone, popular holiday tours abroad completed. Hardly, it seemed, had the first coachload of jolly British campers had time to turn their grey faces towards the *sole Italiano* before the whole lot were swept into the sea by floods. We took a rented villa in Marina di Massa some years ago, overlooking a Mediterranean that pounded and raged for most of the three-week holiday. Each suppertime our landlady-cum-maid, no doubt nettled by our scathing comments on the weather, retaliated with macabre statistics concerning the number of Englishmen who had got themselves drowned that day off our stretch of coast. It was a source of some humiliation to us that the island race was chiefly famous in those parts for dashing like Gadarene swine into the

Rescue at Sea

water whenever the danger flag was hoisted – seldom, if ever, to be seen again.

Happily, it fell to me to restore some vestige of our national dignity by carrying out a rescue at sea. At high tide and on a calm day, one could wade out from the beach, swim a few strokes across a dip and reach a broad ledge where the shallow water was warm and clear. Occupying the villa below us was an Italian couple, the wife pear-shaped and timid, the husband suggesting by his pallid torso and tendency to go into a crabby handstand whenever anyone was watching that he was a sedentary worker of athletic aspiration rather than achievement. One afternoon on the beach, he persuaded his wife, who couldn't swim, to let him carry her on his shoulders across to the ridge. She was reluctant, he was noisily confident. It was only when he walked steeply down into the sea and disappeared from view that he realized, too late, that the whole enterprise was based on a miscalculation.

Feeling the water lapping around her knees, the wife began to scream, at the same time tightening her grip on the man's head by clasping his nose. I was returning to the shore at a stately breaststroke when the momentary appearance of the man's face, purple and with the bulging eyes flashing mute distress signals, caused me to alter course and steam to the rescue. Having with some firmness prised the woman from her husband's head, it was simple to steer her, now limp and buoyant, to the safety of the land.

As sea rescues go, it was unspectacular. But it was something, in the prevailing circumstances, for an Englishman to have prevented an excitable Italian lady from drowning her husband in six feet of water, and I still feel that, before castigating her loudly for her lack of cooperation, he could have said thanks.

But then, you can't have everything. The temperament that can, in a moment, lead Italians into and out of comic-opera situations such as this is not likely to foster the stiff formalities.

For our visit to Portugal some years later I took elaborate precautions. By good luck, I had some work in Portugal earlier in the year, and I visited the little fishing village we had chosen to reassure myself – and my family – that it was everything the brochure claimed. I noted the blissful quietness, the quality of the local food, the almost Scandinavian scrupulousness of the sanitary arrangements. This last was especially important. In Italy we had been persecuted by a temperamental lavatory cistern, in Spain the water supply failed whenever it rained, a perversion of the normal provisions of Nature which I never fathomed. When I got home from my working visit, I was able to cheer everyone up with my report. I should have been warned perhaps by the fact that, while they sing incessantly about April in Portugal, there is a certain reticence about August in Portugal. On the coach from Lisbon airport to our hotel, the lady courier broke the news that, owing to an unprecedented drought, the water in the village would be cut off from noon until 7.30 the following morning, and we would be wise to fill the bath before going out for the day. It was a strong ploy, rich in dramatic possibilities, most of which came to fruition in an astonishingly short time. On the very first night, a friend with whom we were to spend the holiday returned to his room after a long session at the bar and, in his efforts not to disturb his wife, slipped in his stockinged feet and sat fully clothed in the bath. A few mornings later, I was roused from a deep sleep by an agitated knocking on my door. I opened an eye in time to see one of my slippers float past on a swift current, rounding an island of sodden underwear with a navigational instinct I had never suspected. The floor was two inches deep in water, and the knocking on the door was by the lady from the room below who had begun to take the overflow. Fortunately, she had previously made the same mistake, forgetting to ensure, before she went to bed, that the bath taps were turned off. She even helped me mop up with bath-towels.

These were routine enough occurrences which any hack script-writer could have thought up without much effort. He might even have conceived the funfair which, after the first week, set up on a derelict plot across the road from the hotel and shattered our evening peace with disseminated music and announcements. But I fancy he would have left it there, satisfied that to convert a somnolent fishing village into a sort of alfresco amusement arcade was a fair day's work. At this point the celestial doodler sprang to his feet with his cry of triumph, and there was indeed this trick cyclist on a tight wire appearing on the stroke of midnight. His act, which we never actually saw but which we could follow from the hysterical commentary even under a defensive screen of four pillows, consisted of riding on a two-stroke motor cycle up a tight wire stretched at a gradient of about one-in-four. As he revved and goaded his machine, every inch of his progress was described with mounting excitement by the commentator over the tannoy. At the height of the din, there was a triumphant cry of 'Viva Portugal!' and an ear-splitting national anthem. Reaching the top, the rider had dexterously unfurled the Portuguese flag.

Diaries

[Between 1974 and 1980 Humph kept detailed diaries. Never intended to trawl the deep recesses of his soul, they recount his often humorous observations of his day-to-day life.]

1974

In the big outside world news broke on Christmas Eve that the oil-producing countries propose to double cost of oil immediately. Petrol bound to go up to 50p a gallon in New Year, with likelihood of a further increase by end of 1974 to £1 a gallon. Worked out (on new calculator!) that if this happens, a band trip to Manchester for a car doing 25 miles to the gallon will cost £16. This obvious economic problem apart, I rather relish the idea of 'motoring' going into reverse, with the return of the bicycle, if not the horse. A few years' respite from 'growth' and 'progress' would benefit everyone. But I fear that scientists are at this moment working day and night to think of ways of sucking the North Sea oil fields dry with indecent haste.

Tuesday 1 January

Drove back from Barnstaple, starting at about 11.15. The new Volvo is running well and doing over 35m.p.g. on two-star petrol. New Year's Eve seemed more subdued than usual. The hotel was running a dinner-dance – I had supper in solitary state at 7, sitting in a vast decorated ballroom at a table festooned with crackers. It must have looked like a scene from a far-out German movie, especially as I was served by no less than three waitresses and two waiters! The band were first of all refused admission, then put into the unused restaurant and offered a meal at the dinner-dance price of £3 per head. After the second threat to check out *en masse*, they were offered a more down-to-earth meal at £1.50 but it took two bottles of champagne (from me) to induce anything approaching the party spirit. The manager, a great, grey (and drunk) sea-lion, greeted me with a tale of how well other bands had done. Since the 'other bands' were Victor Sylvester Jnr and Sidney Lipton (!!!) [Popular Big Band leaders] I felt we were unlikely to compete and was broadly speaking right. Not helped by said manager staggering onstage in middle of 'party' set to announce that a 'sneak-thief' (he pronounced it 'sneef') was stealing handbags. You never saw a dance-floor empty more quickly!

Wednesday* 2 *January

The much-dreaded three-day-week will really begin to make itself felt today. I find a widespread scepticism as to its necessity. It's a strange situation – most people distrust the government but show no sign of veering towards the Labour Party – what happens next? When anarchy comes, can Enoch Powell be far behind? Quite a number of people seem to share my hope that a fairer, less grasping and more purposeful society will emerge from it all, but the government seems not to have tuned-in on this wavelength at all. There was something nostalgic about Christmas shopping in hurricane-lamplight. I seem to remember from childhood ironmongers' shops with hurricane lamps but it might be imagination. At first I thought that T.V. shutting down at 10.30 was an unmitigated blessing, but alas, most of the programmes which I most enjoy – relaxed interviews with musicians or artists, political or journalistic discussion, films about creative people – have been dropped and for some inexplicable reason, old movies seem to hog the limited time.

Thursday* 3 *January

Daily Mail has 'scare' headline about a possible all-out strike in the mines. Also a report of a speech by Peter Shore (Secretary of State for Trade) predicting that Britain's total reserves will have run out by the end of 1974. Find myself remarkably calm in the face of a possible drying-up of freelance work as the crisis deepens. Life is certainly exciting!

Sunday 6 January

Watched sparrows trying to get at the wire cage of peanuts outside the study window. Occasionally one tries to emulate the acrobatic perch of the blue-tit and finds it not quite as difficult as thought! The presence of our cat Liza doesn't seem to inhibit the birds.

Tuesday 8 January

Ghastly night with protesting stomach – unfair, as I had nothing to eat after 5.45. Severe attack of the horrors about unemployment in February, bankruptcy in March! Matters not improved by Liza purring like a motorbike a few inches from my ear. Put pillows over my head to shut out the noise, found that her head was under it too, purring now deafening! Very funny letter from Mama about Christmas at Loders [Sister Diana's house in Dorset]. 'We started dinner one night with caviar – a tiny little pot each for seven people. I made a mental calculation of the cost and rushed upstairs and sent £5 to Help the Aged as a peace offering! Caviar means nothing to me anyway – kipper paste is more in my line!'

Saturday 12 January

Talked last night to one of the Manchester jazz scene's favourite 'characters' – known to me only as 'Spanish'. He works as a freelance chef (was at Pino's Edge Hotel when I stayed there, as I discovered when I saw him drive up for work to the front entrance in huge Bentley), and apparently earns a fortune in the season, takes it easy in the winter. He wears hand-made suits in a Capone-era style, sports a goatee beard and Salvador Dali moustache and at the Bamboo Club – has all his £ notes changed into (specially kept) half crowns and old pennies because he doesn't agree with decimal currency.

Tuesday 15 January

Went in at 6.30 to Bull's Head – Barnes. Mick Pyne (piano) has gastric flu, Eddie Harvey rushed in from Hertford to deputize. Very successful session, have rebooking on 19 February. At the end a young man with beard and medallion came up, asking about a broadcast I did years ago, talking about a drummer and Ravel's

Bolero. 'That was Ludovic Kennedy,' I said. 'Really?' he cried. 'Yes,' I said. 'You know Ludovic Kennedy....' 'Of course!' he said. 'Who does he play with now?'

Sunday 20 January

Practised calligraphy in the morning using new pens. Large lettering is v. difficult, although rough cartridge paper helps to give distinction to a faulty line. I am practising writing without lines because I prefer a page in which lines which are slightly out of true are rectified or counter-balanced as the writing progresses. Old manuscripts show that the scribes of old were much less meticulous than the formal calligraphers of today. Words were cunningly and artistically curtailed if a line turned out to be too long; each individual letter had its life, so that all 'a's, 'm's or 'e's were not necessarily identical; and spacing was often idiosyncratic, so that if the loops of a 'g' or 'y' invaded a line below, a space was left to accommodate it. Thus writing was a matter of design and movement rather than mere measurement.

Monday 21 January

Back at 11.45 to find the Bosch repair man booked for 12 already here (let in by David [Son], who was off school for O-level 'mocks'). The washing machine, a monument to German efficiency, had to have a 'brake' fitted some time ago in order to prevent the spin-dryer from revving so fast that the machine rocked off its mounting and set off round the bathroom like a Dalek. Now it appears that it will no longer work with the brake and it has been taken out again.

Tuesday 29 January

Very good article in *The Times* by Bernard Levin (every article that says what one has been saying oneself for weeks must be a 'very good article'!). He says that a society that spends fortunes on devising butter that will spread straight from the fridge doesn't deserve to survive. He shares my feelings that talk of the same old wasteful and avaricious 'boom' mentality returning when North Sea oil flows is unacceptable.

Thursday 31 January

The new sub on *Harpers* dealing with my piece is called Laura Pank – she rang this morning asking for my April article – very early, but have promised it for Monday. Apparently she rang last night asking for 'extension D' – after some puzzling, we realized she was reading off the 'ex-D' against my number at *Harpers*, meaning ex-directory! Hmm.

Saturday 2 February

Went to the Public Library, got out the last volume of Michael Foot's biography of Nye Bevan, and the first volume of Arthur Netherest's biography of Annie Besant. Don't know much about her, other than what I've gathered from reading about Bernard Shaw. Also took out Tom Gourdie's book on handwriting and an anthology of articles called *The Calligraphers' Handbook*. Gourdie says, as others have done, that my writing should slope forward at an angle of 7°. When I try this it tends to fall flat on its face!

Tuesday 5 February

In to B.B.C. at 5 to record a *Sounds Familiar* show – Barry Took in the chair, Arthur Askey, Patricia Hayes and Alan Coren on the panel. As an old mate, John Cassells, is now producing it, I found questions much more slanted in my direction. Was able to remember all four members of the Ray Ellington Quartet, added that I think R.E. is best jazz singer Britain ever had. Cue for Barry Took to introduce R.E. as the guest! While I was there I was provisionally booked by Dennis Gifford for a T.V. show involving cartooning and by John Cassells for six *I'm Sorry I Haven't A Clue* programmes. The Derek Nimmo show for next Sunday is postponed due to a strike at the B.B.C.

Thursday 7 February

Wrote letter to *The Times*: 'Sir, I have just received a form from the London Borough of Barnet, addressed to The Occupier and followed by my full address. The first question asked me to supply 1) Name of occupier in full and 2) address of occupier. Since the penalty for withholding information is a fine not exceeding £100, I solemnly copied out the address to which the questionnaire was sent in the first

Humph appeared on Clue *for 36 years as chairman and as a panellist on many other quizzes. This is a humorous cartoon of a fellow panellist on one such show, Clement Freud.*

place. The form then required my signature as Occupier *and my address*. They now have confirmation in triplicate that the house which I occupy and my address are indeed one and the same place. If there's anything else they'd like to know, I hope they'll know where to find me. Yrs etc.'

Saturday 9 February

Received a letter from a publicity company addressed to Mr Humphrey Littleton, inviting me to a party at Ronnie Scott's to congratulate Mr John Dankworth on his C.B.E.. Answered in formal script: Mr Humphrey Littleton – known for some time as Humphrey Lyttelton – regrets that he cannot attend the party at Ronnie Scott's on 12 February, 1974, owing to a previous engagement. He regrets that he will not be able to congratulate Mr John Dankworth personally on the twin honours of receiving the C.B.E. and of having his name spelt right.'

Letter this morning which shows that one can say nothing in a radio programme which will not offend someone. Subsequent to my (and Billie Whitelaw's) lighthearted remarks on dog mess (Mon 4 Feb), a blind lady writes pointing out the hazards to blind people. It seems she was in church and knelt in some.

According to the T.V. news, a poll to appear in tomorrow's *Observer* gives the Tories an 8 per cent lead. Anything can happen between now and the 28th, but the trouble is I don't know what result I want! A Tory win, however big, will alter nothing on the industrial front, and by summer they will have had to bring in some ferocious measures. A Labour win might make them so unpopular after a couple of years that they'll never get in again.

Monday 11 February

My letter appears in today's *Times* (cf. 7 Feb).

Wednesday 20 February

In the evening the Labour Party candidate and his agent came round – breezy pair radiating the slightly inefficient enthusiasm that reminds me of the old C.N.D. doings. They talked me into playing trumpet on their parade on Saturday. Jill [wife] gave them rather hefty Scotches and thought they went off rather tiddly. They got as far as the drive, where the agent discovered he had dropped his car key. It was 10 minutes before he found it in the living room! While discussing the music on Saturday they wondered if someone could bang a big drum. 'I will!' cried my daughter Georgina – then, a minute later, '…but I'm a Liberal.'

Meal in from Vijay's. [Indian Restaurant on Willesden Lane - still going strong.]

Saturday 23 February

Bruce Turner arrived at 10.30, by which time I had prepared my son David's bass-drum with a John Mills poster Sellotaped on the blank side and a rope 'sling'. Bruce, G. (with tambourine) and I drove to Hadley Green. No one there at 10.45, but eventually people began to converge. I called for a volunteer to bang the drum, eventually found a tall man in a flat cap who, once he had got the sling over his head past his pipe, caught on quickly. We stood – a motley crew of long-time Labourites, shaggy youths, excited girls and children – outside Robert Carr's [Conservative M.P.] house and sang 'The Red Flag', then set off through Barnet. Hard going at first, trying to blow with cold lips and uneven ground. Our 'band' was myself, B.T. on alto, the candidate's brother on (classical) clarinet, a folk guitarist and Georgina with her tambourine. The repertoire was limited – 'Maryland', 'The Saints', 'John Brown's Body', 'We Shall Not Be Moved' and 'Why Are We Waiting?' being the chief stand-bys, which we played in rotation for 3 miles from Hadley Green to Oakhill Park! The people from the Do-It-Yourself shop turned out to wave as we passed. At one point, during 'John Brown's Body', Georgina came across and said 'Why don't we sing "Glory, Glory, Hallelujah, Edward Heath's a bit peculiar"?' Odd coincidence – a woman in the Labour Party van on the way home said, 'You wouldn't remember me – you were unconscious last time I saw you!' She was on the scene of our car crash near Colchester in 1956 – actually worked in the timber works from which the lorry came. It was she who rang Mama at home!

Read about Etonians (my nephew Henry included!) pouring water on Joan Lestor [Labour M.P.] in her campaign, sent telegram to Joan – 'Best wishes and wholehearted Old Etonian support for your campaign.'

***Wednesday* 6 March**

Drove in to 34 Wimpole Street at 4.30 to see a specialist, John Musgrove, about my persistent nosebleed. The real Harley Street touch – big desk, plushy carpet, exquisite furniture, with J.M. looking as if he had just come from a wedding. He was surprised to find that I have any nose left after the innumerable cauterizations which I have had – there's apparently a danger that it will make a hole in the partition between nostrils. He has given me a spray with some new drug that strengthens veins and stops bleeding – from reading the leaflet it appears to have been invented to cope with bleeding from all kinds of horrific ailments, and nosebleed is a useful by-product. Consultation cost £8.40 – wonder how they calculate the odd pence.

Thursday 14 March

A large, fat-faced cat, a tabby affected by rust, has for the past two weeks taken up residence here. Jill unwisely allows it into the living-room in the evenings – it's very bad tempered and thoroughly unlikeable.

Tuesday 26 March

Michael Killanin, now Lord K. and President of the Olympics Committee, came to say hello in the bar – haven't seen him since he was a pupil at my father's House and I was about ten. Concert [Dublin] was an enormous success – the Jim Doherty Big Band of Dublin started off, then the team from Ronnie Scott's and finally my band, with Peter King sitting in for the finale. Huge ovation and euphoria all round. After the concert we were all invited to the Tandoori Rooms by proprietor Michael Bull, an Irish–Pakistani from Kenya ('I came over years ago so I'm not a Kenyan Asian!'). Meal was good – Rib of Beef Rickshawboy was a vast hunk of deliciously spiced steak, but came surprisingly with courgettes and chips! Sat next to M.B. who bent my ear somewhat about food-writing.

Wednesday 27 March

Got back to the hotel at about 3, got up at 8.30 to assemble for journey home. Dave Green, who was concerned about getting an early plane for a gig in Hampshire at 10.30 and who had left the theatre immediately after the concert to get a good night's sleep, had turned up at the Tandoori Rooms in the small hours roaring with laughter, full of Guinness and saying 'Stuff the gig!'. He had, however, checked out of the hotel in the early morning to catch the 8.30 plane. We arrived at the airport at 10.30 to find the airport shrouded in fog and Dave still there. Our own plane was an hour late taking off. Spent a boring time in the departure lounge. D.G. got off just before us at noon, but when we reached Heathrow he was still there – the airline (Aer Lingus this time) had once again smashed the neck of his double-bass. Result of the day's events – two missed gigs and a smashed bass. Accident-prone is an understatement for D.G.

Friday 29 March

Gig was at the Halifax Civic Theatre, a cramped old-fashioned building, more like a town-hall than a theatre. It was a firm's dance demanding 'party' things like the hokey-cokey etc. – a sad contrast after concerts like Dublin, but paying more! At one point the social secretary, flushed with fright, came on to give away spot prizes. Among them, trying to be too subtle by half, she called for the first person to bring up a set of plastic teeth – meaning a comb. In a flash the stage was besieged by outstretched hands holding damp and glistening false teeth.

Saturday 30 March

A beautiful spring day, for part of which I dozed in the sun. The fish in the pond are now active, a frog and a newt have made an appearance and the blackbirds in the garden are in operatic form, one of them holding a conversation with itself, assuming at times the heady chirrup of a smaller bird. Ours is no longer a quiet garden, but I noticed this afternoon that the greatest din came from a veritable army of lawn-mowers on manoeuvres.

Wednesday 3 April

To Shireff's Wine Bar & Restaurant at 12.15 to meet Johnny Mercer (American songwriter) for lunch. Mercer small and bald but otherwise with the 'pixy', gap-toothed slightly Chinese look of the old photographs. We talked a lot about jazz musicians and got on well, I think. He made one or two odd remarks about racial matters which didn't really sink in until afterwards. About Nat 'King' Cole, he 'handled himself with great dignity and sense, *didn't get fresh* but wouldn't take anything from anyone'. About his childhood in the South, 'in the summer we had coloured people all around diggin' the potatoes, catchin' the fish, helping in the house. We couldn't give 'em anything except a cup of tea and a biscuit or something – (and with a smile) and we lynched a few, too, when they got out of line.' Sarcasm? Satire? Whatever it was it left T.C. and myself momentarily uncertain what line to take next! He's clearly an intelligent and cultured man, but I shall try and find out on Friday if he has a nostalgia (*vide* 'Lazybones', 'Moon River', 'Old Music Man') for the South of the old, pre-disturbance days.

Friday 5 April

Paralysed with nerves over Mercer interview, made usual firm resolve never again to take on jobs which involve nervous strain. Interviewing is not my metier – I can't master the art of listening eagerly to what the interviewee is saying while at the same time thinking of the next question. We assembled in a hospitality room at the T.V. centre at 4.45, Mercer arrived soon after, with his wife Ginger. After a session of 'make-up' we perched on a rostrum and launched into a marathon chat. I had covered foolscap sheets with questions, dredged them up with, I hope, no visible sign of desperation for an hour and a half. J.M. rose superbly to the occasion, came up with all his stories and we got everything in the can in one session of chat. Acquired one gem from my conversations with him – viz that Jack Teagarden never wanted to go into music – he wanted to be a railroad engineer like his father. When he was given his first trombone he cried!

Tuesday 9 April

Worked most of the day on *Harpers & Queen*. Bored stiff with writing about restaurants. Am toying with the idea of finishing the food-writing, but Jill fears it may put an end to the outings. There has been a steadily increasing warm spell for the past week, must now be rated a heatwave. Bad – usually means a poor summer.

Wednesday 10 April

Got up at 6.45 to finish off *Harpers & Queen* article. Sent letter to Fiona Macpherson resigning from the restaurant column. Explained that I am simply tired of writing about food. Only one thing in life more enjoyable than taking on a new job and that is giving up an old one! As soon as the letter was written I felt relieved – at the moment I feel like giving writing a long rest. Shall continue to take an interest in the restaurant scene, but, as I told F.M., I am coming to be known as H.L. the food-writer and occasional trumpet-player.

Got in an Indian meal from Vijay on Willesden Lane. Have discovered that the prawn bhoona with chapathi makes a nice alternative to the curries to follow masala dosai.

Saturday 13 April

There have been two blobs of frog-spawn in the pond this year, and Georgina brought one back from Wormley. One batch was 'laid' under a stone in the margin – starved of water, it looked like caviar. I took the stone away and filled the pond to cover it – it remains to be seen if it will flourish. One of the remaining blobs 'hatched' a couple of days ago, tadpoles have dispersed in the pond. I transferred the other to the aquarium where they will develop unmolested.

Sunday 14 April

Arrived home at about 11.30.

Spent a relaxed day in beautiful weather – blue sky and sunshine, but quite a chilly breeze. When Jill and Georgina went riding, I took my bicycle and went on a long ride – down Elmbank Road, along Mays Lane, up Barnet Lane to Totteridge then turned right past the ponds, home via Hendon Wood Lane. Totteridge Ponds look nice now, teams of volunteers having cleaned them up in recent weeks. I find cycling quite easy after a break of about thirty years – upper legs get a bit stiff, but I don't get puffed.

Georgina had her Easter Egg hunt at 2 – clings on to this rather absurd routine although it's now entirely a solo affair.

Wednesday 17 April

Finally contacted Fiona Macpherson about the *Harpers* situation. She confessed that she has been avoiding me because she has been 'in a state of cold shock' since she got my letter last Thursday. She accepted the fact with great regret as my column has 'such a huge following', but understands the reason.

Thursday 18 April

Fiona Macpherson rang early in the morning to say that she had spoken to Marcus Morris about my resignation and that she had been chided for not trying harder to keep me. He wants to see me when I'm next in and may well offer more money. Have agreed to think over the possibility of keeping on with the Restaurant page and perhaps doing an occasional hotel column. Will take the opportunity of asking for more money as £60 now covers expenses and leaves no salary at all!

Tuesday 23 April

To the Bull's Head at Barnes for session in which Pete King deputized for Bruce Turner who has a week in Denmark. Good session and packed out – I recall the landlord, Albert Tolley, saying when we first approached him that he didn't think the band would go at the Bull's Head. To be fair he now regularly pays £10 extra for a full house.

Friday 26 April

Jill going off for the day to Badminton with Audrey Williams, fought a premonition of an accident.

Audrey Williams rang at 9.30 to say that Jill was just leaving their house on the way home – in some pain as she fell when crossing under a jump, sprained her ankle and passed out. They had to hold her up to prevent her flopping into a bed of stinging nettles. The premonition explained! J. arrived home limping badly with a swollen foot. It appears that she jumped down a slope on to a concealed stone. She had great difficulty getting off to sleep, gave her two Codeine which did the trick.

Monday 29 April

Worked on two programmes at home – one for Duke Ellington's 75th birthday, one for next week – Ellington again, in case he runs out of breath completely while I'm in Germany. Went in at 4 o'clock to be photographed by Thames Television walking into the B.B.C. (an insert for the *Today* programme on 100 Oxford Street).

Wednesday 1 May

On to the B.B.C. to record my film review for *Kaleidoscope*. It was in the form of an interview with presenter Peter France, so was quite painless to do. Resisted temptation to fall in with his 'Italia Arte mimetic' style of jargon, babbled on in my own way. Producer seemed very pleased with it, wants me to do some more. As Stephen [son] said, 'that's another one to add to the "musician-broadcaster-journalist-cartoonist-nature-lover-food-writer-bandleader" list!'

Evening at home getting ready for German week.

Sunday 5 May

Early start at 10.30 to travel about 300 miles to Cologne. Boring journey through endless agricultural prairie. Got to Cologne at 5.30 after a journey through grey drizzle. So far in three days we have played to 1,300 people – not an impressive score. I wonder how long W. Germany will remain a sort of cultural blotting-paper, soaking up jazz-band tours. Checked into the Hotel Kolpinghaus, quite a smart hotel but cheap, thanks to it being run by some religious body. Hadn't been in the room long before Christian rang through to say that according to the contract we had to be at the hall by 6.30 (it was then 6.40) so could we come at once. Mad rush on to coach which then spent twenty minutes trying to find the Rheinpark. When we arrived we found that we were playing in a sort of Battersea Gardens – it was by now pelting with rain, and all the entrances to the park were locked. Eddie, our burly, taciturn driver, got the coach at an oblique angle across the road and held up about 300 yards of traffic both ways. When we finally got in we found that we were playing in an outdoor theatre – a cold wind blew across the stage and an audience of seventy sat huddled in the rain, their black forms outlined against the misty concrete background giving an odd surrealistic effect. Very difficult to keep the instruments in tune. In the second half, the audience came up and sat round us on the stage. Very cosy. After the concert we were taken by some local musicians to an alleged Portuguese restaurant called Don Pepe – no more Portuguese than I am. Fair goulash soup but main dish was a plank-like rump steak and chips bubbling in hot grease.

Monday** 6 **May

Fair night, though woken early by other guests bellowing in the corridors – Spaniards, Japanese and the like. Didn't have breakfast, after last night's grease-up. The activities of the band in the morning give a good idea of our various proclivities. Dave Green (bass) and Mick Pyne, being Hitler freaks, went to look for records of speeches from World War II to add to their collections (Mick Pyne also collects war-time entertainment shows like *Bandwagon*, *Itma* etc.). Kathy Stobart and Tony Mann make a bee-line, hand-in-hand, for the nearest department store whenever we reach a new town, buying floral enamel casseroles, knitted 'folk-lore' egg-cosies etc., most of which can be bought cheaper in England. Bruce Turner wandered about for an hour or so then went to look for a vegetarian restaurant, having lived up to now off pickled salads, cheese and raw carrot. I went into the hotel restaurant (recommended with one knife-and-fork in Michelin) with Christian and Eddie and had the best – the only – meal of the tour. 'Indian curry soup' (a hot pea soup) followed by vast fresh 'Müllerin' trout with plain boiled potato and salad. On the way to the Post Office to get stamps, passed an antique bookshop with a portfolio of German and Japanese calligraphy from an exhibition in 1962. Prints, but beautifully reproduced on good paper, the German samples being show-pieces – 'labyrinths etc.' – by scribes of the 16th–17th century, the Japanese being by a modern calligrapher. It costs £5 which means I can get ten framed examples for 50p each.

Ate egg and bacon in hotel before the concert. Played to about 400 in a nice auditorium. Tony Mann had his usual foreign tour 'party night' in the hotel afterwards, got well oiled. Meanwhile Eddie the driver was getting drunk in a local casino, lost £283 and had to be bailed.

Tuesday** 7 **May

Eventful journey – left at 12 o'clock to travel to Herne, and discovered after thirty minutes' travelling that I had left my suits behind at the hotel. We had to travel some way along the motorway before we could turn round. On the way into Kamen the coach bumped a car and there was a twenty-minute delay while the drivers exchanged details. When we called at the hotel the proprietress came out to claim 20DM from Eddie, our driver, who seemingly threw up all over his room and left without reporting it. While we were waiting in the central car park, two old ladies got on the bus, thinking it was public transport.

Thursday 9 May

Got up at 8, packed up for travelling as we have no coach. At breakfast, 'Freddy', who is to produce our record, arrived to take us to the studio. Dave Green in poor shape, Mick Pyne in a foul mood. In a small Volkswagen bus and Christian's car, we drove out of Hamburg into the countryside, seemingly forever. Eventually we arrived in a village and drive up to a small villa. This is where the recording studio is, a small garret on the first floor, long and so low that Dave's bass must be in the middle of the room or it hits the sloping ceiling. On the face of it, it looked a disastrous set-up, with everyone stretched out the length of the room and separated by screens. However, as soon as we started to play it was clear that the acoustics were ideal. It took till about 11.30 to achieve a sound (one microphone per person so it can be 'mixed' afterwards) and we then recorded 'In-Swinger', 'Toot'n' in Kamen' (new name for 'Quelque chose français'), 'Talk of the Town', 'St Louis Blues' and 'New Bad Penny Blues' in one take! 'One for Buck' took two and 'Georgia Mae' three. I don't think I have ever played so well on a record – chops were in good shape and the sound seemed to be good. In fact it captured the whole band in good form.

Wednesday 15 May

Worked at home in the morning. Jill had a phone call from Mrs T.-S., mother of Stephen's girlfriend Liz. It appears that a former French boyfriend called Bernard has been pestering Liz ever since a holiday in France last year, refusing to take '*non*' for an answer. The phone call was to say that his mother rang Mrs T.-S. at 6a.m. to say that he had left home heading for England where he threatens to shoot himself if she doesn't relent. 'It's possible', Mrs T.-S. added, 'that he has a gun.' The upshot is that I must pick them up tonight from school as Mrs T.-S. doesn't want Liz to come out to us (where she is staying) on public transport. I don't expect Stephen relishes getting shot up in a crime of passion either. How exiting parenthood is!

Having got them safely home, I turned in my tracks and drove in to the Paris Studio, Lower Regent Street, for the first in another series of *I'm Sorry I Haven't A Clue*. Barry Cryer, Tim Brooke-Taylor and Graeme Garden were on it as usual but Bill Oddie has declined to do another series so was replaced by Willie Rushton. Never met him before but by coincidence he is on the 'Who Said That?' quiz with me in Southampton tomorrow. The story of *I.S.I.H.A.C.* is an extraordinary one – we did the pilot show in 1972, everyone agreed that it was too self-indulgent and dreadful to get off the ground. Months later a B.B.C. 'high-up' heard the pilot, fell about and insisted it should go on. This is its third series. Tonight's two shows were pretty good with some new 'rounds'.

Friday 17 May

Spent the morning doing accounts. I sometimes wonder if this business of reconciling bank statements etc. is habit-forming. Would I go on doing it week after week if I won £500,000 on the pools? Keeping one's nose ahead of overdraft limits is certainly one of life's great challenges! Certainly there is a certain satisfaction, when one closes the book after totting up all outstanding in and out payments, in knowing that one is £228 on the credit side.

Session in the evening at the City University Union, part of the North London Festival. It's organized by B.B.C. producer Graham Tayah who also runs the sessions at the New Merlin's Cave. Two years ago we played the same gig, sharing the bill with Sandy Brown (who guested with us) and the then unrediscovered George Melly. S.B. took over my band with all the symptoms of megalomania, G.M. ended the evening unable to rise from all fours. Half the audience threw up, the other half kept up a stentorian chatter which made music-making redundant. Before the final jam session I strode resolutely off the bandstand. 'Where are you going, Humph?' cried Graham Tayah over the P.A. 'Home,' I said, and left. This time there were fewer people and it was a slightly more sober occasion, despite being written up in the *Observer*.

Sunday 19 May

Writing this up in the garden, as the last few days have been moving towards heat-wave conditions and today is perfect – hot but with a gentle breeze, clear sky with wisps of white and some aeroplane graffiti (whatever happened to sky-writing?). With the warm weather the pond has turned into pea-soup, rather unsightly but said to be good for the fish. I haven't done a census on the fish lately but I think there are about fifteen of all sizes – half the original stock. It seems to be an optimum number as there were virtually no deaths this winter.

Monday 20 May

Opening my letters in the studio I found one which was from Number: 506511, Name: Millhench. It read: 'Dear H. – Thanks a million for the ray of sunshine through the grey provided by your super 8–9 spot on Mondays. My little 'Trani' at the cell window provided a most welcome treat for the boys on 'G' wing during your show. I don't know if you play requests at all but if not you may like this one yourself anyway. J. Johnson and K. Wilding (sic) playing 'Surrey with a Fringe on Top' (great trip that). Whatever, it's all very welcome sound...Regards, Ron.'

Despite the familiarity I have never to my knowledge met Ronald Millhench of the Wilson forgery case!

Tuesday 21 May

The news is currently dominated by the situation in Belfast. An organization called the Ulster Workers' Committee brought all poorer workers out on strike against the 'power sharing' Sunningdale agreement a week ago. Now the strike has become general. Len Murray's brave attempt to lead the shipyard workers to work was a flop and evoked terrifying antagonism, much of it from Protestant housewives transformed, under sectarian stress, into harpies. Can any solution be found short of a civil war, which would, in the short term anyway, establish a 'victor'? The *Guardian* had an effective cartoon

showing the Ulster military group as a small boy saying in front of anxious parents, 'I'll just stop breathing and die – and then they'll be sorry!'

Worked indoors most of the day, sending off V.A.T. forms, answering letters etc. etc.

At the Bull's Head in the evening a doctor who comes regularly to the sessions suggested that my back symptoms sound like the beginning of disc trouble. Suggested that I apply some home therapy ('traction') by hanging from the frame of a door by the fingertips. As he is about 5 foot 2 he can probably do this – at full stretch my arms outstrip the door frame by about a foot and I should have to kneel! Will try it from the garage loft. Might have to go to an osteopath to have the skeleton re-hung.

Once more a very good session at the Bull. Rumour has it that Albert Tolley, the landlord, is due to retire. Not every musician has got on with him – with his vast stomach and forearms to match he's everyone's idea of the autocratic publican, but he has given seven nights a week employment to musicians for many years and it will be a sad day if the Bull abandons jazz.

Thursday 23 May

My birthday, a suitably 'low profile' event. As I am out this evening we are having a 'Queen's birthday' at a later and more suitable date. Started work on an obituary for Duke Ellington in case of the worst happening. According to today's papers he has gone back into hospital with pneumonia so everyone is on the alert.

Friday 24 May

Georgina came in at 12.30 to say that she heard on the news that Duke Ellington has died. The 1 o'clock news confirmed it. The end of an era. Those who survive from the pre-war era – Hines, Basie, Hampton, Goodman, Wilson – can only be regarded now as stragglers. It transpired during the day that he has been having treatment since January for cancer in both lungs. Didn't feel quite the same personal loss as when Louis Armstrong died, no doubt because Duke was a harder man to get close to – and this applies to his music too, which doesn't have quite the same personal impact as Armstrong's playing and singing. Ellington somehow appeared more self-sufficient. Despite the fact that his band had deteriorated dramatically during the last year or two and his own writing talent seemed close to exhaustion, it's impossible to conceive of the jazz world without him. Is it time we acknowledged that it's all over? Like a star millions of light-years away, the light of jazz will no doubt glimmer for some time, hiding the knowledge that the star itself is extinct. Where are the giants now? Gillespie plays intermittently, Miles Davis makes his trivial journey into electronic fashion, Monk has run out of creative steam.

Tuesday 28 May

Letter with a lot of useful bumph from Mr Jacklin of the Soc. of Scribes & Illuminators. It looks as if it will be worth joining as a lay member, with the possibility of perhaps entering for a competition in the future to see what standard I can reach. There's also useful information in the form of summaries of lectures – on quills, paper etc.

On to the Playhouse Theatre to record two more *I'm Sorry I Haven't A Clue* programmes. Same team as last time – Brooke-Taylor,

Rushton, Cryer and Garden. The games went better than last time, perhaps due to a larger studio audience. Dave Lee, who will tell anecdotes before, during and after rehearsals, played the songs (with crucial words buzzed out), but with 1¾ hours recorded we have plenty in hand. Showed them my letter from Ronald Millhench, Willie R. determined to reveal it in *Private Eye* and cause yet another scandal!

Tuesday* 4 *June

Have started on the mammoth task of cataloguing my record collection in a card index – the only way to discover what I have in the shelves. Began with Count Basie, combining it with the preparation of an obituary programme.

Wednesday* 5 *June

Took a trembling Stephen in for his first A-level exam, then went on to a meeting of the R.S.P.B. Reserves and Conservation Committee. I say little at the meetings but as most of them appear to be jazz fans I hold forth afterwards on non-ornithological subjects! From the conservation standpoint a major contemporary problem seems to be the accidental burning of heathland by farmers – two Dorset heaths, nesting sites for fifty-five Dartford warblers (pairs), went west in April.

Friday* 7 *June

Went in to Fulham where a lady called Gabrielle keeps a stock of calligraphic materials in her flat. Her business, called Falkiner's Fine Papers, originally dealt solely in hand-made and 'special' paper, but she was asked by the Society of Scribes and Illuminators to stock other materials as well. So I was able to buy turkey and goose quills, a scalpel, several boxes of Mitchell inks, a Chinese ink-stick and a Chinese stone, with tray and well hollowed out, for rubbing down ink. She doesn't stock reeds, but on the way home I collected a sheaf of garden canes from the D.I.Y. shop which should be ideal.

Saturday* 8 *June

Letter arrived from the Society for Italic Handwriting with membership form enclosed. The twice-yearly bulletin has perked up considerably since my father used to get it in the 'fifties – now pocket-sized with a smart cover. In it, I found a letter from a man in Bristol asking for samples of 'everyday Italic hands' to keep his collection up to date. Shall write to him taking him up on the offer to reciprocate – for *my* collection.

Spent some of the day experimenting in quill-making. First efforts made out of turkey and goose quills not bad, tho' it seems to be important to get the bend of the quill curving towards rather than away from the body, otherwise it twists the pen in one's hand. Rubbing down ink from a Chinese ink-stick seems to be more appropriate to an ancient, slow-moving civilization than the modern rat-race. In other words, it takes one hour to make a tablespoonful! Never mind – it's a relaxing occupation.

Played in the evening at 100 Oxford Street – a glum place nowadays with the bandstand halfway between the two bars, to ensure minimum attention. Furthermore, the piano was diabolically out of tune. I made one or two caustic remarks about it over the microphone, which annoyed Ted Morton who was the director on duty. At the end he insisted that it is a 'very good piano' which is tuned every Wednesday (for a seven-night-a-week workload!). He claimed that the piano is subject to extremes of temperature – all the more reason why it should be tuned more often. A man who brought some Americans down said, 'Correct me if I'm wrong, but I have a feeling you prefer playing in your old style.' 'You are wrong,' I said.

Wednesday 12 June

Duke Ellington's memorial service at St Martins-in-the-Field. Met at 9.30 for rehearsal in the crypt. The event, hastily put together, could have been a disaster but was in fact triumphant. A special choir opened with a 'Gloria' with brass accompaniment. Gerald Lascelles read the lesson, Rev. Austin Williams had composed some special prayers, Derek Jewell (jazz critic) gave a very good address and, interspersed among these verbal tributes, the band played 'Come Sunday' (w. choir, 'In a Mellotone', 'Creole Love Call', 'Mood Indigo' (a superb unaccompanied harmonica introduction by Larry Adler, singing by Cleo Laine, trumpet by me), 'Never No Lament' and a final 'A Train'. The band sounded good and by the end of 'Lament' several people were tentatively applauding. At the end, when the clerics had left in the customary procession, the band's 'A Train' held everybody standing in the church, and Ian Hall encouraged an off-beat handclap which was taken up all round. The result was a joyful spontaneous anthem which must have got through to the old boy upstairs!

Straight on afterwards for a front-line rehearsal at Ronnie Scott's Club, running through the Buck Clayton arrangements which we record next month with Buddy Tate (American saxophonist) tenor.

Thursday 20 June

Letter from Mr Constant of Keynsham, Bristol, written in a 'running' Italic handwriting which makes mine look as if it's written with a policeman's truncheon! He says that he tends to write 'waywardly', altering a lot within the style and switching from Platignum to Osmiroid and back again. If that is 'wayward' what is my switch from fountain pen to metal nib to quill?

Friday 21 June

I went straight on via the B.B.C. to Basildon for a concert at the Arts Centre where we have often played before. Bruce Turner showed me a cheque which I gave him last Saturday dated 'M. Pyne 1974'. I do this occasionally when under stress – Bruce's comment: 'Made a fool of me in front of the bank-manager, dad!'

Quill pens are a partial success. The difficulty is to cut a sharp enough chisel edge to the nib to make satisfactory thicks and thins.

Tuesday 25 June

Got home after the programme last night to find Jill fuming. Someone – and the finger points at me – left the bottom door of the freezer open on Sunday night and all the food – meat, poultry, fish – was partially thawed. A salvage operation had to be mounted to save and refreeze all but the potentially lethal stuff! It is a triumph of contemporary design that if one bangs the upper door, the lower one springs open! We managed to retrieve most of the stuff but it won't keep for long so I fancy we shall be eating freezer food for the next few days.

Monday 1 July

After the programme I went to the Hilton Hotel to confer with the German team who will produce the extraordinary T.V. show on which we appear on 17 July. Peter Kirk M.P., Bill Davies of *Punch*, Edward Heath and Spike Milligan are the cast so far, and their thoughts on Germany and the Common Market will be punctuated by music from us.

Tuesday 2 July

Went in at 12.30 to collect Buddy Tate from his hotel to go to the Pye recording studios to record the Buck Clayton album. Buddy looking very fit and sharp in tartan trousers but suffering from lack of sleep, having just come in from Montreux after a late night. Went straight to the studio and got under way at about 2.20. It took a bit of time getting used to the set-up and we started by making several 'takes' of 'Out-Swinger', quite a difficult up-tempo number featuring the two tenor saxophones. 'Steevos' proved a bit easier and went pretty well OK, as did 'Swinging Scorpio', although by this time the sustained high B-flat ending was proving troublesome for bruised lips and we had to do an 'edit' ending. Recording is exceptionally tiring, for the good reason that when one has run through a tune twice and recorded three or four 'takes', one has blown the equivalent of a condensed half-concert. The most notable thing about Buddy's playing is the colossal 'Texas' sound, full-throated and rich in overtones. He was perhaps not on top form, being tired, but nevertheless we have three good 'takes' in the can.

Wednesday 3 July

Afterwards we went straight to the Festival Hall for rehearsal before the Louis Armstrong anniversary concert. A gathering of old friends – Bill Coleman at seventy, looking as young as ever but suffering from angina which clearly affected his breathing; Helen Humes now 'five-by-five' but singing her heart out even at rehearsal; and Earl Hines (also seventy now) with an improved wig (the last one looked like a black cat asleep on his head) and looking tired but still magnificent. Alas, Bill C.'s playing, though with flashes of the old soaring fluency, is now very uncertain. His doctor says he can still play 'but not too often', and I feared once or twice that he might drop dead there and then.

Sunday 14 July

Watched self interviewing Johnny Mercer in *Omnibus*. Didn't like it at all – I looked sluggish, pasty-faced (too much make-up) and groping for words. And after ninety minutes non-stop I'm not surprised. But Jill thought it was OK. Mercer spoke well (some tribute, I hope, to my prompting).

Wednesday 17 July

Up at the crack of dawn to take the horsebox to Edmonton for its M.O.T. test. Got there at 9, reported to reception then joined the queue in Lane Four. Not too long a wait before I reached the starting line. A rather leery-looking man checked the horn, washer, internal switches and the outside, then wandered off saying, 'All right so far.' Then an elderly man checked the underneath in a service-well while I responded to instructions ('Rock steering, foot-brake, handbrake etc.') over a small loudspeaker. After that he emerged from under the lorry ominously bearing a tin mug. Sure enough they all left for their coffee break, leaving us roasting for twenty minutes. When it came to the testing of lights etc., I tested the flashers without the ignition on, man said, 'Your indicators have packed up – you need a new unit.' Momentary horrors. Despite squirting the windscreen washer when he said, 'Dip your lights', I got it through the test.

To Thames T.V. at 1 o'clock for the T.V. show – sandwich lunch in the green-room, then band-call to rehearse with Adelaide Hall and Norma Winstone. Wracked with nerves all day as indeed are all the production team.

Thursday 18 July

The programme went surprisingly well – all the music was good and accurate, with both Addie and Norma rising splendidly to the occasion. The chat, too, went according to plan, with plenty of good stories. Most of the speakers afterwards lamented that there was no time to go into it more deeply.

Friday 26 July

On arrival at Beaminster I spotted what looked like a wader on the edge of the lake. It flew off and perched on an oil-drum in mid-lake. Dashed back to the cottage to get my binoculars and found two green woodpeckers feeding casually on the lawn, watchable for several minutes. The small wader was gone when we got back but I later identified it as a common sandpiper, probably *en route*. We came home to a plebeian meal of sausages, baked beans and fried potatoes.

Thursday 1 August

Letter from Stephen! He's having a 'really good time' in scorching heat. 'We've visited a nudist beach near San Tropez and I beared (sic) my naughty bits for a short while but decided that the heat may reap serious effects and smartly covered them up again.'

Friday 9 August

Nixon has resigned. I didn't sit up until 2a.m. to watch his resignation speech but there has been pretty full coverage all day. He was hardly contrite, giving as his only reason for retiring the fact that he no longer had 'a strong enough political base in Congress'. Evasive to the end! At night they showed an extraordinary spectacle, Nixon's farewell to his staff and cabinet in the White House. In grim fascination it matched the final court scene in *The Caine Mutiny* – in fact there was a Queeg-like quality about the impromptu speech which rambled on in maudlin fashion about his mother and father, 'greatness' coming from adversity etc., and in which he increasingly looked a shambles of a man – sweat glistening on the upper lip, eyes practically shut and, every now and then, a ghastly attempt at a grin. The pantomime went on when he arrived at his home in California, stepping off the plane with arms raised as if to a hero's welcome. It remains to be seen whether the profound anger of many Americans about Watergate has been assuaged by this extraordinary departure. I doubt it.

Monday 12 August

After dinner, all the men assembled in the library (which is joined to the drawing-room by huge [open] folding doors, so we and the ladies were virtually at opposite ends of the same room!). There we sat like a lot of black crows on a telegraph wire when in came Harriet [niece] looking like a radiant Joan of Arc and saying, 'Can I have some port?' 'What on earth are you doing here?' said Bobby [brother-in-law], to receive the rhetorical answer, 'Up with Women's Lib!' It was shortly followed by Susanna, Anthea, Lucy [more nieces!] and Jill, who was faced with the alternative of staying put with the conventional matrons or joining the demo! The party improved dramatically from then on!

Wednesday 14 August

Spent all morning sorting through the letters – one from Buck saying that he is making a steady recovery, one from Jane Laurence [niece], neatly-typed since she was at time of writing working as a secretary in Montreal with access to a 'super typewriter'. Two letters from my cheerful pen-pal in Portland gaol – one certainly doesn't enquire in these circumstances what the man is 'inside' for, but it is only natural to be curious! He writes with such fervour about jazz – his particular favourite is Thelonius Monk – that I hope our correspondence is proving therapeutic.

Tuesday 20 August

Got up at 7.30 with the idea of leaving for Dorset at about 8.15. Wandered out, half asleep, to bring in the mail and locked the front door behind me! Two house keys inside on the bed. Luckily I had gone out with a car key. After trying for forty-five minutes to open the weak dining-room window latch with an unwound wire coat-hanger (I got it in the top and hooked round the latch, but my careful paper wedge was too effective.), I drove off in dressing gown and pyjamas to phone Jill from the Arkley Hotel call box. Two draymen unloading beer looked faintly surprised but nothing more. Jill was engaged, so drove home, then remembered that jerseys, trousers etc. from the cleaners were still hanging in the back of the car, so dressed in the courtyard. Phoned Jill again from the Frosts' (Arkley P.O.) and told her why I wasn't halfway to Loders (I had heard the phone ringing in the house while I was attempting to break in and assumed rightly that it was her). She confirmed that David has a key to the kitchen door, and as all my things except the shirt and trousers I was wearing yesterday are still in the car, she suggested that I should drive down leaving the house apparently impregnable – which I did, arriving at about 1. Hot sunny day again, so did nothing except sit in the garden. Made a successful sauce hollandaise to go with white cabbage at supper.

Saturday 14 September

Left Swansea on the 11.52, due in at 3.25. Took advantage of a British Rail scheme to make use of the largely empty First Class coaches on Saturdays. Owners of Second Class ticket can transfer to First by paying an extra 50p. Had compartment to myself until, I think, Cardiff, when Leo Abse M.P. and his wife came aboard. At Newport, one extra passenger embarked – dishevelled, in a crumpled blue suit with long walking-stick and big rucksack. Not a hiker, but Michael Foot, looking like every idealists' notion of a Labour Cabinet Minister. I had a nostalgic B.R. lunch, unchanged over the years – packaged vegetable soup, newly-cooked but rather parsimonious steak and kidney pie with roast potatoes, carrots and beans, and pear-cum-peach melba. Regretted that I didn't choose lemon sponge pudding – B.R. are best at school dinners. When I got back to the compartment, Michael Foot and the Abses had got together and were enjoying stentorian political gossip, on which I eavesdropped unashamedly. Had I been an opponent or ill-wisher with a hot-line to the *Daily Mail*, I could have had a field-day. Learnt quite a bit about the domestic life of the Woodrow Wyatts, Foot's belief in getting union people into the management side of industry – and the day the Abses found a tramp living in their Rolls Royce. Train was twenty minutes late, taxi-man in Paddington said 'No, sir – I don't particularly want to go to Golders Green' and drove off. Got another reluctant cab outside. Gig for R.S.P.B. at Palmers Green.

Sunday 15 September

Postscript on yesterday. When the train reached Paddington, Leo Abse said goodbye to Foot with 'see you at the barricades' – Foot replied, 'It might well come to that, the way things are going!' Then as an afterthought he called out to them, 'D'you want a lift?' They accepted. I followed them off the train, visualizing a sleek ministerial car but he went straight to a travel-stained old banger, slung the ministerial rucksack in the boot and drove off. V. impressive.

Wednesday 18 September

Harold Wilson has announced an election on 10 October – coincidence that my last visit to Cornwall was the day before the Feb. election.

Friday 20 September

The promoter who is organizing the Geoff Boycott Testimonial at Easingwold rang up the Colin Hogg office yesterday to say that he had only sold forty-seven tickets and could he cancel. Colin said yes – so long as he paid the full fee! He agreed to go on with it, saying that he believed it to be Boycott and not the band which is unpopular!

Monday 30 September

Woke in the morning to find that the bedroom curtain stops six inches from the bottom of the window and elderly chambermaid doing the laundry in the yard outside my ground-floor room had an unrestricted view of my recumbent form.

Saturday 5 October

Got back from Worthing at about 11, in time to sally forth on behalf of Mr Alfred Dubs and the Boreham Wood Labour Party. Bruce Turner has to go and see his daughter so can't be there. I arrived just after 12 o'clock to find the banjo-player of last week and the one-legged tenor saxist anxiously awaiting me. They had a snare-drummer with them and a proper big drum with a chubby youth to play it – unfortunately he was a jazz fan so banged on the off-beat throughout. We marched from the Crown to the Red Lion and back. Rather more overt hostility than in Barnet – the newsagent opposite the Red Lion came out and urged a woman-driver to 'run the bastards down!'. Afterwards I went with the Labour Party team first to the party H.Q. (the agent's home where her mum made tea) then to a pub where I noticed that most of the canvassers took off their rosettes before going in. Like the Barnet man they have a slender hope of getting in. Noticed Alfie Bass carrying a banner on the parade.

Tuesday 8 October

Harry Carney died today and the final full-stop has been put to the Ellington band. There can be no posthumous Ellington Orchestra tours now. Harry had been with the band for forty-seven years, and for most of them his baritone-sax sound, more than any other single ingredient, identified the band. His main influences were Coleman Hawkins and Adrian Rollini – Hawk for the top of the instrument, Rollini for the bottom. And Hawkins was the model for all his heavily-tongued, chuntering up-tempo work.

Thursday 10 October

ELECTION DAY! Took Stephen to the polls early as he won't be back later, and recorded my vote for John Mills at the same time. The political polls have been remarkably steady over this past week, giving Labour a lead of around 9 per cent. It looks good (though obviously not 9 per cent good!) but I will be happier when all the votes are in and Labour has its majority. Crisis permitting there is then a chance that we might have another big socialist step forward à la 1945.

Went on the air at Capital at about 10 – in the studio were Sarah Ward, the presenter, with a news man announcing the results and two 'commentators' interpreting them. In the lull between results, we played with Elkie Brooks singing songs. There was also a pianist-cum-singer called Paul someone who sang good songs of his own composition and played appalling ragtime that sounded like Gershwin on a bad day. It was an enjoyable, relaxed blow, quite unrehearsed. Meanwhile the results promised a Labour win but it soon became clear that early forecasts of a 20–30 majority were not going to be fulfilled. When I got home at five o'clock, it seemed likely to be five!

Friday 18 October

A full and extraordinary day. Did some tidying-up round the house in the morning, while Jill was at her English class, then caught the 2 o'clock train to Swansea, where I am to introduce an R.S.P.B. film show by the Wales office at the Brangwyn Hall. Jotted down my 'speech' during the journey, working 'in the dark' as I didn't know what sort of audience to expect. In search of one ornithological anecdote decided to inflate Mick Pyne's comment – 'It's Hitchcock!' – on seeing squadrons of geese fly in from the fields at Loch Leven into a story. With a huge audience of about 1,400, many children among them, I sounded (to me) long-winded and verbose. Just before I went on, an elderly man introduced himself just as I recognized him – Norman Bowen, one of my old friends from Port Talbot days! Saw him again in the interval and we had a chat about the old days.

Caught the 12.23 sleeper home, getting some sleep!

Wednesday 30 October

Postponed going out for supper till after the screening of the Ali–Foreman fight. Ridiculously exciting, with Ali allowing the ferocious Foreman to punch himself out then knocking him out in the eighth round.

Sunday 3 November

Spent the day working on my programme. Buck arrived after it, called by to see him at the Green Park Hotel – he looks a lot thinner and smaller, but very fit and sharp, in magenta slacks and matching shoes.

Thursday 14 November

Back from Shoreham through what amounted to a tornado-lashing wind, thunder and lightning, huge hailstones. Got to the Beeb ten minutes late, to record some comments on George T. Simon's book on Glenn Miller. Called it 'a boring book about a boring man' and expressed amazement that a man of such little charm and personality should have become a legend with devotees all over the world. Will probably have the G.M. Society down on my neck!

Friday 15 November

Cooked some of Mr Wood's sausages for my supper – they are just about the only ones I have tasted since the late 'thirties which have that peppery 'pre-war' taste. Left home at 7.30 for cricket club dance at Bassingbourn.

Tuesday 19 November

Session at the Bull's Head, with Peter King added on tenor sax to play Buck's arrangements. Hoped that Buck would be back to be there, but dubious, as he was returning from Paris and France had a general strike! Rehearsed at the Bull at 2.30, got through them all quite quickly. Popped out for a snack – when we got back in time for the session, Dave Green said he'd seen Buck outside. He was walking up and down outside hoping to come in after we'd started and surprise us! Tremendous session, Buck absolutely knocked out by our interpretation of his arrangements. Doctor from Surrey gave me a brace of pheasants.

Friday* 22 *November

While we were playing at the Seven Dials last night the IRA bombed two pubs in Birmingham, killing nineteen people and severely maiming many others. There is likely to be a 'backlash' over this – not helpful to the situation in general nor to our Belfast trip in particular. Georgina is very apprehensive about my trip to Belfast, Jill, I think, less so. I don't seem able to work up much trepidation – there is no precedent to date for the molesting of showbiz events or persons, and I suppose the experience of being actually aimed at and fired upon in wartime blunts one's sensitivity to danger.

Saturday* 23 *November

To Belfast! Collected Buck Clayton at 10.45, drove to London Airport for the 12.50 flight. Very heavy security at the airport – no baggage is allowed in the cabin at all, and everything is searched thoroughly. Some of the musicians – notably Tony Mann – are very nervous but I don't rate the risk very high – theatre and concert events are going on all the time in Belfast and seem to be immune. Anyway I am interested in seeing things for myself. The flight is uneventful and we land at about 2 o'clock. A deputation from the Queen's Festival Committee is there to meet us with three cars – two to go direct to the Russell Ct Hotel, one to take Tony M. into Belfast to choose a drum kit. Kathy went along to hold his, by now, trembling hand. Our car, driven by a lady called Betty, was stopped at an army road block a mile or two from the airport, and searched thoroughly. Soldiers looked very tense – what a bleak and rotten job, especially as it was pouring wet! They drove us by a roundabout country route to Belfast. The hotel has a 'frontier' gate at its entrance, and we were thoroughly searched and frisked before we could pass through.

Met up with Buddy Tate in the hotel grill room, agreed, at Buddy's suggestion, that we would feature him in the second half in the Clayton arrangements. They picked us up again for the concert –

strict security again at the gates of the university. The first half went down v. well – we put in our usual second-half show-stoppers ('Don't Get Around Much', 'Creole Love Call') and got a long ovation at half-time. We started the second half with Buddy Tate, introducing Buck at the same time. Solly Lipsitz came by in the interval, also several local musicians – everyone seemed very grateful that we had come over 'at this time'. It seems a lot of entertainers from the mainland won't go near the place. After the concert McCarthy (once a text-book anarchist sans identity-card, ration book etc., now a text-book entrepreneur with cigar) hustled us off to a 'party' in the university common-room – with drink pinched from the band-room.

Wednesday** 27 **November

A Busy Day. Went into Euston station (The Stephenson Room) for an R.S.P.B. committee meeting, having first called in at Dr Freudenthal's to have my tooth facing glued back on. He took an impression with a view to fitting a new one. Felt more at home at the R.S.P.B. meeting, as a result of having met several of the staff and members at Functions like Palmers Green and Swansea. An interesting meeting revealing, among other things, that there is a Mafia-type organization called the Great British Natural History Co. which traffics in bird and animal corpses for taxidermy.

Sunday** 1 **December

Baked a loaf of bread – two to be exact, from a recipe in the Kenwood mixer book. The Kenwood has a sort of Captain Hook device which does the ten-minute knead in three minutes. Not sure this isn't taking a lot of the fun out of it. They say ten minutes' rigorous kneading gets rid of a lot of aggression! Not having proper bread tins I just made a couple of outsize buns – very exciting to watch them swell and turn golden in the oven!

Monday** 9 **December

Drove into the Aldwych to Bush House, to be interviewed by Melvyn Bragg in a programme called *Heroes*. I had chosen, from 'history', Duke Ellington, from fiction, Michael Henchard in *The Mayor of*

Casterbridge and from my own life, G.W.L. I didn't think I did any sort of a job on it at all, but both the producer and Bragg seemed pleased with it.

Tuesday 10 December

A drama has arisen over tonight's Butterfly Ball which has developed into a big headache. Some time ago the agent organizing the ball rang to ask if I could 'create' a special Dragonfly Dance to be included in the programme – to which the guests could dance with their dragonfly masks. I have devised a medley in waltz-time of 'Poor Butterfly' and Duke Ellington's 'Black Butterfly'. A few days ago we were told that we would also have to accompany Ronnie Corbett in cabaret. It was agreed that, as he only had half-an-hour to fill, we would play him on and back one song. Last night I spoke to his musical director, George Michie, who informed me that Ronnie Corbett insisted on the band rehearsing *every* one of his five or six numbers so he could choose which, if any, he would use. All morning the phones have been humming between the Hogg office and Corbett's management, wife, M.D. etc., also the promoters, committee etc., with Corbett threatening to walk out. I did likewise but agreed to rehearse as much as we can at our rehearsal this afternoon.

To Kathy Stobart's house afterwards for rehearsal. My 'dragonfly' concoction sounded quite effective. At 5.30 Geo. Michie arrives and we run through Corbett's arrangements. Real Blackpool pier stuff. At Biba's later (in the room that used to be the roof restaurant at Derry and Tom's), we are directed to a backstage corridor which has to serve as a green room for the Scots Guards string orchestra, us and innumerable staff.

A message comes back that David Frost would like to see me at the top table – but I am busy discussing the cabaret music with Ronnie Corbett, who has decided that all he wants is a play on and one song – re: what was first mooted before all the hysterics! Eventually I meet up with Frost in the star dressing-room – he greets me with 'Hello, Sweet Prince!'.

Friday 13 December

The car has completely stopped again – in Marylebone this time. Had to phone Lex-Brooklands to collect it (leaving keys under the bumper) and get a hire car to pick me and Georgie up at the school. David emerged from school in 'drag' having taken part in a school sketch. In the taxi on the way home the driver said 'A very unusual school, that'!

Saturday 14 December

Went down to Harold Perry's at 1 o'clock to pick up another hire-car to keep me going over the weekend – a Cortina saloon this time.

Made bread in the afternoon by way of relaxation. Have contrived a recipe for wholewheat bread with 2lbs of wholewheat, 1lb of white flour, 1oz fresh yeast, 1½ pints of warm water, a tablespoonful of salt, teaspoon of sugar. Once kneaded the dough has *one* rise lasting about 1½ hours – then straight into the oven after a quick knead. This makes a very *tight* bread which lasts a long time.

Saturday 21 December

Christmas seems to dominate life at this time and most days are spent making car excursions for various odd jobs. Cooked rabbit stew for supper with one of the rabbits given to me by pig-farmer Tom last Saturday, onions, white wine.

Sunday 22 December

Went to Barnet church for carol-singing and lessons at 6.30. Georgina enjoys singing carols so we chose a church which was likely to have quite a large congregation so the singing would be reasonably hearty. Not a bad service with a procession of local worthies reading the lessons, a good organist and fair choir, once early nerves were overcome and pitching settled down. I would have liked more congregational hymns and even lustier singing – but I suppose I was spoiled by Eton College chapel. The experience of singing good hymns and psalms fortissimo in a congregation of 500 basses and baritones is one that has survived subsequent agnosticism. But why don't Church of England hymn-books and carol-sheets include the music? All that cowlike groaning in unison when we could be harmonizing! Georgina was very nervous, having never been into a church before, but soon discovered that there was no elaborate mystique to be mastered. Even so, she got very worried if I was slow in standing up or kneeling down, fearing that I was going to draw attention to myself! On the way out, as I was thinking 'how nice and anonymous!' the vicar grasped my hand – 'A pleasure to welcome you, sir – you must come and give us a tootle some time!'

Wednesday 25 December

CHRISTMAS DAY. 'Stockings' at a respectable hour these days – about 8.45, after Nana had been roused from her bed in the living room. Stephen and David had token stockings to keep Georgina company.

Sunday 29 December

Christmas card this morning from Barbara Stonehouse! The significance of the exclamation mark is that a drama has been enacted over the past few weeks (which hasn't found a place in this diary) involving John Stonehouse M.P. who disappeared some weeks ago from a beach in Miami. He left his hotel to go for a swim and vanished mysteriously. Since then there has been mounting rumours and speculation in the press – was he drowned (no clothes or body materialized), murdered by the Mafia or what? Barbara Stonehouse has appeared on television several times expressing the belief that he is dead. Then, a few days ago he turned up in Australia, having assumed a new name (two, to be exact – Markham and Mildoon). He was arrested for entering Australia on a false passport, held for a few days in prison and is now released pending a decision about his future. Questions abound – has he been involved in fraud? Did B. Stonehouse know he was alive all along? Has he gone off his nut? We shall see. Meanwhile Mama rang tonight having just heard from Patricia that Henrietta [daughter] gave birth to a boy on Christmas Day, which makes me a grandfather!!!!!

Tuesday 31 December

Looking back to the beginning of this diary, I find that many of my forebodings came to nought. Indeed, for the band it has been a better than average year, and freelance jobs came in steadily after the year got under way. Against this, inflation roars on, and petrol has, in the course of the year, gone up from around 50p a gallon in January to around 73p a gallon in December. Over the course of the year restaurants have found things difficult, especially the expensive ones – the Caprice (to which I never went) closed in December, and there are rumours that the Mirabelle is in trouble. Towards the end of the year, firms that have been household words for years either closed down or needed shoring up. Aston Martin packed up, British Leyland and Burmah Oil had to have Government money. Due to the bad summer and the farming situation (beef etc. having to be kept till prices go up), hay, which began the year at a few pence a bale, ended it at an incredible £3 per bale! Straw is also expensive and hard to get – to the gratification of the R.S.P.B., who have seen the destructive habit of straw-burning decrease dramatically this year. The latter part of the year has been dominated by the economic future on the one hand and the escalation of I.R.A. violence, notably in this country, on the other. In the summer, the Tower of London, in the autumn, Guildford and Woolwich pubs, in the winter, the slaughter in Birmingham, the pillar-box bombs in London, Selfridges, Harrods, Edward Heath's house – then an eleven-day Christmas truce, extended by a fortnight at the time of writing.

1975

Wednesday 1 January

New Year's Eve Dance at Southend, for Garon Agencies, which turned out to be a firm recently taken over by the Walker brothers (Billy and George of pugilistic fame). I drove down full of dread, expecting to have to soldier thru' a night of the 'Hokey Cokey' and 'Knees Up Mother Brown'. George Walker came in at the end and booked us there and then for next New Year's Eve.

Friday 3 January

Norma T.-S. arrived – a majestic talker who scarcely drew breath all evening! I had met her before when she ran the concert I did at King Alfred School and remembered that she has a considerable squirrel fixation – they kept banging in through the kitchen window, knocking over milk-bottles. Tonight we heard all about 'Bustle', 'Fatso the Second' etc., complete with conversations she is supposed to have with them. The young ones took the micky ruthlessly but she didn't seem to notice. She is apparently an expert on dolphins as well as squirrels. Phew!

Saturday 4 January

On the crisis front we heard yesterday that the Post Office has applied to put first-class mail up to 7p! Went shopping in the morning, brought two two-pound bread-baking tins, a good thick chopping-board and a pastry brush. In the afternoon, while Jill and Georgina were at the stables, I decided to have a bash at shortcrust pastry, so made a flan case and put in chopped ham, onion, grated cheese and Carnation evaporated milk, from a recipe in my *The Love of Cooking* book. It came out well enough for Georgie to wolf the lot.... Made two brown loaves.

Wednesday 8 January

Left home at 2 o'clock to drive to Cleethorpes, for the gig at the Beachcomber Club which I did at almost exactly the same time last year. A man called Alec Toyne came back in the interval saying that he was with me at Salerno – he stayed backstage through the whole interval recalling the campaign in minute detail – remembering nicknames like 'Stammering Sam' and 'Agony Payne'.

Thursday 9 January

Back from Cleethorpes in just over three hours. Ever since before Christmas the weather has been exceptionally mild and they say that officially it is Spring, the technical definition being a prolonged period of 43° or over, during which grass continues to grow, buds don't become dormant, birds begin to sing and pair up. There is now a regular dawn chorus, and last weekend Mr Jenkins, our gardener, came up and cut the grass! As a result of a run of warm, mild winters, 'foreign' birds escaped from aviaries have survived in this country. This winter, since November, I have regularly seen between three and five parakeets around the garden! They fly round in a 'flight' like doves, making a spectacular din.

Friday 10 January

To Leicester in the evening for a concert at the de Montfort Hall. Boasted to Roy Williams (trombone) about my parakeets.

Thursday 16 January

Left Haverfordwest. Got home in good time – under five hours to London outskirts, including one stop for petrol, one to phone Jill and one to be nicked for speeding!

Friday 17 January

Drove, with Bruce Turner on board, to Huddersfield. Checked in at about 6, and at 7.30 went down to the dining-room for a meal – the restaurant manager said that there were only three tables set aside for residents, all the rest being booked by parties. As the three tables were engaged, I could not eat until one became vacant. Grumpily ordered sandwiches in my room, which took thirty-five minutes to arrive. While waiting, I wrote a rude letter to the Saxon Inn's operations manager. The dance was a Mayor's Ball in Huddersfield, notable for the fact that, as I was singing 'I wish I could shimmy like my sister Kate, she's shakin' like a jelly on a plate', a lady with a formidable frontage, largely uncovered, jiggled past the bandstand – the first I saw of it was when everyone standing round started laughing.

Saturday 18 January

On the way back to the hotel at 3a.m., ran into a patch of black ice and had to do some fancy rally driving to bring the car to a halt facing backwards, without hitting the kerb.

Monday 20 January

Session for the 'Louis' prog. at 2 o'clock, interrupted for a short time by a Mrs Jenny Banner who had written to me asking if she could take some photos of me with a view to painting my portrait. It seems that she was at Camberwell with me – as Jenny Somerville – but I didn't remember her.

Thursday 23 January

Climbed up on the roof in the afternoon to put on new stuff – Aquaseal, a sort of pitch black goo which is supposed to repel water from the cracks. In the evening there was a sudden thunderstorm with pelting rain – and it came through the roof worse than before!

Stephen back in the evening – picked up a meal from Vijay. Excruciatingly hot chicken Madras!

Friday 24 January

Spent a large part of the day listing my records in a minute book – so many are now coming out that they get lost in the shelves.

Saturday 25 January

Got up on the roof again to try and sort out the leak – now have a theory that the stripping which I put up last year is concentrating the rain in one spot. Have torn some of it away and we shall see.

Thursday 30 January

Up to Birmingham for an appearance on the Terry Wogan 'chat show', *Wogan's World*. Interviewed with Lord Soper and woman's mag. editor Audrey Slaughter. Have always been a fan of Lord S.'s – thought he seemed rather weary and discouraged – not on-stage, but in the green-room beforehand. He says the Methodist church has declined almost to vanishing point. The interview was, like all such, ineffectual. One always looks forward to saying something pithy and fresh, always ends up going over old ground cursorily explored by 'researchers'.

Wrote to Mr S.G. Finnemere, the Probation Officer who put me in touch with Ken Meale last year. K.M. comes out next week after two years, and I have been trying to contact Teddy Layton down in the Southampton area to get him (Ken) introduced into the jazz scene down there – it might help him.

Tuesday 4 February

The Conservative Party held its election today for the leadership – three candidates are standing: Edward Heath, Margaret Thatcher and an outsider, Hugh Fraser, who seems to have stepped in to scupper Heath. The party seems to have been hard up for obvious leaders ever since Harold Macmillan. I can't see la Thatcher catching the public imagination with that dreadful 'hooray' drawl.

During the break between rehearsal and session, heard on the car radio that Edward Heath has been surprisingly defeated in the Tory Party poll by Margaret Thatcher who got 130 to his 119. Before nightfall, he had stepped out of the fray. Can't help feeling sorry for him, tho' he clearly fought a steely campaign.

Thursday 6 February

The Tory Party leadership affair has turned into rather a farcical scramble, with Thatcher now opposed by Willy Whitelaw, James Prior, Sir Geoffrey Howe and Peyton, whose first name I can't recall. As a Labour supporter, I favour Whitelaw, who strikes me as absolutely hopeless – a bumbling, waffley image with no muscle whatsoever. Is this whole charade a preliminary to Enoch?

In the Tory Party election, there's a rush to capture the 'kitchen sink' territory. Margaret Thatcher appears in the papers collecting the milk from the doorstep, Willie Whitelaw appears washing up a saucepan.

Sunday 9 February

Another clear, blue day. Spent the day from noon onwards cooking – have had the notion of making Cornish pasties for some time – took the plunge. Filling needed more seasoning – especially much more pepper – but pretty successful. Listened to my 'Louis' programme at 2.30, *Wogan's World* at 6.15. Latter not bad – got a few laughs!

Chicken for supper.

Saturday 15 February

Back home at 1 o'clock. Go to the T.V. Centre to rehearse for Parkinson. Was on with Billy Connolly, 'The Big Yin' from Scotland, very popular up there but not well-known in England. On the show he had the audience roaring – they were all his fans from North of the Border! Sat behind the set wondering what on earth I was going to do! (Discovered afterwards that both Parky and researcher Graham Lindsay thought the same!) Gift of the gab plus adrenalin came to the rescue – plus some helpful questions from Parky. Got in some Louis and Condon stories, did my 'George Arliss', 'Walter Brenhan' faces, muddled through! Band had two numbers – did 'Rain' and 'Toot'n in Kamen'. Heard the transmission – sounded good.

Tuesday 18 February

Am already sick to death of Mrs Thatcher who is being hailed by the public as a saviour without yet having said or done anything. The dreaded 'media' has been hard at work building her up and this week's Gallup Poll has two-thirds of the sample opining that she will be a good leader of the Tory Party. The same poll wipes out the Labour Party's lead of 14 per cent last month and gives the Tories a 4 per cent lead now – all on the strength of promotion and publicity worthy of a new sex-symbol! The papers call her 'Maggie' – I never saw anybody less like a Maggie. Maggies are rather sloppy, comfortably down at heel, with the forelock adrift. La Thatcher looks permanently as if she has just emerged from under the dryer.

Wednesday 19 February

Head off at 8 o'clock for Birmingham, where we rehearse at 10.30 for *Pebble Mill at One*. Settled on 'Harry Looyah' as the main piece, 'Rain' as the play-off, which in fact we did in full. Went up to the club before the show, had a meal of chilli stew. We shared the programme with a 10-foot-high wooden clock, a display of glass ships in glass bottles, a discussion on premature induction and Diana Dors, who now looks like Christopher Soames in drag. Went afterwards with the boys to a so-called erotic movie called *Emmanuelle*. If that is erotic, Dors is still a 'sex symbol'. Pitiful stuff, but it passed the time and I had a doze.

Monday 24 February

Another busy Monday. Sorted out my programme in the morning, went in to the B.B.C. at 12.45 to do a 'Talk Till Two' for Kay Evans. Last time my 'other half' was the legal lady Nemone Lethbridge. This time it was a vast lady in net stockings called something-or-other Binchy, whom I have often heard being volubly Irish on *Woman's Hour* but hadn't connected with a well-upholstered six-footer.

Went straight off afterwards to Dean Stanley Street to do a stockpile 'obit' on Ella Fitzgerald – it went off surprisingly well considering I am not a committed Fitzgerald fan.

Tuesday 25 February

Wrote *Punch* article in the morning. Tore out *Guardian* picture of Crown Prince Deependra (sic) and sent it to Miles Kington at *Punch* – just for fun – listing some other members of the family. The soldier Journeysendra, the priest Worldwithoutendra, the rally-driving playboy Bigendra and the neurotic Witsendra.

Thursday 27 February

Had a chat with our neighbours the Frosts about the parakeets (see 9 Jan.) – they say that two escaped from an aviary in Mill Hill last June, nested in fir-trees near us and hatched seven young, of which six survived.

Friday 28 February

Replied to a letter from the Principal of the Royal Northern College of Music asking me to be on the advisory committee of the British Council, with special reference to jazz. Declined the invitation, ostensibly for the good reason that my unpredictable life rules out regular committee meetings, however widely spaced. I also feel that I don't want to get involved in arbitrating over the fate of other musicians.

Sunday 2 March

Message from my sister Diana that Mama is ill. Rang her up – apparently M. had a bad night, doctor diagnosed pneumonia. On the phone she sounded strange – speech v. slurred and voice lower than usual. But she seemed alert and talked for quite a while.

Monday 3 March

Back from Swansea. Message from Di to say that, after I spoke to Mama yesterday, she had a relapse and went unconscious. Fortunately Elspeth Hamelman and Mrs Larriman were there and sent for the doctor, who had her moved to the Ipswich Surgical Home, a private nursing home. Di went up last night, stayed (freezing) at Finndale. The specialist at the hospital (according to Di, who rang Jill this evening) is worried that Mama now sleeps a lot, cannot easily be roused. Di thinks it may be the sleeping pills which he has given her.

Tuesday 4 March

Settled a few things in the morning, then drove off to Ipswich to see Mama. Took about three hours in bad lorry traffic, getting Di's rather obscure directions wrong. Found Ma better than I expected – very lopsided in the face and ill-looking, but quite *compos mentis* and making wry jokes in a slurred and unnaturally low voice. It seems quite clear that she has had a fairly mild stroke which has for the moment paralysed her left side. Rose [sister] arrived not long after me, is staying for a day or two at Finndale.

Sunday 9 March

Spoke to Helena [sister] on the telephone – Mama is making a good recovery from her small stroke, now gets up every day. In passing, H. disclosed that fact is wittier than fiction – the Nepalese Chief of Staff is called Surrendra!

To Cardiff for a concert at the New Theatre. About 300, the same, apparently, as for Barber and Bilk recently.

Monday 10 March

Back from Cardiff. Went straight into town, picked up a new cheque-book at the bank, three tickets for *Macbeth* from the Aldwych Theatre, two Gene Schroeder records from the B.B.C. – and David

NO WOMAN, NO CRY...
One evening while playing Canasta
My hostess produced some warm pasta
Poured it over my head
And jovially said
"How's that for an albino rasta?"
Humph
CANASTA

H.L. being witty over lunch.

and Georgina from school. Am putting in a short piece on Gene in tonight's programme. He came on the scene too late to be one of the readily-quoted piano masters. What he did had largely been done by Jess Stacy, Joe Sullivan, Joe Bushkin and others – his strong card was his consistency and the perfect rapport he had with Condon-style Dixieland bands. I liked him when he toured with us in Eddie Condon's band – a big, saggy, squashy-faced man, always friendly, funny in a quiet way but with no ambition to be a jazz 'character'.

Tuesday 11 March

Had lunch at the Gay Hussar with Jeremy Robson [publisher]. Victor Sassie [owner] was in characteristic form, prescribing the meal with great deliberation – 'Listen to me – I'm telling you how to eat....' In mid-meal, Michael Foot walked in, greeting people on all sides as he walked through the room. I discovered that J.R. is another Leftie, used to write for *Tribune*.

Tremendous session at the Bull's Head with the band in top form, fresh from a string of concerts.

Wednesday 12 March

A really foul day, grey, dank and chilling. Spent all of it doing my V.A.T. accounts. Watched the John Conteh fight in the evening – Harry Carpenter was superb, backing Lonnie Bennett right up to the point at which his face fell apart. In an interview afterwards he kept telling a remarkably unmarked John Conteh how hard Bennett was hitting him in the face.

Thursday 13 March

Set off early for Ipswich where we are to combine a visit to Mama with lunch at Robert Carrier's Hintlesham Hall.

Back at the Ipswich Surgical Home, Aunt Sybil and Roger Fulford called in with Di. Mama was brighter, but Jill and I cringed at the patronizing nurses, calling her 'dear' but refusing to put her back to bed till she had had her lunch.

Monday 17 March

Returned from Birmingham at about 11 o'clock, in time to prepare the programme. Heard last night on Peter Clayton's programme that Sandy Brown (clarinettist) has died. He had been very ill with a mysterious blood-pressure complaint a few years ago, but the news came as a shock. Awkward decision has to be made as to how much time I should allocate to him in the programme – I played an hour of Tubby Hayes when he died, but only three samples of Gene Schroeder last week. In the end plumped for about forty-five minutes, using seven records – included our 'Four's Company' which Wally and I made with Sandy and Al back in the 1950s. A nice little piece.

Tuesday 18 March

It now transpires that Sandy Brown's 'blood pressure' complaint was in fact a heart attack, and he had several since. On Saturday morning he phoned his doctor to say 'This is it'. The doctor said he would get him into hospital but Sandy said 'What's the point?'. He had some friends round to watch the Rugby International on T.V. and died during it.

Thursday* 20 *March

Went with Jill and Georgina to *Macbeth* at the Aldwych Theatre. Nicol Williamson as Macbeth, Helen Mirren as Lady Macbeth. A stark production, with actors who were not in action sitting around the perimeter like athletes in a gym. Helen Mirren, dumpier than I expected, was malevolent enough but the sleep-walking scene seemed rushed and lacking in drama. Williamson was powerful in parts – but a great actor can literally alter his shape – q.v. Olivier – and N.W. remained too stringy and round-shouldered. At times he was just too reminiscent of Alastair Sim at his scroogiest!

Friday* 28 *March

Start of the Easter holiday – everything will now be shut for about a week! Had the idea of (at last) getting some work done on my book, but a holiday spirit pervaded, so I baked some bread instead. Made two white, two wholemeal loaves, deep-froze one of each. Also made a cheese and onion flan, using Prewitts wholemeal bread flour. Expected it to be heavy, but it was really v. light and edible.

Thursday* 3 *April

Went in to Les Ambassadeurs Club to attend the awards party for the 1974 Glenfiddich Awards – I had an invitation some days ago, so studiously veiled that I suspected that I may have won one of the prizes – chatted over drinks with D.G., Mrs Clive Jenkins and C.J. himself (he was one of the judges). Then came the awards – prize-day at school – and when D.G. announced that the winner of the Food Writer of the Year award had won it before, Pamela Vandyke-Price, who was sitting next to me, gave me a congratulatory biff on the arm. Though I resolutely resist taking food-writing seriously, I was quite pleased to be the first to win the F.W. award twice. Now I have the inelegant pot for another year, plus another gold medal, a dozen Glenfiddichs and a v. welcome innovation, a cheque for £200. Talked to Clive Jenkins afterwards about Port Talbot. He was born there and his Aunt Mamie lived in Tan-y-groes St.

Friday 11 April

Session at Guildford in the evening – in the main hall of the University of Surrey.

The dance was run by the Round Table. The man in charge of the band was head of Surrey C.I.D. – a hefty copper who, when pouring champagne for the band said, 'It won't be any good – it fell off the back of a lorry.'

Tuesday 15 April

The Budget on the television interrupted my work. Was relieved that Denis Healey didn't clobber the self-employed any more, other than in a general way. Income tax has gone up 2 per cent (tuppence in the pound), V.A.T. at 25 per cent goes on a big range of luxuries and a tax on fags, beer and wine goes up considerably. Am disappointed that he didn't take V.A.T. off the arts. It would help us keep our fees down.

Saturday 19 April

Spent the morning packing for weekend trip to Exmouth and Ringmer. Have just got the horsebox re-taxed, so refilled the radiator and started it up – battery flat! Took it down to John Britten's and had a hefty booster charge put in for an hour. Hope it holds. Left at 1.45 for Exmouth via M4 and M5. Almost there when the back portion of my exhaust fell off. It'll be a noisy trip tomorrow! Checked into the Devoncourt Hotel, a geriatric establishment. I was by so much the youngest in the dining-room that I felt like a juvenile. Gig at Samantha's – a discotheque, which is my least favourite venue – harsh lights, brash décor, noisy intermission music and thuggish bouncers. Forgettable. Sat in lounge writing this up in the morning. An old lady across the room dozed, occasionally talking to herself in a posh voice. Ten minutes here is argument enough for euthanasia.

Friday 25 April

Back from Oldham and just enough time to call in at home for my suit before driving on to Teddington studios for two programmes in *The Quick on the Draw* programme. The new anchor man is Rolf

Harris, replacing Bob Monkhouse. Michael Worsley was there, brought me a couple of pounds of Cumberland sausage from Newcastle.

Sunday 27 April
Had a monumental cook-up all day, while Georgina was at a pony club show with Jill (she won two blue rosettes for 2nd place). I made about twelve more Cornish pasties for the freezer, using leeks instead of onion. Also two open flans with cheese, leek, mushroom and egg. V. successful.

Thursday 1 May
Yesterday the Vietnam war came to an end – a latter-day Thirty Years War. Most commentators talk of it as a defeat for the west – which in terms of the American involvement, it undoubtedly is. But in the context of the Indo-China situation how can one talk of victory or defeat? Is regimentation under communism 'worse' than poverty and corruption under S. Vietnamese capitalism? Saigon seems to have become quite a stink-pot under the American influence.

Saturday 3 May
Did some shopping for Germany – bought a Bullworker, which is an apparatus for toning up the muscles. Buck Clayton had one when he came over here. It's a good way to exercise in ten minutes, tho' I have no ambition to acquire the Charles Atlas shape of the man who demonstrates them in the brochure. Had Cumberland sausage and red cabbage for supper.

Monday 5 May
Got up at 6.30, finished packing and left for Heathrow at 7.30. Mr Jones of Acme Car Hire is picking up the children for school, as Jill was leaving early to drive to Cirencester to look at a horse. Took my car to Heathrow, picking up Dave Green en route. While he was loading up the bass, his small son appeared at the door, looked at me

suspiciously, said 'You're a Humphrey' and took the milk indoors!* Had serious trouble with the people at Lufthansa about Dave's bass. They flatly refused to let him bring it in the cabin, he flatly refused to put it in the baggage compartment and for a while it looked as if we wouldn't catch the plane. In the end compromise was reached. Flight left at 10.55, arrived at Köln at about 12.15. Hopeless service on the plane – four dry biscuits the only refreshment. Concert was reasonably well attended but full of early-teenage kids – a characteristic of subsidized German concerts. Ate afterwards in a Balkan restaurant.

* ref. a contemporary T.V. advert about a Humphrey who steals milk.

Wednesday 7 May

Dreadful night – workmen began hammering and drilling above my room at 7a.m.. Dozed off again but not for long. Am exercising regularly with my Bullworker – very hard on the arms but makes one feel v. fit.

Concert at the Münsterhalle, a huge barn with a shocking echo. Felt a bit nervous at first, especially as we were sandwiched in between Ken Colyer and Chris Barber, and Germany is heavily trad-orientated. After a cautious start the audience warmed to us and we ended with an ovation. At the end a reporter asked me, 'What part of America are you from?' When I said we were English he said, 'But you play American style.'

Sunday 11 May

Left Münster at 12, sans breakfast – a bad mistake as we reached Bonn at about 3 to find the hotel was in a tiny suburb and everything was shut. Found one patisserie open which sold crispbread, butter, Kraft cheese spread and apple pie, so made a meal of that. Slept out of boredom rather than fatigue, having had a beer and a game on the pin-table. Concert w. Ken Colyer – we opened each half with forty mins, going on first because the Colyer bus broke down and they were late. Good acoustics, our band stole the show. Promoter wanted a jam session but it didn't happen.

Monday 19 May

Picked up my mail from the Beeb. It contained a letter from Gabriella Norris, wife of Maxwell Norris, who wrote to me often two or three years ago about Louis etc. He became quite a close correspondent whose letters I have kept. One, right after Louis's death, described his depression not only at the death of his old friend and 'guru', but also because his wife of twenty-nine years, Gabriella, had walked out a year ago in a 'disturbed' state. They must have been reconciled, because he was out walking with her on 17 April when he was killed by a car!

Wednesday 21 May

Left at 2 o'clock to drive to Wrexham, via the M1, M6, Newcastle-U-Lyne etc. Checked in at the Wrexham Crest Motel, asked if I could get a sandwich. They said yes, in the restaurant. Went upstairs, changed, came down and asked for a sandwich in the restaurant. They said, 'We're shut between 6 and 6.30 – but you could have had a cooked meal half-an-hour ago'! These big chain hotels are staffed by idiots.

Saturday 24 May

Main focus of the day was the Duke Ellington Memorial Concert at the Royal Festival Hall. Have always loathed the place and today was no exception. Spent 1½ hours rehearsing for the sound system, and in the event the sound was appalling, with the B.B.C. Radio London complicating matters. Elkie Brooks guested with the band, sang v. well. We shared the prog. with Chris Barber's Band. Good finale with dancer Will Gaines.

Another cat arrived! – a small, black and heavily pregnant kitten which Jill has taken over from a girl called Linda at the stables. The kitten is called Fifi – she doesn't know her own width, so gets up on shelves and walks along knocking everything off.

Tuesday 3 June

Postscript to last night's *Today* programme – chatted in the green-room with Bill Grundy who has the temperament and appearance of an irate bull-dog. I have a sneaking respect for someone who seems so little concerned with being liked! Inspired by an almost non-stop intake of large Scotches, he radiates a sort of bluff malice.

Wednesday 4 June

Went to a R.S.P.B. committee meeting at the St Ermin's Hotel, Caxton Street at 11. Discovered after all these years that the Wilkinson who is the Hon. Treasurer of the R.S.P.B. is the son of Denis Wilkinson who used to teach me classics at school! See a likeness now. It was D.W. who came into class in tears the morning after Munich.

Made a large kedgeree for supper.

Thursday 5 June

Referendum day. Voted NO at 9.30.

Friday 6 June

At last a warm, sunny, summery day – sat out most of the day in the garden, coming in from time to time to see the results of the referendum. It was a foregone conclusion from the first result and the subsequent saturation coverage by both T.V. channels turned into a long-drawn-out bore.

Sunday 8 June

Took the 9.30 train to Dorchester to visit Mama who is at Loders. Train very late, took about three hours. Di met me at the station. Mum now reminds me of a spent battery, very perky and full of humour at first but soon fading into sleep or confusion. She now says 'I'm off home this week' as a matter of routine, tho' I can't foresee any possibility of it at present.

Tuesday 10 June

Session at Gonville and Caius College (where did Gonville come from?) Cambridge. May Balls are not what they used to be. Nowadays you get taken to a college room, left there with the playing times and expected to take it from there. I remember dances years ago in the pre-showbiz days at universities when one was received by the committee and literally inundated with champagne. We did manage to get chicken salad and Spanish bubbly in our 'cell', which was special treatment.

Saturday 21 June

To Islington to play for the Young Socialist Summer Fair (arranged by Vanessa Redgrave). Nice atmosphere w. street theatre, colourful stalls, events going on all day. Singer Maggie Nichols fixed our bit. Corin Redgrave and Robert Powell there, compensated Bruce Turner for not having the chance to touch V. Redgrave's hem!

Monday 23 June

Went on to R.J. Jones Studios in Wimbledon for a double recording-session. Got under way very quickly and recorded 'Take it from the Top', formerly 'A Good Buzz', 'Big Ol' Tears', 'Madly', 'Sprauncy' and 'Lion Rampant' before lunch. Had lunch at nearby Indian restaurant. Elkie Brooks arrived after lunch with her M.D., Dave. I gave her my new words for 'Very First Kiss' – she liked them better than her own – a relief, as I like them better, too! She learnt them off while we remade 'Lion Rampant', a better version than the rather tired one before lunch. Then we did 'Kiss' which came off very well and 'We Fell Out of Love' which came off even better. To get plenty of material we recorded two Ellington songs w. Elkie – 'Oh, Babe! Maybe Someday' and 'Don't get around much…' and my own 'Rain', making a total of ten numbers!

Monday 30 June

Recorded an hour-long programme on Louis Armstrong for Radio Three. Was able to concentrate on Louis's musical contribution on trumpet – stressed his uniqueness in regard to rhythmic feel, 'compositional' improvisation and feeling for drama. Did I overlook Bix? Have always felt that his contribution was on a smaller scale, not, until the late 'twenties, completely free from the jerky, dotted-quaver rhythmic style of the early-'twenties dance-bands.

Tuesday* 1 *July

Recorded first of the *I'm Sorry I Haven't A Clue* programme. John Junkin was deputizing for Tim Brooke-Taylor who is still on holiday. Unfortunately he was teamed with Willie Rushton, who tends to wait for inspiration rather than plunge in. So the result was a bit slow. Simon Brett is the new producer – pleasant, bearded and rather inspiring to the teams.

Friday* 4 *July

To the Royal Festival Hall in the afternoon to rehearse for tonight's concert. Band much improved on the arrangements since 14 June, and all the numbers felt comfortable. Clark Terry turned up to make a guest appearance on the show – greeted me with a huge bear-hug. Likewise Wild Bill Davison, who doesn't seem to have changed at all since I toured with him in 1957. Concert not, for me, as good as rehearsal but OK. Clark played a dazzling set, Bill was pretty good too.

Monday* 7 *July

Met Major Donald Miles-Marsh of the R.S.P.B. Appeal at Grosvenor House – he looks not unlike actor Ronald Fraser, believes that 'eyeball to eyeball' is the best way to get people to contribute to a charity. I see what he means! He certainly got me to agree to be chairman of a showbiz panel which I know I shan't have time to attend.

Wednesday* 9 *July

Went into Lime Grove in the afternoon to do the programme with Ludovic Kennedy and Mike Farebrother, whom I haven't seen since 1938. Then I remember him as a fearsome fast-bowler and something of a smoothy. He hasn't changed, apart from a stone or two in weight and a military moustache – still the same staring blue eyes. He is headmaster of a private school, and looks the part. He brought along his Head of Music, which was fortunate because we were called in to play the Midweek Theme, and M.F. reads no music. In fact, he plays v. inaccurate amateur cocktail piano and it took some time to choose a number which would suit his limited repertoire and Ludo's basic drumming! In the end we played 'Whispering', in which I closed my ears to disparate tempos!

Session at the Bull – packed like sardines!

Tuesday 15 July

Went in to Radio London at 9.30. Yesterday Suzy Barnes played one of my records – 'Clarinet Marmalade', on which I play clarinet! This came in the middle of a bit of chat in which I explained laughingly that I do everything on radio – panel-games, disc-jockeying, reviewing – other than play my trumpet. Otherwise the records are dire musical wallpaper. The chat in between is dilatory and impossible to enliven – painfully contrived over-the-garden-wall waffle, of no conceivable interest to anyone. This is surely radio at rock-bottom. In fact, radio in general strikes me as being currently at rock-bottom. Radio One is unspeakable. Radio Two anaemic, Radio Three impossibly smug and cosy and Radio Four obsessed with belly-laughs and belly-aches. Where is all the news, background to the news, jokey games and talk of abortion and piles in the *creative* radio? Went in at 5 o'clock to make my contribution to the waffle – two *I'm Sorry I Haven't A Clue* recordings. Tim B.-T. is back, show much better.

Thursday 17 July

Final session of *I'm Sorry I Haven't A Clue*. I'm not sure that this game hasn't finally run its course – this has been a good series with better games than before, but there have been moments when it floundered. I shan't be sorry if it expires. I'm rather tired of people coming up and saying 'I enjoyed your programme the other day' and finding out that they mean this bit of nonsense!

Tuesday 29 July

Early start again for the second editing session at Wimbledon. Mixed the Elkie Brooks tracks and the remaining instrumental, 'Rain'. Elkie's came off superbly – 'Very First Kiss' and 'We Fell Out Of Love', both my own tunes, sound beautiful. E.B.'s musicianship has become formidable – she learnt the two quite difficult songs in a very short time and didn't make a single slip. The only reservation I have is about her diction – but the two engineers said that they understood every word, so maybe I'm hypersensitive as the lyricist.

Tuesday 12 August

I got up early (8 o'clock), went into Bridport to get the papers, sausages for supper, mincemeat to make pasties and this pen, an Osmiroid with a selection of nibs.

Wednesday 13 August

I spent much of the day preparing and cooking Cornish pasties – some for supper, some to keep. With fresh onion, carrot and potato from the garden, they were delicious.

Thursday 14 August

Went over to Beaminster early in the morning to do the shopping, buying chicken-breasts from Trocian the butcher for supper. During this first week I've been reading Iris Murdoch's *Under the Net* – having read her A *Word Child* (from the Literary Guild) a couple of months ago. A 'good read' but I'm not too happy about her plots. People tend to walk out into London streets to look for long-lost acquaintances and find them walking in Kensington Gardens within the hour! *Under the Net* is full of it – one coincidence after another.

Monday 18 August

A fair start to the day, with sunny intervals. Georgina wanted to come into Bridport early with me, so I woke her at what I took to be 8.40 from a bleary look at my travelling clock. When we got into Bridport we discovered from the town clock that it was 7.55! Got the papers, drove out to have a look at the sea at West Bay before human pollution had got under way – it looks quite a pretty little bay with a sweep of sea beyond it, but the candy floss and souvenir stalls ruin it. Back at the cottage we walked down to the stream at the bottom of the kitchen garden to see what birds were about. Flycatchers, green woodpeckers both in evidence. After a lazy morning watching the

Headingley Test Match, felt sluggish so leapt on my bicycle and pedalled over to Beaminster. It's a six-mile pull, and there was a brisk shower of rain halfway, but still find cycling exhilarating and sang uninhibitedly on the downward free-wheel flights.

Monday 25 August

Finished off tidying up the cottage, got the packing done and the horsebox packed up. At about 9.30 I took Georgina over to Beaminster where she is going to stay until next weekend.

Back at Loders we said goodbye to Mama, Di, etc. I gave James a cheque for £5 as a godfatherly present (when I was his age the standard tip used to be 10/-).

Tuesday 26 August

Started work at painting the windows and woodwork in the dining-room, Jill having got it all going yesterday evening. It was another steaming day, so I painted in the courtyard with the sun on my back.

Sunday 31 August

Fair night, tho' rather cold as the wisteria has grown in through the window. Left at 10.25, called in to see Mama. Her new companion, the Empress Eugenie (Eugenia Coorea), is tall with a pleasant, squashy face and faintly eccentric. Looks promising.

Monday 1 September

In at 6 o'clock to studio B6 to record 'My Life in Jazz' (what a ghastly title!), followed by my tribute to Cannonball Adderley who died of a massive stroke a week or two ago. Not being too well up on Adderley's music, I was a little worried about the selection of music – but it came off very well, especially through the bit of urbane chat from Cannonball which I included.

Friday 5 September

New batch of R.C.A. recordings from last year's Nice Festival are very disappointing...a lot of badly-organized jam sessions with incredibly sloppy playing. Could hardly find a decent track among about five L.P.s! At lunchtime, went out to get a replacement roll of wallpaper, and in the afternoon finished the wallpapering in the dining-room – it looks very good now, although the hardboard wall has bulged inone or two places from the moisture. But it has a pleasant, cottage-y look.

Thursday 11 September

Drove over to Lytham St Annes, bird-watching en route, to call on Les Dawson. He lives in a large colonial mansion with wife and three children – 'Nobody pays any attention to me – I just wander about.' Tea in a vast kitchen made by Les, who is looking after smallest daughter while his wife is at the hospital with eldest daughter who has cut her eye.

He had a series of hilarious stories about his Do It Yourself exploits – how he gave his lawn alopecia with weed-killer, how he collected pebbles from the beach for wall decoration, set them in concrete in wooden frames – and then couldn't lift them!

Monday 29 September

First-class post goes up today to 8½p – second increase this year (see 4 January).

Rose rang last night to say that Mama had a relapse last week, is much weaker. She and Helena go up there today to assist the Empress Eugenie, who is taking the strain. Shall go there tomorrow.

Tuesday 30 September

At 11 Jill and I set off for Finndale to see Mama. We had a bucketing downpour all the way which slowed up the traffic in between the dual-carriageways. So we arrived at 1.30, went straight in to see Mama. At first sight it was clear to me that she has had a further stroke – she is now right back at the point at which we found her last March. It now remains purely a matter of how long she will hang on. Nature (or the Creator, as she would have it) is not good at making an end. Went in to see her at 3.30, rather shaken by her horrific appearance as she slept. Her face seemed to be melting!

Drove home, went straight off to play a 'Tribute to Duke Ellington' concert at the Desborough Hall in Maidenhead as part of the Windsor Festival. Very full house, extremely enthusiastic.

Wednesday 1 October

Have the feeling this isn't my week. Decided to help out by reversing Jill's car so she could get in with the horsebox, reversed it into my car, denting the engine bonnet. She prides herself on keeping the outside scratch-free, tho' the interior is like a badger's set!

Friday 3 October

Disastro! The cold really broke today, streaming from eyes, nose, everywhere, and it has spread to a cough. Had a short doze in the morning which got rid of the headache. Watched golf on television in the afternoon.

There has been a big drama all week at the Knightsbridge Spaghetti House where we used to eat *en famille* until they sang 'Happy Birthday' at Georgina on her 8th birthday and put her off. Three black gunmen burst in last weekend to rob the place, messed it up and retreated with six hostages into the store-room where they have been ever since. The police are camping in vast numbers outside, waiting and seeing!

Saturday 4 October

Spaghetti House siege is over, the gunmen having given themselves up. One of them (the leader, Frank Davis) shot himself inexpertly in the stomach.

Monday 6 October

The start of another quiet week – the music business is currently in the doldrums. The fall-off in bookings which I anticipated at the beginning of 1974 seems finally to have arrived. From all sides the stories come in of musicians and bands looking all ways for gigs. Apparently the session musicians are really feeling the pinch now, mainly due to drastic cut-backs in the radio and T.V. studios. Our November and December look dire this year, with a dearth of private parties. Someone said to me the other day 'Why should the rich be cutting down?' to which I said 'That's how they became rich in the first place'.

Saturday 11 October

La Thatcher acclaimed yesterday by the Tory Party – a good speech, I suppose, for the Tories, but I can't stand the voice, and bromides about 'greater opportunity' and 'more freedom to spend what we earn' are surely easier said than done. A thought – if she becomes P.M. we shall have two Queens!

The *Observer* Magazine is running a series called the Women of Britain. Read today a short profile of Kathy Stobart, mentioning that she now plays in 'Humphrey Lytelton's Band'. Wrote immediately to the *Observer* Mag. Editor suggesting that a fitting recompense would be for them to pay me to write a piece for their 'Dissent' column on the habit of casually misspelling names.

Monday 13 October

Helena rang from Finndale to say that Mama has been in a deep sleep all day, seems to be nearing the end. I was going to Finndale tomorrow, rang Helena late at night to say that I will go – she seemed pleased.

Tuesday 14 October

Dropped Georgina at school, set off almost at once for Grundisburgh. As soon as I arrived, Helena said that Mama had woken at 4 o'clock and had been conscious ever since. When I went up to see her she had her eyes open but looked very, very weak and barely able to speak. Mary has stayed on at Finndale, Diana arrived at lunchtime. Rose is coming over tonight. The Empress Eugenie has gone to her cottage, feeling herself '*de trop*'. She has taken Rosa with her, which is a relief as people are coming to the house all the time and Rosa is a compulsive barker.

Must confess I felt somewhat '*de trop*' myself as the day progressed. The sisters are a formidable team – Mary is doing all the nursing, Di all the administrative organizing, Helena sitting with Mum, holding her hand. It's a matriarchal family – I remember my father sending occasional postcards saying 'For God's sake come down soon!' not entirely in jest!

Wednesday 15 October

Worked most of the day on my *Harpers* article, thrashing out every word painfully – worked reasonably well.

Thursday 16 October

Letter from *Observer* Mag. Editor taking up my suggestion that I should do a 'Dissent' piece on misspelling.

Battled away at the *Punch* article on drink snobbery. Am writing it on the line that the world is divided into booze snobs and booze slobs. Appallingly tired, found every word a struggle, wrote about four pages, some of it OK, some terribly stodgy. Expect the article will turn out to be a good one – these giving-birth pieces usually do.

Friday 17 October

Drove off to Weston-Super-Mare, checked in at the Royal Pier Hotel – a fearful geriatric centre with strict rules. 'Dinner commences at 7p.m. sharp', 'Rooms must be vacated at 11a.m. sharp' etc. Recalled that in the old days they used to 'light' the resident band, but leave the visitors with full lights. They did the same thing tonight and atmosphere was nil.

Phoned Jill at 10.30 from the hall. Helena had just phoned to say that Mama died at 8 o'clock. Phoned Helena from Weston-Super-Mare right after Jill's phone call. Mama died very quietly having been virtually unconscious for three days.

Monday 20 October

Heavy going with the programme today, hard to pick good records. Ended up with a whole programme on the blues.

Tuesday 21 October

Got to Finndale at 11 o'clock. Took about the same time as the A1 route from home i.e. 2½ hours. Don't know why, but was rather surprised to find that Mum's body was upstairs – Elspeth

Hammelman came over to keep Mrs Jacobs company while the coffin was carried out by Mr Farthing and his men. But Mrs J. came up from the kitchen and watched it leave. An odd cortege to the Ipswich crematorium – sleek Mercedes hearse, me and Rose in Diana's rather mudstained car, Mary and the vicar in Helena's minute green Citröen 'frog'. The ceremony was quiet, efficient and quite unmoving – as Mama herself found it when Fa was cremated. Happily they now dispense with the ludicrous and theatrical moment when the coffin used to rumble off through a hatch. Now the vicar presses a button and curtains glide across. Pretty farcical. Lunch at Finndale, spent afternoon chatting with the sisters. Nana arrived today.

Wednesday* 22 *October

Drove to Jeremy Robson's house at Child's Hill. Left car there, went to St Pancras with him in a mini-cab. 8.48 train to Sheffield where I am to be one of the speakers at the *Yorkshire Post* Literary Lunch. Have to follow Robin Day, Nadia Nerina and Michael Bentine! Petrified to see that it's a huge room with tables stretching away into the distance. Over 500 people there, most of them women in flowered hats. Sat between two businessmen's wives, made conversation between bouts of nerves. Robin Day spoke well, funny for two-thirds of his speech, briefly solemn about T.V. and its responsibilities. Nadia N. chatted amiably about the ballet and Michael B. went stark staring mad. I trotted out my Ludovic Kennedy story. Seemed to go down all right. Returned on the train with Jeremy Robson and Bentine, who talked without drawing breath from Sheffield to St Pancras.

Thursday* 23 *October

Left in convoy for Grundisburgh for Mama's memorial service. Buffet lunch at Finndale House – big turn-out of grandchildren. The service was, for some reason which I can't put my finger on, less moving than Fa's, tho several of the hymns and most of the prayers were the same. The vicar (Schofield) made mincemeat of the words, mouthing them like Boris Karloff overacting. But then he always did.

Back to Finndale for tea and chatter. Sat alone at Fa's desk for a few moments, suddenly felt very sad. Over tea, everyone milled about in the drive outside – Aunt Helena (whom I haven't seen for years – still manages to look like a 'flapper' at seventy-odd), Uncle Robert, the Gasgoignes (two generations) etc. Richard came up with some solicitor's document when I had hands full of tea and cake. Am most pleased that Mama has apportioned to me the contents of his study, including the books, and the vast roll-topped desk behind which I can still see him poring over some painstaking bit of script or writing. Don't know how it will fit into our little house.

Friday 24 October

Took it easy for the rest of the day. The week provided ammunition for my 'misspelling' article – Di gave the news of Mama's death to *The Times* on Saturday. On Monday the 'Deaths' column announced the death of Pamela Lyttellten. They printed a correct one on Tues, but on the same day wrote of a Pamela Lyttelton in the Court Circular.

Monday 3 November

Compiled my programme at 7.45 while waiting for Georgina to get ready for school – based it on 'jazz and church music, worksong etc.', good thing it came easily as today sees the launching of my book and the day is a round of radio interviews to promote it. First call is at 12.30 for the *Woman's Hour* 'Talk Two' spot. Meet up with Kay Evans and Sue MacGregor in the studio, then go to hospitality to wait for Benny Green, who never turns up – he has forgotten about it and is at home in Kings Langley, beyond reach of the studio. Result – I get fifteen minutes of interview on my own, with excerpts from three tracks on the record, go straight on afterwards to the 'p.m.' studio for a rather stuffy interview with Gordon Clough, who hasn't read much of the book. His introduction speaks of 'Humphrey Lyttelton, who refers to himself as Old Etonian, ex-guards Officer- ?' etc. etc. I take a whole chapter to derive that sort of hyphenated description! Straight on from there to a Radio One studio where a young man says, 'I'm sure you're here for a good reason but who are you?' So I introduce myself. Am interviewed by a mildly patronizing young man and give him a flow of instant chat which will be edited for a 'Newsbeat' spot tomorrow – watch our *Nationwide* piece.

Tuesday 4 November

In to London Broadcasting's studios in Gough Square for interview on their 'News Break' programme. Interviewer is Clive Rosslin, a nice mild man with a red hairpiece *who has read the book*! Result is a good, bright interview, rounded off by a track with Elkie B. – 'Oh, Babe! Maybe Someday.' Go on the *Punch* 'At Home', a conglomeration of literary and show-biz folk pretending to like each other. Chatted with Wal Fawkes, Miles Kington, Parky (rather gleefully appalled at the cut-off of our *Nationwide* piece)' Jack Trevor Story, David Taylor – his dad, the only father-and-son team in *Punch*'s history, and Bill Grundy who told me with glee that he listened to the radio all day yesterday, heard me tell the same Louis Armstrong Story twice with similar comments. Told him that both questioners asked the same question and there is only one Louis Story in the book! Bill Davies dragged me away from a conversation with Barry Took to 'meet' Clement Freud. 'Clement, have you met Humphrey Lyttelton?' he said. 'Yes,' said Freud and there the meeting ended.

Wednesday 5 November

Took Georgina to school early in order to get to the B.B.C. on time at 9.30, for the Pete Murray Show – got there at 9.29 to be told that I wasn't on until 10.45. Went to the bank to fill in time. Good interview with P.M. who had no prepared questions, just said 'you tell me what you want to talk about'. Pete in accident-prone form – called Elkie 'Books' and 'Bricks'. Afterwards picked up J. Robson and went to Sackville St for a book-signing session at the Arts Council Bookshop.

Thursday 6 November

After the book-signing, went in to the *Kaleidoscope* studio to be interviewed by Paul Vaughan about my book – once again got over

the point that it's a humorous book. Later in the evening listened to the interview and to George Melly reviewing it – unbelievably pompous, took me to task for not revealing more of myself in the book! 'Humph plays life very close to his chest – I don't think anyone really knows....' Melly certainly doesn't – I can't recall having ever spoken to him for longer than five minutes. 'Amiable' was the word he used, the fat fool.

Friday 7 *November*

Day off...wrote letters all morning, tidied my desk, which has been in chaos for weeks. This period of authorship is always a bit depressing – the preliminaries are over, the book is out, the launching interviews have been done and it all goes quiet! Am I the first author to go into W.H. Smith's to see if his book's on the shelves? I bet not! Looked in at Barnet's Smith's yesterday and saw two copies rather tucked away in the new books section. Thought of taking one out to look at and then putting it back on the top, splayed out like David Niven's book.

Wednesday 12 *November*

A book-signing session at Claude Gill's – usual performance with self sitting in the window rather like one of those Hamburg prostitutes, and customers peering at me, then the book, then back at me, then hurrying off to buy the book they came in for in the first place!

Thursday 13 November

To Finndale House, where all the sisters were assembled. The purpose of the convocation was to allocate and mark up all the contents of the house, and Di had acquired different-coloured stickers for the purpose. After lunch we all set off on a sort of treasure hunt, laying claim to whatever caught the eye 'if nobody else wants it'! It was all amicable and giggly but I couldn't work up a lot of enthusiasm – it felt a bit 'vulture'-ish. However, there's no doubt there are nice *and* nostalgic things which we shall be giving a home. Where, I don't quite know, as there is some quite large furniture. V. tired by the evening.

Saturday 29 November

A small explosion shook the house this evening at about 9.30. Jill said it was a passing juggernaut. I thought it more like a bomb. An hour or so later the T.V. news announced that a six-seater plane had crashed on Arkley golf course. It belonged to Graham Hill – was he on board?

Sunday 30 November

Yes, he was – the plane crashed near the second green with Graham Hill and all the members of his car-racing team. There was thick fog at the time, and the mystery is why they didn't divert to Luton where it was clear.

Thursday 11 December

Birmingham Mayfair Suite, a 'Top Rank'-type ballroom on the Bullring. The dance was for a Round Table, the President of which kept dashing up to say, 'Give them some real jazz.' Halfway through the second set, a couple came up and said, 'Can you give us a different tempo, please?' 'Such as?' I said. 'Not jazz,' the woman said.

George Roper, the 'wellies' man from *The Comedians*, did the cabaret spot, said afterwards it was the worst audience he'd ever played to – not hostile, just noisy and thick.

Monday 15 December

Paid an extra 50 per cent on my room in order to stay on until 6 o'clock. Wrote any number of letters and my *Harpers* article. Among the letters was one to Willi Landels, editor of *Harpers & Queen*, resigning again! This time I think it will stick, as Fiona Macpherson is no longer there to talk me into carrying on. Have suggested Larry Adler to take over, and taking him at his word.

Thursday 18 December

Went across to have a brunch at the Golden Egg in New Street – remember having had a meal there with Stephen when we went to the John Lee Hooker/Jack Dupree concert eight years ago. Very pleasant service – asked for a lightly done egg and the waitress came across specially to ask if it was all right. Had meal in the Rajdoot – not quite as good as the Bristol branch, but good. Hilarious Indian doorman said, 'I believe you are a very famous person, a Lord even!' He reeled off a list of well-known customers – Jimmy Melly, Tony Cooper etc.

Club was packed with a private party of food-salesmen. A cockney comic called Jimmy Jones (who does West Indian jokes on *The Comedians*) has been added to the bill for the last three nights. His manager sent his regards – it's George Webb!

Monday 22 December

Over the weekend a letter arrived from Willi Landels, accepting my resignation, welcoming my suggestion of Larry Adler and asking me to contact him. Also a letter from Mr Mowles in Ipswich asking me to send details of my bank account, meaning that moneys, as they call them in finance circles, are impending. Sent a copy of my book off to Ken Meale, who languishes in Winchester Jail. The Christmas shopping rush is under way with a vengeance – I seem to be behindhand this year.

Thursday 25 December

Up at 8.30 to preside over 'stockings'. Jill says I perpetuate this ritual for children of twenty, seventeen and twelve for my own benefit, and she's probably right! Buying oddments for the stockings adds to the chore of Christmas, but, as David says, it starts the day off well. This year Stephen had about seven things, David eight and G.

about eighteen. Helped Nana prepare lunch – a good turkey, from Mr Woods, with all the usual filling.

Monday 29 December

Looking through G.W.L.'s papers, found a good tract on handwriting by Alfred Fairbank, with lots of good, reproduced examples.

At midnight last night the new Sex Discrimination Bill came into force. In my business the only effect that occurs to me is that Ivy Benson's All Girls Band is now illegal!

Tuesday 30 December

Diana rang this evening to say, among other things, that the rather dotty Mrs Pack whom I showed round Finndale and seemed poised to buy it, is reported dead in today's *Times*. Jill is now convinced that Finndale is not only haunted but has a curse on it too!

1976

Saturday 3 January

Got up in the morning to discover that last night's storm reached the dimensions of a modest hurricane. Two of our forked fir-trees lost one fork each – one fell on Jill's car, one on mine. No damage, as the branches broke the fall. More sadly, one of Mr White's pines next door, the backcloth for much of my sedentary bird-watching, had been snapped off a third of the way up. At the back of the house, our summerhouse had been gently pushed six feet backwards off its concrete base, as if by some firm, strong hand. According to the news, the wind in places exceeded 100 m.p.h. and eighteen people were killed.

I went off on my own to Helena's supper-party. Didn't know many people but met several congenial characters including Tim Rice, a fellow musician-hyphen-panellist who is now a close neighbour of the Lawrences [sister's family]. Tall, mild and curiously square for the co-composer of a revolutionary pop musical.

Monday 5 January

Up early-ish to go to the bank, then set off for Southampton for a programme on Southern Television called *The Brandon Exchange*. In the green-room before the prog. saw a man whom I vaguely recognized. It turned out to be a man called Fraser White, who nowadays is the graphologist for B.B.C. and I.T.V. I argued with him about handwriting – he has the graphologist's belief that calligraphy destroys 'character'. The only 'character' I see in mean and illegible handwriting is that of a rude pig who can't be bothered to make himself understood. He asked me for a sample of my writing – then called it 'semi-calligraphy' and, as such, not much use to him. Piffle!

Tuesday 6 January

An uneventful day. Found a book called *Elizabethan Handwriting* full of samples of just that. The pre-Italic 'secretary hand' looks decorative in its spidery way, but to the twentieth-century eye is totally illegible. For example, the 'h' had a short ascender and long descender and thus looks more like the modern 'g'. With the addition of Wilfrid Blunt's *Sweet Roman Hand* and Aubrey West's *Written By Hand*, both from G.W.L.'s study at Finndale, I now have the basis of a good bibliography on the subject.

Thursday 8 January

Larry Adler rang this morning – he has agreed to take over my restaurant column, wants to have lunch with me to talk about it. Am meeting him at the Press Club in Fleet Street on Monday at 1 o'clock. Rang *Harpers* urging them to tell Larry that I am neurotic about my telephone number – if he blabs it again. *Harpers* rang again later to say that the Thames T.V. people wanted me to appear on *Today*, talking about *Which* magazine's theory that one can live and eat quite healthily on £2 a week. Pleaded absence, got them to send Larry along instead.

Friday 9 January

Dentist – I miss old Freudenthal's Jewish/Austrian philosophizing, usually carried on when my mouth was full of cotton wool and gurgling machinery. Once he had to remove a nerve from a tooth, an excruciating performance since the lower root cannot be anaesthetized. At the end of the operation, when I was on the way down from the ceiling with my legs still tied in a knot, he held up the little wire-worm nerve in his pincers and said, 'On such slender threads does human life depend!' I nodded sagely.

Saturday 10 January

Cheque arrived from Mr Mowles of Barclays Trustee Office in Ipswich which for the moment relieves all pressure, leaving me in the black. It will take some time to get used to solvency after what must be nearly eighteen years of chasing from behind. Can't recall having been substantially or permanently in the black since we bought the house in '58/59. I suppose it was cheek to embark on the house purchase with £1,700 in the bank and a first instalment of only £2,000! But at least we've been in it for eighteen years!

Monday 12 January

Rattled off my programme in the morning, then went in to Shoe Lane to have lunch at the Press Club with Larry Adler. He appeared from the back of the Club looking athletic, having just had a game of tennis with Eliot Richardson, the retiring U.S. ambassador. I suppose that just as a person of high rank can't accurately be a snob, so someone who knows *everyone* can't really be a name-dropper! After a drink in the bar we were joined by his wife-to-be, Lady Selina somebody, who writes for the *Daily Telegraph*. Larry picked my brains, not v. fruitfully, about *Harpers*. Asked rather apprehensively if attending openings and launching parties was considered 'unethical'. I said 'not unethical, but pointless, as you get no impression of a restaurant from an official opening'. Should I worry that I am not gregarious and clubbable?

Tuesday 20 January

Took Georgina in to school, came home to change then drove up to the Paris Studio in Lower Regent Street to do the *Quote...Unquote* game. Other contestants were Alan Coren, Larry Adler, actress Diana

Quick. Latter almost as nervous as me! The question-master was Nigel Rees, who also devised the game. Had contrived some ghastly puns – was quite pleased with 'The vampire's deceasing is final' for Dracula's last words, but it was the gag that died! On the other hand, Queen Elizabeth's words re the interfering Raleigh – 'Walter, Walter everywhere, he never stops to think' got a round of applause! It's a reflection on my literacy that I came third in the programme which was mainly from books, first in the one which derived mostly from newspapers! Larry had a rush of verbosity to the head but was especially good on his showbiz quotes, most of which he appears to have heard in person. His opening remarks to the studio audience informed them that he was off right after the broadcast to have a vasectomy. At the end of the show I wished him well (publicly) with the quote of Churchill's when told that his flies were undone – 'Dead birds don't fall out of nests.'

Friday 23 January

Drove up from Newcastle-u-Lyme at midday, met Steve Voce [journalist/friend]. Went along the road for a quick businessman's lunch at a local restaurant before driving off to the Wildfowl Trust place at Martin Mere. It's another Slimbridge, with a collection of duck and geese laid out around the main building. I find these 'tame' collections boring, so was glad that we headed out to the flats. Incredibly cold but was rewarded easily with a sight of a fieldfare and a very close-up stonechat. Wasn't much warmer in the hides – the icy wind whistled in through the slits and froze the fingers to the binoculars. Spotted two shovellers, some knot and, walking back, a fine redwing with very red markings.

The Voces came with me to the session at Formby – a packed British Legion Hall, band (The Panama Jazz Band) with banjo and occasional tuba. Very good session, atmosphere redolent with nostalgia right down to a geriatric punch-up!

Monday 26 January

Dealt with my programme early in the morning then drove out to Sandy Lodge to meet Trevor Gunton re a 'showbiz' branch of the

'Save a Place for Birds Appeal'. At least, that's what I thought I was going to do, but as soon as I arrived, most of the senior staff converged in the common room and it transpired that I was guest at a lunch. Met Ian Prest, the new director, also Cecil Winnington Ingram, a scholastic-looking man with a stiff neck whom I have seen often at Council meetings but never really spoken to. I had hoped to get out of some of the commitments into which I was talked by Major Miles-Marsh in our 'eyeball to eyeball' meeting last year. But after a prep-school-type lunch in the hall (seven present besides me) I found myself agreeing to do the same thing all over again! Undertook to write to sundry stars asking them a) to be on a 'showbiz' panel and b) to perform at a possible gala evening or two later in the year. Hmm.

Friday 30 January

Drove down on the coast road from Blackpool to have a look at the birds in Fairhaven Park, Lytham St Annes. A pretty chilly day but saw large numbers of purple sandpipers and bar-tailed godwit – worth the visit.

Saturday 21 February

Arrived home at 2 o'clock to find two parcels awaiting – the new *Good Food Guide* and my new binoculars (by mail order) which have a zoom attachment which increases magnification from 15 to 35. With a 7 aperture it's a smallish field of vision, but will be very useful for identification.

On *Parkinson*, M.P. introduced Stephane Grappelli as 'a man who in any self-respecting history of jazz would have a chapter to himself'!!!! Hyperbole is the word, I think. The self-respecting history would have to be eight foot wide! Once again Stephane and Yehudi Menuhin carried on like a couple of old ladies, swapping sickening flattery. What Clive James would call the week's Bad Sight!

Monday 23 February

Went in at 5 o'clock to Bush House to be interviewed for a 'profile' that will go out eventually to every corner of the globe! A lady with intense black eyes conducted the interview – put my back up somewhat by insisting that I have had an 'easy life'. I argued back strenuously that 'an easy life', if such a thing exists, depends on temperament and not on circumstances. Some go to public school and benefit, others are emotionally crippled by the same experience, and so on. Gave the example of Louis Armstrong who quite genuinely looked back on a deprived, harsh and violent slum life in New Orleans as a sunny, totally joyful experience. Temperament again.

Tuesday 24 February

Letter from Buck yesterday. He has started to practise again, says he sounds 'awful' but is taking things steadily.

Tuesday 2 March

Started forming a new trumpet embouchure to cope with the tooth trouble. Have discovered that I can play with the front teeth clenched together, a system which takes any pressure on top and bottom teeth together, with no 'rocking' involved. It will take a bit of getting used to, but I think it'll work.

Friday 5 March

Dave Green brought me a cassette of the V.E. Day broadcast in which commentator Howard Marshall refers to 'a trumpet down there' and there's a snatch of trumpet-playing ('Roll Out the Barrel') which is quite definitely and recognizably me! Incredible that this has been lying there in the archives for twenty-nine years without me having the faintest notion that it had ever been recorded!

Saturday 6 March

Derby. Dinner last night – in a small side room because of banquets in the main restaurants – was uneatable. In the morning, the receptionist rang my room at 10.30 and said 'Can you give me any idea *when* you'll be leaving?'! As soon as possible, I thought, and after tea and biscuits I went off to drive down to Tewkesbury and a nearby reservoir, where I tried out my new 'zoom' binoculars. They work pretty well once you get the knack of focusing them – saw goosander in a small flock, also redwing, fieldfare, reed-bunting. Bitterly cold, but then that's become the pattern of 1976.

Tuesday 9 March

Went to the bank to pay in the weekend's cheques, then dashed across to 100 Brompton Road to look over the script of the Teleton advert which I am putting my name to. It looked O.K. Drove straight home so as to be there when they came to install my free Teleton equipment. 'They' arrived at 4 o'clock – one rather smartly dressed man who hadn't brought any leads! He went into Barnet hi-fi shop to get some, and while there stepped off the pavement to make room for an old lady and walked straight into a Belisha beacon. Came back looking marginally less dapper. The machine looks and sounds very good – quite good enough for me.

Friday 12 March

At 9.15 this morning there was a fire practice in the hotel! An alarm bell went off outside my room and reception rang to say 'Please vacate the hotel immediately'. Got up, crammed everything into my bag, staggered down a back staircase in total disarray in time to meet about fifty bright and breezy members of staff walking back in! Checked out quickly.

Tuesday 16 March

Harold Wilson resigned this morning. No specially urgent reason – he just decided the time was right to bring up a successor in time to run into an election. Apparently he told Queenie of his intentions months ago. He gave a jovial Press Conference, wreathed in pipe-smoke and radiating relief. A ludicrous man but I've always liked him, discounting all the talk of 'deviousness' – compared with corkscrew Macmillan he has always been the nearest thing to the human definition of a straight line. Those who rant on about his 'second-rateness' have an unhealthy nostalgia for 'great men'. Most great men of recent times have contributed a fair measure of disaster, not excluding Winnie. History will probably say of Harold that he kept the ship of state reasonably afloat through potentially catastrophic times.

Sensational session at the Bull's Head with Pete King and Alan Jackson depping for Kathy and Tony – superb drumming from A.J. produced a meaningful gleam in the band's eye. Unspoken thoughts! Crowd wall-to-wall and ecstatic.

Wednesday 17 March

Tedious morning on V.A.T. accounts, adding lengthy columns of figures. Should do it with a quill pen perched on a high stool!

Must be going gaga. Alan Coren just called from *Punch*, said, 'It hasn't arrived yet!' I said, 'What hasn't arrived?' 'Your piece on French cooking.' I had no recollection of any such piece. 'Oh yes, I rang you two weeks ago and you promised it by the sixteenth. It hasn't arrived yet.' Promised it by tomorrow lunchtime!

Friday 19 March

To Milton Keynes in the evening for a concert. Drove (by map provided by the promoter) to a wilderness which will one day be the new city of M.K. Brand new hall (attached to school) in a clinical block of buildings in mid prairie. Pig-farmer Tom came across for the show, says that for farmers it's been 'another mild winter'. For the rest of us it has been a long, chilly drag with very little respite since January! Also there was a Brian Driscoll who introduced himself as 'the correspondent from Parkhurst' – remembered him writing to me from a prison near Aylesbury. Nice handwriting – not surprised to hear he was a forger!

Tuesday 23 March

Letter from the Borough Council saying that 'a recent inspection of the trees on (your) property indicates that two large and three small Elm trees are dead, diseased and insecurely rooted and may fall when subject to wind pressure'. It's the dreaded Dutch elm disease, I'll be bound. Anyway, they have to come down forthwith. In fact, they don't play much of a part in screening as they have no lower branches or foliage – but I expect it will leave a gap on the skyline.

Thursday 25 March

In the afternoon went in to the B.B.C. to take part in the programme *Mr and Mrs Parkinson*. Had no great hopes for this half-hour chat. Parky is hooked on yarns about crumby dance-halls, duff digs and fun and games on the coach – and Mary P. announced at the outset, 'I could go on listening to musicians' stories all night.' I couldn't, and found most of the chat pretty boring.

On from there to Broadstairs (Ted Heathsville) for a dance at the Grand Ballroom – a scruffy old hall in a backstreet, pure Parkinson-fodder. Fair crowd. M. Pyne, furnished with coffee by an obliging staff, got stroppy, called them Mafia and had to apologize. They all belonged to one Italian family!

Tuesday 30 March

Second ballot for the Labour Party Leadership. Healey did abysmally, and Callaghan pipped Michael Foot by eight votes. It looks as if Lucky Jim is going to make it, as it's what the great British public wants – a universal uncle who will meet every awkward question with 'God bless my soul!'. I would like to have seen M.F. in – a Prime Minister in the old mould, with high principles, wide interests and a reforming urge. We shall continue to sink slowly into the doldrums under Jim.

Monday 5 April

Lucky Jim – or rather Sunny Jim – predictably won the Labour Party poll and is now Prime Minister. It'll be a change to have someone in the hot seat whom most people *like*. A commentator on the radio said today that it is only in the South and Home Counties that Wilson is disliked and mistrusted – in the North he is enormously popular.

Dropped the Glenfiddich Award Trophy into the P.R. man's office at Charing Cross – not sorry to be shot of it; it still looks like a metal douche and its tarnishing and blackening over the months is a constant reproach.

Tuesday 6 April

Spent much of the day battling with ideas for the *Punch* article and cursing the fact that *Punch* and Alan Coren have my phone number.

Friday 9 April

Session in the evening at Oxford, for the Lord Mayor's Ball – we are having a dire run of excessively boring dances at the moment. This one was peopled by crusty ancients who sat round glaring balefully at the band. One of them came up and said, 'Why don't you try the Glen Miller approach? It's much less noisy!' The supporting band was a twenty-piece semi-pro affair churning out Glenn Miller arrangements, and it was deafening!

Sunday 11 April

Did some more wall-papering in the bedroom – a very difficult corner with a strip light, a mirror and two square light switches to negotiate. Had to do a bit of patching, but it wasn't bad.

Wednesday 14 April

Back from Liverpool, having had breakfast in the rotten Zodiak bar with Dave Green. He is currently suffering from a painful ache in the shoulder and back which is getting him down – sounds as if it might be the fibrositis from which I suffered some years ago. We were living at Belsize Park then, and I had to go to the Middlesex Hospital from a session at 100 Oxford Street, so great was the pain. Next day I stayed in bed and we called in our genial Irish doctor – the last time we ever had a 'family doctor' in the old-fashioned sense. Dr Slattery ('Slattery will get you nowhere' was our uncharitable motto) pronounced that I had fibrositis and went on, 'If you ask me what that is, I can only say that it's something wrong with the fibres!' Slattery was a great Leftie – we used to meet him looming about on C.N.D. marches.

Wednesday 21 April

Had a message from the G.P.O. telephone supervisor telling me that a Mrs Krahmer had been trying to contact me urgently and giving me a number to ring. It was Greta Krahmer who wanted to tell me that Carlo died yesterday, aged sixty-two. He had cancer of the liver, an odd end for a strict vegetarian who never drank or smoked. When I first came out of the army in 1946 he introduced me into the jazz world and I spent a lot of time at their home in Bedford Street, eating rather unappetizing meals of nut cutlet and salad. Sad.

Thursday 22 April
Left early in the morning to drive to Wimbledon for recording. Session went extremely well – in fact I think it is my best effort on record yet. The trumpet tone which I have been cultivating in recent months came over well on the playbacks – it has different shades and can open out on particular notes, giving ballad-playing an extra dimension. Instead of going back over the discarded material we tried some completely new things . . .

Tuesday 27 April
Down to Worthing for a solo session at Danny Moss's Club. The club has been in the doldrums since Christmas, didn't exactly emerge from them tonight. Met some friends of the Mick Mulligans who said that Pam has Hodgkinson's Disease, which is an incurable form of cancer. Right on top of the news about Carlo, it depressed me considerably.

Tuesday 11 May
20 *Questions* session in the afternoon. Odd to be on it after listening to it for years. G.W.L. always listened, seething with irritation at the slowness of the team.

Saturday 15 May
Back from Birmingham in the morning, got home in time to grab some clothes and go into the Television Centre for the 2 o'clock rehearsal of the *Who Said That?* show. Stricken with nerves which get progressively worse as the recording approaches. Meet all the fellow participants one by one – Lady Antonia Fraser, femme fatale of the literary and theatrical world but looking like a rather vague and detached aristocratic schoolmistress. Ned Sherrin, our chairman, as chesty as a pouter-pigeon and literally compressed into an elegant waistcoat. Nice, though – unexpectedly congenial. Sheridan Morley, twice as large and as blandly noisy as he appears on television, and

Jonathan Miller who wondered why I don't still play Trad! Might as well have asked him why he doesn't persist with his 'smelling armpits' sketch. The first show went better than I expected, especially as much of the quiz was low-brow and to do with showbiz or current affairs. Indeed Morley and I won by two points! Second one more relaxed still. Think it will be all right!

Saturday* 22 *May

To Leigh in Lancashire for a session at the Library, where we played before, surrounded by John Bratby paintings.

Sunday* 23 *May

Over to Steve Voce's at about noon – he cooked a positively lethal spaghetti bolognese for lunch – afterwards we abandoned the idea of schlepping across to Martin Mere for bird-watching – it was a windy day – so we stayed in and listened to tapes etc.

Monday* 24 *May

Letter from Nat Pierce in the morning – starts 'I was so pleased to receive your letter and can't stand your penmanship'! Good story about Jimmy Rushing recording the 'Big Brass' album – they sat him facing the band with two big screens in front of him. 'He spread these walls of Jericho apart and there he sat on a high stool facing us about 15 feet in front of us...we recorded the whole album like that with Rush screaming at us and us screaming back at him.'

Saturday* 29 *May

Heavy day. Went off to the Television Centre for No. 2 in the *Who Said That?* series – this time my partner was the feline basso profundo Lady Isobel Barnett, and Lady Antonia's partner was the science-for-the-masses whiz-kid James Burke. Not crippled by nerves this time, but expected the opposition to wipe the floor with us. Unexpectedly won the first game with a wide margin, drew the second thanks to Ned Sherrin giving us a mark each for naming each of the seven dwarfs! Lady A.'s children in the audience were livid!

Monday 31 May

After brief respite yesterday, off again on a double gig. Wavendon at 12 o'clock for an afternoon session at the Wav. Festival. Lord and Lady Dankworth were just leaving for a Festival Hall Rehearsal when I pulled up the drive. Session was being recorded for B.B.C. transcription. So we had B.B.C. sound-men fidgeting about all the time, plus the need to play stuff not already on Black Lion recordings. In the middle of 'Creole Love Call' – a strong one for a possible record – Bruce Turner's daughter aged two ran up to the stand and, at the quietest moment, pulled her skirt up over her head, presenting a bare tummy. Audience fell about, performance fell apart!

Tuesday 22 June

Up to Newcastle for our appearance at the Newcastle Festival – check into the Swallow Hotel – go almost at once to the Central Hotel where George Melly and I are to do a verbal double act. Overriding a prize berk of a chairman we do a lighthearted chat show, tho' I think George hankered after something more contentious. The concert is at the City Hall, still an insanitary old dump with atrocious acoustics. Could hardly refrain from bursting out laughing when the Feetwarmers walked in – dear old fuddy-duddies like John Chilton and Colin Bates done up like Chicago gangsters with wide pinstripes and stetson hats. We do the first hour then leave to thunderous applause. Ate with Dave at quite a good restaurant called Moors, then walk to the Central Hotel for a short and quite fruitless jam session with a very drunk Melly. Chilton gets v. stroppy with the local organist – have to apply diplomacy.

Saturday 3 July

Drove back from Langton Matravers, went almost straight off to Enfield to open Norman Hudson's R.S.P.B. Open Day. Sweltering hot day again. Instead of making an opening speech, played a 'bird' selection of tunes – 'Skylark', 'Red Red Robin', 'White Cliffs of Dover' and 'Bye Bye Blackbird'. Steve Hemmings was there from Sandy, suggested to him that an open-air band session in the afternoon next summer would be cheaper than an evening concert.

Tuesday 6 July

On from the B.B.C. to the Fairfield Halls, Croydon, for rehearsal for concert with Alex Welsh, Ruby Braff, The Lennie Hastings Trio (The Louis Armstrong Anniversary Concert). When Ruby arrived he was in a mellow mood, far from the holy terror who is alleged to have scorched his way around the country, cursing promoters, audiences and accompanying bands! Played beautifully, tho'. Didn't do badly myself, also joined Ruby with Alex for some numbers.

Wednesday 7 July

Slept very badly – in fact hardly at all. Have rarely let a job get on top of me like this Montreux affair [documentary]. Why? No confidence in the producer, for a start. He knows nothing about jazz, will rely on me too heavily to do his job as well as mine. Got off to airport, after two or three miles remembered my passport. Eventually got on flight, wrote my introductory words out on an 'air-sickness' bag, memorized them. Then into a minibus and a mad career from Geneva to Montreux to catch the 'New Orleans Boat Ride'. Swotting up on Billy Cobham during the journey, as he is said to be on the boat. He wasn't, but Buck Clayton was, a fact which raised my spirits considerably. Buck had brought me over a plastic bust of Louis, now circulating in the U.S. – hideous, but it's the thought.... On boat, interviewed Festival boss Claude Nobs, Atlantic-records boss Nesuhi Ertegun – both pleasantly garrulous. Sat in with band who invited me to do the evening show.

Thursday 8 July

Don Sayer (film producer) called at 9, woke me from a deep sleep – 'can you be down in two minutes'! Went down to reception, where he told me, in effect, that he wanted me to film at Chillon Castle at 11.30. Would I, in the meantime, 'lay on' interviews with Art Blakey, Joe Zawinul etc. for the afternoon. I explained (for the third time) that one doesn't 'lay on' Art Blakey, especially if he has just flown in after a long flight. I told him that if he wanted interviews, he should have cameras on hand during and after the concerts and take what comes.

Exhausted and v. depressed and worried. Time only to snatch a bath, then back to Casino. No sign of D.S. or any film crew, went into the hall to hear 'Weather Report'. Balm to the spirit! A superb and uncomplicated band-show, beautiful music. Had thought of pulling out of interviews on grounds of exhaustion but now felt stronger. D.S. had at last got the message (he arrived at the Casino at 9.45, after a 'splendid meal') and went off to lay on Joe Zawinul himself. Joe turned out to be an old-time fan of mine who 'has always regarded me as the God of European jazz'!! Nerves evaporate, get a fair interview. By midnight I am totally whacked and hear a short bit of Jazz Messengers. I fall asleep in corner of artists' bar where our interview camera is set up, wake up after forty-five minutes to find T.V. lights on, Art Blakey 'in situ' waiting to be interviewed. Comb dishevelled hair and go straight into interview. Another surprise – Blakey greets me like a brother, talks unprompted for ten minutes! To bed, suffused with relief.

Friday 9 July

Re-do first link at airport, get on plane, drive straight from Heathrow to Plymouth for gig with Alex Welsh Band in Big Top Theatre.

Saturday 10 July

Postscript on Montreux. On Thursday night, waiting for Joe Zawinul to appear for his interview, I approached a man whom I thought to be Joe and introduced myself. Clearly *he* thought he was Joe, for he batted no eyelid when I congratulated him on the band's show and talked to him about the interview. He asked for twenty minutes in which to greet his newly arrived wife, then would gladly do the interview. Indeed when Don arrived with the real J.Z. and said, 'Right – let's go!' this man got up to come across. I could do nothing but ignore him, and he left, no doubt mystified. Who was he? And if he hadn't had to greet his wife, what would we have talked about? How long would it have taken me, on camera, to find out that he wasn't J.Z.? A good interview question – 'Who are *you*?'

Wednesday 8 September
Got down to decorating – have decided on Sand Gold walls in the living room, not white as originally planned – it will look v. good with white woodwork.

Sunday 12 September
Long drive to Market Rasen – said to myself that the car was running v. well for 95,000 miles, it promptly repaid my confidence by flashing the red ammeter light to show that it wasn't charging. Arrived in sploshing rain at M. Rasen racecourse with ten minutes or so of juice left in battery! Dismal scene, no people. Pig-farmer Tom turned up, helped rustle up a garage man, who proved useless. Did gig in the clubhouse to 100 people. Afterwards Tom towed me (at 60 m.p.h.) 100 miles to his local garage where I left car.

Monday 13 September
Lift from Tom back to London!

Saturday 2 October
Quiet day. Mr Jenkins has picked the quinces – a bumper crop of about forty or fifty. Shopped for ingredients for pickling, marmalading etc..

Sunday 3 October
Made a couple of slabs of quince paste in the morning.

Tuesday 5 October
Went in at 3.30 to B.B.C. Maida Vale to rehearse some new things for a B.B.C. *Jazz Club* recording. Have got out 'The Bear Steps Out', 'Only for Men' and 'Blue Mist', ran them through. In the actual recording they came off well. I worked hard to get the band pitching into them for the sort of rousing audience response that it needs. 'Blue Mist' especially is going to be an asset in concerts.

Wednesday 6 October
Letter this morning from Charles Wilson, the R.S.P.B. chairman, thanking me for my services from which I assume that my stint as a

council member is over. Have never really got into it – was like a diffident schoolboy at the meetings, totally tongue-tied! My most successful role has been in blabbing about the Society in interviews etc., and opening bazaars. Can continue to do that.

Thursday 7 October

The deal for Poland, which we visit this month, is shrouded in cloak-and-dagger conspiracy. We are to be paid in pounds here, on our return, by the British Council. The Polish money which we collect over there must be handed over in the darkest secrecy to the British Council representative in Warsaw – but only after we have made an elaborate show of spending it! At least this means that we shall have free expenses!

Friday 8 October

Mortgage rates up today in response to a new bank rate of 15 per cent. Comment by miners' leader Joe Gormley, in a frontal assault on the English language, 'It leaves the Labour Party subject to knocking the hell out of.' Watched la Thatcher droning through a speech to the Tory conference – her routine standing ovation was nearly wrecked by a chairman who did a gross caricature of an idiotic Tory. 'Previous Tory leaders have been respected, but never before has a leader of the party been both respected and loved!…and you are loved!!' He then led the assembly into 'God Save the Queen' – but forgot that the 'mike' was on and bellowed what sounded like a tuneless solo.

Letter this morning from artist John Bratby asking if I would sit for him for one of a series of portraits – my co-subjects will apparently be Tom Stoppard, Reggie Maudling, Johnny Speight, Ken Russell, Barbara Castle, Sir Monty Finniston and Sir Charles Forte! Wrote back accepting.

Tuesday 12 October

Straight off after lunch to York via Northampton, where I call off at the Magnus shoe place for some outsize shoes. Being a mail order firm it's only a small terraced house in a residential street with a wily Scotsman in charge – but stacks of shoes from size 12 upwards. Went to town and bought five pairs! He now has my fitting and I need only send off for more in future.

Monday 18 October

Have heard that Larry Adler has been sacked from *Harpers* after eight months – the news given in the William Hickey column in the *Daily Express*, which implies that the parting was fairly acrimonious! They give the reason as being too frequent mentions of Lady Selena, but I suspect that, by harping on lesser-known places, most of them in New York, he lost the interest of the advertisers. In every 'media' job it's important to recognize one's true function – I've always held that the job of even a specialist broadcaster on a 'popular' channel is to deter lonely people from diving headfirst into the gas-oven. A columnist in a glossy who repels the advertisers is heading for unemployment.

Tuesday 2 November

'Back to school' with the *Sorry I Haven't A Clue* team. Same lot – Tim and Willie (sound like characters from an old comic), Graeme and Barry. Feel that this should be the last series – am beginning to be a little bored with it. Programmes didn't go badly, tho' everyone was a bit rusty.

Friday 5 November

Labour Party has suffered two heavy defeats in by-elections yesterday, at Workington and Walsall, the former seats of Fred Peart and John Stonehouse respectively. They held Newcastle South with a reduced majority. Great speculation now as to how long they will last. The spectre of la Thatcher at Number 10 looms larger.

Tuesday 9 November

Heavy day. Left home at 12.45 to go to the Beeb in order to do an interview with Belfast re our forthcoming visit. A lady called Gloria interviewed me over the phone – her first question, did it take long to persuade me to come to Belfast. 'As long as it takes to say "Come to Belfast",' I said. The fact is I feel no personal danger whatsoever – as with Poland, I find going to a place where something, however unpleasant, is actually happening is a nice, stimulating change from sitting in a mainland Britain that is slowly sinking into the mire. On to a viewing of Don Sayer's Montreux film – he has produced a good film, with action shots of self, Getz, Weather Report, Witherspoon, Shakti, The Newport All Stars, Buddy Tate, Blakey, Sarah Vaughan, Odetta etc. etc. Should be good. On to two good *I.S.I.H.A.C.*'s.

Monday 15 November

Met at Belfast by Peter Jupp who is one of the festival committee and books the jazz groups. This time we had a bus to take us into town. All the security arrangements seem more permanent this time – very solid-looking road blocks etc. In the centre of town, we passed a side-street in which a store was burning briskly – but in the adjoining streets people walked around quite unconcerned.

Gig in the Guinness bar a sensational success.

Tuesday 16 November

Waitress called my room at 8.30 to ask if I wanted breakfast. Receptionist called at 10 to ask if I would speak to Ulster T.V. – so capitulated and got up! Beautiful day. Lunch in the cafeteria, then a question-and-answer session at the Harty Rooms, where I waffled away in answer to questions in almost incomprehensible Irish, with Buddy listening enrapt. Afterwards, Buddy and I played a few blues choruses for Ulster Television.

Wednesday 17 November

Succumbed to the blandishments of the breakfast lady and went down at 8.30 with jacket and trousers over my pyjamas. Wasn't worth it – the fried eggs were dried up. Back to bed for an hour then down for the airport call. Drove to the airport in two cars – our driver divulged that the reason that all access roads bar one are closed is that, a short time ago, two fifty-pound bombs were discovered on the runway, waiting for the London plane. Oh well. Shared the plane with the Rev. Ian Paisley and Gerry Fitt – coming to Westminster for some crucial voting, no doubt.

Monday 29 November

Hefty drive back from Whitley Bay, leaving at around 10.15. Drove straight to the Albert Hall for rehearsal for the Schools Prom. Am introducing the two 'swing' bands, from Doncaster and Darlington, and playing a piece called 'Jacob Jones' with the latter. Quite good bands, including some members of the National Youth Jazz Orchestra.

Tuesday 30 November

Today the builders (Colin Goulden) start in earnest – they arrived at about 9 o'clock and set about ripping off the roof. The weather held off until 4 o'clock when it belted down, so they had to complete the felting and battoning in a hurry.

Had to leave at 2.30 to get up to the Albert Hall for rehearsal with today's band, the Ringsdale School Dance Band.

The concert itself was if anything better than last night's. The audience, again near-capacity, was more attentive and certainly my introduction went better – I illustrated the point that jazz skills are no less demanding than 'classical' with the story of Stephane Grappelli meeting Menuhin, quaking with fright at this confrontation with the maestro but saying to himself after four bars of 'Limehouse Blues', 'I am the maestro now!'

Wednesday 1 December

Postscript on last night: hung around at the end, but didn't go to the party at a nearby hotel – too tired. In the interval, Robin Ray and I were summoned to the royal presence of Princess Alexandra in a small room where drinks and refreshments were being served. Remarked to R. Ray that Angus Ogilvy [husband of Princess A.] was at Eton – a small boy who was allowed to listen to our sessions if he sat in a corner and shut up – now here I was making deferential conversation, if not actually bowing and scraping!

Sunday 5 December

Appalling night – gale-force wind and drenching rain. Woken at 2.45 by sound of cascading water. It was pouring in at each corner of the house, i.e. into corridor and Jill's room. Mobilized every pot and pan, brought it under control and got some sleep.

Tuesday 14 December

Went in early to the Sulgrave Boys' Club in Shepherd's Bush to rehearse for the Les Dawson show. Met Les, producer Vernon Laurence and director in the coffee-bar. Upstairs two armchairs were in situ representing the set for our Holmes and Watson sketches. After some preliminary giggling, we start running through the sketches, rehearsing moves etc. All finished by lunchtime.

Thursday 16 December

Took Georgina into school early, then set off up the M1 for Leeds, for the Les Dawson show recording. Car went on the blink en route. Got to Yorkshire Television just before one. Had lunch in the canteen, amongst the rustic cast of *Emmerdale Farm*, among others. During lunch one of the writers for the show, David Nobbs, joined me. He lives in Barnet, in a house previously owned by the fuss-pot who runs the Barnet camping shop! Marched behind me on a Labour Party march once. After lunch I dressed up in my Sherlock Holmes gear – Hack suit with waistcoat, white shirt, silver tie, coaching coat with cape and deerstalker hat. Met up with Watson in the corridor – we couldn't start rehearsal at once owing to a 'dispute'. Les revealed afterwards that it arose from a domestic row between an alcoholic high-up at Y.T.V. whose estranged alcoholic mistress, a video-mixer at Y.T.V., had been banned from the show by him and had complained to the union. Eventually it was settled and we rehearsed and recorded our pieces with much hilarity. God knows how it will turn out!

Early-ish bed but at 4.30a.m. the hotel caught fire. I awoke to find my room full of smoke. In the corridor a man wearing skimpy vest and pants told me that it was all right – the inmate next to him had set fire to his bed, bedside table and telephone!

Tuesday 21 December

A day spent to-ing and fro-ing from shops. We are slightly ahead with presents this year, with several of them already wrapped up. But there still seem to be a thousand things to be bought.

Wednesday 22 December

Drove in to Waterloo to meet Nana off the 12.20 from Bournemouth – it was twenty minutes late.

At supper, a small but startling crisis. Nana suddenly said, 'I feel a bit funny, Jill' and then went ashen and passed out. After a minute she came round a little then went pale and glassy-eyed. Having no phone I ran to the call-box in Glebe Lane and, having failed to find our invisible Indian doctor in the phone-book, dialled 999. An ambulance was promised at once. I then ran back home to find Nana restored to colour and consciousness, apparently completely recovered. Both she and Jill were appalled that I had an ambulance on the way, but there was no stopping it, so I went to wait outside. When they arrived I apologized for having apparently brought them out on a false alarm. 'Don't say that, you're a fine fellow' was the surprisingly reply. The two men came in, looked Nana over, had a glass of Glenfiddich and then offered to drive her along to Barnet Hospital for a check-up. 'I'll take your arm,' said the elder ambulance man. 'And call me Charlie,' said Nana! At the hospital they said 'Nothing to worry about' and she came straight home. Jill thinks nonetheless that it was a mini-stroke – the glassy stare and twitching of the hands suggested it. But it need not be more than a warning.

Thursday 23 December

Colin Goulden and one of his men came in for a Christmas tot at midday – between them they demolished several pole-axing glasses of Glenfiddich and Polish vodka respectively. I gave him the rest of the malt whisky to take away for their colleagues.

Friday 24 December

Tomorrow we start on a four-day official holiday which most companies and factories are extending to a ten-day holiday! Our phone, which went off last Monday, is still off and a voice in the engineer's department informed me glumly that we 'might be lucky' and have it fixed today. My bet is that we shall be incommunicado until the New Year. Meanwhile 1976 has seen the biggest Christmas spending spree since the invention of money!

Picked up a turkey (nett weight 18lbs) and a ham from R. Wood – also 3lbs of sausage meat and 3lbs of sausages. Total cost, £28.

Saturday 25 December

Christmas Day. Stephen came in quite late last night and likewise David – and fortunately Georgina no longer gets up at the crack of dawn! I told the children last year that Christmas stockings would dwindle to mere socks this year, but Jill has taken over with the result that everyone had a stocking this year, myself included!

Monday 27 December

In the evening watched the Montreux film on television – my appearance on the screen was greeted with cackles of laughter from Georgina. Such is fame! The film looked pretty good to me but I've no doubt that the jazz buffs will complain about it and scotch all possibility of the Beeb taking the series.

Friday 31 December

Went in early to leave my car at Brooklands – they won't start on it until Tuesday but it will save a hassle for Tuesday when I have to go for a sitting for John Bratby.

1977

Monday 3 January

Last day of holiday, praise be! Britain still snoozes as if all were well with the world – and us. In the morning I went up into the loft to try and clear up a bit before the builders come in tomorrow. I didn't turn up any long-forgotten treasures, just a few bags of old toys, a (useful) cache of empty jam-jars, several cat baskets and suitcases, innumerable instrument cases and a plastic bag full of the old pieces of tissue paper which I used for my boxes two or three years ago.

Today's 'new look' lunch was chicken with dauphinoise potatoes – Jill rather overdid the quantity. I'm not too sure that a full meal in the early afternoon will help on working days – but when is the best time for a full meal? The fittest octogenarian I ever knew was Dorothea Vaughan, a celebrated and trim Eton widow who ate practically nothing but medlars.

Learnt that Errol Garner has died at fifty-three.

Tuesday 4 January

Got up at 9 in the expectation that we would be inundated with builders at any moment. But they didn't come early! I drove with two empty Calor Gas canisters to the caravan centre at Stirling Corner. 'Yes,' said the man at the counter, 'we do supply refills – but I haven't got any till the end of the week. We have to let 'em get over the holiday.' '*!?? the holiday!!' was my unspoken reaction. Went into the Glebe Lane phone box, rang John Bratby to confirm that he is expecting me for a sitting this morning. A flat, deep voice, economical with words, replied, 'Yes.' I then rang the Telephone Manager's department and was, frankly, rude. I don't suppose it will make any difference. Nana has been prevailed upon to stay until tomorrow so I set off at 10 for Blackheath and John Bratby's studio. What was it about his dimly-recalled reputation that daunted me? Is he temperamental, explosive, awkward, mad? All I can actually call to mind is his rather involved romantic life as reported in the gossip columns. Indeed, last Friday's *Daily Mail* reported in the Nigel Dempster column that he has just agreed to hand over his Blackheath studio as part of his divorce settlement with the former Mrs B. He is clearly still in possession. A card on the big studio door had a crossed-out message for *Forum* magazine (he writes porno pieces with illustrations for the rude mags), and one for 'Dear P.' whom I take to be the Mrs B. to be. Shuffling steps answer my ring on the bell and there was Bratby, a prematurely grey and bowed figure, not florid as I expected (influenced by his pictures, no doubt) but a chalky monochrome. We went into the studio and stood about for some minutes while he threw out questions about me and music – presumably summing up my personality in the process. The studio was ablaze with Bratby canvases and at one point he asked me disconcertingly what my impression of the paintings was. The portraits I saw – Michael Horden, Graeme Garden, Leonard Rossiter – were recognizable but not representational – almost like Bratby flowers with human faces. After a while I perched on a high chair and he started painting. He doesn't use a palette but squeezes a selection of colours down the right-hand side of the canvas. All the time he threw out quite probing questions – he was fascinated by my theory that Louis had no consciousness of his own artistry and aimed at something lower than his actual achievement. He likened him to Van Gogh, who started by trying to paint pretty representational pictures which his talent wouldn't let him realize.

Finished a marathon sitting, sustained by one coffee and two choc biscuits, at 4 o'clock.

Wednesday 5 January

I rang John Bratby at 9.15 to tell him that he could have a shorter sitting today from 11 o'clock. He is one of those people who conclude a conversation, whether phoned or direct, as soon as it reaches its natural conclusion – just by saying 'Good-bye'. After dropping Nana off at Waterloo, drove on to Blackheath and sat for J.B. for an hour or two until he suddenly stepped back and said, in effect, 'Well, thanks for coming out again – good-bye.' I don't know if the portrait, literally encrusted with paint, looks like me – to me it has a strong likeness to Helena and even more to nephew Aubrey! An open mouth explains why he kept me talking with seemingly probing questions but clearly didn't listen to a word!

Meanwhile, life in the purely mechanical sense is grinding to a halt. Our phone is still dead and there seems no immediate hope of its resuscitation in the near future. And the supply of Calor Gas canisters has collapsed – I called in at the Calor Centre at Wood Green on the way home from Bratby and the glum man behind the counter offered no hope, merely shrugging and holding up two crossed fingers!

Thursday 6 January

Today, Thursday, a day of cold, discomfort and bad news, the first two caused by the plasterer working in the bathroom with the courtyard door open. Apparently they have a faulty bag of cement which means that the job took much longer than it need. The bad news came a) from the phone manager, who said that we must take our turn with 600 other people to have the phone repaired, b) from the Calor Gas people who say that supplies are chaotic, c) from Lex-Brooklands who say that my car may have deep-seated engine trouble and d) from the *Melody Maker*, whose 'Raver' column this week pans the Montreux film in offensive terms, referring elegantly to Humph Bleedin' Lyttelton. Tempted to answer it, but what the hell? There is no reasoned corrective for bad journalism.

The good news is that two nuthatches turned up on the peanut dispenser outside my window this evening.

Friday 7 January

Relatively speaking, a good news day. Ray Coleman, editor of the *Melody Maker*, has apologized abjectly for the 'Raver' piece. He says he was away when the proofs emerged, or he would have stopped it. Lex-Brooklands still have my car but don't think that the engine is at fault. And at long last the telephone has been restored, by an engineer specially sent into the area to sort out the mess.

Saturday 8 January

Was chatting with Mr Williams of the Heron Stores in Hendon and he too has noticed that builders never seem to bring even elementary tools of their own. Jill is cross with ours for filling, without a 'by your leave', new pony's drinking buckets with cement. Bought a new gas fire and was then allowed two refill bottles – this sort of scavenging for supplies is reminiscent of wartime! Discovered, on returning from a clothes-buying trip to Marbers with Georgie, that OUR PHONE HAS BEEN CUT OFF AGAIN!! God Almighty!!

Monday 10 January

The plumber arrived at 8.45, explaining that he would have come in yesterday but his car broke down. We have always referred to him as Billy, but Colin Goulden revealed the other day that it is in fact a nickname for him in the building trade, short for Billy Liar!

Spent the morning compiling my programme with a large section devoted to Erroll Garner. With him the problem is to achieve variety – he never really fitted comfortably into a band, and a succession of the piano solos could be stodgy. Unearthed some good things – a hilarious 'Alexander's Ragtime Band', the great Pasadena 'Blue Lou' with Wardell Gray, and a 1944 jam session with Charlie Shavers etc.

Tuesday 11 January

Colin Goulden called in this evening and we went over all the decoration details for the bathroom. We are gradually making headway, Billy Liar having fixed up one bath this morning before leaving at midday 'to take his daughter to hospital'. J. noticed that he took tools and a spirit-level with him!

The telephone is connected again.

Session in the evening at the Bull's Head with Joe Temperley, looking just the same as ever. I was saying to him how the years roll back whenever he rejoins the band and added, 'Any minute now John Picard will walk in with his trombone.' Five minutes later John Picard walked in with his trombone! The music was a bit of a queue-up jam session, but it went down hugely. Kenny Graham turned up, so both my favourite grizzly bears were there!

Friday 14 January

Anthony Eden died today – it seems a long time ago (twenty-one years, to be exact) that Jill and I boo-ed him outside 10 Downing Street. A genuinely tragic figure, I suppose.

Peter Finch died, too, of a heart attack – he was sixty. On *News at Ten*, Reginald Bosanquet, perhaps overcome by these momentous events, was drunk as an egg, could hardly get his mouth to say the right words.

Friday* 21 *January

Straight into Shepherd's Bush and The Sulgrove Boy's Club for rehearsal for the Les Dawson show next Wednesday. A long-winded affair, going over the 'Bad Penny Blues' sequence and the Western Brothers sketch again and again. It's not really my 'thing' but the only way is to fling oneself into it. Dear old Les has no idea of how to play 'Bad Penny' and I have to play it in D to help him out. Dennis Waterman of *The Sweeney* is on the show – knee-high to a piss-pot, like most people who look burly on T.V. Les told me the story of a sewage farm operative who went on a firm's outing to Blackpool and was overcome by the fresh air…it took seven buckets of shit to bring him round!

Saturday* 22 *January

The saga of the pop-up plugs continues. I am beginning to feel nostalgic about our old rubber plug on its broken chain!

Monday* 24 *January

Wrote to Mr Kenneth Lamb, head of B.B.C.'s Public Affairs department, finally accepting the invitation (originally from Sir Charles Curran), to join the Beeb's Central Music Advisory Committee. Shall hate it, although the chairman is my old chum George Lascelles (now Harewood) with whom I stood shoulder to shoulder on the mat before the C.O. at Chelsea Barracks in 1946 on the many occasions when he had spent a late night at the opera and I had been at the Nuthouse – and both of us missed breakfast parade.

Wednesday* 26 *January

Up at the crack of dawn to drive up to Leeds for the Les Dawson show, for which my call is 12 noon. Drive straight to the studio, then sit around while Lynsey de Paul and Dennis Waterman run through their songs with the band which is later introduced by Les as 'the late Geraldo Orchestra'! Eventually get to running through 'Bad Penny

Blues' – consternation among the writers (Barry Cryer and David Nobbs) at Les's contribution. Over the lunch break we have a confab in which I make the point that having to transpose the number to D affects my performance. There is concern that Les will take offence, so we search for a compromise. Meanwhile, Vernon Lawrence, our chubby producer, jumps in with both feet and tells Les that it's not working. Les takes it like a lamb, suggests an alternative ending to the sketch. Thenceforward, the afternoon is spent with run-throughs. I have a plump, bearded dresser with nervous, fidgety fingers who scrabbles me into my dress suit for the Western Brothers sketch – I end up looking like a *palais* bandleader.

Saturday 29 January

Arrived back to find electrician Bob Goulden in discussion with Jill about our still short-winded hot-water tank; he told her that, contrary to Billy Liar's vehement assertion, our new one is not fitted with the longest available immersion heater. There is one of 3'6" which will reach to the bottom of the tank, solving the problem of the chilly bottom.

There are bubbles under the wallpaper in both bathrooms, and grit under the wallpaper of one of them. Hmm.

Gig in the evening at the Green Shield Country Club. Set off in the direction of Harrow, consulted the *A to Z* and fetched up ten minutes away, next to Suzanne's Riding School! Smart room, customers straight from suburban Wifeswapsville.

Sunday 30 January

Fatuous front-page piece in the *Daily Mail* yesterday about a dinner given by Jim Callaghan for U.S. Vice-President Mondale. Suggests it was a lavish spread which shocked the Americans, one of whom was quoted as saying, 'If the British taxpayers got to hear of this, the government would be overthrown.' What was the menu? Consommé, sole, duck with apricots and profiteroles, with wines admittedly fine, but presumably from governmental cellars where they would benefit the taxpayer very little if they were left to turn to vinegar! Last night, fools rang the L.B.C. phone-in ranting about it, one even asserting that, in America, they give visiting V.I.P.s hamburger and coke! Will anything ever cure the British media of deep-seated frivolity?

Saturday 5 February

Had a bath last night – was cold before it was completely full. Life is becoming obsessed with immersion heaters! Is it not possible in 1977 to get one hot bath out of a domestic tank?

Letter this morning from (Sir) Rupert Hart-Davis. He is now preparing for publication the 600 letters exchanged by himself and G.W.L. between 1955 and Fa's death in 1962 – wants my approval in principle. He says they may run into two or three volumes! He also thinks that, at the time, G.W.L. had a sneaking wish that they might one day be published.

Wednesday 9 February

Ludicrous surprise in the post this morning – the quarterly issue of the *Society for Italic Handwriting Journal* arrived, and I have won the handwriting competition! The judge said, 'Possibly not the best writing in the group, but it best fills the conditions – a fluent natural italic handwriting that is cursive and vigorous. I like this hand, the more so if it is as rapid as it looks. Joins from the cross of the t would limit the length of a few of them and keep them at the right height.' Am ridiculously pleased! The prize is £5.

Friday 11 February

Drove off at 5.30 for Cambridge. Checked in at the University Arms. Pig-farmer Tom came across from Kimbolton, gave him a meal in belated repayment for the tow he gave me last autumn from Market Raisen. In the interests of science tried a half-bottle of an English wine which is made in the Biggleswade area, called Gamlingay. Surprisingly dry and flinty.

Saturday 12 February

Drove up in the early afternoon to the Ouse Washes, a big reserve area just north of Ely. On either side of the river Ouse there are dykes or

walls built to allow the river to flood in controlled areas rather than all over the Fens. The road to Wenley was flooded, drove to the Wildfowl Trust Refuge, bought a ticket for the observatory, then the warden (called Josh Scott) came out and said, 'Are you the Humphrey Lyttelton?' Owned up, got a key to the member's room. Afternoon's score, a stonechat, a short-eared owl, a host of whooper and Bewick swans, two barn owls, pochard, pin-tails etc.

Thursday 17 February

Met at the Douglas airport by Jim Caine – middle-aged, excitable, be-spectacled and wearing a rather daft fur hat. Hair-raising drive to the Villiers Hotel, because he would bang his foot on the brake whenever anything moved. Bud Freeman was staying at the same hotel, on holiday, and came to the concert at the hotel. I was playing with the Merseysippi band and the first set went particularly well. Bud reported to me later (embroidering, no doubt) that a lady at a table next to him said about me, 'Doesn't he look handsome! And sexy, too!! If he plays one more blue-note, I'll just have to leave!'

Friday 18 February

Up at a leisurely hour, as the plane back to the mainland is not till mid-afternoon – walked around Douglas. Back at the hotel, met Bud Freeman in the hall and was well and truly button-holed. At one point he put a delicate finger to his left-eyebrow and said, 'Humphrey, pardon me for asking a personal question but do you have a title?' Like many foreign anglophiles he is also a portentous snob! But I like the old boy and when it comes down to brass tacks, he has been a very important jazz voice, level-pegging with Hawkins in the early days of the tenor sax.

Wednesday 23 February

Headed off in the early afternoon to bird-watch at Bridgewater Bay. Not a great day – drizzle and grey skies. It was low tide at the bay so such birds as there were – mainly whimbrel – which are to the curlew what whippets are to the greyhound – were at rather long-range. Looked around for a glimpse of white-fronted geese, said to abound here, but couldn't see any. Bridgewater Bay Nature Reserve is a restrictive rather than a demonstrative reserve – i.e. 'keep out' rather than 'come on in'.

Saturday 26 February

Drove over to the Minehead area, following instructions in *Where to Watch Birds*. Went first to Porlock. Tried to reach Porlock Marshes down by the shore, but the footpath was too muddy and there didn't seem to be much about. Beautiful day but very cold. Scenery v. Continental, especially the view of Dunster Castle on a round, furry hill above Minehead. On the Strand in Minehead itself the ambience was trippery, but two miles along the coast at Dunster I found a space for parking the car overlooking the shore. Bird city! A huge colony of widgeon, lots of shelduck, oyster-catchers, whimbrel, ringed plover, a redshank or two, some sanderling, I think, and goodness knows what else. On way back past the Quantocks saw a heron at close quarters.

Sunday 27 February

Before the concert a manic jazz enthusiast called Jack turned up in the band-room, reminded me that he had written to me at the Beeb asking if he could introduce the show. 'It's up to you,' he said – and when I said OK, he was in a midnight blue dinner-suit in a jiffy!

Friday 18 March

Politically, the omelette appears to have hit the fat. Last night, in a division on the Government's spending cuts, the Labour side abstained from voting altogether, to avoid a more meaningful defeat. Lady Thatcher has today tabled a vote of censure, and on the party alignments as they stand, the Government could well be defeated, and we shall have a General Election. I don't think my feet are yet quite up to slogging through Barnet on another electioneering parade!

Tuesday 22 March

I have a firm feeling now that a deal is about to be struck between the Government and the Liberals. I am for it – and so, surprisingly, is the City of London. Yesterday, when it seemed there might be an election, shares dropped sharply. Almost everybody seems scared stiff of the very thought of Thatcher at the helm!

Sunday 3 April

A fine day, but still rather cold. Spent much of it practising script-writing and labelling all my pens according to the grade of nib.

Have now bought a W.H. Smith's artists' pad with a chequered guide sheet for writing practice. Am going to try and acquire a good formal hand, especially with a broad nib. Would like to be able to produce a good-looking manuscript.

Monday 4 April

A hefty day among the records, with three programmes to do – my regular *Best of Jazz* programme, a *My Kind of Jazz* programme for the B.B.C. World Service and another cassette to record for British Airways at Emison.

Tuesday 5 April

Boring post. One cheque from the Beeb. Some twit in the *Guardian* suggests that it would be a good way of bringing down the postage charge if there were only three deliveries a week! I am at one with Samuel Johnson. 'A thought strikes me – we shall receive no letters in the grave.'

I worked most of the day on my review of Derek Jewell's book on the Duke, which is now taking shape. It's a good book and I shall have to say so even if it adds another millimetre to the circumference of an already inflated head! Saw Peter Clayton last night who interviewed him on Sunday – he asked him how he got so close to the Duke when others failed. 'Well,' he said, 'his entourage told him "here's someone you can trust"'!!! My alternative theory is that it was sheer neck.

Friday 8 *April*

Spent the whole afternoon and evening clearing up the garden work-hut – a mammoth job after about four years, and one which disturbed some mammoth spiders.

In the evening, watched the first part of a T.V. series called *Roots* in which an American black called Alex Haley has traced his ancestry back through slavery to Africa. Soft-pedalled scenes on the slave ship, but still hair-raising. Late at night watched the first of the six *Jazz from Montreux* programmes. The critics will pan it, I have no doubt – for choice of artists, the necessity of cutting etc. It featured Art Blakey's Jazz Messengers and the Newport All Stars. The former very good with an absolutely superb drum solo, a complete African drum band in itself.

Saturday 9 *April*

There is something about Easter Saturday that induces spending! I seem to have gone through a startling number of green men – on a topside of beef, innumerable cans of spray paint, Easter Eggs for all and sundry, some carpentry tools etc., etc., etc. Spent an hour or two in the back hut spray-painting the two chests-of-drawers which I bought yesterday – took a while to get it quite right, so that it didn't drip.

'My' edition of Tony Palmer's *All You Need Is Love* on tonight. The T.V. items in the Press have made great play with the fact that I wrote the script, although all the other programmes have been similarly based on essays, which is all that 'scriptwriting' means in this instance. The woman in the *Daily Mail* said that the programme on 'swing' is introduced by Humphrey Lyttelton, 'surely more associated with jazz'!!!!

Wednesday 13 *April*

Day spent in a variety of jobs – wrote a bit more of the Bix Beiderbecke chapter for my book, cleared out the summerhouse.

Brought in the draughtsman's desk from the summerhouse, used it in my study for calligraphy-practice this evening.

Sunday 17 April

Prepared the supper (braised beef) in mid-morning, put it in the electric casserole for slow-cooking. Then spent most of the day up in the hut, making pots – knocked up three good ones, left them in the summerhouse to dry overnight.

Watched the fourth episode of *Roots* this evening. The episodes on slavery make one wonder how black Americans have restrained themselves from rising up *en masse* and tearing whitey limb from limb. As it is, *Roots* has apparently been a smash hit on American T.V!

Friday 29 April

All-day meeting of the Central Music Advisory Committee of the B.B.C. – my first. Went straight on from King Alfred's to the bank, then had an 'English breakfast' in the Quality Inn to fill in time until the meeting convened at 10.45. Met up again with my old Chelsea Barracks chum George Harewood née Lascelles, who is chairman of the Committee. Always liked him – very unpompous and a good laugher. Others on the committee are Stephen (now a 'Sir') McWalters, whom I remember at Eton as a formidable clever colleger, Richard Ponsonby (at school with me, too!), Anthony Hopkins, Andrew Lloyd-Webber (another 'new boy'), Vilem Tausky, like a wily old elephant, Donald Swann etc. Committee secretary is Roger Carey, who…was at school with me(!).

Thursday 5 May

After supper, watched the David Frost–Richard Nixon interview. First impression – two gibbering madmen talking together, so garbled was their grammar. But by the end, Frostie got control. Nixon absolutely *pathetic* – a broken crook, Captain Queeg at bay.

Tuesday 10 May

A dreadful day. By the early-morning post a letter arrived from the Private Secretary at 10 Downing Street, in a dignified envelope marked ON HER MAJESTY'S SERVICE and 'Prime Minister'. O Gawd, I thought, and O Gawd it turned out to be – it is 'in the P.M.'s mind' to submit my name to the Queen for a C.B.E.! Have always said that I would turn down any such award and turn it down I shall, but when it actually comes to it, it's not so easy. Have not said anything to Jill about it as I must make the decision myself. The whole idea makes me feel ill. Arguments against are unbeatable – in the jazz world it would be put down to the Eton-Guards bit. In the Press it would reinforce my 'establishment' image. If it means anything, I haven't done anything to earn it, if it means nothing, what the hell? And strongest argument of all, I don't want the fuss.

Wednesday 11 May

Symptom of the financial times – jobs are being withdrawn or cancelled at an alarming rate. Dublin fell out last Sunday (the Irish promoter very sorry but had sold no tickets and would have lost his shirt). Today, Exeter College, Oxford on 27 May pulls out for some undisclosed reason – and this was a May Ball with a whole host of bands and acts! And we have had Nottingham and Portsmouth who wanted to cancel at two or three days' notice, not to mention any number of 'firm' pencillings which suddenly evaporated. Dublin and Oxford have agreed to pay a cancellation fee, but that's not really the point. Very unsettling, a jumpy date-book!

Wrote off turning down my medal – took the plunge after reading Graham Collier's biography of 'John and Cleo' in which he says that cynical musicians have speculated on who would have got a 'gong' first – H.L. with his blue-blood Brigade of Guards connections or J.D. with his friendship with Princess Margaret.

Sunday 15 May

A busy day. Left home at 12 to go into the New Merlin's Cave. I agreed some time ago with Graham Tayar to do one of the lunchtime gigs with Bruce Turner's band. Why? To recapture the youthful days of lunchtime sitting-in, I suppose. I failed in this respect, of course – should have gone there on the tube, in baggy clothes, hugging trumpet-case on the knee! Big crowd. Enjoyable little blow, at the end of which Tayar went round with a couple of pint glasses for a collection. S.J. Perelman was in the front row. An undertaker with the grippe would have presented a livelier aspect.

Wednesday 18 May

Concert at Eton – an extraordinary affair. I got down there at about 7.30, met Hugh Phillimore who is promoting. Have to implore him not to go on calling me 'Sir' – it makes me jump. There is a jolly punk-rocker with an ear-ring who has set up a massive sound system which amplifies the echo twenty times. When the band arrives we have a sound test which gets it roughly right. At starting time we walked on to a wild standing ovation! Owing to Sunday House rules we could only do 1¼ hours between 8.45 and 10, so we played through with no break. At the end further wild scenes. Nephew Julian was bobbing about in the 2nd row.

Saturday 21 May

A startling event at the hotel in the small hours – an urgent knocking on the door with much shouting and the distant blowing of a hunting horn. It was 4.30a.m., as I discovered when I rang the night porter and asked irately what was up. It was a Dutch coach party being roused for a 5a.m. departure! Good God!!!

Monday 23 May

My birthday...fifty-six today – quite old, I suppose, though 'you're as old as you feel' is a truism. Can't remember feeling any different at eighteen, with the exception of one's sense of smell which becomes dull. I am now often aware that a smell is there, but can't say exactly what it is. Otherwise, fit as a fiddle. Spent most of the day working on my programmes. In the evening, Keith Stewart brought in a bottle of red wine which we all drank out of paper cups. Otherwise a non-festive day – I have a 'Royal birthday' later.

Wednesday 25 May

Spent most of the day reading through and sending off to Yorkshire the manuscript of the G.W.L.–Rupert Hart-Davis letters. Found one quotation that is repeated, several mis-typings – William Tample, Cosmo Cantaur and 'dull dricket'. Observed to R.H.D. that 'dricket' is not a bad name for the desultory game that I sometimes watch on T.V.

Friday* 27 *May

On the way back last night, took the Sunderland road by mistake, had to make a detour and ran out of petrol on the A1(M). Luckily there was an emergency phone about 100 yards away. The man at the other end was very solicitous, tried to save me money by suggesting that I should walk to the Washington Service Station 3½ miles away. Opted to send for a gallon from the nearest garage. While I was waiting to hear if they had contacted one, a police car pulled up with one policeman on board. He contacted the emergency station on his radio, said a can of petrol was on its way, would take half-an-hour. When it arrived, the young garage-man had such a bad stammer that it was almost another half-an-hour before he could tell me that it would cost £5. Cheaper than I expected – down south they would have rooked me for £15. It took four minutes to drive to the hotel.

Saturday* 28 *May

Very hot day. Did some cooking with the Magimix – made a large quiche and a bacon and apple pie. (When I was buying pie dishes at the Heron Stores in Mill Hill this morning, an old, painted Jewish lady was carried in by two young men, having apparently had a stroke outside. She was slumped like a sack of potatoes and had been overtaken by total incontinence. If she died, it would be considered a normal, peaceful [if inconvenient] death. But wouldn't being run over by a bus or shot by a burglar be more dignified?)

To Oxford at 7 for a dance, once cancelled but later reinstated. The reason turned out to be that the expensive tickets for the college ball didn't sell so they cancelled – but decided to run a public ball at 75p a head when they learnt that they would have to pay cancellation fees! Shared a 'rest-room' with a rock band who lent us their sound equipment and two 'roadies' to set it up. A slapstick farce began each set, with two fat, hairy little men chasing leads all over the stage! Band received rapturously by a predominantly young audience.

Sunday 29 May

Fell asleep briefly on the M40, and after a second of oblivion woke to find myself heading straight for the back of Dave Green's car. This night driving must stop!

Thursday 2 June

Party at Les Ambassadeurs for A. & M. records and the launching of Elkie Brooks's album. We were booked to do a set in which Elkie would sing. Got there at 5.30 for sound rehearsal, but the sound people hadn't got the mikes set up before people started arriving. Fairly typical 'pop' party well patronized by free-loaders. Elkie sang well with the band, but the guests talked inevitably throughout.

Tuesday 7 June
Jubilee Day

Went into the T.V. Centre at 10 o'clock for rehearsal. A scene of total chaos, and naturally enough we didn't do much until mid-morning. All the presenters – Frank Bough, Michael Barratt, Bob Wellings, Dylis – or Dilys – Morgan and Valerie Singleton – very relaxed and chummy. The whole studio set out like a fairground, and our job, apart from our opening and main numbers, is to provide what they call 'stings' – i.e. thirty-second endings which will give the impression that we have been playing all the time when the cameras return from Outside Broadcasts. In all the bustle we have time only to run through the opening. Then up to the canteen for a snack. Hanging about in the studio, talked with author Leslie Thomas and cartoonist Mel Calman, who have a chat spot on the show. Also Alan Price, who has written a ''60s' song....

At 1.05 we went on the air, having waited for H.M. to finish her 'walkabout'. During rehearsal this morning, caught a glimpse of the Queen taken unawares by a camera and looking dreadful – drawn and grim, reminiscent in her wooden features of 'Granny' Queen Mary. However, when she was out among the populace she perked up considerably. Our show roared along at a hectic pace – Alan's song very good, all the presenters incredibly calm and professional, notably Frank Bough who, with his sports experience on *Grandstand*, is a past master at this sort of 'What happens next?' presentation. Our pieces went smoothly, except that Bruce T. didn't come in on cue in 'Mezzrow' despite frequent rehearsals – lazy old bugger. His stock reaction to a chiding is to blow raspberries and repeat 'Gnat's pee, gnat's pee' over and over. At the end of the show the floor manager suddenly cued us and said, 'Play something!!' The Queen was late emerging from the Guildhall lunch and we had to stay on the air. So we launched by reflex action into a 12-bar blues and played it for five minutes. Afterwards, Tom Gutteridge dashed up and said, 'You saved the show!'

Up in the hospitality-room over a cold buffet, sat with Alan P. and Bob Wellings to watch the procession. Impossible not to be overwhelmed with patriotism. Back in The Mall, the police handling of the crowds pouring in was almost balletic – formation dancing on a grand scale! They lined out across Admiralty Arch and St James's, waited until a few hundred people had massed behind them and then moved forward in a block, to be replaced by another line. The shot from the top of Admiralty Arch showing the huge blocks moving forward was awe-inspiring and only topped by a subsequent shot from Buckingham Palace looking out over a crowd which stretched without a gap right back to Trafalgar Square. Light relief was provided by some asinine commentary – e.g.: 'I think that the tide of all human life is at Charing Cross,' 'Horses' hooves' (intoned in a ceremonial voice over a shot of the coach-horses) and, on the crowd massing outside Buckingham Palace, '…and Queen Victoria, *sitting there*…' !!

Tuesday 14 June

En route for home, go to a shop where, according to Windsor and Newton's, they sell woodcarving tools. It's called Tiranti, is just off the Tottenham Court Road and, sure enough, had all the equipment. I bought a canvas roll-up bag with a dozen tools plus a hefty, bottle-shaped mallet and a couple of sharpening stones.

Friday 17 June

Flew out of Gatwick at 8a.m. for Edinboro'. The programme we are to do is called *Jazz Concert* and is part of a series. We have Marion

Montgomery as guest with us – no sign of her on the aeroplane, aroused hopes (didn't get on last time) that she might miss the show. Taxis meet us at Edinboro' Airport, take us straight to the Gateway Studios. We meet producer Andy Mahon, rehearse our numbers – 'Toot'n' in Kamen', 'It's a Thing', 'Lookin' for Turner' and 'Mezzrow'. Check into the Mount Royal Hotel during the lunch break, then back for a pub-lunch in the boozer next to the studio. After lunch, Marion M. arrives with her accompanist-cum-M.D., who turns out to be the youthful and congenial Brian Miller. This time we get on well with M.M., who 'rattles' (her word for 'rabbits') cheerfully in her pronounced Southern accent. Her numbers are 'Kansas City', a ballad ('I Love Him So'?) and 'Bill Bailey' – we did busked backings to the first and last. Supper in an Italian restaurant up the road. Show went well – heard the sound playback after. 'It's a Thing' started in a shambles, rest OK. Back to hotel dog-tired, hassle over my room which was occupied. They had given me the wrong number. Flaked out.

Sunday 19 June

A very long and enthusiastic review of *Salute to Satchmo* by Derek Jewell in the *Sunday Times*.

Left at 1 o'clock to drive to Billingham, checking in first at the Crest Motel in Middlesbrough. Got to the Forum Theatre in Billingham just as George Chisholm arrived from the station. Alex and his band were already there, so we had a chance to rehearse some of my 'presentation'. We put in some of the solo spots with Alex's band, and got the introduction fixed up. There were 'tabs' in the theatre, so Alex led the band into the opening bars of 'Wonderful World' and I did the emotive opening announcement. It worked a dream. There's a very good spirit emerging in the show, with everyone keen on improving it.

Monday 20 June

P.S. On the way to the Beeb from Emison, went to the timber merchants in King Street Hammersmith which the wood-carving shop recommended, and bought a plank of timber with a name like a plastic. They said it was good.

Wednesday 22 June

Another day off. At last, the South East of England has heaved off the Continental quilt of cloud which has enshrouded it since last Thursday. I spent the morning filing and putting away records. Went into the bank in the afternoon to pay in and pick up a new paying-in book. They gave me one of those standard, flimsy affairs which are *useless*.

Took the plunge this evening and laid the first chisel on the block of wood which I bought on Monday. Got the hang of it quite quickly – it's exciting getting even a crude shape out of it.

Tuesday 28 June

Spent a large part of the day painting playing cards on hardboard for Jill's riding-club competition on Thursday – a 'gambler's' event in which the riders go for the high cards on the hardest jumps. Watched a bit of Wimbledon in the afternoon – Nastase went out of the tournament in a welter of four-letter words. We now have Punk Sport. In the first England–Australia Test a couple of weeks ago, four-letter words were as plentiful on the pitch as pigeons – all from the Australians, one of whom, David Hooks, got out at 61 and walked off the field intoning 'F...!' to himself and, ultimately, to the world at large.

Wednesday 29 June

My certificate for the Society for Italic Handwriting competition arrived at long last – with my name spelt wrong! Mrs Sturdy, the club secretary, wrote a covering letter apologizing for the slowness and asking rather tentatively if the name is spelt right. If not, she will send a replacement.

Monday 4 July

Down from Sandbach, got home at around 2, found a letter and cassette from Steve Voce, the latter being my Montreux set with Buddy Tate and Jay McShann.

Left pretty well straight away for rehearsal at the Royal Festival Hall. En route, the faithful TLM 835M suddenly died on me – no power, no nothing. Left it in a side-turning and got into a passing cab.

At the Festival Hall, ran through some of the 'Satchmo' programme for Acker's benefit. At interval time, we were taken up to a 'reception' to meet Princess Anne. She began each conversation with, 'Is it hard work down there?' (as if we were miners!) but responded in a relaxed and un-spiky way to general chit-chat. Roy Williams fixed her with an eagle stare and asked, 'Do you like jazz?' but got no precise answer! Arthur Thompson was at his fatuous worst, saying almost within H.R.H.'s hearing, 'I'll tell you something – she's a *very very* nice girl!' In the backstage corridor he said to me, 'Don't worry, you're going to get the O.B.E. this year.' I said, 'Don't be silly!'

Thursday** 7 **July

Last night I drove over to Eastcote to pick up the records bequeathed to me by a Mr E. Burton. He contacted me at the Beeb some weeks ago saying that he has suffered for years with angina, was about to go into hospital for an operation, and, if the worst happened, he would like me to have his record collection. A week or so ago, a Vera Vincent, who has lived with him for the past few years, wrote to say that he died on Jubilee Day, having declined after all to have the op. I already have some of the records, but there are some welcome albums that fill gaps in my collection – the prize being a complete set of the Mezz-Bechet King Jazz recordings in a handsome album and in mint condition. But there are also bound volumes of magazines and cuttings as well as several books.

Took my car into Lex-Brooklands this morning for a mammoth service – its first for 20,000 miles! It has now done 123,163 miles. Will it survive a service or fall apart at the first touch of a screwdriver?

Friday** 8 **July

Dance in the evening for the Dragon School in Oxford. Vast number of Dragonians turned up, Derek Nimmo among them. Lady said to me, 'When were you heah?' 'Pardon?' I said. 'When were you heah, at the Dragon?' 'I wasn't here,' I said. She, rather sadly, 'Not heah?' As we left at the end, Stan Rogers was singing 'Rock around the Clock'.

Tuesday 19 July

A day doing this and that, but nothing of much significance. In the evening, had David's birthday meal – at a Cantonese Chinese restaurant in Swiss Cottage called the Green Cottage. Got the old-fashioned schoolboy giggles when I phoned to book the table and Chinese waiter read my carefully-spelt-out name back as Mr L.Y.P.T.E.L.P.O.M. To Georgie's mock horror and eventual collapse, I insisted on announcing myself on arrival as Mr Lyptelpom. In this dour world it's important to seize every opportunity for childishness.

Tuesday 2 August

Took it easy today, working through the papers on my desk. The great controversy this year is about an Australian T.V. tycoon called Kerry Packer who is launching a series of 'Super-Tests' in Australia this winter. Kerry Packer is a singularly unattractive man who, as Wally 'Trog' spotted in one of his mini-cartoons, looks as if he is wearing a nylon stocking-mask.

Friday 5 August

Wrote a long letter to Steve Voce – sent him a copy of a page from the *Journal of the Society for Italic Handwriting* which arrived this morning. In a review of a book on *Interpreting Handwriting*, Theodore McEvoy writes, 'The author holds that Italic is nearly always taken up to compensate for some physical deformity or to mask some defect of character which would otherwise have been detected by the graphologist, ('Touché,' I cry,) but it is hard to believe that Michelangelo, Titian, Bebvenuto (sic), Cellini, Katherine Parr, Lady Jane Grey, Elizabeth I and Humphrey Lyttelton, to name a few, wrote Italic for this reason.' I wrote to Steve, 'All right, so no one will ever trace the development of jazz trumpet through King Oliver, Louis Armstrong, Roy Eldridge, Dizzy Gillespie and Humphrey Lyttelton, but how about this for compensation? Especially as the almost invariable mis-spelling of my name has been transferred to poor Bebvenuto!'

Sunday 7 August

One of those daft days. Started yesterday searching my desk for my A.A. membership card, which I last saw on top of the desk. Looked in my leather bag, couldn't see it. Today, a look through all the pigeon-holes in the desk developed into a virtual spring-clean that lasted all day. I threw away a ton of paper, cleared all the desk drawers and my table – no sign of it. Went down the drive, sorted out all the stuff in the car – nothing. At the end of it all, with my room *and* the living-room Hoovered, I looked again in my leather bag. It was in there. Don't quite know when we shall leave for Dorset, if at all. The fact is that Jill does *not* like holidays – and I am getting rather lukewarm myself! One needs the holiday to recover from the hassle of getting away. Georgina will probably go off to a friend's next year, so the era of holidays will finally be over.

Monday 8 August

We are obviously not going to get off today – Jill has phoned the vet who has confirmed that if Thaddeus gets at the lush grass down at Beaminster he will risk laminitis, which is apparently a rush of blood to the feet. So Jill has to arrange for him and Skylark to be looked after.

I decided to make a holiday visit up to the West End. Went into my Haymarket bank and arranged for a bank draft for $44 to send to the Pentalic Corporation for my pens. While I waited for them to organize it, I went to Poole's the Pen Shop in Drury Lane and browsed around among the Mitchell's nibs and Stephen's Ink bottles. Came away with Tom Gourdie's *How to Improve Your Handwriting*, two penholders, two cut Quills, a(nother) pen set by Osmiroid and an Osmiroid Indian ink fountain pen. Then to the bank again to pick up the dollar draft. On the way home I called in at 63 Poland Street and bought some paper. Posh stuff.

Wednesday 10 August

After the usual trials and tribulations we got off en route to Dorset at 3 o'clock.

A dreadful night – throbbing headache not improved by all the cats romping about in a first-day-of-the-hols mood.

Saturday 13 August
In the garden doing my wood-carving. Am just completing a stylized barn owl which has come off quite well.

Sunday 14 August
A dull, hazy day but dry and quite warm. I had a solitary swim in the morning. Otherwise we sat about indoors – self working on my owl – until 2 o'clock. Then we took Nana to a place called Parnham House near Beaminster – an old house open to the public where a furniture designer called John Makepeace has his workshop, also on view. I picked up several small off-cuts for my wood-carving. Nana rang Jill last week in a state of some envy, as her chum Mrs Ecclestone had been taken by someone out to tea. 'Nobody takes me out to tea,' was the theme. So we bought her a cream tea as soon as they began to serve it in the Oak Room! I went down at 6 to bird-watch around the kitchen garden. Two nights ago I saw several of what I took to be wood-warblers – small, pointed, with a strongly yellowish look. Last night, a green woodpecker, tonight fly-catchers.

Friday 19 August
Letter this morning by the second post from Buck Clayton, sounding very cheerful. 'I can now play several choruses of a ballad which is something I wouldn't dare do six months ago because I didn't have my tone back nor my vibrato, but now I do have it and baby please believe me, I'm damn glad of it.'

Saturday 27 August
In a torrential downpour yesterday which washed out the second day of the Oval Test and flooded the Finchley Road at Whetstone, our roof leaked in Jill's room – from the gulley from which Billy Liar cut away all the zinc and felt overlap. Colin Goulden will have to be summoned after the holiday.

Monday 29 August
Session at the Reading Festival this evening – a postscript to the Pop Festival, the litter from which is still ankle-deep over a hundred

acres. The organization seemed to have sagged with relief and exhaustion by the time I arrived and I sploshed around in the mud in search of a band-room. It was in a caravan near the stage. In the artists' bar – a packed tent – met up with Elkie Brooks and her manager Alan – we went into the restaurant and talked over the programme, joined by Peter Clayton, who is compering the evening. The bill consisted of a procession of trad bands, topped by Ken Colyer, followed by us and Elkie, then Chris Barber and Jimmy Witherspoon. Somewhat to my surprise, our opening band set caused a minor sensation. Then Elkie came on and stopped the show stone dead. Uproar! Chris with his stiff, theatrical, carefully contrived 'excitement' stood no chance, and as 'Spoon' churned out the same old songs, voices still shouted, 'Elkie!'

Thursday 1 September
Jill still very depressed – it sounds like actual clinical depression (which I have had only twice, years ago), the sort which descends upon one like a grey cloud in the morning. Perhaps it is induced by the family growing up and away. Naomi Inwald has rallied round with the name of a psychiatrist who specializes in depression, may be able to help her pull out of it when it descends.

Saturday 3 September
Back from Burton at lunchtime, went with Jill in the afternoon to the Mill Hill antique fair to have a look round. A minor disaster befell – one of the stallholders recognized me, passed the information to another who had on sale an old wind-up gramophone and one of my 78s. She put it on and I was dogged by my own music. We bought a pink grape dish and a teapot and jug.

Wednesday 7 September
A fine, sunny day, spent most of it writing chapter on Jelly Roll Morton for the book.

To the Richard Lytteltons in the evening. Richard is up and about but is very thin about the face and neck and looks frail. Judith gave us 'dry sherry' from a bottle which turned out to contain vinegar. To tell or not to tell? I told. Richard ate with us (very lightly), stayed up talking till we left at 11.

Thursday 15 September

Lay in until 11 or so, walked into the town to look at the shops, market etc. Drew money from bank, had a Dover sole at a Berni's Inn for lunch. Was about to settle into a chair in front of golf (Ryder Cup) on T.V. when I was overcome by an urge to get out into some fresh air. Drove ten miles or so to Bakewell then two miles south to a dale along the river Derwent. Walked and bird-watched, saw fly-catchers, blue-tits, marsh or willow tits, long-tailed tits. Back to the hotel feeling rather pious. Bigger crowd at the Aquarius, set went down well.

Tuesday 20 September

For a week the nation, not to say the world, has been exercised over the fate of a giraffe called Victor which did the splits while trying to mate and has since been unable to get up. Ideas have poured into the zoo where the mishap occurred as to how the beast might be lifted. Today, the Royal Navy fitted it with canvas trousers and winched it into an upright position, whereupon it died of shock. The *Evening Standard* headlined its demise on the front page in crisis print!

A vast juggernaut lorry had overturned on the M1 (just after Watford Gap) shortly before I reached it, so it took me three hours instead of two to get home. A night off, but dire T.V., including an in-concert view of The Rolling Stones on *The Old Grey Whistle Test*. I can still see no vestige of talent, only massive exhibitionism. But nowadays, exhibitionism *is* the talent, *vide* George Melly. Incidentally that old buffoon is currently plugging his new autobiography: volume called *Rum, Bum and Concertina*.

Thursday 22 September

In the evening, did quenelles for supper – they don't work well with frozen fish, maybe because of the extra moisture. But the great thing about fish is that, so long as it is fresh, it is always edible!

Sunday 25 September

A spectacular take-off, as our plane to Dublin had to hold back on the runway to allow Concorde to take off before us. As it got under way, the noise almost shook our plane to bits, but it was short-lived and it was quite impressive to see it rise from its own smoke-cloud like a swan in flight. The Burlington Hotel is bedlam. While I am waiting at the porter's desk to order a cab, an American voice complains that she can't get the T.V. to switch on. 'You just turn the little wheel at the top and pray that somethin' 'll happen,' was the porter's advice. I can't get a cab, so call the theatre to get someone to collect me. En route, make enquiries about Mike Butt, who last time gave us a superb meal at his Golden Orient restaurant after the concert. I have been telling Alex and the guys all about it, but rumour has it that he is shut on Sundays. But he will be at the theatre, so we'll see. Sure enough he arrives at the same time as I do, apologizes for being closed on Sundays, but looks promisingly undecided. The Olympia is sold out, concert gets an uproarious reception. Afterwards we repair to the bar which is full of effusive Irishmen. A local trad bandleader presses an album into my hand – the first album by an Irish jazz band. Then the good news spreads – Mike Butt has agreed to open up his place and see what he can 'knock up from the fridge'. The result is a fine hotchpotch of rice, lamb, beef and prawns, all beautifully spiced. Most of the team (less George and Bruce) are there and we sit around till all hours.

Thursday 29 September

'Salute to Satchmo' at the Fulcrum Theatre. Good concert. Backstage afterwards a man with a beard invited me to visit the Eton Jazz Club. It's held at a pub called 'The Christopher' – it used to be a house called the Old Christopher where I was born!

Tuesday 4 October

Have been working in spare moments on a 'Salute to Satchmo', a head of Louis poster, drawn with Georgie's wax eyebrow pencil.

Sunday 16 October

The Voces had to go off early to a christening – I spent the early part of the day in their living-room, writing letters. Have had a letter from Robert Morley asking me to contribute to an anthology of 'clangers' or dropped bricks for a charity (autistic children). Have thought of the faux pas at Diana's party when I said to cousin Viola, 'The last time I saw you was at your parents' wedding.' Duly sent it off to R.M.

In the afternoon, Steve and I went bird-watching for an hour or so down at the docks. The area looked like a cross between a gravel-pit and a bomb-site, but when we walked out alongside the pools, we saw redshank, a solitary dunlin and numbers of turnstone in their rather tatty grey-brown winter plumage.

Thursday 20 October

Letters this morning from Steve Voce and Buck Clayton. Steve says that on the Monday morning after I left him, he went into his office. His manager came in to talk to him, suffered a sudden loss of memory and had a mental breakdown right there and then. A boy working for Steve arrived with his wrist slashed, having tried to kill himself the previous night with a drug overdose. No sooner had he been packed off to hospital than Steve discovered that a representative whom he took on a couple of months ago has been fiddling the books. And finally, one of his female van-drivers (with whom he has been wrongly accused of having an affair) came to tell him that she had written off her car while drunk *and* had been charged for refusing to take a breath-test! Apart from that, he says, 'it's been a fairly uneventful day at the office.'

Our roof over Jill's room leaked badly tonight. I rang Colin Goulden, who says he paid out some money to Rick the Tiler to come and repair it.

Tuesday 1 November

Georgie woke us at 7.30 with a tray of tea and toast and an anniversary card. I gave Jill her teapot – a great success! I took G. in to school, then we got ready for Uncle Richard's memorial service at St Michael's, Highgate. When we got to the Grove, a lot of people were already streaming across to the church. In the end there was a huge congregation, largely consisting of people who looked nearer to death than Richard three weeks before he died. Harold Macmillan, now as slow as a tortoise, read the lesson, peering closely at a small book held right up to his nose. From where we sat at the back he was barely audible. Diana and Rose were there. Talbots and Fords loomed craggily, and Riddells were thick on the ground. Strange to see Mary, beetle-browed, dumpy and rather dowdy, with whom I was agonizingly in love at the age of ten. After we got home and changed we drove (again) to Highate, delivered a bag of quinces for Judith (forgotten this morning).

Friday 4 November

Some power-workers in Yorkshire and the Midlands are on unofficial strike and there are spasmodic blackouts – there was one during our celebratory meal on Wednesday, but it didn't seem to affect the kitchen, and for twenty minutes or so we sat in romantic candle-light.

Monday 14 November

The firemen of England start a total strike this morning. They want a 30 per cent rise, Merlyn Rees (Home Secretary) will only allow local authorities to offer 10 per cent. So we may all go up in flames at any moment. Troops with ancient 'appliances' called 'Green Goddesses', for some arcane reason, are going to try and avert a holocaust. I drive back from Sandbach expecting at any time to see orange flames on the horizon, but all is quiet.

Sunday 20 November

I spent much of the day compiling a letter to Voce. It started, 'Let me guess – a) you have been savaged by Wild Bill Davison and have gone down with chewing-gum poisoning or Wrigley's Disease,' and continued in that vein up to letter z.

Sunday 27 November

Drove out in the morning to Berry Head just beyond Brixham. A bright day but raw and cold. On the cliffs, about 100 feet below the top, there was a small colony of sleek black-and-white guillemots. Back to the hotel for lunch – roast beef and a sort of turban of Yorkshire pudding.

Slightly disappointing concert at Bryanston School, where I remember doing a storming concert two or three years ago. Tonight, the hall wasn't completely full and the boys who were there looked bored and half asleep. Apparently one entire House was barred from the concert as part of a punishment for mass shop-lifting.

Thursday 1 December

An offer has come from Australia for George Chisholm, Alex Welsh and myself to go and do a 'Salute to Satchmo' there next August. Ten concerts in twenty-one days, will I quote for it. No, I won't, a) because it is quite wrong to sell a package that omits Bruce Turner, who will undoubtedly be deeply offended, b) because I don't see any fun in loafing about for eleven out of twenty-one days and c) because I don't really want to go to Australia. Anyway, I can't consider deals like this hurriedly after a long journey.

Both George and Alex broached the subject of Australia. Seemed to be pressurizing slightly. To no avail.

Sunday 4 December

I took the morning easy, read the papers (no *Observer* – the printers are on strike). The big news story this week is President Sadat's diplomatic visit to Israel. It seems the first sensible thing that has happened in that area for years, but other Arab states are already gnashing their teeth over it. Meanwhile, the firemen continue on strike – and people are beginning to take it for granted.

Friday 16 December

Concert in Manchester, at the Royal Exchange Theatre.

Concert a weird affair. We sat on stools in a circle, each bathed in a pool of coloured light. Tony Coe (brilliant) and Tom Whittle (superb) guested. I didn't overwork, but it was very successful.

Saturday 17 December

I opened my speech to S.I.H. by saying, 'My father was, politically, a man of staunch conservatism. One day I asked him why he took the *New Statesman* on a weekly subscription. He said, "Because I think it's a good thing to keep anger alive! By the same token I think it's a good thing to keep humility alive – and I know no better way of doing that than by buying a straight-edged pen and joining the society of italic handwriters, with or without the capital initials"....' After the speechifying, met several of the heavy guns of the contemporary calligraphic world – John Shyvers, Berthold Wolpe, Nancy Winters.

Sunday 18 December

Early start for Blindley Heath, where we do a lunchtime session at the Red Barn. Dr White showed up with two brace of pheasants – my 'Christmas box'!

Tuesday 20 December

First thing on arrival, a cup of tea, then up to the ballroom to check on the amplification. It's now my theory that the only way to get the band playing softly with good internal balance is to dispense with microphones whenever possible. So when I saw four mikes ranged out ready to be connected up, I contacted Keith Mooney, the guv'nor, and suggested that he put them away in a cupboard. When we went on to play (after a crippling four-course meal) I proved my point. And a lot of people at the end said it was the best jazz night ever, because it was so *soft*.

Wednesday 21 December

Another good concert. Got involved in the bar with an elderly punter called Fred, whose 'date' for the night was a motherly old lady called Louie whom he met four years ago in the Isle of Man and with whom he has an annual assignation. As he got drunker and drunker he kept turning to me blearily and rasping, 'I'm not going to bloody make it, am I.' Louie looked on, patently relieved.

Thursday 22 December

Shopping most of the day, with varying success. Also bought some bird magazines from which I made up an 'owl' Christmas card for Dave Green – part of a long tradition which began when I first did an owl-like caricature of Dave in Switzerland.

Sunday 25 December

CHRISTMAS DAY

A leisurely morning with no stockings for the first time. Delicious turkey with champagne and a nice Hermitage white wine from Layton's. I decanted my medlar ratafia. David and Georgina sampled it – luckily it's not very strong but has a good apple flavour.

Saturday 31 December

So that's it. I suppose it can be said to have been a good year – certainly for Sunny Jim, who is currently riding high with a strong pound, falling inflation and a lead over Thatcher in the opinion polls. And I can't complain either – the Satchmo shows have provided a good deal of work in better-than-average conditions – i.e. maximum of 'exposure', minimum of discomfort.

1978

Thursday 5 January

We got up late to the sound of clomping on the roof – the men had arrived to repair it. They have to replace the inadequate 'edging' or 'flashing' which Billy Liar messed up a year ago. Most of his handiwork has been littering the garden since the storm on 23 December.

I have been resisting for some time pressure to get me to go to Australia with the rest of the 'Satchmo' stars in August. Originally the idea was for ten concerts in twenty-one days. Alex and George were keen, Bruce was excluded. I said no, because a) it was too long, b) because it was disastrous to the team to leave out Bruce. Now it's two weeks. Bruce is in, I have said OK.

Wednesday 11 January

Letter from Fiona Sturdy of the S.I.H. enclosing a stack of printed Christmas cards designed by Lewis Trethewey (for his own use) which he promised me for my collection when I opened the Camden exhibition. She said the exhibition has aroused a lot of interest but 'we haven't made it with the Press'. I rang Peter Clayton, who said I must be psychic – he had just put the last full-stop to an article for Sunday's *Telegraph* on the exhibition, so that will cheer them up.

Monday 16 January

Altogether fratchy evening – concert was run by an officious and butch lady who busy-bodied about backstage finding out where our future dates are so that she can offload her 'souvenir programmes' on to them as she has already done at Stratford-on-Avon. At one point she said heartily, 'Humph looks as if he just got out of bed!' Roy W. says I froze her. Full concert. Pig-farmer Tom with his son, Tom, there, very thin and yellow-looking after a month in hospital with an enlarged heart. He brought me three rabbits. Also there, Brian Driscoll, former-convict-gone-straight who interviewed me for amateur T.V. after the concert.

Tuesday 17 January

I went to Lex-Brooklands to pick up my car which is running smoothly and softly after 143,000 miles!

Friday 3 February

Life is currently mildly obsessed with scavenging for petrol, but the threatened 'shortage by the weekend' doesn't seem to be materializing. By the end of the day I have enough to reach Barrow – i.e.: a full tank and 2 gallons in a can.

Sunday 12 February

Forage for petrol – found a Mobil garage without a queue and filled. That's one thing about these temporary shortages and crises – they lower one's aspirations wonderfully. Filling a tank or negotiating a snowbound pass provides a greater sense of achievement than writing a thousand words of a book or playing a good solo on 'Take the "A" Train'!

Monday 13 February

A National Opinion Poll in the *Daily Mail* puts Mrs Thatcher 11 per cent ahead of the Labour Party as a direct result of her 'we'll stop immigration' speech last week. She is a crook – most commentators agree that nothing significant can be done except wait for time to slow down the process, which it is beginning to do.

Tuesday 14 February

Edward Heath has made a speech denouncing la Thatcher's views on immigration, saying that neither she nor anyone else can do any more to slow down immigration.

Wednesday 1 March

Have started a stiff diet – am now about 15 stone 10, hope to lose a stone at least. Worked on accounts, V.A.T. and my book through the day.

Carshalton Hall – Good crowd. Have been doing a lot of practice at home, working on chords etc., from sheet music. So my lip is in good shape. Feeling very empty after a couple of days of severe diet – had a scraggy steak in the bar next to the hall.

Saturday 11 March

Got on the scales this morning, discovered to my mild alarm that since I started my carbohydrate-free diet on 1 March I have shed about 11lbs – a pound a day.

Tuesday 14 March

Theatre Royal – not quite full, but a good house. Acker deputized for George, played well. A nice, uncomplicated man.

Tuesday 28 March

Came back on the Tube. Just before we pulled into Barnet I had a sudden torrential nose bleed. Held it off until I got off the train, then walked out with handkerchief clapped to the nose. The Gents on the platform was useless – no lock-up compartment. Walked out into the car-park which was empty. Bent over the grass verge and let it flow. Two loathsome children came by – 'Ooh, look 'is nose is bleedin'.' 'All right,' I said, 'go away, go away!' The mother walked past without a sideways glance. I clambered out of sight into the bushes, still pouring. Got in a dreadful state, handkerchief drenched. A railway official came by below, asked if I was all right. I pointed at my nose and mumbled. At last it stopped, but I was a sight. Cleaned up with wet grass, but caught sight of myself in a shop window en route to the bus stop – gory! Loo by the Wood Lane bus stop had been vandalized, no paper or towels. At last, a bus and home.

Wednesday 29 March

A busy morning before leaving for Stockport. Had another big nosebleed at around 10. Jill rang Mrs Khyroyan (one of our two doctors) who said she could arrange for me to see a specialist in Barnet in two weeks! Through my diary of 1974 I tracked down the name of the Wimpole Street specialist who treated me last time – John Musgrove. Rang him and his secretary agreed to leave a prescription for the nasal spray that cured me last time – Epsikapron.

Friday 31 March

Nosebleed in the morning – neglected my spray yesterday. It took about half-an-hour to stem it. When I set off for Liverpool I plugged the nostril with cotton-wool soaked with Epsikapron.

Saturday 1 April

A bad night of intermittent sleep and severe toothache. Rang Steve Voce at 10.30 and he rang a doctor friend who agreed to see me and prescribe an antibiotic. Steve came round and picked me up and we drove to Bootle. The doctor was a nice elderly Scot called Jim McMaster. Prescribed Amoxycillin, which Steve popped over to a chemist to get. While he was out I asked 'Jim' to do my blood-pressure, in case this lies behind the nosebleed. He strapped on the tube and inflated it. 'How old are you?' he asked. I told him fifty-seven. 'Your blood-pressure is 140 over 90.' 'Is that good?' I asked nervously. 'It would be good for a man of twenty-seven,' he said.

It was the only good news of the day. On the journey across to Sunderland, the pain was excruciating. It took 3½ hours at the end of which I was gibbering.

Wednesday 5 April

A disaster day. Had a nosebleed at 10 when I got up. It took about forty-five minutes to stem. Went out later in the morning and when I got home at about 12.45 another bleeding started – and this one would not stop. After an hour, Jill drove me to the Barnet General Hospital, where a bevy of nurses administered to me. The staff nurse plugged my nostril once the bleeding had stopped, told me to go home, don't bend down, don't drink hot drinks, take it easy. J.M. said that on no account could I fly to Prague tomorrow – the packing must stay in for forty-eight hours and he will see me on Friday. So Prague is off. At 8, after sitting motionless all afternoon, I ate some lukewarm soup and another deluge started. I couldn't stop it, so back to Barnet General. A different scene – I was left bleeding profusely with a nurse wearily holding ice to my head. Eventually a doctor stemmed the flow with yards of plug. But I had been bleeding for two hours. Felt rather feeble.

Thursday 6 April

Went down to Barnet General at 9.30 to see a specialist at the E.N.T. clinic. Looked a sight with a lint pad taped over my nose. Had to wait for an hour in the 'paddock' – the usual collection of noisy kids, harassed Mums, suffering men, stoic old ladies. Eventually got in to see an Indian specialist who went through the whole history. When I told him that the pack had been in without incident for twelve hours, he said, 'Better not to shift it.' His idea was to leave the pack in till Saturday morning then get it removed at Casualty and Bob's your uncle. I explained to him that, in my experience, Bob would almost certainly *not* be my uncle. So he agreed that it would be best if I left the pack in and saw John Musgrove in the morning as planned. Went home and sat about like a piece of priceless and fragile porcelain, in dread of a sudden flow.

Friday* 7 *April

Had a good sleep, woke at 9, stayed in bed until 11.45, rather nervous about the nose holding out till I got to Wimpole Street.

Jill drove me up to Town. Tenterhooks as John Musgrove reeled out the packing (which is apparently called B.I.P.), but the nose didn't pour. He located the spot – he thought – and once he had dried up some seepage, he applied 'the red hot poker' (his own words). He asked me to wait next door while that settled, and who should be sitting there but Jimmy Young, waiting to go in for some indeterminate complaint. When he emerged I went back in and J.M. cauterized further with silver nitrate. 'I *think* we've got it,' he said finally – but the next fourteen hours will tell.

Saturday* 8 *April

1 o'clock came and went without nasal disaster, so with luck the cauterization has 'taken'.

Sunday* 9 *April

In defiance of John Musgrove, went off to do the two gigs at Blindley Heath and Crowborough. Roy Williams, provisionally booked in case I couldn't make the gig, came along to take off some of the strain. I sat on a bar stool to conserve energy. Big audience at the Red Barn. I managed the two forty-five minute sets all right, in fact the lip stood up well.

Crowborough was held this time in the Crest Hotel – a better room with fair acoustics. Felt very tired by the end but little wonder. At the Red Barn, Doc Duggie White said it would take up to two weeks to recover from the blood-letting. But today's outing was a good psychological boost.

Tuesday* 11 *April

Budget Day – a day spent tidying my desk and getting things in order. Listened to – or rather watched – Healey's 13th Budget. The Tories seem to be in a cleft stick, grumbling about high unemployment but at the same time advocating a higher *spending* tax that would put up prices and unemployment.

Thursday 13 April

Got a long letter off to Graeme Bell outlining our Satchmo show. When we all discussed the Australian tour a few weeks ago, Alex Welsh said that in his view we would only need Graeme's rhythm section (Roy says this is typical – A.W. is terrified of anything new and of playing with unfamiliar musicians). He'll get a shock if Graeme responds to my suggestion of a two-front-line with myself and Alex alternating *plus* some ten-piece arrangements!

Tuesday 25 April

Back to school for the *I'm Sorry I Haven't A Clue* team. Willie Rushton wasn't available for this one, was replaced by Jonathan Lynn, who is the producer (and member of the cast) of the play in which Graeme Garden and Tim Brooke-Taylor are currently appearing. There is a new producer called Chris Perkins, otherwise the show is as usual. Surprisingly we had quite a large audience at lunchtime, and everything seemed to go well. Picked up the information from a somewhat gloomy conversation among the Phoenix Theatre cast that their play is doing badly – was it wise for them to plug it incessantly in a programme (two, to be exact) which doesn't start until the end of August?

Monday 8 May

Wrote to each member of the band outlining my ideas for a new band.

An afternoon with Don Sayer at Kensington House, looking at the Montreux films for which I am to do the commentary later this month. Not a bad set, though one whole half-hour of deteriorating Ella Fitzgerald is too much.

In the Commons, the Government was defeated by eight votes on a Tory amendment to lop a further 1p off the Income Tax. A window-dressing operation by Thatcher's lot.

Tuesday 9 May

Rather a lethargic *I'm Sorry I Haven't A Clue* for me – couldn't get the brain going. Willie Rushton was back in the team, which livened things up. Afterwards I did some shopping for clothes. Visited my Jewish chums at Norman's, who wielded the tape-measure and revealed that my waist measurement is down to 40", my neck measurement down to 16?!! This means that I have to re-kit completely. Bought £180 worth of gear, mainly lightweight, pale-coloured jackets with assorted trousers, socks and shirts. On the way home I breezed into Marbers, where Georgie gets her jeans, and bought two pairs of corduroy trousers, jeans-style. This is the first time I have been slim enough to buy anything there – in fact, I have not been waist 40" since the end of World War II!

Wednesday 10 May

A second warm, sunny day running! Has the weather gone stark, staring mad?

Thursday 11 May

I had a chance to chat briefly with Malcolm and Mick Pyne – the latter seems quite happy about drawing in the boundaries of his style. He admitted that sometimes he has felt *too* free.

Saturday 13 May

The thirteenth started well – drenching with rain with my car's wipers bust. The roof has been leaking again and the phone went dead yesterday afternoon. I phoned the engineers and the man on duty said it's an underground fault, will take at least two or three days!

Went at 6 o'clock to Oxford for a gig at the Randolph Hotel – a University Charity Show, run by undergraduates. Things haven't changed – the young 'hooray' students threw themselves on to the dance floor and thrashed about like drowning men, exactly as they did twenty-five years ago. Quite an easy blow. Not an ounce of hospitality – and that *has* changed over the years. In the early 'fifties one was almost forcibly fed with food and drink!

Tuesday 16 May

A much livelier *I.S.I.H.A.C.* this lunchtime.

Thursday 25 May

A whole day closeted with Don Sayer at the T.V. Centre, doing the 'voice-overs' for Montreux. We do six programmes, all put together by D.S. He axed Earl Hines from the series in favour of the very commonplace Marva Josie until I made him send over to Geneva and get a Hines contribution back!

Saturday 27 May

Another glorious day. Got back home at 2 – caught Jill unawares setting up a fish tank for my birthday. So we fixed it up together – a freshwater tank with two shubunkins, one of those black characters with Pekingese eyes and an exotic silver fish with chiffon attachments. The water is a bit cloudy now – dust from the gravel floating about – but it should clear in forty-eight hours. Jill also bought an oxygen pump which hums away merrily behind the photo albums and keeps a continuous aeration going.

Tuesday 30 May

Bust-up day for this series of *I'm Sorry I Haven't A Clue*. Rather chaotic programmes – uncontrollable adlibbing from the lads. Drinks all round in the pub afterwards, then I went to the bank, and on to Jeremy Robson's office to hand in my mammoth chapter on Bessie Smith. We had a long talk about the book (*Best of Jazz*) – it really does look as if it may come out in the autumn. He is flatteringly enthusiastic about all the chapters so far.

Thursday 1 June

The full story of my new band having appeared in the *M.M.*, two drummers have emerged from the woodwork as I hoped. One is an old acquaintance, Tony Allen, who used to work for Monty Sunshine years ago. Roy W. has worked with him lately, says he has come on a lot. The other drummer is called Alan Cox, not known to me or, as far as I can make out, to anyone else. He says that Alan Jackson and Martin Drew will know of him. Will enquire further.

Friday 2 June

To Cardiff for 'Salute to Satchmo' at the New Theatre. Old George Chisholm was back in the show after his two-month layoff. Looks pretty well, but very, very nervous about playing. I expected him to be playing weakly but he did well, pipping out all the high ones and doing his full comedy routine.

Tuesday 6 June

When I got home, I dashed off a three-page hand-out announcing that the 'new' band will be doing a show called 'Basin Street to Harlem' from September onwards. Dropped it in at Kwik Kopy to be copied by tomorrow.

Wednesday 14 June

D-day today! D for dentures, disaster? Woke up early in the Cambridge hotel with a severe attack of the horrors. Even if one is not a trumpet player, there is something symbolic about the top front teeth. The last line of defence when fists and feet have failed! Fortunately, once I left the hotel, things happened with a rush – home, straight up to Wimpole Street into the surgery, into the chair. The actual extraction was quite painless under local anaesthetic – out of the four teeth, only one – front incisor, stage left – caused David Solomon a bit of a tussle. The denture was put in immediately and my worries evaporated instantly. It fitted perfectly, had none of the feeling of resisting gravity that I feared. Felt so confident that I went with David and Colin, his freelance mechanic, to the coffee-house in Marylebone High Street, and chomped on a mushroom omelette.

At supper, I told Jill and Georgina, who hadn't noticed anything. Georgina said, 'Can we change the subject?'

Thursday 15 June

Did some practice last night – the 'miracle' continues. Managed to play quite easily over the whole range, although it seemed that the tone is missing. But considering the myth that no teeth equals musical disaster if not extinction, I am obviously in no great trouble.

The job tonight at the Royal Academy was the real test. I did quite

Humph demonstrating his art college training in this artwork created for the original edition of his book Best of Jazz.

a lot of practice at home during the day, with similar results to last night. Roy Williams was booked for tonight in case I needed to take it easy. As it happened, things went well and I found that I could get a decent tone. As a result I went for it without letting up, on the principle that if I survived a heavy 'blow' tonight I shall be able to cope with Woolwich on Saturday. Very sore by 2.15, but survived!

They gave us a good meal at Burlington House and the gig was quite enjoyable, although it didn't achieve the abandon of the old Royal College 'do's' in the 'fifties that Hugh Casson was aiming for. Too many young squares, not enough elderly ravers like Sir Hugh.

Monday 19 June

Rehearsal day, to audition the applicant drummers. Alan Cox came in the morning – a young, 'cool', probably very nervous man, pleasant to talk to. We did an hour's playing to give him a good work-out. Quite a good player but with a dragging beat which pulled all the fast numbers down to a medium tempo. Also his fill-ins were limited, indicating that he needs more experience.

For the lunch-break we repaired to the Champion in East Castle Street, saw drummer, to discuss our verdict. Everyone agreed that he was not quite up to it.

After lunch, listened to Tony Allen – a different proposition, full of experience in traditional bands such as Monty Sunshine's. He pounded away quite effectively, but rhythmically he was stuck in the naïve traditional mould. Bruce Turner thought he was 'swinging'! Dave and Mick, who would have to work with him in the rhythm section, were not impressed. So it's back to square one.

Saturday 8 July

Flew off to Istanbul on the 8.50 British Airways flight. Got there at 12, but the Turkish time is two hours ahead. Met by Ian, a young Scotsman with funny magnified eyes behind his glasses – of the British Council. Bruce T. and I arrived bursting for a pee, so Ian took us in his car to the British Embassy, which of course exists for this very purpose – the relief of British nationals abroad.

Met up with the rest of the band at the Sheraton Hotel. Had a wash and brush up, then Ian collected us to drive over to the Castle where the concert is to be held. It overlooked the Bosphorus, and the concert arena is just below the main tower. We were there to do a sound check, but a) the sound people weren't there and b) an elderly piano-tuner commandeered the instrument and demanded that we should hush.

We hushed without further prompting to a little restaurant on the waterfront with Ian in charge. The main feature of the meal was Turkish 'hors d'oeuvres' ('*mesa*'?) which consisted of an almost limitless procession of small dishes (stuffed this and that, meatballs etc., etc.) all of which, according to Ian, will appear on the bill if one doesn't send some back. Our lads sent some back, Dave G. declaring – as he does with any food that rises above the ordinary – that it was the best meal he ever had. Grilled fresh fish followed – very nice. We drank raki, the Turkish version of Pernod, which Bruce Turner took to on the strength of its similarity to aniseed balls.

Huge crowd at the concert. Superb floodlit setting, but appalling amplification, with one speaker emitting a loud hum. In the second half we used no amplification. At the end, many members of the audience beseeched us with passion not to use it tomorrow.

Sunday** 9 **July

Ian arranged for us to have the use of the minibus for some tourism at 12.30. The young Turkish British Council (or Istanbul Festival) man and the Turkish film-star of a driver took us first to the Topkapi Palace, now a museum. The manifestation of grotesque wealth – golden caskets, jewel-encrusted daggers, thrones on which there is barely room for one more precious stone – very soon quenched my curiosity, but I found a room with Islamic manuscripts which were much more up my street. Stupendous illumination.

We then went on to two mosques. Scattered figures (male) went through an elaborate praying routine on the opulent carpets fenced off from the tourists. The women pray in pens remote from the centre of activity. Outside, a man selling postcards was missing from pelvis downwards, sat and 'walked' on a leather pad roughly where his jeans' belt would have been.

Another good concert, though we had to use mikes because the concert was recorded for radio.

Wednesday** 12 **July

To Montreux, arriving at Geneva about 11.30. Met by Don Sayer. In the musicians' bar I interviewed two members of the U.S. student band (one called something Battenburg!). Bill Evans (very easy), a voluble Esther Phillips and a reticent Philly Joe, who didn't want to talk about himself because he's written it all in a book.

Thursday 13 July
Hang-about day until the evening, when D.S. is intent upon getting more interviews, including Dizzy. Interview in hotel garden with Humphrey Whirlwind for B.B.C. overseas. The whole idea is mad – nobody ever got a worthwhile chat in three minutes of recording. Tonight's bill included Ray Charles with Dizzy, Hank Crawford and Micky Roker. Utter disaster. The artists' bar was closed for 'security', and officious stewards turned away all comers. I was in the concert hall listening to Dizzy when Humphrey Whirlwind dashed in to say, 'Don Sayer wants you at once – he's got a Brazilian for you!' The Brazilian was Gilberto Gil, and I had to interview him in the middle of the foyer.

The Ray Charles set was a shambles – it was quite clear that he and the band hadn't even met before the show, let alone rehearsed. On the very slow numbers R.C. set such an irregular tempo that neither Roker nor Duvivier could pick it up – the result e.g.: was 'Georgia… (long instructions to the drummer) … Georgia … (more chat) … the whole day through … (cry of 'Please play it slow!')….' At the end of the night I blew up, refusing to chase round after Dizzy hour after hour. Stormed off to bed.

Friday 14 July
Made a quick getaway from Montreux, driving to Geneva Airport in a Festival car with Dizzy and six cases of Badedas which he proposed to ship home to the U.S. Luckily I was on a different plane so didn't get held up.

Saturday 29 July
Jill, Georgina and I left home at about 9.30a.m. to drive down to Dorset for Lucy's wedding. A very hot day so I wore my lightweight safari suit. I wasn't out of place – at one point I said to Belinda [niece], 'This isn't a wedding, it's an amateur production of *The Boy Friend*!' Most of the young men on the groom's side were in white suits. Julian himself had a white Indian 'smock' and white slacks, eliciting alongside Lucy naughty comments about Persil. Nephews and nieces there in force – a handsome lot, especially on the female side.

Friday 18 August

Still up in the air – landed in Perth, met at the airport by some men in dark glasses who could only be either big agents or small men in the Mafia. One of them was Peter Korda, our promoter. We are introduced to a slight, nervy-looking man called Peter Woodward who is our road-manager. We check in at the Sheraton Hotel, very posh. Had a short doze, went up the road for a Chinese meal. Very good, but one has to discover that one dish – sweet and sour pork, say, or king prawns – is a complete meal in itself. I ordered three! Picked up at the hotel.

Saturday 19 August

Jetlag took its toll and I woke up at about 4 o'clock. Took the opportunity to ring Jill, got through via the exchange in about ten minutes. It was about 9p.m. in London. Snoozed off again till mid-morning. Last night, arrangements were made for us all to go to a club outside Perth to sit in with a local band. In fact, the arrangements involved *two* local bands, and there was a certain element of tug-of-war between the two. In the end, the judgement of Solomon prevailed – we decided to visit both clubs. The first was at the Ocean Hotel outside Perth. Nice, Chicago-style band led by a quasi-Lee Marvin on trombone and with a good lady singer. A.W. came on with self, Roy and Bruce, dictated the numbers, including the inevitable 'Struttin' with some Barbecue'. After three Chicago-style numbers I called 'Rose Room' in A flat and beat it in before he had a chance to argue.

Tuesday 29 August

Went out early to a music shop and bought the John Sangster 'Hobbit' Suite and two Bob Barnards. The mammoth journey begins. Apart from having to change planes at Sydney, and getting off for a leg stretch at Singapore (good souvenir shop) and Bahrain (a Henry Moore vista of sleeping Arabs on all the seats), it was seemingly days aloft.

Wednesday 30 August

At Singapore airport I bought some souvenirs – all quite reasonable quality – a couple of little oriental pots, and a tar-paper parasol with dragon design which reminds me of childhood. At least they haven't started producing them in plastic. At Bahrain I was feeling so blown out that I walked purposefully up and down the transit room to work off the dead-horse feeling. I think the secret of long-haul air flights is to turn away all but one meal in three and virtually fast while aloft.

On arrival in England, I squeezed in a recording for Emison on the way home – they had to have it by the end of the month and I couldn't fit it in before we left. Then home.

Thursday 7 September

First concert with the new band at the Corn Exchange, Ipswich. Incredible luck – the backdrop and P.A. speakers were vermillion, matching the red baize which I stuck on the music stands yesterday! We got there two hours early, rehearsed all the special bits – the 'Basin Street' intro, riffs on 'Fidgety Feet', 'Memphis Blues', 'The Fish-Seller'. It all paid off. The band literally roared into the first set, and maintained the excitement all night. Fabulous reception, and over drinks afterwards, the committee rebooked us for early next year.

Tuesday 12 September

Packed-out session at the Bull's Head – Doc Duggie White was there, looking thin but otherwise reasonably fit. He has cancer, allegedly severe. At the end of the night he said, 'This might be the last time I hear the band.' When I raised an eyebrow he said, 'I'm going to retire and clear out – I don't know where.' A deep one.

Band played fantastically. Apparently, there were as many turned away as got in. Elkie Brooks and husband Trevor were in for the second set. Knocked out by the new band.

Thursday 14 September

By second post, a letter from Steve Voce enclosing a Photostat of a letter to him from Buck, who was ill again last February with liver trouble and is now on the wagon. I wrote to him asking him to do me two arrangements for the new band.

Did some quite hefty digging in the garden, levelling out a new terrace around the two 'formal' ponds.

Sunday 17 September
Did a little more digging etc. in the garden in the morning, getting the new terrace marked out for Mr Jenkins next Friday.

Monday 18 September
Back from Birmingham. Put my Australian programme together – good stuff from Bob Barnard and John Sangster, programme had a very original sound throughout.

Tuesday 19 September
A tedious day, preparing for rehearsal tomorrow. The situation is frustrating at the moment – the band is rarin' to go, but winter bookings are incredibly slow – *nothing* is happening, and November and December look very bare. I suppose the late autumn 'summer' with temperatures in the low seventies isn't helping to get rid of holiday lethargy.

Sunday 24 September
Did some digging of the new terrace. Message from Chesham High School to say that 'someone' left a clarinet there. Didn't even have to look in my car! Will pick it up tomorrow.

Tuesday 3 October
Rehearsal at 4.30 for B.B.C. Jazz Club. The acoustics in Maida Vale 3 are dire – it is impossible to hear oneself except for a distant tinny sound from the far end of the instrument. I was thrown, felt the lack of a warm-up and the responsibility of a 'new' band. Result – I played like a fool, making mistake after mistake. Afterwards Peter Clayton, Keith Stewart *and* Robin J. dashed up to enthuse about the band.

Friday 6 October
A surprisingly long (four-hour) drive from Ashington to Widnes – or rather to where I check in. Stopped off en route at Hexham to buy Cumberland sausages. They seem no longer to come in yard-long lengths, but in the guise of ordinary bangers.

Saturday 7 October

Spent a leisurely day with Steve V. The tapes of yesterday are sensational – his engineer got a fine balance, and even the massed-band jam session at the end sounded good.

Saturday 14 October

The paving stones arrived from Goddard's. I laid them in position in the somewhat vain hope that Jenkins will cement them in when he comes next.

Sunday 15 October

A lukewarm review by Miles Kington in the *Sunday Times* for our Chichester concert – the band 'didn't catch fire' etc. I happen to know he only heard the Bud Freeman set – will tackle him tomorrow.

Tuesday 17 October

A hectic day – the fish-pump bust, I decanted them (the fish) into a bowl, where they began to look rather uncomfortable. I polished off my V.A.T. accounts in the morning. In early afternoon, Jill and I went over to Enfield and bought a larger tank with lid and stand, plus a £35 pump and filter. Got home, started to assemble it, found the bag of accessories missing, it was 5.30, so I rang Wildwoods in haste, as the fish were by now gasping. The youth who sold us the stuff said sorry, and he would put them in the post. Jill rang back and said no, wait there and we'll pick them up. I roared over to find a very cross Bill Heritage, with a new pump at the ready. The new aquarium looks good.

Wednesday 18 October

A marathon day.

Record session began badly, for me especially – no lip, addled brain. We got a quick 'take' of 'Spreadin' Joy', then ran into snags with 'Black and Blue' – never could play that arrangement! With a break for an Indian meal we slogged on till 5 o'clock, recording as much as possible. In the end we did 'Spreadin' Joy', 'Black and Blue' (in bits), 'Ugly Duckling', 'Mable's Dream', 'Tishomingo Blues',

'The Fishseller', 'Blues My Naughty Sweetie', 'Honeysuckle Rose', 'James' – and – 'If I Could Be With You', '100 Years from Today', 'When Your Lover Has Gone', 'Diga Diga Do' and 'East St Louis Toodle-oo'. Fourteen tracks in all. Don't suppose we'll get 'em all in.

Staggered on to Chesterford for a surprisingly fresh blow with the Savoy Jazz Band.

Friday** 20 **October

Charity gig at London University – an extraordinary concert, but the 90 per cent house, who (which) coughed up £5 a ticket, sat through about four hours, beginning with an hour of solo Alexis Korner, followed by an hour of unaccompanied Neville Dickie. When we went on I was surprised to see anyone left! But they sat through an hour of us, with an hour of Melly to finish! There was a reception (sparse in every respect) beforehand at which Mrs Neville Dickie allowed, nay, encouraged, her vile poodle to crap on the floor. She covered the offending pile with a cake box, where it rapidly stank the party to a close.

Thursday** 26 **October

All day at R.G. Jones's, Wimbledon, mixing the album. Horrible two-hour journey in. Anticipated a tough struggle to get ten top-class tracks, but as soon as I heard 'Tishomingo Blues', realized that I might have misjudged the session. 'Blues My Naughty Sweetie' was another single 'take' that sounded fine. By 5 o'clock, we had fourteen tracks, obviously we won't be able to use them all. The main edits were in 'Mable's Dream' and 'Black and Blue', although the latter was far less fraught with disaster than I recalled and I got away with one 'insert' that reduced about six fluffs to one. Came back with a cassette.

Friday** 27 **October

At the Kendal Hotel afterwards I primed the band with a bottle of champagne and then found a quiet corner in which to play them the cassette. In advance they clearly didn't believe the tape was anything special – Dave Green said he thought the session was hurried, and

Malcolm said he hadn't felt very happy with it. As I expected, their spirits rose rapidly as the tape rolled. By the end, euphoria, not entirely due to the champagne!

Thursday 23 November

Message in the p.m. from Alan Jackson, who has a week's work in mid-March. Can he do it? I rang him to explain the position – that we are selling the band as it is, that to have musicians blocking off dates in advance would be hopeless and that I have already discouraged Mick Pyne re Ronnie Scott. He still sounded doubtful, said, 'Yeah, but I don't like to turn down work – we might not get anything in that week!' Sat down and wrote to all the band, explaining the amount of work that's going into the band and suggesting a six-month trial with no deposits, no blocking dates. My new avowed policy is 'no festering boils – lance them immediately'.

Sunday 26 November

Made bread in the morning – turned out well – typical all-wholemeal loaves, not very puffy, but tightly-packed and with a nice, biscuity crust.

Tuesday 28 November

Jeremy Thorpe 'trial' in full swing, with unbelievable revelations every day. There doesn't seem to be one member of the extraordinary cast who has told the truth about anything, Thorpe included.

Was sitting at my desk chewing something this morning when something went snap and one of my ersatz front teeth detached itself. I was able to lodge it back in, but later forgot and lost it (swallowed? bounced away on the tile floor?) while nibbling a medlar! Got spare pair out of the car – will now *have* to get used to playing with them. Practised hard.

Wednesday 29 November

Down to Brighton for a solo gig at a pub called the Adur (pronounced Ada, apparently a river). A glass of champers in the guvnor's flat upstairs then into action. Teeth OK – in fact, initially they felt an improvement on the others, but by the time the second 'set' had declined into a loud jam session with two trumpets I felt the strain!

Thursday 7 December
The men arrived this morning to start on the roof – a small, bustling man in charge who was up and down the ladder like a squirrel. Looks a more businesslike team than the last lot.

Thursday 14 December
Fine clear day, but no workmen! Rang Goddard's, who said the chief tiler's car was broken down at Luton and he couldn't get in.

Friday 15 December
Seven men arrived this morning to do crash work on the roof to finish it. But torrential rain beat them off by early afternoon. Apart from yesterday, there hasn't been one rain-free day since they began.

Saturday 16 December
A solitary tiler turned up at noon with a small son in tow. It became clear that the boy was doomed to sit in the car in freezing cold while Dad combined work with baby-sitting, so I suggested that he should come indoors. At first he shook his head dumbly but when I said that I would be busy elsewhere and he would be on his own, he agreed.

Sunday 17 December
The double at Blindley Heath and Crowborough. Dr Duggie White was at the former with his daughter. It transpires that he is doomed with bone-cancer – appalling for a doctor who knows what is in store. He is currently under heavy drugs, which make him look fit but puffy around the face. In conversation, too, he has lost the 'edge' that he used to have. He gave me a brace of pheasants.

Later, the Crowborough gig was absolutely packed out – played without amplification and you could hear a pin drop!

Monday 18 December

Work on the roof is getting slower and slower now – two dozy men wandered up today but didn't do much.

Can't remember the exact details, but in this forthcoming week Jill and I made frequent sorties to Brent Cross for Christmas shopping. It hasn't been too crowded – indeed, by midweek it began to look like Christmas Eve, with few people and emptying shelves.

Did two programmes tonight, with a 'special' for Christmas Day. Decided to devote it to 'pop' jazz – i.e.: recordings that made the charts. Started with Acker's 'That's My Home' which after all this time sounds very good. Recalled that someone on *Juke Box Jury* referred to his vocal as 'Louis Armstrong without the gravel'.

Tuesday 19 December

Went straight to McCarthey's in Victoria (recommended by Alan Milford) to try for some silver candlesticks for Jill. At first they said they had none, but just as I was leaving, the distinguished-looking old gent behind the counter beckoned me into a back room and showed me a pair that were being kept for someone who hadn't returned. So he offered them to me, first for £120, then for £110 – 'the price we would ask of Mr Milford!'. They look magnificent but they are too big and ornate.

Thursday 21 December

Petrol panic has suddenly started again – the drivers have been on a go-slow for a day or two, and today the news got out. Result – lengthening queues all day long. In the evening I drove out to London Colney – last time the Moynihan Services had no queues. This time it did, but I had a full tank when I drove off an hour later. A man alongside my pump filled up, unbelievably with 60 gallons – £48 on the clock. He wasn't lynched – we all just watched with our mouths hanging open. Must have had extra tanks fitted.

The new roof leaked this afternoon!!! It poured in at the bottom end of the dining-room beam. Jill rang Goddard's, the man who answered said he would be round shortly, never turned up.

Friday 22 December

Up at 7.30 and straight over to the Clarendon Garage at Borehamwood to queue for petrol in Jill's car. Only half-a-dozen cars ahead of me, but even when the garage opened at 8, it still took half-an-hour to get to a pump.

Sunday 24 December

Christmas timing is better this year – a Sunday Christmas Eve means that everything *has* to be bought by Saturday. Today was quite quiet. In the afternoon I got the stocking presents together and finished some wrapping up.

Monday 25 December

Got up at a reasonable hour – 8.30-ish, put Georgina and David's stockings outside their doors. Pottered about getting the lunch ready, tidying etc. in the morning. Jill and G. went off to the Strangeways knees-up. J. came back slightly 'merry'. Stephen came over at about 1.30 – the new hot-plate came into its own – we were ahead of ourselves in getting the lunch ready. Jolly lunch.

Presents afterwards. J. liked her candlesticks. Stephen and David etc. left at 6. Quiet evening. Morecambe and Wise were pathetic – victims of the I.T.V. blight.

Thursday 28 December

Cloudburst in the evening, water bucketed in from both valleys. Drafted a rude, not to say offensive, letter to Mr Smith of Goddard's. Will re-write and type it tomorrow so that he gets it when the firm deigns to return from holiday.

Saturday 30 December

Sent off irate letter to Goddard's re roof.

Sorry to find Callaghan scattering silly showbiz O.B.E.s in Wilson style – Tommy Steele is OK I suppose, but Olivia Newton-John??? She acknowledged the award graciously 'from her home near Hollywood'!

Sunday 31 December

Day of total disaster! Slept badly, waking up at 4a.m. worrying about snowdrifts. Dozed off again, meaning to get up at 6.30, but woke at 7. Dressed in ten seconds, picked up horn and uniform and went off. Car door was frozen solid, had to dash back and boil a kettle to release it. Snow was plentiful but not much drifting. Drove off steadily, but by the time I reached Mill Hill Circus, my temperature gauge had soared into the red, and I was boiling over. Took the lid off the filler too soon, scalded my hand. When I set off again, the needle stayed high but stable so I assumed that the thermostat had jammed and drove on. Got to Gatwick at 9.15 with little real trouble. All the guys were there except A.J. and Roy who arrived later, A.J. without his drums – thought they were being provided. We rang Guernsey, laid a kit on. We needn't have bothered. As we sat around like refugees, periodical announcements were made expressing hopes that the airport would be opened at 12, 2 and 4. It was opened at 4, but our flight had been cancelled at 3.45. Utter gloom all round. Several of the guys had turned down other New Year's Eve jobs, but only Mick and, to a lesser degree, Dave, seemed to imply that it was somehow my fault!

Laborious drive home. Watched the New Year in with Jill and Nana, keeping deep depression at bay with champagne.

1979

Monday 1 January

FREEZE – Snow seems set for some time – not till March, I hope, as in 1962–63! Took G. over to the farm.

Got back to be told by Nana that water was dripping into her room above the bed. Went up in the loft, found a small burst in the copper pipe to the washing machine. Did a crafty D.I.Y. repair with tinfoil, plastic and string binding. Did the trick.

Tuesday 2 January

Nana has been agitating for some days to get off home – there is a party for all the Wild Life workers tomorrow and she doesn't want to miss it at any price. Jill couldn't get through to Waterloo so I drove her in at 11.30 on the off-chance. The departure board was an almost total blank when we got there at 12.15, but, if it hadn't been so freezing cold, it would have been quite like an exciting game of chance watching the boards flipping over rapidly to return to a blank or announce a departure.

When I got home, heard a tell-tale splashing noise from the garage. Found another burst, just at the joint of a tap above the washing machine. At first water squirted out in several streams, but when I fiddled with it, it came adrift and the water gushed. I had to stick a length of hose over it so that it ran away on to the lawn.

Wednesday 3 January

FREEZE continues – bad night listening to water gurgling along the pipes above our head. A man from the tiling firm arrived at 8.30 and said, 'Where's the leak?' I thought he was the plumber and babbled incoherently. Nothing's emerged from his visit – with its layer of snow the roof was invisible.

A lot of one's day nowadays is spent simply surviving, e.g. at about midday all the cold taps went dry – Jill went up into the loft and discovered that the tank was empty. The water running away from the garage burst drew off pressure from the mains. Had to go and stuff cloth into the broken pipe-end to staunch the flow. Then there was the pond-ice to be thawed with a kettle to get oxygen to the fish.

Thursday 4 January

Another freezing day. There is still nasty talk of strikes – the lorry drivers are already half out and once again a petrol-tanker drivers' strike seems likely.

Roof men arrived, poured hot water on to the offending valley which came straight in on to my head as I breakfasted. 'It looks as if we've got trouble,' the foreman said. 'You're telling me!' I replied, dripping.

Friday 5 January

'Panic buying' is once again the watchword. 'Housewives' are alleged to be besieging the shops for frozen-food.

Still bitterly cold – queued for an hour at the garage at Stirling Corner to fill up my car. Used a bit to drive in to the Pizza-on-the-Park for a session in honour of Wild Bill Davidson's 73rd birthday. He is over with his wife Ann on holiday – most of the musicians at the party were trumpeters – Alex Welsh, Digby Fairweather, Alan Elsdon, self. We all took turns to sit in with Bill, who was in good form.

Saturday 6 January

A thaw is being promised by the weather men, but there's little sign of it today. I tucked an overcoat round the engine and left it to hibernate until I actually *have* to use it. I was frozen through when I finished. Sat and wrote all afternoon – it keeps panic at bay!

Sunday 7 January

Thaw – at last, woke to a symphony of assorted drips as a rainfall brought snow from the roof and loosened the icicles. I suffered a day of extreme nervous apprehension regarding the strike situation, not helped much by the Sunday 'heavies' – the *Sunday Telegraph* speaks of a State of Emergency and imminent collapse of industry, the *Observer* is more optimistic, suggests that the petrol strike is on the point of settlement. It all hinges on the Esso, Shell and B.P. vote tomorrow morning, about which there are hopeful noises. I'm not so sure – madness spreads quickly and I fear the worst.

Monday 8 January

Woke early again today, with a sharp attack of the willies.

Spent most of the day preparing my programme. Message to ring Tom Seabrook in the morning – he is coming to town this evening, offered a) to drive me in from home, b) to bring two brace of pheasants and c) to let me have four gallons of petrol!

Drove (on strength of lifting of petrol threat) to Brent Cross, where Jill bought some houseplants.

Met Tom at the King's Head – he had brought ten gallons of

petrol!!! Wouldn't accept payment, except to be allowed to sit in on the programme.

Tuesday 9 January

Didn't get much writing done today – did accounts in the morning, looking for (and to some degree, finding) silver linings in the financial situation. The B.P. men have joined the Esso-Shell drivers in accepting 15 per cent, so the petrol problems will diminish. But the lorry drivers look like making their strike official.

Jill and I went to lunch in Arkley Lane. Afterwards dashed into Lime Grove to do a three-minute obit of Charles Mingus, who died in Mexico a few days ago.

Wednesday 10 January

Not much traffic about – petrol is still short, and quite a lot of garages are still shut. The lorry drivers' strike is getting worse and a rail-strike is threatened next week. Hey ho!

Thursday 11 January

Jobs are beginning to roll in. But on the industrial front things still look bleak. In the course of the day the lorry drivers' strike became official – not a bad thing in itself, as the government can now deal with the T.G.W.U. centrally.

Saturday 13 January

Starting up again with the band tonight – have suffered chronic depression throughout the long lay-off, and a blow, even at the 100 Club, will do me good. On the way in I collected thirteen Wild Bill albums for my programme on Monday.

In the event, it was quite a good session at the 100 Club. Wild Bill Davison was down there, had a sit-in for a set of about forty-five minutes – a marathon for him. We played 'Blues My Naughty Sweetie' in B". All through my solo I could hear a voice complaining to all and sundry, 'How do you like that – asks me up to play and then picks the wrong f..... key!'

Monday 15 January

Tonight's programme went well. I was able to play a lot of Wild Bill records that were not the usual 'Chicago-style' bash – including a lovely 'You Take Advantage of Me' with a Czechoslovakian band that played in a dated, Pasadena Roof Orchestra way, which brought out all the latent Bix in Bill's playing. A strange man, basically very nervous and lacking in confidence – I wonder if he ever got over the Teschmacher affair [where Wild Bill was involved in a fatal car accident that ended the life of clarinettist Frankie Teschmacher] – Dan Sawyer told me that as a result of the accident and one or two other hassles, he lost his union card throughout the 'thirties, and was only able to play small gigs in and around Milwaukee. All the bluster and brashness conceals nerves – he admits to getting 'the shakes' frequently before, and sometimes during, stage performances, hence all the sitting down.

Saturday January 20

Had breakfast with Steve and Jenny before setting off across country for South Shields. Went via the M62 and the A1 – slushy going but made it in just over 3 hours which is about normal.

Sunday January 21

Ordered the *Observer* and *Telegraph* this morning, sat in bed reading about how I couldn't have got across the Pennines yesterday. Moral: read all about it a day late.

Monday 29 January

Prepared two programmes – one general one for tonight; one on Charles Mingus for next week – turned out well, especially the Mingus which, despite the fact that I am not an expert on his music, built up well and by the end had a real 'lump in the throat' quality.

Monday 5 February

Back home, had a meal then slept solidly from 3.30 to 5.30, had to dash straight off to the Gordon Craig Theatre, Stevenage. It's a nice auditorium, but the dressing-rooms would not be unduly drab in Pentonville!

The concert was not well-attended but it was well up to par for the house, and the band played very well. Pig-farmer Tom was there, helped me sell some records.

Thursday 8 February
V.A.T. day. Filled in two quarters' accounts and gave myself a sick headache.

Friday 9 February
Rang Mr Norman Howells at the Velindre Working Mens' Club in Port Talbot – my old stamping-ground – who thought it might be nice if I could bring 'my group' there for their 50th Jubilee in November. I said I'd do what I could.

Monday 12 February
Scottish Tour – set off at 10.30 through thick slush, which fell overnight. The journey from Birmingham to Glasgow is just on 300 miles, but it seemed quite painless.

Wednesday 14 February
Intended to have an early-ish night and to do some shopping in Inverness this morning, but stayed up late with the guys in the hotel lounge, so did no more than pop into a delicatessen called Tarragon to pick up some oatmeal-crusted cream cheese called Caboc, recommended by Jim.

The drive down to Blairgowrie seemed longer than its 100-odd miles (one is spoiled by motorways). On arrival, went to the pub where 'The Gig' functions nightly. Couldn't get much sense out of the lady in charge, but was eventually taken down the road to the chalets where we are all supposed to be put up. Shown *one* chalet with a doubled-bedded room, a twin-bedded room and one with double-decker bunk beds – for all seven of us! 'Acker Bilk and Chris Barber bands loved it here,' I was told. Not for me!!! Drove into the town and checked into the Angus Hotel, no great shakes but better than camping out! Got provisions, had a snack lunch, then went to the chalet to see if the guys were settled in – only Bruce there, the others had checked into the Angus too! Depression lifted once the gig started – a packed 'pub' audience of jazz fans, raving.

Thursday 15 February

Concert at the Adam Smith Centre, two doors away from the hotel. Before tea, we all went along to do a sound-check for B.B.C. Scottish radio, who are taping the show for two broadcasts. In the evening, while I was warming up, a message arrived that a Mr Tom Gourdie was downstairs to see me – Tom Gourdie, calligrapher-in-chief for Scotland!!! Round, scholarly man, gave me an inscribed copy of his *Improve Your Handwriting* book. Sell-out concert.

Friday 16 February

The Tom Gourdie package had a beautifully-written letter enclosed. A prize for the collection.

Saturday 17 February

Checked out of the Golden Lion early – at about 10a.m. – for the drive to Whitehaven via Glasgow and Carlisle. Stopped off in the latter for lunch. Bought 6lbs of Cumberland sausages at Dewhursts ('Passing through again, Mr L.?').

Sunday 18 February

Have given up reading papers for last two weeks – marvellous! No gloomy forecasts, no inaccurate weather reports – it has had the same effect as giving up smoking or going on a diet.

Friday 23 February

Civil Servants' Strike.

Ferocious letter in red print from the V.A.T., threatening instant distraint of my goods and chattels. Had to add up all the irrelevant totals necessary to fill in the forms. Got it all ready for posting, when I heard on the radio that the striking civil servants are to pull the plugs on selected computers, including the main V.A.T. computer at Southend!

Thursday 1 March

Down to Ash to play in a small jazz club outside Yeovil. Club was small but full, and we played a good session. Afterwards played darts with the guys. On returning to my hotel at 2.15, couldn't get in. Rang the night bell for minutes, then went round to the back of the building and roused a receptionist from the staff quarters. She came down, hurriedly dressed, to say that *she* couldn't get in from the staff quarters either, and that she was worried because the porter 'is an elderly man'. Minutes later, she roused another, more senior receptionist, and we all stood round in a freezing wind wondering whether to send for the police. Suddenly I spotted geriatric porter inside, creaking through the hall with a tray of tea. I rapped on the door and he hurried out. 'What's up – is the bell not working?' I said that it had, for forty-five minutes, worked well enough to rouse everyone in the hotel but him. 'Oh, no,' he said, 'oh no, sir, – you see I have this bleeper which bleeps whenever the bell is rung.' The senior receptionist reached over and pressed a thumb on the bell, which pealed out without eliciting a responsive bleep. Consternation!

Sunday 4 March

Rehearsal at 3.30 at the T.V. Centre for panel game *Blankety-Blank*. I am on with David Jason, manic comedienne Faith Brown, cockney model girl Lorraine Chase, manic impersonator Johnny Moore and slinky actress Kate O'Mara, with the other panel (they're recording two shows) including Roy Hudd and Nicholas Parsons; we watch a recording of another show, to get the hang of it. As the panellists have to match words guessed by contestants, it's the only quiz in which it is wrong to think up a witty, subtle or original answer!

Saturday 10 March

Got the car back, picked up a Cortina from Mr Hallam at Perry's, off-loaded the gear from my car then took it to Chalk Farm, where I intended to leave it outside until Monday – but Don Martin was there and took it in. He was doing some private work on AML 445H (my old car) which has been resprayed a handsome metal blue and has done 148,000 miles.

Monday 12 March

We are playing at the Bridgend Leisure Centre. A former Caterham recruit in my company – now a stocky, grey pomposo – came backstage with two friends and they presented me with a box of locally-made model soldiers – the real tin ones.

Thursday 22 March

Lunch with Peter Korda at the Bistingo in the King's Road to talk about a possible Aussie tour in 1980.

Stephen came over for a 'birthday' meal with G. and we watched the British Academy Awards, a role in which (the announcing of the Best Film Music award) I turned down last week (too scared and too old to take on unnecessary nerve-wracking gigs). Andrew Lloyd-Webber now my stand-in!

It looks as though a General Election may be in the offing, with Thatcher lurking in the wings. Dreadful to contemplate, but if we are to have Dr Johnson's poodle at No. 10 we might as well get it over with!

Thursday 29 March

The Government lost the vote of confidence last night by one vote, so we are in for an election.

Charity session at Canvey Island for the International Year of the Child. I did two sessions, one with a noisy pseudo-modern band, with a manic skin-head in 'bovver' boots on tenor, the other with a traditional band led by one John Lancaster, with Hugh Rainey, former banjoist, on trumpet – good, too. Maxine Daniels, looking like a tea-lady, sang with the first band – and very well too. Haven't seen her for twenty-odd years, since she had a nervous breakdown soon after working with us (not the reason!). 'I'm a tea-lady now,' she said.

Friday 30 March

News came over my car radio at 3.15p.m. that a car bomb had exploded at the House of Commons, killing the driver. After much speculation, it was further revealed first, that the victim was an M.P. and then, that it was Airey Neave, the Shadow Minister for Northern Ireland. His car blew up as he drove out of the Commons underground car-park.

Played tonight at the Camden Festival 'Jazz Band Ball' at the restaurant St Pancras Town Hall, opposite Wally Fawkes and Graham Tayar's Crouch End All Stars. Clive Jenkins [trade union leader] was there, hanging about in front of the bandstand like a fan.

Tuesday 3 April

Session at the Bull's Head – an eventful one. Black American singer Joe Lee Wilson sat in. He now lives in Brighton with his wife, Jill Christopher (English) and they were brought along by Viv Bonner and husband Paul – J.L.W. wanted to meet me to say thanks for featuring his record on my show. He sang 'In a Mellotone' and some blues – very good.

Kenny Graham (on the wagon and slimline) and Alan Price looked in.

Wednesday 4 April

Denis Healey presented his makeshift Budget – it contained a lot of technical stuff about allowances, but nowt of interest. Sir Geoffrey Howe, who always looks to me like a huffy prefect, rewarded Healey's restraint with a petulant attack, which might have been effective had he not fluffed every punch line. I wonder how the election will be affected when it dawns on the public that, outside of Thatcher, the Tories are almost totally anonymous. Whitelaw – a blustering prawn; Prior – apoplectic; St John Stevas – a dilettante oozing insincerity. As for Rhodes-Boyson, do we really want Mr Squeers in charge of education? In fact, Dickens created most of them, none less than the odious Reg Prentice.

Thursday 5 April

The Barnet Labour Party, personified by Robert Crick, has asked me to march for victory on 21 April. I have said yes – I like the atmosphere of those chaotic outings.

Friday 6 April

Visit this morning from my friendly neighbourhood tax-collector, demanding a mere £1,000. A jolly man, roaring with laughter.

Monday 9 April

The election campaign starts up in earnest. Jim did quite a good Press conference on T.V., looking straight into the camera instead of simply orating into thin air. La Thatcher, pictured over the weekend buying carrots in Chelsea (what a charade), has haughtily announced that she will not start campaigning until Wednesday. Meanwhile there is much Press bewilderment about the conflicting polls – the average over the whole range is 13 per cent, which is uncomfortably high. I shall be surprised if it stays as high.

Saturday 14 April

The first warm, sit-in-the-sun day of the year! Did a lot of shopping this morning – in case our prodigal sons return over the holiday! Sat in the garden this afternoon – the temperature reached 72 degrees!

In the election, the polls now begin to agree that the Tories are about 10 per cent ahead. I see in my 1974 diary that they were 8 per cent ahead at about the same time. I think it's going to be an exciting finish.

Saturday 21 April

Out on the streets of Barnet at 11 o'clock – the same team as we had in '74 turned up, including Bruce T., whom I rang yesterday, and one-legged Ed and his alto, a tenor-player and the bearded banjoist whose strings lasted as far as Timothy White's this time. We had some young drummers this time on snare and makeshift tom-toms, and they provided quite a lively rhythm-section. Not so many people as on former occasions, but I think that local agent Robert Crick is a bit easy-going nowadays. About fifty, I would say. This time we marched through Barnet, then hopped by car down to the Odeon to play them past.

Sunday* 22 *April

Drove to the Festival Hall at 1 o'clock to play in the 49th anniversary of the *Daily Worker/Morning Star* combined. Quite a good house.

Saturday* 28 *April

Back from Nottingham and then on almost at once to Hatfield to take part in a march for the Labour Party. This march was different from Barnet's in that it took place around the new town shopping centre, weaving in and out of arcades. Roughly the same band as at Barnet, with one-legged Ed on alto, Roy James (or is it Ray) on tenor, Bruce on clarinet, Dennis on banjo, and a rhythm section of three boys-brigade-type drums.

Monday* 30 *April

Woke up mildly depressed, probably a reaction after the enthusiasm of Saturday and the subsequent unpromising polls. Why should I care – I will probably be 'better off' under the Tories, and should react to affairs like the showbiz team – who paraded on the platform at a meeting of Tory Trades Unionists presided over at Wembley by Thatcher yesterday. But I prefer everything about Labour, left-wing and all. The free-enterprise, stand-on-your-own-feet, you-too-can-be-a-success-in-business philosophy presupposes a 'slave' substrata to clear sewage, provide water and electricity and generally do the dirty work.

Spent the day working on the programme – a good one. Cheered somewhat by the news late tonight of a new N.O.P. poll giving Labour a .07 per cent lead!! But do we trust the *Daily Mail* not to have cooked the results to spur the Tories and halt Labour?

Thursday* 3 *May

Election Day – a long haul ahead so took it easy most of the day – Jill and I went up to vote at lunchtime. I wore my red rosette in a final gesture of defiance.

Results began to come in at about 11.30. At first, things looked indecisive – one of the Glasgow constituencies came in first, showing a swing to Labour. This, the now snowy-haired David Butler told us, is what we expect up there. Robert McKenzie is now manic in front of his gadgets, including the now legendary Swingometer! On the strength of the final polls, he predicted a Tory win by about 4.5 per cent, with an overall majority of about thirty to forty. When the London results began to come in, things looked grimmer than that, with huge swings in East London of over 7 per cent. But it soon became clear that North and South of Britain were at odds – small swings in the North of England, a swing *to* Labour in Scotland, but a Thatcher South. Not much drama – Tory Teddy Taylor lost in Scotland, and there was a moment of Greek tragedy when Jeremy Thorpe heard of his crushing defeat in North Devon. Otherwise we saw Thatcher being acclaimed (and boo-ed) in Chelsea, North Finchley and (no boos) Smith Square; Callaghan smiling wanly and then being returned at Cardiff amid a shambles as Pat Arrowsmith and the 'Troops Out of Ireland' people demonstrated noisily; and Steel bravely contemplating the end of Liberal hopes yet again. Sad to see La Belle Helene ousted at Welwyn and Hatfield, but she picked up 25,000, which can't be bad.

Thursday 10 May

Slept like a felled ox.

Gig for charity at a school for disturbed and handicapped children in Mickleover, rang Jill in the interval, to hear that white fungus has struck our indoor aquarium – one fish dead, the others seedy.

Charity raised about £400 on the door alone.

Friday 11 May

Spent the day in the lounge of the Notts-Derby P.H., punctuated by a meal and endless crossword puzzles. Whole place a-buzz with commerce – and business-people make boring watching! Rang home to find that another goldfish has passed on to that great Goldfish Bowl in the sky.

Monday 14 May

First of a new series of *I'm Sorry I Haven't A Clue*. I got to rehearsal at 11 o'clock, which was much too early. The teams – the usual ones of Barry Cryer and Graeme Garden v. Tim Brooke-Taylor and Willie Rushton. Geoffrey Perkins, the producer, didn't give me the cue cards until the last minute, and as the deadline approached, I felt strongly that some of the games were under-rehearsed and might come unstuck. I was right – all-in-all both programmes were pretty disastrous, with great acres of uninspired waffle. Have resolved that this series will definitely be my last.

Tuesday 15 May

State opening of Parliament – watched it on television. Slightly grotesque pageantry, like a rather overplayed and pompous historical play. Queenie made no attempt to look interested as she ploughed through the Queen's Speech. A catalogue of Tory measures, most of which put the clock back twenty-five years – private medicine, private schools, Laura Norder etc. will all get the money. On radio from Parliament, Thatcher sounded frightful – hectoring, shrill, domineering. The news which will eventually put the cat among the pigeons is that there is a strong likelihood of Britain taking on nuclear 'flying bomb' (Cruise missile) bases.

Monday 28 May

Can't fathom the succession of flops in recent days – Hull, Guernsey, Eastbourne, Swadlincote, Ipswich. All eggs. Surely, Thatcher can't be affecting things as quickly as that. It would be nice to have a real packer soon, to restore confidence. Everyone is having the same problem.

Tuesday 29 May

Went up to London at 10.15, dropped some copy into Kwik Kopy for our publicity, paid in at the bank in the Haymarket, then met Don Porter, journalist from Adelaide, and did an interview with him in the Captain's Cabin. Then I took him into the Paris Studio to witness the capers one jazz musician gets up to! Not a bad session of *I'm Sorry* etc. though I'm certain it's on its last legs.

Fox-watching in the evening; we have a fox which comes to the terrace at about 10 every night to collect bones etc. which Jill leaves out. Watched it for several minutes, as it is not apparently shy of appearing in the full glow of the kitchen lights. It's no mangy suburban scavenger, but a fine red specimen.

Thursday 31 May

Jill was out when I got home, but when she got back from the hairdressers', she said the rain had come in the whole length of the dining-room ceiling and in the corridor. We are still waiting for the tilers to come and re-do the valleys. If they take this long when they haven't been paid, the mind boggles as to what would have happened if I had settled their bill.

Wednesday 6 June

Our organizer friend – called, unusually, Handel something-or-other, who went to school with Ed Taylor – took us for a pub lunch, then to the museum, where a local artist called Robert Littleford had an exhibition. Lord Rhodes tipped him for future success, so, I bought one for £95 – a street scene superbly painted in water-colour and full of light. Met the artist, a former dustman, completely self-taught.

Saturday 9 June

In the morning, on the recommendation of the Crest hall-porter, I drove thirteen miles *westward* to Wighton, where a butcher called Fox allegedly makes the best Cumberland sausages. He may do – but he had sold out by the time I got there. Met a man in the High Street who used to book us at the Coachhouse; as we walked, he pointed to a man across the street – 'That's Melvyn Bragg's father!' I bought 10lbs of Cumberlands at Harrison's, said to be second best.

Sunday 10 June

Left Sheffield at 11, drove straight down to Midhurst, checked in at the hotel, where my expensive room entailed walking with a permanent stoop, like Groucho Marx. Quaint and olde-worlde, for which one pays, I suppose.

Monday 11 June

The European elections have come and gone. In Britain the turn-out was about 30 per cent, to the outrage of the politicians, who used words like 'disgraceful' and 'abysmal' as if the apathy had nothing to do with them.

Tuesday 12 June

Budget Day. Big question is – by how much will Sir Geoffrey Howe raise V.A.T.? It was hard enough getting work when it was at 10 per cent. By 4 o'clock we knew the worst – the new rate is to be 15 per cent!! Income Tax comes down to 60 per cent for top men, 30 per cent for the rest of us and the higher rate level is raised from £8,000 to £10,000. Petrol is predictably the main victim of additional tax, with a combination of extra duty *and* V.A.T. adding 10p a gallon – so the £1 gallon is now a firm reality. It looks to me to be an ultra-Tory budget – indeed, the *Sunday Telegraph* last Sunday put it on the line by asserting that if only the rich can in future afford to drive, there is rough justice in that, since the rich 'are usually the most talented or enterprising people in society'. Codswallop! One may as well say that sewage workers or power men are 'the most important or indispensable', and so on....

Wednesday 13 June

At St John's (where we played three or four years ago) there was an officious young Jobsworth on security who wouldn't let us into the main hall without our passes, even though we were carrying our instruments ready to play. Roy chewed his ankle but he wouldn't relent. As we remonstrated, another elderly official in a top-hat said to me, 'Well, you wouldn't get into the B.B.C. without a pass!' I said, 'I do just that every Monday, because they know who I am!' 'Well, I don't know who you are!' he replied. Hmm.

Thursday 14 June

Dropped my corrected proofs for the Quiz book into Batsford's at 11.30, paid in at the bank then into the Paris Studio for *I.S.I.H.A.C.* – another very weary one with the teams not sounding very enthusiastic. Funnily enough, the contract for the book of *I.S.I.H.A.C.* arrived today – it would be strange if it all petered out just as the book came out.

Wednesday 20 June

Very hot day, up in the 80s. Didn't do very much, other than tie up the 31 January V.A.T. return and sit in the garden, listening to the two Prudential Gold Cup cricket matches – England beating New Zealand, the West Indies beating Pakistan.

The jury is out in the Jeremy Thorpe case. I have a bet with Jill that he will get off and emerge from the Old Bailey waving that silly hat to the applause of the crowd.

Thursday 21 June

Drove in to London to do the last *I'm Sorry I Haven't A Clue*. Willie Rushton has lit off on a cruise, sending the producer a telegram two days ago saying simply, 'No can do Thursday'... so we had a little gnome called Denise Coffey who turned out to be very good.

The Thorpe jury is still out after thirty hours. It rained at about 4.30, and the temperature plummeted.

Friday 22 June

The Thorpe jury returned today, and as I predicted, all four were found not guilty. I also predicted that he would emerge waving that silly hat, to the plaudits of the crowd. It was even worse than that – he went to his (or his mother's) London flat and emerged, with wife and mother, on to a balcony, arms aloft. It was the worst exhibition of bad taste I ever saw. David Holmes at least had the dignity to leave hurriedly by a side door.

Went in the afternoon to Wildwood fishery, bought two pumps for fountains and several fish.

Saturday 23 June

Back from Reading. Jill reported that some of the fish have already died. Could have been shock – this clammy weather is not ideal for transferring them. Went over to Wildwood again, bought twenty small fish and more vegetation.

Wednesday 4 July

Session at Bourne End – tiny little pub-room in village near Marlow. Who should be there but Lyn Dutton, whom I haven't seen for twenty years – well, fifteen then. Not much changed and still talking with funny put-on voices. He looked pretty fit, but has apparently had three heart attacks, two severe, and now suffers from angina.

Saturday 7 July

Went in at 2 to the Festival Hall for rehearsal.

In the evening, a good audience turned out – somewhere around 1,500, I would guess. Our set went well. Joe Lee Wilson got the audience going with some very un-avant-garde audience participation. Then the finale, which was rough as hell but went like an express train and raised the roof. Joe Lee's wife Jill very effusive afterwards over my having given Joe this 'break'.

Sunday 8 July

Patchy night, waking periodically with the damn 'Jubilee' trumpet part stuck in my head!

Sunday 29 July

All round it was a rather sloppy concert – I think the number one priority after the hols is to pull the carpet out from under the band and get everyone concentrating again. We tried out the Kenny Graham number for the first time since the recording – what with two days of recording and mixing I know my part backwards but the guys had to struggle with it from the music and it was full of mistakes. Nevertheless it got a huge response from the audience.

There was a note in my band-room from Adelaide Hall saying that she would be along. She has friends in Mold with whom she stays. She came to the last Satchmo show and I got the impression then that she would have liked to sit in, so I intercepted her in the interval and invited her to sing one or two. After some mock horror at the idea, she agreed. In the second half she sang 'That Old Feeling' and recovered well from starting in a too-high key. 'I Can't Give You Anything But Love', with self doing the verse, brought her a huge ovation.

Tuesday 7 August
Started ripping up water mint from around the pond, to clear the decks for building a new rockery. By evening, despite sporadic rain, had the turf up and a space cleared.

Wednesday 8 August
The new pond area comes on apace. We went to the Watergardens and bought one 'squid' pond – deep and squiggle-shaped – and two shallow 'waterfall' ponds, plus a pump. Continued with the work in the evening, sank the pond, built York stone steps....

Thursday 9 August
The rains came, deluging down all morning. Got out in the afternoon to do some more work on the mound. Jill bought a salmon trout. I made a hollandaise sauce, got it right at the third attempt.

Monday 20 August
Back to work in the sense that I had two programmes to do tonight. Made a last visit to Enfield to pick up fish food and a few more plants.

Programmes went well – picked up a huge amount of mail, much of it regarding *I'm Sorry I Haven't A Clue*, with people begging to know the rules of the spoof game 'Mornington Crescent'.

Tuesday 11 September
Bull's Head session: K. Graham was there, heard 'Fickle Fanny' for the first time. He said, 'The grammar's right but the punctuation's wrong.' He meant that we should emphasize the 12/8 feel and play it less jerkily. Unfortunately it is already on record, but I think we played it better then. Joe Temperley, over from the States, sat in on soprano and played beautifully.

Wednesday 12 September
Session at the Haymarket Theatre, Basingstoke. Difficult place to find – I mean Basingstoke, not the theatre. The ring-road seems to bisect the town, and there are signs to Upper Town Centre, but none that I could see to Lower Town Centre!

Nice little theatre with a reasonable audience of around 300 (capacity 400), which they say is over par for the course in this theatre. Alan played superbly and the band recaptured the spirit and enjoyment of its earlier days.

Friday 14 September

Warm, sunny day, sat out with account books and calculator doing V.A.T. accounts. The awful thing is that I have grown to *enjoy* all this V.A.T. nonsense, in much the same way that I grew to enjoy polishing boots and stamping the feet as a recruit at Caterham. My account books are a model of lucidity!

Sunday 16 September

A beautiful day, with the sky a very deep blue and almost cloudless. Spent the whole afternoon in the garden, cleaning out the ponds. Of the two identical terrace ponds, the left-hand one has one orfe and three small goldfish in frequent view, the right-hand one has two orfes and two small goldfish (plus a 'fry', an orfe I think) which skulk out of sight all day. Strange.

Monday 8 October

Day of phoning, to contact John Barnes (saxophonist) about the tour. At first he said he couldn't do the Middle East as he had booked a holiday then, but later agreed to do it, and join the band. He'll be an asset.

Saturday 13 October

Rang artist Robert Littleford in the morning – he said he has just had an exhibition, sold everything, but will give me free choice of the next bunch in two months' time.

Monday 22 October

Had to leave at 12 to drive to Sheffield for a broadcast show from the Big Top Theatre in Norfolk Park. That's just what it is – a circus tent which John Barnes has played in before – in Portsmouth. He does his first job with us and swings! We did a good set. George Melly did the

Humph 'doctors' a photo of a reception at 10 Downing Street.

second set with John Chilton. Melly wore his ridiculous Stetson – short, fat men shouldn't wear large-brimmed hats – they look like mushrooms.

John B. told me he heard from Max Jones that my old producer friend Denis Preston has died. I knew (also from Max) that he had had a bad operation – he in fact had cancer of the oesophagus, and he never really recovered from its removal. I know one has to expect friends and acquaintances to die off, as one gets old, but it's a bit early! D.P. was always a hypochondriac, began walking with a stick years ago in case he had a sudden heart attack and fell over.

Sunday 28 *October*

Long journey back from Carmarthen. Made mistake of staying on the M4 into London, expecting it to be empty. It was blocked solid by a massive T.U.C. pro-abortion demonstration against a new Tory members' abortion bill, due soon. Apart from groups of aggressively 'butch' Women's Libbers (who apparently – and in my view justifiably – took over the head of the march from Len Murray) it could have been any demo from 'Ban the Bomb' to 'Hands off Java', the first one I ever joined, back in 1947 or 8 – why, and against whom, I can't recall.

Thursday 6 December

Lazy day, slept for two hours in the afternoon. In the evening, went to a party (fund-raising) at Bill and Marguerite's. When we arrived, Jill and Georgina disappeared with host and hostess into the kitchen, leaving me teetering about like Monsieur Hulot [French film character] in a roomful of strangers.

Thursday 13 December

Went up to town in the morning to do some Christmas shopping – went to Hatton Gardens. Found a magic shop nearby and stocked up on jokes etc. for Christmas stockings. At 12.45, to Thames T.V. to meet Michael Houldey and see the *Late Night Elk* film due out next Thursday. A very pregnant Elkie Brooks arrived late. Good film with a lot of good jazz singing, including my 'We Fell Out of Love'. Lunch at the White House afterwards – did some heavy grafting with a plump Austrian called Oud who is an A.T.V. big wheel.

Friday 14 December

In the evening went out to a cheese and wine party. Funny do. Among the guests was a rather tiddly businessman who asked, 'What do you do?' 'I'm a musician.' 'Really, what do you play?' 'Trumpet.' 'Oh? In what group?' 'I have a band – Humphrey Lyttelton's Band.' '*Really*? You play in Humphrey Lyttelton's Band?' 'I am Humphrey Lyttelton!' Consternation!

Sunday 16 December

Went up to the B.B.C. in the evening to record a Christmas edition of *I'm Sorry I Haven't A Clue*. Barry Cryer has a skin complaint and can't make it, so John Junkin deputized. We record about 1½ hours for one forty-five-minute programme. Seemed to go very well – a full audience helped. Xmas feature was a series in the 'late arrivals' that made up the words of 'White Christmas', e.g. 'Emma Dreaming, Arthur White, Chris Muss' etc.

Tuesday 18 December

Session at the Cavern Club in the city – a crowded room which looked very good from the stage – rather like a sort of superior Condon's Club. Malcolm E. couldn't make it – a touch of flu. In keeping with the surroundings Roy, Bruce and myself did a Condonesque first session, playing a great many tunes which we don't usually play. I enjoyed the first set which swung along easily.

1980

Friday 4 January

Gig at the Ling's Centre – they now set the rather cold theatre as a jazz club, with tables and an improvised bar, and the overflow in the seats. A good idea – we had a healthy overflow and the session went well. Talk in the band-room about the international situation – heard Dave telling Bruce that he is now a Communist sympathizer. Since 1974 he has been a socialist, a Liberal and a *Daily Telegraph* Tory! Tom Seabrook was at the gig, gave me pheasants and rabbits.

Sunday 6 January

Fine dry day, not too cold, so took the opportunity of cleaning out my car, discovering all kinds of objects that I thought were lost.

Monday 7 January

Out of practice at the microphone – will have to work up some special features to ginger the programme up.

Thursday 10 January

There's something to be said for being without a car. Spent a day trying to get the junk out of my study. Have decided that I can get rid of about 50–100 records that I'm never likely to play or need for research – it'll make room in the shelves and pay off a few bills. The band business is going through the doldrums – nothing new, as without the Middle East Tour, the rot would have set in as far back as November. The cause? First V.A.T., then the cost of petrol, both putting up the fees one has to charge. Put the idiotic local government cuts on top and that's it.

Monday 14 January

Concert at the Redgrave Theatre. Nice little auditorium, with the stage scenery for *The Reluctant Debutante* in situ. Not completely full but they were happy. Two old acquaintances showed up. One was the R.A.F.-whiskered ex-assistant-editor of the *Daily Express* who once interviewed me regarding a regular jazz column on the *Express* – which I turned down for some pompous reason! The other was Guy Rich, erstwhile British diplomat in Berne whom we met back in the 'sixties. We have all remembered him since for his superbly British capacity for brushing aside every crisis with the words, 'It'll be all right'.

Friday 18 January

Left at 1 o'clock to drive up to Blundellsands, checked into the hotel. Over to Steve Voce's for a supper cooked by him – not spaghetti, thank goodness, but pork chops.

Saturday 19 January

Breakfast at Steve's – he always cooks a vast heap of sausage, egg, bacon, tomato, mushroom, fried bread etc., etc. Got off at 11.30, bursting at the seams. Home at 3-ish.

Not a bad crowd – about 200, I should guess. The local Tory M.P. (Sidney Chapman) made a welcoming speech – I don't know if he knows that at election times I go out on the streets trying to unseat him! Seems a good man, though – does a lot for the Bull project.

Sunday 20 January

Up to Town at 1p.m. to do a recording of *Looks Familiar*. At the buffet lunch beforehand, Denis Norden, who has had flu, said, 'One of the nicest things about my three days in bed was dipping frequently into Lyttelton-Hart–Davis Volume II.'

Out to supper with Stephen at an Indian restaurant in Euston – we thought they said 'improbably' the Belle Paris, it turned out to be the Bel-Poorhi or some such. Nice vegetarian food.

Saturday 26 January

Concert at the Alfred Beck Centre at Hayes, Middlesex.

My last recollection of the A.B.C. was a poorly attended 'Salute to Satchmo' concert in '78. Hadn't much hopes for tonight in the light of the slump and seemingly, negligible publicity. Surprise, surprise, an excellent house and enormously successful show. It is a hard thing to say, but there's nothing like the spectre of unemployment for concentrating musicians' minds.

Sunday 27 January

The successful mood of last night was continued tonight at Crowborough where once again we had a good crowd. These successes are important at this time – for my morale and for that of the band. If work continues to be scarce, the more good words going around the better!

Sunday 10 February

Newspapers are full of the crisis that la Thatcher's government is facing. There are rumblings from unexpected quarters – in mid-week the *Daily Mail* (Andrew Alexander) opined, 'The Iron Lady has got metal fatigue!' And in today's *Sunday Times* Ronald Butt has an important dig at her. Meanwhile, the steel strike goes on, now in its fifth week.

Wednesday 27 February

Session at the Firefly, Bourne End. Last time we had shepherd's pie in the interval – this time they gave me a personal pie with H.L. on the pastry lid.

Friday 29 February
Spent the day at R.G. Jones's in Wimbledon, mixing and editing the new record, with Alan Bates. Went there full of apprehension about the numbers we didn't hear back – were they all usable? One by one we pieced together nine excellent tracks. The one I was most concerned about, 'Sir Humphrey', turned out to be one of the best, and Kenny's 'Ladyless and Lachrymose' with Roy soloing is a gem. Went to the pub round the corner with Alan B. and had toad-in-the-hole (writing this watching T.V.).

Ended up with the best album we've done – came away with a cassette.

Monday 3 March
Took a swipe in my programme at a listener who heard me say something a week or two back about Erroll Garner's 'inimitable style – that has been imitated by more pianists than you've had hot dinners', took it seriously and sent it in to *Private Eye*. They in turn published it in their 'Colemanballs' column dedicated to fatuous remarks made over the air. Referred to them all as irredeemably humourless twits.

Monday 10 March
Had to go up to the Beeb at 4 for a meeting with Helen Fry re a *What Makes Me Laugh* programme, which I'm doing in April. Offered her a selection of Benchley, Trollope, Fats Waller, Patrick Campbell, P.G. Wodehouse, Jack Sheldon and Arthur Marshall to start with!

On to the Best Of Jazz studio, to find an apologetic letter from the 'humourless twit' of last week who had checked my Erroll Garner comment with his wife, who also thought it was serious. He says the joke is on *Private Eye*, who paid him £5 for his contribution!

Thursday 13 March
A splendid row has blown up over the Government's determination to discourage our athletes from going to Moscow. They now say that athletes in the civil service or services won't get any additional leave to compete. Now a Civil Service Union says it will pull a lady

long-jumper out on strike for the duration of the Games, and pay her wages.

Lunch at the B.B.C., ostensibly with Managing Director Aubrey Singer but he was away so Douglas Muggeridge took the chair. I sat between Robert Ponsonby and Monica Sims who, despite having met and chatted with me at her party last week, asked me about the summer school I run at my house – taking me to be John Dankworth! During lunch, I overheard Douglas M. saying to Beryl Bainbridge, 'I'm not sure whether to address you as a writer or an actress!' These B.B.C. high-ups should really peep out of their offices occasionally.

Sunday 16 March

Two shows at the Royal Exchange Theatre under the title of 'Three Decades of Humph'. The past was represented by George Webb, John Picard and Wally Fawkes. My band did a short first set of about forty-five minutes, then we had a longer second half with the guests. Wal played very well, quite recovered from his chronic stage-fright. The Voces came over for both sets – second half completely sold out. I was completely whacked by the end, having been on stage for almost four hours.

Monday 17 March

Margaret Thatcher got her vote in the Commons for a boycott of the Moscow Olympics, but 200 M.P.s didn't vote, and basically the 168 majority represented the view of the Tory Party. It still looks as if the athletes will go. And so they should. To me, the argument that Western abstention will let the Russian people know of our disapproval is childish. The Kremlin propagandists will have no trouble in telling the people that they are being snubbed and insulted by the nasty Americans and British, uniting them and the Kremlin is communal affront.

Tuesday 25 March

A busy day. Up to the B.B.C. at 12.30 to do an over-the-line interview with Liam Nolan in Dublin. Met up after all these years with Mark Bonham-Carter, who talks just like his mum, Lady Violet, and whose face is now W.H. Audenesque with wrinkles.

At 6.45, went on the John Dunn show for an interview – nice and easy. Then to the 100 Club for the Charing Cross Road Appeal show – the band went on for an hour and tore the place up, with all the new arrangements scoring heavily in the orgy of Dixieland. Stayed on for the jam session which included old Benny Waters, still blowing strong.

Wednesday 26 March

Listened to Sir Geoffrey Howe's Budget speech and watched the predictable reactions on television. It was an incredibly boring speech, a list of technicalities rattled off without expression, humour or life. Superficially it wasn't very significant – a few p on here, a few off there. But the nub lies in the vastly increased 'cuts', the increased prescription charges, the detaching of social security benefits from the rise in inflation. There was also the 'promised' £12 reduction in s/s benefits for strikers' families.

Saturday 5 April

To London Airport at 9.30, stopping off to put in the records for my programme at the Beeb and to buy a few Easter Eggs. Took off for Dublin at 12.15.

Concert started with us half-an-hour late. Band did a superb one-hour set, all inspired by the return of Dave Green – looking, incidentally, much fitter after his six weeks off.

Back in the hotel, had a steak supper, then sat in the hall watching the world go by – and a rum world it was. A girl in tight-fitting white came in followed by a man who set upon her and carried her off like a cave-man. She had to be rescued and given recuperative coffee by the staff. A man in a crumpled businessman's suit emerged from the restaurant with his paper napkin still tucked like an apron in his trousers. It attracted everyone's attention, including the staff, who pointed it out to him. 'I know,' he said, 'my zip's broken.' All this watched by a midget family perched on a sofa – they had been there all day without moving, except for the midget daughter, who from time to time took a ride in the lift, but only as far as floor two. She couldn't reach any higher.

Tuesday 8 April

Rang Fiona Sturdy of the Society for Italic Handwriting to give her a title of my address to the A.G.M. on 24 April. I suggested, 'Beware of the Scribes' from St Mark – it leaves me free to talk about practically anything! Am daunted by the news that I am expected to speak for forty-five minutes!

Gig at the Bull's Head, marred in the first half by the piano mike being too loud – we all complained and Mick reluctantly turned it down. Bruce, J.B. and A.J. made a shaky effort at Kenny's three-alto piece.

Thursday 17 April

Did the Buddy Bolden session this evening. I got everyone to the Maida Vale studios at 6 o'clock for rehearsal. Yesterday I wrote out the themes we are going to play with the exact phrasing that I shall use, so that we shall get the correct, unison ensemble sound. My idea is to base the phrasing on the Original Dixieland Jazz Band/Keppard eight-to-a-bar feel, with the front line playing in unison except when very obvious harmonies or fill-ins present themselves. In the event, things went better than I could possibly have expected. By 7.30, when we started recording, we had a good, authentic sound. John Barnes caught on especially well, blew a lot of unison stuff in the very high register, which made a kind of 'string' sound – very effective, as Bolden virtually supplanted the swing bands. 'Home Sweet Home' was a real lump-in-the-throat affair, played slow in funeral-march style. Everyone was elated by the session and not only because both Russell D. and David Perry produced bottles of Scotch.

Monday 21 April

Worked for much of the morning on my address to the Society for Italic Handwriting on Thursday. Am getting very nervous about it – the bits I wrote yesterday are OK but it doesn't hang together.

Tuesday 22 April

Up to the Beeb at Maida Vale to sit in on the editing session for the Buddy Bolden programme. The Bolden Band numbers still sounded pretty good, although, to me, the strain of maintaining the archaic idiom shows through from time to time.

Straight on up to Liverpool for a gig with the Blue Magnolia Band. Called in at Steve Voce's beforehand, took him along to the pub the other side of Liverpool ('The Coffee House') where the gig was. On the way, my car began to make strange whirring noises when I changed gear, especially in first and second gears. Steve thought it might be some minor symptom of wear. Hmm.

Roaring session with the Blue Magnolias – a jolly traditional band full of quite good musicians. Good atmosphere with lots of audience participation and a fair old heat. Enjoyed it.

Thursday 24 April

Was going to put my car into Lex-Brooklands but decided, as it has got no worse, to get home and do some more work on my speech. Was going to copy it all out but realized that there would be no time, so ended up with a varied bundle of notes. Not 100 per cent pleased with it, but am no longer in a cold panic. Went in early at 6-ish in case I couldn't find the place. Few people there when I arrived but eventually there were about fifty. They started with Society business, chaired by nice, suave Philip Cranmer, flanked by Fiona Sturdy and Treasurer Donald Fell. In fact, most of the company looked like devout handwriters – the men like schoolmasters or postal clerks, the women grey and cropped.

Quite a number of scribal bigwigs in the audience – Berthold Wolpe, Nancy Winter, Kenneth Yates-Smith, Philip Nairne and daughter Fiona etc. Was worried that my speech wouldn't last the usual forty-five minutes, but needn't have worried. I read my speech which went down well, generally, with some encouraging laughter. Then we had a discussion which was very lively and went on till about 9.30. Afterwards Lady Cholmondeley said it was the best meeting they had ever had, and Berthold W. said much the same. Euphoria all round so it must have been all right. Supper afterwards at P. Cranmer's.

Monday* 28 *April

Letter from Steve Voce saying, among other things, that he has heard from Buck enthusing about our versions of his arrangements, which Steve sent him on cassette. He (Buck) says, 'Humphrey really has a great band now – every one of those guys swings his ass off.'

Saturday* 3 *May

Gig at Radley School, near Abingdon – scene of the Eton School Orchestra's epic performance of Ravel's Bolero in 1938. Got there at 6, set up and then went to the music master's (Alan Dowding) house for a buffet supper. Good concert, though the hall had an echo like Cwm Bychan lake! Public-school concerts are treacherously flattering to the ego – we walked offstage through the audience to a standing ovation.

Thursday* 8 *May

The thirty-fifth anniversary of my tootling outside Buckingham Palace on V.E. Day.

Today's *Daily Express*, still cock-a-hoop over the Iran Embassy 'victory', seems to be hinting today that Mrs Thatcher should parachute into Iran to rescue the U.S. hostages.

Saturday* 10 *May

Back from Southampton. Listened en route to *Any Questions?* The team, including Jean Rook and Lord Willis, all agreed that the 'victory' at the Iranian Embassy made them 'feel proud to be British'. What an odd and rather disturbing sentiment – to be proud of those who behaved efficiently, courageously, level-headedly, yes. But why should Jean Rook, far from the event and not involved, feel proud? Because Britons have shown the world – and particularly the Americans – how to do it? Because we taught the 'wogs a lesson they'll never forget' or simply because a Boy's Own Paper episode has recalled glorious wartime days? Are the South West Iranians proud of their 'lads' too? Seems to me that the revival of expressions of jingoism are writing the foreword to World War III.

Tried out my new Wok this evening – with pork chops marinated in soya sauce and pepper etc. and mixed fried vegetables.

Made some metal frames today for the ponds, to thwart a heron which is breakfasting off the ponds of Arkley. Ron Parsloe at the D.I.Y. shop, after three heart attacks, has fallen off a scaffold and broken both legs.

Saturday 24 *May*

Picked up at home by Chris Durdin of the R.S.P.B., who looks fifteen but must be older. He drove me to Chelmsford, getting lost no more than three times. The fête was in a vast field, but a healthy number of people turned up. I opened it by playing a handful of 'bird' songs on the trumpet, was followed by the town band, Scottish dancers, a kite-flying demonstration and P.T. by girls from a police-training school whose formidable thighs turned pork-pink in the prevailing cold. I bought a couple of prints by Tunnicliffe for £2.50 each (framed), some porcelain pots by local craftswomen (or craftspersons) and some teacloths. Duty done, left for home.

Monday 26 *May*

Had to leave early to go to Wavendon, for the Festival afternoon session. It's an odd session – posh families converge and picnic on the lawn, unleashing ill-behaved children in all directions. In our first set I had valve trouble – the third valve stuck solid, wouldn't budge. I had to use Mick's cornet until the interval when I purged the horn with hot water and flushed out half a rusty paper-clip. After the interval, I told the audience that they could now relax but I couldn't – I was worried about where the other half was!

Tuesday 27 *May*

Letter-writing day – wrote to Steve Voce enclosing a cassette, which I made the other day, of my S.I.H. speech. I propped up the microphone on a pillow in our bedroom and literally 'orated' my speech into it. It sounded splendidly pompous. Wrote to Buck suggesting that he should write an original number, as his tribute to Louis Armstrong, for the Festival Hall concert. Had a rather sad letter from him today, indicating that he is coming to terms with the fact that he will never play up to his own standards again, 'I'll be an old man who keeps on practising'…'It's a challenge, but I'm getting rather tired of being challenged.'

Wednesday 28 May

Went with Jill to the Wildwood fish-farm to put one of our fountain pumps in for repair. Bought ten goldfish to try and cheer up the big pond, which is dominated by the two surviving orfes; they seem to have lost interest, looming about morosely among the water lilies when they should be cruising up and down.

Saturday 31 May

Spent the morning pondering on my reaction to the M.U. strike and especially the union's decision to 'instruct' presenters who happen to be M.U. members to come out. To me, the principle involved is that a union cannot issue orders with regard to activities over which in normal times they have no jurisdiction. How could I be protected against 'victimization' legal action etc. after or during the strike when the union has no control over the contracts, pay and conditions of broadcasters? A moot point, and I intend to moot it.

Friday 13 June

To Durham, for a gig at the University – we arrive at the hall and are shown to a band-room in the living quarters – in the room below there is the sound of mayhem, with wild bellowing and the sound of smashing wood. It is the 'pop' group Matchbox, flushed with recent success in the charts, demolishing their room. Discover in the course of the evening that they are getting £1,200 plus a specified six bottles of brandy and four dozen lagers!! Our set (costing £100 all-in) goes down sensationally and the organizers look rueful.

Sunday 15 June

Back from Disley, short time at home then in to Ally Pally for our appearance at the *Morning Star* beano (called 'Beat the Blues'). Called for 5.30 for a sound-check, found a majestic shambles in progress – car-parking was an assault course in itself. The grounds were teeming with the most unprepossessing gangs of skinheads,

Hell's Angels, punks etc. Onstage, plump, tousled communist ladies were supposed to organize the musicians – Dick Heckstall-Smith's 'Big Chief', a Polish flute-and-bass duo, Annie Ross with Harry South etc. and us – in sound-checks but nothing happened. So we had to hang about for two hours before we went on. By that time the punks had come into the big hall – and once the band had settled in, we had them all pogo-dancing in the area in front of the stage. Only one, a cropped youth in a grey mac, protested by standing in front of John Barnes howling, 'SHU.U.UT UP!!!'. He then spat at me, which I took as a punk accolade. At the end, they all punched the air shouting, 'Umphrey. Um-phrey'.

Monday 16 June
Old Duggie White, dying of bone cancer, was at the Ally-Pally 'do' last night, game as ever, but looking very old and weary despite a massive blood transfusion today to see him through a last holiday in Portugal. He carries a little fold-up seat, and used it to hold at bay some punks who tried to get onstage, then fled, to his great glee.

Tuesday 17 June
Long drive up to Stockton-on-Tees for a session at the Fiesta Club. The place is a typical 'Northern Club' in Norton, just outside Stockton – all glitter and gilt. Quite a few people in, including George Butterworth. He will bang one on the shoulder with 'Eee, yer booger!' or 'Bloody magic!!'. His wife is long resigned to him making a mighty fool of himself, says he's a mouse all day!!

Saturday 12 July
Stayed over at the Swindon P.H., got up early and drove to Heathrow to catch a plane for Holland and the North Sea Festival. Travel with Monty Sunshine's band, including Micky Ashman, now hugely fat. We go from Amsterdam by bus to the Hague, check in at the Benair Hotel, Festival H.Q. just alongside the hall. I am dog-tired, but the foyer is so teeming with familiar jazz faces (familiar mostly from record-sleeves) that I become a teenage jazz fan once again and stand or sit around rubbernecking. In the hotel restaurant met up at last

with Nat Pierce, a big, nervous, friendly man whose voice is familiar to me from the cassettes through which he used to correspond with Steve Voce. While we sit talking, Buddy Tate comes in, looking surprisingly well after his accident in a hotel shower. He turned on the shower at 'cold' and was knocked over – and out – by a jet of steaming-hot water. He must have hit his head because he was briefly unconscious, during which time he was badly scalded by boiling water. His hands are now mottled by skin-grafts and some show on his face. But he is playing again and seems on the mend. Exchanged bear-hugs with Joe Lee Wilson, introduced myself to Jake Hanna, who is a compulsive wise-cracker. The hall itself was turgid with people. Heard a bit of the Concord All Stars with Warren Vache.

Tuesday 29 July

I go in to collect my car, which costs £144 for a new fuel pump. What doesn't cost £144 nowadays? Anyway, like an old, stray sheepdog that won't go away, the car is back with me, cleaner than it has ever been before!

Sunday 3 August

Spent the day tidying up the hut in the garden, a jungle of dumped oddments, rusty carpentry tools, assorted battens of wood, screws and nails of all sizes, cobwebs, moth's hideouts etc.

Monday 15 September

Writing and practising in the a.m. To the Beeb in the afternoon to take part in a 'pilot' quiz called *Jazz Score*. Benny Green is the chairman, self, Annie Ross, Ronnie Scott and George Chisholm the panel. Eric Sykes was the surprise guest. I always like working with B.G. because there's plenty of laughter about.

Chat with Eric Sykes in the pub. A nice, friendly man. Told me a good story about Deryck Guyler in Rhodesia – bomb scare in the hotel one night. Eric took no notice, had a bath, everyone else evacuated, including the staunchly Catholic Guylers, she clutching a bible – sent him back up nine floors for his washboard!

Thursday 18 September

Left at 1.30 for Oldham – to Salford Arts Gallery to open Robert Littleford's exhibition. Got there before anyone else, had a good look round. Beautiful paintings, the best yet, with some superb pictures of the Square in his home village. I picked three choices for my 'fee'...eventually plumped for a painting done on the Oldham–Huddersfield road. Robert arrived soon after me – hair like a flue-brush, enjoying it all madly. Good turn-out of people. I made a short speech.

Monday 22 September

Rehearsal at the Bull's Head for our Croydon concert on 1 October, with Kathy Stobart and Wally Fawkes.

There was an atmosphere of gloom at the Bull – Albert retires tonight, and the new man has done the 'new broom' act and fired all but one of Albert's staff. So there were tears and lamentations in the air.

Sunday 12 October

Gig at Tonbridge School. Left at about 4.30 to drive down. Reception in the headmaster's office beforehand. Met one 'contemporary at Eton', one 'second cousin by marriage', one 'old friend from Sandhurst'. The latter conducted a conversation by repeating one's answers to his questions. 'Do you travel much?' 'Quite a bit.' 'Ah, quite a bit...yes...yes.' Concert was very successful and the band played well.

Wednesday 15 October

Jim Callaghan resigned today. For once he's got the timing right – it would have been fatuous to hang on. Now it looks like a contest between Healey, Shore, Silkin and maybe Foot. I rather favour Shore, with whom I worked on a Gaitskell committee years ago. But I expect it will be Healey.

Saturday 25 October

Business is beginning to look up now, although gigs are coming in very late. Things now look set to tick over, at least, until the end of February.

Left at 3 to drive to Chichester for the Festival. This year the concerts are being compered by Anna Ford.The hospitality at Chichester is very good – plenty of handlers to shift the gear, and a green-room with free wine and a buffet. Crisis when Wally, overcome by the vision of la Ford, dropped his clarinet and smashed the mouthpiece. Borrowed mine but it didn't work so he played soprano throughout.

Monday 3 November

Did a little work on my Jack Teagarden chapter, but the book is going very slowly. Volume II is much harder – to select sixteen or so 'giants' is going to be invidious. Have now done Louis, Hawkins and Fats, most of Lester Young, some of Teagarden. Will certainly have to do Art Tatum, Roy Eldridge, Charlie Christian, B.G., Dickie Wells, Billie Holiday, Lionel Hampton, Benny Carter, Johnny Hodges, Django Reinhardt. Then the third volume will have to cover the bands of Ellington, Basie, Lunceford, Benny Goodman, Chick Webb, John Kirby, Condon/Freeman, Muggsy, Bob Crosby and any other big or small combos that need doing.

Tuesday 4 November

American Election Day – sat up watching the T.V. coverage till about 12.15 when it became apparent that Reagan had won – can't get steamed up about it. Most commentators agree that it will make no great difference, and if we have to look at a face on our screens on and off for four years, Reagan's is less dreadful than Carter's. Meanwhile Denis Healey has won round one in the Labour Party leadership, so it's now Healey versus Foot.

Thursday 6 November

Back from Nottingham, watched *Afternoon Plus* with an interview with Michael Foot, who might well be next leader of the Labour Party. Have great admiration and, at long distance, affection for him, but wonder if he is good vote-fodder. To me the world is divided into

Nature's Prefects and Nature's snotty-nosed kids, and M.F. seems to me to belong irrevocably to the latter – irreverent, contentious and with a recently-acquired tendency to giggle in mid-tirade.

Sunday 16 November

To Oldham by 4p.m. in order to pick up my Robert Littleford paintings from Salford Art Gallery. Excited as a schoolboy! Took 'em to the Bolton Crest and propped them up on the dressing-table. Then went to the Grange Arts Theatre with them and propped them up in the dressing-room. All the guys bar Bruce enthused about them. Bruce said, 'Don't understand about photography, Dad'!!

Thursday 20 November

A heavy day promoting the Penguin edition of *Best of Jazz Volume I*. Left the car on a long meter in London and met the representative of Penguin – a nice young lady with hare's eyes. Our first stop was at Capital Radio, where I was interviewed for half-an-hour by Brenda Marshall and Alan 'Fluff' Freeman – good questions and I talked them into the ground. Then into a hire car and off to Gough Square, where I chatted for an hour to one John Simcock, an erstwhile traditional trombonist (with Dave Keir) turned classical musician turned fisherman. His questions were a bit verbose but we ranged over my whole career and a review of the book will be tacked on to it.

After this a hire car whisked me to Covent Garden where we assembled in a cafe in the new 'market' shopping centre. Then we set up not far from the Penguin bookshop and played a half-hour set to a crowd of about 200. Piano and bass were a bit low but otherwise the acoustics were good and the response very good. I then signed about 150 books. Picked up fish and chips on the way home.

Wednesday 26 November

Tom Seabrook is dead – apparently collapsed and died at home on Monday. Feel very sad about it – he was a good, undemanding friend of the band's, and set such store by coming along to shows in the Cambridge-Peterborough area. Saw him only last Saturday week when he gave me some pheasants. He did have serious trouble with an enlarged heart a few years ago, and has had to take it easy, leaving the heavy farm work to his sons. Helen, his wife, says that the doctors have told her that in a couple of years' time he would have been very slowed-down and in constant pain. Wrote her a letter today.

Tuesday 9 December

The news today dominated by shooting of John Lennon in New York. He had given an autograph to a young alleged fan from Hawaii who later shot him 'for scribbling his signature'. The list of 'pop' martyrs continues to grow – Presley, Marc Bolan, Jimi Hendrix, Jim Morrison, Brian Jones, Janice Joplin, Keith Moon etc., etc., now Lennon.

Monday 15 December

Very tired tonight, did something I've never done before – completely dried up over the name of Horace Silver. Got away with it simply by saying, 'I've gone blank,' and joking through, but it's always a chancy combination, adlibbing and fatigue.

Wednesday 17 December

Message at the Beeb to contact Peter Clayton. He has heard from Tony Middleton that Keith Christie has died – presumably of cirrhosis. Realized on the way home that I have lost my first Old Boy.

Tuesday 23 December

Keith Christie's funeral at the West London Crematorium at Kensal Green at 11 o'clock. Parked outside and walked across. A large gathering of musicians. Ian had a large cassette recorder with him through which he played Bechet's 'Blue Horizon' at the end – it sounded tremendous in the resonant acoustics. Keith loved Bechet.

Wednesday 24 December

Christmas Eve…

The worst Christmas Eve panic for years – everyone has been taken by surprise that food shops and small shops other than chain stores are due to shut tonight until next Monday. Most of the day spent doing last-minute shopping for food.

Monday** 29 **December
Spent most of the day working on my tribute to Keith Christie tonight. The difficult thing is that he did virtually no recording after he left Ted Heath. Heard in the course of the day that, contrary to expectation, Lennie Felix died early this morning. He was hit by a car shortly before Xmas after leaving a club – it overtook on a zebra crossing and hit him. He had been reported semi-conscious and reacting well last night, so his death was unexpected. Will have to 'do' him in two weeks. Very sad – the old faces are dropping like flies. I think the Keith obit went all right – lots of very good music.

Big Butter and Eggs Man

A lot of exquisitely bad taste is acquired in childhood. At my school, first thing in the morning, we were given a glass of milk and a ginger biscuit to sustain us through the pre-breakfast lesson. With that same careful deliberation with which a gourmet lemons an oyster and inhales it from its shell, we used to suspend the biscuit in the milk until it was pliable and then suck it ferociously – an exercise that successfully ruined the taste of the milk and subverted the combined efforts of Messrs Huntley, Palmer, McVitie, Price, Peak and Frean to produce a biscuit that was firm in texture and crisp to the bite. It's my belief that inside every *bon viveur* who sniffs his wine, crackles his cigar between the finger tips and purses his lips over a *coquille St Jacques* there is a *mauvais viveur* who still relishes a soggy ginger biscuit when backs are turned.

It's no accident that it was the Americans who actually invented a word – to dunk – for the splendidly barbaric habit of using the liquids to soften up the solids. My outstanding gastronomic memory of a tour of the States some years ago is of a Jumbo Butterscotch Sundae experienced within a day or two of my arrival. It came to the table in a huge glass chimney, and consisted basically of five blobs of vanilla ice-cream submerged in a gallon of molten toffee. I don't know how you react to sweetness, but I tend to loss of vision, throbbing in the ears and a curious itching on the inside of my skull. Halfway through the Jumbo Butterscotch Sundae I lost consciousness altogether. It was the nearest I've ever been to a 'trip'.

As a small boy I very nearly met a premature end eating one of the most delicious desserts I have ever encountered. It was at my grandfather's country seat in Cambridgeshire, where every meal amounted to what would now be regarded as a banquet. The sweet in question was remarkably simple – just a blob of cream whipped to a consistency so light that a suppressed sneeze would have blown it off the plate, and sprinkled with an equally light topping of powdered chocolate. Gasping with delight, I inhaled the chocolate into my windpipe, where it brought all respiratory activity to an abrupt halt. Meals at Babraham Hall were based on the Victorian principle that children should be seen and not heard, so there was no question of drawing attention to myself by jumping up and making asphyxiated noises which would have interrupted the adult conversation. At that stage there hadn't been much of a life to flash before my eyes, but the brief process had begun when a gulp of ginger pop shifted the plug and I lived on to become something of a connoisseur of sweet courses.

Connoisseurship is attained by experiencing the worst as well as the best, and years in boarding-school introduced me to plenty of the former. Tapioca, Semolina and Sago may sound like a Latin American dance team to you, but I recall them as abominations categorized by my late father as 'wet doll stuffing' – revolting in texture, sickly in taste and as enticing to the eye as a bucket of wallpaper adhesive. Fortunately they, along with rice pudding, blancmange and junket, turn out to have been merely facets of the punitive, character-building purposes of boarding-school education, as I have rarely met any of them in adult life. Occasionally I have been reminded of their awful texture, as cold and clammy and unpromising as an executioner's handshake, by a lemon mousse that has lingered too long on a sweet trolley, acquiring a skin thick enough to repel all insults.

On the face of it, touring musicians, like commercial travellers, are unsound consultants when it comes to food. They spend a large part of their lives exploring the very depths of British culinary practice. In otherwise civilized towns, they have stayed at hotels in which dinner *ends* at 7.30 and where, thenceforward, the only choice is between seedy snack-bars or a Chinese restaurant in which to order 'Sweet and Sour' is to embark on a dispiriting game of Hunt the Pork.

They know what it is to choose between night-starvation and a transport 'caff' where the troughs in the charred bacon hold enough grease to maintain a heavy lorry from Penzance to Perth. In the course of duty they have eaten alleged food which seems to have been hand-knitted, carved out of balsa wood, barbecued by blow-lamp or assembled in a laboratory. They can perhaps best be summed up in a story told by the late bandleader Mick Mulligan. A man goes into a transport café and orders egg, sausage, bacon and chips. 'But listen carefully,' he says, 'I want the egg fried to the consistency of celluloid round the edges, with the white barely formed and the yolk hard and powdery. The sausage must be charred black and hard on the outside, but should be pink and lukewarm at the centre. I would like my bacon burnt to such a fragile consistency that it will disintegrate at the first touch of a fork, and in each valley of its contour must lie a pool of fat. The chips, on the other hand…' At this point the burly café proprietor interrupted. 'Come orf it, mate, I 'aven't got time to do all that!' 'Why,' says the man, 'it didn't take you long last night.'

After years of taking pot-luck in this way, I was considerably startled therefore when Hugh Johnson, once described rather surrealistically as 'one of the world's great palates' and then editor of *Queen* magazine, wrote asking me to contribute their restaurant reviews page. Nothing brings out the latent poet in all of us more readily than food. Men who would endure the rack and the thumbscrews rather than wax lyrical in public over a woman will, at the drop of a romantic place-name, make absolute fools of themselves about meals long ago consumed and digested. Good-foodmanship plays a large part in it of course. To describe, with a profusion of foreign words, some exotic dish experienced in distant parts is to reveal oneself in a single paragraph as a person of culture, discrimination and wide travel. I therefore accepted. It began as a 'guest' article for one issue only, and like the aunt who comes for a weekend and stays a lifetime, I ended up for the best part of eight years.

'Those who can, do – those who can't, teach,' said George Bernard Shaw in a notorious and characteristic half-truth. 'Those who can't, criticize!' is an amendment moved by generations of *artistes* whose pride has been ruffled by adverse comment.

During this time, I persuaded myself that, being no sort of a chef, I should at least learn how to bake a loaf of bread. I had no ambition to become a fresh-loaf-every-morning baker, though the therapy derived from pummelling a lump of dough for ten minutes (known more technically as 'kneading') while imagining it to be the face of someone you particularly dislike had its attraction. Having produced one or two objects recognizable as loaves only because they resembled nothing else on earth, I had an experience that scared me away from the whole business.

Part of my technique, having in the early stages introduced yeast into the dough mixture, was to put the much-kneaded lump (there, that's got the standard pun out of the way) into a loaf-shaped baking tin and pop it into an airing cupboard for an hour or so, to rise or, as they say in the trade, 'prove' (reading the rest of this book alone will reveal the habit of craftspeople of all kinds to separate themselves from the rest of us with meaningless jargon). At this point, I have to reveal that at the time we – or more specifically my late wife Jill – played host to twelve cats. Don't ask. For logistic reasons connected with our house alarm system, they had to be herded into a corridor and locked away whenever we went out. The airing cupboard was in that corridor.

One day, when the mixing and pummelling was over, I had put the tin in the cupboard and turned my attention to things at the other end of the house. Meanwhile, unknown to me, Jill went out on a shopping spree, having locked the corridor door and put the key in her handbag. When she returned hours later, she was mildly surprised to find me in a state of high anxiety. Hurriedly unlocking the door, and quite unaware of what particular phase in the bakery process I might have reached, I opened the cupboard. What confronted me briefly can best be described as the culinary equivalent of John Wyndham's Day of the Tryffids. From above the now dwarfed tin a face, huge, pallid and featureless, stared back at me for a second or two. Then, with a sound that I can only write as 'Phlot!', it collapsed back into the tin, peppering me with doughy shrapnel in the process.

Many years ago, a wartime acquaintance told me a rather indelicate story about an English friend of his who once visited an expensive Parisian brothel. Speaking no French, he ordered at random from a 'menu' of specialities, having no idea what to expect. He was ushered to an upstairs room and left on his own until, after a few minutes, a lady entered, scantily dressed as a waitress and wheeling a well-stocked trolley. Formalities having been exchanged, she proceeded to plaster him where, under the circumstances, he most expected it with whipped cream, trifle and chocolate mousse. At last, crowning the edifice with a maraschino cherry, she announced saucily, 'And now, *chéri*, I am going to eat eet!' After a moment's contemplation, he waved her aside. 'Oh, no – it looks too good. I think I'll eat it myself.'

For someone who had always taken a cursory interest in the technicalities of *cuisine* there was a lot to learn. And that takes practical experience as well as a handy gastronomic dictionary.

For instance if you go to places where they do French cooking, you will probably find on the menu something called *poulet grand'mère*. In Haute Cuisine, this will mean chicken sautéed with a rich brown *grand'mère* sauce added at the climactic moment of cooking. In Provincial, Regional or Country cooking, on the other hand, the same words will convey chicken cooked in casserole with wine and vegetables and as like as not served by a *grand'mère*, probably wearing bedroom-slippers. In Basse Cuisine, the title that should go officially to a high percentage of British restaurant food, it will simply mean that the chicken is *grand'mère*.

There is another category which, for strict accuracy, should be mentioned. It is Cuisine That Is As Haute As Can Be Expected Under The Circumstances, and it is quite commonly encountered in

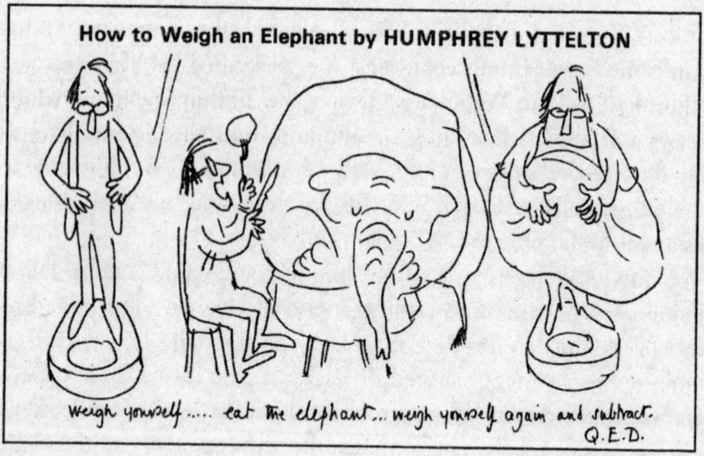

London, especially in large restaurants of some pretension. It usually implies a good, even distinguished, chef trying to apply classic standards to a menu that is too large, a clientele that is too diffuse, a time schedule that is too cramped or ingredients that are too sub-standard.

How to Weigh an Elephant by HUMPHREY LYTTELTON
Weigh yourself ..... eat the elephant ... weigh yourself again and subtract.
Q.E.D.

It was 1948 and my first working visit to France. On the esplanade at Nice, the day after the grand opening of the First International Jazz Festival at the Opera House, a fan dashed up to me, grabbed me by the shoulders and hit me full in the face with, ''Amfree, last night you were *formidable*!' With the last syllable, he emptied his lungs and I went down like a felled ox. I was only unconscious for a second or two, but thought it wisest to stay down for the full count, lest he had taken the opportunity to reload.

Poor man, he meant well, and it is nice to know that, whatever may have happened to him since, he has at least lived a life immune from the ravages of arthritis, asthma, typhoid, wind colics, obstructions of the kidney, spider's bite, consumption, intestinal worms, athletes' foot, embolism and the unwanted attention of vampires. That immunity, according to the remarkably unanimous opinion of physicians and herb-lorists through the ages, derived from the lethal ingredient with which he had laced his lunch that afternoon in Nice. In a word, garlic.

Today, my vulnerability to his onslaught may seem strange. A re-run of the episode now would be a very different story, I can tell you. There's a Greek restaurant just down the road from my house which serves a delicious houmous, two spoonfuls of which, according to my family, would have sent my French enthusiast reeling *and* scorched the paint off every parked car within range. But the pre-war British fare on which I was brought up knew nothing of garlic, other than as just another unmentionable practice indulged in by unspeakable foreigners. No whiff of the stuff was permitted to permeate the pages of *Mrs Beeton's Cookery Book*, on which all well-bred eating, from country-house lunches to public-school dinners, was founded. Garlic was just another of the facts of life for which my expensive education left me ill-prepared.

Despite the noticeable advance in British food, most of the stuff we pay to devour is alien rather than indigenous. There are two ways of approaching foreign food. (Actually, there are three, but we'll leave out 'all upset tummies begin at Calais'.)

I can best define them as the dedicated and the pragmatic. The dedicated eater, visiting a national restaurant of whatever denomination, aims to immerse himself in the gastronomic culture of the country concerned. He is the one you will find grappling bravely with chopsticks, wincing over undrinkable local wines and suppressing the instincts of a lifetime in the face of raw fish. His motto is 'When in Rome, eat as the Romans do', and if some convincing joker were to tell him that in some areas of Rome they eat the table mats, then eat them he will, cork, Canaletto reproduction and all.

The pragmatic eater's motto is less high-minded. It is 'Sod the Chinese, if I want chop suey and chips, I'll have 'em!'. While not admitting to a craving for that particular dish, it is an attitude with which I have some sympathy. To put it crudely, our colon was not designed for culture nor our taste buds for tourism. There is a story that Bishop Gore, an eminent theologian in the early part of this century, was in America when Grapenuts first came on to the market as a new breakfast cereal. At breakfast in a hotel, the new product was proudly set before him. He gazed down into the bowl for some moments and then spoke, enunciating each syllable with scathing precision. 'Gravel! I positively refuse to eat gravel!'

For myself, I positively refuse to drink turpentine. Not long ago, I took home a bottle of Greek *retsina*. Having broached the bottle and battled through a glass of the stuff, I left it on the draining board in the kitchen. Next day, feeling strong enough to have another try, I went to find it. Seeing me looking around by the sink, our daily came to my assistance. 'Are you looking for that bottle? I put it in the garage with your other painting things.' And in the garage is stayed.

You can put me down then as a pragmatic eater. If I go to a specialized restaurant, it is for the same reason that I go to any restaurant – to have a good meal of my own choice, not to endure purgatory and emerge feeling like an issue of the *National Geographical Magazine*.

Clear in my mind is the memory of a little restaurant in a backstreet in Algiers back in 1943, when the genial *patron*, showing broken teeth in a welcoming smile beneath his black, brigand's moustache, set before me a local dish looking like baked tennis socks and tasting indescribably of *je ne sais quoi*. (Actually, *je sais quoi* perfectly well, but *je ne veux pas* mention it in polite company.)

That was during the war. Since then, on sundry tours when playing concerts has been the primary purpose and eating has to be fitted in when and where possible, I've had plenty of opportunity to investigate the cuisines and customs of other nationalities from unusual angles. My thoughts about Dutch food were coloured irrevocably by an incident in 1948, when I first took my band to play in Amsterdam. In those days, foreign tours were run on a shoe-string, and for economy we were housed in an improvised dormitory at the top of a tall house owned by one of the young promoters. On the first night, after the concert, we underwent a reaction understandable, if not excusable, in a group of red-blooded young English men suddenly released from ration books, licensing laws and Spam. In short, we took Amsterdam apart. Dawn was breaking when we clawed our way up the narrow stairs to our communal pad.

Two hours later, our Dutch host, anxious that his accommodation should make up in hospitality what it lacked in the finer comforts, brought us breakfast. Each of us in turn was nudged and prodded into consciousness to be confronted with a large plate around which were arranged several slices of dark, close-textured bread of the pumpernickel variety. On each slice was a different item of food – on one a square of cold beef, on the next a slab of cheese and then, in rotation, apricot jam, gherkin, some kind of pressed meat and finally, and quite incredibly, a wedge of fruit cake.

WAITR
"I think that man's playing anonymously!"

Linger for a moment on the sensation. The mouth feels like the ornithological equivalent of a Rachman-style basement in Paddington that has just been vacated hurriedly by two parrots of feckless disposition and untidy habits. In place of the clear, cool and mobile brow of yesterday is now a rusty, creaking visor behind which a large animal suspiciously like an adult porcupine has clearly moved in for the winter. A binding substance made seemingly of axle-grease, brown sugar and ash-tray scrapings prevents the eyelids from parting to admit the unwelcome light of day. When they do finally open enough to let in a shaft of vision, the cringeing gaze alights, with a slow-dawning horror, on a still life of dry bread and fruit cake.

It was, all in all, a mutually educative experience. We learned of the importance of bread in the domestic economy of Holland, while our host was offered a quite unique insight into some of the more expressive and creative aspects of the English language. The matter, alas, did not end there. Later in the day, when with restored spirits we set off in search of steaks and schnitzels, he insisted on being our guide. He took us straight to what looked like a Lyons Corner House and asked with bland innocence: 'What kind of sandwich do you like?' With his limited command of English he was spared from knowing just how close he came at that moment to being pitched into the canal with his feet encased in a ballast of rye bread.

We once played a three-week engagement in Berne, in a rather posh nightclub. At the end, the owner came to our dressing-room to say a formal goodbye. He made a speech thanking us for coming and regretting that the attendances had not reached his expectations (on most nights it would have needed a tyre-lever to prise an extra person into the place). His peroration was rather moving. 'In Switzerland we are famous for our watches and our cheese. Because business has not been so good, I cannot thank you with watches, so…' and he went over to a cupboard and flung open the door, revealing a stack of cheeses the size of mini-car wheels, '…I thank you with cheese!'

To the Swiss, cheese is a national symbol. It represents industry, thrift, self-reliance, all the things of which they are most proud. They will not only thank you with cheese, they will entice, impress, reprove and even threaten you with cheese. I know of several national dishes – especially those involving chillies or cayenne pepper – which can assume to the unwary all the characteristics of a rather nasty practical joke. But surely the Swiss cheese *fondue* is alone in actually posing a threat to life. I hardly dare touch the stuff myself, having been warned on so many occasions that a swig of the wrong sort of drink will solidify the molten cheese into a cannonball somewhere in my alimentary canal, sending me plummeting to the ground and probably through the floorboards.

Some years ago at the end of a Swiss tour, Joe Temperley, who was then playing baritone sax in the band, rounded off an afternoon of festive sightseeing by sitting down to a *fondue* backed up by several large glasses of chilled beer. He caused consternation in the restaurant. Every time he lifted the beer glass to his lips, people waved their arms and cried 'No, No!' as if he were a prospective suicide poised on a ledge. One total stranger, signalling frantically, sent over to his table a glass of the medically approved *kirsch*. My friend downed it with a genial cry of 'Cheers!' and took another mighty swig of beer as a chaser.

Joe didn't actually plummet. Indeed, when he met us for the journey home, he was already so near the ground that there was no margin left for plummeting. His face had assumed the most extraordinary hue that can only be compared to the northward view of a south-bound baboon, and he had such difficulty with his breathing that we were almost persuaded to send for a man with a stomach-pump. In the event, high altitude seemed to do him good and he recovered slowly during the flight, but was still so mottled and crimson on arrival in London that a fellow-musician suggested he go home with him for an hour or two to regain a more natural colour before he confronted his wife. It was just his bad luck that the fellow-musician's Swedish wife, forewarned of a guest, hurriedly prepared a welcoming meal consisting almost entirely of cheese.

Maybe I have undervalued the role of the travelling minstrel in the service of gastronomy. Certainly we have lacked neither enterprise nor courage. I count it a benign gesture of Providence that, in the last war, I was sent overseas into the firing line and not left at home to suffer the torture of Woolton Pie. This, you will recall, was a thrifty but nourishing concoction of such easy-to-produce ingredients as turnip, parsnip, swede and the like, done up to look from the outside like a sort of Shepherd's Pie.

Some people grow up to relish the pet aversions of their childhood. When I was a boy, parsnips made me gag. Today, the throat contracts and the eyes water at the very sight of the typewritten word on paper. I am told that, as in Woolton Pie, there are ways of cooking par…geeeaaarght…those things which make them not only edible but delicious. That line of subterfuge cuts no ice with me. I still recall the frightful shock when, as an eight-year-old, I crunched my teeth into an artichoke which had been treacherously dolled up to look like a roast potato. No, I'm sorry, but when I contemplate a turnip or any of its subterranean relatives, I find it hard to believe that Lord Woolton was on our side.

Come to think of it, about the only childhood afflictions from which I have made a complete recovery are spinach and curry. Even with spinach I go a bit queasy if they purée it up like baby-food. Perhaps it's cheating to mention curry, since until the Indians arrived the word denoted a sorry Anglicized mess, depressing khaki in colour and spiced only with a few dejected raisins. I was really quite old when I discovered that genuine Indian curry is as richly-hued as the back end of a baboon and after a messy meal leaves the tablecloth looking like a Turner seascape.

Much valuable exploratory work in the field of Indo-Pakistani restaurants was done in the past by touring musicians caught up in a backlash against insipid hotel meals and hamburger bars. I was, literally, in the front line at the height of this movement. Part of my band's stage show was a version by vocal trio of 'The Whiffenpoof Song', in which my two saxophone players and I would converge on the front microphone to sing 'We are poor little lambs who have lost our way, baa…baa…baa!'. Joe Temperley and Tony Coe were both in the throes of acute Madras Curry addiction at the time and, huddled together as we were in close harmony, the first 'baa' used to hit me like a sirocco. We always gave each 'baa' the full value of a dotted minim, and the second one was timed to catch me just as I came up for air. By the third, it was clear to those in the remotest corner of the auditorium that the lead singer was suffering some kind of paroxysm and that only his arms draped in a clubman's embrace around his colleagues' shoulders were preventing him from slumping to the floor. I soon discovered that the only way to meet this problem was to get to an Indian restaurant first and work up a counterblast. In this way I gained sufficient experience, if not to tell other people what they should like, at least to know what I like.

On the other hand I have never really got to grips with vegetarian food. Vegetarianism is rife among musicians, and I have been through all the familiar arguments. Freddy Grant used to insist that if God had meant us to eat meat, he would have given us sharp teeth. He treated my argument that God gave us steak knives instead with less consideration than it deserved. The final rift came when he pressed me to eat a sort of wholewheat rock-cake made, he assured us, from specially chosen health-giving ingredients. They were solid oatmeal rocks, practically impossible to crack with the teeth. He had made it himself and it was as solid and inpenetrable as oak. 'If God had meant me to eat that,' I said, 'he would have given me teeth like a hacksaw.' Freddy's panacea for almost every ill under the sun was a form of self-inflicted torture called a 'vital bath', which, as far as I remember, involved splashing the tenderest portions of one's anatomy with freezing water. Should this fail to produce a cure, he was ready – and fully qualified – to administer a colonic irrigation, a manoeuvre with rubber tubing and funnels the details of which we needn't go into here.

I was once attendant upon Duke Ellington at his suite in the Dorchester Hotel when he was having breakfast. It was four o'clock in the afternoon when, in the other world of offices, factories, cricket grounds and suburban households, everything stops for tea. But the Duke was having breakfast. It consisted of fruit juice, steak with salad, cheese, fruit salad and coffee, and he ate it – if I may borrow a dimly-remembered technical term from schoolroom physics – not in a series but in parallel. In other words, he cleared the way with a gulp of fruit juice, took in a slice of steak, followed it in rapid succession with a liberal spoonful of fruit salad and a wedge of cheese, washed the lot down with coffee, then went on to another permutation.

He only finished half the huge steak. The other half he wrapped carefully in a paper napkin and put in the fridge. Billy Strayhorn, his friend, collaborator and chancellor, saw my eyebrows go up. 'Duke knows something about touring in England,' he said. 'He likes to put something by for the middle of the night.' 'What happens in hotels where they have no fridge?' I asked. 'He puts it out on the window ledge.'

Here, I thought, must be the patron saint of all touring jazzmen, a man who combined a keen and idiosyncratic appreciation of the good things of life with a healthy regard for self-preservation. He loved music, words, food and laughter.

I had always regarded myself as a pretty fair trencherman until the day in Leeds, of all places, when I witnessed a gastronomic duel between two visiting Americans. One was Bobby – valet, hairdresser and general factotum to Duke Ellington, as bald and bulky as a Japanese wrestler. The other, 'Little' Jimmy Rushing, blues-singer extraordinare and the original Mister Five by Five – tipping, not to say demolishing, the scales at twenty-odd stone. Ordering the meal was an auction, each one outbidding the other in the number of pork chops and fried eggs he proposed to eat. I suspect that the outcome was a draw, though I have no clear memory. My mind was too busy boggling at the statistics – sixteen pork chops, ten fried eggs, several hundredweight of chips, two office blocks of apple pie and enough coffee to float them home across the Atlantic with a full Royal Navy escort and all flags flying.

Jimmy Rushing always insisted that his size had nothing to do with over-eating ('I was born fat,' he told us), and it's true that on tour he often kept going on the lightest of snacks for days on end. But from the few occasions when we saw him perform in championship style, it was clear that some heavy training was going on in secret. I took him to an Italian restaurant once after a session at my club in Oxford Street. He was in the mood for some serious eating and asked me to order him the 'best steak in the house'. Misjudging his taste I ordered him a prime fillet which so depleted my budget for the evening that I had to go myself for the cheapest thing on the menu. This was a plain escalope of veal, which arrived hammered so flat that it overlapped the edges of the plate. Jim looked at his steak, which was ten times thicker but covered a much smaller area of the plate. With a rueful expression he looked back at my great floppy sheet of escalope. As the host I felt it incumbent upon me to alleviate his obvious disappointment, so we swapped plates with mutual satisfaction.

Touring America, or Britain for that matter, with American musicians is not the best way to learn the finer qualities of American eating habits.

It is hard to imagine any circumstance which could inspire longing and nostalgia for the type of British all-night transport caff known to initiates as 'Ten Thousand Flies Can't Be Wrong'. But, hurtling around the Eastern States in a Greyhound bus in 1959 I found myself more than once yearning for the 3a.m. taste of egg, bacon, sausage and chips – not because it's a nice taste, but simply because it's a *taste*.

American roadside fare is never gruesome, as ours can be. Indeed, it goes to the other extreme. The most appetizing thing about it is the menu. Southern Fried Chicken in a Basket sounds absolutely delicious until you find out that it takes alert eyesight and a highly developed sense of touch to distinguish the chicken from the basket. And Pot Roast! What visions of succulent meat in rich gravy and firm vegetables that conjures up, and how bleakly disappointing is the square of scrubbed, sandpapered, disinfected and waterlogged teak which arrives in its place!

Doubtless some of the eccentricities which I have noticed in the eating habits of visiting American musicians can be explained by the tastelessness of so much of their own café food at home. When I drove Marie Knight, a handsome and formidable gospel-singer, around Britain some years ago on a tour, she clearly regarded our food as positively sinful.

In desperation I took her to the Leofric Hotel in Coventry, where the French restaurant was, something of an oasis in the Midlands. I ordered her the best steak in the house, and when it arrived, she called for meat sauce – the bottled kind which will restore a blackened penny to mint condition in ten seconds flat – and obliterated the steak from view. Seeing my lower lip trembling, she explained that *small steaks have no taste*. To Americans, size is an important factor – a steak is not a steak if it does not overlap the side of the plate.

Delivered by Hand

I have for some time lived in a state of embarrassment at the reference, in potted biographies from *Who's Who* downwards (or upwards, depending on your point of view) to 'calligraphy' as one of my hobbies.

The word 'calligraphy' itself is defined in the most up-to-date dictionary that I possess as *1. handwriting, esp. when fine or pleasing 2. the art of handwriting*. It comes from the Greek words *kallos* (beautiful) and *graphia* (writing), and the Greeks, never ones to leave loose ends hanging in the breeze, also give us a dictionary word for bad handwriting – 'cacography', from *kakos*, meaning 'bad'.

Calligraphy and cacography – it should be as simple as that. But, ironically, as a result of the Arts and Crafts movement of William Morris from which so much good has since flowed, the word calligraphy has been elevated to the level of high art, describing the highly-trained and immaculate work of latter-day scribes.

In this respect, I am *not* a calligrapher. I dare say that, given a fair wind and limitless time, I could produce something indistinguishable from that sort of calligraphy. The difference is that it would take me a fortnight, at the end of which I would be waist deep in crumpled sheets of paper and two-thirds of the way towards a nervous breakdown; your scribe, on the other hand, would have had it done in an hour and settled down to bottle up his ink and clean his nibs with the placid and, dare I say (bringing sour grapes into play), slightly smug expression of a mediaeval monk.

I'm well aware that the words now jumping from the page make me sound like an old buffer huffing on about current standards. In mitigation, here is a brief exchange plucked from the published correspondence between my father and the publisher Rupert Hart-Davis which shows that there's nothing new about cacography, neither are those of high rank and expensive education immune from it.

> GL: Did you ever get a letter from Monty James? [M.R. James, former Provost of Eton and author of ghost stories.] I once had a note from him inviting us to dinner – we guessed that the time was 8 and not 3, as it appeared to be, but all we could tell about the day was that it was not Wednesday.
>
> R.H.-D. in reply: I never saw Monty James's writing but doubt if he could have been more illegible than Lady Colefax: the only hope of deciphering her invitations, someone said, was to pin them up on the wall and run past them!

As an Eton schoolmaster, my father was in the habit of going off with colleagues around Christmas time on a two-week golfing holiday. Finding, as he often did, that his friends, while excellent company on the fairway, were marginally less so during the long winter evenings, on one occasion he took with him a penholder, a box of assorted Mitchell nibs and a copy of Edward Johnston's *Writing & Illuminating & Lettering* to while away the evenings. When he came home, he had transformed his wiry, barely legible scrawl into an elegant italic script.

From the letters he wrote to my mother (throughout their life together, they corresponded every single day when one or other of them was away from home) this seems to have happened between 1926 and 1927 when he was in his early forties. I was five years old then, living a separate nursery life on the top floor of our big house. It was therefore several years later that I became aware of his enthusiasm for italic handwriting.

I must confess now that much of my education was received in teenage, not through the class room, but from the thoroughly reprehensible habit of going into my father's study in his absence and reading the letters scattered over the surface and in the drawers and pigeon holes of the huge Edwardian roll-top desk at which he sat in his study at Eton College and, after his retirement, at Finndale House in Suffolk.

The letters were not alone. I would find also the sundry implements of a hobby which he practised, in every sense of the word, for the rest of his life. There was always a carpenter's pencil handy, a flattened oval in profile with a straight-edged lead that could be honed on.

We quite soon began to notice that a certain dottiness accompanied his new enthusiasm. For example, though not one for field sports himself, he cultivated the acquaintance of gun-toting friends and relatives in order to cadge from them quantities of twelve-bore cartridges. These he would prise open with a penknife, at great risk to life and property, to get at the buckshot before it became irretrievably dispersed in the carcasses of the surrounding wildlife. Thus harvested, the shot would be put into a small glass jar which he kept always at hand on his desk. He had received a tip-off that the best way to keep a steel nib in pristine condition was to agitate it frequently and vigorously up and down in a jar of buckshot.

Other eccentric items of impedimenta were to follow. He bought broad nibs and from then on, all the little notices around the house – lists of telephone numbers, drawer labels, reminders to switch off lights and so on – were written in careful script. On one particular day in 1936 we found him trying to saw through the thick hide of a twelve-bore shotgun cartridge with a penknife. We had absolutely no warning. There had been no history of that sort of thing in the family – well

Dear Steve
Sent mine off yesterday
and here yours comes today
James Rushing, almost.

It always happens like that, eh? I posted it on the way to a gig last night, so it had gone beyond recall this morning — Anyway, as an exercise in fantasy it was fun, tho' I over-looked the possibility of you being embroiled in Jewell v. Dance (they even <u>sound</u> like the ugly sisters!) At least a hundred people have assumed that Stanley's reference to D.J.'s "Etonian friend" meant me, but I can't be bothered to do anything about it. Am too absorbed in the spectacle of critics locked in internecine strife!

Why doesn't Jewell go for his eyes? Thanks for the tape.

Better get this off now
Cheers — Humph

P.S. Am having fun with contrasting nibs, as you can see —! And 'creative smudging', too! To hell with liquid paper!

Letter sent to Steve Voce in which Humph uses the full range of nib sizes in a calligraphic medley!

there was Uncle Albert, of course, but oddities such as his were far removed from the sinister tinkering with gunpowder and shot in which my father was discovered.

The truth eventually came out. My father was suffering from a disease variously known as Johnston's Disease, Cockerell's complaint or – Italic Fever. In lay terms, he was in the early but already incurable stages of Good Handwriting. It can't be said that there was much history of *that* in the family. From the odd letters that hung about tables and desks in our house when I was a child, I gleaned that my male forebears corresponded in a spindly code consisting largely of wavy lines of varying length which offered a rough inclination of the shapes which the words would have formed had there been any actual letters to form them.

By contrast, the females tended to write, as they spoke, in an extravagant Edwardian style full of explosive stresses and ejaculations, like the barking of large, friendly dogs. '*Beloved* Hermione – I am *simply devastated* to learn of your *Quite Ghastly* motoring accident – *too awful* and what a *Perfect Swine* of a man to suggest that it was *your fault*! You are to *drop everything* and come and stay *at once*, you *Poor Darling* etc. etc.…'

It's not difficult to visualize the resulting page in which ascenders, descenders, cross-strokes, commas and thick underlining overlapped each other in an orgy of angular confusion, like the twigs, boughs and trunks of a storm-stricken forest.

My father and Wilfred Blunt (then art master at the school) co-led the drive to better handwriting at Eton. It should be said that the focal point of this activity was in a schools competition set up and endowed by the then President of the Society for Italic Handwriting and a keen learner himself, the Marquess of Cholmondeley. I am not clear as to how samples obviously from Wilfred Blunt's collection came into my father's possession, other than that, like collectors in other fields, they would exchange items that were surplus to requirement. Blunt's letters reveal the way in which sedulous study of formal italic script can give shape and fluency to everyday handwriting, however hurried or spontaneous. Blunt was friendly with his opposite number at Harrow School, Maurice Percival, and in contrast with the rivalry between those two establishments on the cricket field, and indeed in conversation whenever both were mentioned in the same breath, Blunt and Percival were fellow protagonists when it came to first learning and then teaching italics.

Early in the 'fifties my father joined the newly-founded Society for Italic Handwriting whose prime function was, and still is, to bring together those with an interest in calligraphy of the informal kind. Despite an Italic renaissance in the immediate post-war years, there was a need to unite against the advance of the barbarian ballpoint, and the letters in the Society's journal resounded with camaraderie and desperate courage. 'This letter', wrote a correspondent in 1956, 'is being written with a converted Osmiroid pen fitted with a nib consisting of a piece of polythene from a cycle feeding-bottle tube, a section of an old table-tennis ball and half a paper clip.' For a while in our house it was wise to hide the ping-pong set and lock up your bicycle.

When my father first went down with calligraphy I was away at school, most of the time, and anyway I proved healthily resistant to the virus. My first experience of any kind of handwriting instruction was at private school where several pages of 'copy-book' were a regular punishment. The model was a standard copperplate and the texts were solemn precepts which, I suppose, were intended to prepare us for adult life. 'Hack no furniture' is the only line that I recall. While guiding my squittering pen through the loops and swoops of the letters k and f, I clearly absorbed the message. With hand on heart, I can honestly say that no *chaise longue* or chest-of-drawers has, in the past seventy-five years, had anything to fear from me. The punitive copy-book didn't do much for my handwriting, judging by the legible but indisciplined scrawl that I carried into my twenties.

Looking back on it, I suppose it is possible that the germ did penetrate in those early days, to lie dormant until my mature years when it has struck repeatedly with increasing virulence. Indeed, since some of my father's effects came into my possession, it has been rampant. I inherited all kinds of handwriting stuff from my father's desk – boxes of Mitchell nibs of all sizes, several sturdy penholders (a far cry from the miserable, stunted things that are offered today, if you can find them) and a small jam jar of shotgun pellets which some had recommended as a handy way of cleaning metal nibs by dipping them rapidly in and out. The glass jar full of buckshot wasn't specifically mentioned in his will, but I have assumed that it was intended for me and I use it now. There is one drawback which my father either didn't discover or kept to himself. The nib tends to pick up a single piece of buckshot, secrete it somewhere at the back of its throat and then drop it like an inky bomb just as you reach the end of an impeccable page.

I also inherited his handwriting collection of letters which I found higgledy-piggeldy in a drawer long after he died. I have had great fun putting it in order and adding to it over the years. Every so often I would get a letter to my Monday-night-jazz programme on the B.B.C. written in good italic handwriting and I have to confess that it was dealt with very much more quickly than the other run-of-the-mill enquiries as to who played trombone with Louis Armstrong in 1935! A few of these are in my own collection.

It was from my father, then, that my interest in calligraphy derived and it has grown slowly over the years. My problem is that, as an itinerant musician, I am very rarely desk-bound. So I have had to evolve writing implements which are easily portable and can be used without ostentation in hotel lounges and backstage dressing-rooms. Ready-made italic nibs are all very well, but half the fun in calligraphy is making your own pens. So I buy ordinary school fountain pens – Platignum, Osmiroid, you name it, I've got it – and I doctor them in. This means cutting the 'blob' off the tip of the nib (I use Ready-Wilkinson extra-tough scissors with orange handles for this), honing the back of the nib-tip on a smooth carborundum stone to get a 'chisel' profile and lightly rubbing down any rough edges. My favourite 'home-made' pen is a chunky Schaeffer 'No Nonsense' pen, clearly named without my fussy administrations in mind! It's a constant struggle to get materials. Your friendly high street stationer will stock a few decent Italic fountain pens nowadays, but they're usually hidden away behind ballpoint monstrosities disguised as golf-clubs, gardening implements or female extremities.

As for decent penholders, they are things of the past. The only way to get a good, old-fashioned penholder of the right shape and length is to buy a Mitchell pen-set, with ten assorted nibs thrown in. But I buy about twenty penholders a year for various purposes, and who needs two hundred nibs? I've already got six hundred that my father never got round to using. But ask for a single, separate penholder nowadays and they will generally offer you a nasty, warped and stunted piece of plastic that feels horrible to the touch and tastes filthy. I owe my present cast-iron digestion to those noble, erect, firm-waisted implements which one used to chew from tip to bracket as a schoolboy. They looked like ivory, but the story was that they were a by-product of condensed milk, and we swallowed it – literally.

I have, in the throes of enthusiasm, had a go at making my own quills, with some success. But I haven't kept it up. I suppose I was put off when I discovered that those long, sweeping feathers that tickle your nose as you write belong only to the Hollywood historical movies. The true craftsman strips the feather down to the stem, and it stands to reason really. You can't write properly with a pen that's going to roll and heave in the breeze whenever anyone opens the door. But the bald quill is not nearly so romantic.

I will draw a veil over my attempt to make a reed pen!

You might well ask why I have kept doing it in the face of all this. Vanity, I suppose, in that it pleases the eye to let it linger on a handsome page that has been completed without accident. I am not ashamed of this. Life has its own ways of cutting one down to size when necessary. I once used to take an Italic fountain-pen with me to work, so that I could sign beautiful autographs. Once, after a brief signing session, I noticed a small girl and her mother hanging back after the rest had gone. 'Haven't I done hers?' I asked the mother. 'Yes,' she said, 'but she'd rather have a signature.'

As for practice, well, there is surely no limit to the opportunities that modern life provides once you have hurled the typewriter and the ballpoint pen out of the window. Scripts, articles, letters, cheques, official forms – I make an amateur calligraphic meal out of all of them, to the extent that I actually look forward to doing my V.A.T.

accounts! And whenever I settle down to watch *Coronation Street*, I have a writing pad on my lap.

When he launched the Society for Italic Handwriting in 1952, Alfred Fairbank expressed the view that learning to write with clarity, legibility and elegance is, as much as anything, a matter of good manners. On the face of it, this is a reasonable requirement. It goes with the reproof often uttered by the mentor of my early years, Nanny Viggers – 'Don't speak with your mouth full!' At this point, I find myself teetering on the verge of curmudgeondom (my computer spell-check has just had a rather distressing fit), so I will tread carefully.

I think it's safe for me to observe that, fifty-five years on, the concept of 'good manners' has changed and the term itself has, like its close relative 'etiquette', acquired in the public mind a certain quaintness. If we use the word 'italic' too often, it may well suffer the same fate, especially if, in the process, we adopt such unattractive derivatives as 'italicists' for the practitioners of the style. Nevertheless, it remains true that to send someone a letter or postcard written in the epistolatory equivalent of speaking with a mouth crammed with a jumbo cheeseburger plus a side-serving of mixed salad is disrespectful and often unproductive.

Humph